Death and Taxes

The archaeology of a Middle Saxon estate centre at Higham Ferrers, Northamptonshire

by Alan Hardy, Bethan Mair Charles & Robert J Williams

with contributions by

Martin Allen, Paul Blinkhorn, Emily Edwards, Emma-Jane Evans, Robert Francis, Clare Ingrem, Paul Linford, Lisa Moffet, Fiona Roe, Ian Scott, Edmund Simons, Gill Thompson, Annsofie Witkin

Illustration and design
Rosalyn and Peter Lorimer

Oxford Archaeology
2007

Published for Oxford Archaeology as part of the Oxford Archaeology Monograph series

Also available concerning excavations in Higham Ferrers :-
Between Villa and Town, Excavations of a Roman roadside settlement and shrine at Higham Ferrers, Northants
by Steve Lawrence and Alex Smith

Designed by Oxford Archaeology Graphics Office

Edited by Ian Scott

Figures 1, 2.1, 2.2, 3.1, 3.2, 3.16 are reproduced from the Ordnance Survey on behalf of the controller of Her Majesty's Stationery Office, © Crown Copyright, AL 100005569

ISBN 978-0-904220-43-8

This book is part of a series of monographs which can be bought from all good bookshops and internet bookshops. For more information visit www.oxfordarch.co.uk

Typeset by Production Line, Oxford
Printed in Great Britain at the Alden Group, Oxfordshire

Contents

Chapter 1: Introduction and Project Background

Chapter 2: Archaeological background and the research agenda

Chapter 3: The archaeological results

Chapter 5: Discussion

List of Figures

List of Plates

List of Tables

Summary

Between 1993 and 2003, Oxford Archaeology (formerly Oxford Archaeological Unit) undertook a major programme of survey and excavation on the northern outskirts of the town of Higham Ferrers, Northamptonshire, uncovering extensive remains dating from the Middle Bronze Age to the late medieval period. This volume (Oxford Archaeology Monograph No. 4) deals with the Anglo-Saxon and medieval remains. The results of the excavations of the Iron Age and Roman settlements will be published in a separate volume (Oxford Archaeology Monograph No. 5).

Post-Roman occupation began as early as the mid to late 5th century, with a scatter of Sunken Featured Buildings and a few associated pits. No obvious evidence was found to indicate any continuity between the late Roman and early Saxon occupation.

A possible brief interval in the 7th century was followed by the establishment of a large 8th-century complex of enclosures and buildings, along with other structures including a large malting oven. It is argued that this represents the infrastructure of a purpose-built tribute centre for a royal estate, a type of site not hitherto recognised in England. While the quantity of material evidence of this period is modest, the character of it indicates that a wide variety of produce came into the complex and was then redistributed rather than consumed on site. Evidence of other functions of the complex were revealed in the form of human remains – interpreted as execution victims, found in parts of the enclosure ditches.

At around the end of the 8th century the evidence suggests that the complex was abruptly and completely destroyed and the landscape cleared. The chronology as determined by the material evidence was augmented by a programme of radiocarbon and archaeomagnetic dating.

Starting in the 9th century, occupation resumed in the area, in the form of a scatter of farmsteads. Evidence was also found of a substantial pottery industry producing Late medieval Reduced Ware.

Acknowledgements

Any project that extends over more than a decade of fieldwork and post-excavation is bound to draw on the services of many people.

Most importantly we are pleased to gratefully acknowledge the central part played by the Duchy of Lancaster throughout the project. It speaks volumes for the Duchy's appreciation of heritage and the importance of archaeology that it supported the work so generously through the years, right up to and including this publication. The Duchy's initial representative was Ken Parsons, who helped formulate the initial project strategy. His successor, Roger Whalley, saw the archaeological project through the fieldwork stage – his cooperation, patience and forbearance in the face of the increasingly complicated archaeology (and the increasingly complicated archaeologists!) were crucial to the success of the project, and our thanks are profound. Roger was succeeded by Nick Dart, who has overseen the final stages of the project with similar understanding and support.

The cast of archaeologists involved in the projects is long and varied. The project was initiated by David Miles, then director of Oxford Archaeological Unit, and was initially managed by Bob Williams. The later stages of the fieldwork were managed by Alan Hardy. A number of Site Managers have been heavily involved; Klara Spandl, David Score, Steve Lawrence, Emily Glass and Gerry Thacker all deserve our appreciation for maintaining such high archaeological standards in what were sometimes very difficult circumstances.

On the curatorial side the East Northamptonshire Planning authority was initially represented by Glen Foard, who was the architect behind the formulation of a research strategy for the project, and contributed much to the formulation of working hypotheses during the excavations. Latterly, his successor, Myk Flitcroft coped with the increasingly complex project, deftly walking the tightrope between client and archaeologist, between what was and what was not possible, and making valuable contributions to the understanding of the site.

The post-excavation programme drew on the wisdom and skills of a number of people apart from those credited. John Blair and the late Patrick Wormald directed their talents to the Middle Saxon puzzle, ensuring that the archaeological interpretation could fit into the historical and political context of the time. Andrew Reynolds' help in unravelling the puzzle of the woman's burial is much appreciated. Last but not least, Helena Hamerow read the draft text and offered wise and valuable advice.

The original post-excavation programme included specialists' contributions that were superseded by later work. Nevertheless, the efforts of Umberto Albarella of Durham University and Matthew Canti of English Heritage are not forgotten.

The authors are pleased to express their thanks to three metal detectorists who participated over the years, Mick Gardener in the early days, and more recently Mark Davis and John Grey. They contributed significantly to the understanding of the site, demonstrating that it is possible for archaeologists and detectorists to work together for the common good .

Alan Hardy would like to personally thank Paul Blinkhorn and Steve Lawrence for their efforts above and beyond their formal obligations.

To an archaeologist it is always rewarding when the local community lend support to a project such as this. On the evidence of the number of local volunteer diggers (among whom John Richardson deserves a special mention), the attendance both at the site Open Days (one of which took place on one of the coldest days for years), and at the subsequent evening lectures, the community of Higham Ferrers is due a large vote of thanks for their support. Alan Hardy would particularly like to thank Olwen Mayes, of the Chichele Society for her inexhaustible enthusiasm and energy, maintaining the local interest in the site long after the digging stopped. Thanks must also go to Doreen Holyoak, for valuable information on the origin of Kings Meadow Lane.

Alan Hardy
Bethan Mair Charles

Chapter 1: Introduction and Project Background

HIGHAM FERRERS – ITS LOCATION, GEOLOGY AND TOPOGRAPHY

The town of Higham Ferrers is situated along a limestone ridge on the eastern bank of the River Nene, approximately 15 miles east of the county town of Northampton (Fig. 1.1). Occupation extends from the alluvial plain up to the Boulder Clay plateau to the east. Both banks of the Nene valley have been attractive to settlers since prehis-

toric times, both for the productive potential of the land and for the access to a major waterway.

The town lies across the river from Irthling-borough, which has strong Anglo-Saxon connections (not least indicated by its name). A few kilometres to the north is the area of the Raunds Project, site of a major landscape study, which identified intensive multi-period settlement (Parry, 2006).

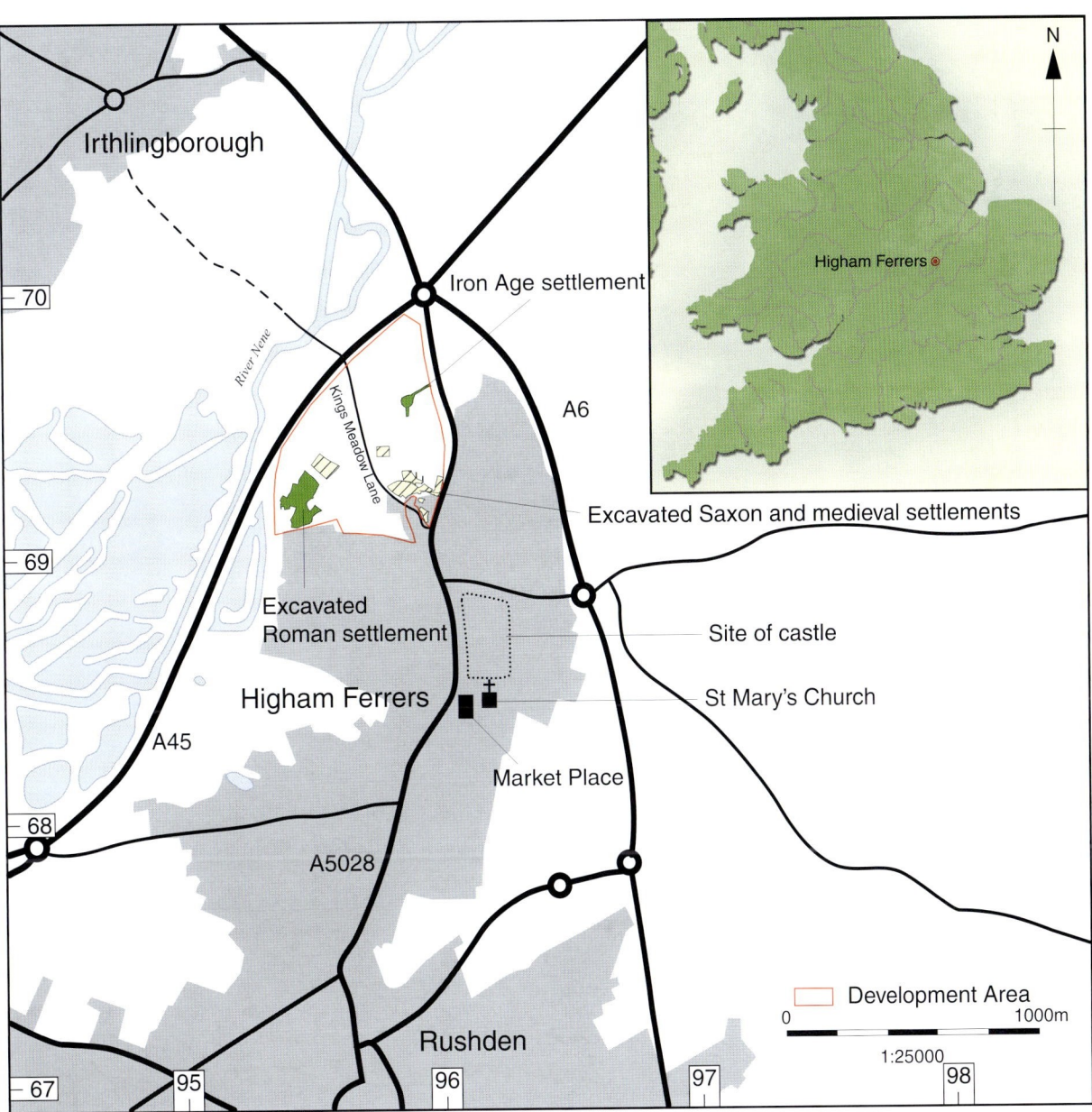

Fig. 1.1   *General location of Higham Ferrers, development area and sites*

The development area enclosing the investigated sites (Fig. 1.2) occupies an area of approximately 42 ha (100 acres) of mixed limestone and ironstone geology on either side of a small dry valley running up from the Nene, varying in height from 35 m to 65 m OD (SP 959694). The valley has historically defined the northern edge of the medieval core of Higham Ferrers, and the valley bottom has been used as a route (now known as Kings Meadow Lane) from the northern end of the town, down towards the river, and across to Irthlingborough.

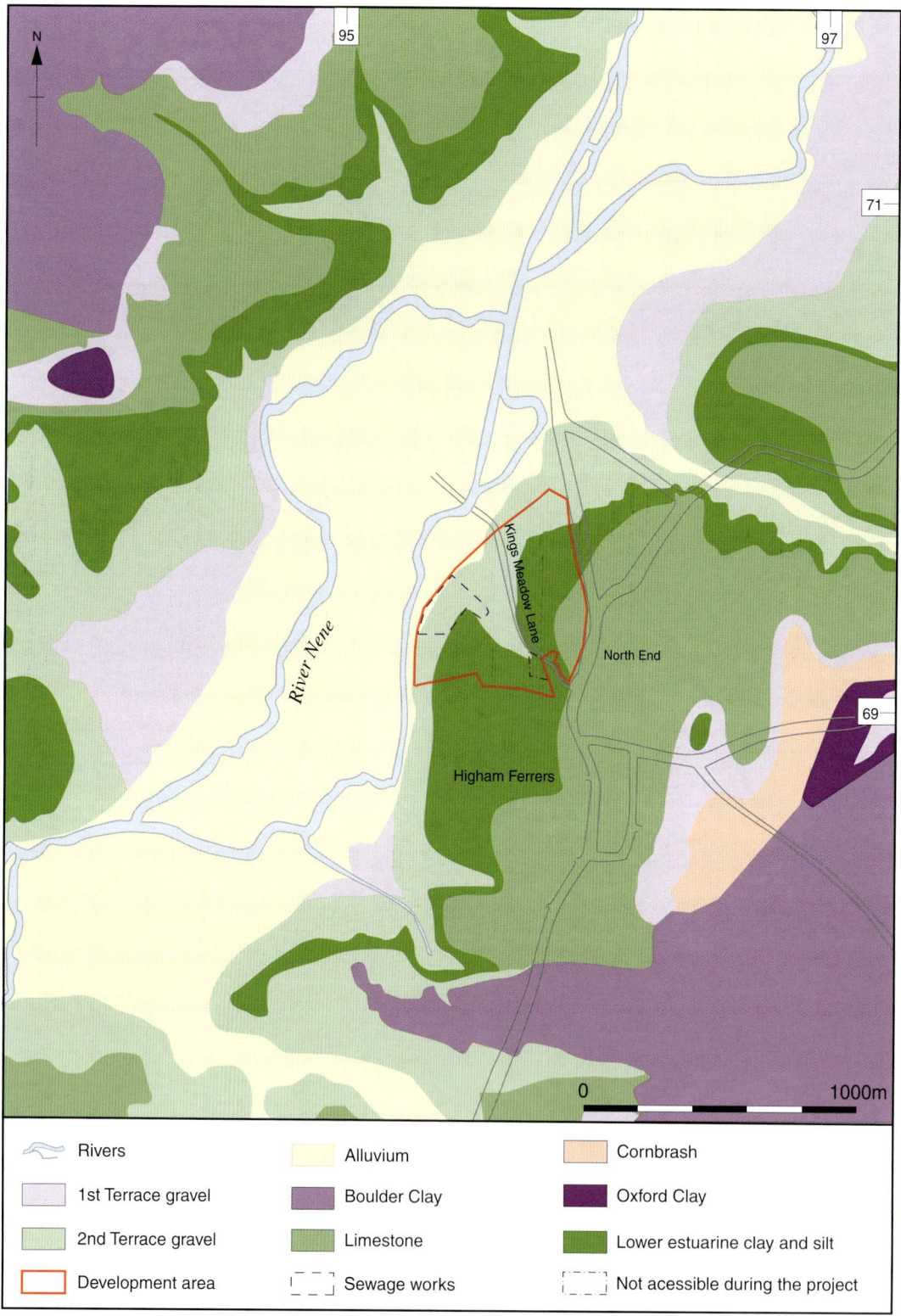

Fig. 1.2   *The local geology and development area*

THE PROJECT BACKGROUND

In October 1988, East Northamptonshire District Council granted outline planning permission to the landowner, the Duchy of Lancaster (DoL), for residential development and recreational facilities on the site (Planning Application No. EN/88/596), comprising an area of approximately 41 ha (100 acres) on the northern outskirts of Higham Ferrers, Northamptonshire (Pl. 1.1).

The initial stages of the project predated the introduction of PPG-16, and consequently the condition relating to archaeology in the original outline planning permission was of limited scope, requiring only that an archaeologist nominated by the local planning authority should be allowed access to the site, to observe the excavations and record items and finds of interest.

The introduction of PPG-16 in 1990, prior to the commencement of any fieldwork prompted a review of the planned archaeological mitigation involving negotiations between the Duchy of Lancaster, English Heritage, Northamptonshire Heritage, and the Duchy's archaeological consultant, David Miles, of the Oxford Archaeological Unit (OAU). The archaeological potential of the site, already suspected from cropmarks plotted from aerial photography (see Plate 2.1 and Figure 2.1), was confirmed subsequently by two detailed archaeological evaluations commissioned by the Duchy of Lancaster (NAU 1991; OAU 1994). This work indicated that the site contained an Iron Age and a Roman settlement of 'county' level of importance, and Anglo-Saxon settlements and an oval enclosure of 'national' importance.

Although the all-party negotiations, working within the new framework of PPG16, determined a much more elaborate archaeological strategy, the funding available for the work was still severely constrained in the early stages, and the project design (OAU 1995) established a rigorously

Plate 1.1   The development area prior to the fieldwork, looking west across the River Nene to Irthlingborough (Duchy of Lancaster copyright)

targeted strategy derived from the perceived potential of the site to contribute to local, regional and national research priorities.

This document envisaged that post-excavation analysis would operate under the same financial constraints as the site work, and was expected to ultimately deliver an article to be submitted for publication to *Northamptonshire Archaeology*. However, while the post-excavation stage of the 1995 fieldwork was still in progress, in 2000, the proposed development by DoL of further parcels of land in the Kings Meadow Lane project put the post-excavation analysis programme on hold, while further fieldwork was undertaken. The very productive results prompted an updated Assessment and Research design (OA 2002), which proposed bringing together the publication in monograph form of the Saxon, medieval and post-medieval archaeology from all of the investigated sites (Sites 1, 2 and 3 in 1995, and Sites 4, 5 and 9 in 2001).

A proposal for further new development by the Duchy prompted more fieldwork in 2002 and 2003, encompassing further areas containing Anglo-Saxon and medieval occupation and a large part of the Roman settlement.

Ultimately, virtually all the fieldwork on all the sites was funded by the Duchy of Lancaster, but the scale and importance of the results from all periods led to the decision to publish the results as two separate monographs, one devoted to the prehistoric and Roman archaeology with the post-excavation and publication funded entirely by English Heritage, and one devoted to the Saxon, medieval and post-medieval archaeology, funded entirely by the Duchy of Lancaster. In addition to the academic publication, the Duchy of Lancaster funded the production of a 'popular publication' in 2004, on the Anglo-Saxon and medieval archaeology (Hardy and Lorimer, 2004).

HISTORICAL BACKGROUND

Introduction

It is fortunate for the purposes of this project that the administrative organisation of Northamptonshire in general – and Higham Ferrers in particular – in the Saxon period has been the subject of some close scrutiny in recent times. In 1985 Glenn Foard, then Northamptonshire's Principal Archaeologist, examined the Saxon administrative organisation of Northamptonshire (Foard 1985). In 2000, the archaeological and historical resource of Higham Ferrers was assessed as part of the Northamptonshire Extensive Urban Survey (Foard and Ballinger 2000). David Hall has also investigated the ways in which the character of Middle Saxon estate administration may be discernible in the layout of the medieval landscape, using Higham Ferrers as an example (Hall 1988, 99-122). In the light of this the following section is essentially a summary of that work.

Early medieval history

At some point in the Late Saxon period, the township of Higham became established in its present position, some distance from the apparent focus of Middle Saxon activity to the north (see Figure 5.6).

The first documentary mention of Higham Ferrers (then Higham) is in 1066, as a hundredal manor held by Gytha, countess of Hereford, but by 1086 William Peverell held 6 hides in Higham. At this stage Higham contained 2 hides in demesne, a market, a mill, woodland and a priest. The regional importance of Higham is emphasised by the fact that only three other towns in Northamptonshire had markets at this time. Foard argues that Higham's late Saxon and early medieval importance resulted largely from its history as part of a large estate, which included the Finedon royal soke, Irthlingborough and the properties originally held by Burgred, King of Mercia (857-874). It is argued that in the 7th century this estate's centre was at Irthlingborough, and that Higham's role may have been as a demesne centre complementing the royal centre directly across the river at Irthlingborough (Foard and Ballinger 2000, 14).

The promotion of its market increased its relative importance, both politically and commercially, and what was a market town grew into true urban settlement by the mid-13th century. This was no doubt helped by the construction and development of the castle (begun in the late 12th century), situated on the north-east side of the town centre.

In 1155 the Peverell family forfeited Higham estate to King Henry II, who gave it to Robert Ferrers, Earl of Derby. It is from him that 'Higham' became 'Higham Ferrers'. In 1266 the Earl of Derby's estates were seized by the King Henry III and granted to Edmund Earl of Lancaster – becoming part of the Duchy of Lancaster. The accession of Henry Bolingbroke, the Duke of Lancaster to the throne in 1327, caused the Duchy – and its lands – to be merged with the lands of the crown. From then on The Duchy and its lands, including Higham Ferrers, were managed on behalf of the crown by a High Sheriff.

Commercial and Industrial Development of Higham Ferrers

By the 13th century there was already a clear preponderance of merchants and craftsmen over agricultural tenants in Higham Ferrers. By 1251, when borough status was granted, only two of the 92 new burgesses were agricultural tenants. The limited status of agricultural tenants in the new borough was clear, and it would appear that then they had become concentrated in the northern end of the borough, which became known as Bond End, and later North End (Foard and Ballinger 2000, 36). Although technically always part of Higham Ferrers, in practise this enclave was virtually a separate community.

Trades practised in medieval Higham Ferrers covered a fairly typical range, with the leather and the cloth industries possibly the most significant, at least until the later medieval period (ibid, 37). The only industry that has yielded unequivocal archaeological evidence is the potting. Fifteenth-century pottery kilns have been located at Bond End, on the northern outskirts of the town (see below Sites 6 and 8). In the Hundred Rolls it states that in 1436 William Potter *'took a messuage not built, together with a selion of land in an adjacent croft, in which croft there is a kiln for making pots and other earthen vessels'*. Repairs to a pottery kiln are also mentioned in 1467 (Sergeantson, 1917, 44).

The process of wealth attracting wealth, and prestige attracting prestige is evident in later medieval Higham Ferrers in the foundation of Chichele College in 1422, (along with The Bede House and the refoundation of the Grammar School) by Henry Chicheley, Archbishop of Canterbury, whose father, Thomas Chicheley had been a burgess and mayor of the town. The college occupied the area of several tenements in the town centre, and, when fully developed, comprised a quadrangular range of buildings surrounding a courtyard.

The later history of Higham Ferrers

Higham Ferrers prospered through the 14th and 15th centuries, seeming to overcome such setbacks as the plagues of the second half of the 14th century and a major fire in 1410. The earliest map of Higham Ferrers by Norden in 1591 (Pl.1.2) depicts a urban core with a market place, church, and well developed burgage plots, but signficantly with no clear trace of the castle; with the demise of the castle in the 16th century, and the Dissolution, the regional status of Higham Ferrers began to suffer. Commercially, the loss of the corn market to rival Wellingborough in the 17th century was fundamental. In 1712 the historian John Morton described Higham Ferrers as *'small and not very populous'*. Evidence of the town's decline is apparent in the number of empty plots shown on the 1737(Pl.1.3) and 1789 estate maps. Cole, writing in the 19th century, spoke of reports of foundations of walls being found in open field to the west and east of the town, implying great shrinkage. It is highly probable, as Foard and Ballinger argue, that medieval occupation probably never extended further than the back lane on the west side of the high street, and it is possible that the foundations Cole reported were actually those of the Roman town, which is known to have extended some distance down the west side of the medieval town (Foard and Ballinger 2000, 36-7).

The lack of population and the decline in artisans and merchants meant a return to a more agricultural regime, and it was not until the 19th century that Higham Ferrers began to expand again, this time on the back of the boot and shoe

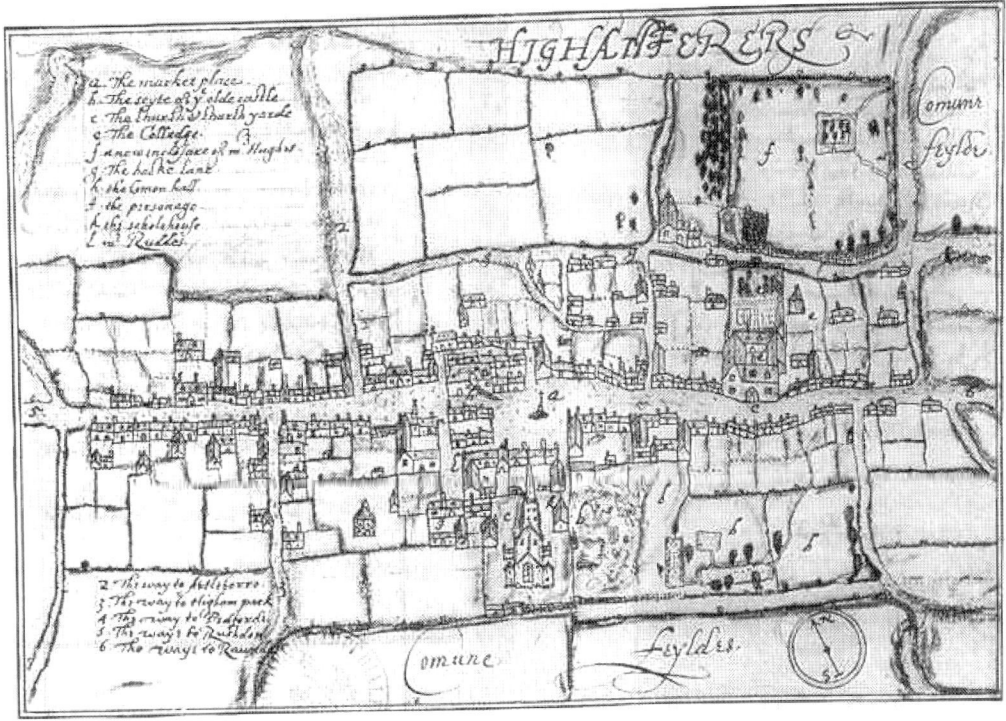

Plate 1.2 Nordens map of Higham Ferrers 1591
(Northampton Record Office, Map 4661, reproduced by kind permission of Bibliothèque Nationale de France)

trade, which became a regional speciality. Initially the proliferation of boot and shoe factories was focussed on the east side of the town, but by the middle of the first half of the 20th century the industry had spread to the area between Kings Meadow Lane and North End, in the shape of Walker and Gunn Ltd. The second half of the 20th century saw further light industrial development around Kings Meadow Lane, but essentially the core of the town around the marketplace and the Church has retained a great deal of its medieval fabric. While Kings Meadow Lane was slightly encroached upon by further light industry, and a sewage farm, in essence the area to the north west of the town, including the Lane, retained its rural character, and its agricultural role.

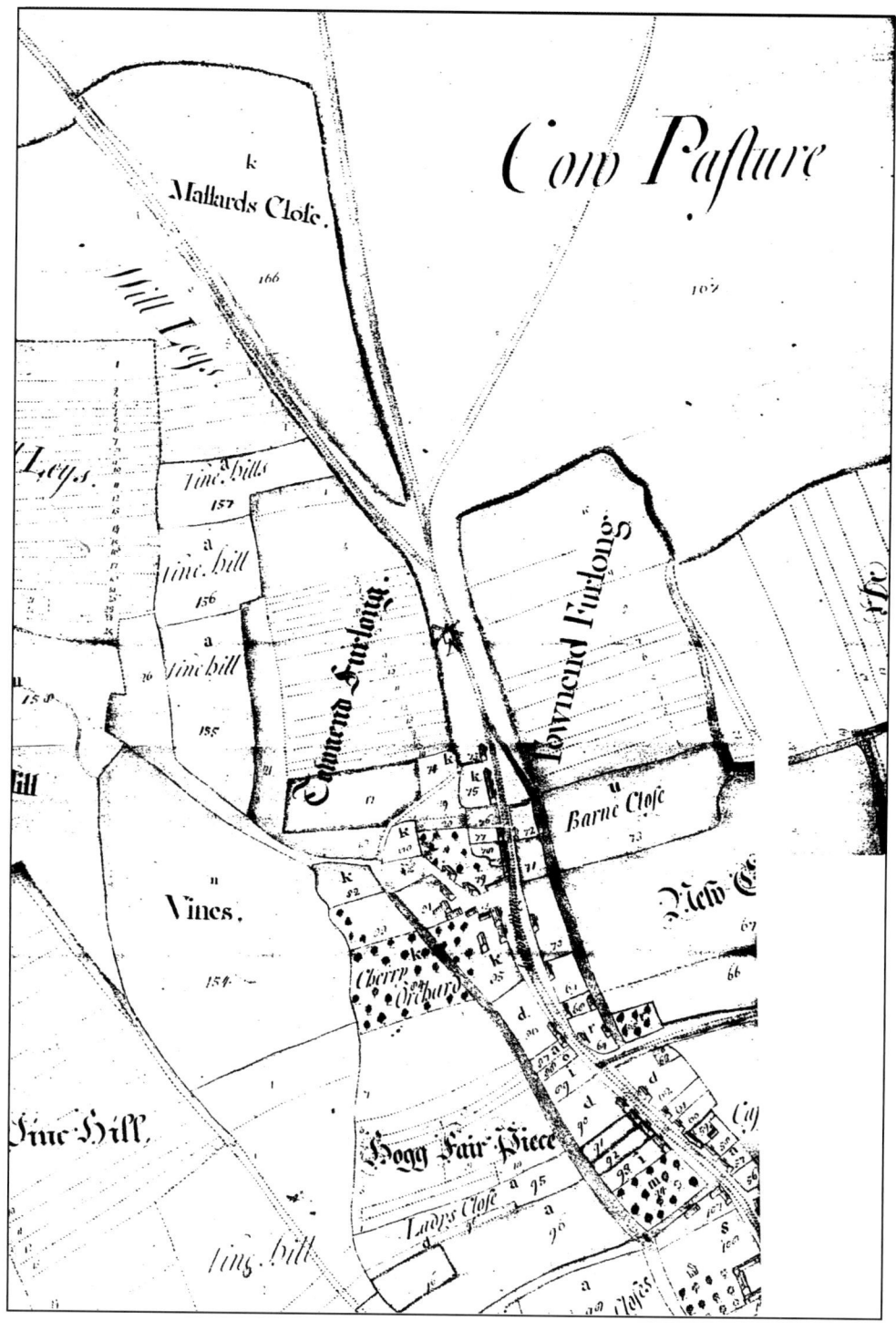

Plate 1.3   Detail from the 1737 estate map of the Kings Meadow Lane area (Northampton Record Office, Map 1004, reproduced with permission of Sir Philip Naylor Leyland Bt. and the Milton (Peterborough) Estates Company)

Chapter 2:
Archaeological background and the research agenda

Until the beginning of the present project in the late 1980's, little archaeological investigation had taken place in Higham Ferrers in modern times, and the results of the work that has been done have not been widely disseminated. David Hall has surveyed the open fields of Higham Ferrers but the results are not published. Rescue excavation was conducted in 1965 by Hall on a late medieval pottery kiln in North End but only the pottery has been published in summary (Hall, 1974). Excavations were conducted on the site of the precinct buildings of Chichele College in 1966 resulting in the exposure of the plan of the college, but no detailed excavation

report has been published. Evaluation trenching took place in the 1990s on the castle site, confirming the scale and state of preservation of the remains of what probably represents the inner bailey (Shaw and Steadman, 1992). Other small-scale evaluations have taken place in a few locations within the town.

The Kings Meadow Lane area remained largely uninvestigated until – prompted by the proposed development in the late 1980s – Northamptonshire Heritage instigated a programme of non-invasive investigation including fieldwalking (Fig. 2.1). Previous work comprised modest excavations in parts of the Roman settlement conducted during the

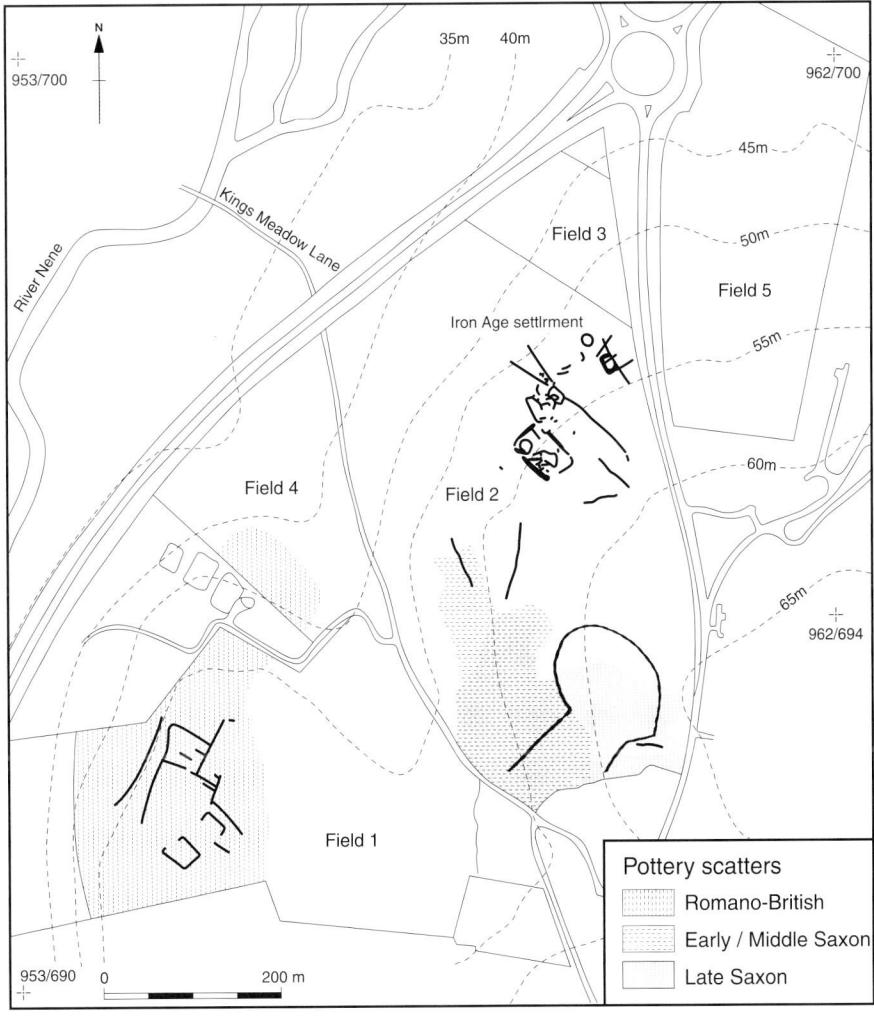

Fig. 2.1 Cropmarks and fieldwalking results in the Area of Kings Meadow Lane (after figure 5 – Medieval Settlement Research Group Annual report 6 1991)

construction of the housing estate to the south of the development area in 1961 (Meadows 1992), and the excavation of a suspected medieval pottery kiln mentioned above (Hall, 1974).

Apart from the programme of fieldwalking across the development area in the late 1980s, further non-invasive investigation in the form of an archaeogeophysical survey was undertaken in two stages by Bartlett-Clark Consultancy (Bartlett 2000 & 2001). The survey (Fig. 2.2) was targeted on the area of the Roman settlement and supported the

inference drawn from the field-walking that there was no major density of Saxon features there, although it did show clearly those features later confirmed as SFBs in Sites 9 and 10.

RESEARCH AGENDA

From the perspective of the late 1980s, when the development project was in its infancy, the importance of this multi-period site, encompassing as it did prehistoric, Romano-British, Saxon and medieval

Fig. 2.2 (a)   The results of the archaeoeophysical survey and the location of sites

archaeology, was already clear. Initial fieldwalking and a close study of the cropmark evidence (Plate. 2.1), followed by an early programme of evaluation trenching (NAU, 1991) showed that the different periods appeared to be represented by broadly discrete areas of archaeological activity, enhancing their potential to each yield uncontaminated settlement evidence.

In the context of the constraints on the funding of the archaeological investigation (see Chapter 1) an approach based upon a scale of research priori-

ties was formulated by Glen Foard in the light of the current national and regional research priorities (1992, developed further in Foard 1994). Broadly, this argued that the Saxon archaeology apparent at Kings Meadow Lane was of national importance, and if not preserved *in situ*, then it at least should be excavated intensively. On the other hand, on the basis of the knowledge at that time, the Iron Age and Romano-British settlements did not appear to offer research opportunities of a unique or nationally important nature. (With the

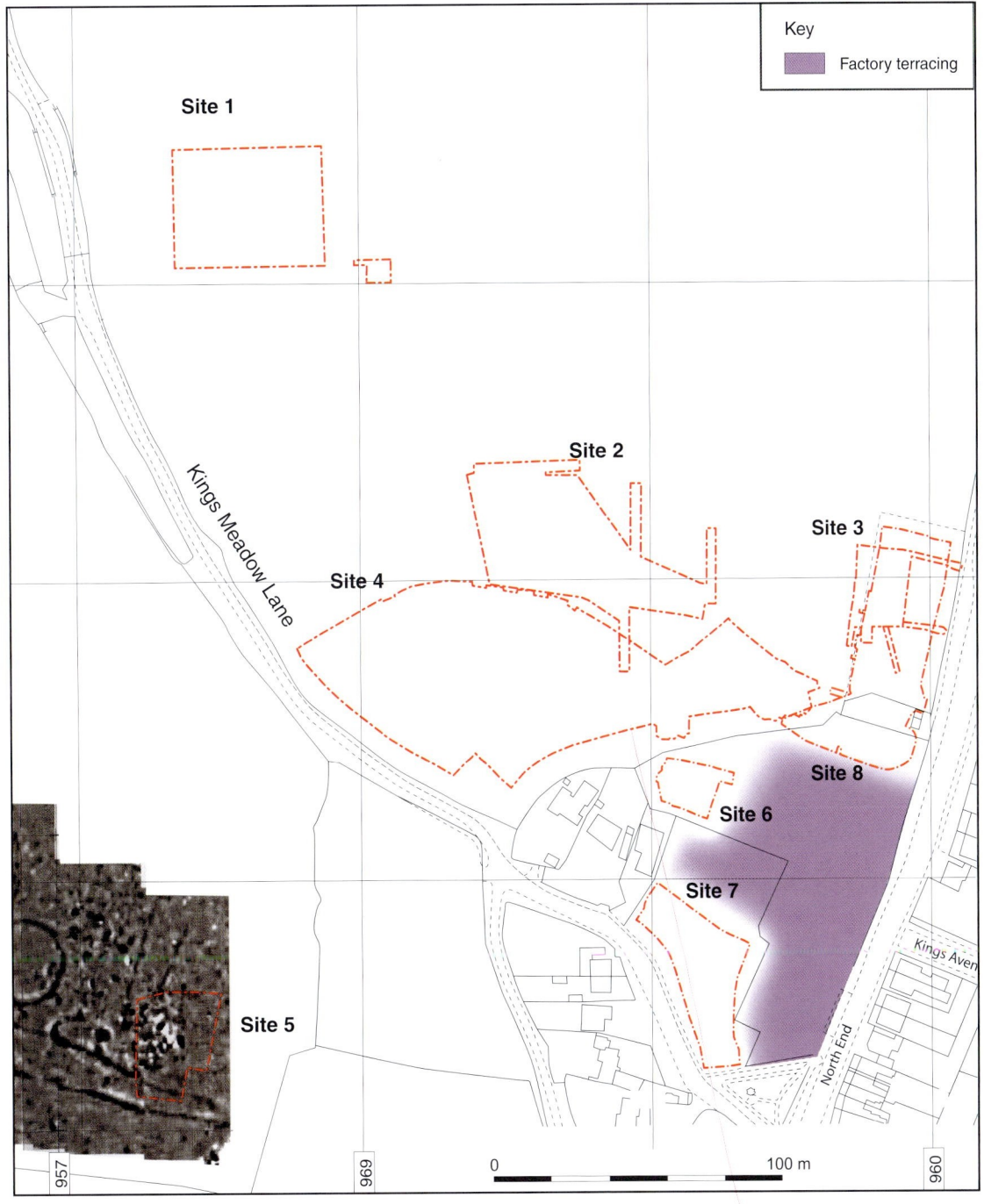

Fig. 2.2 (b)   The results of the archaeoeophysical survey and the location of sites

Plate 2.1   Aerial photograph showing cropmark of the Saxon enclosure
(Reproduced by permission of Northamptonshire Archives Service, © Northamptonshire County Council)

benefit of hindsight, following the excavation of the Roman town that took place in 2001-3, it is clear that the Romano-British settlement is much more significant than first thought. For details of the investigations into the Iron Age settlement and Roman settlement see Lawrence and Smith (forthcoming).

Foard argued that the combination of early and middle Saxon pottery scatters in conjunction with a large, and possibly unique oval enclosure presented a research opportunity of national importance. No closely-dated examples of this form of enclosure are known, although parallels were initially drawn with estate centres such as Yeavering, Northumberland (Hope-Taylor 1977) and Doon Hill near Dunbar (Welch 1992, 49, fig. 30), where two successive timber halls had been built within a polygonal fenced enclosure *c.* 70 m across.

In offering alternative prognoses for this kind of enclosure Foard (1994) noted that oval enclosures had been recorded at the core of a number of Northamptonshire villages/towns such as at Brackley and Daventry, although none had (at that point) been dated or investigated archaeologically. Blair has shown that in the 7th to 9th centuries a large enclosure of some sort invariably surrounded

a minster, separating it from the outside world. They could range from 150 m – 300 m across, and could comprise substantial, if not overtly defensive, earthworks, perhaps augmented by 'a great thorn hedge' as with Wilfred's Minster at Oundle (Blair 2005, 196).

Other possible roles for the enclosure were suggested – a hundredal meeting place, possibly containing some sort of (?pagan) shrine, or more prosaically, a market place. The concept and study of 'market' sites was at this stage still in its infancy, only later being categorised as 'productive' sites, the logic being that the notable amount of metalwork found at these sites (principally by use of metal detectors) implied a focus of exchange or trade (Ulmschneider 2000).

In broader terms, the initial impression from the cropmarks and the fieldwalking (Fig. 2.1) was that the 'enclosure' phase of settlement sat within a continuum of occupation from the 5th century through to the 11th century, and that settlement shifted slightly over time to the east. It is possible that it coalesced around a prototypical green in the angle between two roads Kings Meadow Lane and Windmill Banks. In the early 1990s the concept of the 'middle Saxon shift', first espoused by Arnold and Wardle 1981 (see also Hamerow 1991), was explored. It offered a possible alternative to settlement continuity as displayed at such sites as Yarnton (Hey 1994), West Heslerton (Powlesland 1990), and Catholme (Losco-Bradley and Kinsley 2002).

It was felt therefore that the Kings Meadow Lane project would provide an opportunity to examine the crucial mid to late Saxon period in the context of a developing and migrating early medieval village. Moreover, it was a settlement that, on the documentary evidence, may have derived much of its medieval importance from its elevated role in the Saxon era in the region.

The importance of the Kings Meadow Lane Saxon settlement is enhanced by its relationship to medieval Higham Ferrers itself, a rare example in Northamptonshire of a Saxon village which developed borough status (granted in 1251). It had been suggested that the name "The Bury" – used to denote an area in the north-eastern part of the town on a map of 1789 – is an echo of an original Saxon burgh, and may depict part of its outline (Beresford 1957, 166; Steane 1974, 155). Adjacent to 'The Bury', and some 250 metres from the development area, is the site of the earthwork castle built by William Peverel in 1086. Thus the Anglo-Saxon settlement in the development area may have represented the predecessor of both the burh and the castle and would be a rare example of such continuity. A more recent interpretation by Foard (Foard and Ballinger 2000, 13) has argued against this interpretation pointing out that the enclosed area of such a burgh would be unfeasibly large – larger even than late Saxon Northampton. He argues that the term 'bury' probably relates to enclosed demesne land.

An early and middle Saxon presence at Irthlingborough – directly across the River Nene from Higham Ferrers – was evident from discoveries relating to the re-occupation of an Iron Age hillfort at Crow Hill, just north of the medieval heart of the town. The likelihood that Irthlingborough was the centre of a royal estate is implied by the confirmatory signing of a charter there, by the Mercian King Offa, in 786 (S1184: Chichester, West Sussex R.O., Cap. 1/17/2 (s. viii2)). There is thus great potential in the idea that Higham Ferrers and Irthlingborough could be two elements of the same royal centre.

In a broader context Higham Ferrers is also a key site in regard to regional research aims concerning the origin and formation of villages during the Saxon period, whether evolving organically or established by a higher authority. In addition, the potential importance of the site at Higham Ferrers is enhanced by its proximity to the Raunds Area Project (Parry 2006). The Raunds Area Project investigated a large area of land centred on Raunds and bordering the river to the west and the Boulder clay uplands to the east. The Project surveyed a large area of the landscape, revealing the patterns

and development of early and middle Saxon settlement by means of an extensive investigation, using invasive and non-invasive techniques (see Figure 5.1)

EXCAVATION STRATEGY

Given the long and episodic nature of the project fieldwork – it encompassed ten different sites and a number of evaluation trenches from projects undertaken from the late 1980's to the early 21st century – it is no surprise that the original project strategy changed markedly over the years. Furthermore this was a period when the principle of developer-funded archaeology was introduced and took root. However, is important to bear in mind that, while the strategy was revised and updated inline with perceived archaeological need and available resources at points during the project's duration, the initial research framework was largely retained. Details of the particular circumstances of the investigation for each of the sites can be found in Chapter 3.

NOTES ON THE TERMINOLOGY USED IN THIS REPORT

In a report of this nature, covering a number of sites extending over a large area, and a long time-span, and relating in many of its aspects to the two principal roads passing through or by it, it is convenient for both the authors and reader if unchanging names are given to these features, and indeed, the town itself.

Higham Ferrers was, until the 13th century, simply 'Higham'. The 'Ferrers' part was added by Robert Ferrers, in the mid 12th century. For consistency, the term 'Higham Ferrers' will be used throughout this report.

Although Kings Meadow Lane did not acquire this name until at least the 14th century (and for a time early in the 20th century it was also known as Lovers Lane), it will be referred to as 'Kings Meadow Lane' or 'the Lane', whatever the period under discussion.

In the medieval period the area to the north of the town was a distinct enclave of agricultural tenants. It was called the 'Bond End' until the mid-16th century, when it became known as 'le North Ende'. Confusingly, the name 'North End' is now used for the south end of the road heading north out of the village; the northern part of the road is now known as Windmill Banks, after a windmill that stood on top of the hill in the 18th century. For a time in the 18th century it was also known as Turnpike Road. The road used to carry the A6 trunk route, but that role has now been taken by a by-pass to the east of the town. For the purposes of this report, this road will be termed Windmill Banks throughout the report.

A suitably brief but objective term is necessary when describing the Middle Saxon occupation. The authors feel that the term 'settlement' is misleading and simplistic, and the term 'estate centre' – while valid in the context of the detailed discussion – is ambiguous and arguably too presumptive as an identifying description. Therefore the term 'enclosure complex' will be used as a collective term for the ditches, buildings and other features associated with the Middle Saxon presence.

The archaeological/architectural term 'hall', denoting a rectangular framed building of the Saxon period is in some respects potentially misleading, ascribing – because of the modern connotations of the term – an elevated social status to the building that may not be deserved. However, as a generic architectural term, it has yet to be satisfactorily superseded, and so will be used in this report.

Chapter 3: The archaeological results

INTRODUCTION

Phasing

A single phasing framework has been applied to all of the Saxon, medieval and post-medieval archaeology within the ten relevant sites. The prehistoric and Roman settlement archaeology – predominantly located on Sites 9 and 10 – is excluded from this framework, although the Roman trackway features found in Sites 4 and 6 are shown on the general Phase plan (Fig. 3.1).

The phasing comprises six periods, broadly divided by interpreted changes in site use. Phase 2 is subdivided further into three, although the chronology of those subdivisions is very tentative:

Phase 1:
    Early Saxon: 5th century to late 6th century

Phase 2:
    Middle Saxon: late 7th century to early 9th century
    Phase 2a: *7th century to early 8th century*
    Phase 2b: *early 8th century to late 8th century*
    Phase 2c: *late 8th century to early 9th century*

Phase 3:
    Late Saxon: mid 9th century to 12th century

Phase 4:
    Early medieval: 12th century to 14th century

Phase 5:
    Late medieval: 14th century to mid 15th century

Phase 6:
    Post-medieval: mid 15th century to 20th century

The overall phasing chronology has been determined by a combination of artefactual and scientific dating, where possible in conjunction with stratigraphy and spatial relationships. Inevitably, there are parts of the whole project area where significant stratigraphy was non-existent and spatial relationships were too vague to be useful. This is particularly the case with the western part of Site 2, to the west of the enclosure ditch, and – on the same site – in the area to the south of the buildings. Apparent features were recorded on plan as soil marks but the lack of resources precluded excavation. Therefore it was felt that to place them in a phase would be a speculative step too far. It is almost certain that most of the unexcavated post holes to the south of the buildings are associated with them in some way, but not so clear as to allow confident phasing.

General site conditions

The definition of cut features varied considerably across the eastern sites (Sites 1-8), depending upon subsoil type, and weather conditions. In general, where small features – postholes or shallow gullies, were cut into ironstone or limestone bedrock, they were difficult to define; similarly, where features were cut through silty clay subsoil, their visibility was often extremely variable. As can be seen from Plate 3.6, even large features like the enclosure ditch were virtually invisible in plan in places – indeed, one of the early evaluation trenches was cut across the largest enclosure ditch and failed to identify it. The following summary outlines the circumstances of excavation on each site, in terms of prevailing weather conditions and available resources, and in the light of the overall research priorities (Fig. 3.1).

Sites 1 and 2

These were excavated in the winter of 1994-95. While features were reasonably well-defined after topsoil stripping – despite the low winter light levels – the financial constraints meant that time and material resources had to be targeted on the basis of what appeared to be important at the time. Inevitably, with hindsight, post-excavation has sometimes arrived at different priorities, although overall there is confidence in the interpretation of the archaeology on these sites. Context numbers in the ranges 1200-1400 (Site 1) and 2000-2999 (Site 2).

Site 3

This site was stripped and subject to a very rudimentary evaluation in the winter of 1994-95, and the conclusions drawn from that work were inevitably very provisional and tentative. As nearly all the site falls within the footprint of Site 8, fully excavated in 2003, the latter represents the definitive interpretation of the archaeology of this part of the site complex. Context numbers in the range 3000-3500.

Site 4

Excavated in 2001, this site was the largest single area excavation of the 8 sites. The weather conditions were generally good, although definition of the features after topsoil stripping was still very variable. Context numbers in the range 6000-7999 .

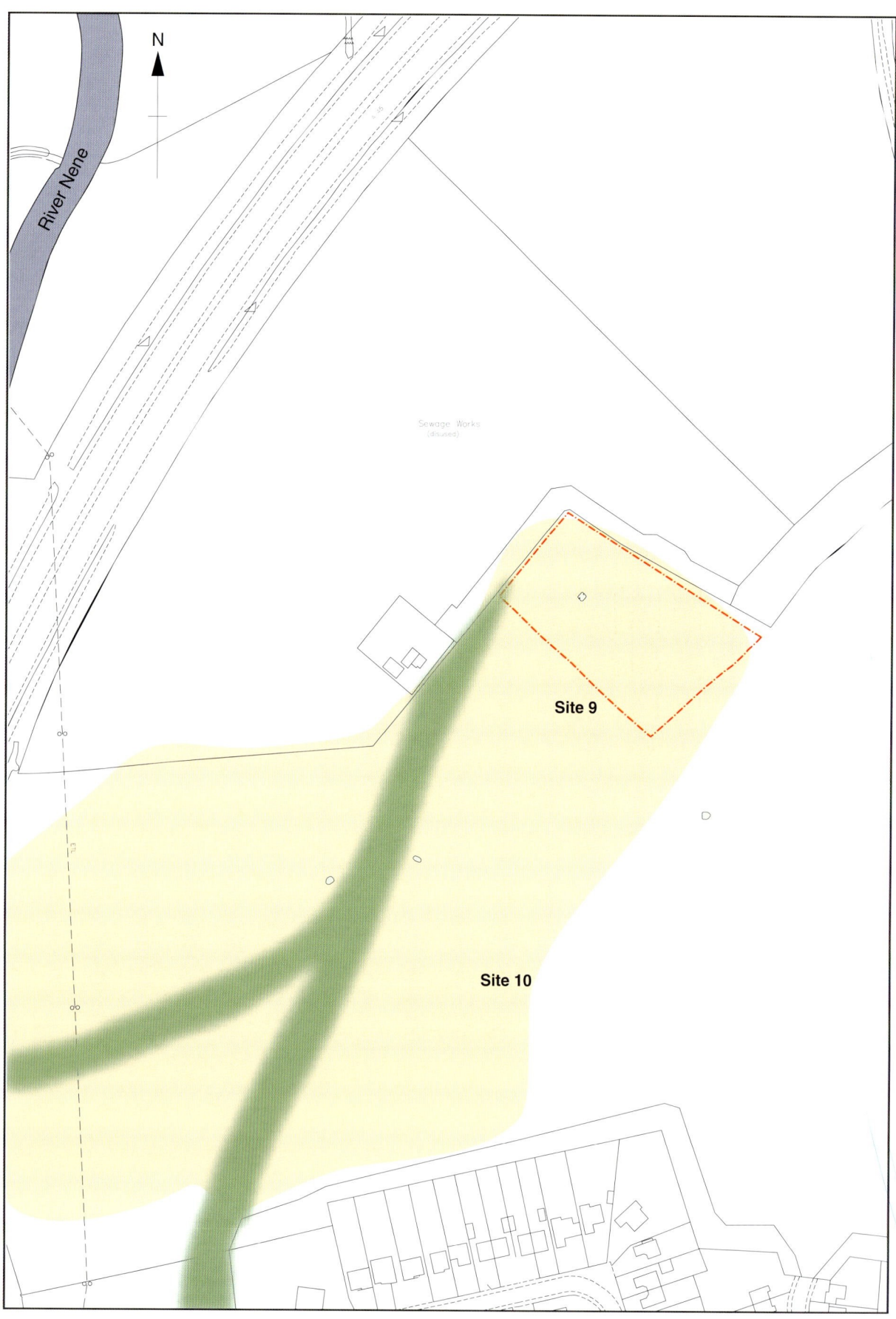

Fig. 3.1a   Phase plan: all Phases

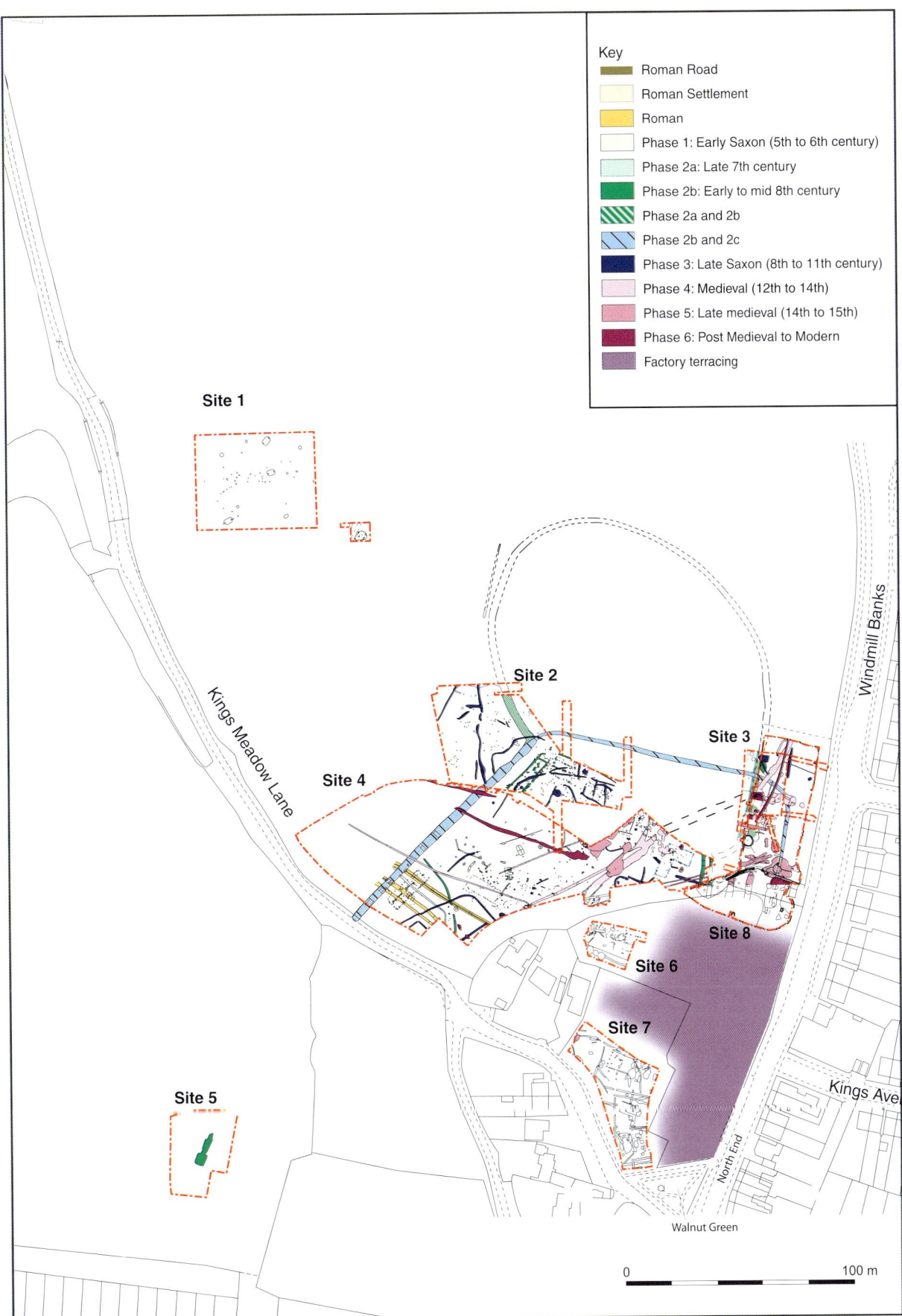

Key
- Roman Road
- Roman Settlement
- Roman
- Phase 1: Early Saxon (5th to 6th century)
- Phase 2a: Late 7th century
- Phase 2b: Early to mid 8th century
- Phase 2a and 2b
- Phase 2b and 2c
- Phase 3: Late Saxon (8th to 11th century)
- Phase 4: Medieval (12th to 14th)
- Phase 5: Late medieval (14th to 15th)
- Phase 6: Post Medieval to Modern
- Factory terracing

Site 1

Site 2

Site 3

Site 4

Site 8

Site 6

Site 7

Site 5

Kings Meadow Lane

Windmill Banks

Kings Ave

North End

Walnut Green

0   100 m

Fig. 3.1b   Phase plan: all Phases

Site 5

Excavated in 2000, this was the expansion of the evaluation trench that first revealed the malting oven. As part of the following year's fieldwork, further trenches were excavated to the north and west of the oven, in an attempt to identify associated features and/or structures. Context numbers in the range 4000-5999.

Sites 6 and 7

These two sites were excavated in 2002, after the demolition of the factory buildings and petrol station on the eastern side of the development area. The weather conditions were good at the time of excavation, but it became increasingly clear that there had been considerable petroleum and/or diesel contamination from the petrol station that had been sited immediately to the north-east of the Site 7 (the corner of one of the backfilled storage tank pits was exposed in the north-east corner of the site). The fumes from the contamination, and the consequent Health and Safety risk, meant that the southern part of Site 7 was abandoned after the initial planning and a small amount of investigative excavation.

While the amount of excavation achieved on Site 7 was less than intended, there is reasonable confidence in the interpretation of the archaeology. The broad layout of the land division from the medieval period onwards is understood, and, given the generally low priority accorded by the research aims to this period, the absence of recovered data is not thought to be critical.

Context numbers in the ranges 9000-9499 (Site 6) and 9500-9999 (Site 7).

Site 8

Excavated in 2003, this site reopened the area first investigated as Site 3 eight years previously (see above). Conditions were generally good, although it was clear that the area had suffered some damage from post-medieval ploughing. In addition the south end of the site had been completely destroyed by terracing for the construction of the 20th-century factory complex (see Fig. 3.1). Context numbers in the range 15000-15999.

Sites 9 and 10

Sites 9 and 10 are produced evidence for Romano-British occupation, which is reported on separately (Lawrence and Smith forthcoming). However a number of sunken feature buildings (SFBs) were found that are reported below (Phase 1). Context numbers in the ranges 8000-8499 (Site 9) and 10000-14999 (Site 10).

PHASE 1 (MID 5th CENTURY TO MID-LATE 6th CENTURY) (Figs 3.2-3.3)

The Phase 1 evidence tended to be concentrated in discrete areas across the sites.

Four SFBs were found on Site 1 together with two pits and a scatter of post holes (Fig. 3.3). Site 4 contained four SFBs and associated features including ditches and pits. To the east isolated SFBs were located on sites 9 and 10.

The features are described by site, but this should not be taken as the chronological order of their construction. The chronology of the settlement is discussed in Chapter 5. All of the SFBs were fully excavated, and environmental samples recovered from the pit fills of those on Sites 1 and 4.

Site 1 (Fig. 3.3)

Three sunken featured buildings were identified in the excavation area along with a single associated pit, and together with another SFB in the small trench to the south-east.

SFB 1253 (Fig. 3.4)

The feature was situated in the small extension area immediately east of Site 1, and was defined by a sub-rectangular pit (1258) oriented W-E, although it became evident on cleaning the area that the north-west corner of the feature had been entirely removed by a modern service trench. The presence of this service trench was not in doubt, but the exact edges of the cut were hard to define, with the result that the stratigraphy of the western end of the section excavated through the SFB was not clear. From the undamaged part of the SFB, the depth of the feature averaged 0.35 m, with a flat base and sharply sloping sides. Two fills were evident: the lower fill (1254) and upper fill (1255), both comprised silty loams with ironstone fragments and inclusions of burnt stone.

Structural postholes – There appeared to be two phases of postholes. At the eastern end were two postholes, 1259 and 1261, of similar dimensions and depths. Two postholes (1278 and 1280) were located near the centre of the SFB. Posthole 1280 cut posthole 1278.

Subsidiary postholes – Five postholes were identified at points around the perimeter of the SFB pit. With one exception (1327), they were noticeably narrower in diameter than the ridge postholes, although they were dug to approximately the same depth. One further small posthole (1284) was located within the north-east quadrant.

Pottery (Fig. 4.1, 7), along with animal bone and burnt stone were recovered from layer 1254. Layer 1255 produced pottery (Fig. 4.1, 6, 8, and 10), animal bone, burnt stone, (SF 57 – NI) and a Cu Alloy and Fe fitting (SF 58 – Fig.4.22, 51)

16

SFB 1256 (Fig. 3.5)

The feature was defined by a sub-rectangular flat-bottomed pit, oriented NE-SW, measuring approximately 2.6 m long x 2.5 m wide. The maximum depth of the pit was 0.09 m, and the edges of the pit were very shallow and poorly defined. The fill (1257) was a reddish brown silty loam with occasional charcoal flecking and small pieces of ironstone. The environmental sample from this material was the only one from all the Site 1 SFBs worthy of analysis (see Moffett, Chapter 4).

Structural postholes – At the southern end was one large posthole (1275), measuring 0.75 m wide x 0.50 m deep containing two apparent postpipes, one large (1274) and one small (1288), both surrounded by a mix of silty clay and ironstone fragments. At the northern end was an elongated double posthole

N

Sewage Works
(disused)

Site 9

Site 10

0   100 m

Fig. 3.2a Phase 1a Early Saxon

(1273) measuring 1.0 m long x 0.50 m deep, which was situated partly within the area of the pit itself. The posthole contained at least two, and possibly three postpipes. Immediately to the north and beyond the pit edge was another posthole (1295), measuring 0.32 m wide x 0.42 m deep. The very shallow depth of the pit meant that there was no clear stratigraphic relationship between the pit fill and the postholes. Finds including pottery (Fig. 4.1.1), animal bone, and a fragment of Copper Alloy (SF88 – not illustrated) were recovered from the pit fill.

Another substantial posthole (1354) was situated approximately 2.3 m north-east of posthole 1295, along the axis of the SFB. Its possible structural association with the SFB is discussed in Chapter 5.

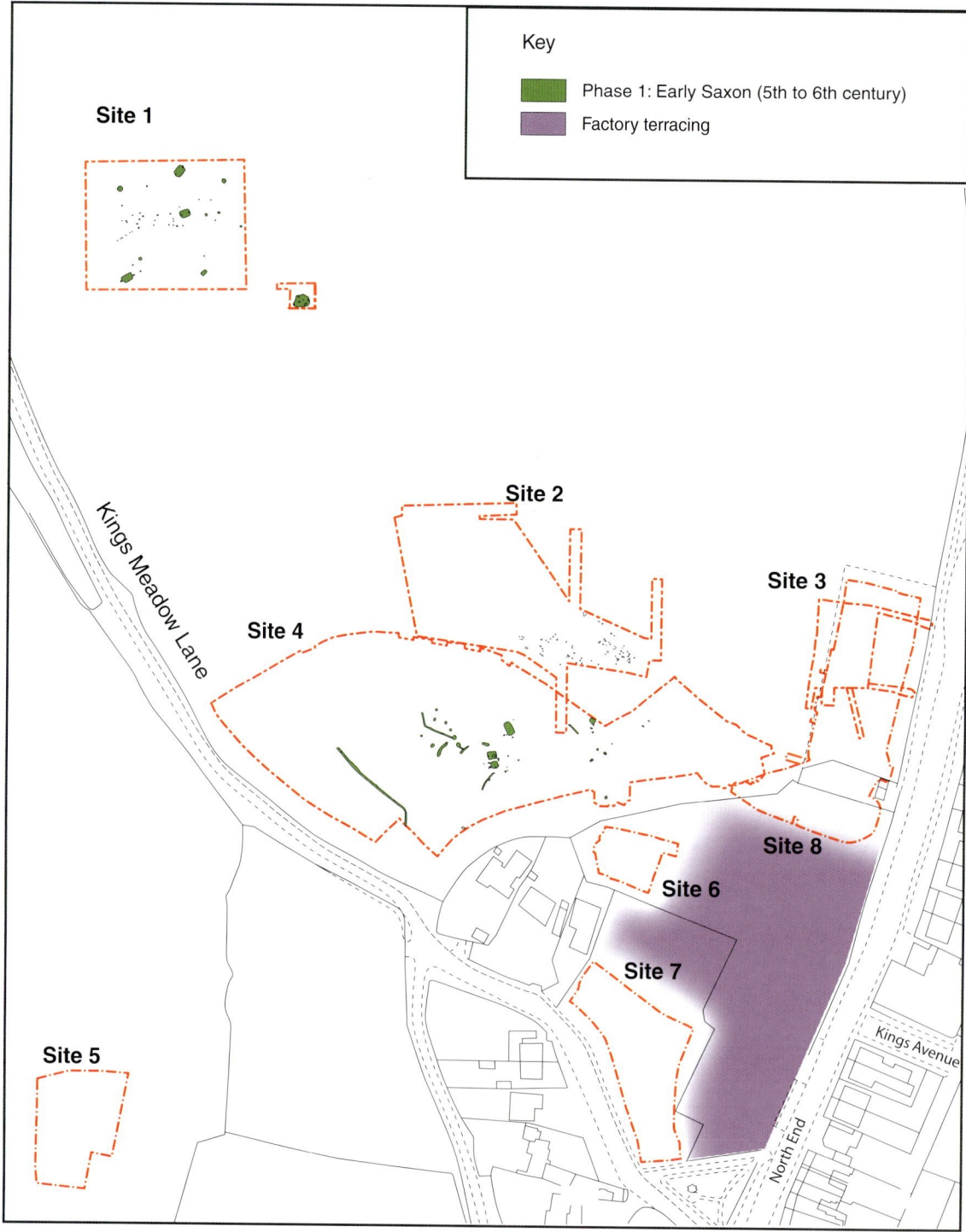

Fig. 3.2b   Phase 1a Early Saxon

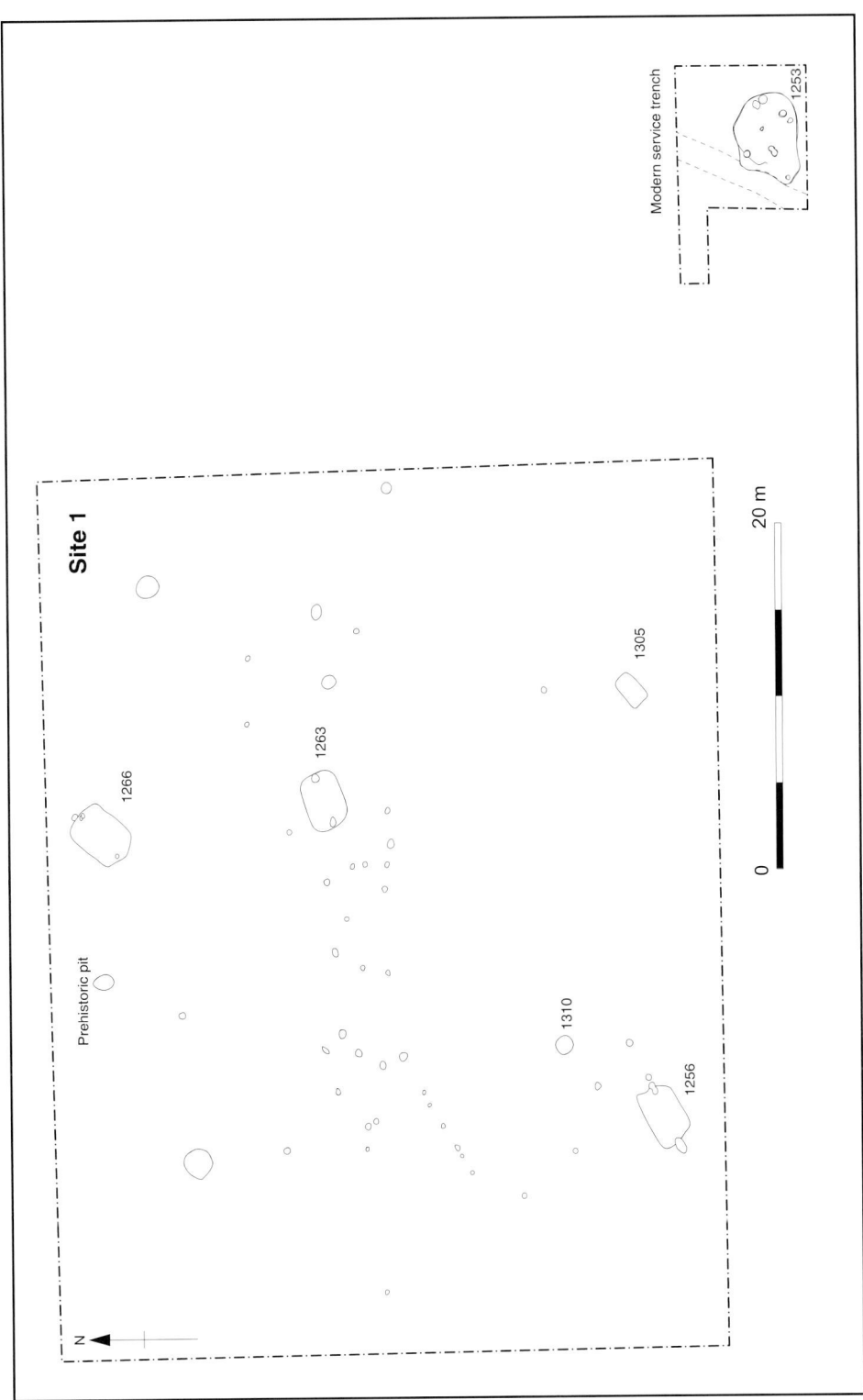

Fig. 3.3 General plan of features Site 1

SFB 1263 (Fig. 3.6, Pl. 3.1)

The feature was defined by a sub-rectangular pit (1264), oriented west-east and measuring 3.5 m long x 2.3 m wide, with a consistent depth of 0.50 m to a flat base. The SFB fill was a silty clay (1268) – with charcoal flecking (1271) in its upper part-mixed with ironstone rubble, which may be evidence of deliberate backfilling. A clay silt layer (1265) overlay fill 1268. A small quantity of animal bone and early Saxon pottery was recovered from all three fills. Layer 1268 produced part of a knife blade (SF 61 – NI) and a Cu Alloy edge binding (SF74 – Fig. 4.17, 50). Another fragment possibly of the same object was recovered from fill 1265 (SF 73 – Fig. 4.17, 49).

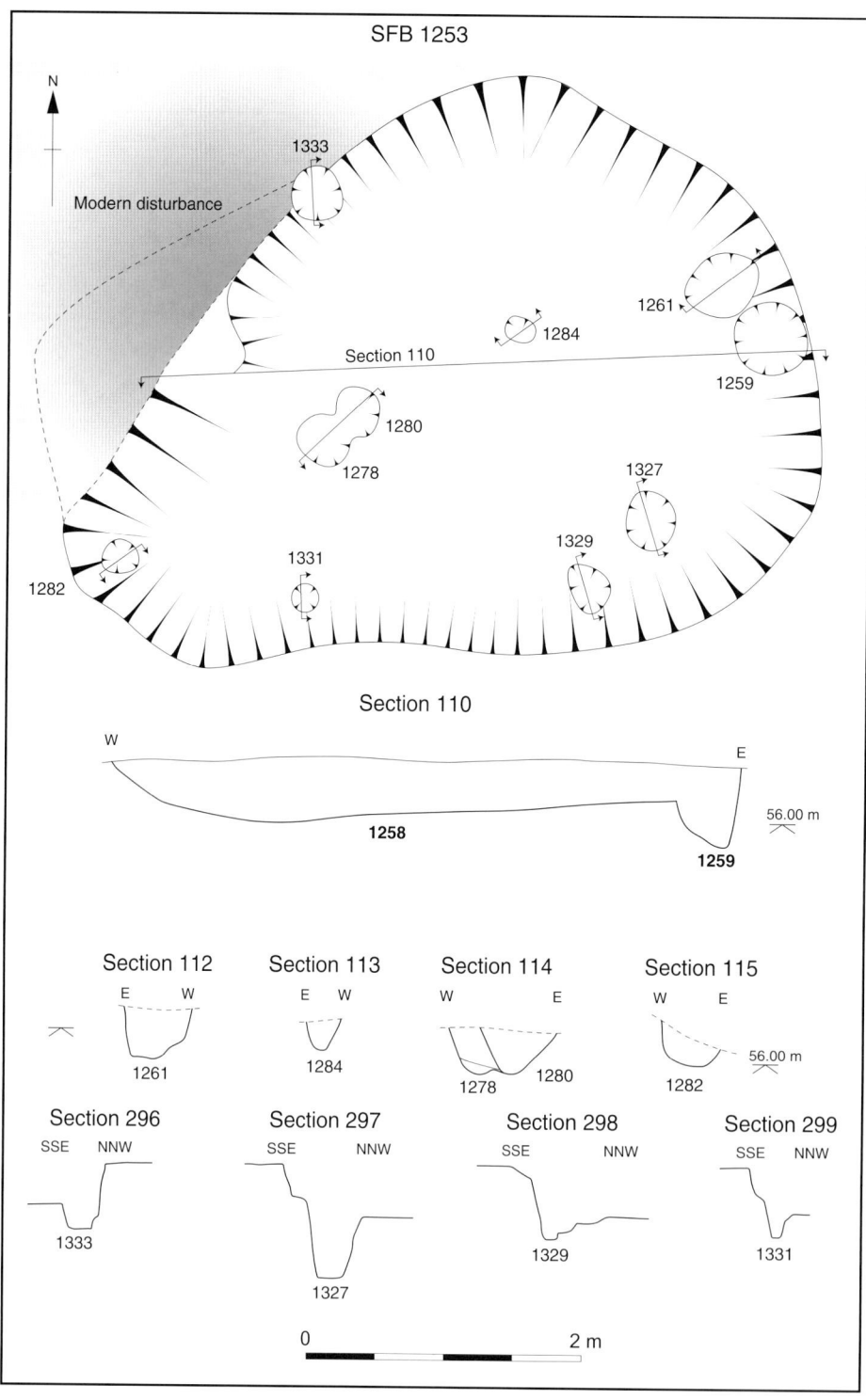

Fig. 3.4   Site 1 SFB 1253

Structural postholes – Two postholes (1276 and 1322) were identified at the west and east ends respectively. Each posthole was cut into the steeply sloping side of the pit and measured 0.35 m wide x 0.90 m deep. Ironstone posthole packing was noted in the western hole.

SFB 1266 (Fig. 3.7)

The feature was defined by a sub-rectangular pit (1270) oriented NE-SW and measuring approximately 3.3 m long x 2.8 m wide. The pit was flat-bottomed, with a maximum depth of 0.32 m. Two fills were recorded in the pit, a 0.08 m deep layer of brownish yellow clay (1297) with occasional charcoal flecks, which the excavator considered to be possibly the disturbed upper surface of the natural subsoil. This was overlaid by layer 1269, a 0.30 m deep layer of grey brown silty clay, very similar to the fills of the three postholes associated with the structure.

Structural postholes – Within the pit, two postholes were identified, cut through the pit's lower fill. The western posthole (1293) was 0.62 m deep x 0.25 m wide. The eastern posthole was 0.24 m wide x 0.64 m deep. A further posthole (1301) was situated just beyond the eastern edge

of the pit, measuring 0.30 m deep x 0.38 m wide.

Finds – From layer 1269 a small quantity of pottery (see Fig. 4.1, 9, 12, and 14) and animal bone was recovered, along with an iron nail (SF64 – NI). The fill (1300) of posthole 1301 also produced pottery (Fig. 4.1, 5, 13, and 17)

Other features in Site 1 (Fig.3.3)

Pit 1305 – This was situated in the south-eastern corner of Site 1. It was sub-rectangular in plan, oriented NE-SW, and measured approximately 2.3 m long x 1.5 m wide. The flat base was overlain by three fills. 1308 was a 0.14 m deep layer of mixed ash and silt, with bone and charcoal fragments. This was overlain by a 0.10 m deep layer of silty clay and ironstone fragments, with some burnt stone inclusions (1325). Sealing 1325 was the 0.20 m deep upper fill of slightly stony silty loam (1304).The upper fill 1304 produced a possible Fe pin fragment (SF 78 – NI).

Pit 1310 – The feature was a shallow dish-shaped pit containing a fill (1309) of silty clay with a high proportion of burnt stone and charcoal, and unidentifiable tree or shrub buds. A small assemblage of pottery and animal bone was also recovered from

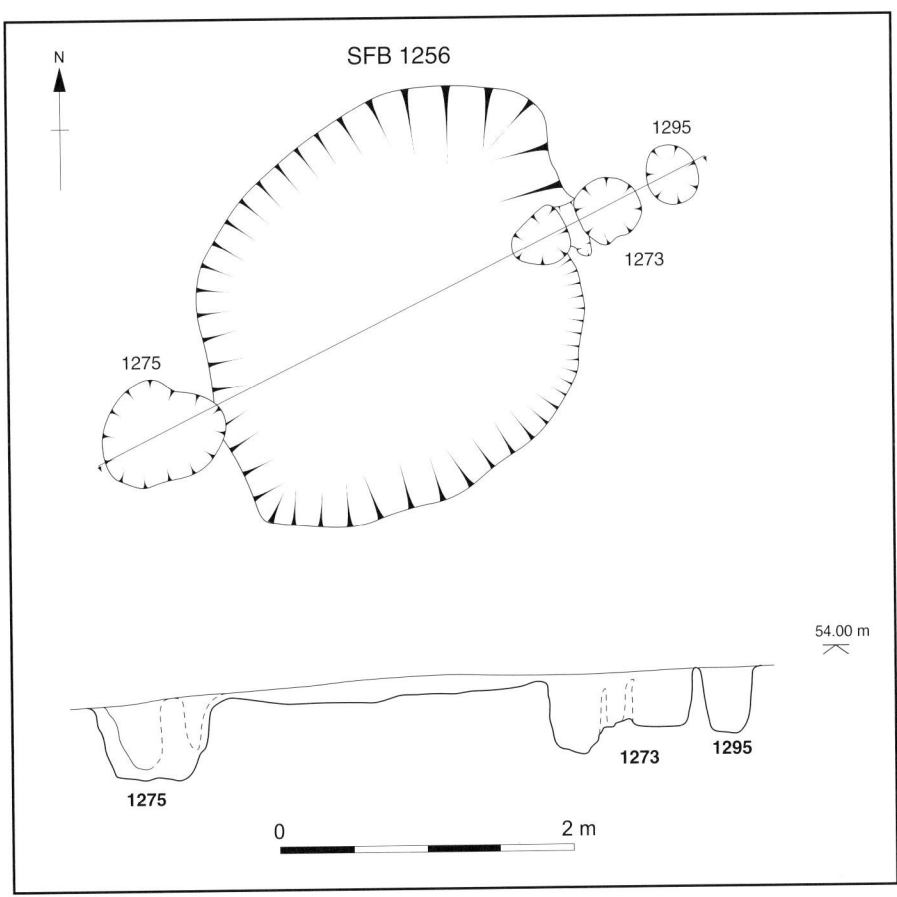

Fig. 3.5   Site 1 SFB 1256

21

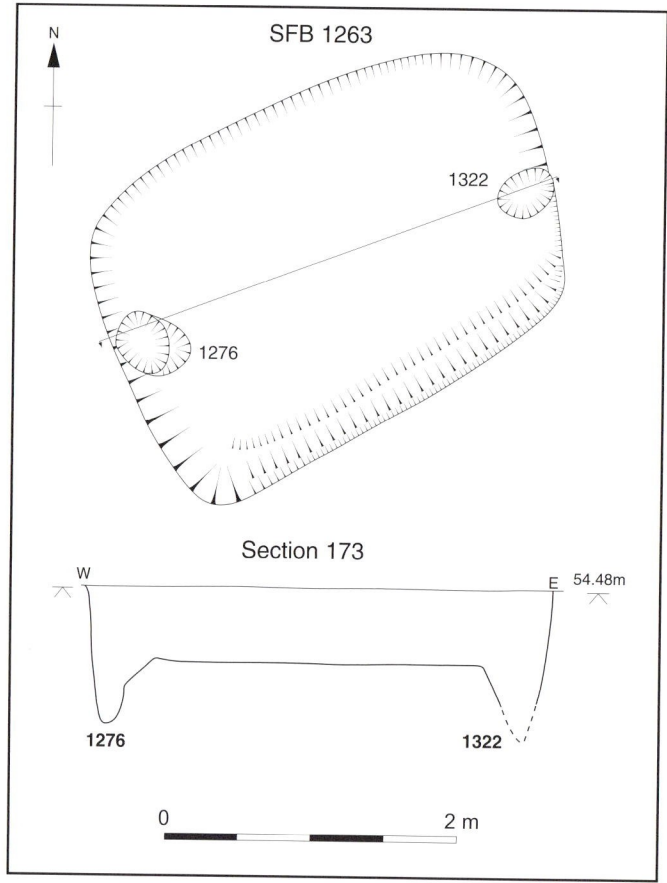

Fig. 3.6   Site 1 SFB 1263

Plate 3.1   SFB 1263 Site 1

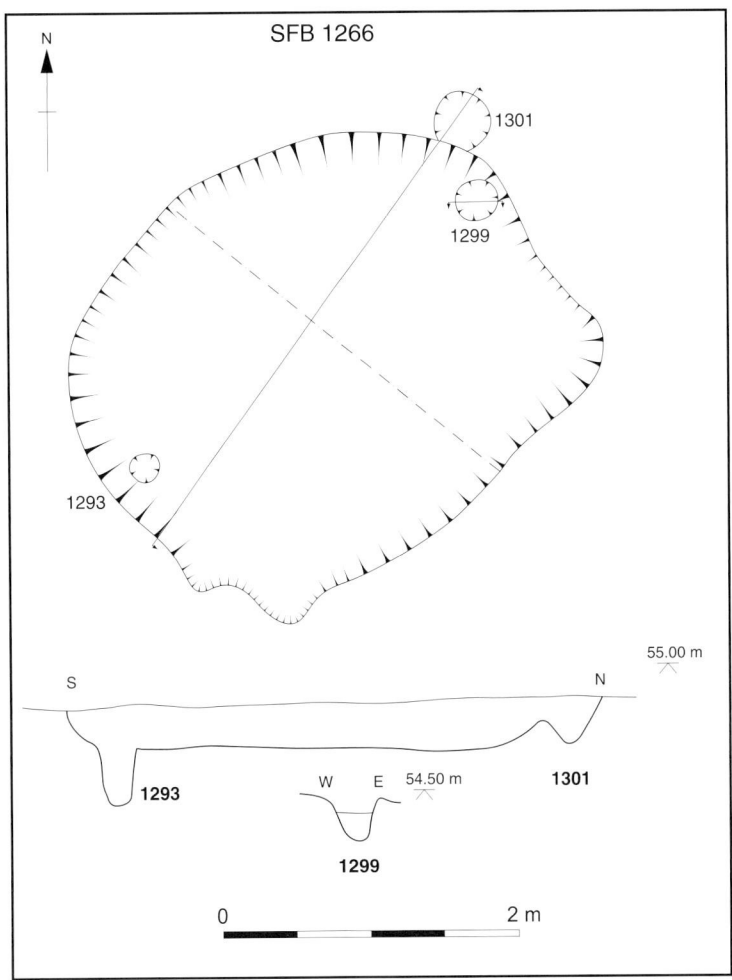

Fig. 3.7   Site 1 SFB 1266

the fill. The pit cut a substantial isolated posthole (1315).

A scatter of discrete features – probably postholes – was identified within the area of Site 1. Only those already cited were investigated; it is assumed that at least some of the rest are associated with the SFBs.

Site 4 (Fig. 3. 2)

Three sunken featured buildings (SFB's) were revealed in the central area of the site, along with a number of associated ditches, pits and postholes.

SFB 6057 (Fig. 3.8, Pl.3.2)

This feature was defined by a sub-rectangular flat-bottomed pit with near vertical sides. It was oriented W-E, measuring approximately 2.9 m long by 2.4 m wide. The maximum depth of the pit was 0.43 m and the fill consisted of dark grey brown sandy loam with charcoal inclusions (6058). The upper fill of the pit was cut by Phase 4 gully 7311. An environmental sample from the undisturbed fill 6058 produced barley and flax seeds.

Structural postholes – A single posthole was revealed at either end of the pit. In the centre was a group of flat limestone pieces, forming a possible postpad. Two more stones were placed on top of the main pad, possibly representing a later adjustment. There were several other similar stones removed from the pit fill in the NW corner of the SFB, which may also represent disturbed elements of the postpad. Recovered finds included 88 sherds of early/mid Saxon pottery (Fig. 4.1, 3, 4, and 15), a bone comb (SF 298 – Fig. 4.19, 36), two Fe nails (SF 351 and 352 – NI), along with 62 g of slag, animal bone and burnt stone.

SFB 6356 (Fig. 3.9, Pl. 3.2)

The feature was defined by a sub-rectangular flat bottomed pit (6356), situated immediately south of, and adjacent to SFB 6057. It was oriented WSW-ENE, measuring approximately 2.3 m long and 2.18 m wide. The maximum depth of the pit was 0.12 m. The fill consisted of dark brownish/grey silty loam (6357). An environmental sample produced a few grains of tetraploid wheat, not normally seen in this country until the medieval period. Given the very shallow depth of the SFB pit in this instance, as Moffett says (Chapter 4), there is a strong likelihood of intrusive later material. A total of 35 sherds of pottery, along with a bone comb (SF 324 – Fig. 4.19, 41), a bone pin (SF 325 -Fig. 4.16, 8), and a small quantity of slag and animal bone, were recovered from the SFB pit.

Structural postholes – A number of postholes, possibly denoting at least one episode of rebuilding, were identified in the pit or close to it.

A pair of postholes (6347, 6358) was excavated at the eastern end of the pit, straddling the pit edge. At the edge of the south west quadrant of the pit four postholes are clustered together. A degree of symmetry is evident in the posthole arrangement at the west end of the SFB pit. Two pairs of intercutting postholes (6419/6421, and 6526/6528) extend from the north-west and south-west corners respectively. Beyond these pairs, two more postholes (6524 and 6364) one on either side were identified. Just to the east of 6524 another posthole 6502 was revealed.

To the east and between SFBs 6057 and 6353 was a series of four intercutting postholes (6564, 6566, 6568 and 6570). Their alignment in relation to the

SFBs, and the presence of a sherd of 5th-century pottery in one of the posthole fills suggest that they are related to the SFBs.

Associated features (Fig. 3.35)

To the south and west of the two SFBs 6057 and 6356 were features which appeared to be contemporary.

Group 7326 – The main group of features comprised 5 pits – roughly equally spaced and extending to the north-west from close to the pair of SFBs 6057 and 6356. Each pit contained a high proportion of charcoal flecks in their fills, although they produced very little datable material apart from 7 sherds (41g) of early to mid Saxon pottery found in fill 6344 of pit 6343. Two of the large pits (6343 and 6168) situated close together are both at the termination of two shallow gullies (6255 and 6352) and may form part of an entrance. Neither gully produced any contemporary dating material. Gully 6352 links to another gully 6522, which also contained a noticeable percentage of charcoal in its fill. The charcoal fill (6344) of pit 6343 was sampled, revealing that the charcoal was exclusively oak (see Thompson and Francis, Chapter 4)

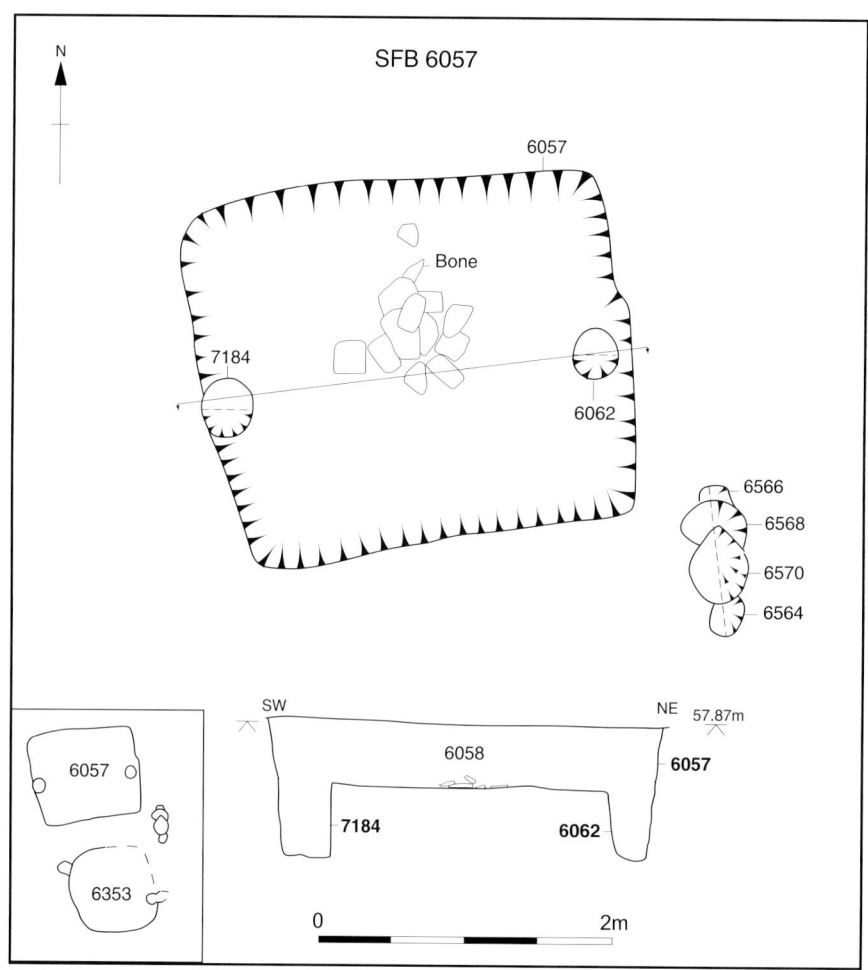

Fig. 3.8   Site 4 SFB 6057

Plate 3.2   SFBs 6057 & 6356 Site 4

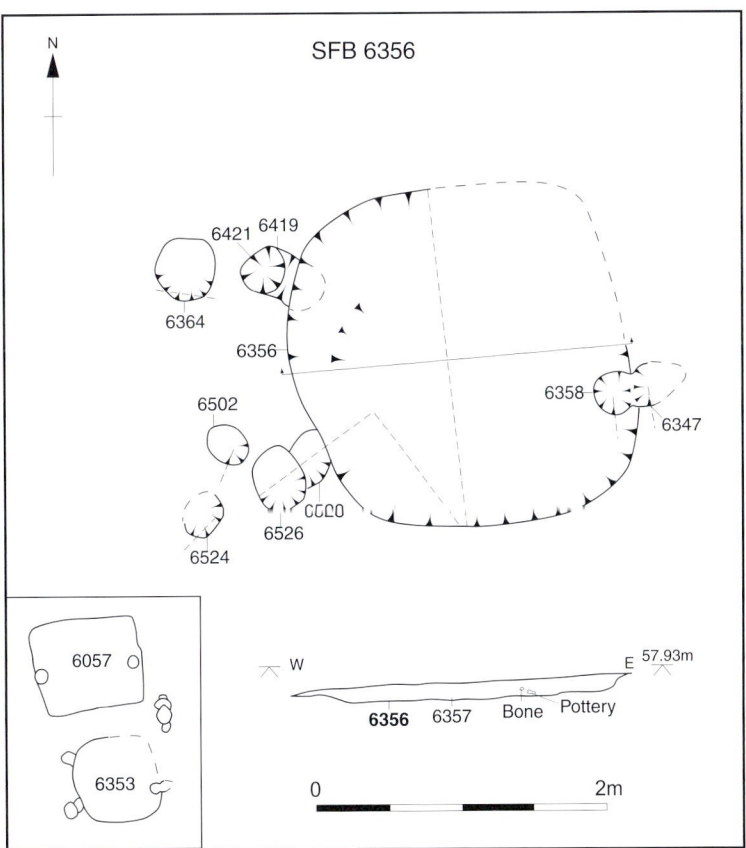

Fig. 3.9   Site 4 SFB 6356

Ditch 7328 – A short curving gully (7328) is considered to belong to this group of features on the basis of its spatial relationship, not its stratigraphy.

Ditch 7306 – Ditch 7306 is located in the south west end of Site 4, emerging from the southern limit of the site on a north south alignment for approximately 5 m before it turns north-west on a NW-SE alignment for 26 m where is it cut by the Phase 2b enclosure ditch. The ditch appeared to run beyond the enclosure ditch to the north-west, but was indiscernible after a few metres. On stratigraphic grounds it must date to Phase 2a or earlier, and its fill was distinct from that of the Roman features in the vicinity. No other Phase 2a features exist in the area, and therefore, it is tentatively assigned to Phase 1.

SFB 6345 (Fig.3.10)

The feature was defined by a sub-rectangular flat-bottomed pit oriented NW-SE, and situated approximately 10 m north of the SFB pair 6057 and 6356. The pit displayed sloping sides, and measured approximately 4.5 m long by 2.35 m wide, with a maximum depth of 0.22 m. The pit fill (6346) was a mid-orange/brown silty loam with occasional charcoal flecking, which produced a few mixed cereal grains from an environmental sample.

Structural postholes – No postholes were identified in the pit, although in close proximity to the pit were four very shallow post holes 6369, 6343, 6367 and 6371 that may relate to the structure, containing mid greyish brown silty clay fills. No datable finds were recovered from these features. A total of 80 sherds of pottery were recovered from the SFB pit fill (6346), along with a bone comb (SF 326 – Fig. 4.19, 37), and fragments of animal bone.

SFB 6630 (Fig. 3.11)

Partly exposed under the northern baulk of Site 4 (and originally exposed – but not recognised – in an evaluation trench), was a probable SFB (6630) with one internal posthole (6641) and a cluster of five others to the south. The recovered early/middle Saxon pottery from the pit fill (6631) and the stratigraphy suggests the feature is of a Phase 1 date, and its depth and shape is consistent with the form of an SFB.

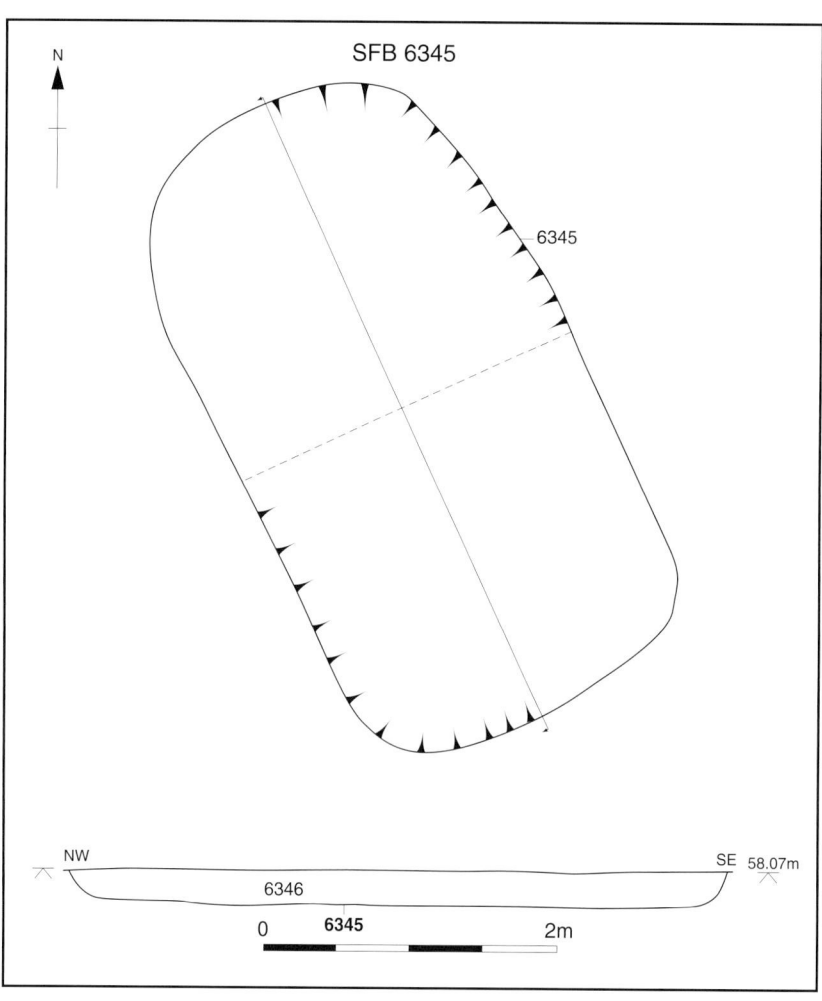

Fig. 3.10   Site 4 SFB 6345

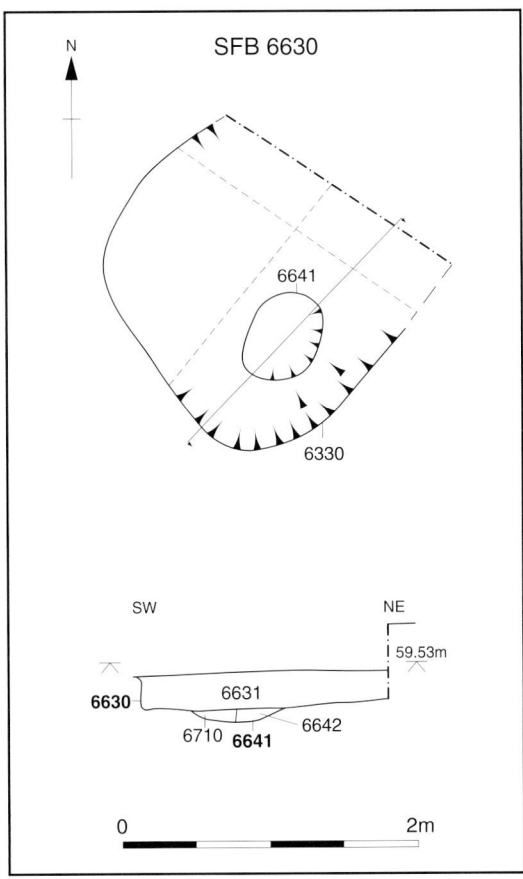

Fig. 3.11   Site 4 SFB 6630

A scatter of small features was identified to the south of SFB 6630, including a truncated gully (7182), and pits 7243 and 7038. Pit 7243 produced sherds of early/mid Saxon pottery, and the fill (7037) of pit 7038 yielded a few mixed cereal grains. It is reasonable to suggest that these features could be associated with SFB 6630.

Sites 9 and 10 (Fig. 3.2)

A scatter of dated Phase 1 features, including three definite and one probable SFBs and a single pit, were identified during the evaluations and excavations that took place in areas of the Roman settlement.

While the presence of complex Roman stratigraphy in some instance made the definition of the Saxon features problematic, there is a high degree of confidence that no significant Anglo-Saxon features have been mistakenly phased as Roman, or vice versa.

SFB 8222 (Site 9) (Fig. 3.12)

A single SFB (8222) and a possibly associated pit were identified within the area of Roman features interpreted as a temple complex. The SFB comprised a subrectangular pit 8222, flat-bottomed and with moderately sloping sides, oriented SW-NE and measuring 3.12 m long x 2.87 m wide x 0.28 m deep. Two opposing quadrants were excavated, revealing patches of compacted natural on the pit base, and two gable postholes – 8262 at the southwest end and 8251 at the north-east end.

The lower fill (8223) of the SFB pit was a brownish grey silty clay containing stone pieces and charcoal flecks. It sealed the fills of both postholes. A significant quantity of 6th-century pottery was recovered from both the lower fill and the upper fill (8256) of the SFB pit (Fig. 4.1, 18, 19, 20). Quantities of similar pottery were found in isolated sections dug into nearby Roman ditches 8292 and 8294. In both cases these are interpreted as shallow pits or depressions in the upper fills of the Roman ditches, but not recognised as such during excavation.

Structural postholes – posthole 8262 measured 0.36 m in diameter by 0.42 m deep, with near vertical sides and a concave base, and posthole 8251 measured 0.24 m in diameter x 0.42 m long x 0.42 m deep. Both postholes contained brownish grey silty clay fills (8263 and 8252 respectively) and remains of limestone packing against the hole edges.

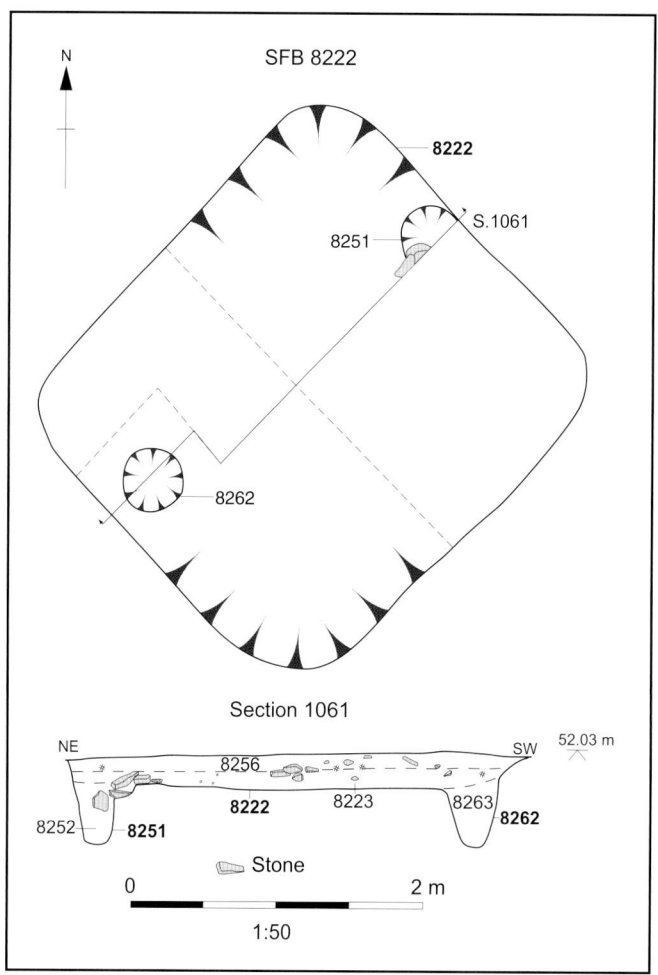

Fig. 3.12   Site 9 SFB 8222

SFB 10212 (Site 10) (Fig. 3.13)

SFB 10212 was revealed in an evaluation trench situated on the NE-facing slope of the Kings Meadow Lane dry valley extending to the east of the Roman settlement. The poorly defined subrectangular pit (10206) of the SFB was oriented W-E and measured approximately 3.25 m long x 2.5 m wide x 0.30 m deep. A quantity of 6th-century pottery was recovered from the fill of the SFB pit.

Structural postholes – Two gable postholes were revealed, 10224 to the west, and 10209 to the east. The former measured approximately 0.35 m wide x 0.44 m deep; the latter 0.30 m wide and 0.40 m deep. The postpipe fill (10208) of posthole 10209 was visible in the surface of the SFB pit fill (10205), suggesting that the post was in place during the infilling of the pit. By contrast, the fill of posthole 10224 was only visible after the pit fill had been removed. Both postholes contained a similar fill, a brownish grey sandy silt, with some small ironstone rubble inclusions.

SFB 12740 (Site 10) (Fig. 3.14)

SFB 12740 consisted of an ill-defined sub-rectangular, or oval, pit (12731), situated on the east side of the Roman road, set within a small courtyard and alongside the remains of a stone building, both of which dated to the 3rd century. The SFB pit was oriented W-E and measured approximately 3.97 m long x 2.14 m wide x up to 0.22 m deep. It was excavated in quadrants producing a single dark grey brown sandy silt fill with occasional limestone/ironstone inclusions. A large quantity of 6th-century pottery was recovered from the fill.

Structural postholes – no structural postholes were found within or in close proximity to the SFB pit. While this fact, along with the generally poor definition of the feature, undoubtedly raises some doubts over its identification as an SFB, its overall (if ill-defined) proportions and the presence of a large assemblage of Early/Middle Saxon pottery lends at least some confidence to the identification.

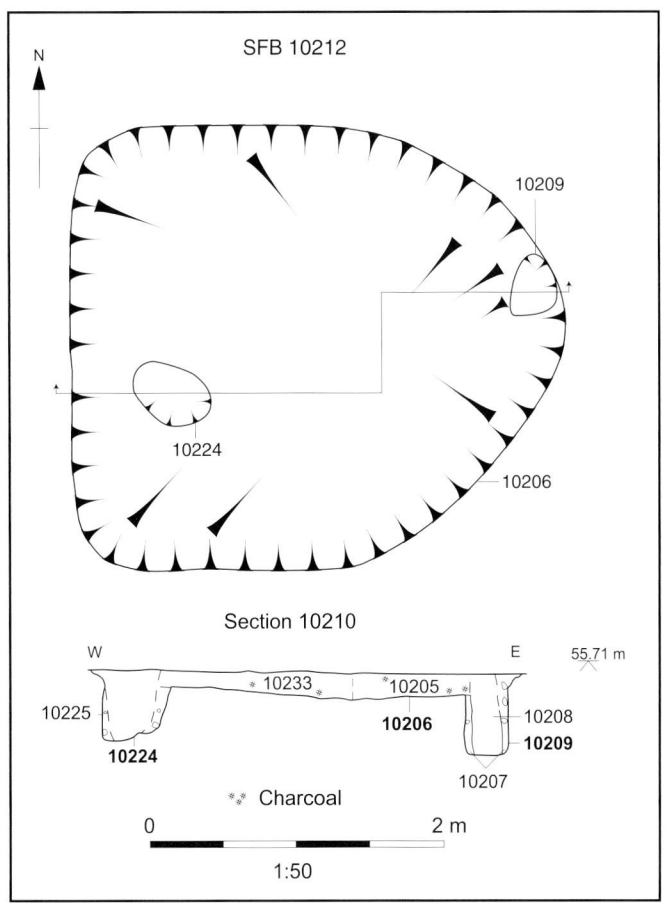

Fig. 3.13   Site 10 SFB 10212

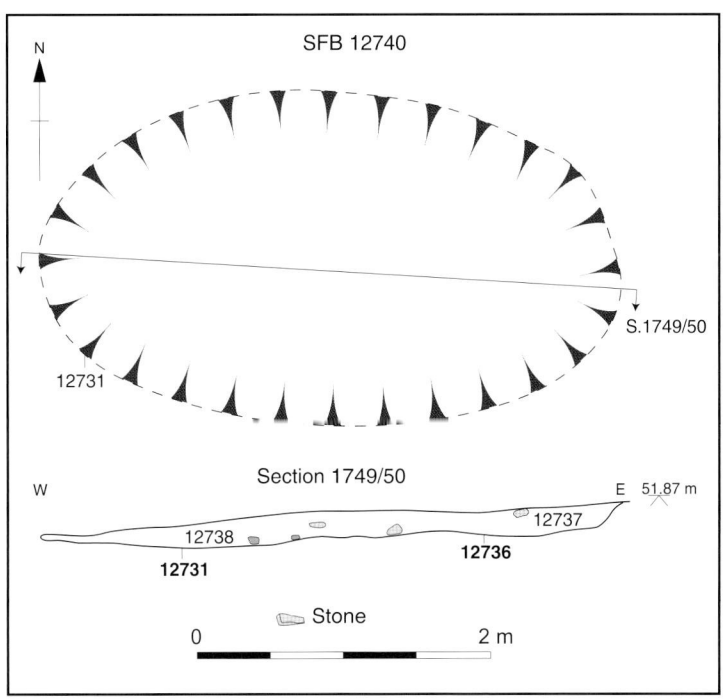

Fig. 3.14   Site 10 SFB 12740

SFB 12800 (Site 10) (Fig.3.15)

SFB 12800 was situated on the western side of the Roman road, within the Roman 'shrine area'. It consisted of a sub-rectangular flat-bottomed pit (12795) oriented NW-SE and measuring 3.84 m long x 3.04 m wide x up to 0.32 m deep.

Structural postholes – a single posthole (12797) was revealed in the south-east end of the pit, set in by 0.70 m from. It measured 0.38 m in diameter x 0.39 m deep. Against the north-west end of the SFB pit was a double posthole (12891/12893). Each part measured 0.28 m in diameter x 0.40 m deep. No postpipe was visible in the fill of the SFB pit, so it is considered that the posts were removed before the pit was infilled.

   The fills of the postholes and SFB pit were similar, a mid-brown sandy silt with occasional ironstone inclusions. Significant quantities of 6th-century pottery were recovered from the pit fill and the fill (12894) of one of the north-eastern postholes (12893).

Other Phase 1 features on Site 10 (Fig. 3.2)

Two pits excavated on Site 10 were assigned to Phase 1.

Pit 10521, a shallow feature measuring 1.20 m long x 0.62 m wide x 0.12 m deep was identified close to the eastern side of the Roman road, approximately midway between SFB 12800 and SFB 8222. Its fill (10522) produced a single sherd of Early/Middle Saxon pottery.

Pit 10221 was shallow and flat-bottomed and measuring 1.80 m x 1.10 m x 0.30 m deep. It was found a short distance south of SFB 10210. The fill of the pit (10220) contained a high proportion of burnt stone and charcoal, and the underlying natural ironstone showed signs of burning in situ. The fill produced no artefactual dating evidence, but, given the absence of Roman features in the vicinity, it would be reasonable to cautiously suggest that this feature is contemporary with nearby SFB 10210.

PHASE 2 (EARLY 8th CENTURY TO EARLY 9th CENTURY)

The main features of this Phase are the horseshoe-shaped enclosure and associated buildings. As already noted, Phase 2 can be divided into three sub-phases. The start and end dates for Phase 2 are based upon the ceramic evidence and radiocarbon dating which suggests a start date of no earlier than

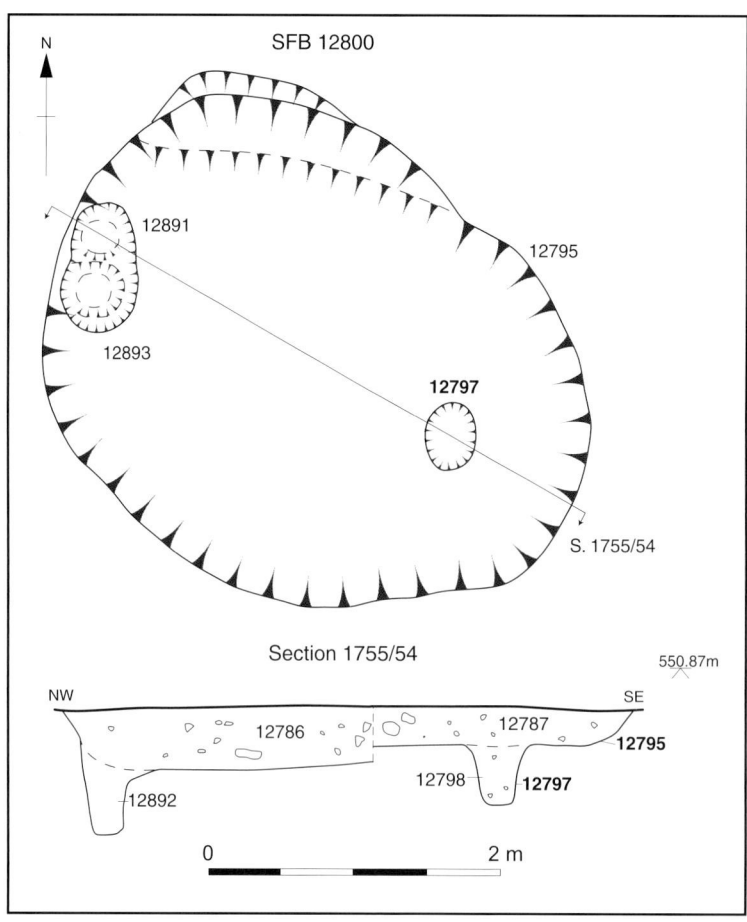

Fig. 3.15   Site 10 SFB 12800

the second half of the 7th-century, but more probably the early 8th century, and an end date of the early 9th century.

The three sub-phases reflect the episodic development of the features comprising Phase 2. They relate to structural changes and were identified stratigraphically. The chronology of the sub-phases is imprecise and more open to variation than that of the overall Phase.

Phase 2a (early to mid 8th century) (Fig. 3.16)

This sub-phase comprises the horseshoe-shaped enclosure (2658 – Site 2 = 15370 – Site 8) in its earliest form, with a rectangular timber building 2664, which is sited in the open mouth of the enclosure. This sub-phase is tentatively dated early to mid 8th century.

Enclosure ditch (Sites 2 and 8) (Figs 3.17-3.18)

The horseshoe-shaped enclosure (2658 – Site 2 = 15370 – Site 8), which was first identified by aerial photography, enclosed an area of around 0.8 ha (2.2 acres). In the initial evaluation, the area was tested by 18 trenches (Fig. 3.17). Eight trenches were sited over the horseshoe ditch, and ten trenches within the enclosed space. None of the latter revealed any contemporary features, and – except for the far south western corner – no contemporary artefacts. The ditch itself showed slight alteration in depth, although this is likely to be due to later variable truncation by ridge-and-furrow cultivation. The original ditch profile, where the recut had not obscured it, tended towards a shallow 'V' shape, and in most sections two or three fills were discerned – of silty clay with varying proportions of

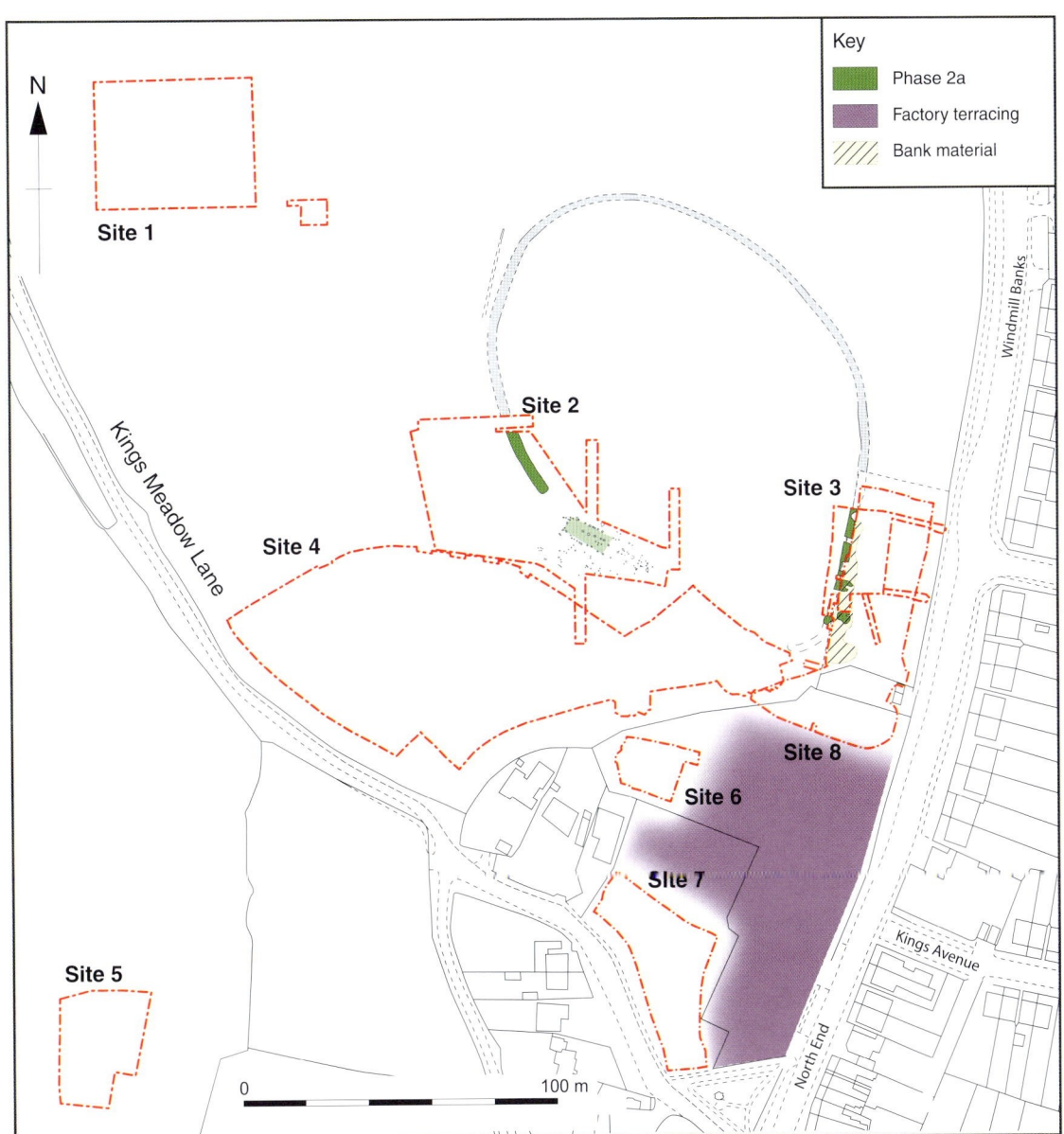

Fig. 3.16   Phase 2a Middle Saxon enclosure

ironstone fragments, depending on the subsoil character in the vicinity.

Only on the eastern side of the enclosure – within the area of Site 8 – was there any evidence of a bank associated with the enclosure ditch. This was characterised as a thin layer of redeposited natural subsoil (15423) up to 0.10 m deep, laying against the outside edge of the ditch, and forming the top fill (Fig. 3.18, Section 2088). A copper alloy dress fitting (SF 4038 – Fig. 4.22, 59) was recovered from this possible bank residue. The object is probably later in date and intrusive. Due to the constraints of the site boundary, only three small sections were excavated into the ditch, and no other finds were recovered.

The western terminus of the horseshoe enclosure was revealed in Site 2. The eastern terminus is inferred to lie within in the unexcavated area between Sites 4 and 8 (see Figure 3.17). Evidence of a possible fence line across the open 'mouth' of the horseshoe enclosure is suggested by a line of postholes extending east from the western ditch terminus, to the north of Building 2664.

Building 2664 (Fig. 3.19)

This building was assigned to Phase 2a as it is stratigraphically the earliest building of the group of three close to the enclosure mouth, although it is accepted that it could belong to Phase 2b.

The rectangular structure measured 12.0 m x 6.0 m in plan, and was defined by a total of 50 postholes. It was oriented WNW-ESE, and situated east of the western terminus of the horseshoe enclosure (see below). The definition of the line of both north and south walls was reasonably clear, with spacing between posts of between 1.6 and 2.2 m and an apparent doorway defined by the space between postholes 2115 and 2117 in the south wall. Definition of the end walls is problematic; a scatter of mostly unexcavated posthole-like soil marks lies to the east of the identified building footprint. Within this scatter it is possible to devise a number of hypothetical end walls. However, not only were many of these soil marks unexcavated, but it is questionable whether they were contemporary,

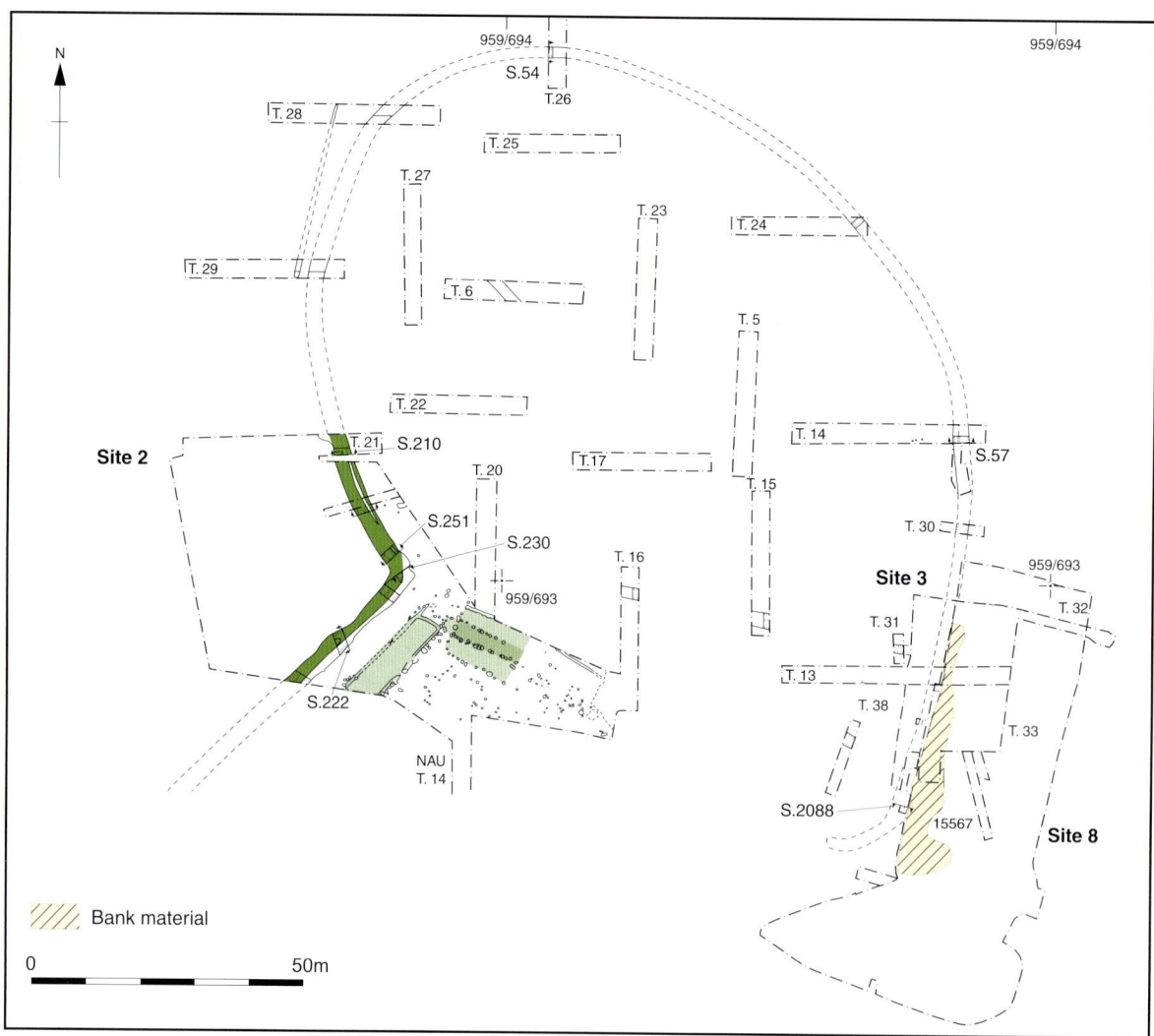

Fig. 3.17 Phase 2 Sites 2 and 8 Enclosure 2658 and evaluation trenches

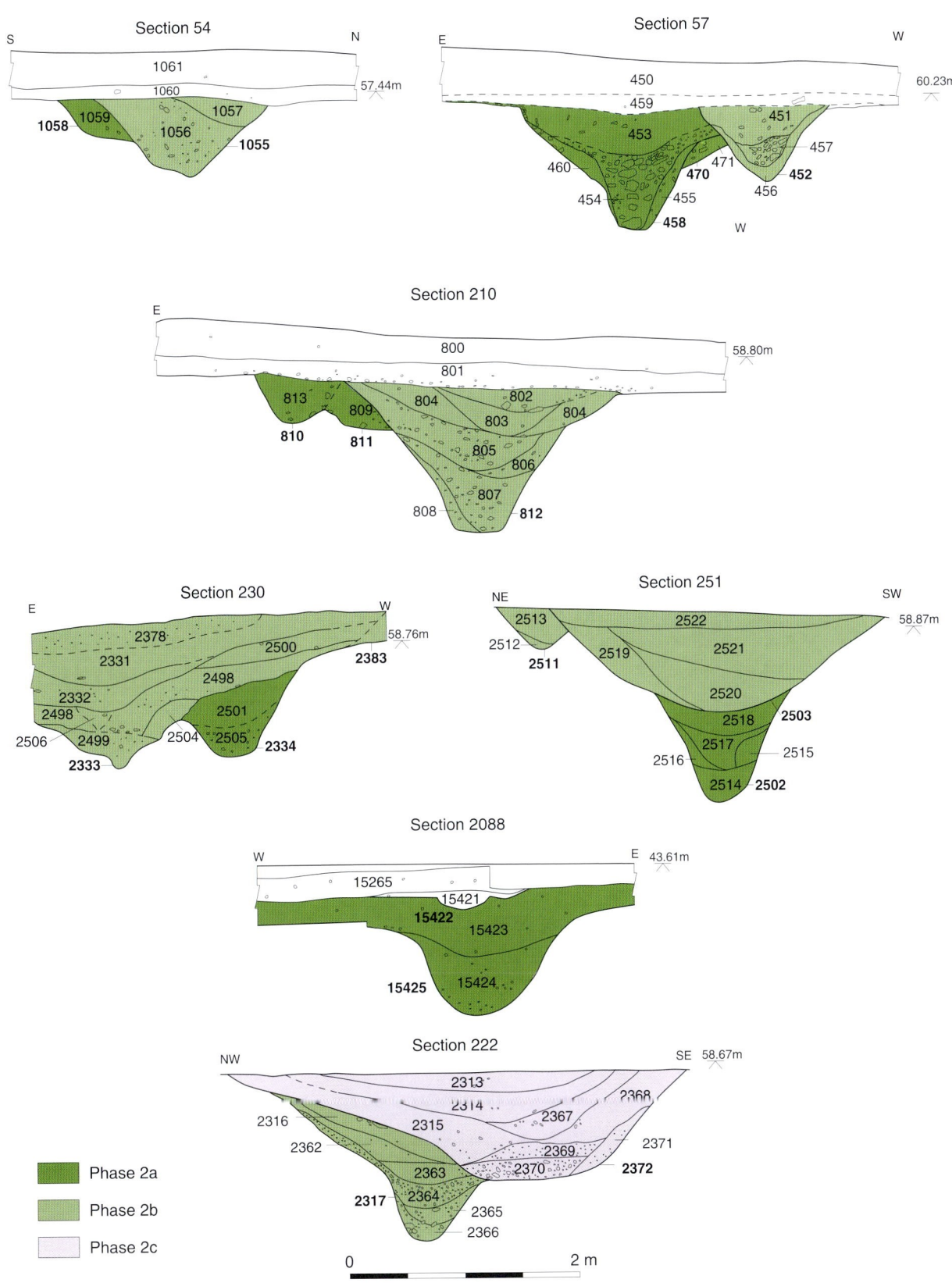

Section 54

Section 57

Section 210

Section 230

Section 251

Section 2088

Section 222

Phase 2a

Phase 2b

Phase 2c

0   2 m

Fig. 3.18   Phase 2a/b Enclosure sections

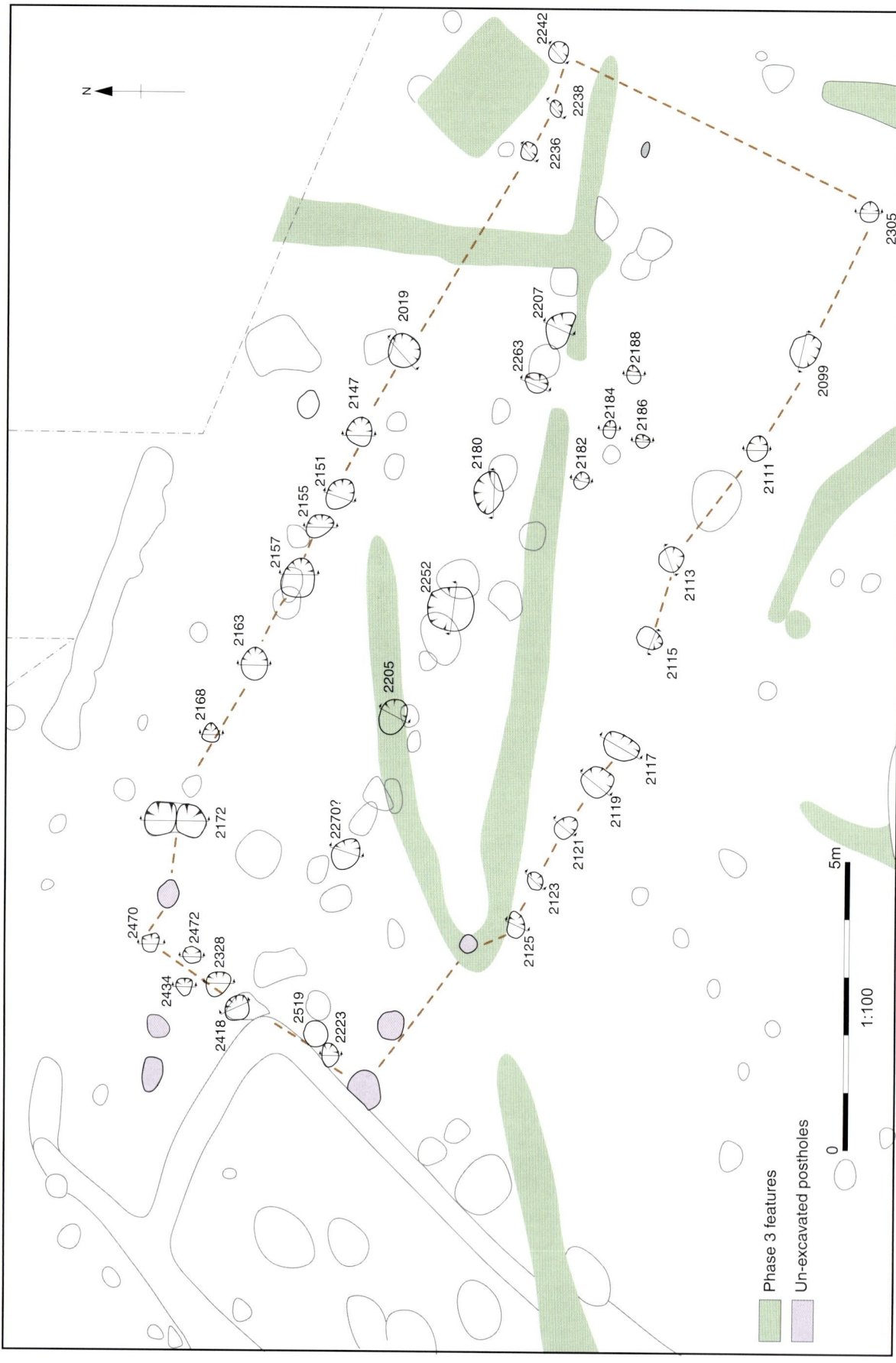

Fig. 3.19 Phase 2a Site 2 Building 2664

considering the proximity of considerable Phase 3 activity in the area. On balance, this eastern area lacks the regular intervals between posts and central aisle posts recorded in the western part, of the building. The interpretation of these features as part of a long building of consistent build is far from convincing. While it is not impossible that Building 2664 could have been some 25 m in length, the irregularity of the posthole scatter makes it more likely that the building was nearer 12 m in length.

Separating the postholes of the west end of the building from those of the two later structures was also difficult. The layout depicted suggests a straightforward end wall, with a possible short extension, perhaps a fence?

Internal features – A line of 6 postholes defined what

appeared to be a central ridge support, and a group of four small postholes formed a T-shaped arrangement to the south of the central line, although its purpose is unclear. No hearth or area of burning was evident. The presence of a quantity of charred grain in one of the postpipe fills (2154) was noted (see Moffett Chapter 4).

Phase 2b (mid to late 8th century) (Fig. 3.20)

The structural changes assigned to this sub-phase comprise the recutting of the original horseshoe ditch together with extensions to the ditch (2317 – Site 2, 7234 – Site 4), to form an extended enclosed space. Associated with this work was rectangular timber building 2665, which the replaced building 2664, and timber buildings 2666, 7023 and 7237, and

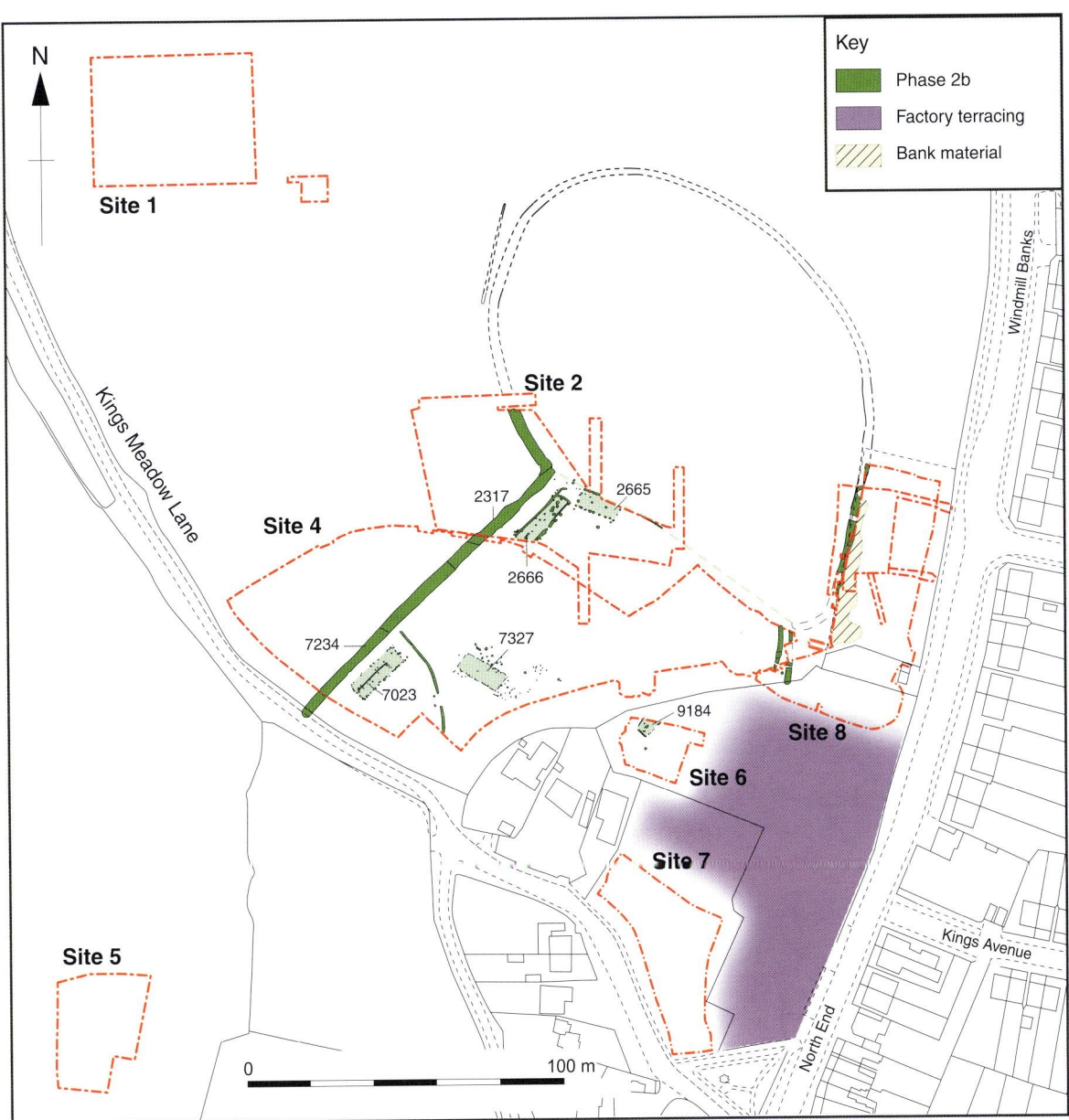

Fig. 3.20   Phase 2b Middle Saxon enclosure extensions

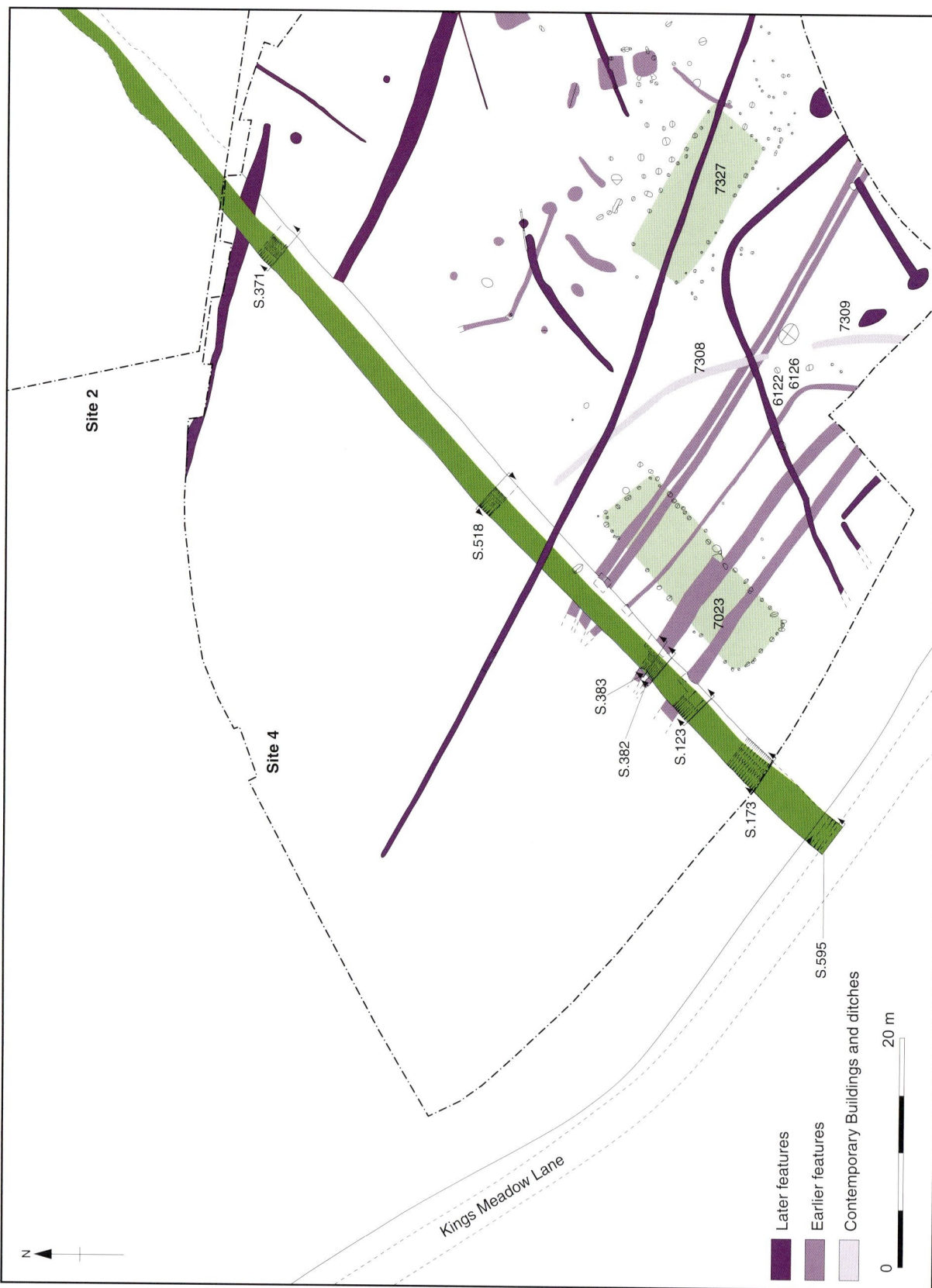

Fig. 3.21 Phase 2b Site 4 Enclosure extension plan

9184. Buildings 2665 and 2666 were set almost at a right angle to one another in the original entrance to the horseshoe enclosure. Buildings 7023 and 7237 were both rectangular, again set at a right angle to one another, and were sited further out from the enclosure, between the extended entrances ditches. Building 9184 was only partially explored and lay some way to the south of the other buildings between the extended entrances ditches. This sub-phase is dated to the mid to late 8th century.

Enclosure ditch (Figs 3.21-23)

Re-cutting of enclosure ditch

At least one recut was evident in all sections of the horseshoe ditch. Generally the sections showed that – where the recut did not exactly match the original ditch line – it was cut along the inside edge of the original. The existence of an external bank in the first phase would clearly encourage the digging of any recut to take place on the opposite side of the ditch.

The recut ditch profile was more variable than the original profile, but in general it was cut deeper. Again, the fills were varying mixes of silty clay and ironstone fragments, with evidence of subsidence of the upper layers, allowing the levelling accumulation of later ploughsoil. Again, finds were conspicuous by their absence from the interior of the enclosure, except in the south-west corner near the building group, and from a single section of the eastern side of the enclosure ditch. At this point (Trench 14, fill 451 – see Fig. 3.18, Section 57), a significant assemblage of mid-7th to mid-8th-century pottery was recovered, along with a notable quantity of cereal remains and relatively numerous fragments of lava quern.

Extensions to enclosure ditch (Fig. 3.21-3.23)

The evidence shows that, at the time the horseshoe enclosure was recut, the opportunity was taken to extend the enclosed area with two straight ditches, one fully revealed running from the western end of the original ditch in a south-west direction towards Kings Meadow Lane. There is evidence that a similar extension ditch ran from the eastern terminus of the horseshoe ditch southwards.

The western extension (2317/7234) was revealed in its entirety, extending from the terminus of the Phase 2a horseshoe enclosure (Site 2) to the edge of Kings Meadow Lane (Site 4) (Fig. 3.21). Nine full sections and one half section were hand excavated through the ditch, representing a 17% sample, and other small sections were excavated to confirm the ditch's relationship with linear features to the east. A selection of the excavated sections is illustrated in Figure 3.22.

Despite its size, the definition of the ditch in plan was extremely unclear. This is considered to be principally because of the similarity between the fill of the ditch and the surrounding subsoil, a similarity that supports the contention that the ditch (in its last phase) was backfilled with the banked upcast from its construction.

For most of its length, the earliest cut of the ditch displayed a marked 'V' shaped profile, with typical dimensions being approximately 2.5 m – 3.0 m wide x 1.0 m – 1.2 m deep. The lower fills of the ditch appeared to be erosion deposits from the upcast, comprising brown or light brown silty clays, with varying proportions of ironstone fragments, depending upon the character of the natural through which the ditch was cut at that point. Near the south-western end of Site 4, section 173 revealed three distinct cuts to the ditch (Fig.3.22). The second cut in the sequence (6327) corresponds most closely to the profile of the original cut elsewhere, and displays the same fill characteristics. The earliest cut (6196) in the sequence does not appear anywhere else, and its single ironstone rich fill suggests it was backfilled soon after its excavation. It may be suggested that this feature is either an early and aborted ditch, or possibly an earlier and unrelated feature.

Generally, finds from the lower fills of the first phase of the ditch were scarce, and comprise a small quantity of bone and a few sherds of early/middle Saxon pottery. The secondary (upper) fills of the first cut of the ditch were generally very mixed deposits, characteristic of backfill. In the sections close to the horseshoe enclosure and in proximity to Building 2666 (Site 2), the fill contained bone, pot and charcoal flecks, reminiscent of dumped domestic debris. Elsewhere the secondary ditch fills contained a few sherds of early to middle Saxon pottery and occasional fragments of animal bone.

The relationship of the western extension ditch with the present line of Kings Meadow Lane was investigated so far as was possible by a narrow section dug against the north-east side of the Lane (Fig.3.22, section 595). This revealed a sequence of post-medieval and modern surfaces and make-up layers over the fills of the enclosure ditch. It was not possible to investigate the stratigraphy under the central part of the Lane, nor on the Lane's south-western side. Consequently, while it is clear that the enclosure ditch extended beyond the extant hedged boundary to the edge of the Lane, it is debatable whether it originally crossed the line of the Lane. This issue is considered further in Chapter 5.

The area to the south of the eastern terminus of the horseshoe enclosure (Site 8) was heavily truncated by the factory terracing and other modern disturbance. Two short lengths of parallel N-S oriented ditch (7317) and (7318/15165) – the latter identified on both Site 4 and Site 8 – were located (Fig. 3.23). Both ditches belong stratigraphically to Phase 2, and it is suggested that at least one, and possibly both of these ditches represented the extension of eastern enclosure ditch, and could have extended as far south as the junction of Kings Meadow Lane and Windmill Banks. A small

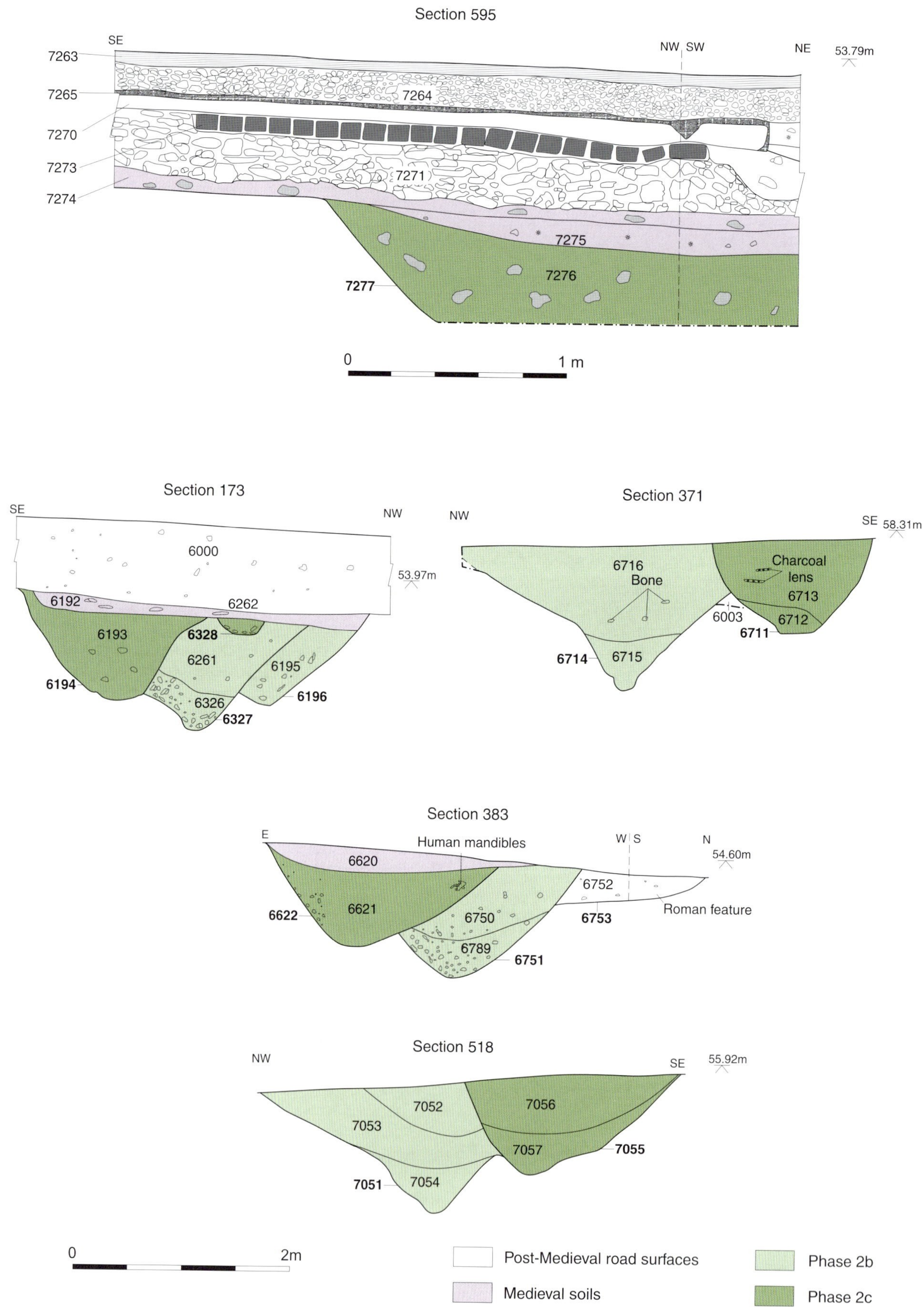

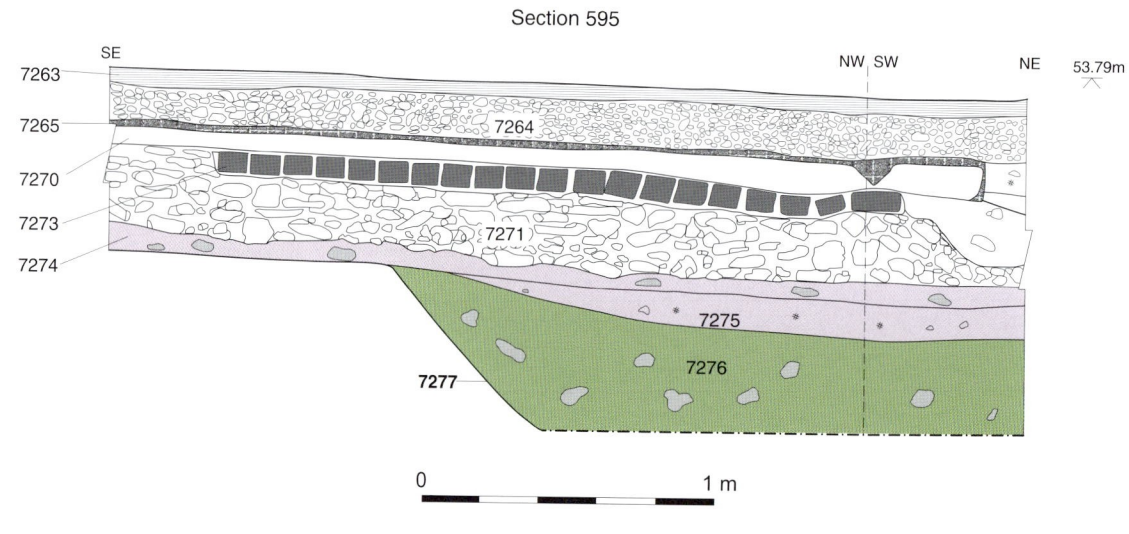

Section 595

Section 173

Section 371

Section 383

Section 518

	Post-Medieval road surfaces		Phase 2b
	Medieval soils		Phase 2c

Fig. 3.22   Phase 2b Site 4 Enclosure extension: ditch sections

amount of 8th-century pottery was recovered from the ditch fills, but perhaps of more interest was a group of 9 bone needles (SFs 4003 – 4011 inclusive; Fig. 4.16, 11,12, and 15), three of them broken but complete, found in the base of ditch 15165. From their position (Pl. 3.4) it would appear that these needles were strung together when deposited. Whether they represent a termination deposit or, more prosaically, were simply thrown away or accidentally dropped is unclear.

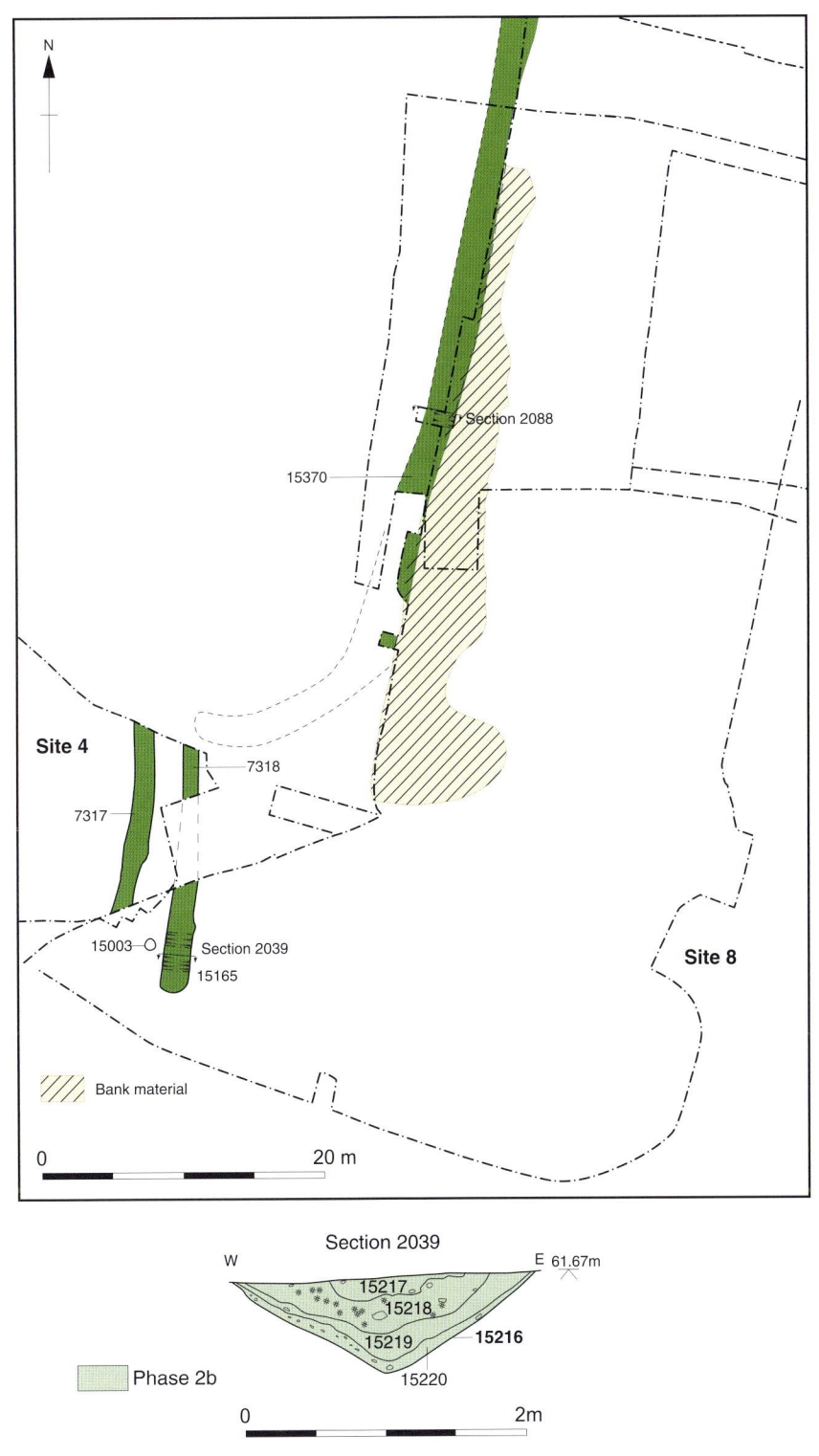

Fig. 3.23   *Phase 2b Site 8 Enclosure extension plan and section*

Plate 3.3   Building 7023 postholes under excavation

Building 2665 (Fig. 3.24)

The structure was defined by a total of 21 postholes, representing a rectangular building that, by its position, was evidently a rebuild of Building 2664 (Phase 2a). The building footprint was shifted to the north-east, possibly to utilise the wall or aisle timbers of the earlier building and to make room to the west for Building 2666 (see below).

The disposition of the postholes in Building 2665 suggests an overall length of 12.0 m x 6.0 m wide, with a 1.0 m wide doorway on the south side, defined by postholes 2179 and 2248). Two substantial interior postholes (2019, 2161) appeared to represent ridge supports. The south, west and east walls were defined by earthfast posts; the partially exposed north wall, by contrast, was represented by an arrangement of a beamslot and postholes (see Figure 3.24 detail). The difference might be due to a variation in design, but it is perhaps more likely that the variable truncation caused by the post-medieval ridge-and-furrow is responsible for this apparent difference. The depth of postholes on the south wall averaged at least 0.20 m less than those in the north wall beamslot, showing that any evidence for a beamslot gully along the south wall could well have been completely removed. As with Building 2664, there was no evidence of an internal hearth within the footprint of Building 2665.

Building 2666 (Fig. 3.25)

This structure was on the same alignment as the enclosure extension ditch (2317) and was sited immediately west of Building 2665. Unlike Buildings 2664 and 2665, the structure was defined by an approximately rectangular arrangement of beamslots and incorporated postholes, giving a total footprint size of 20 m x 5 m. While the south-western end wall was not fully exposed, the terminus of the western wall allows the position of the end wall to be confidently extrapolated. A single doorway was evident in the middle of the eastern side of the structure, defined by an interruption in the beamslot, and at least one large posthole (2330) on the northern side. A noticeable feature was the large disparity in the measurements of depth and width between the beamslots and postholes of the west (back) and east (front) walls of the building respectively. The east wall beamslots were generally 0.10 m–0.15 m deeper, and substantially wider than those of the west or back wall. The line of the ridge and furrow truncation runs across the northern part of the building, so is unlikely to be the cause of this disparity, which is discussed further in Chapter 5.

A scatter of postholes was identified in the building's interior. A central line of aisle posts can be inferred, although there is some doubt which postholes belong to the building, and which postholes belong to Phase 3 (see below). An area of

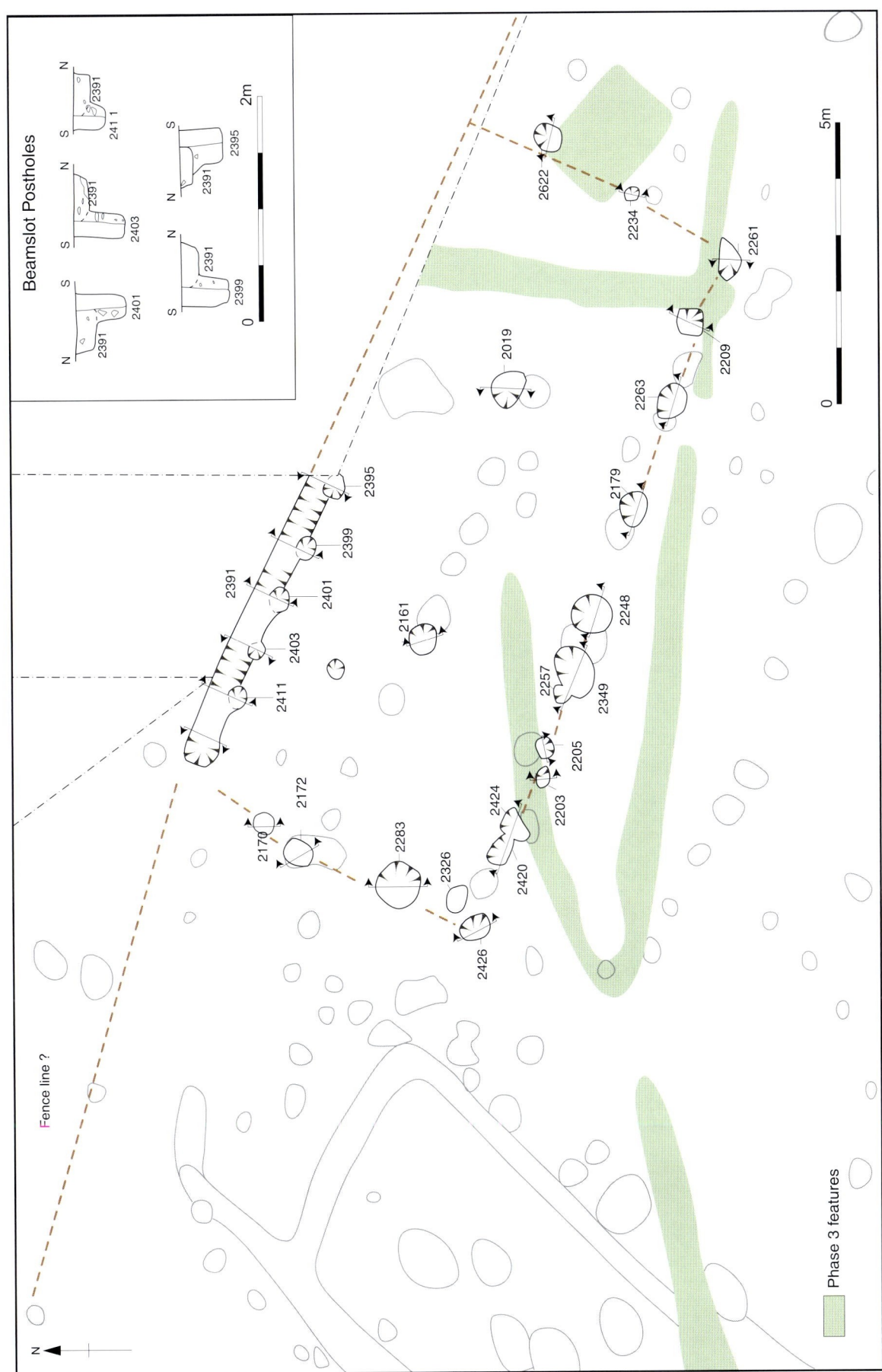

Fig. 3.24 Phase 2b Site 2 Building 2665

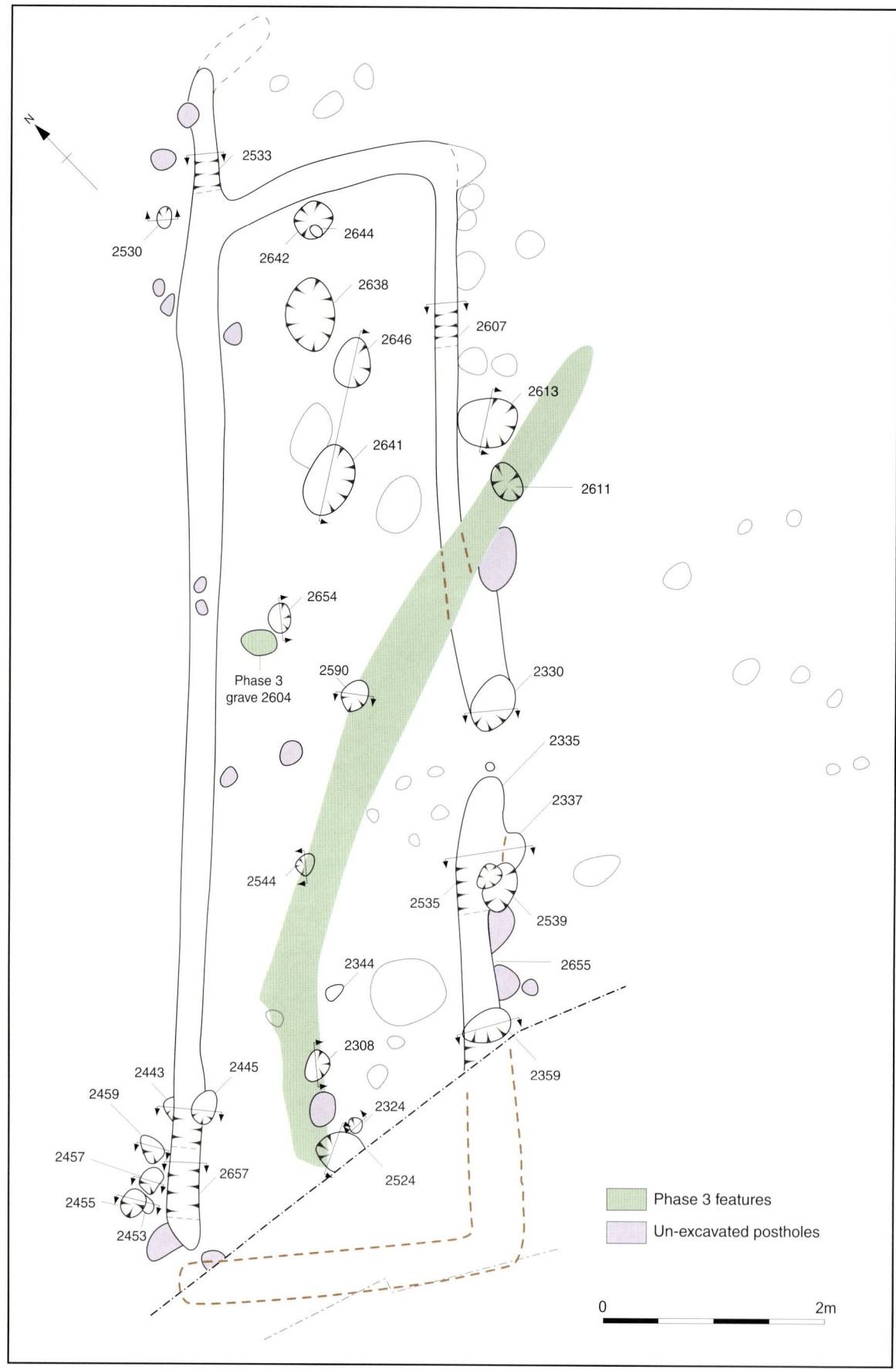

Fig. 3.25 Phase 2b Site 2 Building 2666

burnt subsoil was revealed in the northern part of the building, suggesting the likely position of a hearth. Support for the domestic function of this building comes from the bone, pottery and charcoal flecks in the upper layers of the first cut of the enclosure extension ditch to the west (2317). Grain processing or storage is also suggested by the charred remains from one of the postpipes (2644), at the northern end of the building.

Other structures

In the open area formed by the angle between Buildings 2665 and 2666, a scatter of probable postholes was identified and planned as soil marks, but most were not excavated due to lack of resources (Fig. 3.26). While some alignments with the buildings 2665 and 2666, and the earlier building 2664, are apparent, no clear building outline is evident, although subsidiary structures are implied. However, it should be born in mind that some of these features almost certainly relate to activity in Phase 3, and possibly to later activities.

Building 7023 (Figs 3.27, 3.21, Pl.3.4)

The structure was located close to, and aligned with, the enclosure extension ditch (7234) in the south-west corner of Site 4 (Fig. 3.21). The building was identified by 52 external postholes, defining a rectangular structure measuring 19 m x 6.5 m. Within this footprint were a further 20 postholes and one central beamslot. It is presumed that the west (back) wall originally consisted of more regularly spaced postholes, but that those cut into the fill of earlier linear features were often impossible to see or excavate.

The postholes were of a fairly uniform diameter, averaging 0.40 m, and their depth varied within a range 0.15 m–0.30 m. This variation did not relate to the position of the posthole within the building, but is thought to be due either to the difficulty of digging the posthole in the variable subsoil (a mix of silty clay and ironstone) at this point on the site, or to the variable length of the timbers to be set into the postholes. It was noted that the building was set on a site with a pronounced slope down to the south-west. After initial topsoil stripping, the level

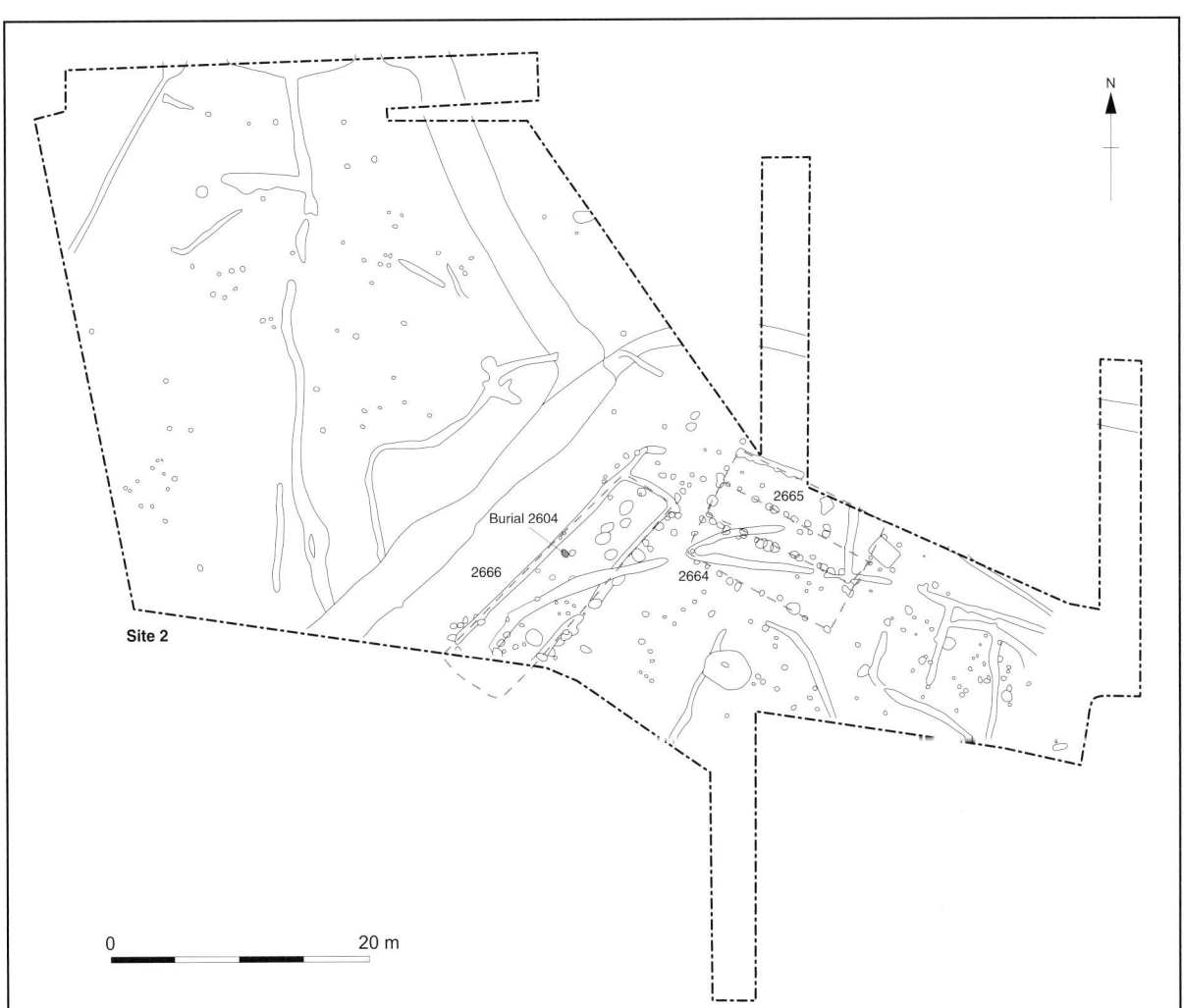

Fig. 3.26   Site 2: General plan of features

Plate 3.4   The set of bone needles in the enclosure ditch Phase 2b

at the highest (north-east) corner of the building was 55.85 m OD whereas the level at the lowest (south-western) corner of the building of 54.67; a difference of 1.18m. This characteristic is discussed further in Chapter 5.

No finds were recovered from the building footprint, and the posthole fills produced just two sherds of residual 6th-century pottery (Fig. 4.1, 16) along with one early 8th-century sherd.

The internal layout of the building suggested some complexity in construction. The southern two-thirds of the building was bisected longitudinally by a 12.5 m long beamslot (7019), averaging 0.20 m wide. A number of interior postholes seem to occur in pairs, straddling the beamslot, for instance 6994 and 6996, and 7008 and 7010. A doorway on the eastern side is suggested by a gap between postholes 6918 and 6920.

By contrast, the northern third of the building's length was evidently different in construction, with no central beamslot, and a generally closer spacing of the postholes, particularly apparent along the front or east wall. Three postholes situated beyond the end wall (6942, 6952 and 6956) possibly represent additional support or bracing for the structure. Only one interior posthole (6980) was identified. A possible doorway for this end 'room' might be defined by the gap between postholes 6934 and 6936.

Neither part of the building revealed any evidence for a hearth, although two small pits (6978 and 7229), both situated just beyond the northern end of the building, contained charcoal-rich fills, indicating that hearth debris was dumped in the area. Charcoal and burnt stone was also noted in the upper fills of the Phase 2b enclosure ditch (7234) to the north of Building 7023.

Associated features

To the north-west of Building 7023 and arcing from the enclosure extension ditch and extending to the south baulk of Site 4 was a ditch (7308/7309) with a gap forming an entrance (Fig.3.21). Both parts of the ditch varied between approximately 0.60 m and 1.0 m wide and averaged approximately 0.20 m deep, with a shallow 'U' shaped profile. Both ditches contained a mid orange brown silty clay fill. A single sherd of early/middle Saxon pottery was recovered from the fill of one of the ditch termini. The gap between the termini of the two ditches contained two postholes (6122 and 6126), 2.4 m apart and apparently defining an entrance into the area containing Building 7023. Both postholes were approximately 0.40 m wide x 0.20 m deep and contained a single silty clay fill, devoid of finds.

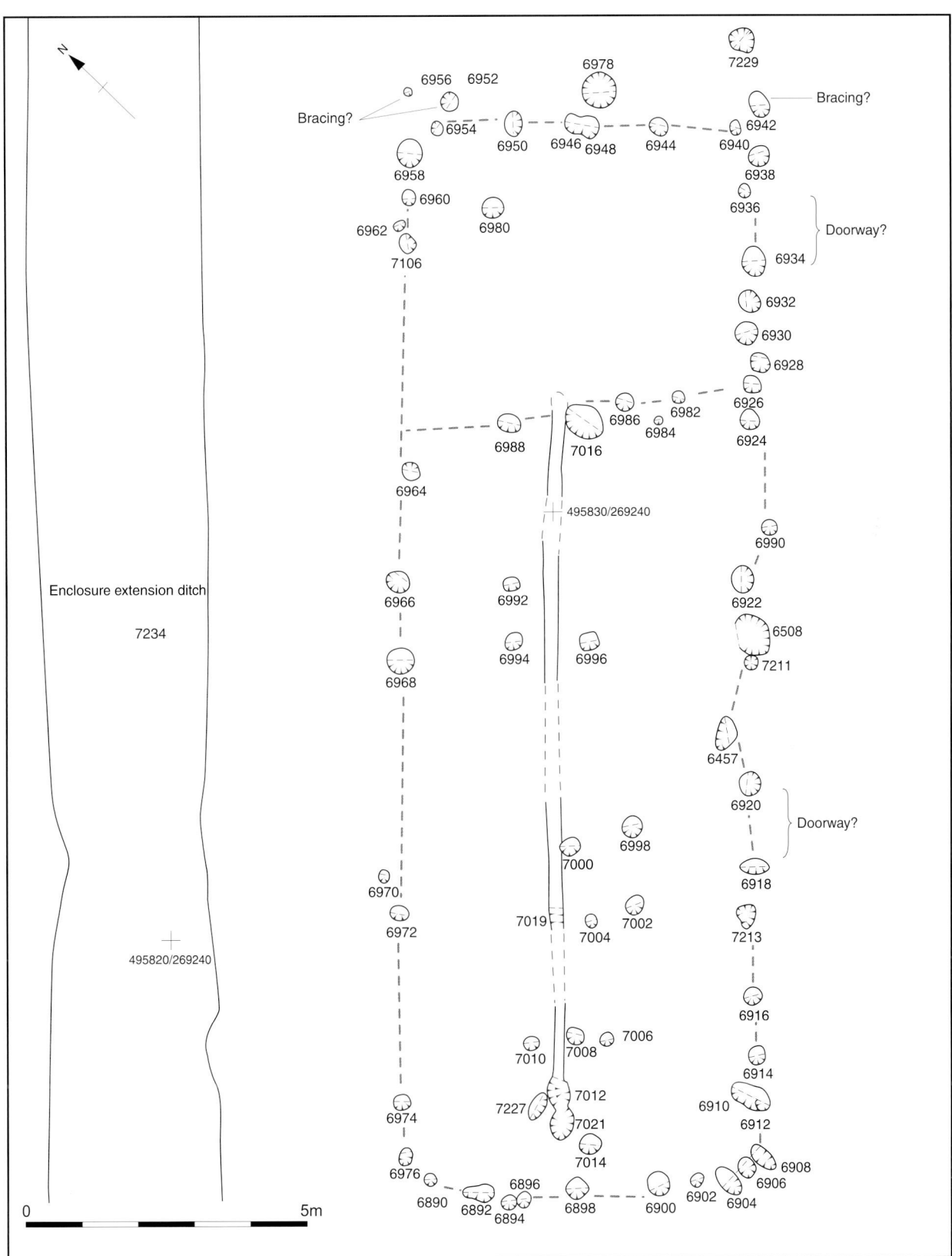

Fig. 3.27 *Phase 2b Site 4 Building 7023*

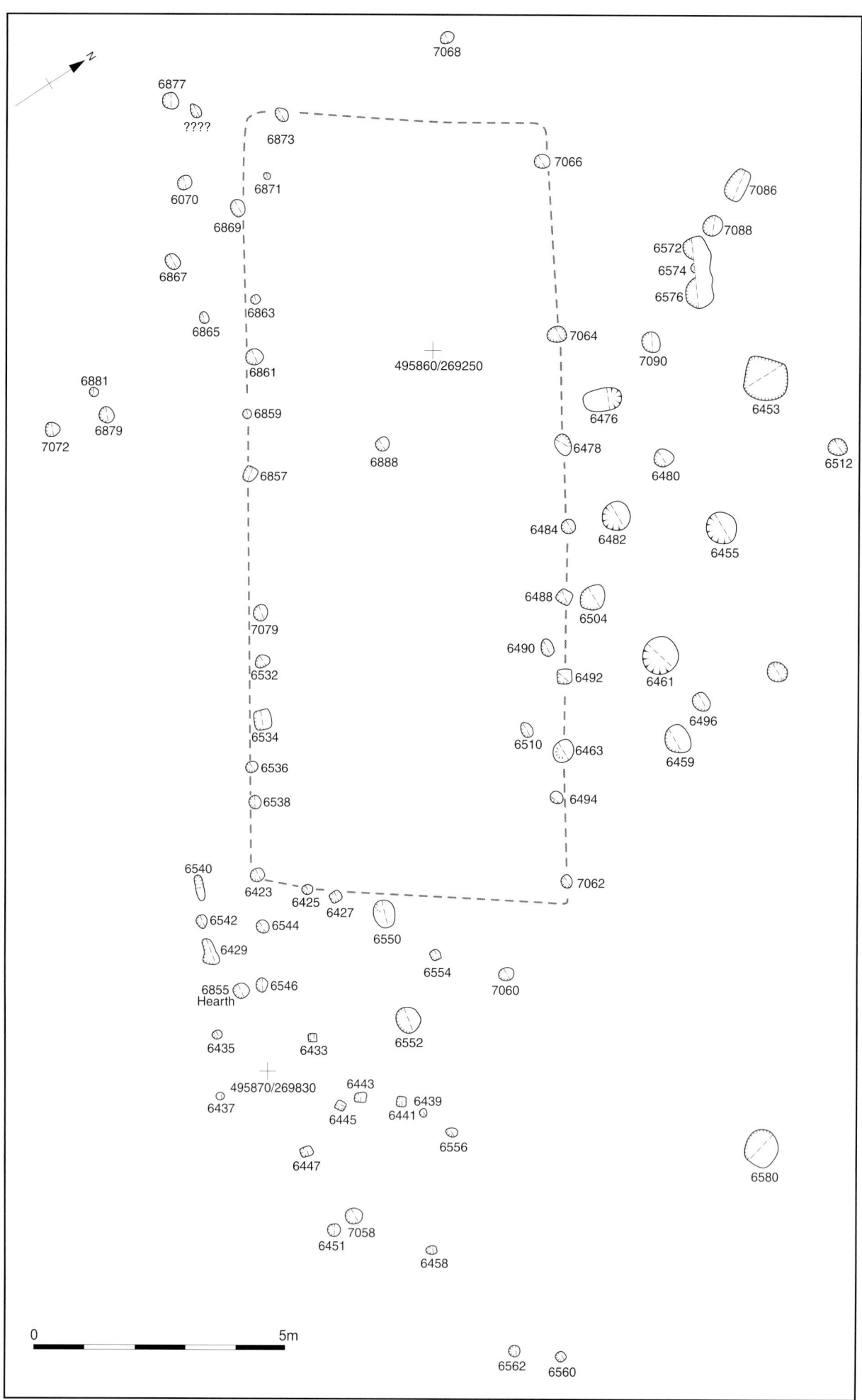

Building 7237 (Fig. 3.28)

This was situated north-east of Building 7023, and aligned approximately at right angles to it. It comprised a total of 26 postholes, defining a rectangular structure approximately 18.0 m long x 6.5 m wide. The truncation by later activity was variable; the north-west end of the building in particular was almost completed truncated. The postholes that survived varied from 0.2 m to 0.3 m in diameter and 0.1 m to 0.2 m in depth, and contained similar fills of brown/grey silty clay. A possible doorway approximately 2.6 m wide was defined by a gap in the otherwise well-defined posthole line along the south-west wall. A single interior posthole was identified, probably representing a central ridge post, and three others were identified within the buildings footprint, close to the line of the north-east wall. These latter features may be associated with the building but equally may relate to the Phase 1 activity to the north (see above).

Datable artefacts from the building were scarce. Only two fragments (7g) of pottery were recovered from the main section of the building. These came from postholes 6484 and 6873 and one fragment dating to the early/mid Saxon period and one to the late Saxon period. A further two fragments (3g) were recovered from posthole 6447 just to the south, and posthole 6476 just to the east of the main building structure. This pottery dates to the early mid Saxon period. Given the proximity of two Phase 1 SFBs, the occurrence of early middle Saxon pottery in the area is no surprise. More significantly, a substantial quantity of grain – principally barley – was recovered from a sample of the fill (6617) of one of the postholes (6616).

A scatter of 22 postholes was identified to the south-east and north-east of the building. Some appear to define a curving fence-line attached to the building's east end. Close to the south corner of the structure was a small hearth (6855) measuring 0.26 m in diameter and 0.02 m in depth. The feature had evidence of in situ burning and contained a charcoal filled deposit and stones reddened by fire. To the north-east of the building was a scatter of post holes and small pits. There is no obvious regularity in the positioning of these features, although the presence of another small hearth, and the overall distribution of the features – respecting the building's footprint – suggests they are more likely to be contemporary with the building than features associated with earlier or later occupation.

Building 9184 (Fig. 3.29)

This structure was partly revealed in Site 6, approximately 60 m south-east of Building 7327. It was oriented NE-SW, approximately in line with the western enclosure extension ditch, and was identi-fied by postholes and a beamslot. These features defined a building 4.3 m wide x at least 6.5 m long. The south-west end wall comprised a beamslot and incorporated postholes spaced at approximately 1.0 m intervals. The north-west wall was identified only by a vestige of a beamslot, and the south-east wall comprised a line of postholes and a poorly defined beamslot. A possible doorway on this wall is suggested by a gap 1 m wide between two postholes, one of which (9131) was substantial in size and contained limestone packing. If it is presumed that the doorway was located at the mid-point of the building, as is the case on all but one of the other buildings in this phase, then the original length of Building 9184 would have been at approximately 9 m.

A single internal feature was identified – a shallow gully oriented on the centre line of the building, possibly representing a beamslot that – as with Building 7023 – could infer a load-bearing ceiling. Interestingly, an environmental sample from the end wall beamslot fill (9060), revealed another similarity with Building 7023, in the make up of the charred plant remains (see Moffett, Chapter 4). A small posthole (9113) was identified close to the west wall, although the presence of a sherd of 12th-century pottery in its fill raises a question mark over its assignment to this Phase.

A single pit (9106) situated approximately 4 m to the south-west of the building produced a sherd of mid Saxon pottery from its fill 9149 and on this basis can be tentatively associated with the building.

Phase 2c (Figs 3.30-3.31)

In Phase 2c the horseshoe enclosure was abandoned. The enclosure extension to the south-west was recut (2653/7330) and extended to the east (2655) and then continued curving more towards the south (15190). The buildings of Phase 2b seem to have continued in use. A malting oven identified some way to the south-west on Site 5 is assigned to this phase. This sub-phase is dated late 8th century to early 9th century.

Enclosure ditch (Sites 2, 4, 8) (Figs 3.31-3.32)

The recut of the south-west ditch extension was fully revealed in plan (Sites 2 and 4) and seen to cut the Phase 2b ditch on the east side, supporting the idea that any bank associated with the ditch would have been on the west side. Where it was examined in the excavated sections, the recut displayed a shallower 'U'shaped profile than its predecessor, around 0.80 m deep rather than over 1.0 m deep, and between 1.6 m and 2.0 m wide. The northern end of the recut extension ditch (2653) now extended to the north and east of Site 2 (as context 2655), and was picked up in two evaluation

Fig. 3.28 (facing page) Phase 2b Site 4 Building 7327

47

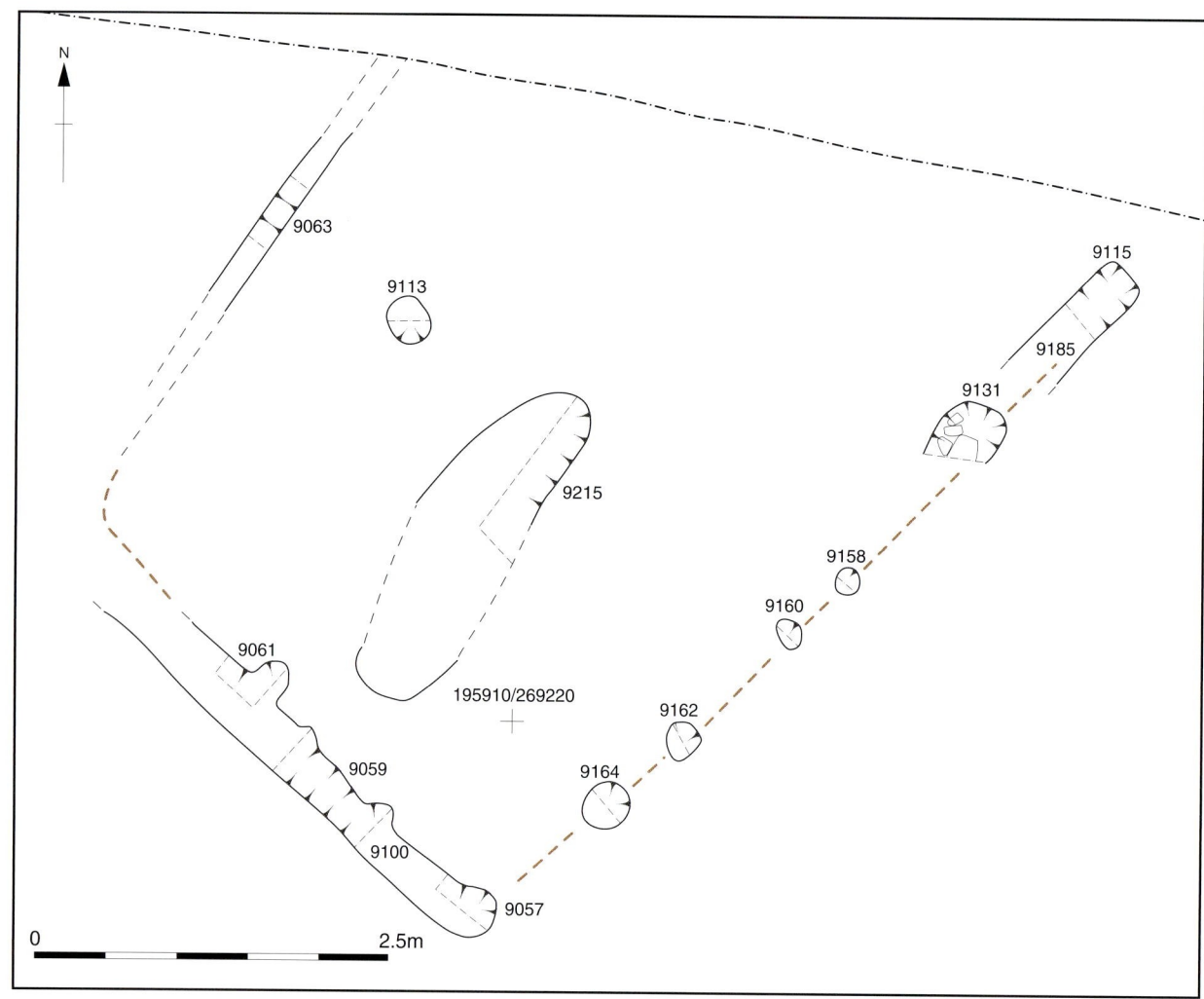

Fig. 3.29   Phase 2b Site 6 Building 9184

trenches that extended north of the site (Fig. 3.32, Section 76). The ditch profile at this point was smaller than that of the western ditch, being 1.5 m wide x 0.70 m deep, although this may be due to the severity of the truncation caused by the post-medieval ridge-and-furrow in this area, perhaps exacerbated by the less-than-ideal excavation conditions on Site 2.

The recut ditch was identified emerging from the west baulk of Site 8 (context 15190), cutting the backfilled Phase 2a/b horseshoe ditch and the associated bank residue (15423). It then curved evenly to the south and, despite severe truncation and disturbance from medieval and later activity, was traced to the edge of the factory terracing (Fig. 3.31). Its profile displayed relatively modest dimensions, being no more than 1.4 m wide x 0.80 m deep (Fig. 3.32, sections 2045 and 2027). The fills of the ditch were in places well stratified, and showed signs of subsidence, so that upper fills, (for instance context 15028 of ditch 15190, which produced a high grain content) are probably Phase 3 accumulations.

The evidence of material culture recovered from the 15 sections cut through the 260 m length of the

Phase 2c ditch varied considerably across the enclosure complex. Finds from the eastern part of the ditch in Site 8 were very sparse, with no contemporary pottery, very little animal bone, and no metal finds. To the north of Site 2, the ditch (Fig. 3.31, Section 76) produced a significant quantity of cattle and pig bone; this may be related to the proximity of buildings 2665 and 2666, or to a building or activity in an adjacent unexcavated part of the area. Where the ditch passed alongside Buildings 2666 and 7023, there were considerable concentrations of domestic debris, broadly in the interface between the lower erosion fills of the ditch and the final backfilling material. In particular, in the ditch alongside Building 7023, finds included a dump of animal bones (principally cattle), and skeletal remains of at least three humans (Pl. 3.5; human bone report Witkin, Chapter 4, and discussion Chapter 5).

Malting oven (Site 5) (Figs 3.33, Pl. 3.6)

The other major structure assigned to this phase is the malting oven (4010), situated on the south-west

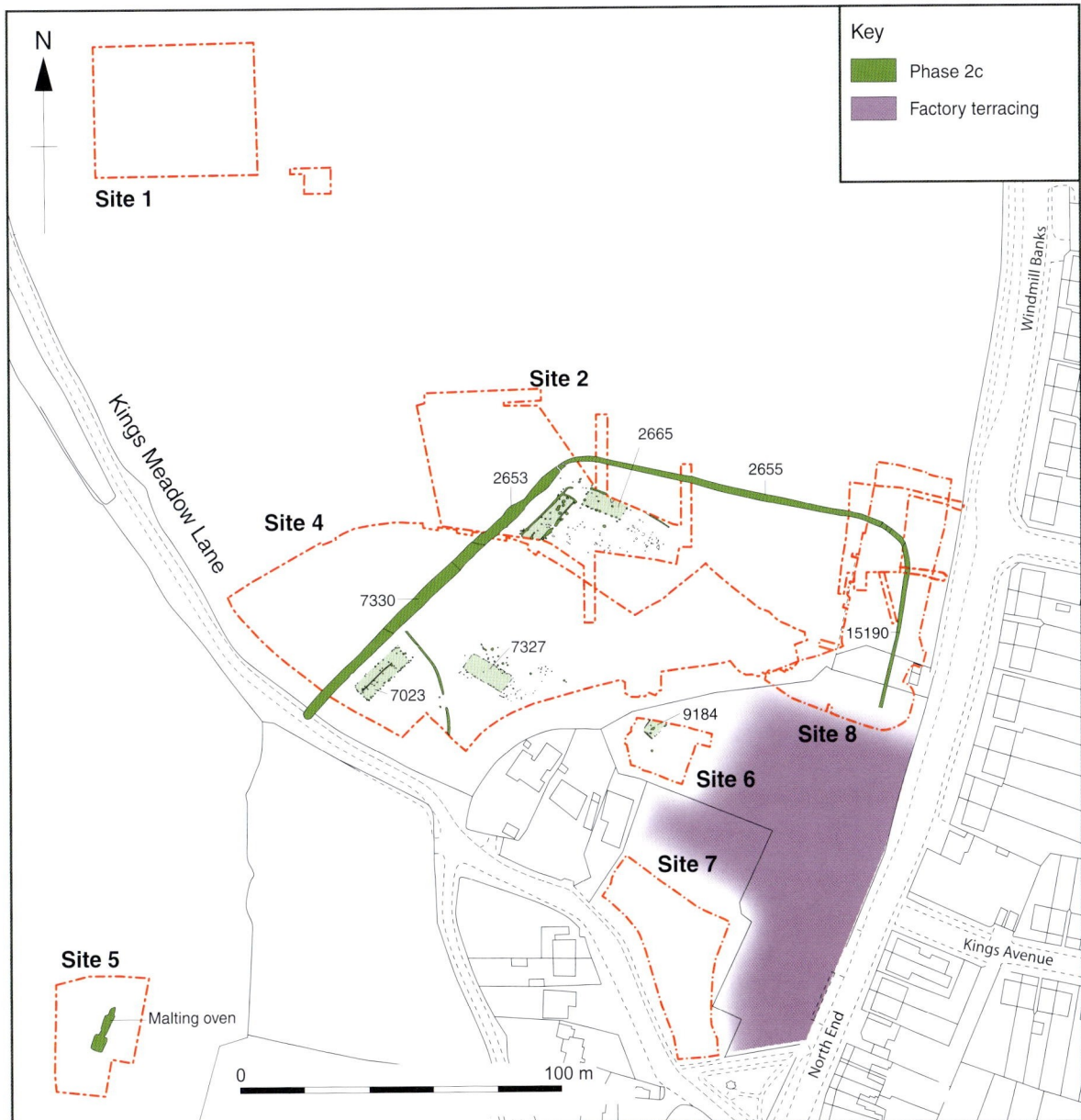

Fig. 3.30   Phase 2c Middle Saxon enclosure, and location of malting oven

side of Kings Meadow Lane, on the ridge extending north-west towards the site of the Roman settlement. The structure was first revealed in an evaluation trench, and later fully revealed by excavation. After examination the complete structure was reburied under a protective layer of gravel and the housing development in this area was redesigned to avoid impacting on the oven remains.

The surviving oven structure comprised a rectangular flat-bottomed pit (4023) cut into the silty clay and ironstone natural (4001) and measuring 2.7 m wide x 3.1 m long x 0.75 m deep. The pit sides were fully lined with coursed rubble walling (4019, 4020, 4021, 4022) averaging 0.4 m wide. The exposed wall faces showed evidence of being subjected to considerable heat. The pit was floored with irregularly

sized stone slabs (4016, 4044). These were sealed by a layer of heavily burnt clay (4017, 4043) from which two small fragments of Early/middle Saxon pottery were recovered. From the north-east end of the rectangular pit extended a 4 m long channel (1023) measuring from 1.2 m wide, where it exited from the pit, to 2.0 m wide at its furthest extent. As with the pit, the sides of the channel were lined with coursed rubble walling (4030, 4031) and again showed evidence of burning. The channel depth averaged 0.45 m to the point where the stone lining ceased; beyond this it decreased to nothing over a further 2.2 m. There was no evidence of stone flooring; the subsoil surface (4028) fire reddened at the pit end, appeared to have represented the floor of the channel. A single large slab of limestone was found

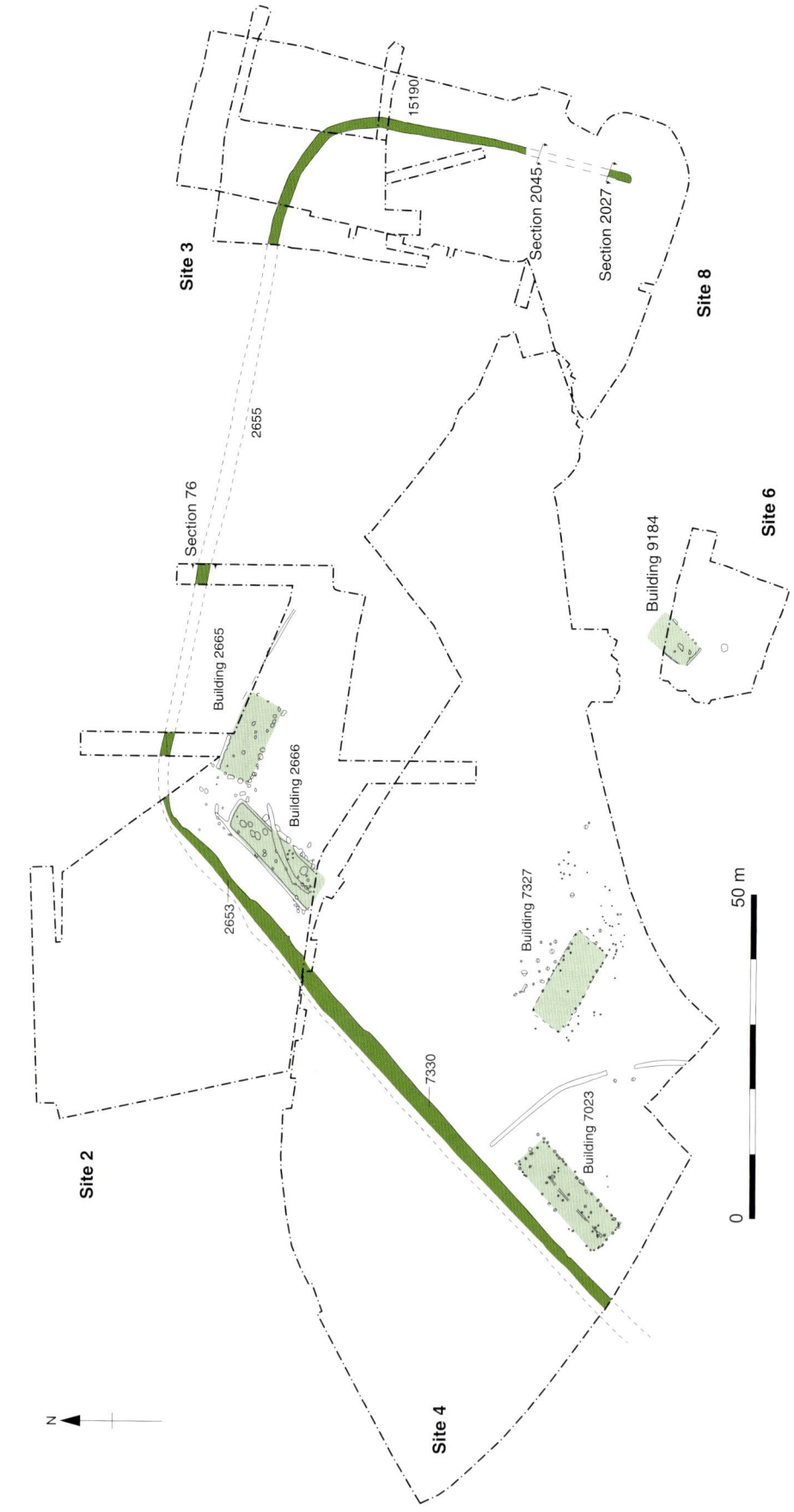

Fig. 3.31 Phase 2c Sites 2, 4, 6 and 8: Enclosure and contemporary buildings

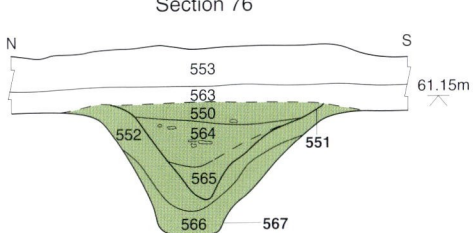

Section 76

N   S

553
563
550
552   564   551
565
566 ——— 567

61.15m

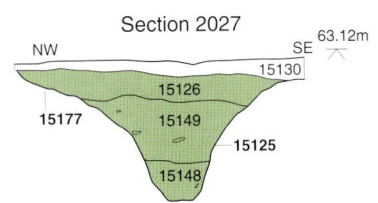

Section 2027

NW   SE   63.12m

15130
15126
15177   15149
15125
15148

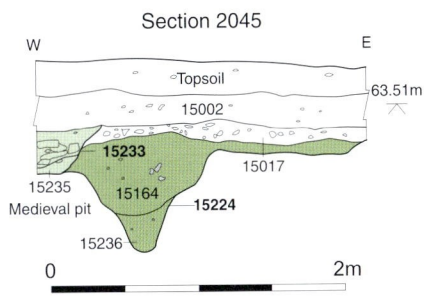

Section 2045

W   E

Topsoil
63.51m
15002
15233
15017
15235   15164
15236   15224
Medieval pit

0   2m

Medieval   Phase 2c

Fig. 3.32 (left)   Phase 2c Enclosure ditch sections

Plate 3.5 (above and below)   The malting oven and detail of flue Phase 2c

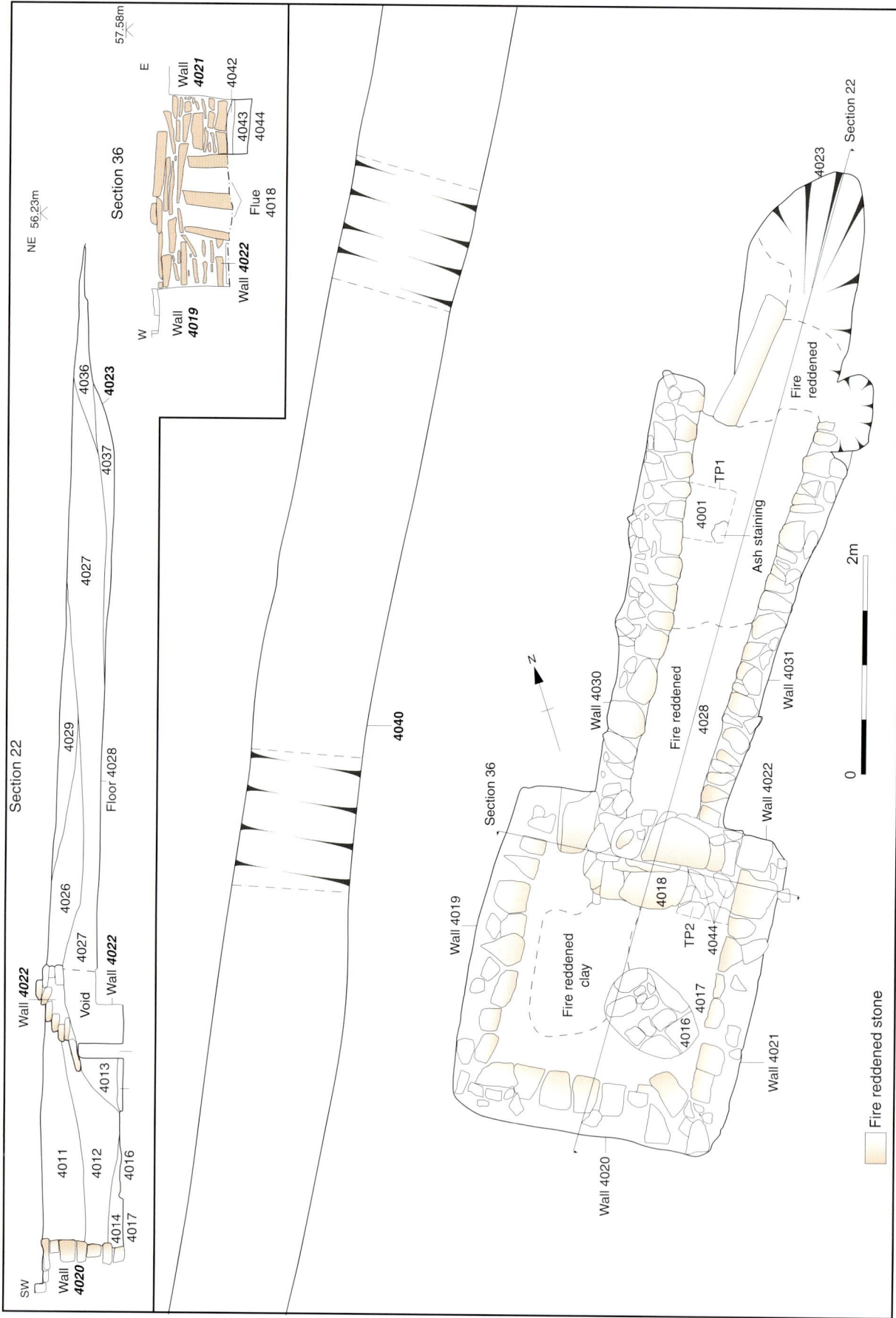

Fig. 3.33   Phase 2c Site 5 Malting oven plan and section

at the open end of the channel. Where the channel entered the pit, the overlying end wall (4022) was supported on three upright stone slabs. These extended into the chamber of the pit itself and were roofed with flat stone slabs (4018) (see detail Pl. 3.5).

The primary infilling deposits in the pit were two layers (4014 and 4015) of ashy silt, both containing a high concentration of charred cereal grain. A sample of this material was taken for environmental analysis (see Moffet, Chapter 4). Sealing deposit 4015 was layer 4013, a sandy silt, that extended into the 'tunnel' linking the pit with the channel and merged with layer 4027 (see below). A small fragment of Middle Saxon pottery was recovered from layer 4013. In the pit layers 4013 and 4014 were overlaid by layer of grey brown silty clay (4012)

containing a large proportion of substantial fragments of structural fired clay. The final layer in the pit filling was 4011, a more silty version of layer 4012, containing a lesser proportion of fired clay fragments. Sample of the fired clay material from layers 4011 and 4012 was recovered for analysis (see below Chapter 4).

A sample of the charred grain from context 4015 within the pit was subjected to radiocarbon dating and produced an AMS date of cal 710 AD–963 AD at 68% confidence, or 662 AD–1014 AD at 95% confidence. This date range fits into the timeframe of the enclosure complex, and suggests that the oven's final use (producing the charred grain) could well have taken place just before the complex was dismantled.

Plate 3.6   Skeleton 6678 in the enclosure ditch backfill Phase 2c

The primary fill of the channel at its open end was an ashy lens (4037). This was overlaid by a sandy silt layer (4036), and both were covered by a layer (4027) of silty clay which extended the entire length of the channel and merged with layer 4013. In turn this was overlaid by layers 4026 and 4029 of mixed orange and brown silty clay. These deposits appear to be the result of deliberate deposition, perhaps the final backfill of the disused feature.

(For a full analysis of the oven's structural clay, and a discussion of the construction, use and abandonment of the oven, see Edwards *et al*, Chapter 4; and for analysis of the charred grain, see Moffett, Chapter 4.)

Associated features

No evidence was found of any structural features within a radius of approximately 5 m from the oven structure. A very shallow NE-SW oriented gully (4032=4040) was revealed running alongside and parallel to the west side of the oven. A possible continuation of this feature (7524) was identified in evaluation Trench 3 (not illustrated) situated 10 m to the north of the oven, which was targeted on two possible linear features identified from the magnetometer survey (Fig. 2.2). The dating of this shallow gully is uncertain, despite its similar alignment to the oven's axis. The few sherds of pottery from the fill are a mix of Roman, late Saxon and medieval. If it is associated with the oven, it does not appear to have had a structural function.

A further evaluation trench (Tr. 2, not illustrated), situated some 10 m to the west of the oven revealed a large, shallow quarry pit (7516). Sample excavation of its fill (7517) produced pieces of fired clay very similar to the oven fabric within the oven chamber, and showing similar wattle impressions. However, these pieces were all very abraded, suggesting they had been weathered before deposition in the pit. A few sherds of late medieval pottery were also recovered from the fill.

PHASE 3 (MID 9th CENTURY TO 11th CENTURY) (FIG. 3.34)

With the demise of the enclosure complex at the end of Phase 2c, the landscape once more became open ground. The evidence for the occupation and activity that developed in the succeeding two centuries is much more scattered and seems to be characterised by a much more modest scale of enterprise in terms of the division of the landscape.

The evidence is for at least two *foci* of settlement or activity. One focus ('South-west group') was represented by a self-contained ditch and gully group at the south-edge of Site 4. To the east of this group is a small scatter of features including beam slots and postholes ('Central group'). To the north and east is a more widespread, but diffuse spread of features across Site 2, the east part of Site 4, and encroaching onto Site 8 ('Northern group').

South-west group (Fig. 3.35)

To the south-west, in Site 4, the evidence was largely contained within a shallow ditch (7307) that extended from the south-west baulk of Site 4 and curved to enter the south east side. Within the enclosure defined by ditch 7307 was an interrupted gully (6017), which seemed to echo the orientation of the 7307, and in the southern corner of the site, a straight gully (7310). A small assemblage (15g) of early mid Saxon pottery and animal bone was recovered from the fills of these features. These gullies varied in size from 0.6 m to 0.9 m in width and 0.20 m to 0.5 m deep.

Immediately outside the enclosure ditch (7307) to the north-east was an irregular shaped flat-bottomed pit (6279) partially exposed against the baulk. The pit measured 1.8 m long x 2.5 m wide x 0.15 m deep, and there was a possible posthole in the base of the pit. The size of the pit, the possible presence of a posthole, all suggest that the feature could have been an SFB similar to those to the north. A small assemblage of late Saxon pot and bone was recovered from the pit fill (6280), along with some animal bone.

Central group (Fig. 3.35)

The scatter of features in this group has little cohesion, and reveal no clear patterns. To the north of ditch 7307 on a rough south-west to north-east alignment was a curvilinear ditch 7325. The ditch measured approximately 15 m long and was between 0.4 m and 0.7 m wide and 0.16–0.45 m deep, and contained a mid grey brown silty clay fill. A total of 10 sherds (43g) of pottery, dated to between 850–900AD were recovered from the fill, in addition to some animal bone.

To the southwest of ditch 7325 and the north and east of enclosure 7307 was a small scatter of postholes and beamslots possibly representing one or more structures. The principal feature is a beamslot (7324) 5.8 m in length, 0.40 m in width and 0.08 m in depth with sheer sides and a flat base. Two fragments of 9th-century pottery were recovered from the fill of the feature. A second beam slot (7142) thought to relate to this feature was identified immediately to the south on a NW-SE alignment. This was approximately 2.0 m in length with squared ends, 0.32 m in width and 0.05 m in depth containing a mid-orange brown silty clay fill.

A small group of shallow pits to the south and west, and postholes to the east of these features, may be related to this focus of activity. They have similar fills (mid to dark brown silty clay) which differ from those of the postholes thought to relate to Phase 2b building group 7327 further to the west. However, given the variable nature of the subsoil in this area, reliance upon the characteristics of fills alone is perhaps not advisable; it is quite possible that some of the features assigned to this group may belong to Phase 2b, or even Phase 1.

A little to the north of beamslot 7324 was a circular, flat-bottomed pit (6054) with straight sides, measuring 0.2 m in diameter and 0.3 m in depth. The feature contained a single fill of mid grey brown sandy silt from which 23 sherds (108g) of pottery dated to the 10th century was recovered, in addition to a quantity of animal bone.

Northern group (Fig. 3.26, 3. 36)

The main evidence for Phase 3 occupation extends across Site 2, the eastern part of Site 4 and into Site 8. It comprises ditches and gullies, buildings and associated features.

Gullies and associated features (Site 2) (Figs 3.26, 3.34-3. 38)

An irregular and extensive complex of gullies and associated features were identified across most of Site 2, clearly post-dating the enclosure ditch and the buildings of Phase 2. Due to lack of resources attention was focussed on the features to the east of the enclosure ditch extension. Features to the west were planned as soil marks but remained largely unexcavated. They are assigned to Phase 3 by virtue of their similarity in form and layout to features to the east assigned on the evidence of stratigraphy and finds to Phase 3.

The central element of the group of linear features was a curving, interrupted ditch (2650/

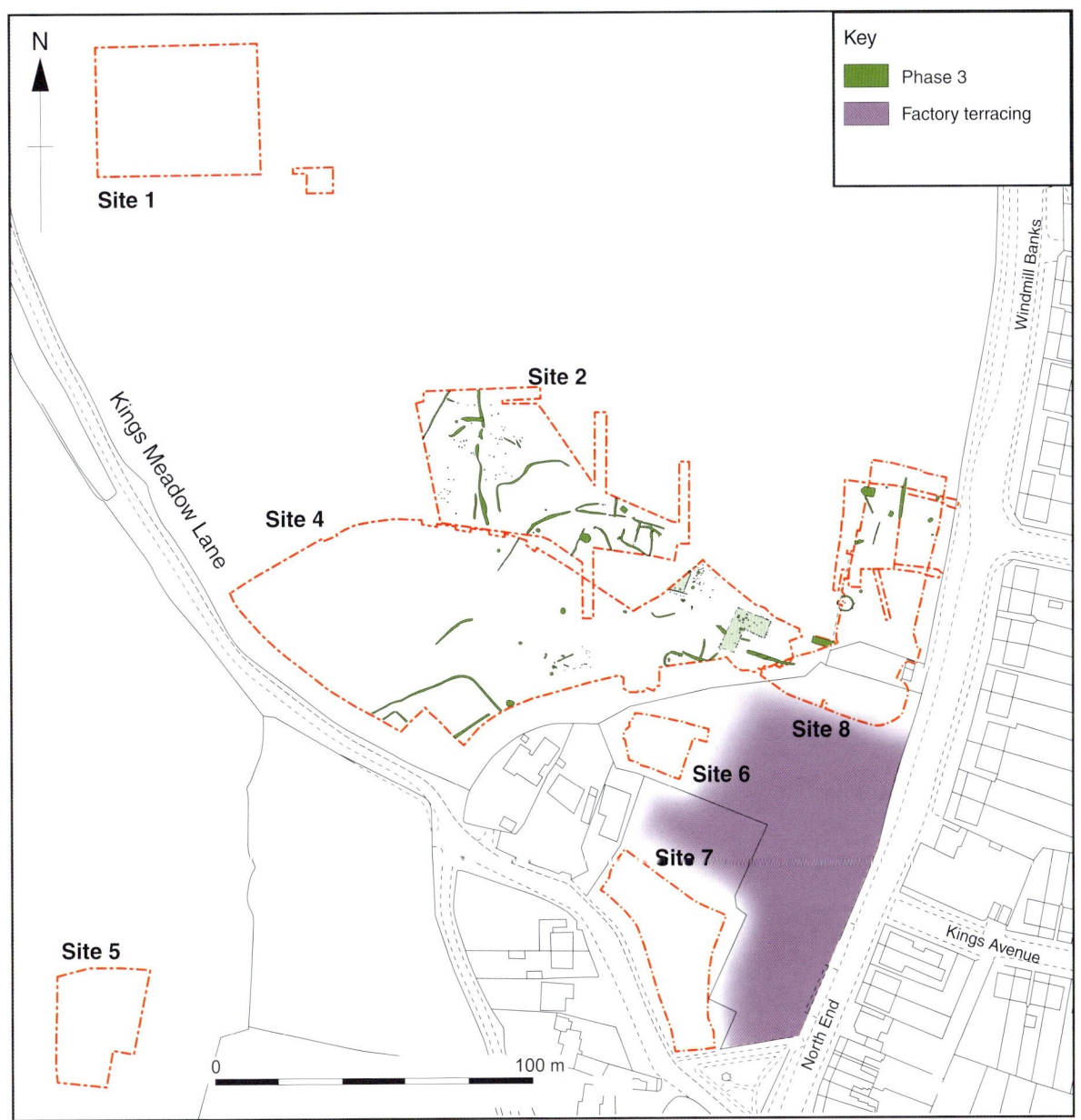

Fig. 3.34   Phase 3 Late Saxon activity

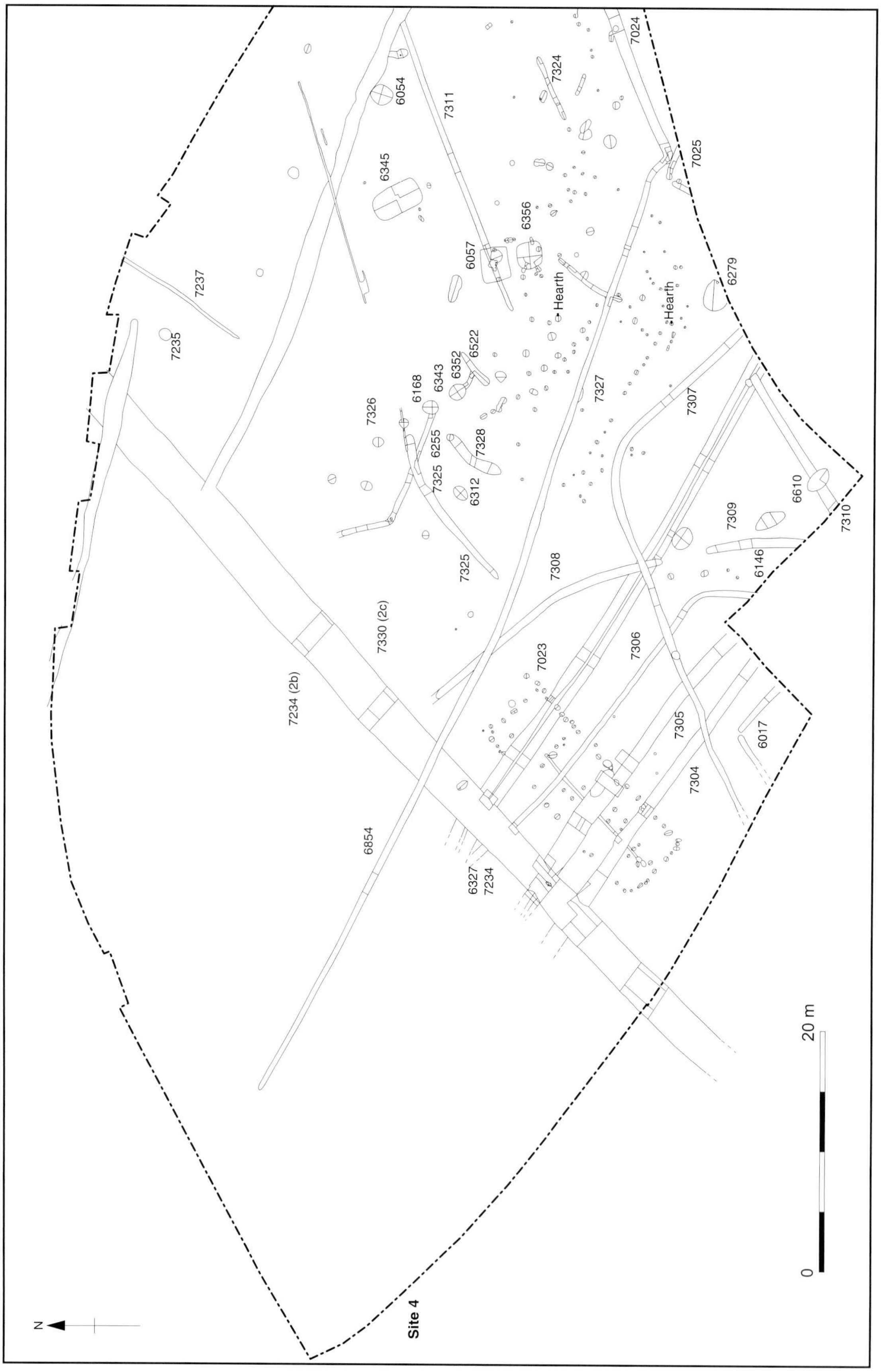

Fig. 3.35 Site 4 (W): General plan of features

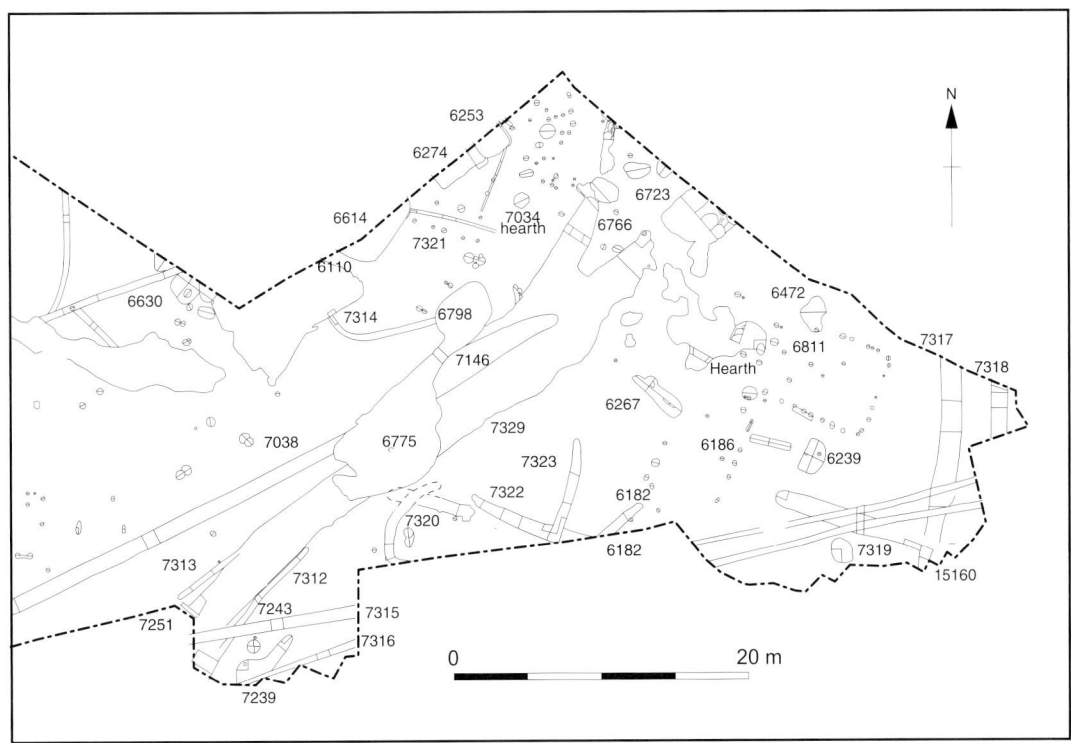

Fig. 3.36 Site 4 (E): General plan of features

2077/2109/2547), running across the site from east to south-west and probably extending into Site 4 in the form of the narrow gully 7237 (Fig. 3.35). The central part of the linear feature (context 2109) appears to represent two divergent stretches of gully, and two postholes 2145 and 2174 continue the line of the northern arm of 2109 to the east. Approximately 4 m to the west of ditch 7237 in Site 4, was an isolated pit (7235) measuring 1.05 m in diameter and 0.2 m in depth containing a quantity of oak charcoal (see Thompson and Francis, Chapter 4), along with fragments of fired clay, animal bone (including pig and horse bones), burnt stone and fragments of an iron knife blade (not illustrated, Cat No. 27), which is a post-medieval form and probably intrusive.

The gap between ditch 2077 and 2650 could represent access into an enclosure, and slightly to the north was a flat-bottomed pit (2008), measuring approximately 2.2 m long x 1.45 m wide x 0.25 m deep. The fill was a sequence of burnt clay deposits and soil, and produced a small assemblage of animal bone, but only one sherd of redeposited 3rd-century pottery. The sides of the pit were cut to form a ledge in places, prompting the suggestion that the pit had been used as an exterior hearth, covered by some form of superstructure. A simpler, and arguably more convincing, explanation is that the pit represents the site of a bonfire, probably repeatedly used. The heat from the fire would have discoloured and granulated the underlying clay subsoil, giving the impression, when revealed in excavation of a shallow pit filled with layers of burnt clay and ash.

To the south of the main enclosure line were a number of small gullies (2010, 2013, 2165, 2651 and 2652) apparently defining small enclosures. Also identified was a large shallow pit (2009), irregular in plan, with a maximum diameter of 3.62 m and a maximum depth of 0.30 m. Despite the fact that the pit fill (2006) produced a similar assemblage of charred plant remains to the gullies to the north, and a single sherd of pottery, it seems most likely that this feature represents a contemporary tree throw. A similar, but smaller pit (2346) was identified to the

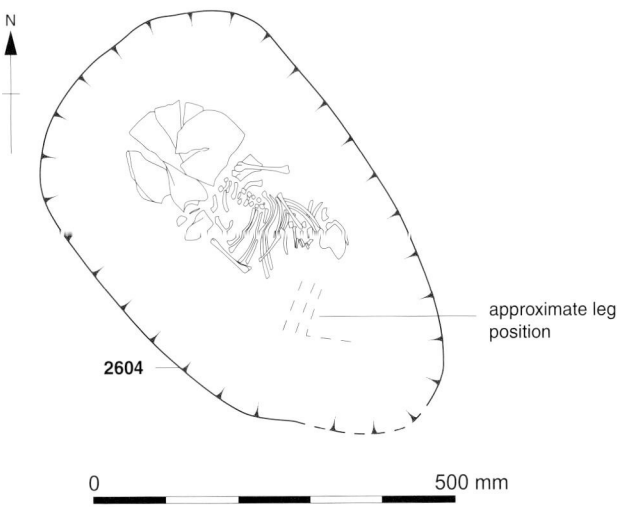

Fig. 3.37 Phase 3 Site 2 Child burial 2591

west, close to ditch 2547. A significant assemblage of charred grain was recovered from fill 2004 of gully 2010.

On the west side of ditch 2547 the rudimentary and disturbed grave (2604) of a child burial (2591) was identified (Fig. 3.37 and Pl. 5.5). The grave was cut was a very shallow oval pit with a rounded base, measuring no more than 0.70 m long x 0.40 m wide x 0.14 m deep. The site of the burial was under an area of post-medieval plough disturbance, which possibly accounts for at least part of the disturbance of the grave and its contents and lay within the footprint of the demolished Phase 2b structure 2666. The burial is described in detail by Witkin in Chapter 4.

Building 7321 (Site 4) (Fig. 3.38)

To the south-east of the pattern of ditched enclosures just described and located against the north baulk of Site 4, was a group of postholes and beamslots defining part of a rectangular structure or building and associated structures or features. Approximately 12 m to the south-east on the same NE-SW alignment is another building 6811 (see below).

The eastern wall of building 7321 was defined by a beamslot (6300) approximately 5 m long and incorporating two postholes (6308 and 6302). The north end of the beamslot was truncated by late medieval quarrying, but posthole 6306 could represent the original northern terminus of the slot. Similarly, the south end of the slot could be indicated by posthole 6594. The northern wall of Building 7321 was represented by a short length of slot (6304) emerging from the west baulk and terminating close to posthole 6306.

The south side of the structure was represented by beamslot 6582, which measured at least 6 m long. Its western end was truncated by late medieval quarrying, and its eastern end was very indistinct due to post-medieval ploughing, although it was still evident that beamslot 6582 continued beyond the junction with beamslot 6300. On either side of beamslot 6582 was a series of postholes – five to the south, two to the north (in addition to posthole 6594). The southern group may have been external to the structure and could very well represent bracing struts for the southern wall.

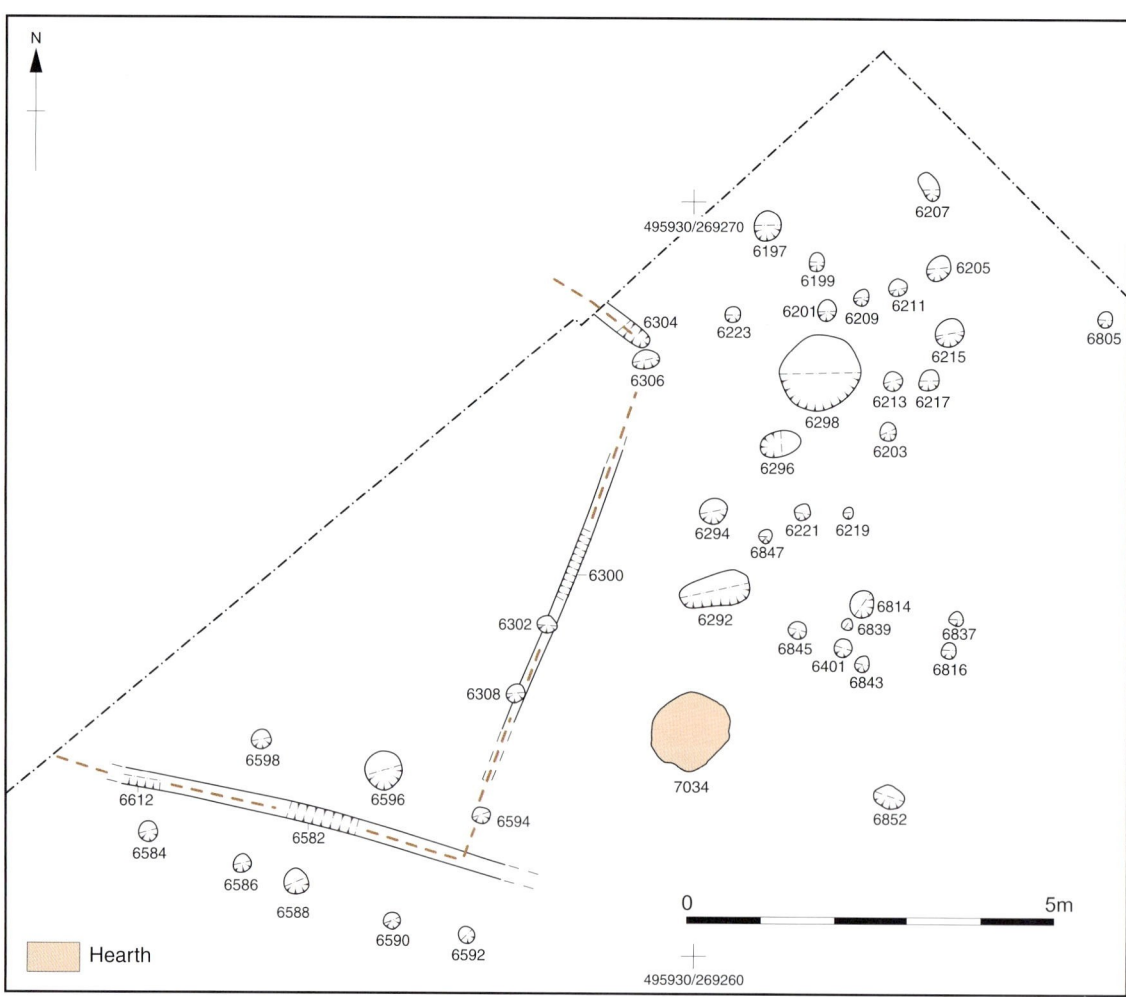

Fig. 3.38 Phase 3 Site 4 Building 7321

Associated features

A number of post holes to the east of this structure are also thought to be related. However, no discernible pattern could be seen. The fill of the postholes was identical to that of the building beam slot and postholes, and three postholes close to the north east corner of the structure contained pottery dated to the late Saxon period. A sub-circular area of burnt subsoil (7034), probably representing a hearth base, was identified near the east side of the building. A sample from the hearth material revealed evidence of barley (see Moffett Chapter 4). Finds recovered from the hearth included burnt stone and pottery dated to the 10th century.

Further to the south of this area were the remains of a curving gully (7314) measuring 0.42 m in width and 0.14 m. Both ends of the ditch were truncated by late medieval quarrying. Eight fragments of 9th- to 10th-century pottery were recovered from its fill. It is possible that this ditch relates to the complex of gullies on Site 2 to the north-west. Two pairs of closely spaced postholes between ditch 7314 and Building 7321 may also be elements within this phase.

Building 6811 (Site 4) (Fig. 3.39- 3.40)

The structure was situated at the east corner of Site 4, and was identified as an arrangement of postholes apparently defining an 'L' shaped struc-ture, although truncation by later ploughing was particularly severe over the north-western part of the structure. The main W-E wing of the building measured approximately 12.0 m x 6.0 m and consisted of 23 postholes, mostly circular, averaging 0.25 m wide and 0.12 m deep. Internally nine postholes and remains of three hearths, defined by shallow depressions in the subsoil (7026, 7076, 7049), were identified. Environmental samples were retrieved from the ashy material (7027, 7077) of two of these hearth features (see Moffett Chapter 4). Hearth 7076 was the only feature to contain finds including a small quantity of burnt stone, slag, fired clay, flint, animal bone and a lead sheet fragment.

A possible annex or additional wing to the building was suggested by an arrangement of 13 postholes and one short gully extending at 90° to the main structure. The fill of these features was different from the fills of main structure and consisted of mid to dark brown silty clay, suggesting that they parts of a separate building episode. The clearest surviving wall line, on the east side of the 'annexe', included a 1.0 m wide gap suggestive of a doorway, between posthole 6096 and gully 6792. In the interior of this wing there were three postholes, two of which (6092, 6098) could relate to the suggested doorway, as they are situated close to either side. A small amount of pottery (3 sherds) from three of the postholes (6092, 6094 and 6096) was dated to the late Saxon period.

Associated features

In the angle formed by the two wings of Building 6811 was a short linear feature (6186), possibly a beamslot. Its fill produced 10th-century pottery, an awl (SF 319 – Fig. 4.16, 2) and a small quantity of iron slag and burnt stone. Further to the east a ditch (7319) was identified, extending for 14 m to the eastern baulk of Site 4, a further 5 m length of the same feature was identified on Site 8 (context 15160). The ditch was up to 1.32 m in width and 0.34 m in depth and contained a mid grey brown silty clay fill. Finds included 9th- to 10th-century pottery and animal bone.

Paddock complex (Site 4) (Fig. 3.40)

To the south-west of Building 6811 was a complex of linear features possibly defining a series of paddocks or small enclosures represented by 4 separate ditches dated from the 11th to the 12th century. The western side of the enclosure was formed by a curving ditch (7320) that contained 22 sherds of 12th century pottery. In close proximity was a short NW-SE ditch (6115), part of which had been identified in an NAU evaluation trench. The relationship between these two features was not clear. Continuing to the south-east from ditch 6115 was ditch 7322, which also produced 9th- to 12th century pottery. Running north off ditch 7322, and towards Building 6811 was a short gully (7323), which produced nearly 400g (61 fragments) of pottery of a similar date. In addition to the pottery and animal bone was a pair of bone handle plates held together with iron rivets (SF310 Fig. 4.22, 63), and a knife blade (SF 318 – Fig. 4.18, 26). To the east of 7323, another small ditch (6182) was identified, which appeared to extend the north-east from 7322 for a distance of 6 m. In contrast to the others features in this group, this gully produced bone but no pottery.

To the north and east of Building 6811 a small group of features was identified on Site 8, north of the line of the Phase 2c enclosure ditch, and this group is assigned to Phase 3. The features included an SFB, and possibly associated ditches and pits.

SFB 15300 (Site 8) (Fig. 3.41, Pl. 3.7)

This was first revealed, but only partially excavated during the evaluation of this area (Site 3). The shape in plan of the SFB pit (15296) as depicted (Fig. 3.41) is a composite; only the eastern part was fully excavated in Site 8, while the western end of the pit was defined approximately in the evaluative work on Site 3. The feature measured approximately 5 m long x 2.8 m wide in total, with near vertical sides sharply rounding to a near flat base. A single posthole (15297) measuring 0.12 m diameter x 0.26 m deep was identified, located against the eastern end of the pit, at its mid-point.

The single grey brown silty fill (15305) of the pit

Fig. 3.39 Phase 3 Site 4 Building 6811

Annex postholes

Hearths

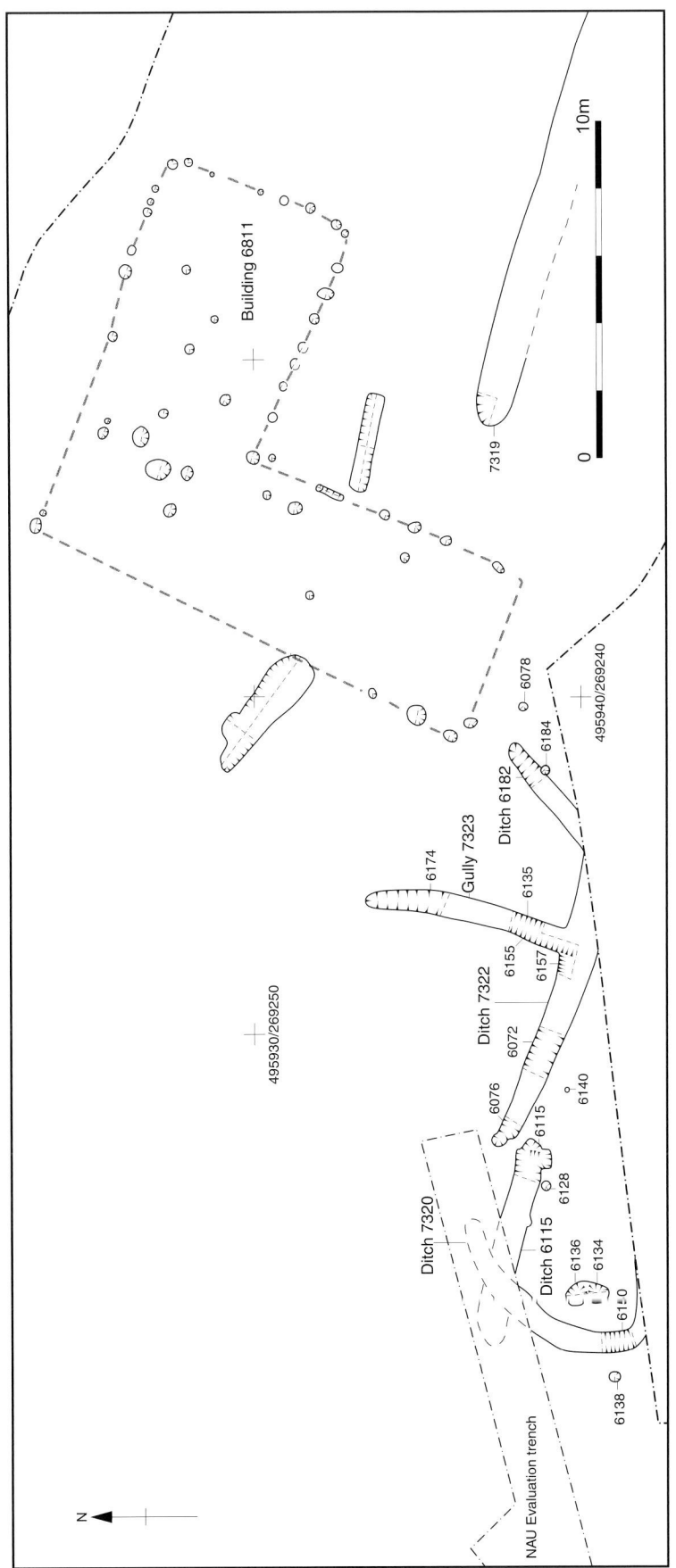

Building 6811

7319

495940/269240

6078

6184

Ditch 6182

6135

Gully 7323

6174

6155

6157

Ditch 7322

6072

495930/269250

6076

6140

6115

6128

Ditch 7320

Ditch 6115

6136

6134

6110

6138

NAU Evaluation trench

N

10m

0

Fig. 3.40   Phase 3 Site 4 Paddock complex 7320 and Building 6811

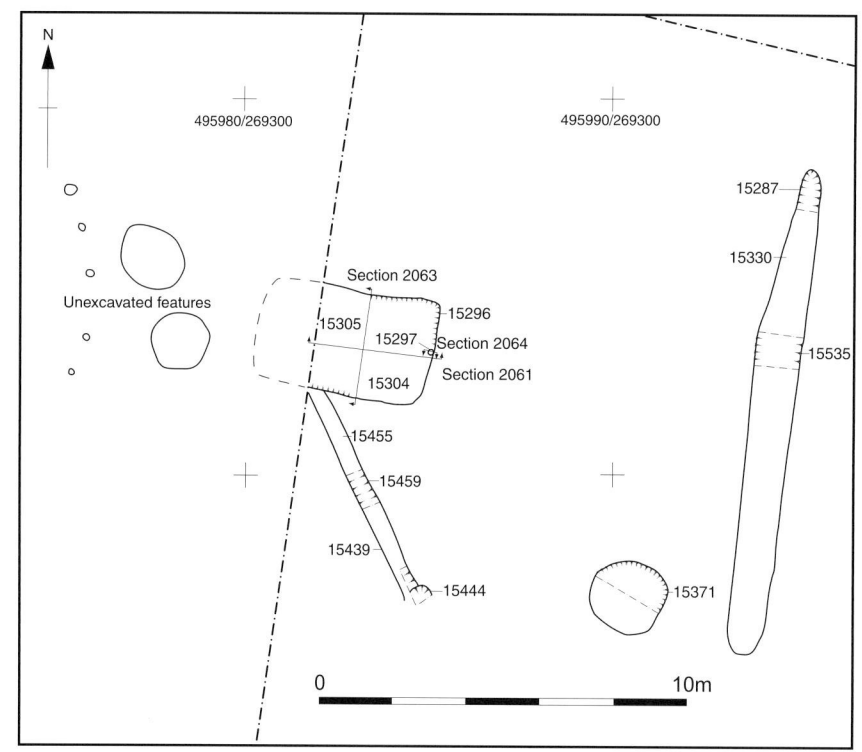

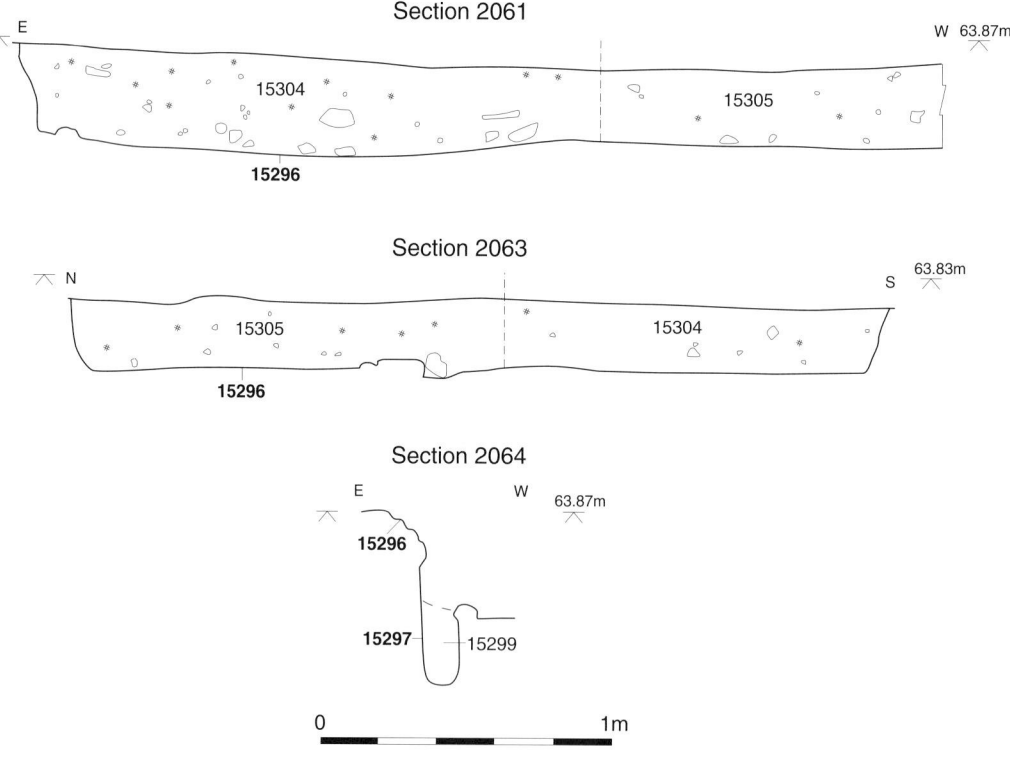

Fig. 3.41   Phase 3 Site 8 Building 15300 and associated features

produced modest quantities of animal bone and late 10th-century pottery, and a single iron object (Fig. 4.22, 64), whose function is unclear. A sample of the pit fill produced a mixed charred plant assemblage, which may well be indicative of later (possibly Phase 4) domestic waste.

Features possibly associated with the SFB included a shallow gully (15455) extending to the south-east, and truncated by later features. The fill of the gully (15460) also produced pottery of the late 10th century. A similar shallow gully (15410), oriented N-S was detected to the south of 15455, and may also be associated. To the east, a 13.5 m long north-south oriented ditch (15330) was identified, measuring 0.60 m wide x a maximum of 0.20 m deep. Its fill contained a small quantity of St Neots Ware.

A number of pits were identified in the vicinity of the SFB; circular pit 15371 was located to the southeast, and produced animal bone, pottery and burnt stone from its three layered fills. A scatter of soil marks, possibly representing two large pits and five postholes, were recorded to the west of the SFB during the Site 3 evaluation, but were not excavated. The north-eastern part of Site 8 was conspicuously empty of features, except for three pits (15256, 15258, 15261), all of which produced 10th-century pottery. While they may be associated with the domestic focus of the SFB pit, it is recog-

nised that they could relate to another focus off-site to the north or east.

Ring gully (Fig. 3.42)

Towards the southern part of Site 8 a ring gully 15365 was identified, close to the western baulk. Posthole 15359, sited at the approximate centre of the ring gully would appear to be associated. Two postholes of similar size (15352 and 15357) were located against the outside of the gully on the eastern side. A small assemblage of late Saxon pottery was recovered from the gully fill. A possible contemporary pit (15462) was identified to the north-east of the ring gully. Its fill contained a piece of daub displaying one crudely smoothed face, but no wattle marks. Given the fact that the pit was cut by a later (Phase 4) drain, the daub may be intrusive.

PHASE 4 (11th -13th CENTURY) (Fig. 3.43)

There appears to be some migration or nucleation of the Phase 3 settlement *foci*, both southwards towards the junction of Kings Meadow Lane and Windmill Banks, and eastwards towards the main N-S road at Windmill Banks. Whereas in Phase 3 the settlement is not sharply focused, in Phase 4 there are two distinct areas of settlement: to the south in

Plate 3.7   Late Saxon SFB Site 8 Phase 3

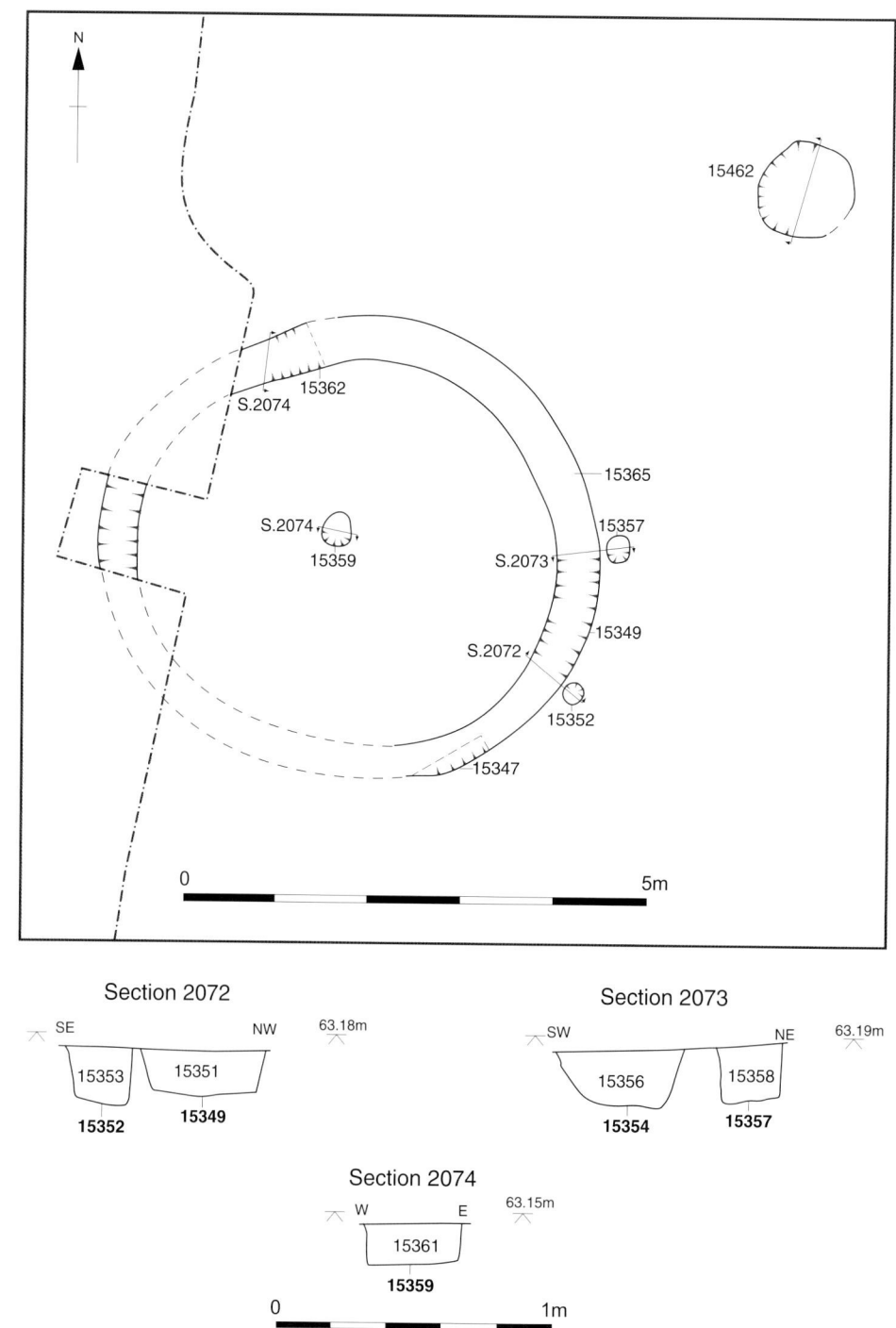

Fig. 3.42 Phase 3 Site 8 Structure 15365 and associated features

Site 7, where the evidence suggests a modest settlement, and to the north, at the east end of Site 4 and in Site 8, where more elaborate structures were found.

Between the two *foci*, plough furrows and field boundaries respect and echo an boundary leading from the Lane in a north-easterly direction towards the N-S road. It is during this phase that the land divisions evident in their developed form in the 1737 map (see Pl.1.3) are first identified archaeolog-

ically. From this point on there is a clear distinction between the agricultural land to the west and settlement (of whatever character) to the east and south.

Southern settlement (Site 7) (Figs 3.44)

The earliest phase of activity comprised an arrangement of linear and curvilinear ditches along with a number of pits. The ditches were principally orientated NE-SW and NW-SE and were relatively

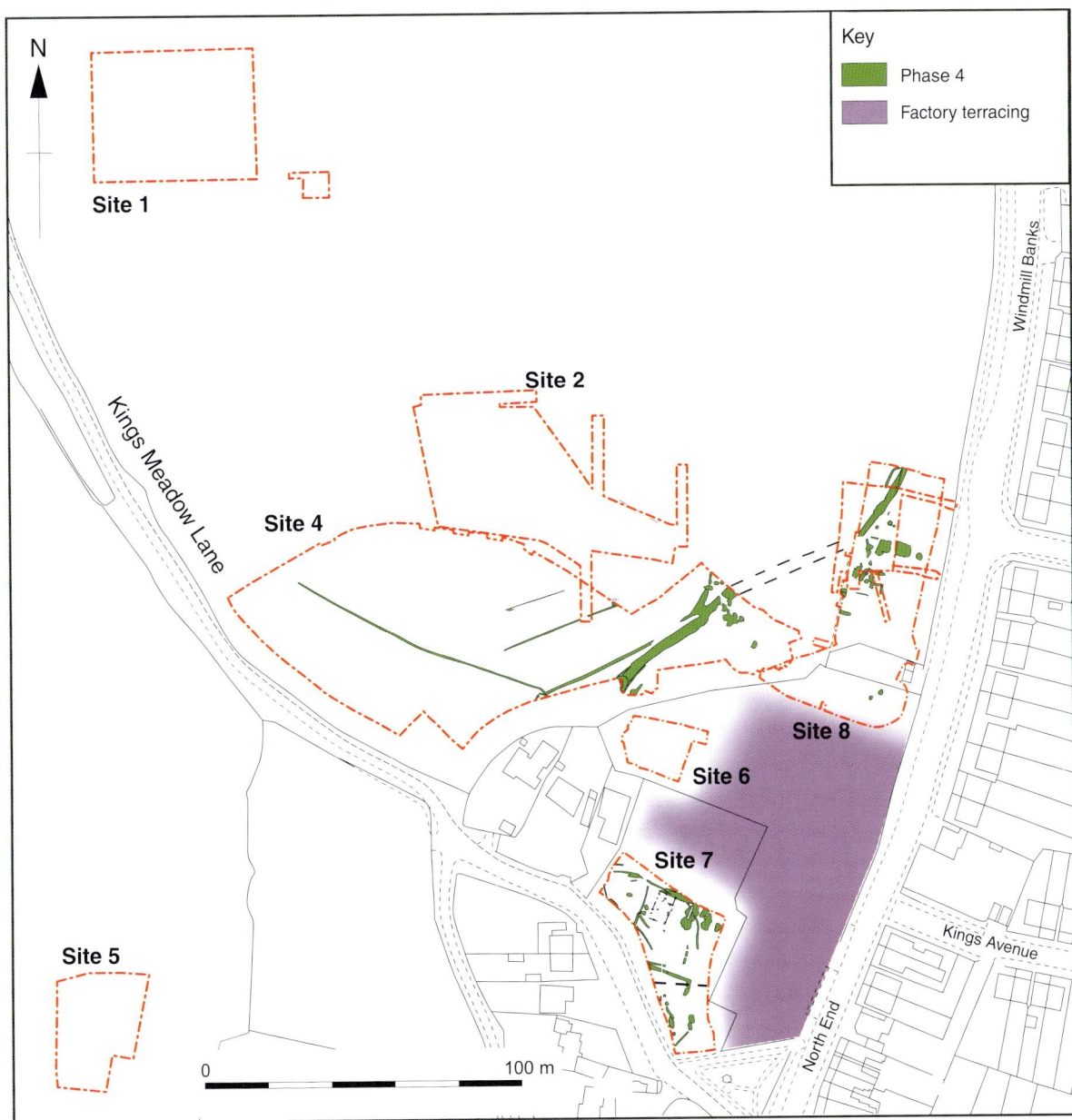

Fig. 3.43   Phase 4 Medieval activity

shallow. They appear to form the remains of two sub-rectangular enclosures orientated NE-SW. Pottery assemblages from the ditch fills were dominated by early medieval sherds. These along with stratigraphic and spatial relationships suggest an early medieval date.

Building 9528 (Site 7) (Fig. 3.45)

Within the westernmost enclosure 11 post-holes and a shallow gully, orientated NE-SW may represent a structure. Sherds of 11th- to 12th-century pottery from these and nearby features suggest an early medieval date for the building. The postholes that were excavated were generally shallow, having suffered considerable truncation. Four postholes

within the building footprint were identified, but their arrangement did not suggest they represented internal aisle posts.

Immediately to the north of building were at least two gullies (9385 and 9389), which may have curved around the east side of the building. To the east of the Building 9528 was a narrow curving gully (9517), which probably represents a continuation to the south-east of ditch 9385. Also to the east were some large pits (9342, 9344 9358, 9515). The pits were sample-excavated, and in general produced modest amounts of pottery and bone. It is suggested that they represent backfilled clay quarry pits, and that the occupational debris they contained was derived from redeposited midden material.

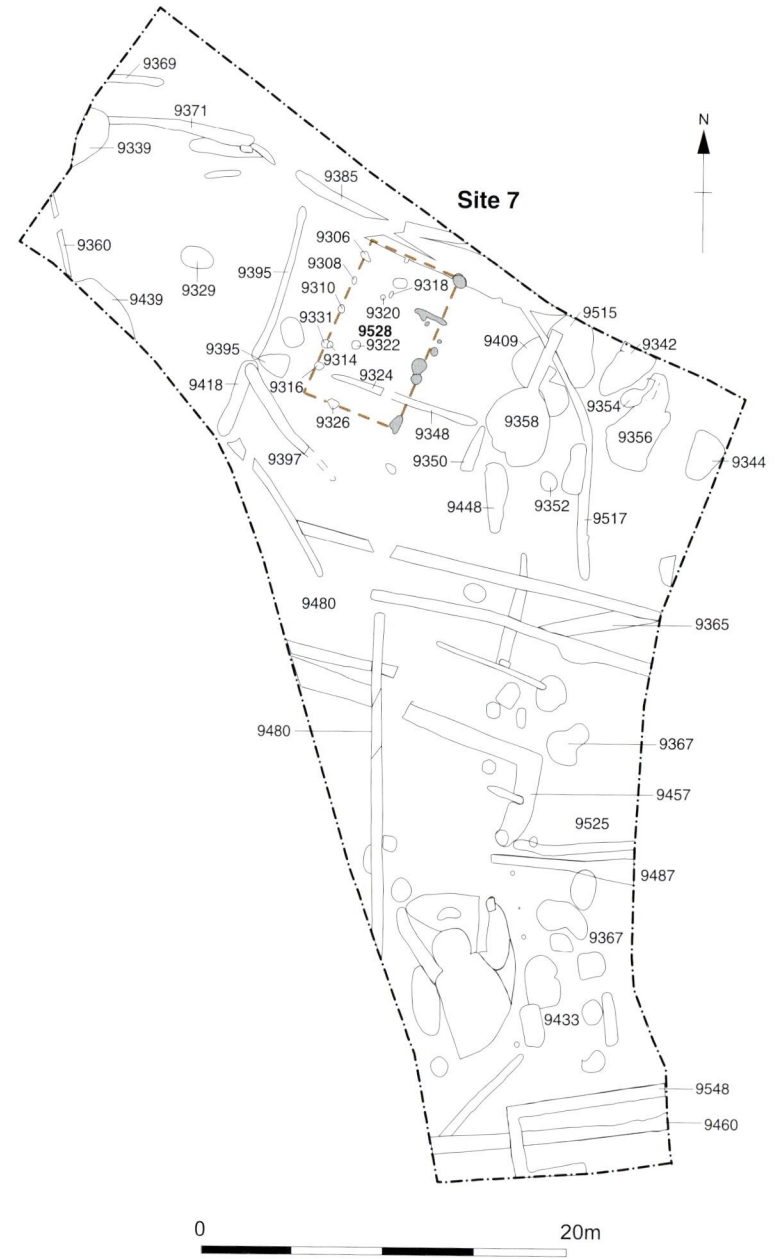

Fig. 3.44   Site 7: General plan of features

To the south-east of Building 9528, a substantial L-shaped ditch (9457) was identified. This was aligned WNW-ESE and had a right angle turn at the SE end. Finds included early medieval pottery and some bone. To the south of ditch 9457 a number of features – principally pits – were identified and assigned to this phase on the grounds of their stratigraphic relationships or the similarity of their fills with excavated features of this phase.

Eastern settlement (Site 8) (Fig. 3.46, Pl. 3.8)

The division between settlement and agricultural land is clearly shown in Site 8, where a large boundary ditch (15320) extends from the northern baulk, curving south-west, away from the line of the north-south road, possibly to reappear in Site 4 as ditch 7329. Ditch 15320 had a fairly steep sided U-shaped profile, and averaged 1.4 m wide x 0.40 m deep. Its fill, 15279, produced a quantity of generally 12th-century pottery along with some animal bone.

An area of concentrated domestic activity was identified immediately to the east of ditch 15320. Unfortunately this was also an area that appears to have suffered considerable truncation by later ploughing, making the reconstruction of the domestic activity unusually difficult. There are numerous structural elements, but not a clear structural pattern.

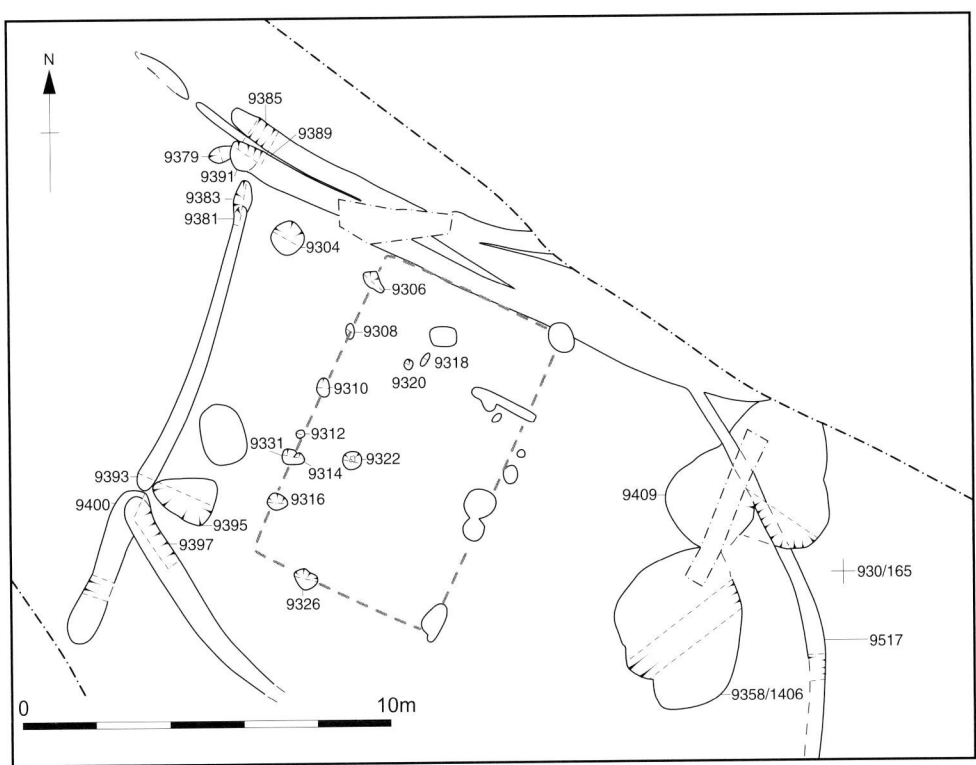

Fig. 3.45   Phase 4 Site 7 Building 9528

Plate 3.8   Structural remains Site 8 Phase 4

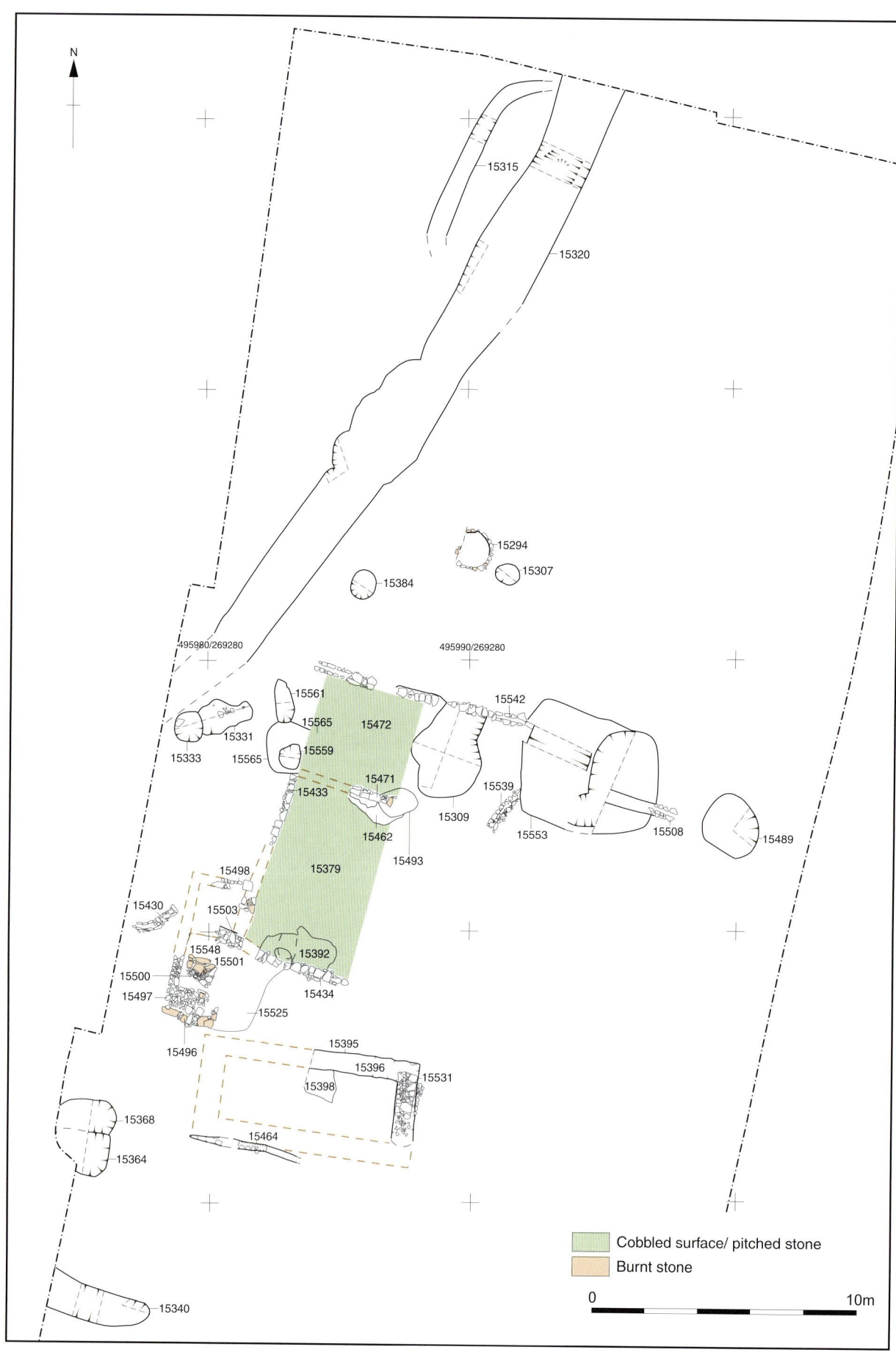

N

15315

15320

15294

15307

15384

495980/269280

495990/269280

15561

15565

15472

15542

15331

15559

15333

15565

15565

15471

15433

15309

15539

15462

15493

15508

15553

15489

15498

15379

15430

15503

15548

15392

15501

15500

15497

15434

15525

15496

15395

15398

15396

15531

15368

15464

15364

15340

Cobbled surface/ pitched stone

Burnt stone

0   10m

The earliest activity is represented by a scatter of large deep pits (15553, 15489, 15309, 15563), possibly originally dug as quarries, and either backfilled in one operation or used as rubbish pits and filled in episodically. Finds in these fills included modest assemblages of animal bone and 12th- to 13th-century pottery, and inclusions of daub fragments. The focus of this activity was located in the middle of the site, with a group of at least three vertically sided or undercut pits (including pits 15309 and 15553) each at least 0.90 m deep. For safety reasons none were bottomed. The presence of domestic rubbish in the pits, albeit not in large quantities, implies a settlement focus nearby.

The quarrying activity in the central part of the site gave way to a complex of structural elements, seemingly related but difficult to understand as a group. The activity focussed around a well-used pitched limestone yard surface (15379), which sealed some of the infilled quarry pits. The northern edge of the yard surface was bounded by a stone-sided and stone-capped drain (15542) which extended for a distance of approximately 9.2 m. The drain was constructed within a shallow trench, so that the stone capping was flush with the yard surface. It was noted that there was no stone floor to the drain. To the west, the drain structure petered out, but to the east it appeared to run into the western side of a large pit (15553). The pit remained largely unexcavated, but it appears to have served as a sump for two other drains (15539 and 15508).

A circular stone-lined oven base (15294) measuring 1.3 m in diameter and 0.10 m in depth was located to the north of the drain. The interior of the oven base was formed of hard-packed and burnt clay (15303). Another oven (15493) was situated on the southern side of the yard surface and survived as a sub-circular spread of superimposed layers of ash and hard-packed burnt clay. An Edward I penny (SF 4032 – not illustrated) dating to AD 1278-1307 was found in this material, and an environmental sample produced fairly abundant cereal remains (see Moffett Chapter 4).

The southern element of this settlement focus was represented by a small rectangular structure (15495) and possibly related surfaces, drains and walls. Structure 15495 was oriented NNE-SSW and measured approximately 5.6 m long x 2.2 m wide. Its walls (where they had survived later truncation) were defined by unmortared limestone rubble footings surviving to a maximum of three courses, averaging 0.40 m wide. The south and west wall footings (15496 and 15497) were reasonably intact. The north wall (15498) was heavily damaged. The east wall was only suggested by short returns of the north and south walls, and it is by no means clear if it extended the length of the building, or if the building was open-fronted to the east. Any clarifying evidence was destroyed by the post-medieval ditch (15283; Fig. 3.53) at this point.

Within the footprint of structure 15495 were the partial remains of a ?hearth floor of pitched stone and limestone slabs (15500), extending over much of the southern part of the structure. Many of the slabs displayed evidence of burning. Crossing the northern part of the structure's footprint was a stone built drain (15503), which appeared to run to a point coincident with the line of the west wall of structure 15495. At this point a further short length of drain (15430) curved away to the south-west. The construction of the two drains differed slightly, suggesting they were not built at the same time, although their location suggests they were part of the same drainage system. Drain 15430 was V shaped in profile, the sides formed of slabs of unworked limestone, with a flat stone capping. In contrast, drain 15503 was box-shaped in profile, with a flat stone-slab floor, vertical stone sides and a stone-capped roof. Where drain 15503 passed through structure 15495, it was noted that the level of the drain roof was some 0.22 m higher than that of the hearth base.

To the east of structure 15495, and butting against both sides of drain 15503 were the remains of a pitched stone surface (15525, 15392) which showed signs of being patched at least once, and levelled with a spread of yellow clay (15527) which showed signs of burning. To the south-east the yard surface butted against the line of a short length of wall footing represented by a very shallow robber trench (15395). This extended east for a distance of approximately 4.5 m, before turning to the south for a distance of 2.5 m in the form of surviving limestone rubble footings 15531, bonded with a lime mortar. No continuation of the wall line was seen beyond what is evident in Figure 3.46, although a very truncated west-east oriented length of stone sided drain (15464) was revealed approximately 3 m to the south of robber trench 15395, and may have run alongside a wall to the north.

Evidence of a later programme of consolidation of these yard areas was found to the north and northeast of Structure 15495. A short length of NE-SW oriented wall (15433) was revealed, comprising a single course of unworked stone slabs, roughly faced to the east. Its appearance suggests it may have revetted a raised area or platform to the west. To the north-east a short length of stone slabs were identified (15471), oriented west-east. This feature was faced to the south and to the north appeared to represent a revetment to a pitched stone surface extending to the north (15472). In the evaluation of this area these two features were linked as one L-shaped feature – the evaluation backfilling and overburden re-stripping appeared to have damaged the fragile remains.

Linear features and Building 7025 (Site 4)

The evidence for occupation in Phase 4 on Site 4

Fig. 3.46 (facing page)   Phase 4 Site 8 Buildings and associated features

comprises almost exclusively shallow linear features, representing land divisions or possibly individual plough furrows. The corner of a possible building was also exposed. It would seem that the area between the settlement *foci* of Sites 7 and 8 reverted to ploughland.

The phasing of the features in this area is uncertain. While their fills produced small quantities of late Saxon (Phase 3) pottery, their stratigraphy, such as it was, and their characteristic straight lines, is in contrast to the less orderly, but more confidently phased Phase 3 features on Site 2 for example. It is quite possible that the late Saxon pottery could be residual, and no surprise that no Phase 4 pottery is present, given the absence of a nearby domestic focus.

A shallow ditch (6854) oriented WNW-ESE appears to have defined the southern extent of the land divisions. It was traced for approximately 80 m from close to the western baulk to a terminus at the eastern side of the site. The terminus of 6854 appeared to have been cut by the terminus of ditch 7024 of similar proportions to 6854 which was oriented WSW-ENE-(7024) and which extended towards the northern baulk, although its northern end was heavily truncated. Ditch 6854 contained a few sherds of, presumably residua,l late Saxon pottery, and ditch 7024 produced both a residual sherd of early Saxon pottery (Fig. 4.1.21), and intrusive sherds of late medieval pottery.

Building 7025 (Fig. 3.35)

Just south of the junction of ditches 6854 and 7024 the north-west corner of a possible building or structure (7025) was exposed. The evidence comprised the termini of two shallow flat-bottomed beamslots (6695 and 6699). The end of 6695 was abutted by a posthole (6697) and another posthole (6707) was situated against the east side of 6699. The only dating evidence from any of the features was a single piece of abraded Roman roof tile. It is arguable that the proximity of the proposed Building 7025 to the junction of ditches 6854 and 7024 is unlikely to be coincidental, and suggests they are part of the same phase of activity.

Parallel to ditch 7024 and approximately 17 to 18 m from was another ditch 7311. This extended from the northern baulk for approximately 39 m towards ditch 6854. The ditch measured approximately 0.5 m in width with a general depth of between 0.09 m and 0.13 m becoming deeper to a recorded 0.23 m at its south-western terminus. Finds included Late Saxon pottery in addition to a quantity of animal bone.

Ditch 7329 (Fig. 3.36), which was a shallow and indistinct feature on a SW-NE orientation, extended across the eastern part of Site 4 for approximately 44 m. At its southern end the ditch was flanked either side by gullies 7312 and 7313, was shallow and had been re-cut on the north western side. Its fill, a dark orange brown silty clay, produced a small quantity

of animal bone and 8 sherds (39g) of Shelly and Sandy Coarseware dated to between 1100 – 1150, slag and a horseshoe fragment (SF 311 – not illustrated). Towards the north-eastern limit of the site the feature became less clear in plan, and its fill, a mid brownish grey silty clay, contained pottery dating to between 1100-1150, animal bone, a further horseshoe fragment (not illustrated) and flint. Any potential stratigraphic relationship between ditches 7329 and 7024 had been destroyed by Phase 5 quarrying (context 6775), but it is believed that ditch 7329 is later in date than 7024. Against the north baulk, ditch/feature 6723 appeared to continue the line of 7239 into the northern baulk, and onwards towards Site 8.

In the north-eastern part of Site 4 two other irregular features (contexts 7146 and 6766) appeared to merge with ditch 7329 from the west. Both 7146 and 6766 were no more than 0.15 m deep with poorly defined edges and furrowed bases. They appeared to be the result of episodic ploughing along the same line, rather than a single construction episode. Along with some animal bone, a range of pottery dating from the 10th to the 12th centuries was recovered from their fills. Other finds from these Site 4 ditch fills included a Clay Spindle Whorl (SF339 – Fig. 4.16, 19), nail fragments (SF 337 & 338 – not illustrated) and an iron plate fragment (SF350 – not illustrated).

In the eastern corner of the excavation area a shallow, flat-bottomed pit (6239) sub-rectangular in plan was identified. It had two finds-rich fills of mid to light greyish brown silty clay. Finds included pottery dated to between 1100 and 1150, along with animal bone, ceramic building materials and two pieces of iron (SF 320 and 321 – not illustrated). The truncated bases of two postholes (6242 and 6244) were identified in the floor of the pit, and may have been functionally related to it.

PHASE 5 (14th CENTURY TO MID 15th CENTURY) (FIG. 3.47)

The later medieval period saw intense industrial activity in Sites 4, 6 and 8, but otherwise the spread of settlement appears to be further confined to only the area near the junction of Kings Meadow Lane and Windmill Banks (Site 7), perhaps reflecting the late medieval contraction of the borough (see Chapter 1).

Site 6 contained the well-preserved remains of Kiln 1 with associated structures, including stone wall footings, stone surfaces and posthole structures, possibly drying sheds. A second, less well-preserved kiln (Kiln 2) was found to the north-east of Kiln 1 on Site 8. This was associated with ditches and a possible limestone rubble surface. To the north of the kiln was a probable boundary ditch 15283, which cut the Phase 4 boundary ditch 15320 and was probably its replacement. To the west of Kiln 2 and north of Kiln 1 a number of quarry pits were located on Site 4. These have been assigned to Phase 5.

Pottery kilns and associated structures

Two kilns were found within the project area, although there is evidence suggesting that there may have been more. Kiln 1 on Site 6 was sufficiently intact and sufficiently fully excavated to allow detailed analysis of the structure (see Chapter 5). The structure of Kiln 2 on Site 8 was heavily truncated but its structure was similar to Kiln 1. An excavation in 1965 immediately to the west of the location of Site 8 revealed a large quantity of wasters and features interpreted at the time as a medieval kiln. This evidence is reconsidered in Chapter 5.

Kiln I (Site 6) (Figs 3.48-3.49, Pls 3.9-3.10)

The kiln (context 9200) was sited in the south-western corner of Site 6, and consisted of a trench that measured 8.20 m long x 3.60 m wide x 0.85 m deep overall. The trench was divided into three sections by thick clay and stone linings (9227 and 9228). The three sections were the central firing chamber and the two stoke pits (9072 and 9082). The central firing chamber (9092) was oval in shape, with an arched flue made from clay (9080 and 9091) at each end. The flues opened into the two stoke pits, (9072 and 9082). Within the firing chamber was a central flat-topped pedestal made of a core of sandy clay with some ironstone rubble. Sealing the

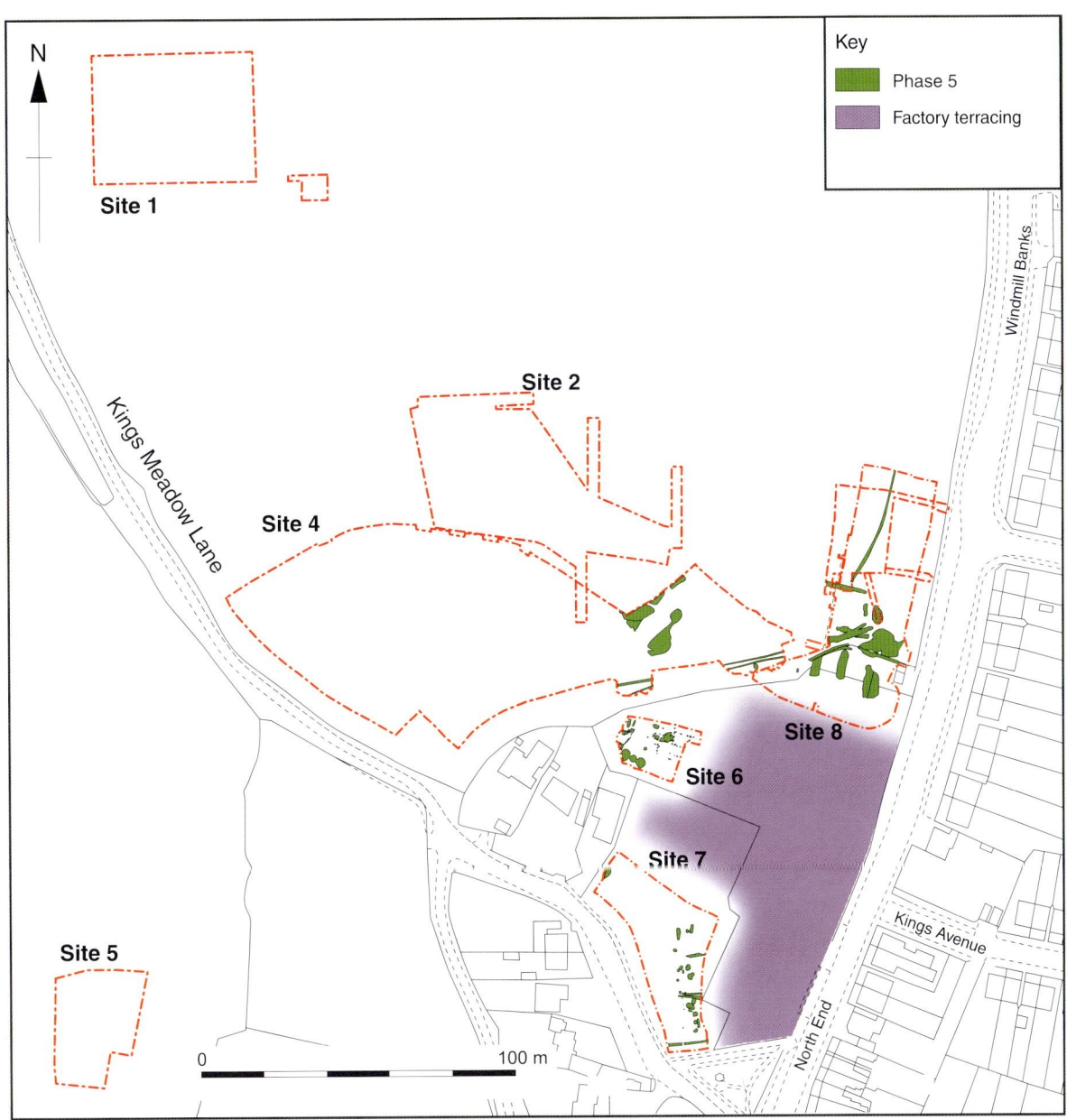

Fig. 3.47   Phase 5 Late medieval activity

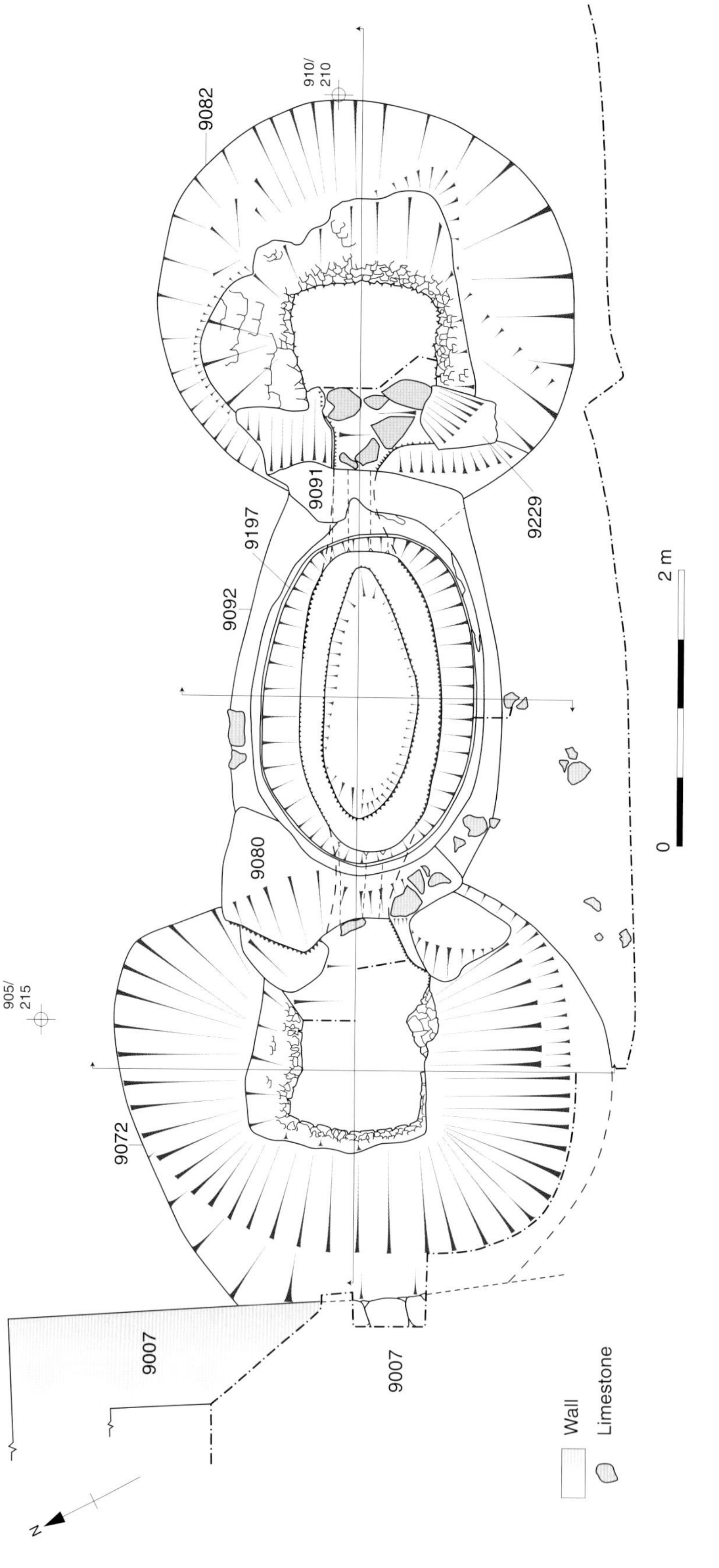

Plan 507

9082

910/
210

9091

9197

9229

9092

9080

905/
215

9072

9007

9007

0   2 m

Wall

Limestone

Fig. 3.48 Phase 5 Site 6 Kiln 1 plan

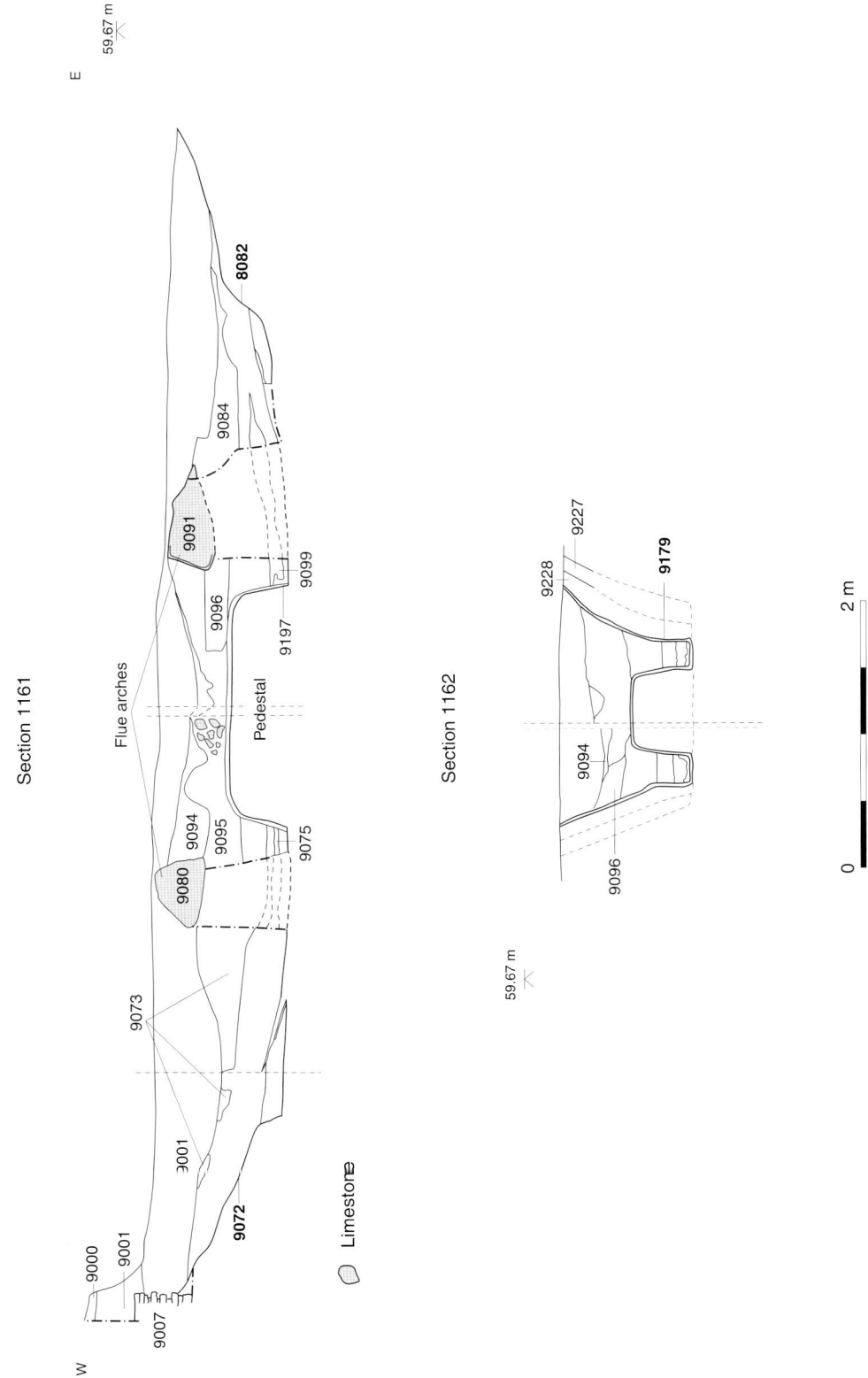

Fig. 3.49 Phase 5 Site 6 Kiln 1 section

Plate 3.9 (above and below)   Kiln 1 on Site 6 after full excavation, and detail of finger marks on chamber wall

inside of the central chamber and the surface of the pedestal was a clay coating between 5–10 mm thick. This appeared to have been applied and smoothed by hand, as finger marks were discernible in places (Pl.3.9). The southern wall of the eastern flue revealed what appeared to be a repair patch of clay lining (9229), presumably replacing a part of the original lining that had fallen away. Further evidence of lining repairs was noted in the central firing chamber. (For consideration of the super-structure and operation of the kiln see Chapter 5.)

Ashy deposits in the base of the chamber and the two flues represented the last use(s) of the kiln. Samples were taken from two of these deposits (9099, 9075; see Moffett Chapter 4). The firing chamber and the two stoke pits were backfilled with a sequence of dumps of dark grey sandy silt with a very high proportion of 'waster' sherds of coarse grey Late medieval Reduced Ware (see Blinkhorn Chapter 4). Within the backfill material were fragments – some substantial – of the collapsed kiln superstructure (eg. contexts 9096, 9073, 9084, 9094). The dumped wasters not only filled the kiln chamber and flue pits, but also extended as a substantial layer over most of the western part of Site 6. The total weight of recovered wasters exceeded 440 kg.

Archaeomagnetic dating – A programme of sampling for archaeomagnetic dating was carried out on the intact central pedestal of the firing chamber of Kiln 1 by Paul Linford of English Heritage (Pl 3.10). A date range of 1395 to 1425 AD (63% confidence), and 1385 to 1435 AD (95% confidence) was obtained for the last kiln firing. This compares with a date range for the pottery typology of AD 1350 to AD 1550. (The full report on the archaeomagnetic dating is included in Chapter 4, together with the associated analytical figures in Appendix 3.)

Features associated with Kiln 1 (Site 6) (Figs 3.50-3.51)

Three limestone rubble footings (9005, 9007 and 9008) were exposed. probably represent parts of two possible buildings. Two footings (9007 and 9008) were partially exposed at the western edge of the site (Fig. 3.51). Each appeared to represent the north-east corner of a structure, and could either represent two separate structures or, less probably, parts of a single structure.

Wall 9008 was situated immediately north-west of Kiln 1 and survived to a height of 0.70 m (7 courses). A small sondage excavated within the exposed building corner revealed a possible shallow NE-SW ditch (9192), pre-dating the wall. Two layers of silty clay (9196 and 9190) sealed the ditch and appeared to represent make-up for the internal floor, which was represented by a trampled surface containing a high proportion of waster sherds (9212). This in turn was sealed by a looser accumulation of kiln waste (9189).

Wall 9007, 3.0 m to the north, survived to a height of only one partially truncated course, and appeared to be set on top of a levelling deposit (9009) of silty clay over compacted layers of pot wasters (9010/9011). This suggests that wall 9007 represents a much less substantial structure, later in date than context 9008, although there is no reason why they should not be broadly contemporary.

The third limestone footing (9005) lay to the east of structure 9007 on a similar alignment. It survived to a length of approximately 5 m, but had clearly been truncated. Like wall 9007 it was insubstantial in build, and only one course in depth. It may repre-sent a boundary wall separating the workshop area to the west from the drying and firing area to the east. Between walls 9007 and 9005 was spread of limestone rubble, representing either demolition of the walls or a rough yard surface.

(Consideration of the features associated with the kiln site found in 1965 immediately north-west of Site 6 can be found in Chapter 5.)

Building group 9230 (Site 6) (Figs 3.50-3.51)

To the north and east of Kiln 1 was an irregular stone surface (9006/9065) associated with up to 40 post holes. The post holes were largely found to the east and south of the stone surface. Apparently associated with the stone surface was a line of four rectangular postholes (9023, 9025, 9052, 9054), with a spacing between centres of 3.0 m. This line of postholes appeared to coincide with the southern edge of the stone surface 9006, which suggests that the posts and surface represents a drying platform sheltered by an open- sided timber superstructure, where newly made pots were dried prior to firing.

The rest of the postholes were circular or sub-circular in plan, and averaged around 0.15 m in diameter x 0.20 m deep. Their arrangement suggests either a single timber structure with defined rooms, or an agglomeration of small sheds or lean-tos, all generally respecting the same NW-SE alignment as the kiln and main workshop buildings.

Kiln 2 (Site 8) (Fig. 3.52; Pl.3.11)

The pottery kiln (15275) was represented by the very truncated remains of a central chamber, with a freestanding oblong pedestal, and two opposed flues, the whole structure oriented WNW-ESE. The struc-ture measured approximately 5.1 m long x 1.6 m wide, which broadly corresponds to the dimensions of the base of kiln 9200 (see Figure. 3.44). The material remains of the firing chamber consisted of little more than a reddening of the natural silty clay defining the shape of the chamber and the outside edge of the base of the central pedestal. Both stokeholes were defined by shallow depressions, each with the remains of a lining formed by unworked limestone blocks (15491, 15492). The eastern stokehole was partly cut away by ditch 15350 (see below). A residue of a dark grey silt with a high percentage of ash and pottery sherds

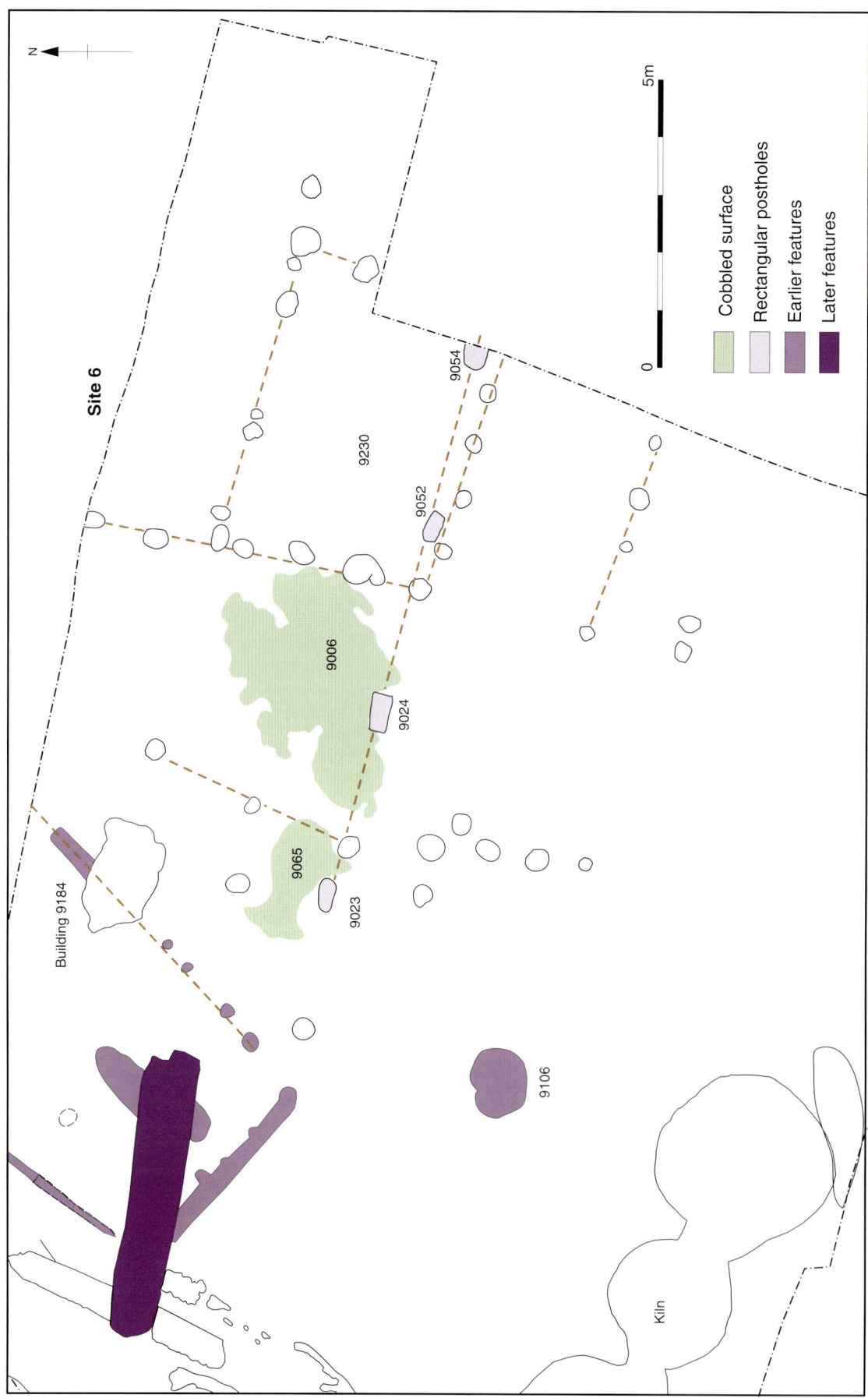

Fig. 3.50 Phase 5 Site 6 Kiln 1 associated building 9230

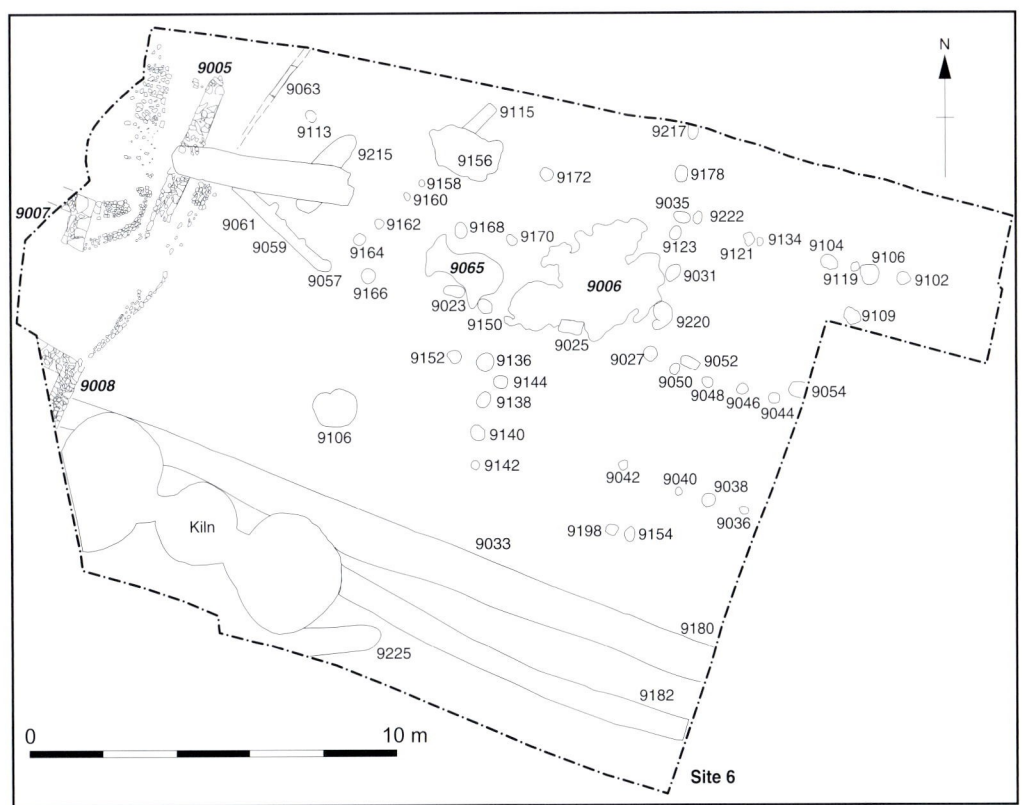

Fig. 3.51 (above)   Site 6: General plan of features

Fig. 3.52 (below)   Phase 5 Site 8 Kiln 2

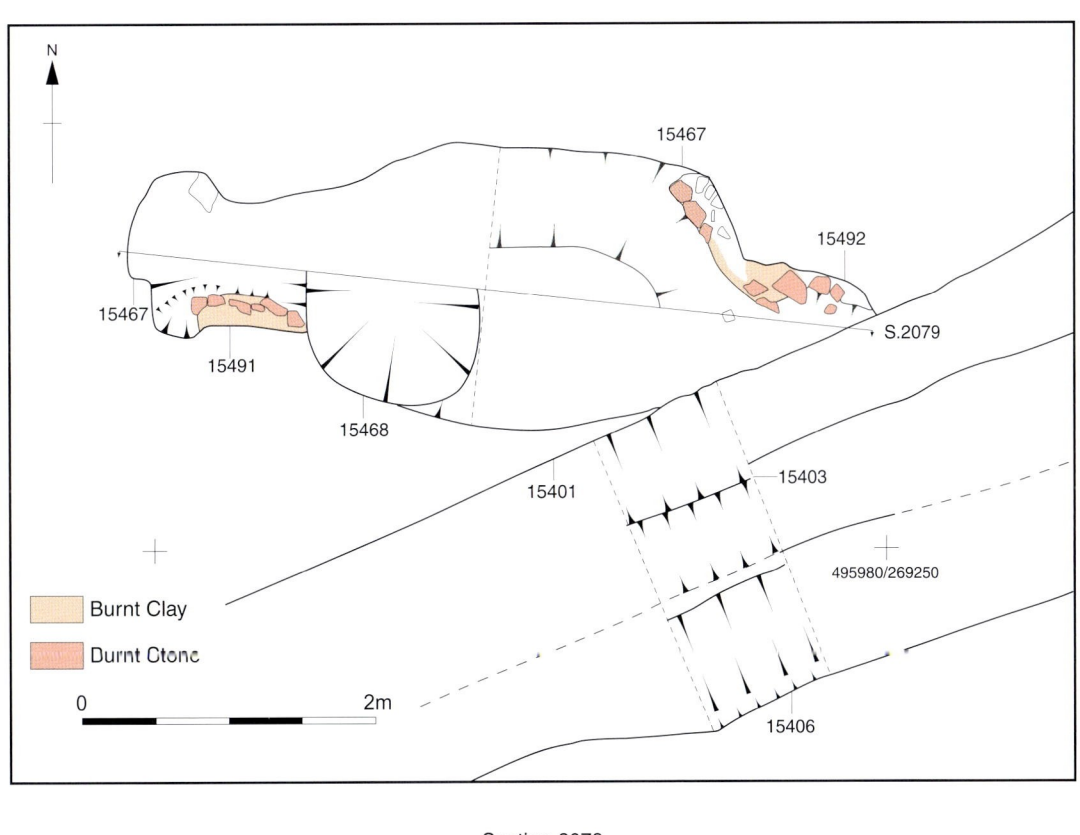

Burnt Clay

Burnt Stone

0   2m

Section 2079

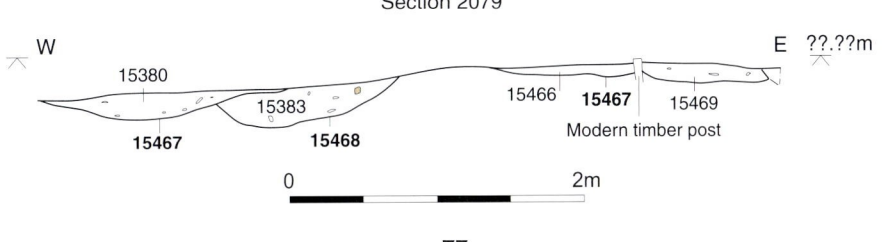

15380, 15469) – was recorded in the surviving bases of both of the stoke holes. A shallow circular feature (15468), measuring 1.2 m in diameter x 0.25 m deep was revealed under the south-west part of the chamber, pre-dating the construction of the kiln. The feature could be unrelated, or possibly a consequence of the kiln's construction.

Associated features (Site 8) (Fig. 3.53)

To the north of the kiln, only two features could be associated with the kiln in terms of stratigraphy. A shallow U shaped ditch (15393) extended west from the baulk for a distance of 10.1 m to a terminus. A very ephemeral linear feature (15323) extended for a distance of 3.5 m between the terminus of 15393 and ditch termini to the east of the kiln. Finds from the feature fill include a Roman coin (SF 4030) and fragments of Reduced Ware pottery. To the north of feature 15393 a narrow curving ditch (15283) extended from the west baulk north-east into the northern baulk. This may be a later redefinition of a boundary first defined by Phase 4 ditch 15320, which was cut by 15283.

An area of approximately 23 sq m of compacted limestone rubble (15523) was exposed to the east of the kiln; set onto this was two small areas of pitched limestone (15222). It is likely that the pitched limestone originally covered all the rubble, and has been truncated by later activity. Although no associ-ated postholes were found, it is reasonable to suggest that this represents a drying platform, presumably sheltered by an open-sided timber superstructure – fulfilling the same function as platform 9006/9065 on Site 6.

To the south of the kiln were the termini of two parallel ditches (15070 and 15180), oriented north-south and spaced 4.5 m apart. Their surviving depth was approximately 0.40 m. The lower fills of the ditches contained reduced ware sherds, suggesting they were open when the kiln was active. The ditches clearly would have continued to the south, and possibly define an access way to the kiln. South of the stone platform and north-east of ditch 15070 was a large clay quarry pit (15197). The absence of cereal remains in a sample of the lower fill (15199) probably reflects the absence of agricul-tural activity in the vicinity at this time. The backfill of pit 15197 had been repeatedly capped by further material, evidently because of subsidence.

This subsidence may have been due to the use of the area immediately south of the kiln as a trackway, giving access onto Windmill Banks. The trackway ran WSW-ENE and was bordered by a sequence of boundary ditches to the north (15350, 15355 and 15360), and to the south two ditches (15047, 15086) – later replaced by limestone walls (15009 and 15010). A gap between these two walls would have allowed access from the trackway defined by 15180 and 15070 to the south. The later

Plate 3.10   Archaeomagnetic sampling in progress on Kiln 1

phase of the trackway appears to post-date the kiln activity, as the northernmost track boundary ditch (15350) cuts the base of the kiln, and the southern ditch and wall sequence cuts ditch (15180). However, as all of these boundary ditches contain large amounts of reduced wares, which are also present in the matrix of the trackway surface, it is reasonable to conclude that the trackway was intended to facilitate the kiln's operation.

Quarry pits (Site 4) (Figs. 3.36, 3.47)

Two linear features (7315 and 7316) oriented SSW-ENE were revealed at the south edge of Site 4 and are assigned to Phase 5. To the north of the ditches was a scatter of deep, steep-sided (or over-cut) pits, concentrated in an area of clay subsoil. These features appear to represent clay quarrying in the later medieval period, although their proximity to one of the denser areas of Phase 3 activity meant that the fills of the pits contained pottery dating

from the 11th century through to the 15th century. The earlier pottery is clearly residual. Some subsidence of the fills evidently took place, because some post-medieval finds were also evident in the upper fills.

In the centre of the site, and partly obscured by later ridge-and-furrow, was one series of pit cuts (6775), extending over an area of approximately 8 m x 5 m. Sample excavation revealed steep or overcut sides and a flat base at a average depth of 1.2 m. A single posthole was exposed in the base of 6775, which must relate to the original excavation of the pit, perhaps supporting an A-frame hoist. Finds included early and late medieval pottery, animal bone, and in the upper fill two fragments of clay pipe. To the north of pit 6775 was a smaller quarry pit 6798 which also produced both early and late medieval pottery and a horseshoe nail from fill 6800 (SF 342 – not illustrated)

To the north of this group of pits a further cluster of quarry pits (6110, 6614, 6274) was partially

Plate 3.11   Kiln 2 on Site 8

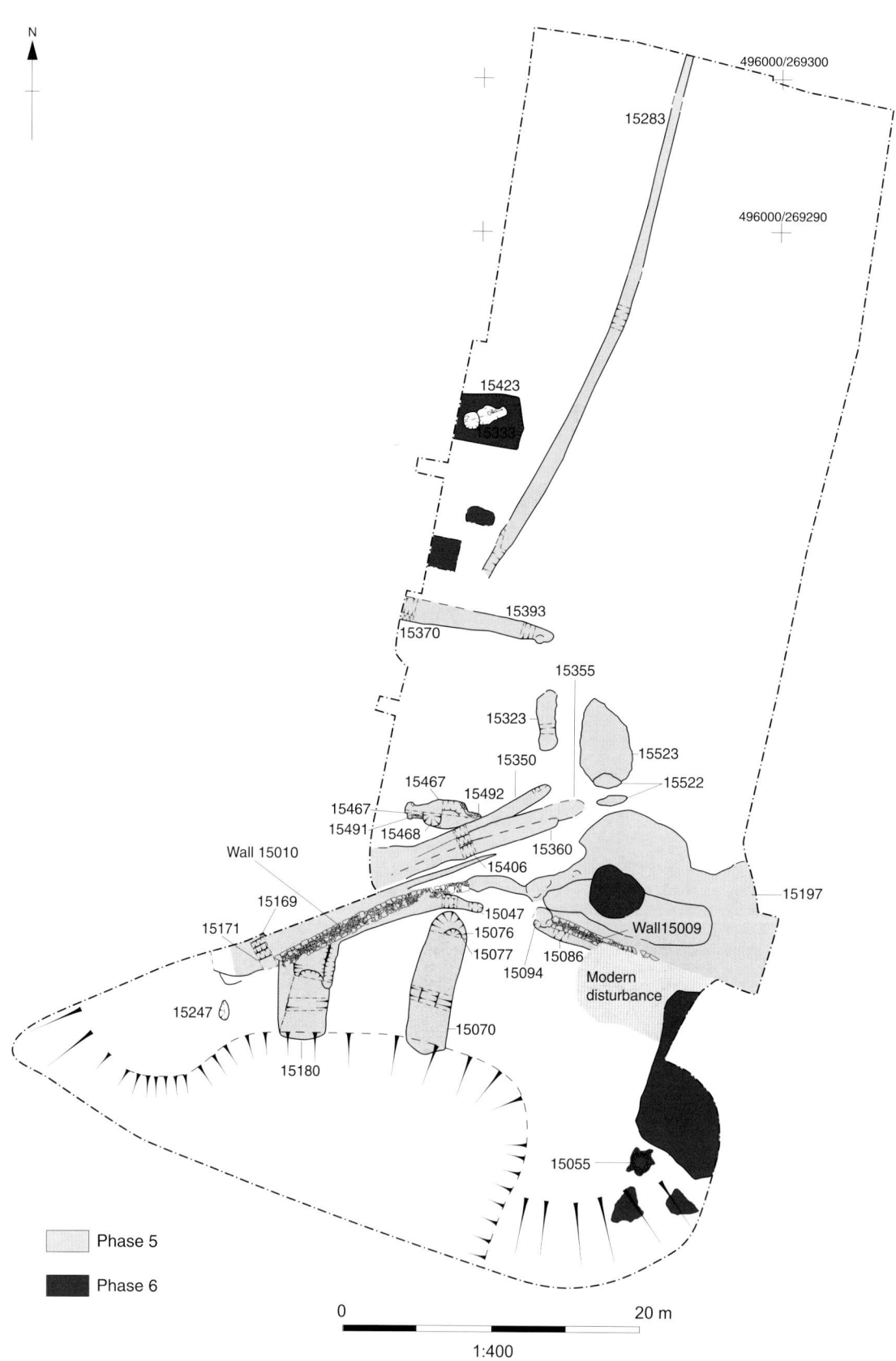

Fig. 3.53   Phase 5 and 6 Site 8 Features

revealed under the northern baulk. Sample excavation produced quantities of redeposited early medieval and Late Saxon pottery and bone, not surprising given the proximity to intense Phase 3 activity.

Pits and linear features (Site 7) (Figs 3.55, 3.44, 3.47, Pl. 3.12)

The corner formed by Kings Meadow Lane and Windmill Banks contained a scatter of pits and linear features that appear to belong to this phase. Only sample excavation was undertaken due to the severe contamination of the area (see above). The spread of activity was characterised by a number of linears (9365, 9525, 9487, 9460,), all oriented approximately W-E and extending from the eastern baulk. They appear to define boundaries, possibly for properties fronting onto Windmill Banks. A broad N-S swathe of pits extended from the southern site boundary, broadly defining a western limit to these linears.

Among these pits was a stone-lined oven base (9367 – Pl. 3.12) surviving as a square stone feature constructed within a flat-bottomed pit approximately 1.8 m wide and 0.34 m deep, with a floor of yellowish clay. A number of the stones within the structure were burnt, but not all of the burnt faces faced inward. This suggests that structure 9367 is the rebuild of an earlier feature, and it is probably not a coincidence that a heavily disturbed and burnt depression was revealed approximately 1 m to the north-west. An environmental sample from the fill of structure 9367 revealed a mix of wild and cultivated plant species, deriving possibly from a managed meadow, the material presumably representing the residue of the oven fuel (see Moffett Chapter 4).

PHASE 6 (MID 15th CENTURY TO 20th CENTURY) (FIG. 3.54)

With the end of the pottery industry, the archaeological evidence indicates that the area reverted to farmland. There was limited evidence of occupation from Sites 7 and 8. On site 7, close to Kings Meadow Lane, there were the stone footings of a small building (9548) and associated boundaries and pits. On Site 8, bordering the main N-S road, a well (15155) and cobbled surfaces were found. On Side 4 two linear features, possibly remnants of ridge and furrow, were found together with two pits, one of which contained modern rubbish.

Building 9548 (Site 7) (Fig. 3.55)

Stone footings (9548) of a post-medieval brick and stone cottage were revealed at the south end of Site 7. This one of the cottages that would have fronted onto Walnut Tree Green, a triangular open space in the angle formed by Kings Meadow Lane and Windmill Banks. The building was defined by 0.70 m wide coursed rubble footings measuring (exter-

Plate 3.12   Oven base 9367 Site 7 Phase 5

nally) 4.2 m wide x at least 8.7 m long. A doorway *c.* 1.4 m wide formed the entrance on the south side of the building. No evidence was found of accumulated internal surfaces, and it is therefore likely that the ground floor was flagged, and that the flagstones were salvaged before demolition. Alternatively, (although less likely), there could have been a suspended wooden floor.

To the north of the cottage a shallow depression (9433) covered an area of approximately 9 m x 6 m. Sample excavation was minimal, but recovered pottery dating from the mid-18th century, along

with many cattle horn cores in a matrix of clay and stone rubble, which spread to the south to form a yard surface abutting the building 9548. To the north, property boundaries possibly relating to Building 9548 were found. These comprised 9480 to the west and aligned approximately north-south, and two unexcavated parallel linears extending to the eastern baulk and forming an angle with 9480. To the north of these features, two shallow linears (9348 and 9350) were found. These formed a right angle and may also be related to this phase of activity, although neither feature produced any finds.

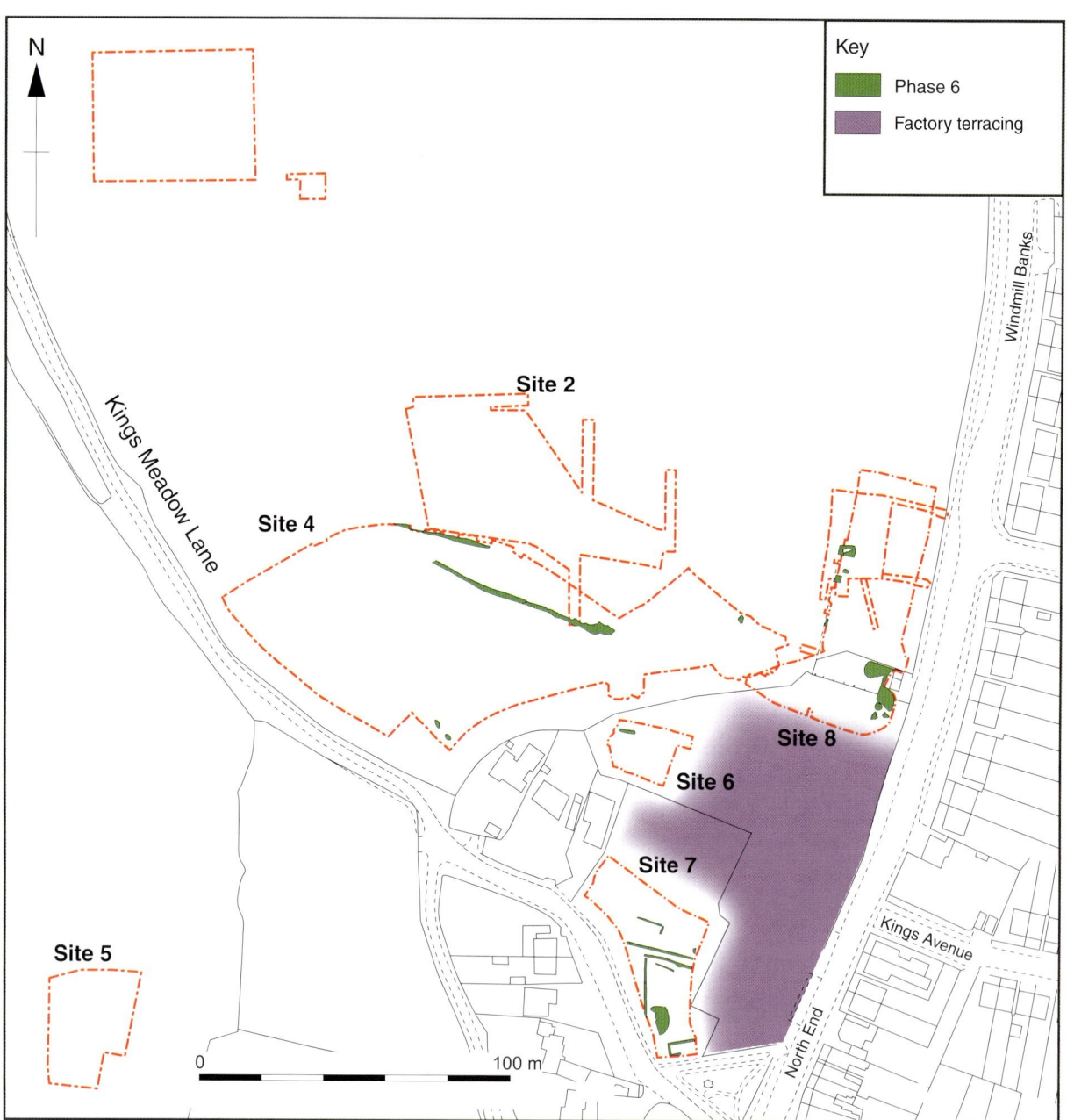

Fig. 3.54   Phase 6 post-medieval

Fig. 3.55 (facing page)   Phase 5 and 6 Site 7 Features

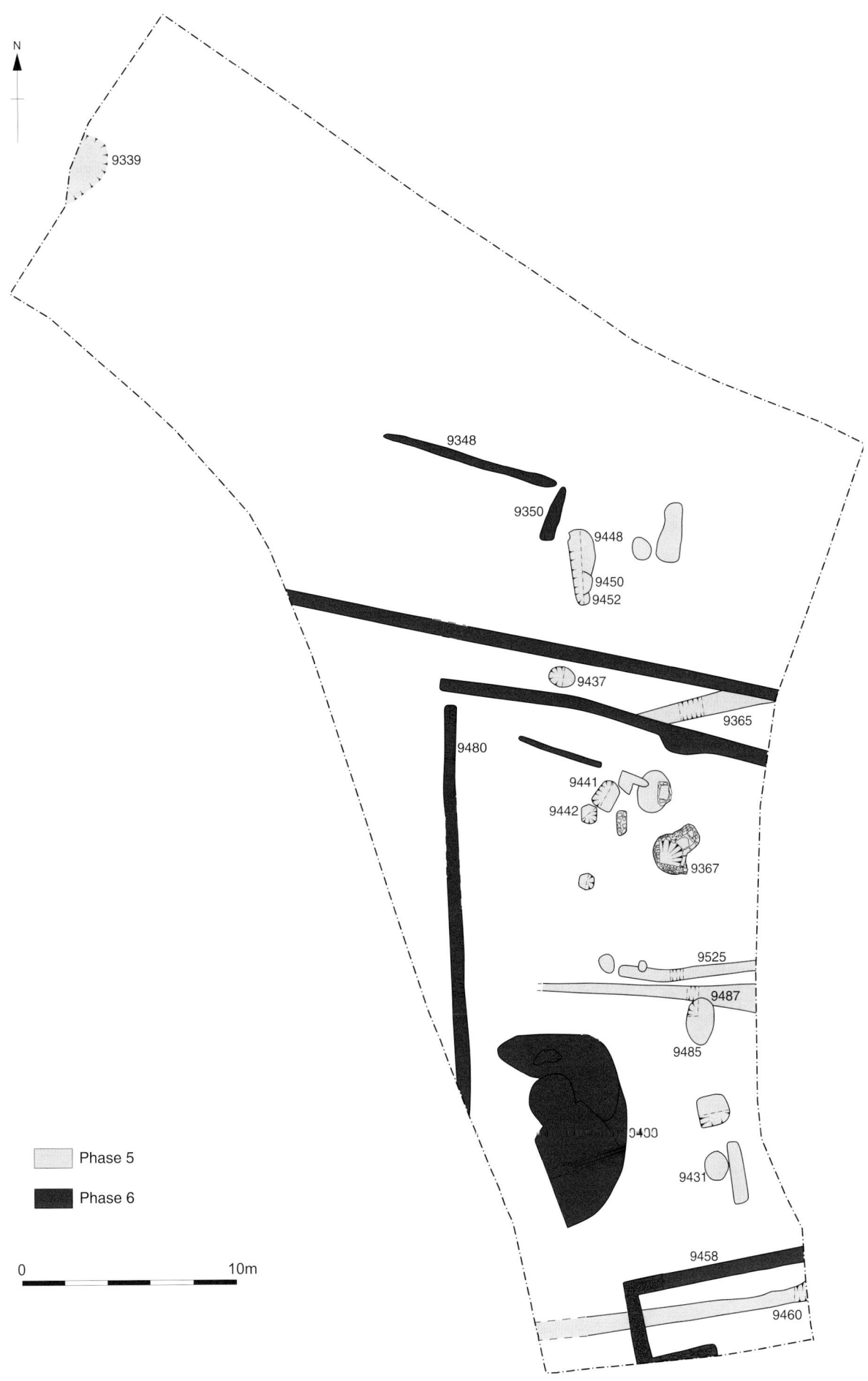

N

9339

9348

9350

9448

9450
9452

9437

9365

9480

9441

9442

9367

9525

9487

9485

0400

9431

9458

9460

Phase 5

Phase 6

0   10m

83

Well 15155 and associated surfaces (Site 8)
(Fig.3.53)

In the south-east part of Site 8 a stone-lined well
(15155) and associated surfaces 15090, were
revealed. Finds from the top fill of the well and the
cobbled surface dated to the 19th century, although
the construction of both features may have been
earlier. The area immediately north of surface 15090
was occupied by a 20th-century electricity substa-
tion, and two recent geotechnical pits were
revealed against the western baulk. The southern
part of the site revealed the northern limit of the
20th-century factory terracing, confirming that at
this point the ground level had been lowered by at
least 1.5 m, removing all archaeological features
and deposits.

Site 4 (Fig. 3.9, 3.35-6)

Two shallow W-E linear features were identified
crossing the centre of the site. From their stratigraphy and uneven and indistinct definition, it is
reasonable to suggest that they represent remnant
ridge-and-furrow of the post-medieval Townend
Furlong (see Chapter 2, and Pl.5.6). Near the south-
west edge of the site, two pits (6610 and 6146) were
found. One (6610) contained a silty loam fill, but no
finds; pit 6246 had signs of intense burning around
the pit rim, and was filled with modern rubbish
including an aluminium watering can. Both features
appear to relate to 20th-century bungalows that
used to stand along the north side of Kings Meadow
Lane; their footprints were not revealed in the
excavation area.

Chapter 4: The material evidence

The first part of the chapter contains specialist reports on the artefacts. The second part contains reports on the environmental evidence and and the final part comprises details of radiocarbon and archaeomagnetic dating.

POTTERY *by Paul Blinkhorn*

Introduction

The report is in two parts; the first dealing with the post-Roman pottery derived from domestic activity from all the sites investigated. The second part deals exclusively with the large quantity of late medieval Reduced ware representing the industrial waste from the two pottery kilns on Sites 6 and 8.

The pottery assemblage comprised 545,553 g with an estimated vessel equivalent (EVE), by summation of surviving rimsherd circumference, of 260.26. It included manufacturing waste from two late medieval kilns, totalling 499,517 g and with an EVE = 224.53. The rest of the assemblage was early Saxon or later, and comprised 4,250 sherds with a total weight of 46,036 g (EVE = 35.73).

The ceramic evidence suggests that there was unbroken occupation at the site possibly from the middle of the 5th century, and certainly from *c* AD 500 until the 12th century. After that, the area appears to have been waste or agricultural land, until the establishment of a late medieval pottery industry at the site, with at least three kilns manufacturing late medieval Reduced ware at the site. After these fall from use, probably some time in the 15th century, the land once again becomes marginal.

Analytical methodology

The pottery – both Post-Roman and Medieval – was initially bulk-sorted and recorded on a computer using DBase IV software. The material from each context was recorded by number and weight of sherds per fabric type, with featureless body sherds of the same fabric counted, weighed and recorded as one database entry. Feature sherds such as rims, bases and lugs were individually recorded, with individual codes used for the various types. Decorated sherds were similarly treated. In the case of the rimsherds, the form, diameter in mm and the percentage remaining of the original complete circumference was all recorded. This figure was summed for each fabric type to obtain the estimated vessel equivalent (EVE).

The terminology used is that defined by the Medieval Pottery Research Group's *Guide to the Classification of Medieval Ceramic Forms* (MPRG 1998) and to the minimum standards laid out in the *Minimum Standards for the Processing, Recording, Analysis and Publication of post-Roman Ceramics* (MPRG 2001). All the statistical analyses were carried out using a Dbase package written by the author, which interrogated the original or subsidiary databases, with some of the final calculations made with an electronic calculator. All statistical analyses were carried out to the minimum standards suggested by Orton (1998-9, 135-7).

Fabrics

The middle Saxon and later pottery was quantified using the chronology and coding system of the Northamptonshire County Ceramic Type-Series (CTS). The CTS does not include Anglo-Saxon hand-built pottery as the variable nature of the material means that each site has to have its own specific fabric series. A total of 1,330 sherds (20,094 g, EVE = 13.19) of Anglo-Saxon pottery was recorded in the following fabrics and quantities:

F1: Quartz and Oolitic limestone. Sparse to moderate sub-rounded quartz up to 1 mm, sparse sub-rounded limestone up to 2 mm, rare ooliths, rare black ironstone up to 2 mm. 219 sherds, 3,433 g, EVE = 2.02.

F2: Sparse quartz up to 1 mm, few other visible inclusions. 347 sherds, 4,964 g, EVE = 4.07.

F3: Granite. Sparse to moderate sub-angular granite lumps up to 2 mm, free quartz grains up to 1 mm, rare rounded red ironstone up to 2 mm. 49 sherds, 582 g, EVE = 0.48.

F4: Chaff-tempered. Moderate to dense chaff voids up to 4 mm, rare quartz grains up to 1 mm. 76 sherds, 864 g, EVE = 1.11.

F5: Quartz tempered. Moderate to dense sub-rounded quartz up to 1 mm, rare red and black ironstone, limestone and organic material up to 2 mm. 508 sherds, 8,201 g, EVE = 3.69.

F6: Limestone. Rare to sparse shelly limestone platelets up to 2 mm, rare quartz up to 1 mm. 5 sherds, 187 g, EVE = 0.11.

F7: Red Ironstone. Sparse to moderate sub-rounded red ironstone up to 2 mm, rare quartz and limestone up to 1 mm. 126 sherds, 2,133 g, EVE = 1.71.

The range of fabric types is typical of sites in the region. Most of the pottery could easily have been made from locally-occurring clays, as most of the inclusions noted can be found in the vicinity of the site. The exception is the granitic wares, which occur in small quantities on most contemporary sites in the county and are likely to have originated in Leicestershire, where outcrops of Mount Sorrel granite are known in the Charnwood forest area (Vince 1995). Clays in that area, with distinctive acid igneous rock inclusions, have been exploited since the Iron Age.

The middle Saxon and later pottery, classified using the CTS, was as follows:

F95: **Ipswich Ware Group 1 fabrics**, AD725-850. 83 sherds, 888 g, EVE = 0.21.

F96: **Ipswich Ware, group 2 fabrics**, AD725-850. 3 sherd, 30 g, EVE = 0.

F97: **Raunds-type Maxey Ware**, c. AD650–850. 148 sherds, 2,584 g, EVE = 0.87.

F100: **T1(1) type St Neots Ware**, AD850-1100. 780 sherds, 5,390 g, EVE = 6.46.

F102: **Thetford-type ware,** AD850-1100. 10 sherds, 338 g, EVE = 0.18.

F200: **T1 (2) type St Neots Ware**, AD1000-1200. 845 sherds, 5,932 g, EVE = 3.85..

F205: **Stamford ware,** AD850-1250. 107 sherds, 778 g, EVE = 1.24.

F207: **Oolitic ware**, AD975–1150. 26 sherds, 611g, EVE = 0.50.

F330: **Shelly Coarseware**, AD1100-1400. 659 sherds, 6,707 g, EVE = 7.13.

F360: **Miscellaneous Sandy Coarsewares**, AD1100-1400. 6 sherds, 86g, EVE = 0.04.

F319: **Lyveden/Stanion 'A' ware**, AD1150-1400. 31 sherds, 569 g, EVE = 1.18.

F320: **Lyveden/Stanion 'B' ware**, AD1225-1400. 15 sherds, 218 g, EVE = 0.12.

F328: **Grimston Ware**, L 12th–15th century. 1 sherd, 4g, EVE = 0.

F329: **Potterspury ware**, AD1250-1600. 61 sherds, 787 g, EVE = 0.04.

F322: **Lyveden/Stanion 'D' ware**, AD1400-?1500. 4 sherd, 70 g, EVE = 0.

F366: **Raunds-type Reduced ware**, ?14th century. 2 sherds, 59g, EVE = 0.06.

F369: **Brill/Boarstall 'Tudor Green' types**, late 15th 17th century. 1 sherd, 1 g, EVE = 0.

F401: **Late Medieval Oxidized ware**, ?AD1450-?1500. 14 sherds, 248g, EVE = 0.18.

F403: **Midland Purple ware**, AD1450-1600. 4 sherds, 346 g, EVE = 0.07.

F404: **Cistercian ware**, AD1470-1550. 6 sherds, 21 g, EVE = 0.15.

F406: **Midland Yellow ware**, 1550–1700. 20 sherds, 212g, EVE = 0.07.

F407: **Red Earthenwares**, AD1400+. 36 sherds, 460 g, EVE = 0.09.

F408: **Rhenish Stonewares**, AD1450+. 3 sherds, 38 g, EVE = 0.10.

F409: **Staffordshire slipware**, AD1680-1750. 3 sherd, 56 g, EVE = 0.

F410: **Tin-glazed Earthenware**, 17th–18th century. 2 sherd2, 7g, EVE = 0.

F411: **Midland Blackware**, AD1550-1700. 1 sherd, 41 g, EVE = 0.

F413: **Manganese Glazed ware**, late 17th–18th century. 2 sherds, 31 g, EVE = 0.

F415: **Creamware**, mid 18th–early 19th century. 1 sherds, 12 g, EVE = 0.

F417: **Nottingham Stoneware**, 18th–19th century. 2 sherds, 26g, EVE = 0.

F426: **Iron-glazed Earthenware**, late 17th–19th century. 9 sherds, 237 g, EVE = 0.

F429: **Staffordshire White Salt-Glazed Stoneware**, 1720-80. 4 sherds, 6 g, EVE = 0.

F1000: Miscellaneous 19th and 20th century wares. 29 sherds, 141 g.

A sherd not covered by the CTS was also noted, as follows:

?**North French Blackware**, 7th–9th century. Fine, grey sandy fabric, darker surfaces with external burnishing and ?rouletting. 1 sherd, 2g, EVE = 0.

Post-Roman Pottery

The Anglo-Saxon pottery assemblage is both one of the earliest and one of the largest from Northamptonshire and the surrounding region. The spatial distribution of the pottery shows that there was a degree of settlement mobility, but that this related to the organization of the site rather than simply being the result of rebuilding of structures as they decayed over time. The middle Saxon assemblage also shows spatial traits which suggest that either the chronology of Maxey ware is in need of reconsideration, or that it had a functional role which was very different to the other contemporary type, Ipswich ware. The late Saxon pottery also shows some spatial traits which offer evidence of the internal organization of the settlement at that time.

Chronology

Early Saxon pottery

The dating of Early Saxon hand-built pottery is almost entirely reliant on the presence of decorated sherds, although there are a few chronologically distinct vessel forms. Sharply carinated vessels, particularly bowls (*Schalenurnen*) tend to date to the 5th century, although later examples are known, while tall, narrow, high-necked vessels tend to be of 7th-century date. The main problem is the identification of groups dating to the 7th century. It seems that the Anglo-Saxons generally used only plain vessels during that time (Myres 1977, 1), but it cannot be said that an assemblage which produced only plain sherds is of 7th-century date. Usually, decorated hand-built pottery only comprises around 3-4% of domestic assemblages, as was the case at sites such as West Stow, Suffolk (West 1985) and Mucking, Essex (Hamerow 1993), so a lack of decorated sherds could be the result of the vagaries of archaeological sampling rather than chronology.

Here, a total of 52 decorated sherds (501g, EVE = 0.45) were noted, representing 3.9% of the hand-built assemblage, and a wide range of decorative techniques occurred, some of which appear to date to the earliest part of the Early Saxon period, that is to around the middle of the 5th century. For example, a sherd from context 1257 has fragments of impressed fingertip decoration and curved lines (Fig 4.1, 1). Myres (1977, 28-30 and fig. 167) found many continental parallels to vessels with such decoration, which he dated to the later 4th to mid-5th century.

A number of other pieces of a similar date were noted. A small jar with well-defined shoulders and linear decoration (Fig. 4.1, 2) appears likely to date to the early part of the early Anglo-Saxon period. Such decoration again has many continental parallels, and many of the smaller vessels of similar shape and decoration from this country are of 5th-century date (Myres 1977, 45). Although 6th-century examples are known (H. Hamerow pers.comm.), on balance the occurrence of a number of other early sherds on this site suggests that an early date for this vessel is reasonable.

A similar date, for the same reasons, can be postulated for two sherds from context 6058, both of which were incised and carinated (Figs 4.1, 3-4). A similar date can be suggested sherd from context 1300 with a slashed carination (Fig. 4.1, 5); it is possibly from a *Schalenurne*, and is also likely to be early. Further sherds that are likely to be contemporary are a rim from a small jar with horizontal combing (Fig. 4.1, 6), and a vessel with corrugated shoulders from context 1254 (Fig. 4.1, 7). The exact form of the latter is uncertain, but bowls in this style were said by Myres (1977, 17) to be amongst the earliest Anglo-Saxon vessels in England, although later examples are known.

A small group of bossed and incised sherds were also noted, and these are most likely to date to the later part of the 5th century (ibid. 39). Four of the sherds (Figs 4.1, 8-10 and 18) had bosses which were pressed out from the inside, while a fifth (Fig. 4.1, 11) also had fragments of two stamps. This seems most likely to date to the early to mid 6th century (ibid. 42). Other 6th-century material occurred in the form of a group of stamped sherds (Fig. 4.1, 12-16, 19-22), some with linear decoration, which can be amongst the latest decorated early Anglo-Saxon pottery (ibid. 20-2).

The rest of the early Saxon decorated pottery assemblage comprises small fragments of incised sherds of uncertain type, and three with rustication (eg. Fig. 4.1, 17). None was dateable other than to within the broad early Saxon period.

Illustrated sherds

Figure 4.1

1   DES8: Context 1257, Fabric 5. Fingertip and line decoration. Dark grey fabric with smoothed outer surface.
2   DES15: Evaluation trench 10, context 4, F7. Rim and shoulder of small jar with incised decoration. Uniform black fabric.
3   Context 6058, F3. Carinated and incised vessel. Black fabric with dark brown, burnished outer surface.
4   Context 6058, F2. Carinated and incised vessel. Black fabric with burnished surfaces.
5   Context 1300, F5. Bodysherd from vessel with slashed carination. Uniform black fabric.
6   Context 1255, F7. Rimsherd from small jar with horizontal cordons. Uniform black fabric, burnished outer surface.
7   DES4: Context 1254, F5. Sherd from vessel with corrugated shoulders. Black fabric with smoothed outer surface.
8   DES5: Context 1255, F5. Sherd with fragment of incised boss. Hard black fabric with 'wet-hand' finished outer surface.
9   DES6: Context 1269, F2. Sherd with fragment of incised boss Black fabric with highly burnished surfaces.
10 DES7: Context 1255, F5. Bossed and incised sherd. Black fabric with smoothed and lightly burnished surfaces.
11 DES16: Evaluation trench 10, context 4, F5. Bossed, stamped and incised sherd. Uniform black fabric.
12 DES14: Context 1269, F1. Rimsherd from small jar with row of stamps on neck. Dark grey fabric with dark brown, burnished surfaces.
13 DES9: Context 1300, F5. Stamped and incised sherd. Black fabric with smoothed and lightly burnished surfaces.
14 DES14: Context 1269, F1. Stamped and incised sherd. Dark grey fabric with dark brown, burnished surfaces.
15 Context 6058, F2. Stamped sherd. Uniform black fabric with burnished outer surface.
16 Context 6923, F5. Stamped and incised sherd. Dark grey fabric with dark brown, smoothed outer surface.
17 Context 1300, F1. Rusticated bodysherd. Dark grey fabric with smoothed outer surface.
18 Context 8196, F7. Bossed and incised sherd. Light grey fabric with smoothed, darker surfaces.
19 Context 8196, F5. Stamped and incised sherd. Black fabric with light grey-brown outer surface.
20 Context 8196, F5. Rimsherd from small jar with stamped and incised decoration. Uniform black fabric with smoothed surfaces.
21 Context 6023, F5. Stamped and incised sherd. Uniform black fabric, smoothed outer surface.
22 Context 6652, F5. Stamped and incised sherd. Dark grey fabric with orange –brown outer surface.

Middle Saxon and later pottery

Each context-specific assemblage of middle Saxon and later date was given a seriated phase date on the basis of the pottery types present, based on the methodology defined in the Northamptonshire County Ceramic Type-Series (Tables 4.1 and 4.2).

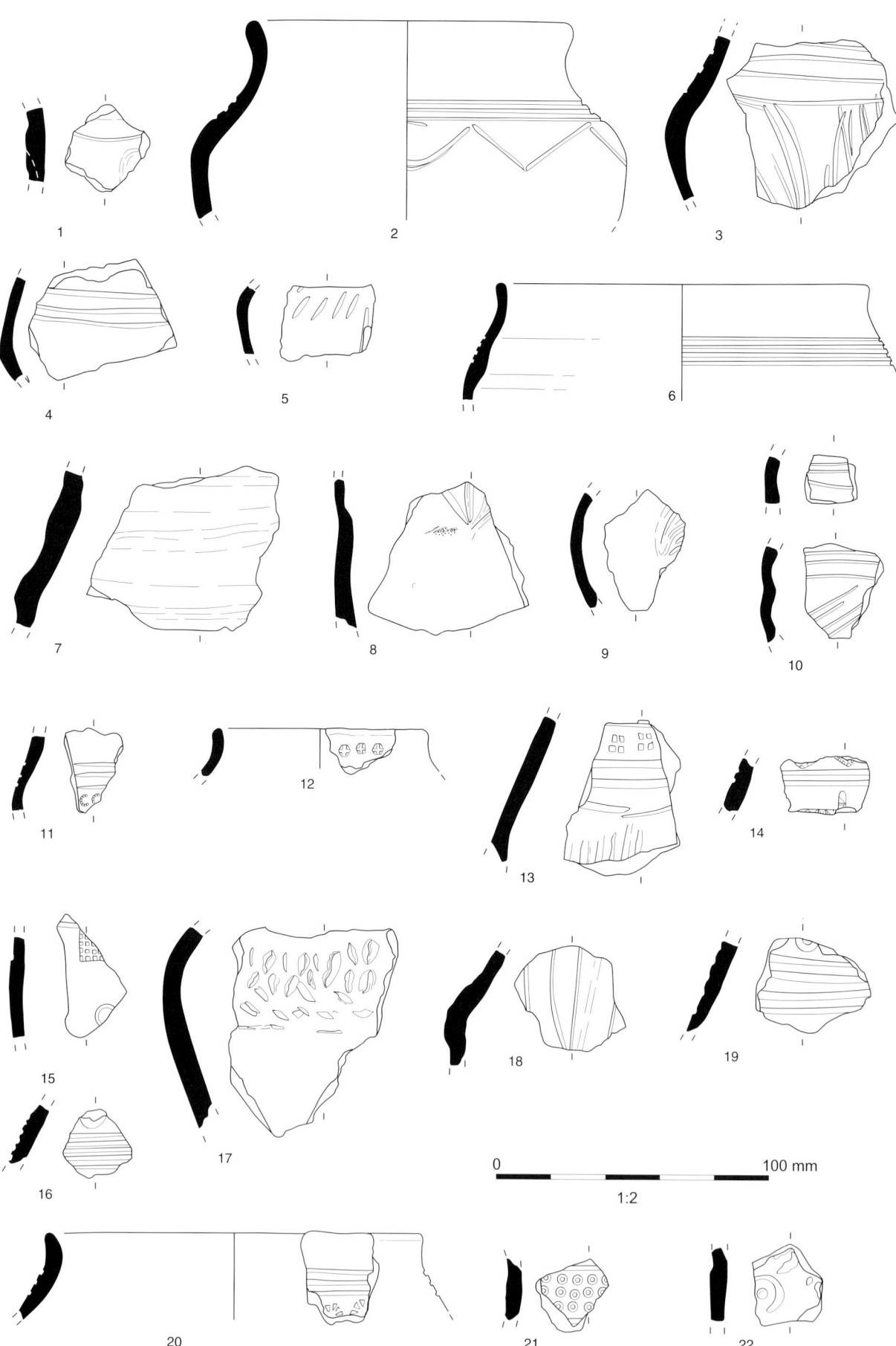

Fig. 4.1 Early Saxon pottery

Table 4.1: RSP Phases and Major Defining Wares for the Post-Roman Ceramics of Northamptonshire c. 450–1100

RSP Phase	Defining Wares	Chronology
MS	Ipswich Ware, Maxey-type Wares	*c.* AD650–850
LS1	Early Stamford ware, T1(1) St. Neots Ware	*c.* AD850–900
LS2	Stamford Ware, Northampton Ware	*c.* AD900–975
LS3	Cotswolds-type Oolitic Ware	*c.* AD975–1000
LS4	T1(2) St. Neots Ware	*c.* AD1000–1100

Table 4.2: RSP Phases and Major Defining Wares for the Medieval Ceramics of Northamptonshire

RSP Phase	Defining Wares	Chronology
Ph0	Shelly Coarsewares, Sandy Coarsewares	*c.* AD1100–1150
Ph1	Lyveden/Stanion 'A' Ware	*c.* AD1150–1225
Ph2/0	Lyveden/Stanion 'B', Brill/Boarstall ware	*c.* AD1225–1250
Ph2/2*	Potterspury Ware	*c.* AD1250–1300
Ph3/2	Raunds-type Reduced Ware	*c.* AD1300–1400
Ph4	Lyveden/Stanion 'D' Ware	*c.* AD1400–1450
Ph5	Late Medieval Oxidized Ware	*c.* AD1450–1500

Pottery occurrence

Table 4.3 shows the pottery occurrence per RSP phase. It shows that there were high levels of pottery deposition at the site through the Anglo-Saxon period and into the early medieval period. Pottery is relatively scarce from phase LS3, but as this is a very short phase (*c* 25 years), this is hardly surprising, and there is no reason to believe that there was an hiatus at that time. By the second half of the 12th century (Ph1), there is a sharp decline in

Table 4.3: Pottery occurrence per ceramic phase, all post-Roman fabrics

Phase	No sherds	Wt sherds (g)	EVE
ES	647	10766	5.96
E/MS	575	8341	6.55
MS	238	3304	0.98
LS1	330	2362	2.83
LS2	335	2721	2.92
LS3	31	662	0.72
LS4	474	2984	1.81
Ph0	999	8225	9.14
Ph1	48	699	1.17
Ph2/0	22	305	0.37
Ph2/2	43	524	0.13
Ph3/2	8	150	0.12
Ph4*	251	2259	1.90
Ph5*	73	892	0.51
Total	4074	44194	35.11

*excludes kiln waste

the amount of pottery deposited at the site, with very little from the 13th and 14th century. Once the site is occupied by potters in the 15th century, pottery (kiln waste aside) begins to occur in reasonably significant amounts. After the kilns were abandoned, pottery deposition again decreased, with the general impression gained that from the second half of the 12th century onwards, the Kings Meadow Lane area was very much marginal in terms of its relationship to the town of Higham Ferrers.

The data in Tables 4.4, 4.5 and 4.6 shows the occurrence of the main fabric types through time. Generally, in the Anglo-Saxon period, residuality is fairly low, suggesting that most groups are well-stratified, primary deposits. This is true of the early medieval (Ph0 and Ph1) groups, but in the 13th-century (Ph2/0) assemblages, over a third of the meagre 305g of pottery of that date is residual Saxo-Norman material. The later 13th- to 14th-century (Ph2/2) groups are only small, but all the pottery appears well-stratified, and the same appears true for the 14th-century (Ph3/2) pottery. The data for Ph4 (early-mid 15th century) suggests very high residuality, but the table does not include the kiln waste. It seems highly likely that the potters would have used their own wares, but there is no way to differentiate between what is waste and what was utilized. It is a fact that there was major ground disturbance at the site with three pottery kilns operating at one time or another, so a greater amount of residual pottery is perhaps to be expected. In Ph 5 (mid 15th to 16th century), there is again much residual pottery, but one or more of the kilns could still have been operating at that time (see below), with the resulting disturbance of earlier

Table 4.4: Pottery Occurrence per middle and late Saxon ceramic phase by weight (in g), major wares only, expressed as a percentage of total weight per phase

Phase	E/MS	Ipswich	F97	F100	F205	F102	F207	F200	Total wt
MS	13.2%	24.8%	62.0%	-	-	-	-	-	3304
LS1	7.0%	0	5.6%	84.7%	1.4%	-	-	-	2362
LS2	4.1%	0	9.8%	76.3%	9.6%	0.2%	-	-	2721
LS3	0	0	0	10.0%	0	0	90%	-	662
LS4	1.3%	2.0%	0.4%	11.5%	3.9%	0.8%	0	80.1%	2984

Table 4.5: Pottery Occurrence per early medieval ceramic phases by weight (in g), major wares only, expressed as a percentage of total weight per phase

Phase	E/MS	MS	LS	F102	F200	F205	F330	F319	F320	F329	Total
Ph0	0.5%	0.9%	3.6%	2.0%	25.5%	4.0%	61.6%	-	-	-	8225
Ph1	0	0	0	0	2.3%	0	56.2%	41.5%	-	-	699
Ph2/0	0	0	0	34.8%	1.3%	0	27.5%	3.9%	32.5%	-	305
Ph2/2	2.7%	0	0	0	1.7%	0	19.3%	2.5%	0	73.1%	524

Table 4.6: Pottery Occurrence per late medieval ceramic phases by weight (in g), major wares only, expressed as a percentage of total weight per phase

Phase	E/MS	MS	LS	EMED	F330	F320	F329	F366	F322	F401	Total
Ph3/2	0	0	0	0	4.0%	0	56.7%	39.3%	-	-	150
Ph4	3.7%	1.8%	9.2%	19.1%	39.0%	4.2%	12.0%	0	3.1%	-	2259
Ph5	5.7%	1.7%	20.5%	0.2%	8.5%	1.9%	2.9%	0	0	15.9%	892

strata. Generally, the data shows a pattern of consumption which is typical of medieval sites in this area of Northamptonshire.

Fragmentation Analysis

The data in Tables 4.7 and 4.8 show the mean sherd weight of the major fabrics in each of the ceramic phases. One of the main points of interest in this analysis is the question of the chronology of the hand-built pottery. It seems that in some areas of the country, hand-built pottery was not used in the middle Saxon period, but it is uncertain if this was the case in Northamptonshire. For example, in East Anglia, most middle Saxon sites that produced Ipswich ware produced very little hand-built material (see below), and in some sites in Oxfordshire such as Eynsham Abbey (Blinkhorn 2003a) there is strong evidence that hand-built pottery ceased to be used in the early years of the 8th century, regional imports aside. At Higham Ferrers, only 34 sherds of hand-built pottery were noted in middle Saxon contexts, and one of these was a decorated sherd of 5th century date, and thus redeposited. The remaining sherds had a mean sherd weight of 13.0 g, which is not much less than that for the same material in earlier contexts, and considerably higher than that from late Saxon and

later contexts, when the material was definitely residual. It would seem therefore that hand-built pottery continued in used at the site during the middle Saxon period, or at least there is no reason to suspect that it did not. Unfortunately, there are no obvious traits in form, fabric or manufacture which could allow these sherds, if they are middle Saxon, to be differentiated from early material.

To further cloud the issue, it is also a fact that residual pottery is not necessarily more fragmented that reliably stratified material. This is demonstrated by the data in Tables 4.7 and 4.8, where some wares, such as the Ipswich ware, Maxey ware (F97), T1(2) type St Neots ware (F200) and Thetford ware (F102) produced the largest mean sherd weight in phases in which they were residual. This is usually a trait caused by the presence of a small quantity of large sherds, and is the case here; the F200 assemblage in Ph2/2, the highest value for the ware, comprises just one sherd, and the Thetford ware from Ph2/0 comprises two handles from a large storage vessel.

Vessel Consumption:
Quantitative and Typological Discussion

The pattern of vessel consumption shown in Table 4.9 is largely one which is generally observed at contemporary sites in Northamptonshire. The

Table 4.7: Mean sherd weight per middle and late Saxon ceramic phase by weight (in g), major wares only

Phase	E/MS	Ipswich	F97	F100	F205	F102	F207	F200
ES	16.7g	-	-	-	-	-	-	-
E/MS	14.6g	-	-	-	-	-	-	-
MS	12.9g	10.3g	16.5g	-	-	-	-	-
LS1	5.5g	0	26.4g	6.9g	16.5g	-	-	-
LS2	4.8g	0	24.4g	8.0g	6.7g	3.0g	-	-
LS3	0	0	0	8.3g	0	0	25.9g	-
LS4	6.7g	29.5g	12.0g	5.1g	7.7g	11.5g	0	6.3g

Table 4.8: Mean sherd weight per earlier medieval ceramic phases by weight (in g), major wares only

Phase	F100	F102	F200	F205	F330	F319	F320	F329
Ph0	4.8g	41.8g	5.5g	7.2g	10.6g	-	-	-
Ph1	0	0	8.0g	0	11.6g	24.2g	-	-
Ph2/0	0	106.0g	2.0g	0	6.5g	12.0g	19.8g	-
Ph2/2	0	0	9.0g	0	5.9g	13.0g	0	17.4g

Table 4.9: Vessel occurrence by EVE per type per ceramic phase, expressed as a percentage of the total vessels per phase

Phase	Jars	Bowls	Jugs	Cylindrical Jars	Cups/Mugs	Total EVE
ES	76.2%	23.8%	0	0	0	5.96
E/MS	64.4%	35.6%	0	0	0	6.55
MS	34.7%	43.9%	21.4%	0	0	0.98
LS1	70.3%	29.7%	0	0	0	2.83
LS2	58.9%	36.0%	24.7%	0	0	2.92
LS3	80.6%	0	0	19.4%	0	0.72
LS4	79.0%	12.7%	0	8.3%	0	1.81
Ph0	66.5%	13.5%	10.3%	9.7%	0	9.14
Ph1	81.2%	8.5%	10.3%	0	0	1.17
Ph2/0	67.6%	0	32.4%	0	0	0.37
Ph2/2	100%	0	0	0	0	0.13
Ph3/2	0	100%	0	0	0	0.12
Ph4	73.2%	18.9%	6.3%	0	1.6%	1.90
Ph5	45.1%	11.8%	0	0	23.5%	0.51

Anglo-Saxon assemblage comprises almost entirely jars and bowls, with small quantities of pitchers appearing during the middle Saxon period and towards the end of the late Saxon phase. In the earlier medieval period, jars dominate, supplemented by smaller quantities of bowls and pitchers, with cylindrical jars, specialist cooking vessels which were in use in the region around the time of the Norman conquest, being represented from phase LS3 – Ph0, their usual period of use (Blinkhorn 1999c). It is the later medieval assemblages that are untypical. Usually, jugs become more common through the medieval period, but this is only true of Ph2/0 groups. The later ones, presumably due to the very small assemblage sizes, do not show the usual pattern, until Ph4, which is once again more typical. The presence of relatively high quantities of cup and mug sherds in the latest medieval phases is worthy of comment. It has been noted before that these sorts of vessels tend to occur in greater numbers at industrial sites, presumably due to the fact that hard physical work was often involved (Blinkhorn 2000, 21). Admittedly, the cup/mug data from Ph5 is actually only from two vessels, and so while the pattern could be a result of the vagaries of archaeological sampling, it may also be significant.

Early Saxon Pottery

In the main, the early/middle Saxon hand-built pottery was in good condition, with a higher than normal mean sherd weight (15.1g), but no vessels were reconstructable to a full profile. This is not unusual for sites of this period in the region. There is little doubt that most early-middle Saxon pottery assemblages from domestic sites of the period are the products of secondary deposition. In particular, SFB hollows appear to have been used as dumps after the structures were abandoned, with the source of the refuse presumably domestic middens of some description. It is highly unlikely to be the pottery which was used in the structures, otherwise, completely reconstructable vessels would be common finds.

The data in Figs 4.2 and 4.3 shows the frequency distribution of hand-built jar and bowl rim diameters respectively. In both cases, there appear to be three favoured sizes, which could be crudely classified as small, medium and large. In the case of the jars, form could be a factor, and there is no certainty that the rim diameter reflects the vessel size, but it is a trait which is worthy of mention as it suggests that vessel functionality could be related to size.

Very little information regarding trends in vessel form was recorded because of the fragmentary nature of much of the Anglo-Saxon assemblage, but it appears that most were simple globular vessels with rounded or flat bases and upright, slightly everted rims, although two foot-ring bases and one pedestal type were also noted (eg. Fig. 4.4, 34-35). The group of pottery from context 6058 (Figs. 4.4, 23-33) is typical; it comprised a group of large rim and base sherds, along with a large number of small rim fragments and bodysherds, some of which appear likely to be parts of the illustrated vessels, but could not be joined.

There were very few early Saxon feature sherds other than rims or bases. Fragments of six lugs were noted, three of which were upright, rim-mounted examples and the others longitudinal types mounted on the shoulder of the vessel.

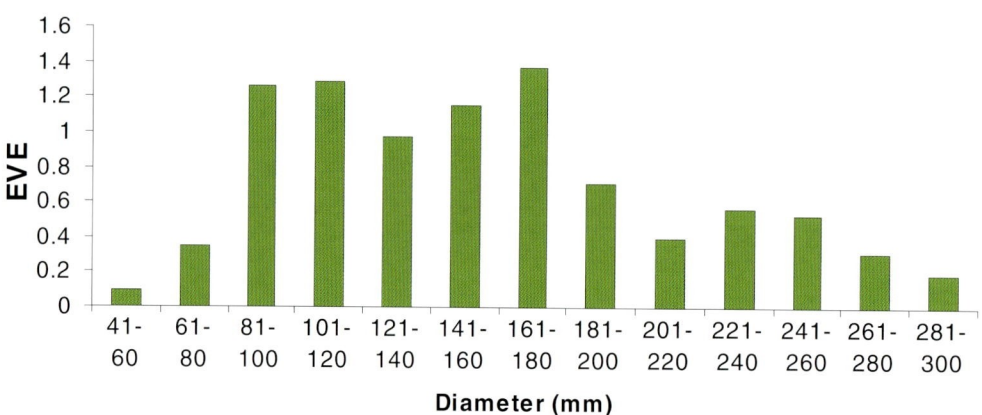

Fig. 4.2 Rim diameter distribution, early/middle Saxon hand-built jars

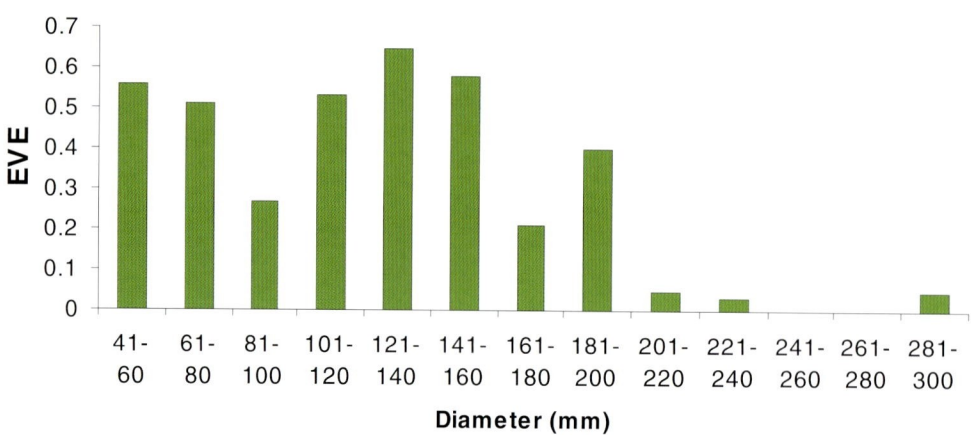

Fig. 4.3 Rim diameter distribution, early/middle Saxon hand-built bowls

Illustrations

Figure 4.4

23 Context 6058, F2. Jar rim. Uniform black fabric with burnished outer surface.

24 Context 6058, F1. Jar rim. Black fabric with burnished dark brown outer surface.

25 Context 6058, F5. Jar rim. Uniform black fabric with burnished outer surface.

26 Context 6058, F1. Jar rim. Uniform black fabric with brown, unfinished outer surface.

27 Context 6058, F5. Jar rim. Uniform black fabric with burnished outer surface.

28 Context 6058, F1. Jar rim. Uniform black fabric with unfinished outer surface

29 Context 6058, F2. Jar rim. Uniform grey fabric with burnished outer surface.

30 Context 6058, F4. Jar rim. Uniform black fabric with orange-brown, unfinished outer surface

31 Context 6058, F1. Bowl rim. Uniform black fabric with burnished outer surface.

32 Context 6058, F1. Bowl rim. Uniform black fabric with smoothed outer surface.

33 Context 6058, F1. Flat base from ?jar. Uniform black fabric with burnished outer surface.

34 Context 6527, F3. Foot-ring base sherd. Harsh black fabric with smooth and burnished outer surface.

35 EMS6: Context 1269, F2. Pedestal base. Black fabric with orange-brown outer surface.

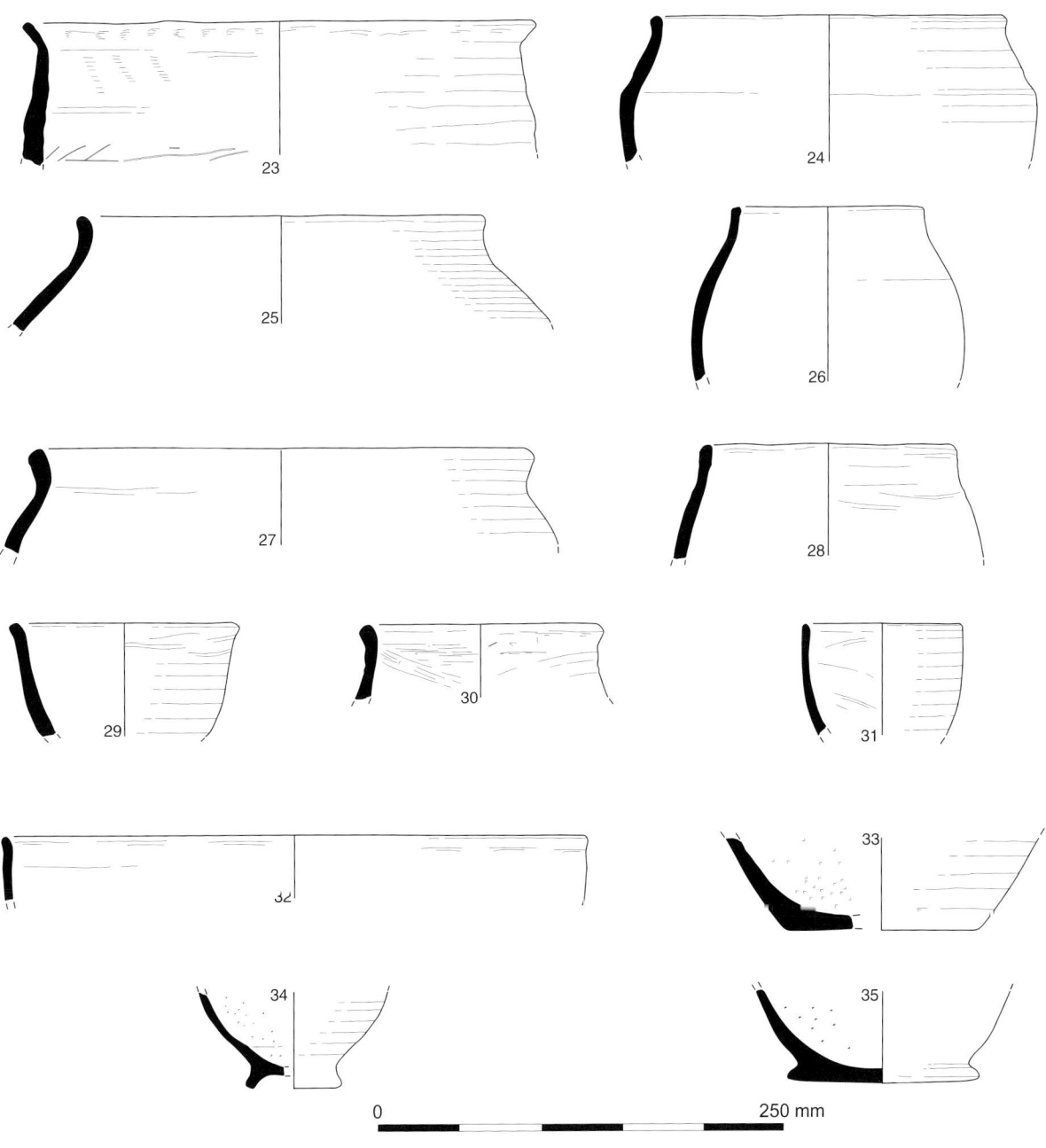

Fig. 4.4 Early/Middle Saxon pottery

Middle Saxon

The Ipswich ware assemblage, as noted above, is one of the largest known from the inland areas of the south-east Midlands. It is also typical of assemblages found at sites outside the East Anglian kingdom in that pitchers and large jars are far more frequent than at sites inside the kingdom, where small jars usually represent 95% or more of an assemblage (Blinkhorn in prep.) It seems likely that pitchers were desirable as vessels – the Ipswich ware potters were the only English makers of such vessels – but that large jars travelled as containers for traded goods.

Only one rimsherd – from a stamped pitcher – was recorded (Fig. 4.5, 36) but a stamped sherd from another vessel was also noted (Fig. 4.5, 37). Stamping was only used on pitchers and large jars (Blinkhorn in prep). The only other feature sherds were fragments of the bases of two vessels, one large, one small. Many of the bodysherds appear to be from larger vessels on the basis of their curvature and thickness.

The Maxey ware assemblage appears to comprise in the main bar-lug vessels (eg. Fig. 4.5, 38), which is typical of the tradition in Northamptonshire. Some rim sherds do not have these features, but they could easily be from such vessels, as the rim forms are generally the same.

The sherd of possible North French Blackware (Fig. 4.5, 39) is likely to be from a jug, although the sherd is too small to be certain of this. It is one of the very few finds of such material in the region, and its significance is discussed below.

Late Saxon and Medieval

The late Saxon pottery assemblage offers evidence that there was continuous occupation on the site from the middle to late Saxon periods. A small assemblage of red-painted Stamford ware was present (eg. Fig. 4.5, 40), and also small jars in coarse fabrics with simple rimforms, some with rouletted decoration (eg. Figs. 4.5, 41). Such pottery is amongst the earliest products of the industry, and was made at the Castle Site kiln in the town. This kiln produced radiocarbon dates suggesting that it was last fired *c* AD 850 (Kilmurry 1980, 134-42).

The rest of the late Saxon assemblage has a range of forms in various fabrics which indicates continuous activity throughout the period. St Neots ware, the most common late Saxon fabric type, shows typical typological traits. Generally, jars in earlier St Neots ware assemblages are smaller than those in the later groups. Here, the LS1/LS2 jars have a mean diameter of 161.4 mm, while those from LS4 groups have a mean of 180.0 mm, and those in the latest group, from the early medieval Ph0, have a mean of 198.1 mm, which is much as would be expected. In terms of form, the whole assemblage is typical of contemporary groups in the region, comprising jars with simple everted forms and bowls with inturned rims (eg. Fig. 4.5, 43). A single spouted bowl was also noted (Fig. 4.5, 44). While

these are a well-known part of the St Neots ware tradition, this example had an unusually large and elaborate spout. The vessel was smoke-blackened on the outer surface, as the spouted bowls often are, suggesting that it was used in cookery. The same comments apply to many of the cylindrical jars (eg. Fig. 4.5, 45).

The Oolitic ware (F207) is mainly represented by a single 'barrel' jar (Fig. 4.5, 42). Such vessels appear to be earliest forms in this tradition, and the illustrated jar is dated to LS3, ie. the later 10th century, the time when such pottery first appears in this area of Northamptonshire. The Thetford ware (F102) also shows traits noted at other sites in the region. Despite being first made in the 10th century at the eponymous Norfolk centre (Rogerson and Dallas 1984), it does not appear in Northamptonshire in any sort of quantity until around the time of the Norman Conquest. At Kings Meadow Lane, the whole assemblage apart from two very small sherds, is dated to phase LS4 or later. The majority of the sherds are from large storage vessels (eg. Fig. 4.5, 46), which again is typical of assemblages from this area of the county, and implies that the contents rather than the pots were the reason for the desirability of the ware.

The early medieval shelly ware assemblage is fairly fragmented, but again appears typical of sites in the region. It is dominated by jars, although some bowls and jugs also occur. Shelly ware jugs (eg. Fig. 4.5, 47) appear to have largely fallen from use once glazed examples began to be made in the 13th century, and that appears to be the case here. Certainly, all the stratified shelly ware jug rims date to Ph0 or Ph1, although the paucity of pottery from the later medieval phases may be a factor.

The rest of the medieval assemblage, the kilns aside, is sparse and fragmented, and apart from those noted it all appears typical of the range of material found at other contemporary sites in the region, and therefore merits no further consideration.

Illustrations

Figure 4.5

36   MSS3: Contexts 2331 and 2332, F95. Rim and upper body of stamped pitcher. Brick red fabric with grey surfaces.

37   MSS4: Context 2624, F95. Stamped bodysherd. Uniform grey fabric.

38   MSS2: Context 451, F97. Rim and body of bar-lug vessel. Grey fabric with pink surfaces, outer extensively smoke-blackened.

39   Context 1271, ?North French Blackware. Bodysherd. Grey fabric with darker surfaces. Outer surface burnished with incised (?rouletted) decoration

40   Context 15132, F205. Bodysherd from storage jar. White fabric with buff surfaces, geometric design in thin red paint on outer surface.

41   Context 15011, F205. Rimsherd from small jar. Uniform grey slightly sandy fabric, diamond-notched rouletting on the outer rim-bead.

42   LSS1. Context 555, F207. Full profile of jar. Light grey fabric with dark, grey-brown surfaces.

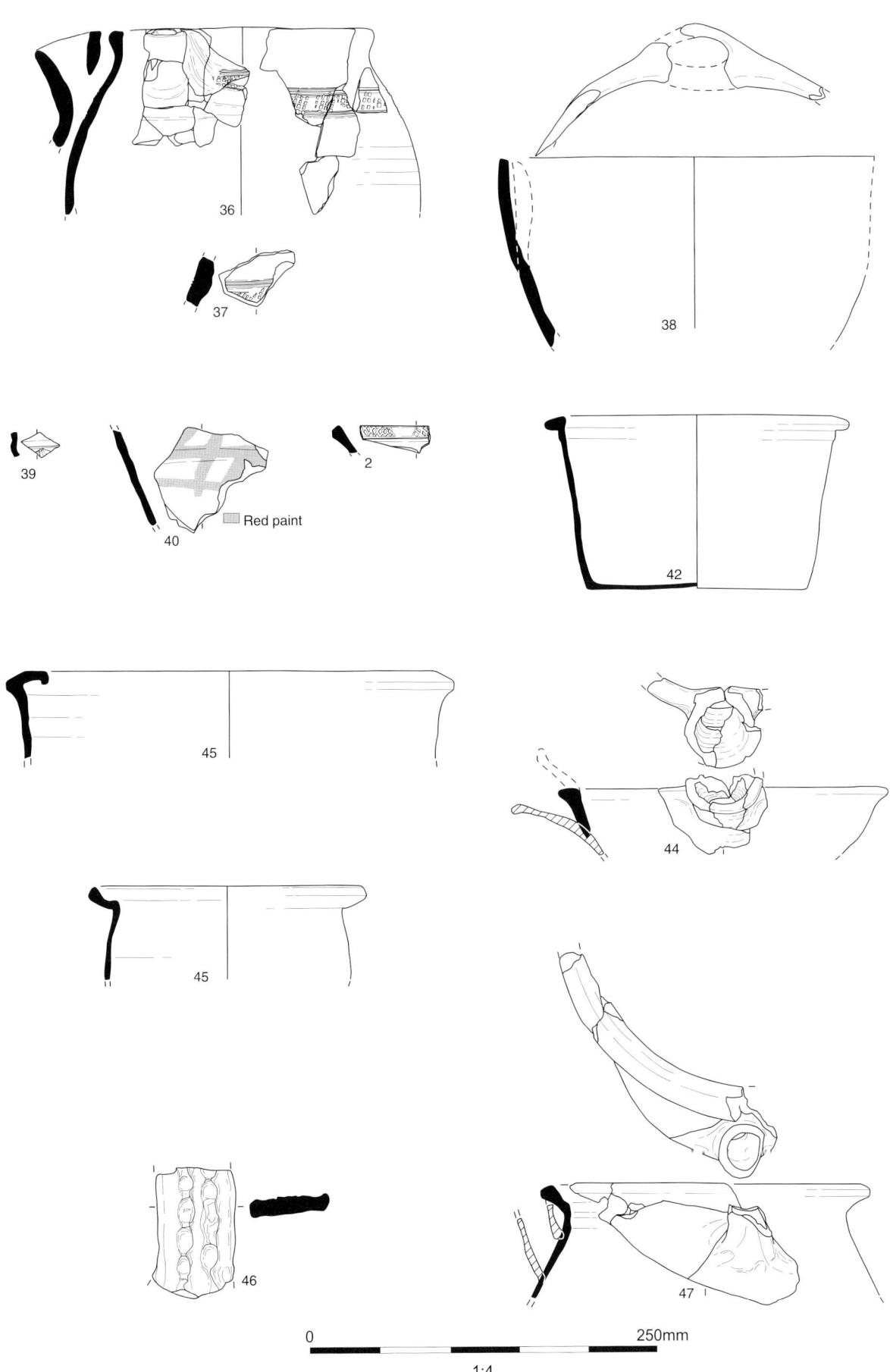

Red paint

Fig. 4.5   Middle and Late Saxon pottery

43   LSS2: Context 2335, F200. Inturned rim bowl. Dark
      grey fabric with pae orange-brown surfaces.
44   Context 6620, F200. Rim and spout from bowl. Grey
      fabric with light brown surfaces, outer surface
      smoke-blackened.
45   Context 6241, F200. Rim from cylindrical jar. Grey
      fabric with brown surfaces, outer surface evenly
      smoke-blackened.
46   Context 15511, F102. Handle from large storage jar.
      Light grey fabric with browner surfaces.
47   Context 15310, F330. Rim and spout from pitcher.
      Grey fabric with orange surfaces.

Spatial distribution

Early Saxon

The distribution of the decorated pottery suggests
that the early Saxon settlement was substantial, and
also that there was not a great degree of mobility in
the occupation *foci* over time, other than that caused
by expansion. The earliest decorated sherds are
almost exclusively from the areas to the north-west
(Site 1) (Fig. 4.1, 1, 5-7) and to the south-west of the
enclosure (within Site 4) (Fig. 4.1, 3-4). It is possible
therefore that the whole area to the west of the
enclosure was settled during the 5th century,
although the lack of features at the western end of
Site 4 means that two separate foci may have co-
existed. An early sherd (Fig. 4.1, 2) was also noted in
Site 3 to the east of the enclosure, although this area
may have been an outlier to the main settlement.
The bossed and incised pottery, probably dating to
the later 5th – early 6th century, occurred mainly in
features in Site 1 (Fig 4.1, 8-10), but a single sherd
was noted to the west in Site 9 (Fig. 4.1, 18) and
another (Fig. 4.1, 11) to the east of the enclosure. The
stamped pottery indicative of a 6th-century date
occurred in Site 1 (Fig. 4.1, 12-14), Site 4 (Fig. 4.1, 15-
16, 21-22) and Site 9 (Fig. 4.1, 19-20).

This distribution pattern suggests that the earliest
Anglo-Saxon settlement at the site was mainly in
the area directly to the west of the enclosure, with
perhaps a less dense occupation area to the east, and
that it started around the middle of the 5th century.
By the later 5th century, the settlement had
expanded westwards, or another separate focus had
appeared, and all these areas continued to be used
through the rest of the early Saxon period.

Middle Saxon

Very little consideration has been given to the
spatial distribution of middle Saxon pottery types at
settlement sites in the past, although some analysis
of spatial distribution was attempted with the
material from the site at Cottenham in
Cambridgeshire. The site produced nearly 49 sherds
of Ipswich ware, along with 'a little' Maxey ware
(Hall 2000, 22), although it seems likely that some of
the material was misidentified. Two sherds
described as 'St Neots ware' (ibid. figs 28.20 and
28.22) are almost certainly Maxey type, with one of
them clearly a bar-lug, and not 'a looped handle' as

described in the text, (ibid. 24). It is unfortunate that
these errors were made, because, had the pottery
types had been properly identified, the analysis of
the spatial distribution of the middle Saxon pottery
could have been extremely helpful in understanding the site.

At Kings Meadow Lane, the distribution of the
Ipswich ware shows that the majority of it was
deposited in Site 2, in or near the buildings at the
entrance to the enclosure, and in the enclosure ditch
itself. A further seven sherds came from Site 4,
directly to the south of Site 2, with just four sherds
coming from features away from this area of the
site. Six sherds were noted in features in Site 6,
which could easily be a peripheral area of the focus
in Sites 2 and 4, together with three sherds from Site
7 and a single sherd from Site 8. A single sherd was
noted at Site 1, but otherwise, the Ipswich ware was
entirely limited to an area to the south of the enclosure.

The distribution of the Maxey ware shows
considerable differences from that of the Ipswich
ware. The largest group by far came from context
451, an evaluation trench *c* 20 m to the north of Site
3. The context is a re-cut of the eastern arm of the
enclosure ditch, and produced 108 sherds of Maxey
ware (1,741 g), over two-thirds (by weight) of the
site assemblage. Five sherds (64 g) were noted in the
eastern half of the east-west ditch that (in Phase 2c)
closed off the mouth of the enclosure, and a further
14 sherds (338 g) came from Site 3 itself, and five
(185 g) from Site 8. This means that just over 90% of
the Maxey ware from the site came from the area in
and around the eastern side of the enclosure ditch.
The rest of the Maxey ware assemblage was thinly
scattered across the areas to the south of the enclosure entrance, apart from three sherds (53 g) which
occurred at Site 9. This means that less than 8% of
the Maxey ware from the site occurred in the area
where nearly all the Ipswich ware occurred.

This distribution pattern is undoubtedly significant, but identifying its meaning highlights one of
the major problems of middle Saxon pottery studies
in the region. The most obvious reasons for the
difference in the distribution of the two middle
Saxon pottery types at this site appear to be either
chronological or functional. If chronological, it
would suggest that the area to the east of the enclosure was a focus which fell from use early in the
middle Saxon period.

A date range of AD 650-850 for Maxey Ware has
gained general acceptance. However, while there is
little doubt that it is a middle Saxon ware, the exact
limits of the chronology have not been rigorously
tested. Recent work (Blinkhorn in prep.) has shown
that Ipswich ware has a chronology of *c* AD725–850,
based on a number of numismatic associations and
scientifically-obtained dates. No such examination
of the dating evidence for Maxey ware from the
south-east midlands has been carried out. The
original definition of Maxey ware came from the
type-site, and the pottery was dated to the middle

Saxon period on the basis of associated artefacts, but no absolute dating was obtained (Addyman 1964, 49). In addition, the Maxey group did not produce any bar-lug vessels which are typical of the tradition in Northamptonshire, but did have vessels with upright triangular lugs (Addyman 1964, fig. 14), which are typical of the Lincolnshire tradition, so it seems likely that the pottery from Maxey is of the Lincolnshire type, and thus different from the material from Kings Meadow Lane.

Since then, several large groups of the material have been excavated, but a firm absolute chronology is still lacking. Two sherds from the assemblage at Chicheley in Buckinghamshire produced thermoluminescence dates of AD780 and AD830, both +/- 15% (Farley 1980, 97), indicating that some Maxey ware from that site may have been contemporary with Ipswich ware. Chalk Lane in Northampton produced a range of radiocarbon dates from phase 2B, with the latest being AD660 +/- 75, although all the stratified Maxey ware came from the preceding phase (Gryspeerdt 1981, 110 and table 2). If the dating is reliable, this would suggest that Maxey ware fell from use by AD735 at the latest. The site at Green Street, Northampton (Chapman 1999, 42) did not produce any absolute dating in association with the Maxey ware. The St Peter's Street site did produce a number of coins, amongst which were a sceatta dated to *c* AD 735 and a penny of Behrtwulf of Mercia, dated to *c* AD 843-8 (Archibald *et al.* 1979, 243-44). Unfortunately, both came from a building which on the ceramic evidence seems to date to the first half of the 10th century, although there appears to be a considerable amount of both residuality and intrusion in the structure (McCarthy 1979, table 11). Maxey ware was present, but the association appears unreliable.

A middle Saxon sceatta dated to *c* AD750 was also noted at St Peter's Gardens,Northampton (Archibald and Metcalf 1985). It occurred in a context from Phase 2 of the site, a period of activity which although did not produce any Maxey ware, did not produce any pottery later than the middle Saxon period except for a single early late Saxon sherd, which could easily have been intrusive. Maxey ware did however occur in the soil horizon through which the phase 2 features were cut, and was the latest pottery type from that phase, suggesting that its deposition pre-dated AD750. The rest of the Maxey ware from the site was redeposited in late Saxon features, so again this would suggest that Maxey ware had fallen from use by the middle of the 8th century.

As noted above, there are a number of sites which have produced both Ipswich and Maxey ware, but the stratification of the two suggests that there may be chronological differences; features tend to produce large quantities of one pottery type with little or none of the other. This was certainly the case at North Raunds (Blinkhorn forthcoming b). Maxey itself produced just nine sherds of Ipswich ware, but 92 of Maxey-type. At Castor, the bulk of the Ipswich ware (156 sherds) occurred in a single pit, but the feature produced only four sherds of Maxey ware, with the rest of the assemblage of that pottery type being unstratified (Green *et al* 1987, 135-6). The site at Warmington, which produced 17 sherds of Ipswich ware did not produce any Maxey ware despite being located in an area where such pottery is well known. Wollaston produced 45 sherds of Maxey ware but just three of Ipswich ware, and very little, if any Ipswich ware is known from Northampton, despite Maxey wares being fairly common. At West Fen Road, Ely, only one sherd of Maxey ware was noted, while there were over 400 sherds of Ipswich ware, but there were also only three sherds of hand-made pottery, suggesting that there was little or no activity before the 8th century. At Tempsford, although much of the middle Saxon pottery was redeposited, contexts of middle Saxon date tended to produce either Ipswich ware or Maxey ware, but rarely both.

All this evidence would suggest that a case can be made for Ipswich ware and Maxey ware having different chronologies, although the thermoluminescence dates from Chicheley would suggest otherwise. However, the date range given for the Chicheley sherds, AD 780 and AD 830, both +/- 15% (Farley 1980, 97), means that they could easily date to around AD 700, and thus would match the chronology suggested by the numismatic and radiocarbon dates from Northampton. On this basis, a case can be made for the bar-lug vessels in the Northamptonshire Maxey ware tradition having a chronology of *c* AD650–750.

If this chronology is correct, then it would suggest that the activity around the eastern side of the enclosure at this site pre-dates the middle Saxon settlement to the south, and that in the period AD650-750, the area which was extensively occupied in the early Saxon period to the west of the enclosure was largely abandoned. This cannot be postulated with total confidence however; there are still too many uncertainties surrounding the dating of Maxey ware to allow it, but there seem to be good grounds for investigating the possibility further, as a clearer understanding of the pottery can only lead to a clearer understanding of the middle Saxon archaeology of the region.

Further uncertainty about the significance of the Maxey ware distribution comes from the question of vessel function. As noted above, much of the Ipswich ware from the site comprised either pitchers or large storage vessels. The Maxey bar-lug vessels, which were designed to be suspended, and therefore were ideal for cookery, may have had a different function from that of Ipswich ware. The different distribution of the two wares may simply be a reflection of areas of different activity at the site. Certainly, many of the Maxey ware sherds were externally smoke-blackened, suggesting they had been used in cooking. The Ipswich ware vessels were not blackened, and it could be surmised that the area in which Ipswich ware mainly occurred was an area where storage and social activities such as drinking and eating took place, and that the area to the east, where the Maxey ware mainly occurred, was a preparation area, and perhaps where cookery took place. This would certainly be of practical value. If, as seems likely, the site had a fairly large seasonal population, then cookery would have had to have taken place on a fairly large scale, and it would have made sense to locate kitchens well away from the main concentration of timber buildings with inflammable thatched roofs. This separation of cooking from domestic structure was common practice in the medieval period. The Maxey ware spread is also in an area which would generally have been down-wind of the main middle Saxon settlement area represented by Ipswich Ware. This would have served to further lessen the risk of fire to the main settlement.

Late Saxon – Early Medieval

The presence of red-painted Stamford ware at this site is an extremely useful indicator because it represents the earliest products of that industry, and can dated to the mid-9th to mid-10th century (Kilmurry 1980, 142). In addition, a few small jars in relatively coarse sandy fabric were noted; these have a similar chronology to the red-painted sherds. These early Stamford ware vessels were almost all from Sites 6 and 8.

The Saxo-Norman cylindrical jars, which were a product of the St Neots ware industry, and which appear to have been a specialist cooking vessels (Blinkhorn 1999c), show a distribution which is almost entirely limited to the eastern side of the site, despite the fact that St Neots ware is found in most areas of the site. In total, sherds from 18 different vessels were noted, of which 11 came from Site 8, two from Site 3 and five from Site 4. As noted above in the discussion of the Maxey ware, the eastern side of the settlement would have been down-wind from all the timber buildings on the site and locating kitchens there would have considerably reduced the chances of fire.

By the medieval period most of the pottery, the kiln waste aside, comes from the eastern side of the site suggesting that by that time a street-frontage ribbon settlement typical of the period had developed.

Assemblage in its local and regional context

The above data shows that the Anglo-Saxon and early medieval assemblage from this site is in the main large and well stratified. It demonstrates that there was significant and prolonged activity during that time, and is by far the largest assemblage ever excavated in Higham Ferrers, although groups of contemporary pottery have been noted recently in other smaller excavations in the town, suggesting that the Kings Meadow Lane area was not occupied in isolation. Either there were other contemporary settlements nearby, or perhaps the sites are parts of

the same large, dispersed Anglo-Saxon settlement. At the early to middle Saxon site at Mucking in Essex, the pottery indicated that the concentration of 5th-century settlement was located some 500 m away from focus of 6th-century settlement, although there were 6th-century outliers in the area of the 5th-century core, and vice versa (Hamerow 1993, fig. 3).

At Higham Ferrers, a group of 12 sherds of early to middle Saxon hand-built pottery was noted at Wharf Road (Blinkhorn 2003b). They included a single small fragment with combed decoration, indicating an early Saxon date. The only other pottery from the site was a single small medieval sherd and some post-medieval material. Early and middle Saxon pottery was also noted at excavations at College Street. Two sherds of Maxey ware were noted at site HFC203 (Blinkhorn 2003c, 132), along with over 100 sherds of late Saxon and medieval wares. The assemblage was otherwise largely Saxo-Norman and early medieval in date, although there also appears to have been a 'peak' in pottery deposition during the later 13th-14th century (CTS Ph2/2). Excavations at another site in College Street (CSHF02) (Blinkhorn 2002a) produced two small sherds of early/middle Saxon hand-built wares, but also around 150 sherds of Saxo-Norman and medieval pottery. The main period of ceramic deposition was the 12th-13th centuries, with very little material deposited between phases Ph2/2 and Ph5.

When the Kings Meadow Lane assemblage is considered in a wider regional context, the late Saxon and medieval material, in terms of the range of fabrics, is generally typical of sites in the northern half of Northamptonshire, but the early and middle Saxon assemblages are worthy of some discussion.

The early/middle Saxon hand-built pottery assemblage of 1,330 sherds is one of the largest in the county, and also in the region. It is on a par with that from Chalk Lane, Northampton (Gryspeerdt 1981, 108) which yielded 1,265 sherds. The latter included fragments of 14 decorated vessels, most of which were stamped and thus likely to be of 6th-century date. The Raunds excavations produced around 7,000 sherds of hand-built pottery, but only a handful was decorated, suggesting that most of the assemblage was of 7th-century date. The site at Dando Close, Wollaston, produced 1,016 sherds, with the decorated vessels mainly stamped, like Chalk Lane, , suggesting that there was little Anglo-Saxon activity before the 6th century. An assemblage of 857 sherds of hand-built pottery was found at St John's Square, Daventry (Blinkhorn 1997, 71), but again the decorated wares were primarily stamped and so of 6th-century date.

Excavations at Brixworth yielded an assemblage of 237 sherds of hand-built pottery (Timby 1995, 90), although only two were decorated. Both the sherds had bosses, and one was incised, so a date of the late 5th to 6th century seems the most likely. At this site, a wide range of decorative techniques was noted, with some sherds (see below) possibly of 5th-century date. Fifth-century Anglo-Saxon pottery is very rare in Northamptonshire; the largest assemblage of that date comes from a single SFB at Stoke Doyle near Oundle, which produced a carinated *Schalenurne,* which is likely to date to the 5th century (Pearson 1994, 102-104).

The identification of middle Saxon (*c* AD650-850) pottery groups in Northamptonshire is generally reliant on the presence of Ipswich and Maxey wares. The local hand-built types may have continued in use during that period, but as yet it has not been possible to confirm this, nor to identify any distinctive wares dating to the period (see above).

Perhaps the most notable middle Saxon sherd from the Kings Meadow Lane site is the possible fragment of North French Blackware (Fig. 4.5, 39). It must be stressed that the small size of the sherd means that the provenance of the piece is not totally secure, especially as there is Roman pottery from the site, but it has been shown to a number of authorities, with the general consensus is that it seems more likely to be a middle Saxon import than a Romano-British sherd. Continental imported pottery is well-attested in the wics of middle Saxon England, such as Southampton, Ipswich, London and York (eg Brown 1997), but it does not seem to have penetrated very far inland, other than at sites in the hinterland of the ports of entry (eg Blinkhorn 2002b), and most of these appear to have been places of some wealth and significance. A good example is perhaps the episcopal complex at North Elmham in Norfolk, thought to be the seat of the Anglo-Saxon Bishop of Norfolk (Wade-Martins 1980). The site produced over half the known continental imports for the whole of rural Norfolk, despite the fact that it produced less than 5% of the total middle Saxon pottery from the same sample set.

In the south-east Midlands middle Saxon imported pottery is particularly scarce, and where it has been identified, the sites appear to have been places of relative wealth and/or power. They are inevitably found at sites that have also produced Ipswich ware. At Castor, the probable site of a nunnery, sherds from at least two imported Blackware vessels were noted (Green *et al* 1987, 142), and at Bedford, a sherd of late 8th- to 9th-century Tating ware occurred in the Midland Road area of the town (Slowikowski 1991). Tating ware is a rare find in England and western Europe generally, and mainly occurs on high-status royal, ecclesiastical or trading sites, such as North Elmham. The nature of middle Saxon Bedford is far from clear, but the Midland Road area has produced an assemblage of Ipswich ware (Baker and Hassall 1979, 154), and its location at a fordable point of a major river suggests that it could have been of some significance in the middle Saxon period. Small quantities of Ipswich ware have been found at a number of sites around the town and in the Ouse Valley generally, suggesting extensive trade in the area in the middle Saxon period and Bedford is an obvious

focal point for that trade. At Chalk Lane, Northampton, Richard Hodges identified sherds which may have been Frankish Blackware, although an English source could not be ruled out (Gryspeerdt 1981, 118). Otherwise, finds of such pottery are extremely rare in the region; the presence of such a sherd at Kings Meadow Lane, if the identification is correct, is a strong indication that it had a status which was considerably above the ordinary.

Ipswich ware has been noted in small quantities at a growing number of sites in the county, particularly in the Nene Valley, but groups of more than a handful of sherds are rare (Blinkhorn in prep). At present the only known assemblages with 10 or more sherds are the group of 17 sherds from Warmington (Blinkhorn forthcoming a) and the 73 sherds from two sites excavated at North Raunds (Blinkhorn forthcoming b). The Kings Meadow Lane assemblage of 86 sherds, representing 16 vessels, is the largest yet excavated in the county.

The Maxey ware assemblage of 148 sherds from Kings Meadow Lane is the largest from the county, and one of the largest from the region. Its Jurassic petrology suggests that it is most likely to have a local source. Maxey Ware is often found without Ipswich ware in association, possibly suggesting different in chronologies for Ipswich Ware and Maxey Ware (as discussed above) or suggesting sites of different status. The sites with Ipswich ware were indulging in long-distance trade, whereas those with Maxey ware were not. In Northamptonshire, sites which produced fairly large groups of both Ipswich and Maxey wares are North Raunds (37 sherds of Maxey), Warmington (12 sherds of Maxey, although all Lincolnshire types) and Dando Close, Wollaston (45 sherds of Maxey and 3 of Ipswich; Blinkhorn forthcoming e). Northampton has produced a number of groups of Maxey ware, although only one probable sherd of Ipswich ware has so far been noted, at Chalk Lane, Northampton (Gryspeerdt 1981, 110). The latter site did however produce 77 sherds of Maxey ware, and excavations at Green Street, Northampton produced 15 sherds of the same material (Blinkhorn 1999a, 56) although all but one sherd was from a single vessel. At St Peter's Street, Northampton (McCarthy 1979, tables 10-17), at least 75 Maxey ware sherds were present, although a full catalogue was not published and the actual total may be higher. Ten sherds were found at St Peter's Gardens (Denham 1985, table 2), along with four sherds which are similar to Ipswich ware, but probably not of that type.

The Kings Meadow Lane assemblage also stands comparison with those from sites from further afield in the region. At Castor in Cambridgeshire the excavation of a probable middle Saxon nunnery produced 191 sherds of Ipswich ware and at least 46 of Maxey ware (Green *et al* 1987, 138; full total of Maxey ware not published), along with seven sherds from an imported continental blackware vessel. Cambridgeshire has recently produced a number of large assemblages of Ipswich ware (eg Blinkhorn forthcoming c), particularly in and around Ely, and it seems that most of the county was within the hinterland of Ipswich. In Norfolk and Suffolk hand-built pottery is rarely found in association with Ipswich ware, suggesting that the latter was manufactured and traded to the extent that it served as the 'local' domestic pottery for the entire kingdom. The recent finds from Cambridgeshire suggest that this was also true for much of that county, although, as noted, large groups of Maxey ware are also known, but as with the Northamptonshire material, the two are rarely found together in quantity. For example, the Ely West Fen Road site (Blinkhorn forthcoming c) produced 414 sherds of Ipswich ware but just one of Maxey-type, whereas at the 'type-site' of Maxey (Addyman 1964, 47-58), 92 sherds of Maxey ware were present, but just nine of Ipswich ware. (The latter were not noted in the original analysis of the assemblage, but were seen by this author at a later date.)

Elsewhere in the region, large groups of Maxey and/or Ipswich ware are rare. In Buckinghamshire, all the known groups of Ipswich ware comprise less than ten sherds, although a site at Chicheley near Newport Pagnell, (Farley 1980, 97) produced 77 sherds of Maxey ware. In Bedfordshire, the site at Tempsford (Blinkhorn forthcoming d) produced 155 sherds of Maxey ware and 56 sherds of Ipswich ware, but most sites produced just a few sherds of each or either type.

It can be seen therefore that the middle Saxon pottery assemblage from Kings Meadow Lane is exceptional for the region, with perhaps only the sites at Tempsford, Castor, and, to a lesser extent, Raunds being comparable. As noted above, the site at Castor is thought to have been a nunnery, and both middle Saxon sculpted stone and a silver sceatta, both rare finds in this area of the country, are known from the site. The exact nature of the site at Tempsford is unknown, as most of the middle Saxon pottery was redeposited due to extensive later activity, a comment that also applies to North Raunds.

This all suggests that the Kings Meadow Lane site was a place of some wealth and importance during the middle Saxon period. Ipswich ware is the most widely-distributed English pottery type of the middle Saxon period, and is found along the east coast of England from Yorkshire to Kent, and as far west as Gloucestershire. The reason for this seems to have been, in the most part, trade passing through the wic of Ipswich rather than the desirability of the pottery other than the pitchers (Blinkhorn 1999b, p 5). It is not a totally reliable indicator of site status, but it seems that the further from Ipswich an assemblage is found, the greater the likelihood that the find-spot is a place of some importance. The size of the assemblage from this site shows that traded goods were arriving at the site on a scale that is virtually unparalleled in the south-east Midlands region, although most was either not consumed here, or was of a type which left no physical trace.

Late Medieval pottery kilns *by Paul Blinkhorn*

Introduction

The first evidence for the production of pottery at Higham Ferrers came from the Hundredal Court Rolls. An entry for 1436 noted that one William Potter *took a croft where there is a kiln for making pots*, and there is a later reference to repairs being made to a kiln in 1467 (Serjeantson, 1916). The first archaeological evidence came from salvage excavations at Kings Meadow Lane in 1965 (Hall 1974) which produced large quantities of waste pottery and evidence of a structure that was interpreted at the time as a kiln. The more recent excavations, covered by this report, produced the remains of two kilns, both producing Late Medieval Reduced Ware (Northants CTS fabric F365), a common pottery type in the south-east midlands in the later 14th-15th century. The vessels are all wheel-thrown, often with knife-trimming on the lower walls, and the fabric is inevitably reduced to a grey colour, sometimes with a red core. It is usually moderately to heavily tempered with sub-rounded quartz up to 2 mm, sometimes with rare to moderate rounded calcareous material (?ooliths) up to the same size. The vessels are usually thin-walled (less than 5 mm), and occasional large flint pebbles up to 10 mm are noted in the fabric. These must have been a point of weakness, and most of those that were noted appear to have caused vessels to break during firing.

The ware appears purely functional to the modern eye; the mainstays of the manufactories were large bowls (pancheons), cisterns and jars, along with smaller quantities of specialist cooking vessels such as dripping dishes.

Late Medieval Reduced ware is one of the two main late medieval pottery traditions of the south-east Midlands, particularly Northamptonshire, Buckinghamshire and Bedfordshire, with the other being Late Medieval Oxidized ware (Northants CTS F401) which is, for all intents and purposes, the same in terms of fabric, manufacture and the range of vessel forms, with the only major differences being that the material was fired to an orange-red colour, and some of the vessels are glazed.

Oxidized ware seems to be a slightly later introduction, and, although the exact chronology is still a little uncertain, it does not seem to have appeared until the 15th century, and perhaps as late as 1450. The difference in colour is purely down to the firing environment. Pots with an iron-rich clay, when fired in an oxygen-rich environment, inevitably have an orange or red colour, while those fired in an oxygen-poor environment are usually grey or black. This is due to the reaction between the iron in the clay and the oxygen in the kiln. There are two oxides of iron; one, which is black, forms in a low-oxygen environment, while the other, more familiar perhaps as rust, forms in oxygen-rich conditions, and it is these that colour the finished pot.

The reason why some potters produced Reduced wares and others Oxidized wares is unclear, but one explanation may be simply economics. A fully sealed kiln, capable of produced reduced pottery, may have taken longer to stack and unload then one with a partial dome and a temporary roof. The latter would have reached the temperatures required to efficiently fire the pots, but would have allowed for more oxygen into the kiln (see below). In an industry that was probably mainly staffed by those at the lower end of the social scale and whose wares were very cheap, such considerations could have meant the difference between success and failure. Certainly, in medieval Britain, few potters appear to have had sufficient wealth and status to enable them to reach the rank of Freeman, and there was never an earthenware potters' Guild (see McCarthy and Brooks 1988, 77).

The excavation of a near-complete kiln and the discovery of traces of another nearby, means that we now have one of the most important and best-understood late medieval pottery manufactories of the period in the south-east Midlands.

Kilns

The kilns themselves are fully described in Chapter 3, and discussed in Chapter 5.

Pottery

Kiln 1 pottery

The pottery assemblage weighed 443,722 g, with the estimated vessel equivalent (EVE), by summation of surviving rimsherd circumference, being 208.09. All the material from the kiln and its associated features was in the tradition of late medieval Reduced ware, which is classified in the Northamptonshire County Ceramic type Series as F365, and broadly dated to the 15th century.

The range of vessel forms comprised almost entirely pancheons, jars, jugs and cisterns, although fragments of a small number of dripping dishes

were also noted. All the sherds were unglazed, and decoration was limited entirely to incised cordons on the shoulders of jars and jugs, and stabbing on jug/cistern handles. A total of 10,450 g of incised bodysherds were noted, as against 304,480 g of plain examples.

The homogeneous and fragmented nature of the assemblage meant that vessel reconstruction was largely impossible, and few profiles were reconstructed apart from some of the pancheons, which are shallow when compared to other vessels. It was not possible to differentiate between jugs and cisterns, as it seems likely that the latter were of the same general form as the former, with the only real difference being the presence of a bunghole near the base. The vessel count, by EVE, was as follows:

Pancheons: 90.86 (45.8%)
Jars: 22.35 (11.3% of the assemblage)
Jugs/Cisterns: 85.22 (42.9%)

In addition, dripping dishes were represented by four handles and two rimsherds. The asymmetrical nature of such vessels makes computation of EVE impossible, but a total of 310 jug handle fragments were noted, which perhaps gives some idea of the relative number of such dripping dishes present in the assemblage, and it should be borne in mind that dripping dishes often had two handles per vessel.

The 429 jug handle fragments were all from single thumb-grooved types, with 46 decorated with stabbing. All spouts (47 examples) were simple pulled lips.

There were 454 fragments from sagging bases, and 169 from flat bases, with one fragment of the latter having thumb-frilling; this was probably from a jug. A total of 26 of the flat bases were attached to vessels with concave lower bodies again probably from jugs.

Bowls/Pancheons- The range of rim forms for bowls and pancheons is shown in Figure 4.6. The numbers (by EVE) and the occurrence of the different the different rim forms are shown in Table 4.10. Figure 4.7 shows the occurrence of bowls of different rim diameters (by EVE) and indicates that the occurrence is broadly unimodal, as is the case with jars

Table 4.10: Pottery Occurrence, Bowl rims, Kiln 1, by type, in EVE

Type	EVE	%	Type	EVE	%	Type	EVE	%
201	8.21	9.0%	209	0.77	0.8%	217	5.05	5.6%
202	19.88	21.9%	210	1.01	1.1%	218	1.78	2.0%
203	6.24	6.9%	211	5.95	6.5%	219	2.18	2.4%
204	0.50	0.6%	212	0.51	0.6%	220	4.94	5.4%
205	0.11	0.1%	213	0.48	0.5%	221	0.20	0.2%
206	13.66	15.0%	214	4.71	5.2%	222	0.24	0.3%
207	1.14	1.3%	215	1.25	1.4%	223	0.39	0.4%
208	1.25	1.4%	216	9.86	10.9%	224	0.29	0.3%

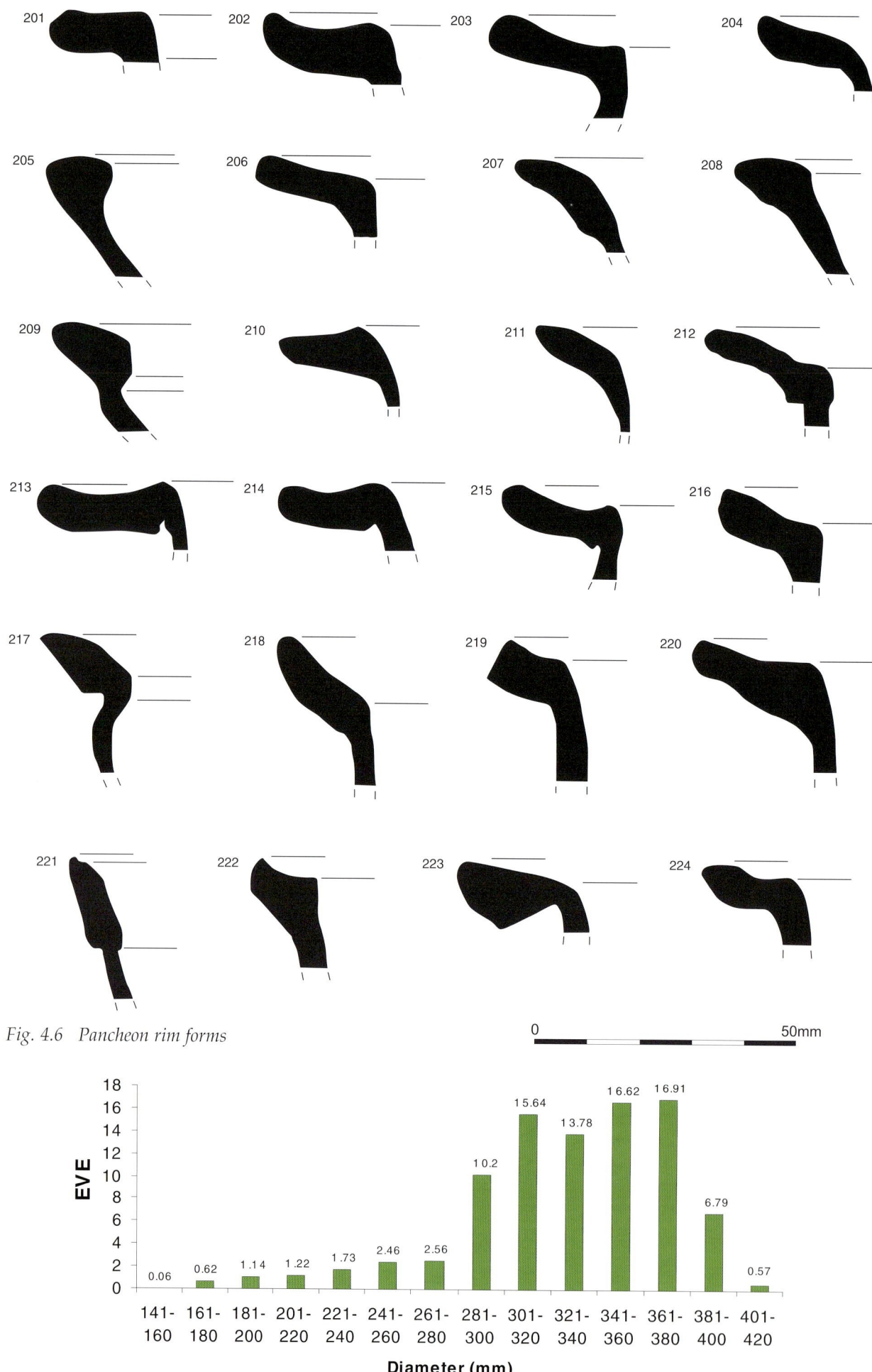

Fig. 4.6 Pancheon rim forms

0 ▬▬▬▬ 50mm

Fig. 4.7 Bowl rim diameter occurrence, Kiln 1, by EVE

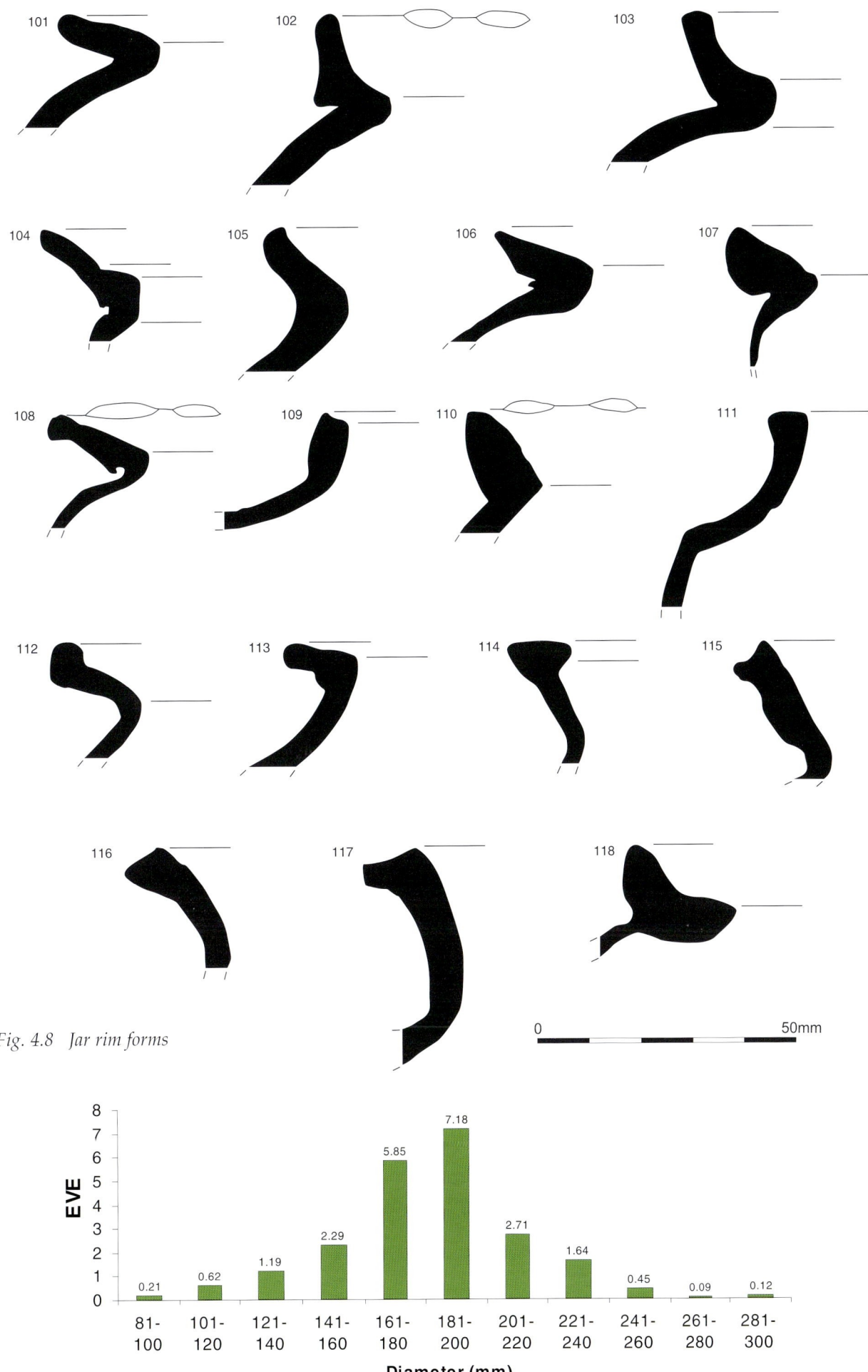

Fig. 4.8   Jar rim forms

Fig. 4.9   Jar rim diameter occurrence, Kiln 1, by EVE

(see below). The mean rim diameter is 339.7 mm, with a standard deviation of 43.7 mm.

Jars – The range of rim forms for jars is shown in Figure 4.8. The numbers (by EVE) and the occurrence of the different rim forms are shown in Table 4.11. Figure 4.9 shows the occurrence of jars of different rim diameters (by EVE) and indicates that the occurrence is broadly unimodal, as is the case with bowls. It cannot be certain that the rim diameter is an accurate reflection of vessel size, but it has been shown that this was the case with medieval pottery from the nearby hamlet of West Cotton (Blinkhorn 1999c). The data from here shows that the rim diameters of the jars had a unimodal distribution, with almost half the vessels in the 160-200 mm diameter range. The mean rim diameter was 196.1 mm, with a standard deviation of 34.5 mm.

Jugs/Cisterns – The range of jug/cistern rimforms is shown in Figure 4.10. The numbers (by EVE) and the occurrence of the different rim forms are shown in Table 4.12. Figure 4.11 shows the occurrence of jugs/cisterns of different rim diameters (by EVE). As with the jars, the occurrence is broadly unimodal, apart from two sherds at the largest end of the distribution scale. The mean rim diameter is 120.4 mm, with a standard deviation of 24.1 mm.

Handles – A total of 310 handle fragments were recorded. They were all variants of thumb-grooved straps (Fig. 4.12), with a number of examples having stabbed decoration. The number of fragments by type is shown in Table 4.13. Four horizontal handles from dripping dishes/skillets were noted. Two were of type 5 and the others of type 6. None were decorated. They are not included in the data in Table 4.13.

Table 4.11: Pottery Occurrence, Jar rims, Kiln 1, by type, in EVE

Type	EVE	%	Type	EVE	%	Type	EVE	%
101	11.36	50.8%	107	0.08	0.4%	113	0.61	2.7%
102	0.92	4.1%	108	0.65	2.9%	114	0.41	1.8%
103	2.34	10.5%	109	0.41	1.8%	115	0	0
104	1.43	6.4%	110	0.16	0.7%	116	0	0
105	0.86	3.8%	111	1.11	5.0%	117	0	0
106	2.08	9.3%	112	0.10	0.4%	118	0	0

Table 4.12: Pottery occurrence, Jug/Cistern rims, Kiln 1, by type, in EVE

Type	EVE	%	Type	EVE	%	Type	EVE	%
301	9.13	10.7%	307	6.09	7.1%	313	1.67	2.0%
302	3.80	4.5%	308	33.46	39.2%	314	0.48	0.6%
303	1.53	1.8%	309	0.51	0.65	315	0.83	1.0%
304	3.83	4.5%	310	1.36	1.6%	316	3.59	4.2%
305	8.49	9.9%	311	3.24	3.8%	317	0.67	0.7%
306	3.28	3.8%	312	2.17	2.5%	318	0.95	1.1%

Table 4.13: Jug/Cistern handle occurrence, Kiln 1, no. of examples.

Type	No Plain	%	No. Stabbed	%	Total	%
1	32	10.3%	0	0	32	10.3%
2	2	0.6%	0	0	2	0.6%
3	8	2.6%	3	1.0%	11	3.6%
4	7	2.3%	3	1.0%	10	3.3%
5	143	46.1%	17	5.5%	160	51.6%
6	76	24.5%	17	5.5%	93	30.0%
7	2	0.6%	0	0	2	0.6%
Total	270		40		310	

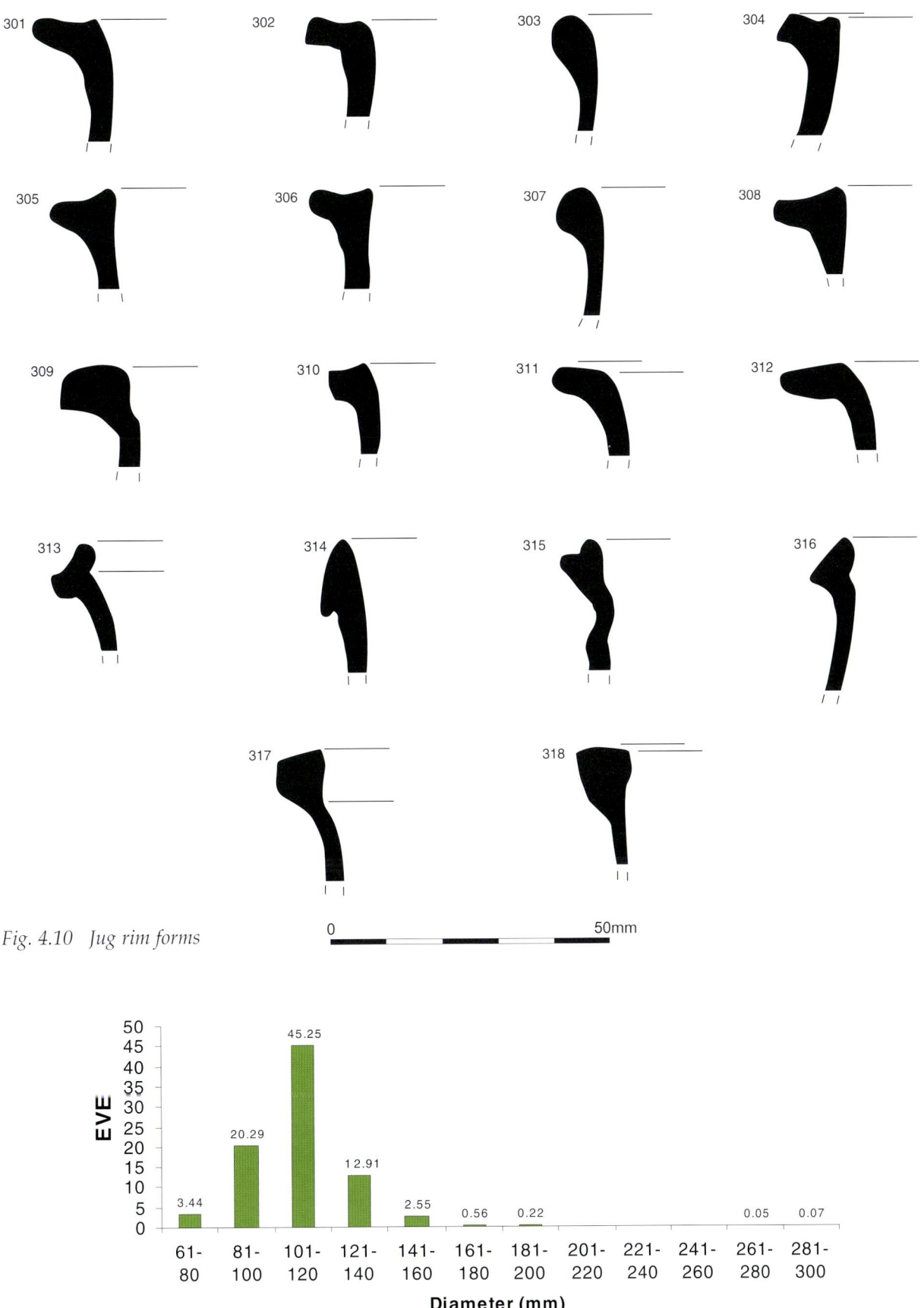

Fig. 4.10   Jug rim forms

0   50mm

Fig. 4.11   Jug/cistern rim diameter occurrence, Kiln 1, by EVE

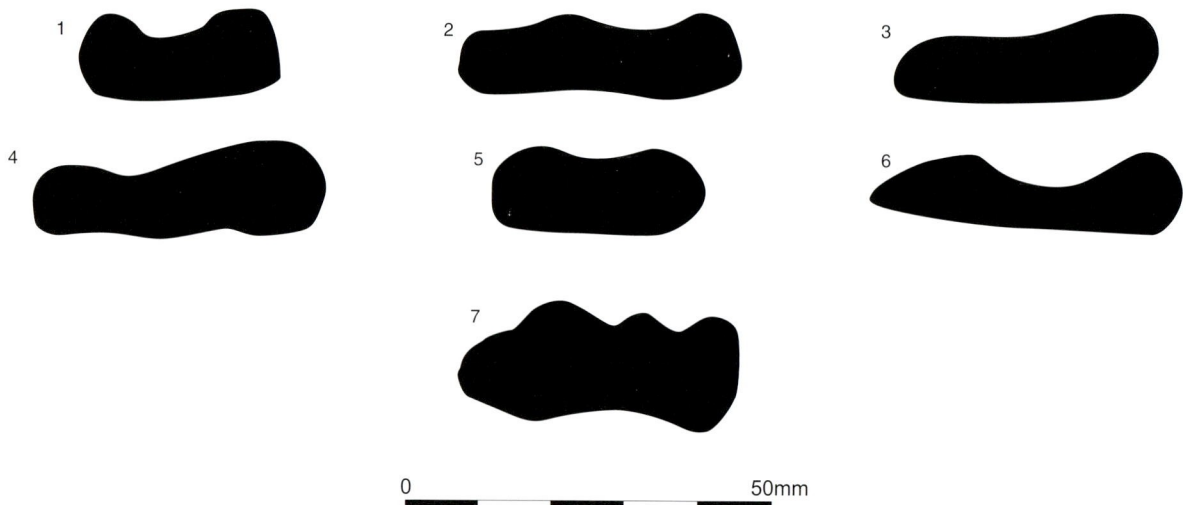

Fig. 4.12   Handle cross-sections

Bungholes – A total of 27 fragments or complete bungholes were noted, giving a minimum number of cisterns. All had an applied, thumb-impressed, roundel surrounding the orifice, with between four and nine thumb impressions. The hole diameter, where it was complete enough to measure, was fairly consistent, ranging from 19-24 mm, with most being 20-21 mm in diameter. The occurrence is shown in Table 4.14.

Spouts – The only type of spout noted was a simple pulled lip, of which 45 examples were noted, all from jugs/cisterns.

Bases – Figure 4.13 shows the distribution of the bases by diameter. Both sagging and flat examples have been combined, and there does not appear to be any differentiation between base form and vessel type. Furthermore, some of the sherds are distorted, and thus their original form cannot be determined with certainty.

The base diameters have a trimodal distribution, with peaks in the ranges 141-160 mm, 181-200 mm and 281-300 mm. It is assumed that these represent jars, jugs/cisterns and pancheons respectively. The lack of full profiles of vessels means that this assumption cannot be confirmed, and there is bound to be overlap between the vessel types. However, of the 16 bowls that were reconstructed to a full profile, all but

Table 4.14: Bunghole Occurrence by orifice diameter, Kiln 1, no. of examples

Diameter	No. Examples
19mm	2
20mm	5
21mm	11
22mm	2
23mm	1
24mm	1

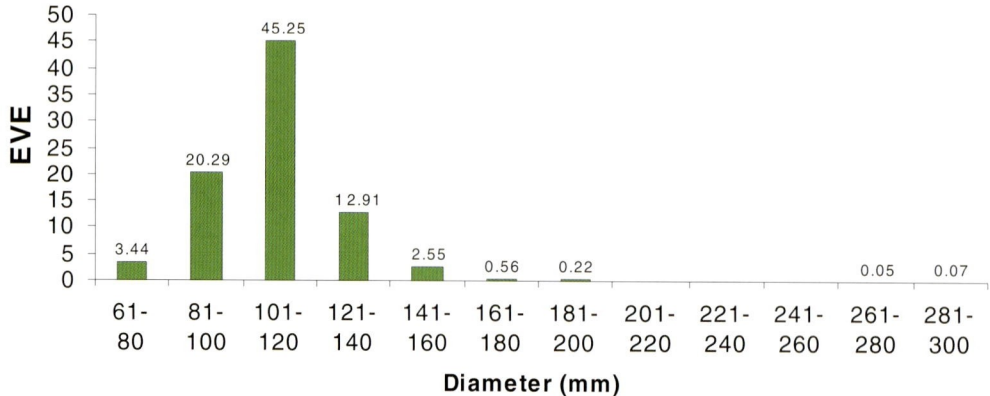

Fig. 4.13   Base diameter occurrence, by number of examples

two had base diameters greater than 260 mm, with the two smaller examples having diameters of 180 mm. Similarly, of the seven bases with cistern bungholes still attached, all but two were in the size-range 160-240 mm, with one larger (300 mm) and one smaller (130 mm), although both may be distorted.

Dripping Dishes – Fragments of the rims of three vessels of this type were noted. All were of a simple upright form.

Kiln 2 pottery

The assemblage of Reduced ware from this kiln and associated features had a total weight of 54,998 g (EVE = 16.35). The reason why so much less pottery was recovered from this kiln is likely to be due to the fact that it did not have any structure below ground level. Most of the pottery from Kiln 1 was recovered from the kiln chamber and stoke-pits.

The range of vessel forms was the same as that from Kiln 1, and the fabrics did not show any great discernible variation. The vessel occurrence (in EVE) was as follows:

Bowls/Pancheons = 5.90 (36.1%)
Jars = 1.04 (6.4%)
Jugs/Cisterns = 9.41 (57.6%)

Bowls/Pancheons – The range of bowl rim forms is shown in Figure 4.6. The occurrence (by EVE) of the different rim forms is shown in Table 4.15.

Figure 4.14 shows occurrence (by EVE) of bowl rim diameters. It shows that, as with the material from Kiln 1, the occurrence is broadly unimodal. The mean rim diameter is 299.4 mm, with a standard deviation of 34.1 mm. This is a smaller mean than for the vessels from Kiln 1, and the size distribution is more restricted, as evidenced by the smaller standard deviation.

Jars – The range of jar rim forms is shown in Figure 4.8. The occurrence (by EVE) of the different rim forms is shown in Table 4.16.

The distribution of rim diameters is not tabulated, because the relatively small assemblage size means that the data has no real pattern. However, the mean jar rim diameter is 212.3 mm, with a standard deviation of 39.6 mm. This does not greatly differ to the same data from Kiln 1 (see above).

Jugs/Cisterns – The range of jug/cistern rim forms is illustrated in Figure 4.10. The occurrence (by EVE) of the different rim forms is shown in Table 4.17

Figure 4.15 shows the jug/cistern rim diameter occurrence (by EVE). It shows that, as with the jars,

Table 4.15: *Pottery occurrence, Bowl rims, Kiln 2, by type, in EVE*

Type	EVE	%	Type	EVE	%	Type	EVE	%
201	1.30	22.0%	209	0	0	217	0	0
202	0.12	2.0%	210	0.19	3.2%	218	0.14	2.4%
203	0.17	2.9%	211	0.39	6.6%	219	0	0
204	0.05	0.8%	212	0.06	1.0%	220	0.68	11.5%
205	0	0	213	0.11	1.9%	221	0	0
206	1.64	27.8%	214	0.19	3.2%	222	0.14	2.4%
207	0	0	215	0.06	1.0%	223	0	0
208	0	0	216	0.40	6.8%	224	0.06	1.0%
	3.28			1.4			1.02	

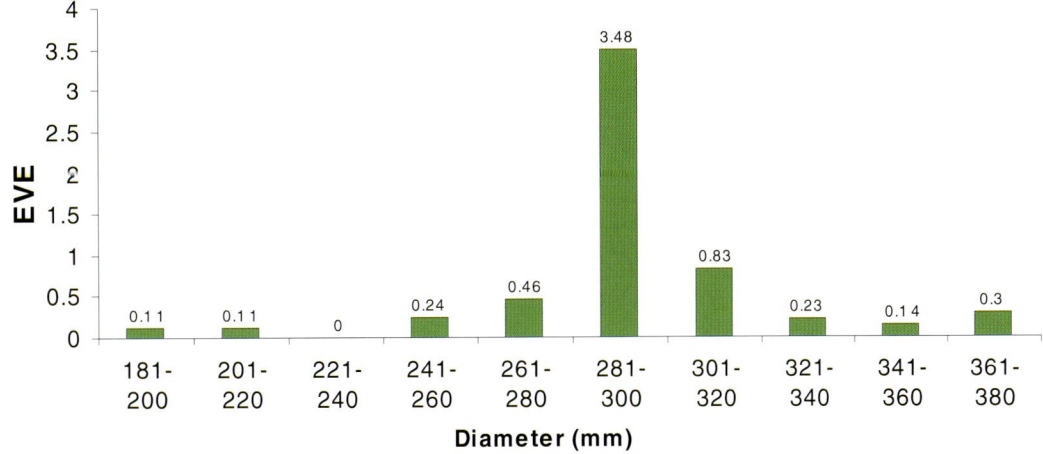

Fig. 4.14 *Bowl Rim diameter occurence, Kiln 2 by EVE*

Table 4.16: Pottery occurrence, Jar rims, Kiln 2, by type, in EVE

Type	EVE	%	Type	EVE	%	Type	EVE	%
101	0.36	34.6%	107	0	0	113	0	0
102	0	0	108	0	0	114	0	0
103	0	0	109	0	0	115	0.12	11.5%
104	0	0	110	0	0	116	0.35	33.7%
105	0	0	111	0	0	117	0.05	4.8%
106	0	0	112	0	0	118	0.06	5.8%

Table 4.17: Pottery occurrence, Jug/Cistern rims, Kiln 2, by type, in EVE

Type	EVE	%	Type	EVE	%	Type	EVE	%
301	0.63	6.7%	307	0	0	313	0	0
302	0.08	0.9%	308	0.57	6.1%	314	0	0
303	0	0	309	0	0	315	0.14	1.5%
304	0.12	1.3%	310	0.07	0.7%	316	0.08	0.9%
305	1.52	16.2%	311	0.81	8.6%	317	0.40	4.3%
306	0	0	312	0.10	1.1%	318	4.89	52.0%

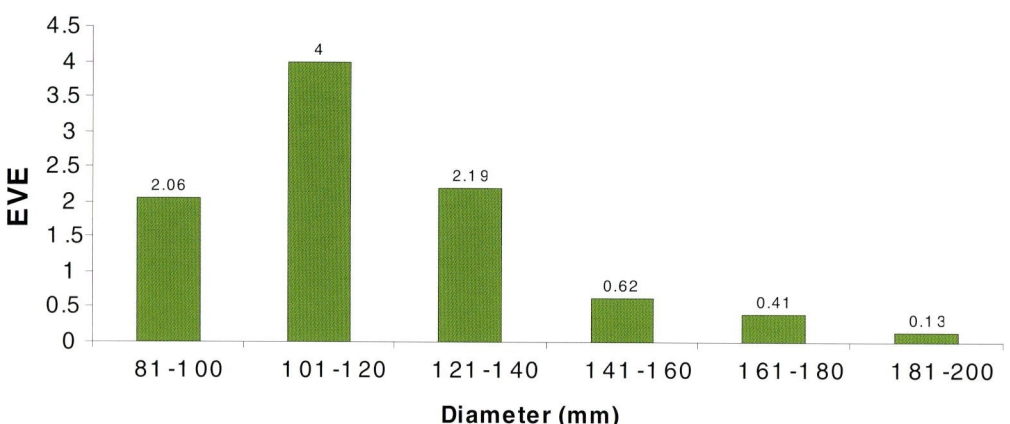

Fig. 4.15   Jug/Cistern rim diameter occurrence by EVE

the occurrence is broadly unimodal. The mean rim diameter is 130.2 mm, with a standard deviation of 23.5 mm.

Handles – A total of 58 handle fragments were noted, all of them undecorated. All were variants of thumb-grooved straps (Fig. 4.12). In addition, two horizontal handles from dripping dishes/skillets were noted, both of type 5. Another unusual variant was an upright loop handle. All the other 55 handle fragments were of type 6.

Bungholes – Fragments of just two bungholes were noted, with both of a similar type to those from Kiln 1, and both had an orifice diameter of 20 mm.

Spouts – The only type of spout noted was a simple pulled lip, of which three examples were noted, all from jugs/cisterns.

Bases – Only seven base sherds were noted. They were all sagging bases, and within the 120–220 mm size range.

Regional Context

The late medieval Reduced ware industry of the south-east Midlands, one of the most important pottery types of the later 14th-15th century, was first formally defined by Moorhouse (1974). Its products are found throughout the region, along with the slightly later (?mid 15th-16th-century) Late Medieval Oxidized Ware industry.

Two Reduced ware manufactories, at Everton (Hassall 1976) and Flitwick (Mynard *et al* 1983), are known from Bedfordshire. In both cases, little or no trace of a kiln was found, but large amounts of waste pottery were noted, and it is all very similar in terms of form and fabric to the material from Higham Ferrers. At Flitwick, 54 % of the rimsherds were from bowls, 32.9 % from jugs/cisterns, 11.4 % from jars and 1.2 % from dripping dishes (Mynard *et al* 1983, 76), although it should be noted that these figures were obtained by rimsherd count rather than EVE. One notable difference from Flitwick is that a small proportion of the pots were glazed (0.9% by weight). No dating evidence was obtained from the Flitwick excavation, but an individual named Henry Potter is known to have lived nearby during the mid-15th century, and there are documentary records indicating that there were clay-pits in the adjoining parish of Ampthill at around the same time (ibid, 75 and 83).

Higham Ferrers has produced the only Reduced ware kilns in Northamptonshire, but a number of Oxidized Ware manufactories are known. Excavations at Glapthorn, near Oundle (Johnston *et al* 1997) examined two late medieval pottery and tile manufactories and their associated out buildings, and also showed that the kilns were also used for lime-burning. The first of these, the 'Leacroft' kiln (Johnston *et al* 1997, 15-24), although built of stone, was otherwise very similar to Kiln 1 at Kings Meadow Lane, being of Musty's type 2c with a central pedestal and opposed stoke-holes, and sunk into the ground (Musty 1974, 44 and fig. 1). The kiln also had an associated building, containing a stone bench, drains and a probable drying oven. The east side of the structure produced a large number of smashed whole pots, which had either been thrown into the structure before demolition, or had fallen from a shelf (Johnston *et al* 1997, 22). Curiously, all these pots were 'seconds', that is, warped or damaged during firing, but still usable. Much of the floor of the building was covered with underfired pottery sherds, seemingly laid down deliberately. Also of note were two large animal ribs which were probably used as throwing formers, and a notched knuckle bone which may have served as a makeshift handle for a 'cheese-wire' used for cutting pots off the wheel after throwing (ibid, 20, fig. 6a). These all came from the demolition rubble over the building.

The dating for the workshop comes from sherds of Cistercian ware and 'Tudor Green' pottery in the upper layers of the workshop floor, suggesting that the pottery was in operation in the second half of the 15th century.

The second Glapthorn kiln, at Gypsy Lane (Johnston *et al* 1997, 24-29), was similar to the first, a type 2c with opposed stoke-pits and a central pedestal, again made of stone, and the whole sunk into the ground. Associated buildings were also identified, but some had been badly plough-damaged, and the rest were largely unexcavated,

but interpreted as a brewing complex that pre-dated the kiln. No precise dating evidence was forthcoming, although one of the pre-kiln structures produced a buckle plate (ibid, 29) which is likely to date to the mid 14th-15th century, suggesting that the Gypsy Lane kiln was operating broadly at the same time as that at Leacroft.

Leacroft produced *c* 1,282 kg of pottery, with the fabric containing abundant, well-sorted sub-rounded white quartz 0.25–0.5 mm in diameter, with occasional red ironstone fragments. The fired fabric was mainly orange, often with a dark grey core, and all the pots were wheel-thrown with knife-trimmed, flat bases. This is absolutely typical of the products of the industry in the region. The majority of the rims (75%) were jar forms, although many, if not most, could have been cisterns. The rest of the assemblage comprised bowls and pancheons (14%) and skillets (2%), along with some ridge tiles. Twenty fragments of fire-bars were noted; none were complete, but they were consistently of a flat profile and 210 mm wide and 40 mm thick.

It was estimated that around 30% of the pottery from the fill of the kiln comprised large sherds which had been fired more than once, and had actually been used for covering the pottery during firing, suggesting that the kiln had an open-topped dome (ibid, 29-31). Musty (1974, 54-5) cited replica firing experiments that showed that this was a feasible way to fire pottery to a serviceable temperature. To produce a reduced firing, the top of the kiln would have had to have been sealed with clay and sods. Therefore, it may be that the major difference between Oxidized and Reduced ware is simply the nature of the kilns.

The Gypsy Lane assemblage was even larger, with 2,032 kg of pot recovered. The fabric was identical to that from Leacroft, and the range of vessels similar, although the proportions differed somewhat. Bowls/pancheons were the most common (66%), followed by jars/cisterns (18%) and skillets and jugs. Four fragments of sgraffito-decorated wall-tile wasters were also recovered. These are the only examples that can be linked to this industry, although examples of a different type of sgraffito wall-tiles are known from Tring (Johnston *et al* 1997, 33). No kiln furniture was noted other than a possible spacer-ring.

The medieval potteries at Lyveden which, like Higham Ferrers and Glapthorne, were located in the north-east of Northamptonshire, were extensively excavated in the 1960s and 1970s. Area D1 at the site (Bryant and Steane 1969, 8 and fig. 2) contained a kiln and associated structure, which was dated to the 14th century on the basis of associated artefacts. The kiln, with a single stoke-pit and double flue is quite different from that at Higham Ferrers, and classified by Musty (1974, 47 and fig. 1) as type 4a (ii) (Lyveden type). At the time, it was the only kiln of the type known. The remains of a rectangular building, interpreted as a potter's workshop, were located next to the kiln, as were two yards surfaced with stone and sherds in a clay matrix. A large dump of waste pottery, a stone slab pavement and an area of cobbles were located just to the east of the kiln. A probable clay-puddling pit was located in the workshop (Bryant and Steane 1969, pl. 5), as were a small collection of potter's tools, including knives, whetstones and fragments of antler and bone which are likely to have been used for forming and decorating pottery (ibid, pl. 7). The products of the kiln, in a limestone fabric typical of the industry, are quite different from those from Higham Ferrers, comprising mainly jars and bowls, and only a single cistern bung-hole.

Excavation of Area J at Lyveden produced a tile kiln and associated workshop (Steane and Bryant 1975, 33-38, figs 12-13 and pls 19-22) dating to the late 15th century on the basis of the presence of Cistercian ware and Tudor Green pottery and two coins dating to the 1460s and 1470s. This makes it broadly contemporary with the Glapthorn potteries. Large quantities of Oxidized ware occurred at the site, but the fabric is slightly different from that from Glapthorn, as small quantities of limestone ooliths were present in the clay, making it highly probable that it was made somewhere in or near Lyveden, as the dominant geology of the area is oolitic limestone. Otherwise, the range of vessels is the same.

The village of Stanion, also in Northants, and near Lyveden, is a well-known medieval potting village. However, most finds have been made at best under rescue conditions, and few of them have been fully published. The two kilns published by Bellamy (1983) are an exception. One kiln was identical to that from area D at Lyveden and probably of the same date (Bellamy 1983, 154-56). It produced pottery of 13th- and 14th-century date (ibid. 156-59). Excavation on the second kiln, although it was limited to part of the stoke-hole and flue, nonetheless showed that it was producing late medieval Oxidized wares (ibid. 159-61), with a fabric very similar to the pottery noted at the tile-yard at Lyveden. The range of vessel types was jars, cisterns, bowls and jugs which are again typical of the tradition.

A kiln at Wood Newton in Northamptonshire was excavated under rescue conditions in 1973 (Mynard 1980). It was badly damaged, but appears to have been a rectangular variant on Musty's type 4, with a single stoke-pit and a central ridge. The bulk of the pottery was Oxidized ware, with the vessel types including cisterns, jars, bowls, and skillets, along with a few odd fragments of costrels, chafing dishes, lids and cups, the latter group in the 'Tudor Green' style, although it is unclear from the report whether these were wasters or merely associated vessels. The excavators dated the kiln to the early 16th century.

The village of Potterspury in west Northamptonshire was making pottery during most of the medieval and post-medieval periods, and, although,

like Stanion, most of the identified kilns were excavated under rescue conditions, a few have been fully analysed and published. A kiln dated to the 14th–early 15th century was excavated there in 1949 (Jope and Ivens 1995). It was a single flue type, with a raised 'stoking place' and an internal platform with radial fire-bars. The pottery was mainly jugs and bowls of typical 'high medieval' type, and bears little resemblance to Reduced or Oxidized ware.

Other, unpublished, kilns of late medieval date are known from the county. At Yardley Gobion, near Potterspury, two probable 15th century kilns were investigated. The only publication is a note (Moore 1974), but they appear to have been single-flue examples fed from a common stoke-hole. The pottery is typical of the 15th century, comprising mainly jugs/cisterns and large bowls, although there was a large variation in colour, and both the kiln and its products are more typical of the Potterspury industry rather than the Oxidized and Reduced ware traditions.

A number of Reduced and Oxidized Ware manufactories are also known from the broader region, although some are merely finds of wasters, with no kiln structure recovered. In Buckinghamshire, a series of finds of small groups of probable wasters have been made at Great Brickhill. For example, Jack Ironcap's Lane (Beamish 1990) produced a range of vessels types typical of the late medieval industries of the region. Bowls and jugs/cisterns were dominant. Great Brickhill appears to have been the source of both Oxidized and Reduced wares, as wasters of both types have been found (ibid, 88-92; Mynard and Zeepvat 1992, 275).

A contemporary pottery, along with a tile-kiln, is known from Latimer in Buckinghamshire (Farley and Lawson 1990). The products are broadly part of the late medieval Oxidized/Reduced ware industry, having a hard sandy fabric and the typical range of vessel forms, although vessels more typical of the 'Tudor Green' and Cistercian ware industries were also present. Both grey and red sherds were noted. The main products of the kiln were jugs and jars, although cauldrons, bowls and skillets were also present, along with a few cisterns, chafing dishes, dripping dishes, costrels, mugs and a bird whistle, and also some of the earliest saggers known from the region. The kiln itself was built within the ruins of an earlier tile-kiln, and utilized part of its structure. It sub-rectangular in plan, with a central spine with radiating kiln bars, and similar to the broadly contemporary example from Wood Newton in Northamptonshire (above). The Latimer kiln has produced an archaeomagnetic date of AD1460-1510 at the 68% confidence level (Farley and Lawson 1990, 53).

Evidence for late medieval potting has also been obtained from Tyler's Green, near Penn in Buckinghamshire, a place best-known for its production of highly decorated medieval tiles. Various pieces of evidence for pottery production were made during field-walking, but no evidence of a kiln has been recovered. However, Oxidized ware wasters were present in the usual form of fragments of jars, jugs and large bowls, some of which were glazed (Hutchings and Farley 1989, 107). The assemblage is given a similar late date to the Latimer kiln, although it could conceivably be earlier on the evidence from elsewhere. There is also likely to be earlier pottery production, since wasters of an earlier, perhaps 14th-century industry with many of the characteristics of the later tradition were also noted (Cauvain *et al* 1989, 115-118), and the Rolls of the Court of Common Pleas have a reference to one John le Pottere, who joined the Vicar of Penn in poaching rabbits in 1350 (ibid, 118).

A number of broadly contemporary potting sites are known to the east of Higham Ferrers. At Colne in Cambridgeshire, test-pitting produced evidence of a kiln and manufactory which produced both reduced and oxidized pottery (Healey *et al*, 1998, 52-58). Both grey and orange sherds were noted, with the range of vessels comprising mainly jars, jugs, bowls and cisterns, along with a few skillets. The assemblage is dated to the late 15th-16th century. Other than at Ely, pottery production in Cambridgeshire otherwise is very under-attested. Cistercian wares kilns and wasters and others of medieval date have been excavated, but the medieval tradition appears to lasted virtually unchanged until the 16th century (Hall 2001, 2), and there is no evidence for the production of vessels which could be regarded as Oxidized or Reduced wares.

To the north of Higham Ferrers, the village of Bourne in south Lincolnshire was also producing large quantities of late medieval pottery, and a 16th-century kiln, complete with potter's workshop, house and clay puddling facility, have been excavated (Moorhouse 1981, fig. 88). The pottery, Bourne 'D' ware, is typical of the late medieval tradition in terms of the range of forms, but the actual pottery, in a smooth mainly pale red fabric with a thin external white slip and glaze is quite different to the more southerly tradition (McCarthy and Brookes 1988, 409).

This brief overview of the known late medieval pottery industries of the south-east Midlands perhaps serves to stress the importance of the excavation of the Higham Ferrers kilns. Very few manufactories of late medieval Reduced ware pottery in the region have produced a kiln as complete as Kiln 1 at this site, and the presence of the other two structures, although incomplete or damaged, helps to show how the industry may have evolved. The late medieval Reduced ware tradition is, at the time of writing, about to be the subject of a major research project funded by English Heritage (Slowikowski forthcoming), and the Higham Ferrers manufactory will be a significant component of that study.

Comparative analyses of the kiln assemblages

There is no way of knowing if the two kilns were definitely contemporary. The archaeomagnetic dates obtained from Kiln 1 suggest that it is a candidate for the old kiln that was present when William Potter took his croft in Higham Ferrers in 1436 (Serjeantson 1916) It is possible that Kiln 2 was the one for which he required clay for repairs in 1467. It is quite possible that both kilns were operating at the same time. We cannot, of course, be certain that William Potter was operating as a potter in the Kings Meadow Lane area, although, at present, there is no evidence for pottery manufacture in Higham Ferrers other than at this site.

The assemblages from Kilns 1 and 2 differ greatly in size. The pottery data suggests that there were some variations within their output, especially with regard to form. It must be remembered that when comparing variations in waster groups from pottery manufactories, the occurrence of the various forms and vessel types is not necessarily a reflection of the output of the site; what is being examined is the pottery that failed to fire successfully, and is not necessarily an accurate representation of the output.

The proportions of the main vessel types do not appear to show much variation, but they were compared using the chi-squared test (eg Drennan 1997, 188-9). The test produced a chi-squared value of 1.41 (2d.f.), which indicates that there is no significance in the difference of the proportions of the three main vessel types observed at the two kilns.

There does appear to be a considerable difference between the ranges of jar rim forms from the two kilns (Tables 4.11 and 4.16). Kiln 1 has a wide range of forms, although there were no rims of types 115-118, whereas these made up the bulk of the forms from Kiln 2. There is, of course, a large difference between the basic quantities of rimsherds from the two kilns, so it is entirely possible that this pattern is simply due to the assemblage sizes and the result due to the vagaries of archaeological sampling. Again the differences can again be examined using the chi-squared test, although the presence of large numbers of rim types with a data value of '0' is problematic, as the chi-squared test cannot confidently be used with data which has a value of 0. To circumvent this, the data from each kiln was amalgamated into two groups, one comprising rim forms 101-109, and the other rim forms 110-118. When these were compared, a chi-squared value of 2.20 (1d.f) was produced. This gives a confidence level of between 80%–90% that there is a significant difference between the two assemblages, although when the strength of the value is tested using Cramer's *V* (for example Drennan 1997, 193), this returns a value of 0.08, which indicates that there is little significant difference, and that the observed pattern is simply due to the large difference is the assemblage sizes.

A similar operation was carried out for bowl rim form occurrence, dividing them into three groups (types 201-208, 209-216 and 217-224) which produced a chi-squared value of 0.22 (2d.f.). This shows that there is no significant difference in the proportions of the various rim forms, with the assemblage sizes again being the most likely cause of the difference.

Finally, the same operation was carried out for the jug/cistern rims. These appear, at first glance to be greatly different, with the Kiln 2 assemblage greatly favouring type 318, which was not the case with Kiln 1. Again, the rim form data was divided into three groups, 301-306, 307-312 and 313-318. This returned a chi-squared value of 16.80 (2d.f.), which gives a confidence level of greater than 99.9%. Calculation of Cramer's *V* produces a value of 0.42, which suggests that, in this case, the difference has some significance. This would suggest therefore that the products of the two kilns show some differences in the area of jug/cistern rimforms.

If Kiln 2 had produced a larger assemblage but with the same proportions of the different rim forms of the different vessels types, then the differences would have been highly significant. This would have suggested that the two kilns were firing the products of two different potters. It is still uncertain whether the two kilns were contemporary in operation or not.

The differences between the two waste dumps can be further examined by comparing the mean rim diameters of the different vessel types. To establish whether any differences in the mean diameters are significant Student's *t*-test can be used (eg Drennan 1997, 132-3). This could establish whether the vessels from one waste dump were generally of a different size to the same vessel types from the other. For the jars, the result is a *t* value of 0.45, which suggests that there is not any significant difference in the mean sizes of the jar rims, but the same test applied to the bowl/pancheon rim diameter means gives a *t* value of 2.19, which gives a significance level of between 0.05 and 0.02, meaning that the differences in the rim diameters of

the bowls is likely to be significant. In the case of the jugs, the calculation of *t* gives a value of -1.25, which has a significance level of between 0.5 and 0.2, meaning that the difference is much more likely to be due to the sample sizes than any significant physical difference in the mean rim diameters.

In summary then, it would appear that the proportion of vessel types in both waster dumps was generally the same. The same basic range of rim forms was noted in both groups, although there were differences in the preferred jug forms between the two kiln waster assemblages. The most likely reason for the observed differences in rim form preference for jars and bowls is the substantial difference in the size of the two assemblages. The difference in the mean rim diameters of the jars and jug/cisterns is again probably due to the assemblage sizes, but the range of bowl/pancheon sizes was significantly different between the two waster groups. This would suggest that Kiln 1 and Kiln 2 were firing the products of two different potters; there seems no logical reason why the observed differences in jug rim forms and bowl size ranges would otherwise occur.

METALWORK AND WORKED BONE AND ANTLER *by Ian Scott*

Introduction

The finds included here are those from sites with Saxon, medieval and later occupation. Table 4.18 shows a summary quantification of the finds assemblage, which comprises 437 metal objects (308 iron, 83 copper alloy and 46 lead), 22 bone objects and two ceramic spindle whorls (Total n = 461). The largest phase assemblage (n = 134) comes from Roman-British contexts, almost all from Site 9. This phase assemblage is omitted from this report, but has been included with the Romano-British Project

Table 4.18: Summary Quantification of metal finds by Phase and Function

Phase	Function Arms	Tools	Transport	Measure	Household	Personal	Security	Door	Window	Structural	Nails
Preh											1
Rom		1	1	1	2	10				2	78
1		2			1	3				1	8
2a		2				1					
2b		9	1		3	2	1				1
2c						1					
3		2	1		4	1					2
4		2	4	1	1	3				1	10
5		1	5			5		1			11
6	1	2	2		3	14	1			3	18
Mod					1						2
u/s	1	6	12	3	4	22		1	1	2	15
Totals	2	27	26	5	19	62	2	2	1	9	146

Table 4.19: Function Codes used in Tables and Finds database

Function Code	Description
Tools	Craft tools, from smithing to textile work.
Transport	Items relating to waggons, carts and also horse gear
Measure	Weights and scales
Household	Household furnishings and equipment including pots and utensils
Personal	Jewellery, items of dress, toilet items and writing materials
Security	Keys, locks and chains
Door	Door fittings including hinges and latches
Window	Window fittings including hinges and grills
Structural	Other structural fittings including holdfasts and staples
Nails	Nails (excluidng hobnails)
Bindings	Bindings and strips with nails or nail holes
Miscellaneous	Bar, rod, strip, sheet and plate fragments, waste products from carft processes including offcuts and melted waste
Query	Objects of uncertain identification
Industrial	Equipment, other than tools, used in industrial processes
Unknown	Objects or fragments, usually small that cannot be identified

material from Site 10 (Scott forthcoming). Small quantities of finds, including residual Romano-British objects, from Anglo-Saxon SFBs were found on Site 10 and these are included in the discussion in this report and selected items (**10, 31-35, 41-42 & 45**) incorporated into the following catalogue.

The catalogue has been ordered partly by chronology – i.e. finds from Anglo-Saxon (Phases 1-3) and Medieval (Phases 4-5) contexts – and within the chronological groups by function. Selected unstratified finds and objects from Phase 6 (16th century to modern) contexts are appended where they can be identified typologically as Romano-British, Saxon or medieval..

The finds assemblage for each chronological block is summarised in table form under broad functional categories, as a means of characterising the composition of each assemblage. (See Table 4.19 for functional categories.)

Bindings	Misc	Query	Unk	Totals
				1
3	23	7	6	134
2	5	7	1	30
	1			4
	4	1		22
	5	1		7
	4	5		19
	8	2		32
	10	3		36
1	8	11	1	65
	2	1		6
2	24	12		105
8	95	50	8	461

Finds from Anglo-Saxon Phases 1-3 (Tables 4.20–4.22)

Saxon contexts produced 82 items, including 30 from Phase 1 contexts, 33 from Phase 2 contexts and 19 from Phase 3 contexts.

The Phase 1 finds are mainly from SFB fills. The SFBs on Site 1 (Table 4.20) produced a limited number and range of finds. SFB 1253 produce 5 objects, including a decorative knob or terminal in copper alloy but of uncertain type or date (**51**), a small clamp or dog (**48**), two nails and short strip of iron. SFB 1256 produced a single small corner fragment of copper alloy plate. The most finds (n = 10) came from SFB 1263 and included the tip of a knife blade of uncertain form (**23**), two pieces of copper alloy edge binding (**49-50**), polished slightly dished copper alloy disc (**52**), three small copper alloy fragments of uncertain function (**53-55**), a nail, a length of rod or bar – possibly a nail stem fragment – and small triangular fragment of iron. SFB 1266 contained a single nail. The number and range of finds from the SFBs is limited and most of the objects are incomplete. Other than finds from the SFBs, finds were recovered from two pits (contexts 1305 and 1306) probably of Phase 1. Both produced a single undiagnostic object.

Two SFBs on Site 10 produced also finds (Table 4.21). The finds from SFB 12740 number eight and include fragments of a composite bone comb (**42**) and a copper alloy bracelet fragment (**32**), a piece of an iron binding or collar and piece of strip with a nail hole, two nails, a fragment of copper alloy wire, and a iron strip of uncertain identification. The bracelet is Romano-British in date. Finds from SFB12740 number only five, but include an ivory pinbeater (**10**), a possible iron finger ring (**31**), two Romano-British bow brooches (**33-34**) and a small hemispherical lead object. The latter could be a slightly flattened pistol ball and therefore intrusive.

Table 4.20: Phase 1 contexts (SFBs and pits): Summary Quantification by Context and Function

Site	Feature	Context	Function Tools	Transport	Measure	Household	Personal	Structural	Nails	Bindings
	SFBs									
1	1253	1252						1	1	
		1255							1	
	1256	1257								
		1265								1
	1263	1268				1[1]			1	1
		1271								
	1266	1269							1	
	Pits									
	1305	1304								
	1306	1307							1	
	Totals		*0*	*0*	*0*	*1*	*0*	*1*	*5*	*2*
	SFBs									
4	6057	6058	1[2]				1[3]		2	
	6345	6346					1[4]			
	6356	6357	1[5]				1[6]			
		6366								
	6630	6631							1	
4	*Totals*		*2*	*0*	*0*	*0*	*3*	*0*	*3*	*0*
	Totals		2	0	0	1	3	1	8	2

1. Cat.No. 23 – knife blade fragment
2. Cat.No. 7 – punch
3. Cat.No. 36 – bone comb fragments
4. Cat.No.37 – bone comb fragments
5. Cat.No.8 – bone needle or awl
6. Cat.No.38 – bone comb fragments

The difference between the finds from SFBs on Site 1 and those on Site 10 is marked. The presence of Romano-British objects in Site 10 SFB fills can be explained by the proximity to the Roman settlement. However, both Site 10 SFBs produced bone comb fragments, which were notably absent from Site 1. The presence of the pin beater in Site 10 mirrors other settlement sites (for example at West Stow: West 1985, Vol. 1, 138-140 and table 59). Although the numbers of finds are limited, there

Table 4.21: Site 10: Finds from SFB (Phase 1) contexts: Summary Quantification by Context and Function

SFB	Context	Function Tool	Personal	Nails	Binding	Misc	Query	Total
12740	12732		1[1]					1
	12733				1		1	2
	12737		1[2]	2	1	1		5
Total		*0*	*2*	*2*	*2*	*1*	*1*	*8*
12800	12787	1[3]	1[4]					2
	12793		1[5]					1
	12794		1[6]				1	2
Total		*1*	*3*	*0*	*0*	*0*	*1*	*5*
Total		1	5	2	2	1	2	13

1. Cat.No. 42 – composite bone comb
2. Cat.No. 32 – bracelet fragment
3. Cat.No. 10 – pinbeater
4. Cat.No. 31 – possible finger ring
5. Cat.No. 33 – RB bow brooch
6. Cat.No. 34 – RB bow brooch

Misc	Query	Unk	Totals	SFB Totals
			2	
1	1		3	5
1			1	1
	1	1	3	
	3		6	10
1			1	
			1	1
1			1	
			1	
4	5	1	19	
	1		5	5
			1	1
	1		3	
1			1	4
			1	1
1	2	0	11	
5	7	1	30	

processing of wool had continued in Phase 2. Two came from Site 2 (**3-4**), and one from Site 4 (**5**). Further heckle teeth were found unstratified on Site 4 (**89-92**). Also a pair of shears of Saxon or medieval type was found on Site 2 from a Phase 6 context (**88**). These may well have been used in wool processing or textile production. The presence of a strap distributor indicates the possible presence and use of horses.

The most notable find from a Phase 2 context is the small fragment of decorated metalwork (**46**) from the enclosure ditch fill (context 15119). This is a hint that the site had high status links in phase 2, but generally the finds suggest a limited domestic assemblage.

Finally there are 20 objects from Phase 3 contexts. There were two nails and three miscellaneous fragments (see Table 4.22). The catalogued finds include an awl (**2**), a heckle tooth (**6**), a horseshoe fragment (**22**), four knives or knife fragments (**25-28**), individual broken comb teeth (**40**), and four objects of uncertain function (**61-64**).

These came from Sites, 2, 4 and 8. There are two objects of uncertain identification (**60-61**) from Site 2. Finds from Site 4 include the awl (**2**), a heckle tooth (**6**), a horseshoe fragment (**22**), a Saxon knife (**26**) of a type datable to the 8th- to 11th centuries, and bone handle plates (**63**) and two nails. There is also a clearly intrusive fragment of a knife of post-medieval form (**27**) from context 7236. The awl may have been used in carpentry or leatherworking, the heckle tooth may be residual from Phase 2, or indicate continuing wool processing.

Apart from a knife blade of good Saxon form (**28**), the finds from Site 8 comprise three objects of uncertain identification (**59, 62, 64**), one of which (**59**) may be an instrusive object of later date, and three miscellaneous pieces.

The presence of a horseshoe fragment indicates the presence and use of horses. To this should be added two horseshoe fragments – a possible Type 2 shoe (**66**) and a certain Type 2a shoe (**67**) – from Phase 4 contexts on Sites 3 and 4 respectively. These could be late Saxon in date. Overall the Phase 3 assemblage is limited in number and range.

Two hooked tags of Saxon type and date (**100-101**) can be identified amongst unstratified finds. These came from Site 4. Already noted are the shears (**88**) and four heckle teeth (**89-92**), which could be Saxon.

Catalogue

Tools (Fig. 4.16)

The tools could all be used in the processing of wool or hides. The shears (1) could have been for clipping wool or for general cutting. The awl (2) may have been used in leatherworking, or in carpentry. The heckle teeth (3-6) are all from combs used in the preparation of wool for spinning. An incomplete example, with teeth held in an iron binding, comes from the Lake End Road West site, Dorney, Buckinghamshire (Scott 2002, 37, fig. 4.5: 5) from an early to

does seem to be a difference between the finds from Site 1 SFBs and those from Site 10 SFBs. The problems of relating the finds from SFB pits to possible uses of the buildings are obvious: the finds generally related to the abandonment or demolition of the structures. However in general terms the difference in the finds assemblages between the two sets of SFBs does hint at a difference in the nature of the occupation in the two quite separate areas.

Finds from later Saxon contexts (Phases 2 and 3) are summarised in Table 4.22. Nails and miscellaneous objects are tabulated in more detail in Tables 4.23 and 4.24.

The 32 objects from Phase 2 contexts include one hobnail, almost certainly a residual Roman object, one nail and ten miscellaneous fragments (Table 4.18). The catalogued objects include three probable heckle teeth (**3-5**), a bone needle or awl (**9**), and a group of eight similar bone needles found bundled together (**11-18**). Other finds include a strap junction or distributor (**21**), a tanged knife (**24**) and knife handle plate (**29**), a pendant hook or hanger (**30**), a comb fragment (**39**) and hairpin fragments of bone (**43-44**), the handle and stem of a padlock, or slide, key (**47**) and two objects of uncertain identification (**58-59**).

The presence of heckle teeth from Phase 2 contexts is of interest as they would indicate that the

Table 4.22: Anglo-Saxon contexts (Phases 2 & 3): Summary Quantification by Context and Function

Site	Phase	Context	Function Tools	Transport	Measure	Household	Personal	Security	Structural	Nails
eval	2b	451								
	2b	452				1				
	3	550					1			
	3	564	1							
Eval		*Totals*	*1*			*1*	*1*			
2	2a	2431	2				1			
	2a	2478								
	3	2084								
	3	2484				1				
Site 2		*Totals*	*2*	*0*	*0*	*1*	*1*	*0*	*0*	*0*
4	2b	6027					1			
	2b	6044				1				
	2b	6654				1		1		
	2b	7053	1	1						
	2c	6712								
	2c	7027								
	2c	7035					1			
	2c	7077								
	3	6156				1				
	3	6160		1						
	3	6187	1							
	3	6402								1
	3	6832								1
	3	7236				1				
Site 4		*Totals*	*2*	*2*	*0*	*4*	*2*	*1*	*0*	*2*
8	2b	15100	7							1
	2b	15101					1			
	2b	15119								
	2b	15218	1							
(3)	3	3003								
	3	15259				1				
	3	15305								
	3	15423								
	3	15486								
Site 8 (and 3)Totals			*8*	*0*	*0*	*1*	*1*	*0*	*0*	*6*
Totals			*13*	*2*	*0*	*7*	*5*	*1*	*0*	*3*

mid Saxon pit. A more complete example with iron binding was found at York (Ottaway 1992, 538-41 & fig 212).

The ivory pinbeater (10) from SFB 12800 on Site 10 is a notable find. Pinbeaters are a distinctive Anglo-Saxon object, but the use of ivory rather than bone is suggestive of high status.

1   *(not illustrated)* **Shears arms and spring bow**, encrusted. Blades missing. Fe. L 110 mm. Site 4; HFKML 01, 6763 sf 341. Ph 4.

2   **Awl**. Possible awl. Tapering rectangular section tang, with broken blade at the other end. Fe. L 70 mm. Site 4; HFKML 01, 6187, sf 319. Ph 3

The following objects (nos **3-6**, see also **89-92**) are distinctive objects and formed parts of heckles (cf almost complete examples from Norwich: Goodall in Margeson 1993, 182 and fig. 134, 1420-1422; York: Ottaway 1992, 538-41, and fig. 212; and Lake End Road West site, Dorney, Buckinghamshire: Scott 2002, 37 and fig. 4.5: 5).

3   *(not illustrated)* **Heckle tooth fragment**. Broken tapering spike of circular section. Could be part of a heckle tooth. Fe. L 58 mm. Site 2; HFKM 95, 2431, sf 87. Ph 2a.

4   *(not illustrated)* **Possible heckle tooth**. Tapering spike, eroded and laminated. Possibly of circular

Misc	Query	Unk	Totals
1			1
			1
			1
			1
1			4
			3
1			1
	1		1
	1		2
1	2	0	7
			1
			1
			2
			2
2			2
2			2
	1		2
1			1
	1		2
			1
			1
			1
			1
1			2
6	2	0	21
3			11
			1
	1		1
			1
	1		1
			1
2	1		2
	1		1
1			1
4	0	21	
14	7	0	53

section. Fe. L 89 mm. Site 2; HFKM 95, 2431, sf 86. Ph 2a.

5   *(not illustrated)* **Possible Heckle tooth**. Tapering spike of circular section, slightly flattened and of sub-rectangular at the wide end. L 91 mm. Site 4; HFKML 01, 7053, sf 348. Ph 2b.

6   *(not illustrated)* **Heckle tooth**. Tapering spike of circular section. Squared and battered at the broad end. Fe. L 116 mm. Site 2; HFKM 95, 564, sf 97. Ph 3.

7   Possible **punch** made from cut long bone. The cut end is chamfered. L 84 mm. Site 4; HFKML 01, 6058, sf -. Ph 1.

Possibly a punch for marking pottery, or perhaps more probably a rough-out for a handle.

8   **Needle** or **awl** made from small long bone. The tip and stem are highly polished. L 81 mm. Site 4; HFKML 01, 6357, sf 325. Ph 1.

9   **Needle** or **awl**. Curved stem of oval section. The section changes near the tip and has slightly hollowed out sides – reflects form of original bone? Highly polished. L 93 mm. Site 8; HFWIB 03, 15218, sf 4022. Ph 2b.

10   **Pinbeater**, made of ivory, and tapering to a point at each end. L 163 mm. Site 10; HFKML 02, 12787, sf 2968. Ph 1.

This is a long example of the weaving tool found in Anglo-Saxon contexts. There are examples from West Stow (West 1985, 125 & figs 191, 7; 210, 13; 246, 15-17) and Lake End Road West site, Dorney, Buckinghamshire (Riddler 2002, 41 and fig.4.10, 10-11).

Catalogue nos 11-18 are all similar bone needles and were found together. They are probably weaving tools, cf examples from Winchester (Keene 1990, vol 1, 233) and West Stow (West 1985, 125, figs 210, 14; 233, 3; 246, 18-24). It is probable that they were deliberately placed as a termination deposit.

11   **Needle** with pierced triangular head. Curved stem of oval section. Polished. L 124 mm. Site 8; HFWIB 03, 15100, sf 4003. Ph 2b.

12   **Needle** with pierced triangular head. Stem of circular section. L 110 mm. Site 8; HFWIB 03, 15100, sf 4004. Ph 2b.

13   *(not illustrated)* **Needle** with pierced triangular head. Stem of circular section. Complete but broken. L 110 mm. Site 8; HFWIB 03, 15100, sf 4005. Ph 2b.

14   *(not illustrated)* **Needle** with pierced triangular head. Stem of circular section. L 108 mm. Site 8; HFWIB 03, 15100, sf 4006. Ph 2b.

15   **Needle** with pierced triangular head. Stem of circular section. L 112 mm. Site 8; HFWIB 03, 15100, sf 4007. Ph 2b.

16   *(not illustrated)* **Needle** with pierced triangular head. Stem of circular section. Stem broken, tip missing. L 100 mm. Site 8; HFWIB 03, 15100, sf 4008. Ph 2b.

17   *(not illustrated)* **Needle** with pierced triangular head. Stem of circular section. L 114 mm. Site 8; HFWIB 03, 15100, sf 4009. Ph 2b.

18   *(not illustrated)* **Needle** with pierced triangular head. Stem of circular section. Broken but complete. L 102 mm. Site 8; HFWIB 03, 15100, sf 4010. Ph 2b.

The two spindle whorls (nos **19-20**) are of forms paralleled at West Stow (West 1985, 139, and fig. 244, 12-13) and Winchester (Woodland 1990, fig. 46, 102, 105 and 112)

19   Domed **spindle whorl** with concentric grooves around circumference. Ceramic. D 25 mm; H 15 mm. Site 4; HFKML 01, 6763, sf 339. Ph 4.

20   Domed **spindle whorl**. Ceramic. D 33 mm; H 14 mm. Site 4; HFKML 01, 7210, sf 327. u/s.

Transport (Fig.4.17)

In addition to the objects catalogued there is a fiddle key horseshoe nail from a Phase 4 context (context 6763, sf 337). The horseshoe fragment (**22**) is undiagnostic, but could be early in date.

21   **Strap junction**, with one complete narrow strap with two nail holes. Part of a nail remains in one hole. There is a neat loop. The second strap is largely missing. Fe. L 58 mm. Site 4; HFKML 01, 7053, sf 347. Ph 2b.

2
7
8
9
10
11
12
15
0
100mm
19
20
0
50mm

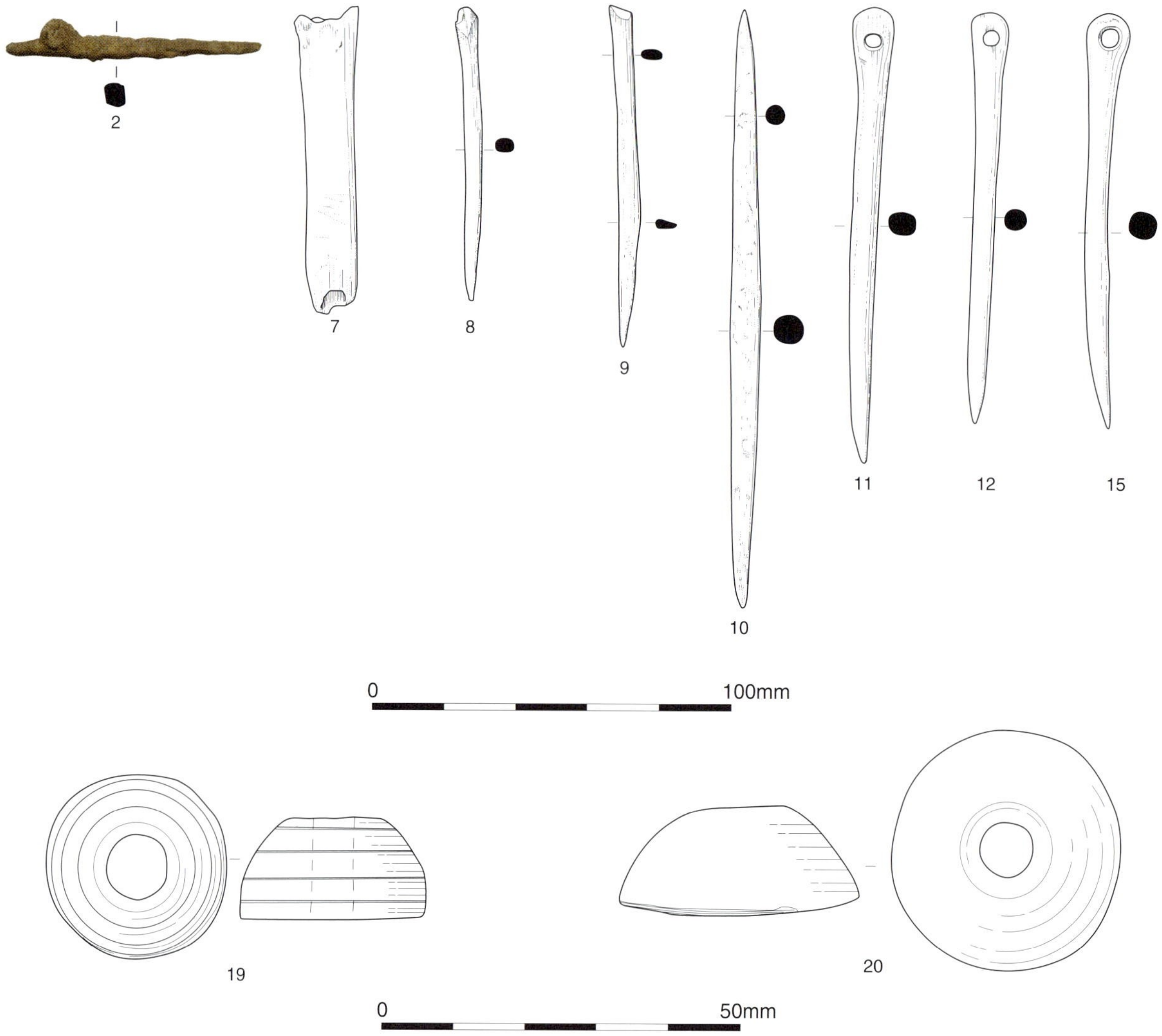

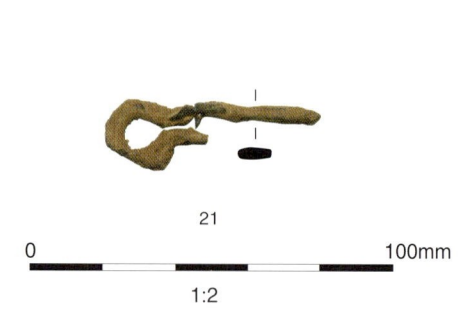

Fig. 4.16 Small Finds – Anglo-Saxon tools

21
0
100mm
1:2

Fig. 4.17 (above) Small Finds – Anglo-Saxon transport objects

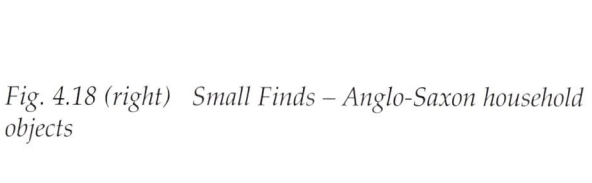

Junction of blade and handle
24
26
29
0
100mm
1:2

Fig. 4.18 (right) Small Finds – Anglo-Saxon household objects

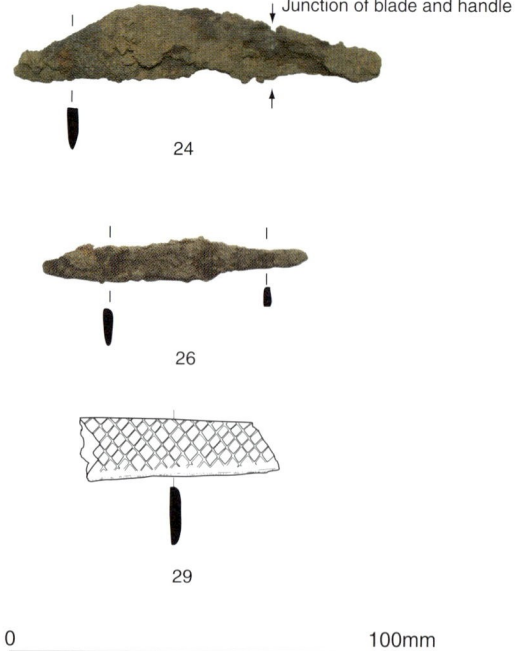

22 *(not illustrated)* **Horseshoe fragment**. Heel fragment from a branch of thin section, no calkin, part of one nail hole of uncertain form. Fe. L 42 mm. Site 4; HFKML 01, 6160, sf -. Ph 3.

Household (Fig. 4.18)

Knives

23 *(not illustrated)* **Knife blade fragment**, comprising tip of triangular section blade. The back and edge curve to the tip. Fe. L 77 mm. Site 1; HFKM 95, 1268, sf 61. Ph 1.

24 **Tanged knife**, with short straight back and angled point. Fe. L 99 mm. Site 2; HFKM 95, 452, sf 92. Ph 2b.

Knife with an angle back blade form (Ottaway Type A2) which according to Ottaway occurs from the 8th century onwards. Most are pre-Norman Conquest in date (Ottaway 1992, 561-64, see esp. figs 228: 2798 & 229: 2809).

25 *(not illustrated)* **Knife, whittle tang**, with broken blade and tang. Gently sloping choil. Uncertain form. Fe. L 30 mm. Site 2; HFKM 95, 2484, sf 94. Ph 3.

26 **Knife, small, whittle tang**. Straight or slightly curved back which than curves down to the tip. Triangular section. Small curved choil. Complete. Fe. L 71 mm. Site 4; HFKML 01, 6156, sf 318. Ph 3.

A knife of Ottaway Type C3, which according to Ottaway are broadly dateable from the 9th to the 11th century (Ottaway 1992, 570, see esp. fig. 234: 2929).

27 *(not illustrated)* **Knife fragment**, from a whittle tang knife with elongated circular section bolster. The bolster and small part of the blade survive. Fe. L 49 mm. Site 4; HFKML 01, 7236, sf -. Ph 3.

Probably post-medieval in date and therefore intrusive.

28 *(not illustrated)* **Knife blade**, with narrow slightly curved back with parallel edge and triangular section. Whittle tang? Tip and tang missing. Fe. L 68 mm. Site 8; HFWIB 03, 15259, sf 4027. Ph 3.

Ottaway Type D blade with convex curved back (Ottaway 1990, 572).

29 Knife **handle plate**. Tapering plate with cross-hatched decoration. Tapering plate with rounded edges. Not finished. Back quite rough. Bone. L 54 mm. Site 4; HFKML 01, 6044, sf -. Ph 2b

Other

30 *(not illustrated)* **Pendant hook** or **hanger**. Tapering strip formed into a hook at one end, and pinched at the upper end, but broken. Fe. L 172 mm. Site 4; HFKML 01, 6654, sf 333. Ph 2b.

Personal (Fig. 4.19)

In addition to the objects catalogued listed below a single hobnail (context 7025, Ph 2c) was found in a Phases 1-3 context. It is probably residual and derived from Roman levels. The foot of a small long brooch (**35**) and a decorated copper alloy hairpin (**45**) were recovered from the spoil heap (context 10508) on Site 10. Although unstratified, both are Saxon types. Also from Site 10 were comb fragments. One group was from an SFB (**42**), and the other (**41**) from amongst a group of finds, including Saxon pottery, in a dark silt deposit (context 10575). A number of objects of certain or probable Romano-British derivation (**31-34**) are included because they were found in the fills of SFBs.

Jewellery

31 *(not illustrated)* Possible **finger ring** formed from a coil of square section wire. Fe. D 21 mm. Site 10; HFKML 02 12787, sf 2967, Ph 1.

32 Possible **bracelet fragment**, comprising thin strip of rectangular section with regular closely set small notches along one edge. One end tapers to a blunt point. ID uncertain. Copper alloy. L 47 mm. Site 10; HFKML 02 12737, sf 3066. Ph 1.

33 **Bow brooch**. Well-preserved small brooch formed from a single strip. Sprung pin with internal chord. A so-called 'Nauheim derivative'.Copper alloy. L 33 mm. Site 10; HFKML 02 12793, sf 3068. Ph 1.

34 **Bow brooch** fragment, comprising catchplate and part of bow. The bow is of hollow curved cross section and has a possible rivet hole. Possibly a 'Nauheim derivative with expanded bow'. Copper alloy. L 33 mm. Site 10; HFKML 02 12794, sf 3083. Ph 1.

35 **Small long brooch**, with lozenge-shaped foot. The head is missing. Eroded. Copper alloy. L 46 mm. Site 10; HFKML 02, 10508, sf 921. Ph 1.

This is a form that dates to the 6th century.

Bone Combs

The comb fragments (**36-42**) are all from double-sided composite combs. It is not possible to establish the length of the combs because the surviving pieces are so fragmentary. See the examples from Lake End Road West site, Dorney, Buckinghamshire (Riddler 2002,) which are dated to the later 7th or 8th century, and from West Stow (West 1985, 127-8 and figs 252-53), which range in date from the 5th to 7th century. The Higham Ferrers examples are predominantly from Phase 1 contexts.

36 **Comb**. Two fragments plus a number of loose teeth. The larger fragment has two half round side plates with slight decorative striations running their length. There are four extant rivets. The teeth are much eroded. Second fragment is part of the end of the tooth plate. Bone. L 59 mm. Site 4; HFKML 01, 6058, sf 298. Ph 1.

37 **Comb** fragments. Four sizeable fragments and a number of small pieces. Two fragments with *in situ* plate fragments are slightly tapered. The plates are notched along the edges. The other two fragments are corners from the tooth plate. One fragment has wider teeth spaced at c. 4 teeth per cm (11 teeth per inch). The second fragment has narrow teeth spaced at 6 teeth per cm (15 teeth per inch). Bone. L 67 mm; W 31 mm. Site 4; HFKML 01, 6346, sf 326. Ph 1

38 **Comb** fragments. Four large fragments and a number of small pieces. There are two side plate fragments, with a decoration of transverse parallel lines in panels. The plates are notched along the edges where the teeth have been cut. The other two fragments are from the tooth plate. One side has smaller narrower teeth than the other. Bone. Side plate fragments: L 49 mm; W 16 mm; and L 23 mm; W 15 mm. Tooth plate fragments: L 18 mm; W 26 mm; L 16 mm, W 17 mm. Site 4; HFKML 01, 6357, sf 324. Ph 1.

39 *(not illustrated)* **Comb** fragment, comprising part of tooth plate, with teeth largely broken off, and two narrow side plates of half round section. The latter are decorated with crosses. Bone. L 55 mm; HFKM 95, 2431, sf 107. Ph 2a.

40 *(not illustrated)* **Comb** teeth. Seven individual broken teeth. Bone. L 19 mm. Site 2; HFKM 95, 550, sf -. Ph 3.

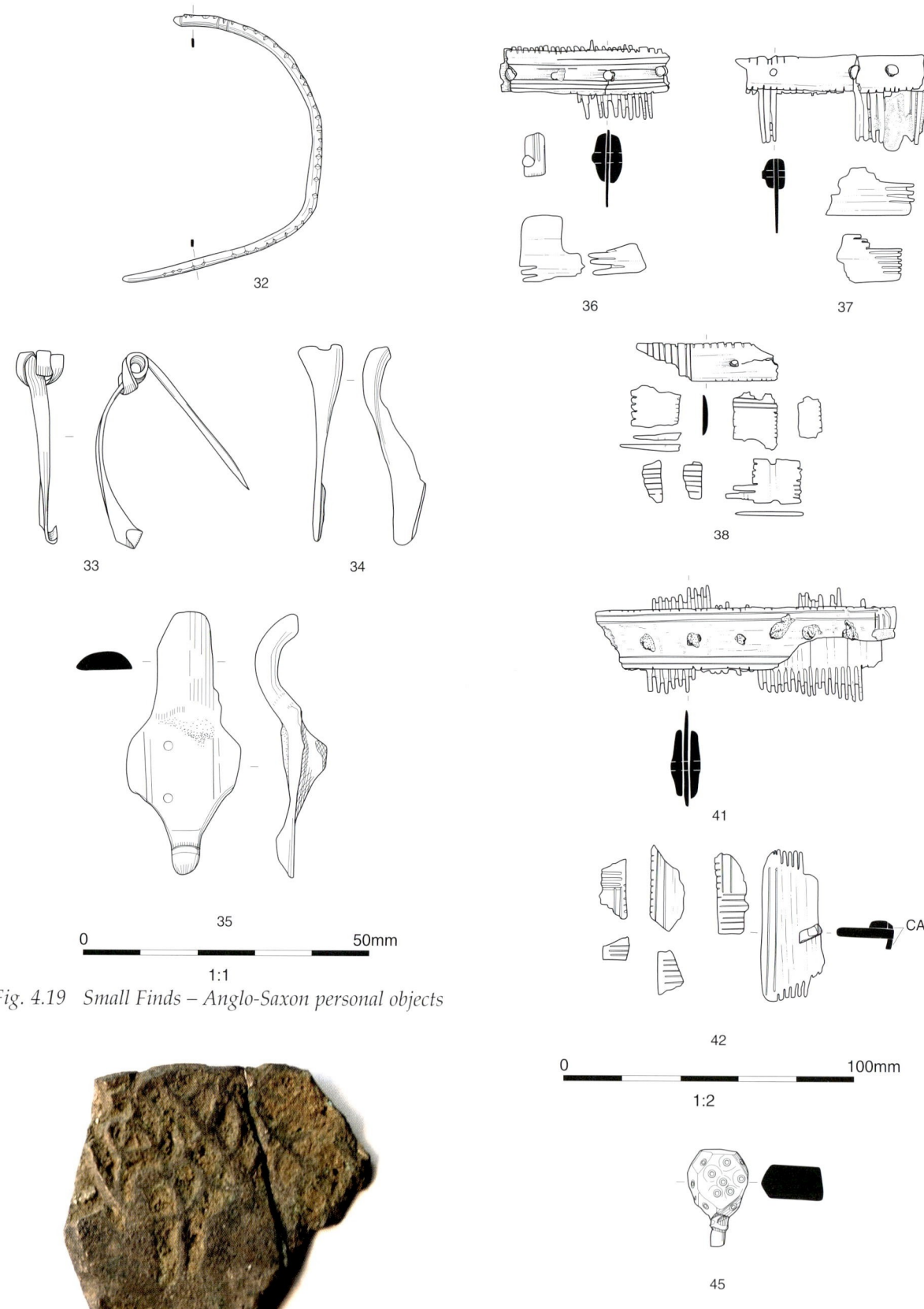

Fig. 4.19   Small Finds – Anglo-Saxon personal objects

Plate 4.1   Small finds – No. **46**, interlace decorated sheet

41   **Composite comb fragment**, secured by iron rivets. L 105 mm. Site 10; HFKML 02, 10575, sf 989. Ph 1.

42   **Composite comb fragments**, comprising end of the double sided tooth plate, part of decorated handle plate and teeth fragments. The comb was held together by iron rivets. W 51 mm. Site 10; HFKML 02, 12732, sf 2921. Ph 1

43   (*not illustrated*) Possible **hairpin** fragment. Tapering stem fragment ending in sharp point. Highly polished. Bone. L 50 mm. Site 4; HFKML 01, 6027, sf 274. Ph 2b.

44   (*not illustrated*) Tip of **hairpin** or **needle**. Circular section. Bone. L 22 mm. Site 8; HFWIB 03, 15101, sf 4023. Ph 2b.

45   **Hairpin** fragment, comprising hexagonal facetted head, and small part of stem. The main facets have five ring and dot motifs, the side faces two ring and dots, and the smaller facets single rings and dots. The stem may have been cut. Copper alloy. L 16 mm. Site 10; HFKML 02, 10508, sf 920. Ph 1.

The head of the pin can be paralleled amongst finds from Hamwic (Hinton and Parsons 1996, 23 form Bb1ii and fig. 9: 4/2, 169/327, etc).

Decorative metalwork (Pl. 4.1)

46   Fragment of **decorated sheet or plate**. Part of a pattern of delicate but vigorous ribbon interlace and a possible roundel survives. The pattern is in low relief on thin plate about 1 mm thick. Possibly originally gilded. Cu alloy. L 15 mm; W 17 mm. Site 8, HFWIB 03, 15119, sf 4014. Ph 2b

Although elements of the ribbon interlace pattern survive the overall decorative scheme is incomplete. The pattern may have been cast, or possibly die-stamped, onto the surface of the plate, and it is possible that the object was gilded originally. The object is difficult to date closely on the basis of the decoration alone, but it could very well have originated in the early to later 8th century, which would agree with the dating of the Phase 2b context, in which it was found. There are similarities to the interlace on the heads of the Fiskerton pin set (Wilson 1984, illustration 33) which are generally date to the 8th century. A recent find of a dress pin from Horncastle, Lincolnshire (Department of Culture, Media and Sport 2001, *Treasure Annual Report 2000*, 40 and fig.55; Treasure ID M&ME 326) is slightly simpler but has similar interlace to the Fiskerton pins and has been dated to the later 8th century. These examples are of much higher quality being of silver gilt and silver respectively. However the decoration of the Higham fragment would fit happily with this Mercian metalwork. The original function of the fragment is uncertain, but it is unikely to be a fragment of a strap end because it is rather too thin in section. Possibly it is a fragment for the head of a decorative dress pin, but more probably it is part of a decorative mount perhaps for attachment to a wooden box or for furniture.

Security

The only item that can be identified in this category is a key.

47   (*not illustrated*) **Key stem**, with expanded head and rolled loop and attached ring. Bit missing. Fe. L 158 mm. Site 4; HFKML 01, 6654, sf 334. Ph 2b.

The form of the key suggests that it is a barrel padlock, or slide, key. The handle form is found in late Saxon/early medieval contexts (eg. Winchester: Goodall 1990, 1005-06, 1020-22 & figs 322-23; York: Ottaway 1992, 673-76 & figs 289-290) as well as later medieval contexts (eg. York: Ottaway and Rogers 2002, 28767 & fig.1453).

Structural

48   (*not illustrated*) **Clamp**, or **dog**. with flat rectangular section back tapering to points at each end. The points are incomplete. Fe. L 43 mm. Site 1; HFKM 95, 1252, sf-. Ph 1.

Nails

The nails from Saxon contexts, in contrast to Romano-British contexts, are very limited in numbers and have been tabulated (Table 4.23). Most come from Phase 1 contexts.

Bindings (Fig.4.20)

49   **Edge binding** formed from thin sheet. Angular in section and slightly flattened at one end. No visible pin/rivet holes. Cu alloy. L 38 mm. Site 1; HFKM 95, 1265, sf 73. Ph 1.

50   **Edge binding** formed from thin sheet. No visible pin/rivet holes. Cu alloy. L 33 mm. Site 1; HFKM 95, 1268, sf 74. Ph 1.

Miscellaneous objects

The miscellaneous finds are tabulated and not illustrated (Table 4.24).

Table 4.23: Anglo-Saxon Contexts (Phases 1-3): Summary of nails

Identification / Comments	Count	Size	Site	Provenance	Phase
Nail, Type 2, almost complete	1	L 54	1 2 3	HFKM 95, 1252, sf -	1
Nail, Type 1, almost complete	1	L 92	1 2 3	HFKM 95, 1255, sf -	1
Nail, Possible Type 1, incomplete, heavily encrusted and laminated.	1	L 47	1 2 3	HFKM 95, 1268, sf 62	1
Nail, Type 1, almost complete	1	L 48	1 2 3	HFKM 95, 1269, sf 64	1
Nail, Type 1? Nail, incomplete and much eroded.	1	0	1 2 3	HFKM 95, 1307, sf 113	1
Nail, Type 1, incomplete. L 47+mm	1	L 47	4 5 9	HFKML 01, 6058, sf 352	1
Nail, Type 1, incomplete	1	0	4 5 9	HFKML 01, 6058, sf 351	1
Nail, Type 1, small. Sample <107>	1	0	4 5 9	HFKML 01, 6631, sf -	1
Nail stem fragment	1	0	8	HFWIB 03, 15100, sf 4014	2b
Nail stem fragment, tapering to point.	1	0	4 5 9	HFKML 01, 6402, sf 345	3
Nail, possible Type 1, almost complete	1	L 27	4 5 9	HFKML 01, 6832, sf 346	3

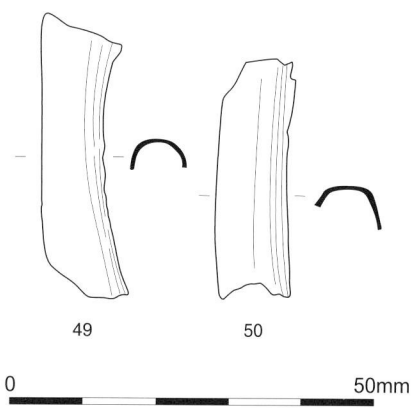

49   50

0   50mm

Fig. 4.20   Small Finds – Anglo-Saxon structural objects

Objects of uncertain function (Fig 4.21)

51   **Decorative fitting**, possibly a terminal. It has a flat back. The lower portion is formed by an angular knob, above is a reeded raised band. The top of the object has a thin curved piece sticking up with iron corrosion adhering. Cu alloy. L 21 mm. Site 1; HFKM 95, 1255, sf 58. Ph 1.

52   (*not illustrated*) **Disc** formed from thin sheet, dished and highly polished. It has a pair of holes near one edge. Function uncertain, but it could be decorative. Cu alloy. D 34 mm. Site 1; HFKM 95, 1265, sf 84. Ph 1.

53   (*not illustrated*) **Small copper alloy fragment**. Comprises thin sheet with a hole, with a second small fragment backing the first. A thin strip attached to the second sheet passes through the front sheet.. L 11 mm. Site 1; HFKM 95, 1268, sf -. Ph 1.

54-55 (*not illustrated*) **Curved thin strips**. The two fragments do not join. The larger fragment is wider at one end and has part of a nail/rivet hole. The shorter length is curved, of uniform width, and no nail hole. Cu alloy. L 96 mm & 40 mm. Site 1; HFKM 95, 1268, sf 85. Ph 1.

56   **Plate** cut from bone. Elongated trapezoid. Unfinished? L 73 mm; W 16 mm. Site 4; HFKML 01, 6058, sf -. Ph 1.

57   (*not illustrated*) **Blade fragment**, heavily encrusted. Thin in section. Possibly chisel blade fragment? Fe. L 44 mm. Site 4, HFKML 01, 6357, sf -. Ph 1.

58   (*not illustrated*) **Tubular object**, tapered at each end. The x-ray suggests that the object contains a bar down the centre – perhaps a tang, and that there are four bands about the object, equally spaced along its length. Possibly a heavily mineralised tool or knife handle? Fe. L 93 mm. Site 4; HFKML 01, 7035, sf -. Ph 2c.

59   **Cast cruciform fitting**. Two arms terminated in knurled knobs, and two have cable decoration and were hinged at their outer ends. Central oval knob. Flat back. Part of a ceremonial collar? Cu alloy. L 22 mm; W 18 mm. Site 8; HFWIB 03, 15423, sf 4038. Ph 2b.

60   **Small hooked fragment**, curved and of square cross-section. Flared and flattened at the end opposite hook end. Cu alloy. L 15 mm. Site 2; HFKM 95; 2084, sf 69. Ph 3.

61   (*not illustrated*) **Tapering spike** of square section. Could be a nail stem or spike. Fe. L 81 mm. Site 2; HFKM 95, 2484, sf 102. Ph 3.

62   **Blade fragment** of triangular section. The back and edge are very slightly curved, and appear to taper towards the point (incomplete). The ?tang is curved.

Table 4.24: Anglo-Saxon contexts (Phases 1-3): Summary of miscellaneous pieces

Identification / Comments	Metal	Count	Fragt Count	Size	Site
Strip, short length, of curved cross-section.	fe	1	1	L 32	1 2 3
Plate, corner fragment	cu	1	1	L 34	1 2 3
Rod or bar. Heavily encrusted and laminated. Possibly nail stem fragment	fe	1	1	L 48	1 2 3
Wire or pin fragment, thin, circular section	fe	1	1	375	1 2 3
Small strip, tapering.	cu	1	1	L 14	4 5 9
Wire fragment, curved. Could be part of a small brooch?	fe	1	1	L 44	1 2 3
Strip, folded	fe	1	1	L 34	1 2 3
Plate or sheet, irregular outline. No visible nail holes.	fe	1	4	0	8
Plate, two joining fragments. One slightly curved edge	fe	1	2	L 54	8
Plate fragment, with curved edge; other edges broken. One nail head extant.	fe	1	1	0	8
Sheet fragments, irregular x 2. No original edges.	fe	2	2	0	4 5 9
Wire fragments, short x 2.	fe	2	2	L 11 & 13	4 5 9
Melted waste, irregular splash.	pb	1	1	0	4 5 9
Plate fragment, heavy, with one slightly curved edge. Encrusted	fe	1	1	0	4 5 9
Strip fragments x 2. One (i) slightly tapered; (ii) one fragment has a pointed terminal with nail	fe	2	2	L 33	8
Thick wire or thin rod	fe	1	1	L 67	8

ID not certain. Fe. L 97 mm. Site 3; HFKM 95, 3003, sf 34. Ph 3.

63 **Handle plates**? Two polished narrow plates. Polished. The plates narrow to each end and are joined by two iron rivets. The wide space between plates suggests that this is not from a comb. Bone or ivory. L 80 mm. Site 4; HFKML 01, 6156, sf 310. Ph 3.

It is unlikely that this pair of joined bone strips formed parts of a comb, because the spacing between them is too great and there is no trace of the notching along the edge of the strips. This notching, which is noticeable on the cat nos **37** and **38** for example, is caused by the cutting of the comb teeth.

64 **Object** with central stem of triangular section. Rectangular flange at one end with elongated slot in the centre. The outer edge is folded up and incomplete. Possibly hinged? The other end comprises a curved strip. Function unclear. Fe. L 106 mm. Site 8; HFWIB 03, 15305, sf 4029. Ph 3.

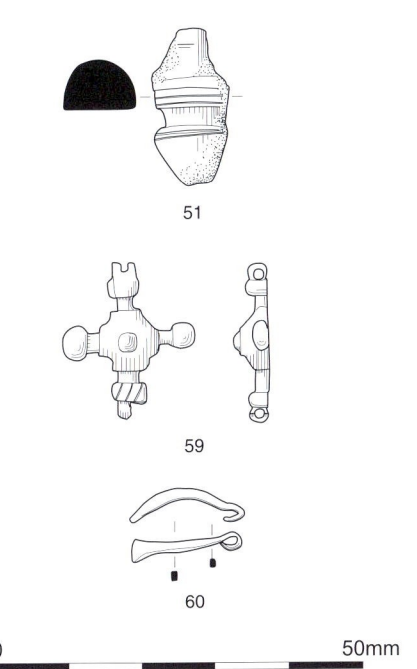

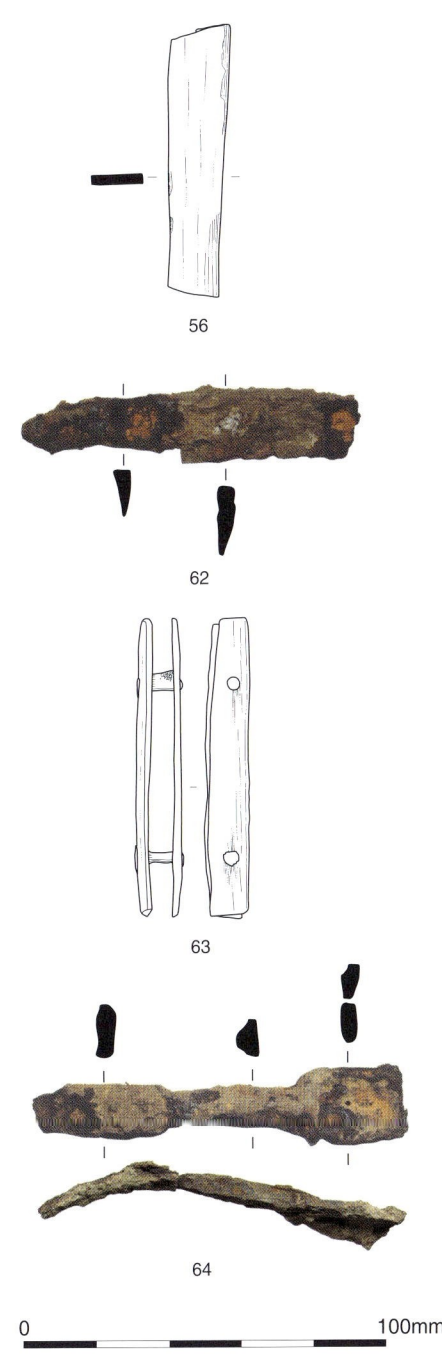

Provenance	Phase
HFKM 95, 1255, sf 57	1
HFKM 95, 1257, sf 88	1
HFKM 95, 1271, sf -	1
HFKM 95, 1304, sf 78	1
HFKML 01, 6366, sf -	1
HFKM 95, 2478, sf 93	2a
HFKM 95, 451, sf 109	2b
HFWIB 03, 15100, sf 4013	2b
HFWIB 03, 15100, sf -	2b
HFWIB 03, 15100, sf -	2b
HFKML 01, 6712, sf 336	2c
HFKML 01, 7027, sf -	2c
HFKML 01, 7077, sf -	2c
HFKML 01, 7236, sf -	3
HFWIB 03, 15305, sf 4031	3
HFWIB 03, 15486, sf -	3

Fig. 4.21   Small Finds – Anglo-Saxon miscellaneous objects

Table 4.25: Medieval contexts (Phases 4 & 5): Summary Quantification by Context and Function

Site	Phase	Context	Function Tools	Transport	Measure	Household	Personal	Security	Door	Structural
eval	5	904								
	5	1105								
Eval		*Totals*	*0*	*0*	*0*	*0*	*0*	*0*	*0*	*0*
3	4	3004		1						
	5	3002					1			
Site 3		*Totals*	*0*	*1*	*0*	*0*	*1*	*0*	*0*	*0*
4	4	6025								
	4	6154		1						
	4	6266		1						
	4	6763	2	1						
	4	7033								
	4	7506								
	5	6254								
	5	6772								
	5	6800		2						
	5	7250								
	5	7289	1							
Site 4		*Totals*	*1*	*4*	*0*	*0*	*0*	*0*	*0*	*0*
5	4	4007								
	4	4009								
	4	5016					1			1
Site 5		*Totals*	*0*	*0*	*0*	*0*	*1*	*0*	*0*	*1*
6	4	9333					1			
	4	9335					1			
	4	9343								
	4	9468				1				
	5	9032		2						
	5	9039								
	5	9402								
Site 6		*Totals*	*0*	*2*	*0*	*1*	*2*	*0*	*0*	*0*
8	4	15366								
	4	15399								
	4	15523			1					
	4	15540								
	5	15007								
	5	15028								
	5	15029					1			
	5	15044								
	5	15064								
8	5	15101					1			
	5	15159								
	5	15172		1						
	5	15188								
	5	15191								
	5	15212								
	5	15246					1			
	5	15456								
	5	15506								
	5	15512							1	
	5	15520					1			
Site 8		*Totals*	*0*	*1*	*1*	*0*	*4*	*0*	*1*	*0*
Medieval		Totals	1	8	1	1	8	0	1	1

Nails	Misc	Query	Unk	Totals
	1			1
1				1
1	1	0	0	2
				1
				1
0	0	0	0	2
2	1			3
				1
				1
2				5
	1			1
1				1
		1		1
	1			1
1				3
	1			1
				1
4	4	1	0	27
1				1
1				1
1		1		4
3	0	1	0	60
				1
				1
	2			2
				1
	1			3
	1			1
1				1
1	4	0	0	130
1				1
	4			4
		1		2
1				1
1				1
		1		1
				1
1	1			2
1				1
				1
	1	1		2
	1			2
	1			1
1				1
1				1
				1
	1			1
1				1
1				2
1				2
10	9	3	0	289
19	18	5	0	68

Finds from Medieval Phases 4-5 (Tables 4.25–4.27)

Sixty eight metal objects come from medieval contexts, 32 from Phase 4 contexts and 36 from Phase 5 contexts (Tables 4.18 & 4.25). Finds from *Phase 4* contexts include eight nails and eight miscellaneous pieces (Table 4.27). There are a pair of shears (**1**), two horseshoe fragments (**66-67**) and two horseshoe nails (Table 4.26) and a possible weight (**69**). The two horseshoe fragments are of an early form which could be residual from Phase 3. The only household item is a knife blade fragment (**70**). There are three single personal items: a copper alloy hairpin (**71**), a strap end (**75**) and a lace chape (**77**). There is one structural fitting: an L-shaped staple (**80**), and two items of uncertain identification (**81-82**). The finds come from Sites 3, 4, 5, 6 and 8.

Finds from *Phase 5* include eleven nails and ten miscellaneous fragments (Tables 1 & 10). There is a blade from a pair of shears (**65**), a hooked attachment from a pair of spurs (**68**) and four horseshoe nails (Table 4.26). There are no household objects, but five personal items. These comprise three buckles (**72-74**), a strap end (**76**) and a lace chape (**78**). There is an L-shaped hinge pintle (**79**). This is small and could be from a window shutter or from a piece of furniture, rather than a door. Finally there are three unidentified objects (**83-85**). The finds come from Sites 3, 4 6 and 8.

A number of objects, which can be dated to the medieval phases on typological grounds, were recovered from later phases or by metal detector. These include a dagger chape (**86**), cast vessel leg (**96**), a circular brooch (**97**), five buckles (**102-105, 107**), a buckle pin (**108**), a strap guide (**109**), two bar mounts (**110-111**), a strap end (**113**), part of a purse mount (**118**), a book clasp (**120**) and a key (**121**).

The range and quantity of finds from medieval phases is limited, but with the emphasis on personal items, it probably represents a domestic assemblage of some pretension.

Catalogue

Tools (Fig. 4.22)

65 **Shears blade**, with parallel edge and back. The back is angled at the tip. The blade is plain with a square blade top. The handle is of oval section, expanded and flattened to form the spring, part of which survives. Fe. L 160 mm. Site 4; HFKML 01, 7289, sf 354. Ph 5.

Transport (Fig.4.22)

Horseshoes

See the typology of horseshoes in the discussion of finds from excavations in London (Clark 1995).

66 *(not illustrated)* **Horseshoe fragment**. Heel from a thin branch with small upset calkin, with single incomplete countersunk nail hole. Possible Type 2 shoe. Fe. L 57 mm. Site 3; HFKM 95, 3004, sf 42. Ph 4.

67 *(not illustrated)* **Horseshoe fragment**. Narrow branch fragment with single round nail hole and oval countersinking. Type 2a. Heavily encrusted. Fe. L 43 mm. Site 4; HFKML 01, 6154, sf 311. Ph 4.

Table 4.26: Medieval Contexts: Horseshoe nails

Identification / Comments	Count	Size	Site	Provenance	Phase
Horseshoe nail, fiddle key nail with worn head.	1	L 29	4, 5, 9	HFKML 01, 6266, sf -.	Ph 4
Horseshoe nail. Fiddle key nail incomplete	1	L 20	4, 5, 9	HFKML 01, 6763, sf 337.	Ph 4
Horseshoe nail. Worn fiddle key nail, clenched stem	1	L 25	4, 5, 9	HFKML 01, 6800, sf 343.	Ph 5
Horseshoe nail. Fiddle key nail	1	0	4, 5, 9	HFKML 01, 6800, sf 342	Ph 5
Horseshoe nail. Possible fiddle key nail	1	L 33	6, 7	HFCF 02, 9032, sf 803	Ph 5
Possible horseshoe nail with expanded head. Eroded and encrusted.	1	0	8	HFWIB 03, 15172, sf -	Ph 5

Fig. 4.22   Small Finds – Medieval tools

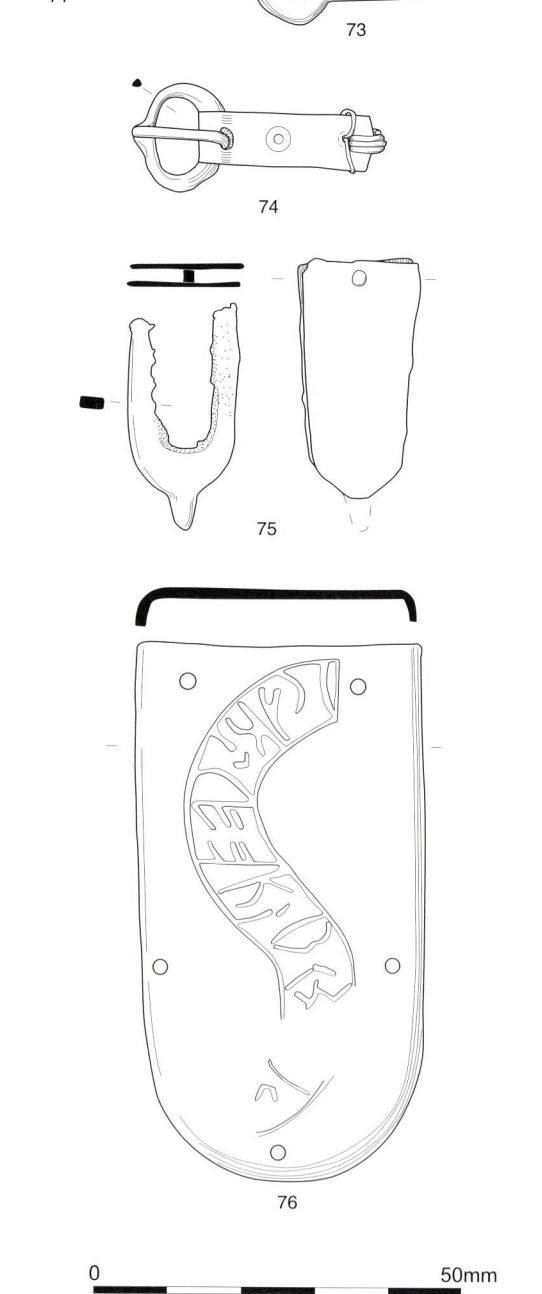

Fig. 4.23 (right)   Small Finds – Medieval personal objects

Horseshoe nails

There were only six horseshoe nails from medieval contexts (Table 4.26)

Riding gear

68 **Spur attachment.** Hooked attachment from spur leather. Fe. L 25 mm. Site 6; HFCF 02, 9032, sf 801. Ph 5.

Cf examples from London (Ellis 1995, 149-50 and fig. 106: 365-371).

Weight

69 (*not illustrated*) Possible **Weight**. Cylindrical with wide central perforation. Pb. L 25 mm, D 25 mm Site 8; HFWIB 03, 15523, sf 4036. Ph 4.

Household

70 (*not illustrated*) Possible **blade fragment**, heavily encrusted. The blade appears to taper and have a triangular section. Fe. L 95 mm. Site 6;HFCF 02, 9468, sf -. Ph 4.

Personal (Fig 4.23)

Hairpin

71 **Hair pin head**, domed, scar only of stem. Cu alloy. D 6 mm. Site 6; HFCF 02, 9335, sf -. Ph 4.

Buckles

72 (*not illustrated*) **D-shaped buckle frame**, with flat pointed pin. Encrusted. Fe. L 36 mm, W 33 mm. Site 3; HFKM 95, 3002, sf 63. Ph 5.

73 **Oval buckle frame** with composite rigid plate. The back and front plates are missing. The forked spacer is extant. The frame is of triangular section. Cu alloy. L 36 mm; W 16 mm. Site 8; HFWIB 03, 15101, sf 4021. Ph 5.

74 **Oval buckle frame** with folded plate, small. There are two rivet holes in the plate. The inner rivet hole has an extant rivet; the outer rivet hole has thin wire passing through it and wrapped around the end and sides of the plate. Cu alloy. L 34 mm, W 14 mm. Site 8; HFWIB 03, 15520, sf 4043. Ph 5.

Strap ends

75 **Strap end**, three piece with forked spacer. Plain outer plates. Single rivet. Cu alloy. L 38 mm; W 15 mm. Site 5; HFKML 00, 5016, sf 37. Ph 4.

See examples from London (Egan and Pritchard 1991, 140-46 & figs 93-6). A late medieval form.

76 **Strap end**, comprising tongue-shaped plate, with lip around three sides. Five nail or rivet holes. Decorated with snake-like motif with rune-like letters incised on face. Appears to be made from modern rolled plate. Cu alloy. L 73 mm, W 39 mm. Site 8; HFWIB 03, 15029, sf 4001. Ph 5.

Lace chapes

77 (*not illustrated*) **Lace chape** with butted seam, and two opposed pin/rivet holes. Cu alloy. L 24 mm. Site 6; HFCF 02, 9333, sf -. Ph 4.

78 (*not illustrated*) **Lace chape** with overlapping seam and one pin/rivet hole Cu alloy. L 24 mm. Site 8; HFWIB 03, 15246, sf -. Ph 5.

Door, window or furniture fittings

79 (*not illustrated*) **L-shaped hinge pintle**, incomplete. For a small drop hinge. Fe. L 59 mm. Site 8; HFWIB 03, 15512, sf 4044. Ph 5.

Structural fittings

80 (*not illustrated*) **L-shaped staple** or holdfast. Fe. L 56 mm; H 39 mm. Site 5; HFKML 00, 5016, sf 38. Ph 4.

Table 4.27: Medieval contexts: miscellaneous objects

Identification / Comments	Metal	Count	Size	Site	Provenance	Phase
Tongue-shaped strip, small	fe	1	L 20	4 5 9	HFKML 01, 6025, sf 239	4
Plate fragment, with one straight edge with a notch.	fe	1	L 39	4 5 9	HFKML 01, 7033, sf 350	4
Bar or rod, heavily encrusted	fe	1	L 63	6 7	HFCF 02, 9343, sf -	4
Waste, flat droplet, formed over a corner or edge	cu	1	0	6 7	HFCF 02, 9343, sf -	4
Waste, offcut. Small tapering strip	pb	1	0	8	HFWIB 03, 15399, sf 4040	4
Waste, offcut Small irregular fragment	pb	1	0	8	HFWIB 03, 15399, sf 4041	4
Waste, small melted fragment	pb	1	0	8	HFWIB 03, 15399, sf 4042	4
Waste, small fragment	pb	1	0	8	HFWIB 03, 15399, sf 4043	4
Bar fragment	fe	1	L 64	1 2 3	HFKM 95, 904, sf 23	5
Plate fragment, with original edges and two nail holes at one end and much eroded at the other, wider end. Curved in cross section	fe	1	L 142	4 5 9	HFKML 01, 6772, sf 340	5
Plate fragment, irregular in outline, and no decoration or nail holes visible on x-ray.	fe	1	0	4 5 9	HFKML 01, 7250, sf 353	5
Ring Plain, heavily encrusted. Diameter 23mm x 21mm	fe	1	D 23 x 21	6 7	HFCF 02, 9032, sf 802	5
Waste, small droplet of leaded bronze?	cu	1	0	6 7	HFCF 02, 9039, sf 800	5
Waste, tapering offcut, folded	pb	1	0	8	HFWIB 03, 15044, sf 4018	5
Bar or nail stem fragment	fe	1	L 65	8	HFWIB 03, 15159, sf 4019	5
Bar or rod fragment	fe	1	L 67	8	HFWIB 03, 15172, sf -	5
Block. Dense block of sub-square section	fe	1	L 36	8	HFWIB 03, 15188, sf 4020	5
Waste, small flat melted fragment	pb	1	0	8	HFWIB 03, 15456, sf 4039	5

Nails

There are only 19 nail fragments from Medieval (Phase 4-5) contexts, and they have not been separately tabulated.

Miscellaneous fragments (Table 4.27)

Only 18 miscellaneous fragments were found. They include 10 iron fragments – mainly bar and plate, but including a dense block and a ring – two copper alloy droplets and six lead fragments. The latter include both offcuts and melted waste. Much of the lead came from context 15399 on Site 8 (Phase 4).

Objects of uncertain identification (Fig. 4.24)

81   *(not illustrated)* **Possible tang** of rectangular section, with remains of bent stem. Perhaps from a drill bit or gouge? Fe. L 89 mm. Site 5; HFKML 00, 5016, sf 27. Ph 4.

82   **Strap fragment**, short, formed from cut thin strip, with two angle cut corners and two rivet holes. Broken at one end. Cu alloy. L 16 mm, W 11 mm. Site 8; HFWIB 03, 15523, sf 4037. Ph 4.

83   **Long bone** cut short, with angled cut faces on either side. L 50 mm. Site 4; HFKML 01, 6254, sf -. Ph 5

84   **Curved tapering antler point**. The cut broad end is polished. The tip still retains its original grooved surface. There is a crudely cut notch around $^1/_2$ of the circumference of the stem near the broad end. Function uncertain. L 43 mm. Site 8; HFWIB 03, 15028, sf 4000. Ph 5

85   *(not illustrated)* **Loop** formed from rod, with short piece of broken strip through the eye. Perhaps a drop-hinge eye? Fe. L mm. Site 8, HFWIB 03, 15159, sf 4018. Ph 5.

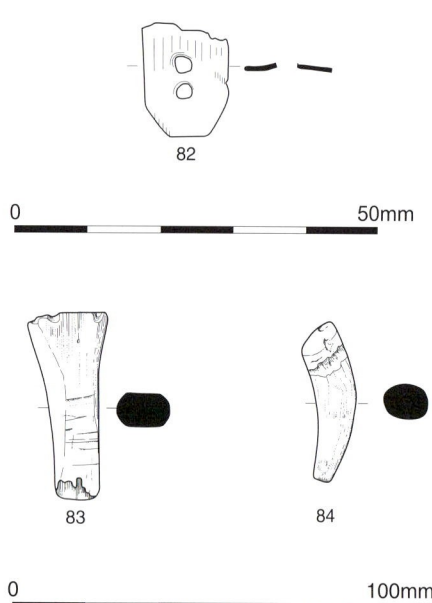

82

83   84

Fig. 4.24   *Small Finds – Medieval objects of uncertain function*

97

88

Fig. 4.25   *Small Finds – Unstratified tools*

Finds from Phase 6 contexts and Unstratified Finds

A substantial number of finds were recovered from Phase 6 (16th century to modern) contexts, and others were unstratified. Amongst these finds are some that can be identified typological as Saxon or medieval, or probably Saxon or medieval and these are catalogued below.

Catalogue

Weapons

86   *(not illustrated)* **Dagger chape** formed from thin sheet, rolled and overlapped. There is a single rivet or pin hole. Cu alloy. L 31 mm. Site 2; HFKM 95, 2001, sf 46. Ph 6.
Medieval. Comparable pieces have been found at York (Ottaway and Rogers 2002, 2904, & fig. 1478).

Tools (Fig. 4.25)

87   Possible **metalworking hammer**. Maybe a cross- or straight, pane hammer. Fe. L 0 mm. Site 6; HFCF 02, 9368, sf -. Ph 6.
Uncertain identification. Uncertain date.

88   **Shears**. With narrow tapering blades of triangular cross-section. The top of each blade is curved with a slight recess. The tips of the blades are broken. The arms are circular in section. Only part of the sprung bow is extant. Fe. L 280 mm. Site 2; HFKM 95, 2001, sf 50. Ph 6.
Medieval.

89   *(not illustrated)* **Heckle tooth**. Tapering circular section spike, encrusted. Fe. L 72 mm. Site 4; HFKML 01, 6125, sf 272. u/s

90   *(not illustrated)* **Heckle tooth**. Tapering circular section spike. Fe. L 100 mm. Site 4; HFKML 01, 6125, sf 244. u/s

91   *(not illustrated)* **Heckle tooth**. Tapering circular section spike. Fe. L 90 mm. Site 4; HFKML 01, 6125, sf 307. u/s

92   *(not illustrated)* **Heckle tooth**. Tapering circular section spike, tip bent into a hook. Fe. L 75 mm. Site 4; HFKML 01, 6125, sf 297. u/s

Measurement (Fig. 4.26)

None of these can be closely dated, but Anglo-Saxon and medieval examples of pendant weights and conical weights can be cited.

93   **Pendant weight** formed from strip folded and hammered to form the lower thicker portion. Pierced for suspension through the thinner upper portion. Pb. L 39 mm. Site 4; HFKML 01, 6030, sf 288. u/s

94   *(not illustrated)* **Possible weight** comprising irregular cone, with thin hole through the centre. Pb. L 27 mm; H 24 mm. Site 4; HFKML 01, 6030, sf 286. u/s [ID 116]

95   **Possible weight**, irregular truncated cone with large central hole. Pb. D 18 mm. Site 4; HFKML 01, 6125, sf 284. u/s

Household

96   *(not illustrated)* **Cast vessel leg**, of heavy leaded bronze. Tapering solid leg, broken off at narrow end. Signs of hammering on one face, and possibly on opposite face. Cu alloy. L 78 mm. Sites 2; HFKM 95, 2001, sf 45. Ph 6.
Late medieval or post-medieval

Personal (Fig. 4.27)

Brooches

Medieval. See in general Egan and Pritchard 1991, 248-55, & figs 160-64.

97   **Circular brooch**. The frame is of flat rectangular section. The face is decorated with plain edgings flanking flat beading. There is a slight constriction where the pin was attached. Cu alloy. D 26 mm. Site 2; HFKM 95, 2001, sf 49. Ph 6.

98   **Disc brooch** comprising flat disc with overlaid thin sheet with embossed decoration. Outer edge is decorated with a pie crust, or ribbed, band, then a concentric groove. In the centre is a slightly recessed panel with an irregular wavy edge. There is a central hole to secure a decorative stud or similar feature. Cu alloy. D 29 mm. Site 4; HFKML 01, 6030, sf 281. u/s

99   **Small enamelled disc brooch**. There are eight fields radiating from a central circular field. The radial fields are defined by fine applied strips of copper alloy. The catch hook and attachment point for the pin survive on the back. Cu alloy. D 21 mm. Site 4; HFKML 01, 6030, sf 315. u/s

Hooked tags

A Saxon type, current from the 7th to 11th century (Hinton 1996, 10), the function of which is not certain, but almost certainly used as some form of fastening for clothing. A silver pair from Winchester may have fastened a garter (Hinton 1990, 548), but others may have been used to fasten purses. The plain example (**101**) is paralleled by examples from Winchester (Hinton, 1990, 552, fig. 149: 1426-27). The example with ring and dot pattern (**100**) is paralleled at Hamwic (Hinton 1996, 9-10, fig. 4: 36/190 & 169/488).

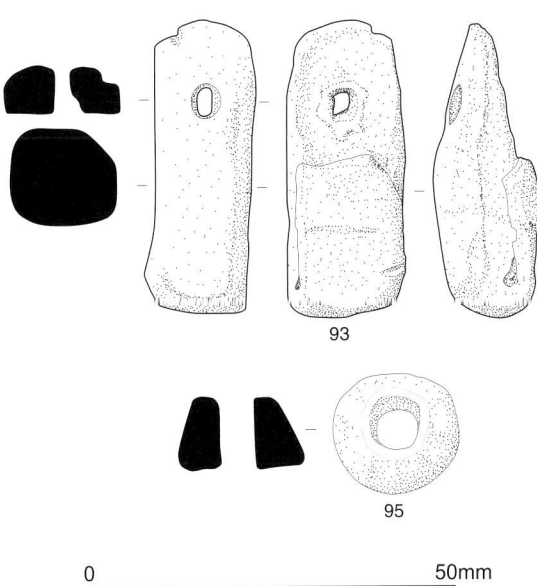

93

95

0   50mm

Fig. 4.26   Small Finds – Unstratified weights

100 **Hooked tag**. Trapezoid plate with five punched ring and dot motifs, two with stitching holes. The hook has been straightened. Cu alloy. L 19 mm; W 10 mm. Site 4; HFKML 01, 6125, sf 203. u/s

101 **Hooked tag**. Plain teardrop-shaped hooked plate with two stitching holes. Cu alloy. L 20 mm. Site 4; HFKML 01, 6125, sf 330. u/s

Buckles

102 **Double loop rectangular buckle** with chamfered or bevelled inner and outer edges. Flat on the back. Cast in an open mould. Cu alloy. L 41 mm; W 28 mm. Site 2; HFKM 95, 2001, sf 53. Ph 6.

This buckle is a late medieval or post-medieval form.

103 **Double oval buckle frame**, with one half largely missing. Cast. Cu alloy. L 29 mm; W 28 mm. Site 7; HFCF 02, 9527, sf -. u/s

An early post-medieval form – see generally Margeson 1993, 28 and fig. 16: 163-73 and fig. 17: 174. See also examples from Camber Castle (Scott 2001, 260, fig. 7.2: 26-28, 31).

104 **Buckle with cast oval frame, and folded plate**. The front part of the plate is decorated with central grooves. The back plate is slightly short with a cut decorated end. Cu alloy. L 34 mm; W 28 mm. Site 8; HFWIB 03, 15130, sf 4015. Ph 6.

Probably medieval or early post-medieval. Not precisely paralleled.

105 **Asymmetrical buckle** with elongated oval loop of square cross section, with rectangular strap loop. No pin nor evidence for one. Cu alloy. L 19 mm; W 30 mm. Sites 4, 5, 9; HFKML 01, 6030, sf 290. u/s

Late medieval or early post-medieval. Cf the examples from Battle Abbey (Geddes 1985, 158 & fig. 49: 17)

106 **Folded buckle plate**, small and rectangular with cast relief decoration. The pattern appears to comprise a sinuous abstract plant motif. The plate is broken at the fold and the back is missing. There are two rivet holes one at each outer corner. Cu alloy. L 25 mm; W 13 mm. Site 2; HFKM 95, 2001, sf 47. Ph 6.

The abstract pattern, with its *Art Nouveau* echoes, suggests that this object may be of late 19th-or early 20th-century date.

107 Possible **folded buckle plate** formed from thin sheet, with chased border of running triangles, and five rivets. Cu alloy. L 27 mm; W 25 mm. Site 5; HFKML 00, 5000, sf -. Ph 6.

Medieval. A comparable piece comes from Swan Lane, London (Egan and Pritchard 1991, 160 7 fig. 104: 756). It is identified as a possible strap end.

108 Possible **buckle pin fragment**. It has punched two ring and dot motifs and a small hole. It is curved at one end. Cu alloy. L 26 mm; Site 4; HFKML 01, 6125, sf 207. u/s

Medieval. Compare with similarly decorated example from York (Ottaway and Rogers 2002, 2896, & fig. 1472: 14334).

Strap guide

109 **Strap guide**. Trapezoid frame with internal opposed lugs. Cu alloy. L 22 mm. Site 4; HFKML 01, 6125, sf 302. u/s

Medieval. See Egan and Pritchard 1991, 231-33 & fig. 149: 1254-65, and Ottaway and Rogers 2002, 2902-03 & fig. 1477: 14378-79.

Bar mounts

The bar mounts from Higham Ferrers have central and terminal lobes and are a medieval form. Examples come have been found in York (Ottaway and Rogers 2002, 2907-09 & fig. 1480: 14437), and London (Egan and Pritchard 1991, 213-15 & fig. 134: 1154, 1157-58).

110 **Bar mount**, with domed centre with large hole, and two tapering arms of half round section. The latter terminate in domed ends, and are pierced with small pin holes. The back of the object is flat and shows filing marks. Cast in a one piece open mould. Cu alloy. L 30 mm; W 12 mm. Site 4; HFKML 01, 6125, sf 200. u/s

111 Possible **large bar mount**. Incomplete, gilded. Cu alloy. L 45 mm; W 18 mm; Site 4; HFKML 01, 6125, sf 303. u/s

Strap guide or belt plate

112 Possible **rectangular strap guide** or **belt plate**, with slight medial grooves/ridges. Two thin fixing arms, one at each end. Fe. L 24 mm; W 18 mm. Site 4; HFKML 01, 6276, sf 323. u/s

No precise parallel known. Broadly comparable objects from Anglo-Scandinavian contexts at Coppergate, York (Ottaway 1990, 688-90 & fig. 297) and from Medieval contexts at York (Ottaway and Rogers 2002, 2902-03 & esp. fig. 1477: 12722) have been identified as strap guides.

Strap ends

113 **Shield-shaped strap end**, small and plain but with a slight raised ridge around edge. Thin sheet at the back riveted to front. Cu alloy. L 17 mm; W 15 mm. Site 4; HFKML 01, 6030, sf 278. u/s

Small short strap end comparable to examples from London (Egan and Pritchard 1991, 146-48 & fig.96: 694-701), and York (Ottaway and Rogers 2002, 2900 & fig.1475: 14362. The Higham Ferrers example is distinctly shorter than the cited examples.

114 **Long narrow strap end**, with rounded terminal. Part of the front face is chamfered. It has a single rivet hole. Cu alloy. L 43 mm; W 7 mm. Site 4; HFKML 01, 6125, sf 306. u/s

No parallel found.

115 Possible **strap end**. It comprises a trapezoid plate, with two rivets, separated by a constriction from curved and ?decorated but incomplete end. There is a thin plate on the back of the trapezoidal plate. Fe. L 34 mm. Site 4; HFKML 01, 6125, sf 216. u/s

Saxon. This fragment is similar to a strap end from Coppergate (Ottaway 1992, 690 & fig. 298: 3792).

Buttons

116 **Small cast button** with quincunx pattern of small pellets on a hatched background. The loop is bent over. Cu alloy. L 12 mm. Site 2; HFKM 95, 2001, sf 44. Ph 6.

Possibly medieval.

117 **Flat disc button**, with thin outer edge, a concentric circular of pellets, a cable border and plain flat circular central portion. Loop on the back. Cu alloy. L 23 mm. Site 2; HFKM 95, 2001, sf 44. Ph 6.

Fig. 4.27 (facing page) Small Finds – Late medieval and post-medieval personal objects

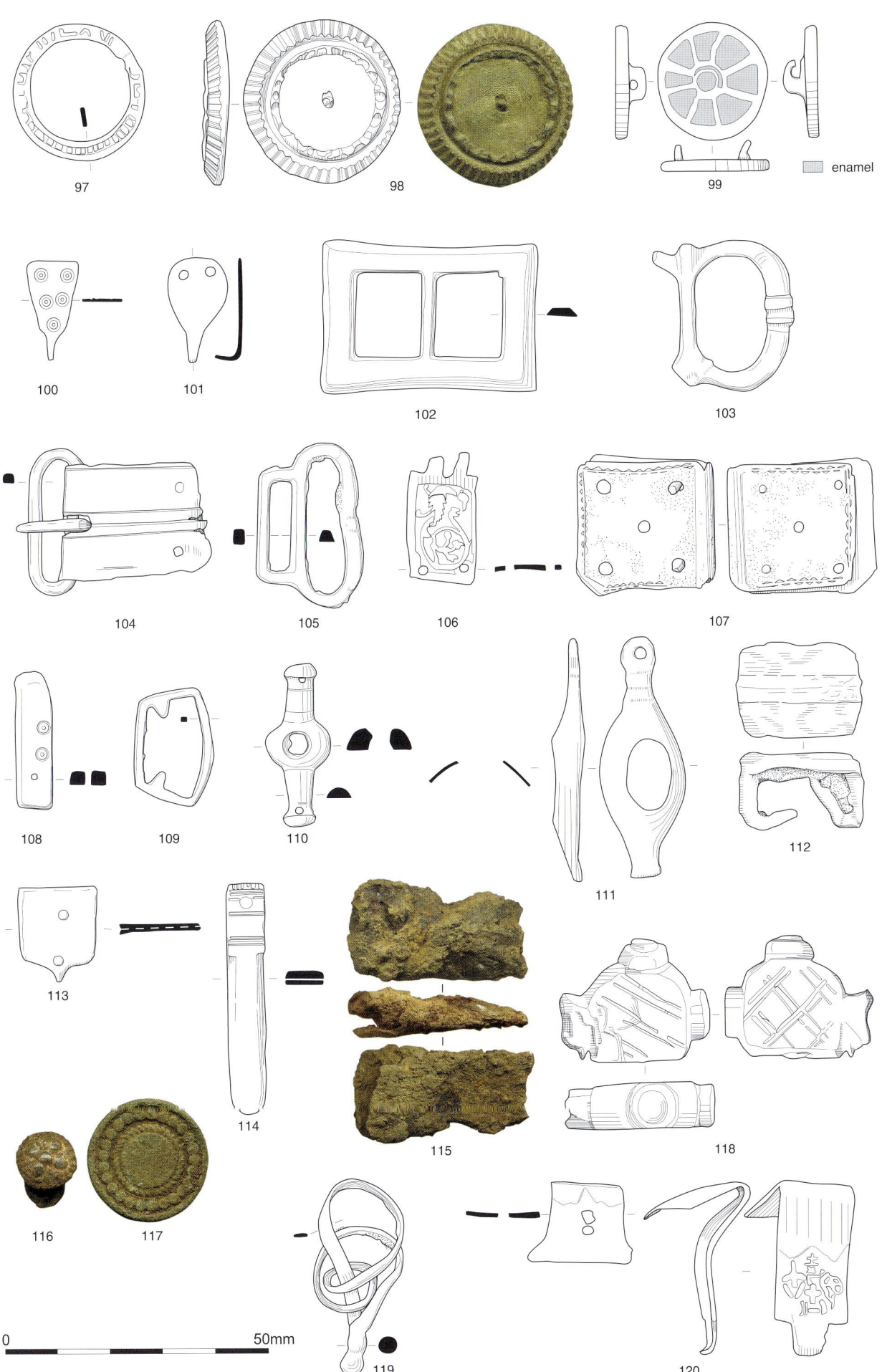

97

98

99

enamel

100

101

102

103

104

105

106

107

108

109

110

111

112

113

114

115

116

117

118

119

120

131

Purse bar

Purse mount fragment, comprising central moulded swivel to which the loop was attached. The spindle is partially extant. Only the stubs of the two arms survive. The object has been cut and hammered. Cu alloy. L 29 mm; H 23 mm. Site 4; HFKML 01, 6125, sf 225. u/s

Late medieval

Possible personal

119 Possible **pendant**, formed from thin strip looped and coils and joined at a knobbed terminal. Cu alloy. L 37 mm. Site 2; HFKM 95, 2001, sf 37. Ph 6.

Book Clasp

120 **Book clasp**, bent. The back plate is missing. There are two closely set rivet holes near the flared end, but no visible rivet, or rivet hole, near the hooked end. The face of the plate is plain in the centre, but textured, with no clear pattern at each end. The plain central section is slightly raised in relation to the textured zones and marked by distinct edges, zig-zag at the hooked end and lobed at the flared end. Originally about 50 mm long. Cu alloy. L 33 mm; W 19 mm. Site 2; HFKM 95, 2001, sf 55. Ph 6. Medieval.

Security (Fig. 4.28)

121 **Key** with solid stem and plain oval bow. The stem projects well beyond bit and there is a stop midway along the bit. The bit is long and has six teeth. Fe. L 190 mm; W 53 mm. Site 8; HFWIB 03, 15260, sf 4035. Ph 6.

Uncertain identification (Fig. 4.28)

122 **Cast fitting** tapering from a swelled end to a knobbed terminal. The widest portion is hollow at the back. Silvered or tinned. Cu alloy. L 36 mm. Site 1; HFKM 95, 1250, sf 31. Ph 6.

123 **Teardrop-shaped drop handle**. Cast, with hollow back. Trapezoid suspension loop. Cu alloy. L 46 mm, W 17 mm. Site 2; HFKM 95, 2001, sf 56. Ph 6. Post-medieval furniture fitting.

124 **Decorative binding or strip**. Thin strip terminating in a crude trefoil, now bent. Originally c 60 mm long. Pb. L 22 mm. Site 4; HFKML 01, 6030, sf 287. u/s

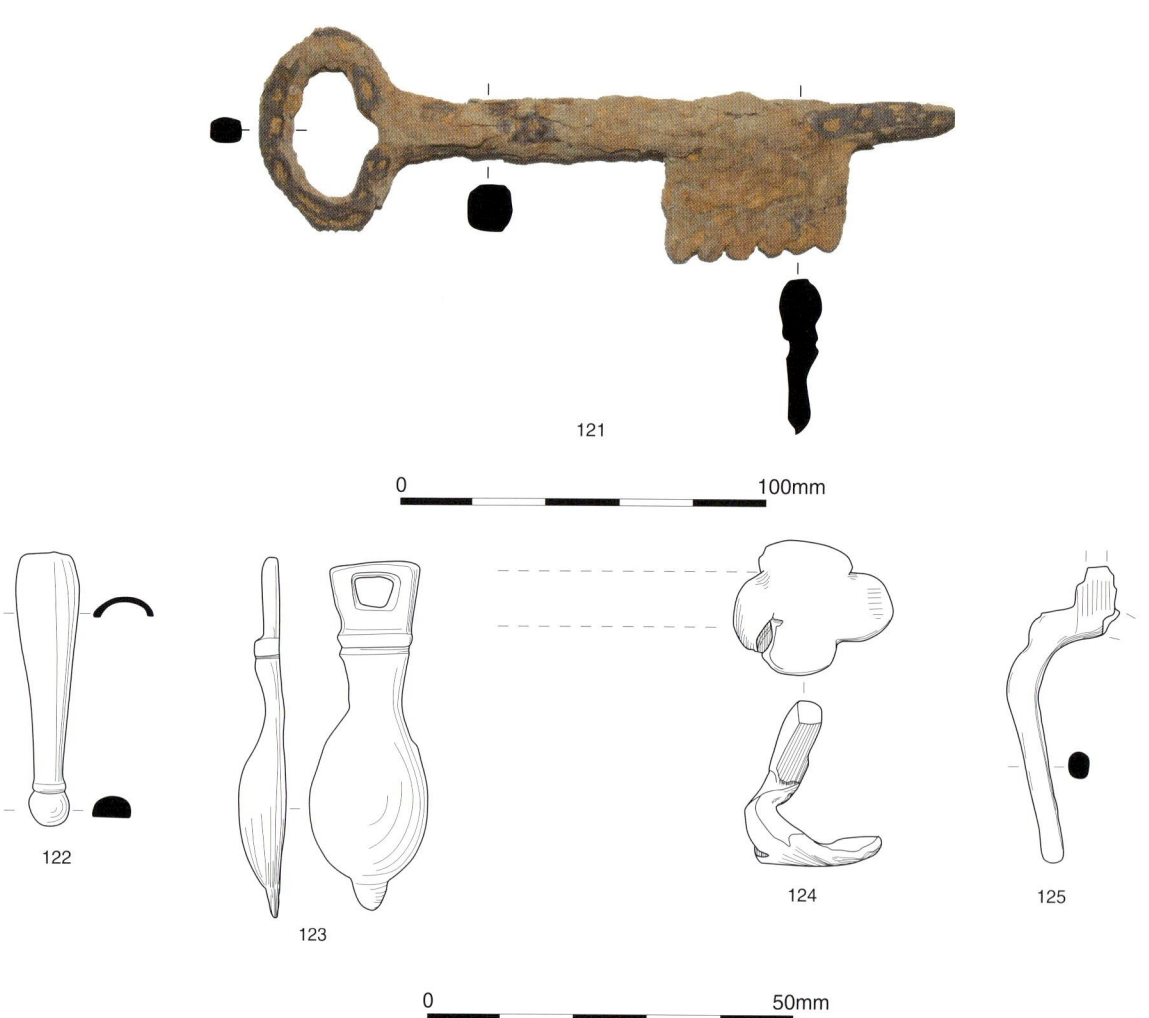

121

0   100mm

122   123   124   125

0   50mm

Fig. 4.28   Small Finds – Unstratified miscellaneous objects

125 Forked object, apparently incomplete. Cu alloy. L 40 mm; Site 4; HFKML 01, 6125, sf 210. u/s

126 *(not illustrated)* **Object** with sub-rectangular stem or handle. One end has an incomplete flat apparently round head, the other end flares. Both ends are incomplete. Fe. L 60 mm. Site 4; HFKML 01, 6125, sf 263. u/s

COIN *(PL. 4.2) by Martin Allen*

The coin from the site (4028) is a silver penny of the St Edmund Memorial coinage, later phase (*c.* 905-917/18), with St Edmund's name on both sides (North 1994, no. 483/1). The repetition of a version of the obverse inscription on the reverse is a feature of many St Edmund Memorial coins of the later (post-Cuerdale hoard) phase (Blackburn and Pagan 2002, 14).

> *Obverse* +SC EADMVDI (S on its side) around chevron-barred A.
> *Reverse* +SCE EADM (S on its side) around cross pattée.
> Weight: 1.25 g. Die axis: 200o.

The St Edmund Memorial coinage was the normal currency of the Southern Danelaw (which included Higham Ferrers) from *c.* 895 to the conquest of the area by Æthelflæd of Mercia and Edward the Elder (899-924) in 917/18 (Blackburn and Pagan 2002). It was quickly replaced by the English coinage of Edward the Elder, and it is unlikely that the excavated coin could have been in use and available for loss later than *c.* 925 (pers. comm. Dr Mark Blackburn).

The coin has been recorded in the Fitzwilliam Museum's online Corpus of Early Medieval Coin Finds from the British Isles 410-1180 as EMC no. 2006.0114 (www.fitzmuseum.cam.ac.uk/coins/emc).

Plate 4.2   Silver penny of the St Edmund Memorial coinage, later phase (c. 905-917/18)

WORKED STONE *by Fiona Roe*

The worked stone assemblage amounts to 14 objects (Table 4.28). There are fragments of lava quern of varied date from 9 contexts, 2 whetstones which came from a middle Saxon ditch and late Saxon gully, and 3 further worked fragments of less certain purpose.

Niedermendig lava

Niedermendig lava does not survive well under certain conditions, which explains to some extent the limited size of the assemblage and the fact that only fairly small fragments were found. Nevertheless there are examples from phases 1 – 4, demonstrating that this high quality quernstone was transported to Higham Ferrers over a long period of time. There is a recognizable rotary quern fragment (6631) from an early Saxon SFB, another four fragments from middle Saxon ditch fills (408, 451, 3035 & 15149) and further small fragments (6268) from a late Saxon pit. There are also small fragments from similar Medieval contexts (6037, 15382). The best preserved piece (3002) was unstratified and this has part of a vertical handle hole near the rim, a feature also seen on querns found at Dorestadt (Parkhouse 1976, 182). A similarly placed handle hole survived on a lava millstone found at Goltho, Lincolnshire (Beresford 1987, 195 & fig 166).

It is becoming clear that Niedermendig lava was imported into England extensively throughout the Anglo-Saxon period and indeed later. Finds have been recorded in particular at sites in eastern England, since these were most conveniently positioned to receive goods from across the North Sea. Quantities of lava were also shipped up the Thames, as for example to middle Saxon Dorney, Buckinghamshire (Roe 2002, 37 & CD). Finds that can be attributed to the early Saxon period are less easy to trace but numerous lava fragments came for example from early to middle Saxon Quarrington in Lincolnshire (Taylor 2003, 255). At Riby Crossroads, Lincolnshire, a site with occupation from the 6th or 7th century, the pieces of lava were again in poor condition (Watt 1994, 283). At Flixborough, Lincolnshire, lava fragments are known to have occurred in middle and late Saxon contexts (Loveluck 2001, 93). The fact that lava does not always survive well could account for the shortage of Northamptonshire Saxon sites where it has been recorded, but it is known to have been found at Raunds (Blinkhorn 1999, 16) and Maxey (now in Cambridgeshire; Addyman 1964, 59). It is notable that on many middle Saxon sites with lava querns, Ipswich ware also features among the finds; these goods (and no doubt other commodities), may well have been transported in the same trading network.

Lava querns are also known from a number of Roman sites, but this aspect of the trade may have ceased before the arrival of the first Saxons, although future work could prove otherwise. Ability to grind corn and make bread would have been a matter of importance to newly arrived immigrants in the 5th and 6th centuries, and so it seems likely that they arrived already equipped with lava querns. They probably also ensured that arrangements were available to supply replacements for worn out or broken querns. In the case of Higham Ferrers, these may have been obtained from Suffolk, since Ipswich ware was also being acquired. However a route avoiding laborious land transport would have been available up the river Nene, perhaps via the port at Kings Lynn. The settlements at Northampton, Raunds, Irthlingborough and Brixworth could also have benefited from river-born traffic up the river Nene, while at Maxey there was a link with the coast via the river Welland. It is becoming clear that many rural communities were able to obtain goods from overseas (Hamerow 2002, 190, 192), and it has been suggested that geography was as important as 'status' for maintaining long distance trading connections (Hamerow 1999, 201). Such trade would not have been difficult to achieve for Northamptonshire sites which, although not near the coast, were linked by river systems to the North Sea.

Other materials (Fig. 4.29)

There are five objects made from other varieties of stone. A whetstone (2020 – Fig.4.29, 2) was made from an iron-stained sandstone probably collected from the local Northampton Sand. A second whetstone (6621 SF 331- Fig. 4.29, 1) of this type was found in the enclosure ditch fill. Other fragmentary pieces of local sandy limestone (cxt 451) and sandstone (cxt 15161), displaying worked surfaces, are of uncertain purpose. A piece of Millstone Grit with a worn surface (1311) may be a re-used rotary quern fragment from the nearby Roman site.

Fig. 4.29   Worked stone – Whetstones

134

Table 4.28 Catalogue of Worked Stone by Phase and Site

Site	Context	SF	Description	Stone	Context type
Phase 1: early Saxon, 5th – 6th century					
4	6631	-	Fragment from rotary quern, weathered, traces of wear on grinding surface; 145 x 97 x 38 mm, 615 g	Niedermendig lava	SFB fill
Phase 2b: middle Saxon, mid 8th – late 8th century					
3	408	-	2 fitting fragments, worn grinding surface; 74 x 55 x 23 mm, 105 g	Niedermendig lava	ditch fill
3	451	-	2 fitting fragments; 60 g	Niedermendig lava	ditch fill
3	451	-	Fragment, slightly concave, smooth surface, may have been utilised? 108 x 78 x 23 mm, 220 g	Limestone, sandy	ditch fill
3	3035	-	1 fragment, weathered; 95 g	Niedermendig lava	ditch fill
Phase 2b/c: middle Saxon, late 8th century					
4	6621	331	Fragment from small whetstone with wear along two long sides; 41 x 17 x .95 mm, 8 g	Fine-grained sandstone, slightly micaceous and iron-stained	ditch fill
Phase 2c: middle Saxon, late 8th – early 9th century					
8	15149	4025	1 fragment with possible grinding surface, worn thin; 96 x 81 x 21 mm, 251 g	Niedermendig lava	ditch fill
Phase 3: late Saxon, 9th – 11th century					
2	2020	-	part of whetstone, rectangular block, well worn; 82 x 45 x 35 mm, 170 g	Sandstone, sandy coloured (iron stained), some feldspar, a little mica, probably local Northamptonshire Sand	gully fill
4	6268	-	6 fragments, weathered; 112 g	Niedermendig lava	pit fill
Phase 4: Medieval, 12th – 13th century					
4	6037	-	1 fragment; 30 g	Niedermendig lava	ditch fill
8	15382	-	6 fragments; 153 g	Niedermendig lava	pit fill
Phase 6: Post-medieval to modern, 16th – 20th century					
8	15161	-	Fragment with apparently worked, flat surface, traces of mortar, uncertain identity; 51 x 33 x 12 mm, 35 g	Sandstone, porous, may be weathered Northampton Sand	well fill
Unstratified					
1	1311	75	Fragment with smooth, worn surface, possibly re-used piece of rotary quern; 86 x 79 x 63 mm, 285 g	Millstone Grit	pit fill
3	3002	35	2 fitting fragments from rim of rotary quern with a pitted surface and part of handle hole near edge; 133 x 85 x 28 mm, 345 g	Niedermendig lava	layer

BUILDING MATERIAL: THE MALTING OVEN CLAY *by Emily Edwards, Edmund Simons and Alan Hardy*

The well-preserved remains of a malting oven represent a unique Middle Saxon survival. Initially located by an untargeted evaluation trench, the structure was later fully exposed (Site 5). After excavation and examination the structure was sealed under a protective layer of gravel, and remains intact within the current housing development.

A detailed description of the archaeological features and deposits associated with the structure is included in Chapter 3. A description and interpretation of the fired clay, and a discussion on the construction, use and destruction of the oven follows.

Dating

In the absence of any artefactual dating or dated typological parallels, the only means of dating the structure was radiocarbon assay. The barley grain found in the oven chamber produced a radiocarbon date of Cal 662 -1014 at 98% confidence – 710 to 963 at 78% confidence. This date range is consistent with the later part of the date range for the estate centre complex.

Assemblage

The fired clay assemblage consisted of a large quantity (84kg) of material recovered by hand from deposits within the oven chamber (4010). All of the clay appeared to be structural, with many pieces showing very clear wattle impressions, and little or no evidence for post-depositional abrasion or weathering. The assemblage is interpreted as fragments of the clay covering of a wicker frame superstructure which had been constructed over the stone foundation.

Methodology

The quantity of material recovered is estimated to represent a randomly selected 10% of the original structure. The material has been grouped by form, and the fragments counted and weighed. (A small quantity of heavily abraded material, almost certainly derived from the same structure, was found in nearby medieval features but has not been included in this analysis). The material from the oven was also examined for evidence of wattle or other impressions of organic and non-organic inclusions. The wicker impressions were measured in order to determine the range of sizes of pieces used. The surviving fragments with wattle impressions were grouped according to size, shape and number of impressions of rods (uprights) and sails (cross pieces). Those with significant (and perhaps informative) flat surfaces were also noted separately.

Dimensions and characteristics of the clay fragments

Many of the fragments were very large, measuring 350-400 mm in length with – broadly – three ranges of clay thickness. The thickest pieces ranged from 60 mm-85 mm, the middle range 35-47 mm and the thinnest fragments from 15-25 mm thick.

Of a total of 428 pieces, 20 showed impressions of rods and sails; 50 showed impressions of sails. Of those with both rods and sails, 14 had convex surfaces and 3 or 4 were concave (the rest being flat). Of those with sails alone, over 35 had surfaces, only 1 of which was concave, 2 convex and three displayed both convex and concave surfaces.

The majority of the external surfaces on pieces were flat, and crudely smoothed while those that were curved were mostly concave (Pl. 4.3.a1/a2, d1/d2, 4.4.j1/j2). A total of 10 fragments displayed impressions of sawn or split oak planks, stone faces or wipe-marks. (Pl. 4.4.e1, f1, g1/g2, h1).

Fabric

Fabric type and level of oxidation were noted. The clay was sandy and contained moderate quantities of shell, chalk, and limestone possibly as naturally occurring inclusions. All of the clay fragments showed impressions of organic material (probably straw), used as a temper to prevent the clay cracking during the initial firing or subsequent use. This would suggest that the oven's construction occurred after harvest – that is, in late summer, a likelihood supported by one piece that bears the clear impression of a fully developed head of corn.

Discussion of the material

Oven Structure and Building Techniques

While the evidence from the clay fragments is by no means complete, when considered in conjunction with the stone structural remains, and the charred plant remains, it is possible to suggest with some confidence a plausible interpretation of construction, appearance, preparation and use of the malting oven.

Construction (Pl. 5.2)

Pit and base

The first stage comprised the excavation of a shallow, flat-bottomed rectangular pit (the oven chamber), with a long, slightly wedge shaped trench (the flue) extending from one end. The base of the pit was floored with unworked flat stone slabs, covered with a thin layer of clay, and the sides of the pit and the trench were lined with unmortared rubble stone walling. No disturbed stone slabs were noted in the overburden or the demolition material in the oven, giving support to the idea that the walls would not have extended much above the contemporary ground surface, if at all, when first built. Where the flue entered the chamber, the walling extended across the opening, and the arch was supported by three flat slabs on edge (see Fig. 3.33 section 36 and Pl. 3.6). It is significant that the arch extended into the chamber itself; this would have directed the hot air to rise through the centre of the chamber, rather than just at the flue end.

Drying platform

There would have been a drying platform, on which to spread the grain, suspended above the chamber floor. This platform could have been a separate element, possibly a wattle hurdle laid flat, but is perhaps more likely that, given the sophistication of the rest of the structure, the platform would have been a slatted timber screen (perhaps similar to a modern wooden pallet) which incorporated a frame resting on the stone walls, after the fashion of a wall plate. Significantly a few of the clay fragments contained impressions suggesting that they were pressed against sawn or split timbers (see Pl. 4.4, g1/g2)

Superstructure

It is almost certain that the clay was collected from the immediate proximity of the oven. A large pit was partially excavated approximately 10 m to the west of the oven. Although it produced some later medieval dating material, it also contained, in its lower fill, some very abraded pieces of fired clay, almost certainly derived from the oven superstructure. This implies that the pit was open at the time of the oven's use.

The framework of the superstructure was woven from wattles and thin saplings, probably of hazel. There was no direct evidence to indicate how the wicker framework was anchored to the stone base. A possible (and simple) solution would have entailed inserting the rods (vertical wattles) into drilled holes in the timber wall plate. Once the top of the uprights had been tied together to form a dome or arch, the sails (horizontal withies) would have been woven into the structure. Some clay fragments displayed sharply concave outer surfaces, with marks of withies in three directions. These could represent parts of the superstructure where the tunnel over the flue meets the chamber dome.

It would have been necessary to provided access into the chamber. In Pl. 5.2 this is conjecturally shown as framed opening, with a removable wooden screen or door, incorporated in the super-structure.

Preparation for use

Significantly the clay floor of the chamber, and the exposed internal faces of the stonework of both the chamber and the flue were reddish in colour, suggesting exposure to fairly intense heat. It is difficult to reconcile this with its function as a malting oven, which would have required only gentle heat (around 70 °C, albeit over a sustained period). Other examples of late Saxon ovens, such as those found at Stafford, demonstrate signs of burning in the flue and at the entrance to the chamber only, in keeping with the presumed *modus operandi* of the malting process (Moffett 1994, 56). To explain signs of intense burning throughout the oven chamber at Higham Ferrers, it is suggested that, once the structure was built, a fire was set within the chamber itself for a few days, to dry out and lightly fire the clay superstructure, thus making it reasonably weatherproof, without setting fire to the wicker framework – no evidence was found that the wattles themselves were burnt.

A single firing in this way still may be too little to account for the intensity of reddening of the oven floor and walls, but if the superstructure was periodically rebuilt (perhaps annually) the oven could have had a number of these 'firing' episodes (Ruth Shaffrey pers. comm.)

Use of the oven

Malting is an important part of making ale from grain. The process today is essentially the same as in the late Saxon period: The barley grain is soaked in water for a day or two, and then spread out on a floor, where it begins to germinate, and the starch in the grain turns to sugar. The grain is then gently heated for a few days to about 70-80 °C, which stops the germination. The resulting malted grain is then milled to produce a grist. This is then added to water and the grain husks raked off. The liquid is then boiled and sealed in casks. Honey is added to sweeten the taste and produce mead.

It is probable that the soaked grain would have been spread out on sacking over the platform within the chamber of the Kings Meadow oven. The airflow would have drawn warm air from a small fire at the end of the flue into the chamber and up through the grain. The large slab of stone found at the open end of the flue may have been used to seal the end of the flue to retain heat within the chamber.

Associated structures

No evidence was found of any associated structure, or structures, either forming a shelter for the oven or representing associated buildings such as storage sheds. It can be assumed that such buildings – albeit probably light and insubstantial – existed, and therefore that they may have been sited outside the excavated area. The very shallow gully close to the west side of the oven (Fig. 3.33), and the scatter of features revealed in the three subsequent evaluation trenches, are enigmatic. The mix of dating material recovered from their fills precludes close dating. The pit identified in the western trench could well be a shallow quarry pit, dug during the construction of the oven; the abraded fired clay and late medieval pottery from its upper fill suggests it remained open after the oven's demise, and filled slowly.

The position of the oven in relation to other features of similar date is worthy of consideration. Its radiocarbon date and its sophisticated structure leave little room for doubt that it can be associated with the operation of the estate complex in its later years. While the oven – a fire risk – would no doubt have been situated well away from barns and domestic buildings, it does appear to tbe excessively far from contemporary structures. It is over 100 m south-west of the rest of the excavated complex. This might suggest that other elements may also have been sited on the south-west side of Kings Meadow Lane. This area had largely been covered by modern housing and light industrial development before the excavation began, and so no further investigation of the area was possible. This theme is discussed more extensively below (see Chapter 5).

Duration of the oven

Clearly the structure was built to process good quantities of grain, but was it intended to last more than one season? The stone oven and flue bases would not be affected by the weather, but it is arguable whether the superstructure would withstand prolonged adverse weather conditions. However, there is no reason why the wattle and daub superstructure could not have been renewed each year. When the structure finally ceased to be used, it seems that it was deliberately and rapidly demolished. None of the clay fragments from within the chamber displayed any signs of abrasion, which suggests that the superstructure was not

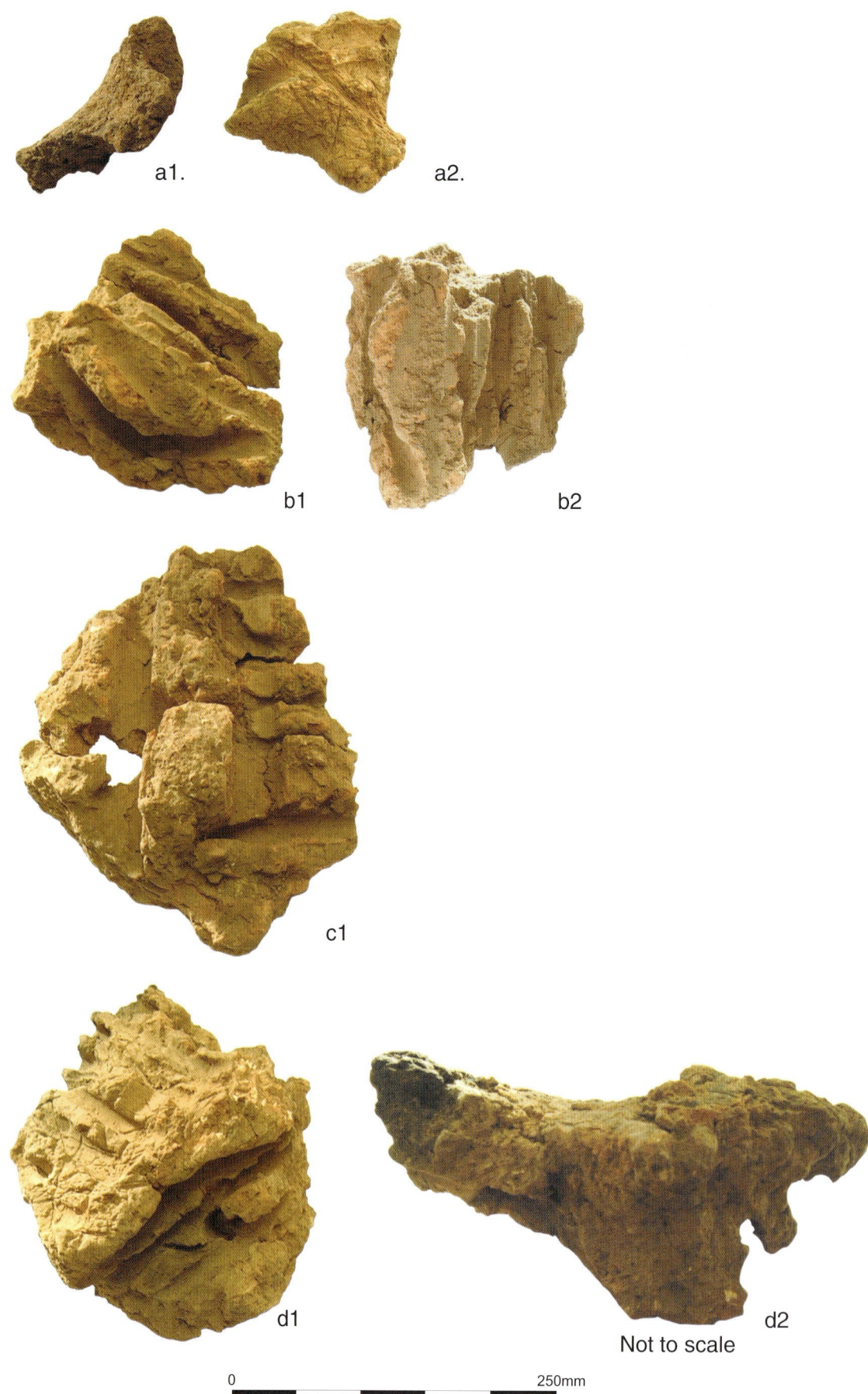

a1.

a2.

b1

b2

c1

d1

d2

Not to scale

0   250mm

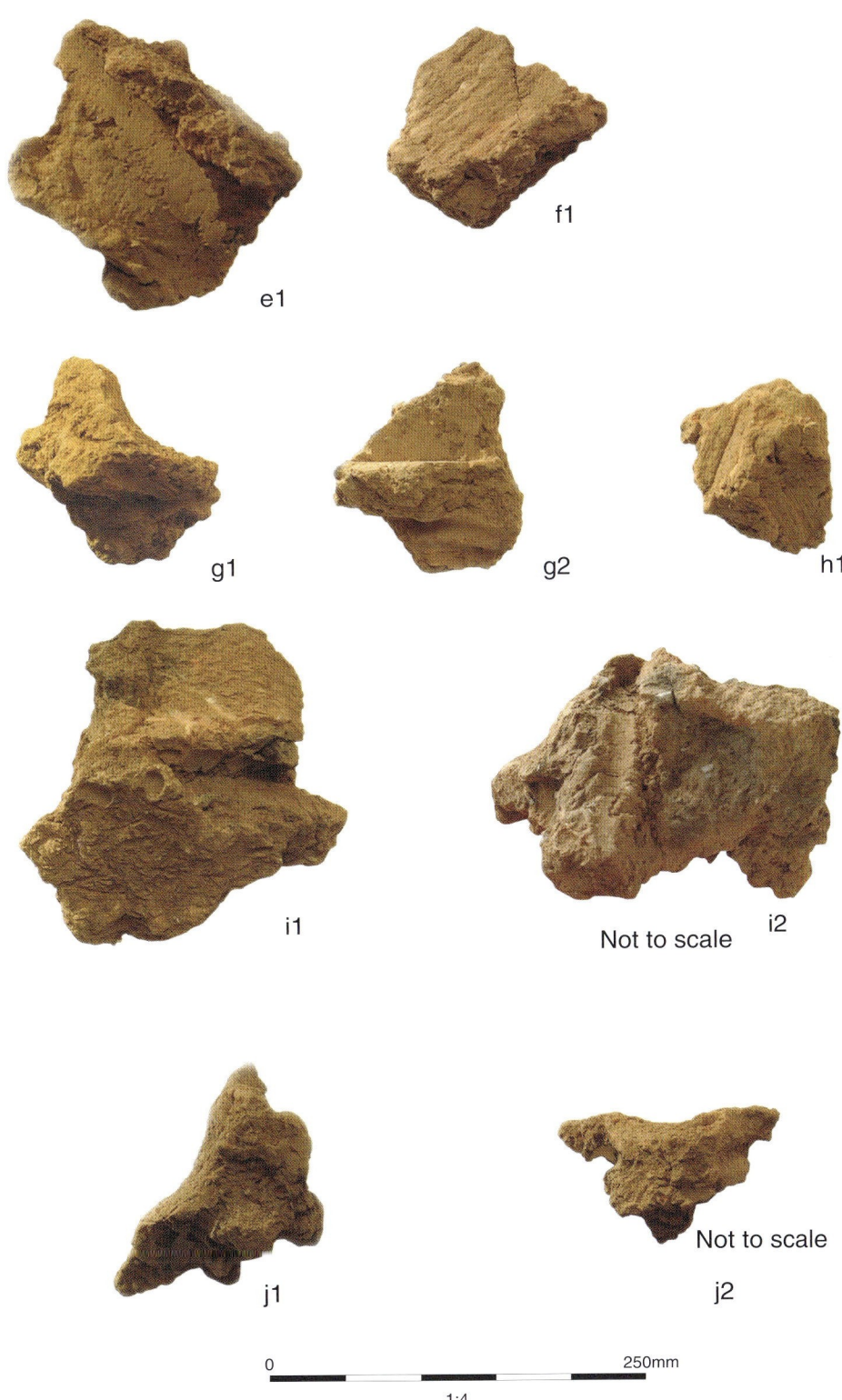

Plate 4.4 (above)   Malting oven fired clay

Plate 4.3 (facing page)   Malting oven fired clay

merely abandoned and allowed to decay slowly. The demolition perhaps took place at the same time as the clearance of the rest of the estate centre.

Similar middle Saxon structures are conspicuous by their absence from the archaeological record in England. A few examples of corn drying ovens have been identified, some reminiscent of Roman 'T'-shaped ovens or likely to be re-used furnaces, as for example in the case of two 8th-century ovens at Gillingham in Dorset (Nenk, Margeson and Hurley, 1991, 221). One of the best examples, albeit radio-carbon dated to the early 10th century, was found as an isolated feature during the excavation of a Bronze Age cemetery at Ewanrigg, Cumbria in 1985 (Bewley *et al* 1992 fig. 4; and Bewley 1987, 233). The oven comprised a circular flat-bottomed stone-lined pit measuring 2 m in diameter, with a projecting flue on one side. Charred oats, barley and wheat in the chamber suggested its use as a grain drying oven, although its use as a malting oven is quite possible too.

Local examples of medieval malting ovens, dating to the late 12th or early 13th century, have been found at West Cotton, Raunds (Chapman, forthcoming). These are of similar build, with a rectangular stone-lined chamber and a superstructure of clay over a wattle frame.

Catalogue of illustrated fired clay fragments (Pls 4.3-4.4)

4.3.a1/a2 'T'- shaped piece of structural clay. Five Sails, width of 17-20 mm. An impression of an ear of corn in addition to several grain impressions. Slightly concave surface.

4.3.b1/b2. Many sails, ranging from 9-15 mm. Includes the impression of a bent hazel rod. Flattish surface. Ironstone embedded within the body of the fragment.

4.3.c1 Sails 10-20 mm in width. Rods 20 mm Consists of 2 large refitting pieces. Slightly concave surface. Clear impression of withies wound around the uprights. Some impressions clearly show the shaped ends of rods.

4.3.d1/d2 Sails 12-15 mm, rods 20 mm. It shows an impression of a hazel rod running in a third direction to the rods and sails, possibly from part of superstructure where the chamber meets the flue.

4.4.e1. Sails 8 mm. Rod 27 mm. An impression that could be evidence of the clay having been smoothed over a join. It appears to have been created by the side of someone's hand being wiped across the clay. 15 mm across.

4.4.f1. Rod 62 mm, whole width not present. Possible impression of an Oak plank. No exterior surfaces present.

4.4.g1/g2. Sails 22 mm, entire width of rod not present. The fragment has a flat, smooth impression forming a 90° angle which could have been the result of the clay being pressed over the edge of a squared timber.

4.3.h1. Sails 10 mm. Rods 25-30 mm. Impressions of a plank or split hazel. No surfaces.

4.4.i1/i2. Sails 9-24 mm. Two fingerprints in the clay. A slightly concave surface

4.4.j1/j2 Evidence of the shape of the oven: A concave surface, indication of a possible basket shape or of clay applied internally.

HUMAN SKELETAL REMAINS
by Annsofie Witkin

Summary

The articulated and disarticulated remains from Higham Ferrers consisted of an adult female, a neonate and the disarticulated remains from a minimum of two adult males. The adult female and the disarticulated remains were all from the deliberate backfill of a ditch. It is argued that these individuals were all probable victims of execution. The skeletal evidence from the female indicated that her body had been displayed until advanced decomposition had taken hold. This is also likely to have been the fate of the two males represented by the disarticulated remains. The neonate most likely represented the surreptitious burial of a stillborn child.

Methodology

Preservation and completeness

There are a number of factors which affect the preservation as well as the completeness of a skeleton. The main factor is the pH value of the soil, but the depth of the burial, the degree of *in situ* compression, truncation and the quality of excavation and post-excavation treatment will also have an effect (Brothwell 1981, 7-9).

Preservation of the skeletons as a whole rather than as individual elements was scored on a sliding scale from 'destroyed' to 'excellent' depending on the amount of erosion and flaking of the outer surface of the bone. Completeness of the skeleton was also scored on a sliding scale from less than 25% complete to 100% complete. Preservation and completeness of the skeleton affects primarily the recording of pathological lesions and metric data.

Skeletal inventory

The skeletal components of the individual were recorded in tabular form as present or absent. Dental inventory was recorded following the Zsigmondy system. Dental notations were recorded using the universally accepted recording standards and terminology (after Brothwell 1981).

Assessment of age

The assessment of age provides the biological age of the skeleton and not the chronological age of the individual. This is because factors such as nutrition and lifestyle have an impact on skeletal growth and subsequent degeneration. Ageing of subadults provides more narrow age ranges since the growth and maturation sequence of children is fairly predictable and uniform.

The neonate was aged by using longbone length (Scheuer *et al* 1980). The adult individual was aged using the degenerative changes of the pubic symphyses (Todd 1920; 1921; Brooks and Suchey 1990) and the auricular surface (Lovejoy *et al* 1985). Both disarticulated mandibulae were aged by dental attrition (Miles 1962; Brothwell 1981).

Sex determination

The sexually morphological differences between males and females emerge after the onset of puberty. Generally, sex can therefore only be determined with any degree of accuracy in individuals aged over *c* 17 years and the differences between the sexes are most pronounced in the pelvis since the female pelvis is adapted to childbirth. Cranial, pelvic and post-cranial metrical measurements were used for the determination of sex. The features from the cranium and the pelvis used for the determination of sex were chosen from *Standards* (Buikstra and Ubelaker 1994). The metric data used for the assignment of sex were the femoral head diameters (Chamberlain 1994).

Stature estimation

Stature was calculated using the regression formulae devised by Trotter (1970) for white males and females. The combined measurement of the femur and tibia was used since it carries the least error.

Pathology

The remains were examined for abnormalities of shape and surface texture. When observed, pathological conditions were fully described and recorded following accepted osteological standards. Throughout life, joints are subjected to wear and tear. This gradual deterioration of the joint surfaces is therefore common in older individuals. Today, up to 85% of individuals are affected by joint diseases such as osteoarthritis (Roberts and Manchester 1995, 100). The changes that take place are new bone formation around the margins of the joint or on the surface itself. Porosity may also be present on the joint surfaces. The aetiology is multifactoral but increasing age, genetic predisposition, lifestyle and environmental factors such as climate all play a part in the development of degenerative joint disease.

Taphonomy

Taphonomic processes involve chemical, biological and physical postmortem changes to the bone. These include colour and shape changes, weathering, carnivore or herbivore gnawing and cultural modifications (Buikstra and Ubelaker 1994, 106). Animal tooth marks are quite commonly observed on human skeletal remains. Carnivorous gnawing is usually located on the trabecular ends of longbones although ribs are also subjected to carnivorous gnawing. Herbivorous gnawing is commonly carried out by rats and rabbits. The characteristic

parallel square-bottomed grooves are often located on site of bony prominences such as the orbital rim (Buikstra and Ubelaker 1994, 98).

Results

Skeleton 6678

The skeleton was situated within the Phase 2c backfill (6621) of an enclosure ditch (7330) dating to the late 8th–early 9th century. The individual was orientated SW-NE – along the line of the ditch. There was no grave cut and the body must therefore have been deposited at the same time as the backfilling of the ditch took place. The skeleton was prone, tightly flexed with the feet directly beneath the pelvic area (Pl. 4.5). The ankles were very close together possibly indicating that they had been bound.

Preservation and completeness

The skeleton was in an average state of preservation but the cortical surfaces of both femora and tibiae were badly eroded. Postmortem breaks were also present on the left femur, tibia and fibula as well as the pelvis. The ribs were also very fragmented. Around 65% of the skeleton was present and the elements missing comprised the cranium, mandible, both arms, hands, scapulae, clavicles, all cervicals, the first thoracic vertebral element, sternum, manubrium, six left ribs and two right ribs, the fourth lumbar vertebra, right patella, all foot phalanges, right metatarsals and most of the tarsals from both feet.

Age and sex

The skeleton was a female individual aged between 30 and 50 years. The somewhat broad age range was caused by the lower age estimate of the right pubic symphysis. However, due to the slight degenerative changes present on the body it is likely that she was aged between 30 and 40 years.

Stature

Skeleton 6678 was 1.62 m tall. This is marginally taller than the national average of 1.61 m for the time period (Roberts and Cox 2004, 390).

Pathology

The degenerative changes on skeleton 6678 were slight and affected the knees and the spine. Schmorl's nodes was also present on the lower thoracic vertebrae and upper lumbars. These are caused by a disc hernia in which the disk protrudes through the vertebral surface causing a defect. These are common degenerative defects and are found in most people over 45 years of age (Aufderheide and Rodríguez-Martín 1998, 97).

Taphonomy

Carnivorous puncture marks were present on the spinal processes of the first and second lumbars of

Plate 4.5   Skeleton 6678 in situ and detail of toothmarks on the lumbar vertebrae

0 _____ 10 mm

skeleton 6678 (Pl. 4.5). Three puncture marks were situated on the first lumbar of which one perforated the process. Only one was present on the second lumbar. The size of the puncture marks indicated that it was a medium sized carnivore (Domínguez-Rodrigo and Piqueras 2003, 1386). The shape of the puncture marks is consistent with the tooth morphology of a dog.

Skeleton 2591

Provenance and preservation

The burial was situated on Site 2, at the north-western edge of the complex of small Phase 3 paddocks. The skeleton was orientated NW-SE and located in a small oval pit (2604) which measured 0.7 by 0.4 m and was 0.14 m deep (Fig. 3.37 and Pl. 5.5). A radiocarbon date of the late 9th to early 10th

century (Cal. 780 AD to 1030 at 95.0% confidence interval) was recovered from the bones. Skeleton 2591 was generally excellently preserved apart from the lower legs, which were poorly preserved. The skeleton was near complete; the only elements missing being the right and left distal ulnae and the distal end of right radius.

Age and sex

The skeleton was a baby aged between 37 and 38 weeks *in utero*. A baby is full-term at 40 weeks and this newborn was therefore slightly premature.

Pathology and taphonomy

No pathological lesions were present on the neonate. Gnaw marks were present on the lower limbs of the neonate (2591) and the left femur was particularly badly affected. Unfortunately, all bones were used for radiocarbon dating before a detailed analysis of the gnaw marks was carried out. It is therefore not possible to ascertain whether the gnaw marks was produced by a scavenging carnivore such as a dog or a fox or a herbivore such as a rat.

Disarticulated remains

Disarticulated remains were recovered within a few metres of skeleton 6678, from the same backfill of ditch 7330. A mandible (sf 355) and a pelvic fragment were recovered from context 6050 and a mandible (sf 356), patella, femur shaft and parietal fragment from context 6621. On the basis of radio-carbon dating, mandible Sf 355 is contemporary with skeleton 6678 and mandible Sf 356 is earlier, possibly dating to the late 7th–early 8th century (see below).

The disarticulated remains recovered from the ditch fills are summarised in Table 4.29; the remains constituted a minimum number of two individuals, both male.

Preservation and completeness

The mandible (SF No. 356) and the patella from context 6621 were complete. The breaks present on all the other bones were old as indicated by the colour of the exposed cortex. There was minimal erosion of the ends of the bones as well as the surface. The femur shaft does however show some slight surface changes consistent with erosion from stones in the soil and plant root tracks.

Age and Sex

Only the mandibles could be aged and sexed. Both were males and mandible 355 was from an individual aged 30-38 years and mandible 356 from a male aged 24-30 years.

Pathology

One small carious lesion was present on the denti-tion of mandible Sf 355. Dental caries is a destruc-tion of the enamel caused by the production of acid from bacteria present in dental plaque (Hillson 1996, 269). The cavities are commonly found in areas where food is likely to get trapped (Hillson 1996, 275).

Small deposits of calculus were present on the right premolars and left lateral incisor on mandible Sf 356. Dental calculus is formed by mineralised plaque, which accumulates on the base of living plaque deposits (Hillson 1996, 225), is a common pathological condition, and is generally related to poor oral hygiene.

Periodontal disease is commonly caused by the accumulation of calculus between the teeth and the soft tissue. This causes inflammation of the soft tissue – gingivitis – which may lead to inflammation of the bone, which in turn would cause bone loss and subsequent exposure of the roots of the teeth. The loss of the tooth would eventually follow (Roberts and Manchester 1995, 56). There are two types of periodontal disease, horizontal bone loss which involves the simultaneous loss in height of the alveolar margin involving the whole dental arcade and vertical bone loss which is localised around an individual tooth or a pair of teeth (Hillson 1996, 263-265). Moderate to considerable vertical bone loss affected the right molars on mandible Sf 355 and moderate horizontal bone loss was present on mandible Sf 356.

One dental abscess was present on mandible Sf 355 which affected the left canine. An abscess may be formed when bacteria enter the pulp cavity through dental caries, excessive attrition or trauma to the crown. An abscess can also occur when a periodontal pocket is formed. When bacteria accumulate in the pulp cavity an inflammation starts which can track to the apex of the root. As the pressure builds up from the continuous accumula-tion of pus, a hole (sinus) forms on the surface of the jaw which allows the pus to escape (Roberts and Manchester 1995, 50). It is at this advanced stage that the abscess is visible and recorded archaeologi-cally. The only dental anomaly present was a congenitally missing or impacted third molar on mandible Sf 356. It is impossible to ascertain the reason for the absence of the tooth without an x-ray.

The mandibular condyles on mandible Sf 356 had slight osteophyte formations at the joint margins. These were very mild degenerative changes.

Slight porosity was present on the superior part of the parietal fragment from context 6621. This type of lesion is known as porotic hyperostosis and is caused by anaemia. The lesions were healed. The aetiology of anaemia is multifactoral and it is impossible to discern the direct cause of the porotic hyperostosis. Causes of anaemia include an iron-deficient diet, parasitic infection, chronic disease

Table 4.29: Summary of the disarticulated human remains

Context number	Small finds number	Skeletal element	Side	Age	Sex
6050	355	Mandible	-	30-38 years	Male
6050	-	Iliac blade	Left	Adult	Unsexed
6621	356	Mandible	-	24-30 years	Male
6621	-	Parietal	Right	Adult	Unknown
6621	-	Femur shaft	Right	Adult	Unknown
6621	-	Patella	Right	Adult	Unknown

and excessive blood loss (Roberts and Manchester 1995, 166-167).

Taphonomy

Mandible Sf 356 had longitudinal cracking present on the body. This is caused by weathering and indicates that the bone was exposed on the ground surface prior to deposition. The surface changes are slight and were recorded as stage 1, the mildest form of weathering seen on bone (after Behrensmeyer 1978).

Discussion

The placement of skeleton 6678 in a ditch must be seen as a deviant form of interment. As such, normal social identity is not expressed, but what is expressed is the circumstance of death and the types of sanctions which the society in question merited the individual (Shay 1985, 226).

The death penalty appears in English law codes from the end of the 7th century. It has been argued that until the 11th century, executed criminals were treated differently and buried separately as if their punishment had not ended with death (Daniell and Thompson 1999, 83). A series of characteristics has been identified which can be used for the identification of execution burials. These include random orientation, prone and decapitated corpses, instances of tied hands and location on, or adjacent to, principal boundaries (Reynolds 1997).

The location of skeleton 6678 within a 'boundary' ditch (Pl. 3.6) and the body position supports the contention that this individual was an execution victim. However, the bones also provide a far more detailed narrative as to what happened to the body after execution and prior to the rather haphazard disposal of the body in the ditch.

The female was missing the arms, head, neck and the 4th lumbar, and in addition there were carnivorous puncture marks on the spinal processes of the first and second lumbar vertebrae. The burial, along with skeletal and taphonomic evidence is consistent with her having been strung up and displayed after execution. The evidence of the ankles being very close together in the burial strongly suggests that the legs were bound together and that she was suspended upside-down. She was displayed in this manner until putrefaction was so advanced that the gravitational pull separated the body at its weakest point which would have been at the waist. This would account for the missing 4th lumbar since the vertebral elements adjacent to the point of separation would have become loosened and one vertebra could easily have become dislodged and carried off by scavenging mammals.

It is not possible to ascertain the exact length of time the woman was suspended before the body separated. The rate of decay is complicated and in this instance it is primarily affected by climatological factors such as humidity, precipitation and temperature (Sledzig 1998, 111). In general, the higher the temperature and humidity the more rapid the decomposition and in very hot humid conditions skeletonisation may occur in two to four weeks. On the other hand, cold weather slows decay and skeletonisation may take up to two years (Sledzig 1998, 111-112). However, given that the bones of the woman were scavenged by carnivores it seems likely that the remains would still have been fleshed. It is therefore possible to give a very tentative time estimate of weeks rather than months.

Assuming the body was suspended upside-down and out of the reach of carnivores, the arms would have been disarticulated through carnivorous activity *after* the upper half of the body had fallen to the ground. Studies of scavenging mammals have established that the sequence of exploitation of a carcass starts with the most meat bearing parts, which are usually the hindquarters followed by the forequarters (Lyman 1994, 147). The same pattern is observed in bone dispersal from carnivorous activity and the bones from the head would be the last part to be removed from the carcass (Lyman 1994, 187). The presence of the legs in the burial also adds to the premise that she was suspended upside-down. Had the whole of the body been accessible to scavengers, either on the ground or while suspended, the legs would have either been missing – like the arms – or there would have been carnivorous teeth marks present on them.

There are substantial amounts of ligaments and tendons surrounding the shoulder joint which makes this a relatively strong structure. The weakest attachment point of the arm to the torso is therefore the synovial joint between the manubrium and the clavicle. It was at this point the arms of the female had become separated from the body and they could have easily been dragged away and consumed elsewhere. However, the pattern of the missing bones from the woman does not follow the pattern of bone dispersal outlined above since it would have been more likely that the head would still have been attached to the torso. As the head was also missing, a more likely scenario may be that the woman was suspended by her feet, with her arms and head within reach of scavenging mammals. In this scenario, the arms and the head could have been torn off the body prior to the trunk dropping to the ground, indeed their activity may even have facilitated the separation of the torso from the hips.

However, what is certain is that the torso was partly eaten by carnivores once it was on the ground. The only elements with puncture marks were the first and second lumbars, consistent with a medium sized carnivore – most likely a dog. This strongly suggests a relatively low level of exploitation of the carcass, which may indicate that the torso was lying on the ground for a relatively short period of time, possibly a day or two. The legs were cut down from the scaffolding and removed together with the torso and the remains of the body was probably placed in an organic container such as a sack and deposited in the ditch. The position of the body in the ditch would therefore have been purely accidental with no premeditated thoughts regarding body position or orientation.

The disarticulated human remains found within the same fill of the ditch are likely to have been remains from other execution victims. The evidence of weathering on mandible Sf 356 indicated that this individual at least had also been displayed after death. Unfortunately, the time line given for the developing stage 1 is rather broad and ranges from 0-5 years for mammals (after Behrensmeyer 1978 and Andrews 1990). However, considering the location of the bones in the ditch and their disarticulated nature, it is likely that all three individuals had been displayed posthumously.

The remains indicate that over a period of time at least three individuals – two males and a female – were killed. The radiocarbon dating idicates that one of the males is likely to be a contemporary of the female and the other is substantially earlier. This suggests that the site was used for executions over a considerable period of time.

The neonate

The later burial of neonate 2591 is also a deviant form of interment. However, the age of the individual suggests that it was born slightly prematurely. The child may have been stillborn, or may have died shortly after birth and before being baptised. As such, the burial appears to be surreptitious and it is possible that the burial was carried out hurriedly since the grave was very shallow.

ANIMAL BONE *by Emma-Jayne Evans*
(with revisions by Lena Strid)

Introduction

A total of 10,149 fragments of bones and teeth were recovered from Saxon, medieval and post-medieval deposits; 643 fragments were recorded at the University of Birmingham by Umberto Albarella and Cluny Johnstone in 1995 during the assessment stage of Sites 1-3, with a further 9506 fragments from the remaining sites recorded by staff at OA.

Methodology

The bones recorded at the University of Birmingham were recorded using the methods described in Davis (1992) and Albarella and Davis (1994). Identification of the bone at OA was undertaken with access to the reference collection and published guides. All the animal remains were counted and weighed, and where possible identified to species, element, side and zone (Serjeantson 1996). Also, fusion data, butchery marks, gnawing, burning and pathological changes were noted when present. Ribs and vertebrae were only recorded to species when they were substantially complete and

could accurately be identified, or were from an identifiable articulated skeleton in which case there could be no doubt as to their species. Undiagnostic bones were recorded as small (small mammal size), medium (sheep size) or large (cattle size). The separation of sheep and goat was undertaken using the criteria of Boessneck (1969) and Prummel and Frisch (1986), in addition to the use of the reference material housed at OA. Where distinctions could not be made, the bone was recorded as sheep/goat (s/g).

The condition of the bone was graded using the criteria stipulated by Lyman (1996), grade 0 being the best preserved bone and grade 5 indicating that the bone had suffered such structural and attritional damage as to make it unrecognisable.

The quantification of species was carried out using the total fragment count, in which the total number of fragments of bone and teeth was calculated, and this figure broken down to the total number of fragments identifiable to each species. In addition the minimum number of individuals (MNI) was calculated using the zoning method (Serjeantson, 1996). The elements used for working out MNI do not include mandibles, ribs, vertebra, loose teeth, tarsals and carpals.

Tooth eruption and wear stages were measured using a combination of Halstead (1985), Grant (1982) and Levine (1982), and fusion data was analysed according to Silver (1969). Measurements of adult, that is, fully fused bones were taken according to the methods of von den Driesch (1976), with asterisked (*) measurements indicating bones that were reconstructed or had slight abrasion of the surface. Withers heights were calculated using Fock (1966), Harcourt (1974), Kieserwalter (von den Driesch and Boessneck 1974, 334), Teichert (1975) and Matolcsi (1970).

Results

The majority of the bone from this site was recovered by hand collection, as shown in Table 4.30. The only species recovered by sieving that were not

Table 4.30: Total number of hand collected and sieved animal bones

Phase	Hand collected	Sieved	Total
1	1338	960	2298
2b	1571	265	1836
2c	1201	544	1745
3	1027	177	1204
4	891	49	940
5	1428	151	1579
6	496	14	510
Unphased	37	-	37
Total	7989	2160	10149

Table 4.31: Domestic animals identified by species and phase

Phase	Cattle	Sheep/goat	Sheep	Goat	Pig	Horse	Dog	Cat	Unidentified	Total
1	158	125	6	3	121	5	3	1	1753	2175
2b	190	189	8	2	189	45	39	26	973	1661
2c	167	64	4	-	54	28	118	-	1261	1696
3	125	97	4	-	59	13	4	-	868	1170
4	104	98	2	-	61	17	57	-	582	921
5	132	165	5	1	72	47	20	4	1110	1556
6	121	40	2	-	18	6	14	-	274	475
U/s	4	4	-	-	3	-	-	-	26	37
Total	1001	782	31	6	577	161	255	31	6847	9691

present in the hand-collected material were the shrew, water vole, vole, mole and mouse. As only these few small mammals are added to the total species list from sieved material, both the hand-collected and sieved material will be discussed together in this report.

The condition of the bone from Higham Ferrers was good, with a large majority (approximately 77%), scoring 2 according to Lyman's grading. This good condition has allowed for a large variety of species to be identified, with approximately 32.5% of the total number of bone fragments being identifiable. Tables 4.31–3 show the species present at this site.

Phase 1: 5th – 6th century

The majority of the animal bones excavated were recovered from this phase. Of the sheep/goat bones, only six could positively be identified as sheep and one as goat, so therefore they will discussed as a single sheep/goat group.

The total fragment count suggests that cattle, sheep/goat and pig were present in similar numbers, with all other species much less frequent. The minimum number of individuals indicates that sheep/goat and pig were most common with an MNI of 4 each, with cattle being slightly lower at 3, although MNI is not a very reliable method when applied to small samples, it is less affected by

recovery bias. However, there is a much greater number of unidentifiable medium sized bones than large bones, which may also suggest that medium sized animals, that is sheep/goat and pig would have had much higher fragment counts than cattle if more of the bone had been identifiable to species, further substantiating the claim that sheep/goat and pig were present in higher numbers than cattle

The majority of the animal bone from this phase was recovered from SFBs, pits and associated postholes as shown in Table 4.34 below.

The age at death of cattle based on tooth wear and eruption stages could be estimated on five mandibles, and gave an age of 8–18 months for one individual, young adult for two individuals, adult and senile animal for the last two individuals. Although this is only based on a small sample, it seems that there were more animals being killed at a young age, most likely for meat production, with some older animals being kept probably for traction. The fusion data also supports the tooth wear data in that there were animals dying at a young age, with a minimum of two animals dying before reaching 1.5 years, and another two at 2–3 years and 3.5–4 years. However, out of all the bones available for assessment of fusion data, only 23.5% were seen to be unfused, suggesting that while cattle were killed at an optimum age for meat production, many had been kept into adult-

Table 4.32. Wild animals identified by species and phase

Phase	Red deer	Fallow deer	Roe deer	Hare	Rabbit	Fox	Badger	Field vole	Vole	Water vole	Mouse
1	3	-	1	-	1	-	-	22	3	3	4
2b	2	-	-	3	-	-	1	2	12	-	3
2c	2	-	-	-	1	-	-	3	3	1	2
3	-	-	-	-	-	-	-	1	1	-	2
4	2	-	-	-	-	1	-	-	-	-	-
5	-	1	-	1	-	-	-	-	-	-	-
6	-	-	1	-	-	-	-	-	-	-	-
U/s	-	-	-	-	-	-	-	-	-	-	-
Total	9	1	2	4	2	1	1	28	19	4	11

Table 4.33: Birds identified by species and phase

Phase	Domestic fowl	Goose	Mallard	Duck	Teal	Swan	Grey partridge	Crane	Buzzard	Crow	Swallow	Bird	Total
1	10	2	-	-	-	-	-	-	-	-	-	8	20
2b	76	5	1	1	1	3	1	-	-	2	1	28	117
2c	4	-	-	-	-	-	-	1	-	-	-	2	9
3	6	-	3	0	-	-	-	-	-	-	-	5	14
4	7	1	-	-	-	-	-	-	-	-	-	6	14
5	4	6	2	-	-	-	-	-	-	-	-	7	19
6	4	2	2	-	-	-	-	-	24	-	-	2	34
U/s	-	-	-	-	-	-	-	-	-	-	-	-	-
Total	111	16	8	1	1	3	1	1	24	2	1	58	228

Table 4.34: Distribution of identifiable animal bones from phase 1

	Sunken feature building	Posthole	Pit	Ditch	Finds reference	Gully	Layer	Total
Cattle	99	24	29	2	3	1	-	158
Sheep/goat	82	14	27	5	5	-	1	134
Pig	81	18	17	4	-	-	1	121
Horse	1	2	1	-	1	-	-	5
Dog	2	-	-	-	-	-	1	3
Cat	-	-	1	-	-	-	-	1
Domestic fowl	6	-	4	-	-	-	-	10
Goose	2	-	-	-	-	-	-	2
Red deer	3	-	-	-	-	-	-	3
Roe deer	1	-	-	-	-	-	-	1
Rabbit	-	-	1	-	-	-	-	1
Bird	2	-	5	-	-	-	1	8
Frog/toad	35	-	25	3	-	-	-	63
Field vole	-	15	-	7	-	-	-	22
Mole	-	-	-	1	-	-	-	1
Mouse	4	-	-	-	-	-	-	4
Shrew	1	-	-	1	-	-	-	2
Vole	3	-	-	-	-	-	-	3
Water vole	-	3	-	-	-	-	-	3
Total	322	76	110	23	9	1	4	545

Shrew	Mole	Rat	Frog/Toad	Total
2	1	-	63	103
2	1	-	27	53
1	-	-	29	42
-	-	-	12	16
-	-	-	2	5
-	-	1	1	4
-	-	-	-	1
-	-	-	-	-
5	2	1	134	224

hood, probably, as the tooth wear evidence suggests, for breeding and traction purposes. The presence of two neonatal bones may suggest the small scale use of milk, or they may simply be natural fatalities.

Butchery marks, most commonly chop marks through the shafts of long bones, were noted, suggesting that animals had been processed for meat and marrow. There is also evidence of skinning on a metacarpal and a proximal phalanx, which along with the meat and marrow production, suggests that the entire carcass was used. There is also some evidence of horn working, in the form of several horn cores which had been chopped at the base.

Withers heights could be calculated on two long bones, giving heights of 1.11 m and 1.13 m. Pathologies were noted on two bones, a pelvis with eburnation on the acetabulum indicative of the bone on bone wear often seen in degenerative joint disease such as arthritis, and the expansion of the lateral aspect of the proximal articulation of a second phalanx, which is often attributed to the stresses placed on the feet during traction.

A number of articulating cattle bones were found in fills of the SFBs, suggesting that they had suffered little or no disturbance once they had been deposited in the (presumably) disused SFB pits.

The age at death of sheep/goat based on tooth eruption and wear stages suggests that two animals died aged 3–10 months, four at 10–20 months, and one at 5–8 years. This young age at death pattern suggests that the majority of sheep/goats were exploited for meat production, with a small number being kept well into adulthood for breeding purposes and wool production. Fusion data also suggests that there were animals dying before reaching skeletal maturity, with 33.3% of the bones available for analysis being unfused. As with the cattle, it is likely that the animals kept into adulthood were used for breeding, and to a lesser extent for wool production. The presence of a few neonatal bones also suggests that sheep/goat were breeding within the vicinity of the site as it is unlikely that such young animals would have been imported.

Butchery marks were only noted on three bones, two of which had been chopped for marrow extraction, and another had dismemberment cut marks, indicating the processing of the carcasses for meat production. As with the cattle remains, withers height could be calculated on two long bones, giving a height of 0.62 m and 0.54 m. No pathologies were noted on any of the sheep/goat bones.

Tooth eruption and wear stages for pig suggest the age at death was immature for two animals and sub-adult for three. Fusion data supports the idea that the majority of the pigs were slaughtered at a young age for their meat, with 81.2% of the bones available for fusion data analysis being unfused. The presence of foetal bones also suggests that these animals were breeding within the vicinity of the site. The high proportion of juveniles in the assemblage is unsurprising as pigs were usually killed for their meat at an early age, and there was little to be gained in keeping them into adulthood.

Butchery marks were only present on one bone, a scapula with cut and chop marks along the edge of the blade. Pathological changes were noted on one pig bone in the form of well healed periostitis along the shaft of a 3rd metatarsal. This 3rd metatarsal was seen to articulate with a 4th metatarsal, a navicular and a cuboid, suggesting they had been not disturbed after deposition. A type 3 non-pathological depression was present on an ulna.

Only five horse bones were recovered from this phase, giving a minimum number of one. Fusion data provides the only ageing information,

suggesting that all the remains are from adult horses. Withers heights could not be calculated from any of the bones present, and no butchery marks or pathologies were noted.

The three dog bones present suggest a minimum number of one, as does the single cat bone recovered. The minimum number of domestic fowl is three, one of which has a spur on the tarso-metatarsus, indicating that it is likely to be male. Cut marks on two bones suggests that they could have been kept for meat, but it is also likely that they were kept for eggs and possibly for cock fighting. The goose bones are consistent with an unimproved domestic form, and one bone bears a cut mark, highlighting their use for meat production.

Red deer is represented by three bones, one of which was a worked fragment of shed antler. Only one roe deer bone was recovered, which suggests that while deer were hunted during this phase, it is unlikely that they contributed a great deal to the diet of the local population. The remaining wild species present, namely rabbit and various small mammals are likely to be intrusive, and to have died naturally rather than being exploited by the human population.

Phase 2: Late 7th – Early 9th century

Sub-phase 2a: Late 7th century to mid 8th century

No animal bones were recovered from Phase 2a deposits

Sub-phase 2b: Mid 8th century to late 8th century

As with phase 1, cattle, sheep/goat and pig dominate the assemblage from phase 2b. Of the sheep/goat bones, only eight were positively identified as sheep and two as goat, therefore these will be discussed together as sheep/goat. The total fragment count from this phase suggests that sheep/goat are the dominant species with cattle and pig following closely behind, whereas the minimum number of individuals suggests that pig are dominant with eight, followed by seven sheep/goats and three cattle. The fact that pig and sheep/goat are more common is further supported by the fact there are a great deal more unidentifiable medium-sized fragments than large fragments, which if they had been identifiable to species would have no doubt increased the minimum number of these animals.

Table 4.35 shows that the majority of the bone from this phase was recovered from ditches, with with limited quantities recovered from pits and postholes.

The age at death of cattle based on tooth wear and eruption stages was estimated for seven mandibles, giving ages of 8–18 months, 30–36 months, young adult, two adult and two senile. Although this is again based on a small sample, there do appear to be slightly more cattle kept into

Table 4.35. Distribution of animal bone from phase 2b

	Ditch	Pit	Post hole	Total
Cattle	176	10	4	190
Sheep/goat	188	8	3	199
Pig	180	5	4	189
Horse	44	-	1	45
Dog	38	-	1	39
Cat	26	-	-	26
Domestic fowl	76	-	-	76
Goose	5	-	-	5
Red deer	2	-	-	2
Hare	3	-	-	3
Badger	1	-	-	1
Bird	28	-	-	28
Frog/toad	20	2	5	27
Field vole	2	-	-	2
Mole	1	-	-	1
Mouse	3	-	-	3
Shrew	1	-	1	2
Vole	-	-	12	12
Swan	3	-	-	3
Crow	2	-	-	2
Duck	1	-	-	1
Mallard	1	-	-	1
Swallow	1	-	-	1
Teal	1	-	-	1
Grey partridge	1	-	-	1
Total	804	25	31	860

adulthood than in the earlier phase, perhaps indicating a greater dependence on the use of cattle for traction. The fusion data also suggests that cattle were being kept into adulthood, with 21.4% of the bones coming from juvenile animals.

Evidence of butchery was noted on many bones, in the form of both dismemberment marks and chops, suggesting the processing of carcasses probably for for marrow extraction. As with the earlier phase there is some evidence of horn working in the form of horn cores that have been chopped through the base, and evidence of skinning in the form of chop marks through a 1st phalanx.

Withers heights could be calculated on five bones, giving heights of 1.07 m, two at 1.11 m, 1.23 m and 1.41 m. Pathological changes were only observed on one bone; a pelvis with eburnation on the acetabulum as with the pelvis from phase 1. A type 2 non-pathological depression was also noted on a mandibular condyle. A number of articulating cattle bones were recovered from a ditch fill, suggesting they had undergone very little disturbance after their final deposition.

The age at death of sheep/goat could be estimated for thirty mandibles using tooth eruption and wear analysis. Four were aged at 1–3 months, six at 3–10 months, eight at 10–20 months, four at

20–34 months, six at 3–5 years, one at 5–8 years and one at >8 years. This age at death pattern suggests that the majority of sheep/goats were being killed, at an optimum age for meat production before reaching adulthood. The presence of some older individuals may represent those kept for breeding purposes or small scale wool production. The fusion data also suggests that many animals were being killed before reaching skeletal maturity, with 39% of the bones available for fusion data analysis being unfused. The presence of a foetal tibia suggests that the breeding of these animals occurred within the immediate vicinity of the site, or that a pregnant ewe was brought to the site and then miscarried or was killed whilst there.

Dismemberment cut marks were noted on several bones, as were chop marks, both indicating that the animals had been processed for their meat and marrow. Withers heights could not be calculated on the sheep/goat bones from this phase, and pathological changes were only noted on a mandible with much expansion of the bone around the premolars, and porosity of bone around the expansion, probably due to an infection.

The age at death of pigs was estimated on twenty three mandibles using tooth eruption and wear stages and gives ages of juvenile for seven mandibles, immature for two, sub-adult for eleven and adult for three. This suggests that the vast majority of the pigs on site during this phase were sub-adult or younger, which is also reflected in the fusion data analysis, with 69.8% of bones used for fusion data analysis being unfused. Dismemberment butchery marks were only noted on two bones. The remains of a partially articulated carcass were recovered from the large enclosure ditch. The carcass was aged as adult using the tooth wear analysis, but fusion data suggests it could not have been more than 3 years old.

The minimum number of horses from this phase is two. Age at death could only be estimated using fusion data, which suggest that at least one animal died around 3–3.5 years of age. The remaining bones were all fully fused. Butchery marks were found on three bones, two astragali, which appear to have skinning marks, and an atlas with dismemberment marks. Horses are likely to have been kept for riding and light traction rather than for their meat, but would more than likely have been slaughtered as they started to decline with age. It is probable that the meat may then have been used, possibly to feed the dogs, and their hides would have been used for leather working.

The partial remains of an articulating adult horse skeleton, comprising twenty-one bones of the vertebrae and forelimbs, was found in ditch fill 2302. Withers heights could be calculated on one bone, giving a height of 1.39 m. No pathologies were observed on any of the horse bones.

The minimum number of dogs is two, one of which is represented by a partial articulating skeleton recovered from a ditch fill (context 1056) and comprises the forelimbs. The only ageing data available comes from one unfused proximal ulna, suggesting an age at death for one animal as before 9–10 months. Two skulls have been smashed in the back in a similar fashion, which may suggest the deliberate breaking of the skulls to access the brain. One incidence of pathology was noted, a mandible with the second molar missing, with the root socket being well healed.

Of the twenty six cat bones recovered, twenty one come from an almost complete sub-adult cat skeleton, recovered from a ditch context 2440. The minimum number of cats is therefore two. No butchery marks or pathologies were noted on any of the cat bones

A large proportion of the domestic fowl bones from this site were recovered from this phase. The minimum number is six, four of which were recovered from ditch 15099. Butchery marks were only noted on one bone, but as domestic fowl is easy to pull apart once cooked, it is not necessary to use knives to dismember the bird during consumption.

The minimum number of goose is one. There are similar minimum numbers for mallard, teal, swan and grey partridge. This phase provides the evidence for the greatest variety of birds being consumed on the site. All were discarded in the enclosure ditch. Two fragments of unworked red deer antler were also recovered from the enclosure ditch, but these may have been brought into the site as shed antler, perhaps found in the surrounding landscape. The presence of hare, badger, crow and swallow, and the small mammals including field vole, water vole, mouse, shrew, mole and frog/toad are likely to be intrusive animals, present as natural fatalities.

Sub phase 2c: Late 8th century to early 9th century

There is a change in the total fragment count of the main domestic species in this Phase. Cattle are dominant, with many fewer sheep/goat fragments, and pig with only a third the numbers of cattle bones. The four sheep bones recovered will be discussed with the sheep/goat bones. There is a minimum of four cattle, three sheep/goats and three pigs. There is also a change in the numbers of fragments recovered with considerably more large fragments recovered compared to medium ones, suggesting that the minimum number of cattle would be higher than sheep/goat if more of the bone could have been identified to species. This contrasts with phases 1 and 2b, which yielded more of medium sized fragments than large.

Table 4.36 shows that, as with phase 2b, the majority of the animal bone is recovered from ditches, most of it from ditch 7330. Much of the bone from pits was recovered from pit 7503.

Age at death for cattle was calculated on eleven mandibles using tooth eruption and wear stages and gave ages of 1–8 months, 8–18 months for two mandibles, 18–30 months for one, young adult for

Table 4.36: Distribution of animal bone from phase 2c

	Beam slot	Ditch	Hearth	Pit	Post hole	Total
Cattle	3	127	-	37	2	169
Sheep/goat	-	37	2	29	6	74
Pig	-	42	3	6	5	56
Horse	1	22	-	5	-	28
Dog	-	117	-	1	-	118
Domestic fowl	-	4	-	1	-	5
Red deer	-	2	-	-	-	2
Rabbit	-	-	-	1	-	1
Bird	-	1	1	-	1	3
Frog/toad	-	23	6	-	-	29
Field vole	-	3	-	-	-	3
Water vole	-	1	-	-	-	1
Mouse	-	2	-	-	-	2
Shrew	-	1	-	-	-	1
Vole	-	3	-	-	-	3
Crane	-	1	-	-	-	1
Total	4	234	12	79	3	320

two, adult for one, old adult for one and senile for three. As with the other phases this age at death pattern suggests that the majority of animals were being killed before reaching maturity, indicating an economy based on meat production. It's likely that the older animals were those kept for breeding and traction purposes. The fusion data indicates that, with 33.9% of the bones used for analysis being unfused, a reasonable number were being kept into adulthood, further substantiating the tooth wear evidence that older animals were being kept for breeding and traction.

Butchery marks were noted on a number of bones, in the form of dismemberment cut marks and chops through the shaft of long bones, indicating the processing of carcasses for meat and marrow. Withers heights could be estimated for five cattle bones, giving heights of 1.07 m, 1.10 m, 1.13 m and 1.24 m for two. Pathological changes were noted on a pelvis, with eburnation and pitting of the acetabulum, characteristic of osteoarthritis. Articulations were seen between vertebra and a sacrum, from ditch 7330, which may represent the disposal of a carcass after primary butchery, with the meat bearing limb bones being taken elsewhere on the site.

Age at death of sheep/goat using tooth eruption and wear stages could be calculated on seven mandibles, with four giving an age of 10–20 months, and three an age of 3–5 years. This indicates that sheep/goat were kept for meat and wool production. With only 14.3% of the bones available for fusion analysis being unfused, it is likely that the herds contained a substantial amount of older animals. These were probably kept for breeding purposes and wool production.

Butchery marks in the form of dismemberment cut marks and the chopping of long bone shafts were only present on four bones. No pathologies were noted on any of the bones, and withers heights could not be calculated from any of the measurements taken.

Only three pig mandibles could be aged, suggesting two immature and one adult individual. The fusion data suggests that 70% of the bones came from juvenile animals, which is unsurprising as pigs are usually killed at a young age for their meat. Dismemberment cut marks were seen on a scapula, but no pathologies or articulations were noted on any of the bones. Articulations were noted between an atlas, axis and two cervical vertebra, suggesting little disturbance after their disposal. An ulna has a type 3 non-pathological depression on the articulation.

The minimum number of horse from this phase is two. One unfused distal tibia suggests that at least one individual died before reaching 1.5–2 years, and an unfused ulna suggests another died before reaching 3.5 years. A femur, humerus and tibia had been chopped through the shaft, probably for marrow extraction. Articulations of two groups of bones were present, a lower hind leg, and an upper fore leg.

The minimum number of dog from this phase is two, with all the bones except eleven being recovered from ditch 7330. The majority of the dog remains are from two articulating skeletons, both from context 6193. The presence of deciduous teeth and unfused phalanges suggests that at least one was a puppy. Withers heights were calculated on both skeletons from context 6193, one giving a height of 0.54 m, and the other giving heights varying from 0.33 to 0.38. This variation in the heights from the second skeleton can be explained by the fact that the dog displays signs of having suffered from rickets, resulting in noticeable length

differences in the bones present. Some elements were more affected than others. Rickets is quite an unusual disease to find in carnivores, and suggests that the dog must have had a poor diet, and was kept indoors for most of its life. Pathological changes were also noted on one ulna from context 6051, which displayed new bone formation around the articulation, possibly the result of a trauma and/or non-specific infection.

The minimum number of domestic fowl is one; the only other bird species identifiable was crane, a bird not uncommon in Saxon times. It is likely that the crane was consumed on site, as these birds would have been eaten at this time, and a single bone of this species is unlikely to be present through natural causes.

The only representation of red deer from this phase was a skull fragment and a piece of antler that had been chopped through the base of the tine and hollowed out. The only other wild mammals present were a rabbit, and various small mammals such as field vole, water vole, mouse, shrew and frog/toad.

Phase 3: Mid 9th century to 11th century

Cattle continue to be dominant in total fragment count in this phase. Four sheep bones were identified, and will be discussed with the sheep/goat remains. There is a minimum of six cattle, four sheep/goats and two pigs. There is more medium sized unidentifiable fragments than large (246 fragments compared to 163), which may increase the minimum number of sheep/goat and/or pig, but it is still fair to say that cattle was the more dominant species. The bones from this phase were recovered from a large variety of features, with pits being the most common for bone deposition.

Age at death of cattle could be ascertained from one mandible, giving the age of old adult. Although

Table 4.37: Distribution of animals bones from phase 3

	Ditch	Pit	Gully	Post hole	Sunken feature building	Hearth	Quarry pit	Beam slot	Layer	Stake hole	Tree throw/ Bowl	Finds reference	Unknown	Total
Cattle	26	35	9	7	8	-	3	1	-	3	2	6	2	102
Sheep/goat	28	28	4	4	5	1	1	3	1	-	2	1	1	79
Pig	12	13	6	0	3	1	-	-	2	1	1	3	-	50
Horse	2	4	-	-	2	-	1	-	1	-	-	-	-	10
Dog	-	3	-	1	-	-	-	-	-	-	-	-	-	4
Domestic fowl	2	2	-	2	-	-	-	-	-	-	-	-	-	6
Mallard	-	2	-	-	-	1	-	-	-	-	-	-	-	3
Bird	1	1	-	2	-	-	-	-	-	-	-	1	-	5
Frog/toad	-	5	-	-	-	2	-	-	-	-	-	-	1	8
Field vole	-	-	-	1	-	-	-	-	-	-	-	-	-	1
Mouse	-	1	-	-	-	-	-	-	-	-	-	-	-	1
Vole	1	-	-	-	-	1	-	-	-	-	-	-	-	1
Total	71	94	19	25	18	6	5	4	4	4	5	11	4	270

tooth wear analysis suggests that only older animals were present, 9.1% of the bones analysed were unfused, suggesting that some young individuals were present also. It is therefore likely that, as with the other phases cattle were used for both meat and traction.

Butchery marks were noted on several bones, primarily in the form of chops through the shafts of long bones. There are cut marks present on a mandible, possibly caused during dismemberment, to gain access to the tongue. Withers heights could be calculated on two bones, giving heights of 1.02 m and 1.11 m.

The age at death of sheep/goat was calculated on five mandibles, giving ages of 1–3 months, 20-34 months and 3-5 years for three mandibles. The presence of very young individuals suggests that the animals are breeding close to the site, and it appears that more sheep/goats were being kept into adulthood in this phase. The fusion data also indicates that 29.4% of bones were unfused, which along with the tooth wear information perhaps reveals a change in the economy to one based primarily on wool production, but with some animals still being killed at an early age for meat.

Dismemberment cut marks and chops through the shafts of long bones suggest that some sheep/goats were being processed for meat and marrow. Withers heights could not be calculated from any of the bone measurements, and no articulations were seen between any bones. One metatarsal has a lump on the shaft, possibly due to trauma.

Two pig mandibles could be aged, suggesting one immature and one sub-adult animal. A total of 77.8% of relevant bones were unfused, suggesting that a large proportion of the pig population were killed before reaching maturity. A large proportion of the pig bones comprise teeth and feet bones, further suggesting that the animals were brought in as whole carcasses and processed at the site. The

presence of foetal/neonatal bones also suggests that they were breeding within the vicinity of the site.

Butchery marks were only noted on one maxilla, probably occurred during dismemberment.

The minimum number of horse is one. One animal was aged at 5.5–7.5 years. One unfused proximal tibia suggests another animal died before reaching 3–3.5 years of age. Two bones have been chopped through the shaft, probably for marrow extraction. Withers height could not be calculated from the measurements taken, and no pathologies were noted.

The minimum number of dog is one. The majority of the remains were recovered from pit 6675, with one bone from posthole 6136.

A minimum of one domestic fowl was recovered, with at least one juvenile present. The only other bird species identified was mallard. The only wild mammals present were various small creatures such as field vole and mouse. There is also evidence for frog/toad.

Phase 4: 12th century to 14th century

The total fragment counts of cattle and sheep/goat from this phase are almost equal, with pig present in fewer numbers. Two sheep bones were identified, which have been combined with the sheep/goat bones for this discussion. The minimum number suggests that sheep/goats are the dominant at four, with a minimum of three cattle and pig present. There are considerably more medium sized unidentifiable fragments than large fragments, further suggesting that sheep/goat and possibly pig were more numerous than cattle during this phase.

The bones are distributed throughout a variety of features, with pits being the most common for bone deposition, as shown in Table 4.38 below.

Age at death could be estimated using three mandibles, gives ages of 18–30 months, adult and

Table 4.38: Distribution of animal bones from phase 4

	Ditch	Drain	Gully	Layer	Pit	Post hole	Quarry pit	Structure	Tree throw	Total
Cattle	36	1	3	1	52	-	10	1	-	104
Sheep/goat	47	-	4	-	36	-	12	-	1	100
Pig	33	-	-	-	20	1	6	1	-	61
Horse	3	-	2	-	9	2	1	-	-	17
Dog	-	-	1	-	55	-	1	-	-	57
Domestic fowl	4	-	-	-	2	-	-	-	1	7
Goose	-	-	-	-	1	-	-	-	-	1
Red deer	1	-	-	-	1	-	-	-	-	2
Bird	2	-	-	-	2	-	1	1	-	6
Fox	1	-	-	-	-	-	-	-	-	1
Frog/toad	1	-	-	-	1	-	-	-	-	2
Total	128	1	10	1	179	3	31	3	2	358

old adult. Fusion data suggests that 20.7 % of relevant bones were unfused, suggesting that cattle were used for both meat and traction. Dismemberment cut marks were noted on several bones, and many had been chopped for marrow extraction. Skinning marks were also noted around the base of a single horn core. This suggests that cattle were used for a number of different products during this phase.

Withers heights could not be calculated from any of the measurements taken of the bones, and no articulations or pathologies were observed. A type 1 non-pathological depression is present on the proximal articulation of a 2nd phalanx.

Age at death of sheep/goat was calculated for eight mandibles, giving ages of 10–20 months for three, 20–34 months for one, 3–5 years for two, 5–8 years for one and >8 years for another. This suggests a mixed economy of wool and meat production. Fusion data suggests that 35% of relevant bones were unfused, further substantiating the tooth wear evidence that sheep were kept for meat and wool. The presence of foetal/neonatal bones also suggests that sheep/goats were being bred within the vicinity of the site.

One bone had been chopped for marrow extraction, and there were cut marks evident on a mandibular ramus, probably caused by dismemberment to gain access to the tongue. Withers heights could not be calculated from any of the measurements taken, and no pathologies were observed on any of the bones.

Five pig mandibles could be aged, giving ages of immature for two and sub-adult for three. Fusion data indicated that 43.8% of the bones analysed were unfused, suggesting that almost half of the pigs were killed before reaching skeletal maturity. Cut marks were noted on several bones, and some had been chopped for marrow extraction. No pathologies were recorded, and only one articulation between a radius and ulna was observed, from ditch 7329.

A minimum number of two horses were recovered from this phase, neither of which could be aged using tooth eruption and wear stages. Fusion data suggests that the horses had reached skeletal maturity before they died. One cut mark was observed on a 2nd metacarpal, which also had pathological changes; it appears to have been fusing to the 3rd metacarpal with bone remodelling, and was possibly caused by infection along shaft. Articulations were observed between a 2nd, 3rd and 4th metatarsal from pit 9439.

The minimum number of dogs is two. The majority of the bones are from an articulating skeleton from pit 15567, and appear to be from an adult dog. There is also a mandible from quarry pit 9344, which has been aged as <6-7 months, and an unfused scapula from pit 9341, possibly of the same age at death. Withers heights could be calculated on the skeleton, giving a height of approximately 0.40 m. No pathologies or

butchery marks were seen on any of the bones.

A minimum number of three domestic fowl were recovered from this phase, one of which was a juvenile bird. A single goose bone, from pit 6267, suggests that geese had been eaten during this phase, although how much they would have contributed to the diet cannot be inferred from a single bone. A fragment of red deer antler and a metatarsal with dismemberment cut marks indicates that the local population perhaps undertook some hunting. The remaining wild animals identified from this phase were a single fox bone and two frog/toad bones.

Phase 5: Late 14th – late 15th century

The total fragment count from this phase suggests that sheep/goat were present in greater numbers than cattle and pig. This is also true of the minimum number of individuals, which suggests a minimum of nine sheep/goats, five pig and four cattle. There is also a greater number of unidentified medium sized fragments than large fragments, which would likely further increase the numbers of sheep/goat and perhaps pig. Five sheep bones and one goat bone were identified from this phase, which will be discussed with the sheep/goat remains.

The majority of the bones were recovered from quarry pits, with slightly fewer from ditches, and the remaining bone scattered over a number of features, as shown in Table 4.39 below.

Age at death of cattle could be determined from two mandibles, giving ages of 1-8 months and 8-18 months. It is difficult to determine the use of cattle from only two ageable mandibles, but the fusion data suggests that 26.6% of the relevant bones were unfused, which is similar to the evidence from earlier phases and suggests that cattle had been kept for meat production, and to a lesser extent for traction.

Butchery marks are primarily those attributed to marrow extraction, but there is also evidence of dismemberment and skinning, suggesting that the entire carcass was used. Withers heights could be calculated for two individuals, giving heights of 1.03 m and 1.13 m. Pathological changes were observed on one bone, a metatarsal with osteophytic lipping and slight porosity of the proximal articulation, characteristic of degenerative joint disease. A 2nd phalanx has a type 1 non-pathological lesion on the proximal articulation.

Age at death for sheep/goats could be estimated using eight mandibles, and gave ages of 3–10 months for one, 10–20 months for one, 20–34 months for three, 3–5 years for two and 5–8 years for one. This suggests that the majority had been killed at an optimum age for meat production before reaching adulthood. The presence of three older individuals may suggest that some sheep/goats had been kept for wool, which is further substantiated by the fusion data, which indicates that 16.7% of bones were fused.

Table 4.39. Distribution of animal bone from phase 5

	Ditch	Gully	Kiln	Layer	Other	Oven	Pit	Post hole	Quarry pit	Sunken feature building	Trackway	Total
Cattle	42	3	5	11	-	1	9	3	55	3	-	132
Sheep/goat	69	4	4	15	2	-	8	2	56	11	-	171
Pig	18	2	2	4	-	-	2	1	43	-	-	72
Horse	18	2	5	-	-	-	1	-	18	2	1	47
Dog	5	-	-	-	-	-	1	-	14	-	-	20
Cat	-	-	1	-	-	-	-	-	3	-	-	4
Domestic fowl	-	-	1	-	-	-	1	-	2	-	-	4
Goose	1	-	3	1	-	-	-	-	1	-	-	6
Mallard	-	1	-	-	-	-	-	-	1	-	-	2
Bird	1	-	2	1	-	-	-	-	3	-	-	7
Fallow deer	1	-	-	-	-	-	-	-	-	-	-	1
Frog/toad	-	-	-	-	-	-	-	1	-	-	-	1
Hare	-	-	-	-	-	-	-	-	1	-	-	1
Rat	-	-	-	-	-	-	-	-	1	-	-	1
Total	155	12	23	32	2	1	22	7	198	16	1	469

Dismemberment cut marks are present on a number of bones, and many have been chopped for marrow extraction. Withers heights could not be determined from any of the measurements taken. Pathological changes were seen on a mandible, with swelling of medial aspect around M1 and M2, possibly due to an infection at tooth roots.

Nine pig mandibles could be aged, giving ages of juvenile for one, immature for two and sub-adult for six. This suggests that all the pigs had been killed before reaching maturity, but the fusion data suggests that only part of the pig population had been killed as juveniles, with 35% of the bones being unfused. Cut and chop marks are present on a number of bones, and an ulna has a type 3 non-pathological lesion on its articulation.

Horse bones from this phase give a MNI of two, although age at death could be calculated for at least five individuals, giving ages of 6.5–9 years, 7–9.75 years, 9.75–12.25 years, 11–20 years and 14+ years. All the horse bones were fused, with the exception of a calcaneus, suggesting one animal died before the age of three. Withers heights could be calculated of one individual, giving a height of 1.37 m. Two sets of left astragalus and calcaneus – one from quarry pit 6798, and the other from kiln 9072 – were articulated. The articulating tarsals from the kiln had eburnation and porosity on their articulations, with extensive new bone growth, characteristic of osteoarthritis. A metatarsal had tarsals fused to the proximal articulation, with extensive new bone growth around the joint, characteristic of spavin.

The minimum number of dogs is two. All the bones are fused, suggesting that all the remains recovered are from adult dogs. Withers heights could be calculated for one individual, giving a

height of 0.38 m. An astragalus and calcaneus from ditch 15158 were seen to articulate.

Four cat bones were recovered, two of which were from juveniles. The birds present from this phase include domestic fowl, goose and mallard, all of which are likely to have been exploited for their meat, and possibly eggs. The wild species are represented by fallow deer and hare, and single rat bone and one frog/toad bone.

Phase 6: 16th – 19th century

A large proportion of the bones from this phase come from pits as shown in Table 4.40 below. Most of the bones are from cattle and give a minimum number of twenty. Sheep/goats were present in fewer numbers with a minimum number of five, and pig have a minimum of only two. The high minimum number of cattle is due to a large number of horn cores, the majority of which were recovered from pit 9342.

Age at death of cattle could only be determined using one mandible, giving an age of 1-8 months. Of the bones used for fusion analysis, only 8.3% were unfused, suggesting that the majority of animals had reached skeletal maturity. As most of the bones are horn cores from horn-working debris, there is too small a sample to infer animal husbandry regimes, but butchery marks on several bones suggest that at least some of the cattle were processed for consumption. One of the cattle skulls recovered has holes in the parietal bone, thought to be of congenital origin. Withers heights could not be calculated on any of the bones present, and no pathological changes were noted.

The age at death of sheep/goats was calculated on two mandibles, both giving ages of 5-8 years.

Table 4.40: Distribution of animal bone from phase 6

	Demolition layer	Ditch	Evaluation trench	Finds reference	Gully	Layer	Pit	Quarry pit	Rubble layer	Structure	Subsoil	Wall	Well	Total
Cattle	28	-	1	1	1	11	77	1	-	-	-	-	1	121
Sheep/goat	2	1	-	7	2	11	15	1	-	2	-	1	-	42
Pig	2	-	-	-	-	7	5	-	1	2	1	-	-	18
Horse	-	1	-	-	-	-	4	-	-	1	-	-	-	6
Dog	-	2	-	1	-	1	10	-	-	-	-	-	-	14
Domestic fowl	-	-	-	-	-	-	3	-	-	-	-	-	1	4
Goose	-	-	-	1	1	-	-	-	-	-	-	-	-	2
Mallard	-	-	-	-	-	-	2	-	-	-	-	-	-	2
Bird	-	-	-	-	-	-	2	-	-	-	-	-	-	2
Roe deer	-	-	-	1	-	-	-	-	-	-	-	-	-	1
Buzzard	-	-	-	-	-	24	-	-	-	-	-	-	-	24
Total	32	4	1	11	4	54	118	2	1	5	1	1	2	236

Fusion data suggests that only 13.3% of the bones were unfused, which, along with the tooth wear data suggests that the majority of the sheep/goat were being kept well into adulthood, perhaps reflecting a change in the economy to one predominantly based on wool production.

Butchery marks were noted on three bones, one with cut marks, and another two which had been chopped. Withers heights could be determine for one individual, giving a height of 0.57 m. No articulations were seen between any of the bones.

Age at death for pig was calculated on two mandibles, giving ages of immature and sub-adult. The sample of pig bones is very small and the evidence for the proportion of unfused bones – only 50% – may not be representative of the age at death of the pig population as a whole. Cut marks were noted on two bones, but no pathologies or articulations were seen on any of the bones.

The minimum number of horse is one. Very little information can be gained from such a small sample, although the presence of a canine tooth suggests that at least one individual was a male. A minimum of two dogs were present during this phase, with four bones from pit 15189 likely to come from the same animal. A minimum of one domestic fowl was recovered, one bone of which exhibited dismemberment cut marks. Goose and mallard were also present, both of which are likely to have been consumed. The remains of a buzzard were recovered from layer 9004. This is more likely to have been a natural fatality rather than the product of human exploitation. The only other wild species recovered from this phase was a roe deer, represented by a single antler fragment, which had been chopped from the skull at the base.

Discussion (Fig. 4.30)

Although none of the bone samples from any phase on this site is large, some interesting conclusions may be drawn as to the use of domestic and wild species from the Saxon and medieval periods at Higham Ferrers. Domestic species are present in varying numbers throughout all periods, with some exploitation of wild species and birds also occurring, suggesting that whilst cattle, sheep/goat and pig provided the majority of the meat for the local population, the diet was supplemented by birds such as domestic fowl, goose and duck, and by the small scale hunting of deer.

During phase 1 and sub-phase 2b, sheep/goat, closely followed by pig appear to have been the dominant species, with cattle less exploited. While cattle probably provided the greatest amount of meat, sheep/goat would have been the most numerous animals providing not only meat, but also milk and wool. The evidence for high numbers of pigs from the Saxon period is not uncommon for this time, and they only started to decline in the later middle Saxon period (Phase 2c) and medieval phases, suggesting that there was no substantial decline in the woodland coverage until the late Saxon period. Phase 2c and 3 saw a change in the balance of livestock species; cattle became dominant and there was a relative decline in the numbers of sheep/goat and pig. However, the medieval period saw a reversion back to the predominance of sheep/goat, which is not unexpected as the wool industry increased during this period. The withers heights of cattle and sheep/goat provide too small a sample for any in-depth analysis, but they appear to be consistent with those expected from the Saxon and medieval periods.

Age at death is commonly used to determine animal butchery techniques, and this site is no exception. Throughout all phases cattle appear to have been primarily used for meat, and to a lesser extent for traction. Pathologies on some of the cattle bones suggest that some animals were suffering from osteoarthritis, a degenerative joint disease often associated with old age. Pathological changes

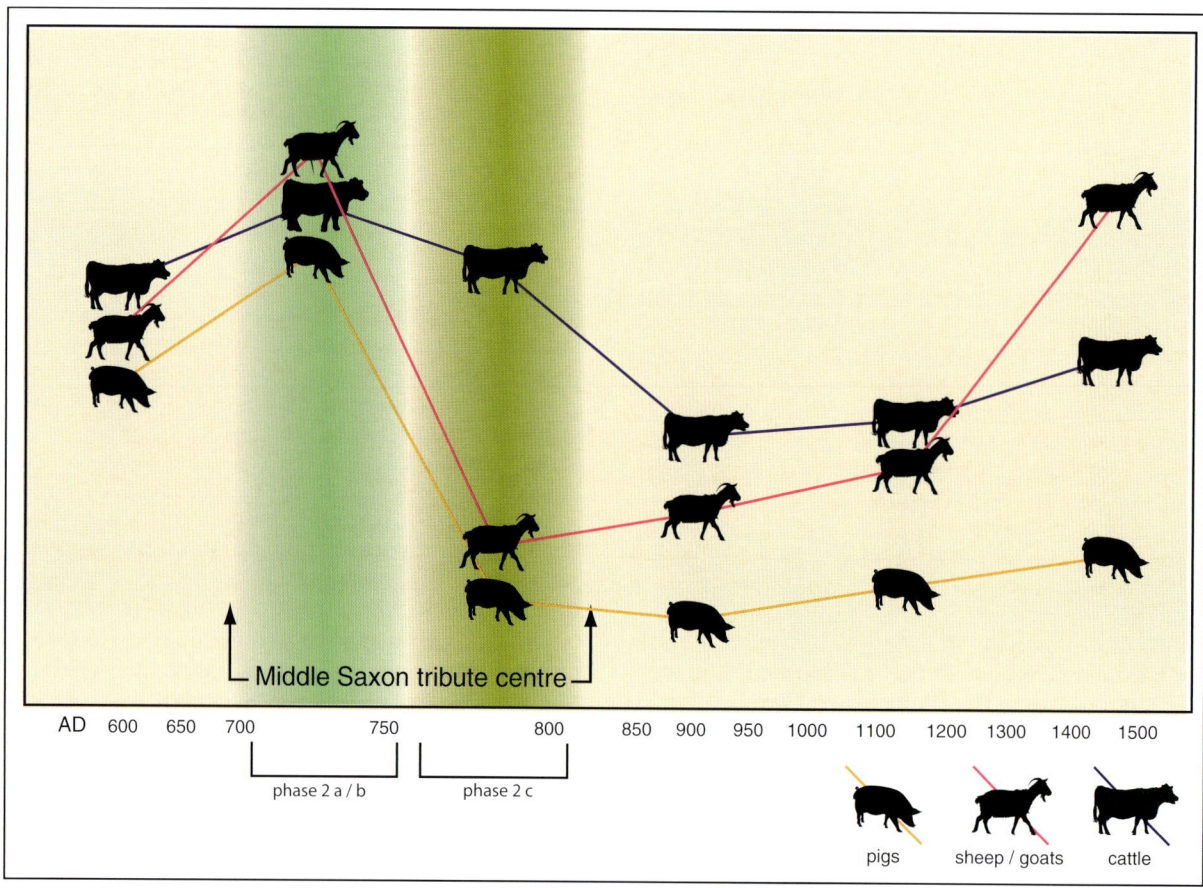

Fig. 4.30   Animal bone occurrence by species and phase

attributed to stress related trauma were also seen on several foot bones, a condition often associated with animals used for traction. There is some slight evidence – the presence of a number of neonatal bones – that cattle may have been exploited for small scale milk production, but these may just as easily have been the result of natural infant mortalities. It is only in Phase 6 that there is any evidence of definite industrial scale animal exploitation. This was a pit (9342) on Site 7, which produced a notable quantity of waste from horn working, although it was only partially excavated,

Sheep/goat also seem to have been primarily kept for meat production, but there is some evidence to suggest they had also been used for milk and wool. As with the cattle, some sheep/goat had been kept into adulthood, which would only have been for breeding and/or wool production. This is particularly evident in phases 2c, 5 and 6, where although the tooth wear evidence suggests that they had been killed at an optimum age for meat production, the fusion data shows a big decline in the number of unfused juvenile bones, suggesting a large part of the population had been kept into adulthood.

The age at death of pig is consistently young throughout all phases, which is not unexpected, as other than for breeding purposes there is little to be gained from keeping pigs into adulthood. There is an increase in the number of adult bones in the later medieval periods, as pig became increasingly domesticated and would have been bred closer to the site, and perhaps in the back yards of individual households, as opposed to roaming in the surrounding woodland in the earlier Saxon periods.

Horse is present but infrequent throughout all the phases, and primarily would have been kept for riding and light traction. Butchery marks on some of the horse bones are likely to represent the use of old animals for their hides, as food for animals and to a smaller extent maybe for the local population. While the consumption of horsemeat was officially banned by Pope Gregory III in AD 732, it is quite likely that horse meat – if available – would have been consumed when times were hard (Hollis 1946).

Dogs appear to have been present throughout the Saxon and medieval phases, which is not uncommon as they would have been kept as guard dogs and for hunting. The butchery of dogs is only evident from Phase 2b; two skulls appear to have been deliberately broken in a similar manner, possibly to extract the brain. However, it is unlikely that dog had been consumed regularly during any of the phases represented at Higham Ferrers. Pathological changes on an articulating dog skeleton from phase 2c are indicative of rickets. This disease is uncommon in carnivores and was probably caused by a poor diet and a lack of vitamin D and by keeping the animal indoors – perhaps as a guard dog. Cats had also been present during phases 1, 2b and 5, and would have been tolerated for keeping down the numbers rodents around the site.

Domestic fowl were eaten consistently throughout all the periods from Higham Ferrers, with goose and duck also complementing the diet. These birds may have also provided eggs, and domestic fowl may have been used for cock fighting. Possible evidence for the hunting of red and roe deer is only seen in the earlier phases, although with such a small sample it is unlikely that deer would have contributed a great deal to the everyday diet of the local population. A single fallow deer bone was recovered from phase 5, suggesting that hunting had added little to the diet of the medieval population. The remaining wild species present, including rabbit, fox, badger and small rodents are likely to have been intrusive and not animals introduced to the site by the inhabitants.

The distribution of the bones varies throughout the different phases, with different types of feature favoured at different times. The majority of the bones from Phase 1 contexts were deposited in SFBs pits, with other pits as the second choice for disposal. The phase 2b enclosure ditches contained the majority of the bone, including a partial horse skeleton, partial dog skeleton and an almost complete cat. It is therefore likely that these ditches were used to dispose of unwanted animal carcasses. Phase 2c also saw the disposal of animal bone mainly in ditches, and primarily in ditch 7330. The material includes the two articulating dog skeletons, one of which had the rickets. These two skeletons were within the same context of the ditch, and may have been disposed at about the same time. Phase 3 saw an increase in the variety of features from which bone was recovered, and an increase in the use of pits for disposal. By phase 4 pits had become the most common place for disposing of bones, a trend which continued into phase 6.

The body part representation of all the domestic species indicates that the animals had been bred and slaughtered locally, with neonates of cattle, sheep/goat and pigs present throughout the various phases, and almost all skeletal elements represented for each phase. There are no obvious patterns in the distribution of body parts around the site (apart from the previously mentioned disposal of carcasses in the ditches), therefore no specific area of primary butchery can be identified. There is evidence that almost the entire carcasses of cattle had been used – the horn, the hide, the meat and marrow – but no specific sites of industrial activity can be detected until phase 6, where pit 9342, which contained a large number of cattle horn cores (MNI = 20), suggested a site where horn working may have taken place.

With regards to changes in husbandry through time on the site, cattle appear to been used fairly consistently for meat and traction, sheep/goat for meat but increasingly for wool production into the medieval period, and pigs consistently for meat, with more localised breeding in the medieval period. These patterns are to be expected from Saxon and medieval sites, but one of the main distinctions that can be noted is the variety and quantity of birds consumed during phase 2b. This phase produced a larger number and wider range of bird remains – both domestic and wild – compared to the other phases. There were domestic fowl, goose, mallard, teal, swan and grey partridge present. This is also the phase when the large oval enclosure ditch and associated structures were at their most developed. The site may have been established as a collection centre where animals could be housed before being moved on or slaughtered. Perhaps this increase in the number of bird bones consumed is a result of a more organised society, one where they are able to make more use of the birds around them, or perhaps it is simply that the birds were brought in by the people coming to the tribute centre with other livestock.

The transition from phase 2c to 3 saw a considerable drop in the total fragment counts of the main domestic species, perhaps an indication of the drop in the local population when the tribute centre went out of use. Whilst the animal bone evidence does not obviously suggest that Higham Ferrers was a high status site during any of the phases, there was clearly more livestock present, and more variety in the diet, during phase 2b.

FISH REMAINS *by Claire Ingrem*

Only contexts of Phases 1, 2b and 2c and 3 have produced any fish remains. A few bones belonging to small animals were amongst the recovered fish remains.

Methodology

The remains were examined at the Centre for Applied Archaeological Analyses (CAAA), University of Southampton following the standard methodology outlined on the CAAA website: (www.arch.soton.ac.uk/Research/CAAA/bones/Methodology.htm)

Data (Table 4.41)

Phase 1: 5th–6th century

Seven fragments of bone were recovered from contexts dated to this phase including two caudal vertebrae belonging to a medium sized (300-600 mm total length) eel (*Anguilla anguilla*). These came from SFB fill 6357 along with a fragment of jaw that was unidentifiable to taxa. A caudal vertebra belonging to a medium sized pike (*Esox lucius*) was

Table 4.41: Fish remains: Species representation according to phase (NISP)

Phase	1	2b	2c	3	Total
Esox lucius	1				1
Cyprinidae			1		1
Anguilla anguilla	2	1	2		5
?cyprinidae			1		1
Fish	1				1
Sm.mammal				1	1
Amphibian	1				1
Unidentifiable	2	1			3
Total	7	2	4	1	14

recovered from SFB fill 6058. SFB fills 6346 and 7037 produced a single undiagnostic fin spine and fin ray respectively. In addition, a single fragment belonging to an amphibian was recovered from context 6344.

Phase 2: Late 7th to early 9th century

Phase 2b – Deposits dated to the mid-late 8th century produced a single caudal vertebra belonging to a medium sized eel (context 6979).

Phase 2c – Deposits dated to the late 8th to early 9th century produced two eel vertebrae (contexts 6193, 7027), one from the anterior abdominal region and the other a caudal bone. In addition, a single anterior abdominal vertebra (context 7027) belonging to cyprinidae (carp-family) was recovered and a caudal vertebra probably also belonging to carp (context 6398).

Phase 3: mid 9th century to 11th century

A single rib belonging to a small mammal was the only small animal bone to be recovered from deposits dated to the mid 9th-11th century.

Discussion

Despite the small size of the sample it does provide evidence that the Saxon and medieval inhabitants at this site were consuming some fish. Eel are catadromous, spending part of their life cycle in freshwater environments and returning to the sea to spawn when they have reached adulthood (Wheeler, 1969). Eel probably would have been available in local rivers and lakes. Pike and cyprinidae are freshwater species (*ibid*), and like eel would have been available from local sources.

In light of the small number of fish bones recovered from the site, it is most likely that their remains represent the small scale exploitation of local fresh water sources. Fish remains are not generally present in large numbers on Saxon sites, but it is not unusual to

find some evidence for fish consumption on sites of the period. Where the range of species encountered has limited, it is been interpreted as representing small scale local exploitation. This seems to be the case here. The presence of pike is interesting because it was considered something of a luxury with its consumption during the later Middle Ages restricted to those of high social standing (Hoffman, 1987).

CROP ECONOMY AND OTHER PLANT REMAINS *by Lisa Moffett*

Introduction

Very few Saxon settlements have yet been investigated archaeobotanically, and fewer still have been fully published. The settlements at Higham Ferrers span an unusually long period of time, from early Saxon to the later medieval, thus providing an unusually long view of a series of changing communities and the arable activities that took place around them.

Methodology

Samples were taken at the discretion of the excavator with advice from the author. Contexts with datable material which contained other occupation material were sampled and contexts which seemed of particular interest were targeted for sampling. Soil sample sizes were generally 40 litres, or less if the fill of the context was less. A total of 94 samples was collected from all of the sites, of which 42 were analysed.

The samples were processed by water flotation in a flotation machine at Oxford Archaeology. The mesh size used to collect the flot was 250μ. The residue (non-floating material) was collected on a 1 mm sieve. The flots were dried and stored in polythene bags. Assessment of the flots for their potential for further analysis was carried out by Dominique de Moulins for sites 1, 2 and 3 (1996), and by the author for all the other sites.

Full analysis was carried out by the author on selected samples as recommended in the assessments. These samples were either fully sorted or a subsample was sorted if the full sample was large. Most of the sorting was carried out by staff at Oxford Archaeology, but a few samples were sorted by the author. Identification was carried out by the author using the modern reference material in the collection at the University of Birmingham and the author's own collection. The results of the analysis are given in Tables 4.42-46 below. The taxonomy follows Stace (1997).

Results

Phase 1 (Table 4.42)

Features sampled from the early Saxon settlement included mainly SFBs, pits and postholes. Most of the samples produced a few fragments of grain, some of which was identifiable as barley or wheat, and a few weed seeds. On Site 1 in particular the amount of identifiable material seemed to be small, while Site 4 appeared to have more charred material.

Samples from five of the SFBs were analysed, from Sites 1 and 4. A posthole fill from one of the Site 1 SFBs was also analysed, and a pit fill from Site 4, although the latter was an isolated pit and may possibly belong to Phase 2a. Two other SFBs were sampled from Site 1 but the samples were very poor in charred plant remains and were not further analysed.

Context 1257 (SFB1256) (Site 1)

This sunken feature building had a fairly limited number of cereal grains, mainly barley with a few oat grains, and a couple of grass seeds. Like the other SFBs from this site the number of items in the sample was low. This is in contrast to the SFBs from Site 4 which show considerably more evidence of crops.

Context 6058 (SFB 6057) (Site 4)

This is the only sunken feature building from Site 4 where the main cereal is hulled barley, which is twice as abundant as wheat. There are only a few grains of oat and no rye, but flax seeds are also very abundant. Flax is grown today for fibre and oil, and the seeds are also used in cooking and often used to decorate the tops of loaves of bread. Different types are now used for fibre and oil and may well have been in the Saxon period. Unfortunately it is not possible to tell different types apart from the seeds alone. Flax is unlikely to become charred as a result of any processing or other activities related to its use, other than cooking. The number of seeds found could represent a small number of capsules, less than those found on one plant. It is possible that flax was used for cooking, including bread. A few capsules, however, may also have been part of general domestic debris which was swept into a fire. No capsule fragments were found but the seeds would probably survive better than the fairly light capsules.

A few large fragments of legumes were found which are in the size range for pea or bean, but they were poorly preserved and could also have been large-seeded wild legumes. A few fragments of hazelnut shell (*Corylus avellana*) are possible evidence for wild food.

A very few chaff fragments of glume wheat, probably spelt, were also present. These are possibly residual from an earlier period, but it is also possible that spelt continued in cultivation in this period.

Context 6346 (SFB 6345) (Site 4)

Wheat was more abundant than barley, with a small number of grains of oat and rye, and a single flax seed.

Context 6357 (SFB 6356) (Site 4)

Free-threshing wheat was the most abundant cereal, with some barley and flax present in roughly equal numbers. Some of the barley grains had germinated but there were too few barley grains overall to draw any conclusions about this.

Context 6631 (SFB 6630) (Site 4)

Free-threshing wheat is also the main cereal in this sample, with a small amount of barley and oat, and a very few grains of rye. There was no sign that any of the grains had germinated and there were no flax seeds or other non-cereal crops found.

A small number of free-threshing wheat rachis nodes were found, including a few identified as bread wheat (*Triticum aestivum*) and two that appear to be a free-threshing tetraploid type (*Triticum turgidum/durum*). Tetraploid wheat rachises were found from a couple of other samples at Higham Ferrers (see below) and were dated to Phase 3, but generally this wheat in known in England mainly in medieval contexts. The presence of tetraploid wheat in this SFB in the 5th-6th centuries raises a suspicion that some material may be intrusive. Further radiocarbon dates from other sites are needed to clarify this issue.

This sample had the highest percentage of weeds, (over 20% of the assemblage) but it is doubtful if this is greatly significant since many of the seeds are of stinking mayweed (*Anthemis cotula*), a plant which can produce many seeds on a single flowerhead.

A single stone of sloe (*Prunus spinosa*) hints at possible collection of some wild food, though it could also have been burned if the thorny branches of sloe were used for a fire.

Context 7037 (Pit 7038) (Site 4)

In this pit hulled barley and free-threshing wheat seem to be present in roughly equal amounts. There are only a few grains of oat and rye, and there are no other crops. This sample had poorer preservation than some of the others, with nearly half of the cereal grains being unidentifiable.

Context 1300 (SFB 1266) (Site 1)

A small posthole on the northern edge of SFB 1266 had no cereal remains though it did have a single large-seeded legume, too poorly preserved to be further identified, which might or might not have been cultivated. The other plants, apart from a fragment of hazelnut shell (*Corylus avellana*), were all weedy species which could have grown in almost any type of disturbed ground, including crop fields, gardens, waste ground or waysides.

Context 1309 (Pit 1308) (Site 1)

This pit produced cereal grains, mainly of hulled barley, but also including some oat and wheat. A single glume base was found which could have been residual. There were a few weeds, but apart from the cereals, the main component of the samples was buds, probably of a tree or shrub. The

Table 4.42: Charred plant remains: Phase 1

	1257	1300	1309	6058	6346	6357	6631	7037	
Context no	1257	1300	1309	6058	6346	6357	6631	7037	
Sample no	10	47	29	118	100/101	103	107	112	
Phase	1	1	1	1	1	1	1	1	
Sample size (litres)	40	40	50						
Total flot size (mls)	75	50	300	250	180	210	80	148	
Amount analysed (mls)	100%	100%	60	125	55	210	40	124	
Items per litre	1	<1	4						
Feature	sfb	post hole	pit	sfb	sfb	sfb	sfb	pit fill	
Crop species									**Common name**
Triticum dicoccum/spelta spikelet forks					2				emmer/spelt
Triticum dicoccum/spelta glume bases			1						emmer/spelt
Triticum spelta L rachises				1					spelt
Triticum spelta glume bases					2				spelt
Triticum turgidum/durum rachises							2		rivet/macaroni wheat
Triticum aestivum L. rachises							5		bread wheat
Triticum cf *aestivum* L. rachises				3					? bread wheat
Triticum sp(p) free-threshing rachises							13	1	free-threshing wheat
Triticum sp(p) free-threshing				2	20	19	163	50	free-threshing wheat
Triticum sp(p)			2	19	30	14			wheat
Triticum sp(p) germinated				1					wheat sprouted
Triticum/Secale						1	8		wheat/rye
Secale cereale L					3		7	4	rye
Hordeum vulgare L rachises								1	barley
Hordeum vulgare L hulled, twisted				5		1			hulled barley
Hordeum vulgare L hulled, straight				2					hulled barley
Hordeum vulgare L hulled	4		8	37	9	6			hulled barley
Hordeum vulgare L hulled germinated					1	3			hulled barley sprouted
Hordeum vulgare L	8		12	3	16	5	17	44	barley
Hordeum vulgare L germinated						4			barley sprouted
Avena sp.	3		5	8	4		29	5	oat
Avena sp. germinated						1			oat sprouted
Avena/large Poaceae					2	1	10		oat/large grass
Cereal indet.	19		11	32	33	31	115	94	cereal
Cereal coleoptiles							1		cereal sprouts
Cereal/large Poaceae culm nodes					2			1	cereal/large grass
large *Vicia/Lathyrus/Pisum*		1		3					vetch/vetchling/bean/pea
Linum usitatissimum L				78	1	21			flax
Wild species									**Common name**
Urtica urens L		1			1	1			small nettle
Corylus avellana L (nutshell fragments)		1		3	2				hazel
Chenopodium sp		2	3	5			9	-	fat hen/goosefoot
Chenopodiaceae						1	9	3	goosefoot family
Chenopodiaceae/Caryophyllaceae		1							goosefoot family/pink family
Stellaria media type						1			chickweed
Spergula arvensis L				9	1	2			corn spurrey
Persicaria maculosa Gray			1						redshank
Fallopia convolvulus (L) A Löve					1		3		black-bindweed
Rumex sp		1	1					2	dock
Malvaceae							1		mallow family
Potentilla sp							1		cinquefoil
Prunus spinosa L							1		sloe
Prunus spinosa/Crataegus thorns					1				sloe/hawthorn
Prunus sp							1		sloe/bullace/damson
Vicia sativa L					1cf		1		vetch

Table 4.42 (continued): Charred plant remains: Phase 1

Context no	1257	1300	1309	6058	6346	6357	6631	7037	
Sample no	10	47	29	118	100/101	103	107	112	
Phase	1	1	1	1	1	1	1	1	
small-medium *Vicia/Lathyrus*					4	2	11		vetch/tare/vetchling
Melilotus/Medicago/Trifolium/Lotus		1	1		2	3			melilot/medick/clover/bird's foot trefoil
Bupleurum rotundifolium L		1							thorow-wax
Daucus carota L						1			wild carrot
Hyoscyamus niger L		1						1	henbane
Plantago major L.					1				greater plantain
Plantago lanceolata type			1						ribwort plantain
Euphrasia/Odontites					4	2	4		eyebright/red bartsia
Galium cf *aparine*						2			cleavers
Galium sp								1	cleavers/bedstraw
Centaurea sp							1		knapweed/cornflower
Anthemis cotula L				13	12	1	37	5	stinking mayweed
Juncus sp								1	rush
Eleocharis palustris/uniglumis						1			spikerush
Carex sp								1	sedge
Poa annua L.					9				annual meadow grass
Bromus hordeaceus/secalinus					1		2		soft/rye brome
Phleum pratense L					7		5		timothy
Poaceae indet	2	1	3		7	4	14	4	unidentified grasses
cf *Claviceps purpurea*			1				1		? ergot
? tree/shrub buds			24						? tree/shrub buds
root/rhizome fragments			2						root/rhizome fragments
Unidentified	3				7		8	2	unidentified seeds & other fragments
Total items	39	11	76	226	183	128	479	220	

buds were damaged by charring and identification was not possible.

Discussion

Given that none of the sunken feature buildings has any evidence to suggest a laid or trampled floor in the base of the pit (Hardy Chapter 3 above and Chapter 5 below) it is possible that most of the charred material is redeposited material derived from backfill after the buildings went out of use. This is not certain since charred plant remains are small and could drop through cracks between the boards of a wooden floor laid over the pit. Over some time it is possible that significant amounts of charred material could accumulate in this way.

The presence of fairly abundant amounts of cereal remains in some of the SFBs is an interesting contrast to the results from SFBs sampled at Barrow Hills (Moffett 2007). There, 30 SFBs were sampled, including 15 sampled only by small 'control' samples to see if further work was worthwhile. Most of the SFBs (including all which were 'control' sampled) produced very small amounts of charred plant remains and all were sparse in cereals. The two buildings which did produce more material had mainly wild plants including weeds of disturbed ground, but also including plants of damp or wet ground, and grassland plants (Moffett 2007). These could have been derived from building materials, bedding, fodder, or even represent handfuls of plants collected and dried for tinder to start fires. Cereals must have been consumed by the inhabitants but there are only a few remains of free-threshing wheat, hulled barley, oats (though this may have been a weed) and field bean to suggest this. A few remains of glume wheats were assumed to be residual from the earlier prehistoric settlement at the site. The buildings need not all have been domestic (and only a few were in use at the same time) but it almost seems at Barrow Hills as if cereal related activities, such as parching or cooking, were taking place elsewhere, or the occupants were disposing of any waste without burning it.

The evidence from the sunken feature buildings at Higham Ferrers, however, at least at Site 4, very much suggest that crops were being used nearby, if not actually in the buildings. Free-threshing wheat, which was probably bread wheat, seems to have been the most common cereal, or at least the one most often exposed to fire. Barley and flax, however are the main crops in context 6058 (SFB 6057), suggesting possibly a different activity or use. Like

Barrow Hills there is a trace of glume wheat, spelt in this case, but so little that it seems unlikely this represents a contemporary crop. Rye is present, and may have been grown as a crop in its own right, but it is poorly represented. Cultivated and wild oats are indistinguishable from each other using just the grains. Very large oat grains might suggest cultivated oats, but the grains in these samples were all of a size which could have been either. Wild oats are often very successful weeds of cereals and may in any case have been tolerated by Saxon farmers who probably had different views from modern farmers concerning what they valued in their crop fields, especially if the weeds were edible.

The composition of the cereal assemblages from contexts 6058, 6346, 6357, 6631 and 7037 (from the buildings 6057, 6345, 6356, 6630, and pit 7038 respectively) suggest a processed and fairly clean crop product ready for consumption rather than any of the waste products of crop processing. Weed seeds vary in abundance from 29% of the assemblage in 6346 to 9% in 7037 and the greatest abundance of chaff was 4% in 6631. Chaff fragments and most weed seeds do not survive charring as well as cereal grains, however, and may be underrepresented. The presence of flax seeds also suggests possible domestic activities. Flax seeds are oily and also do not survive as well as cereal grains, yet in two of the samples flax is relatively abundant. The crops may have become burned as a result of minor spillages when handling, either directly when being prepared, or when being swept into a hearth afterwards. Roasting of cereals can be done to improve the ease with which they can be ground in a quern to flour or meal, and this may also have added some flavour. Hulled barley, (and hulled oat also), if they are to be used for human consumption, need to be either loosely milled, or parched and then pounded to remove the enclosing lemma and palea, a process known as hummeling (Fenton 1978). It is also possible that whole grains, and flax, were used to decorate loaves of bread just as they still are with granary and seed loaves today.

Phase 2 (Table 4.43)

Samples from this phase were taken from the enclosure ditch, the features associated with the buildings and the stone built malting kiln. Some of the samples from the ditch and the building features were relatively poor in charred plant remains and not analysed. In all 18 samples were analysed. There were no samples from Phase 2a.

Enclosure ditch

A fill from the enclosure extension ditch 15218 (Site 8) and a primary fill 15221 (Site 8) from the Phase 2b enclosure ditch both produced similar results. A rather sparse assemblage of cereal remains and weed seeds suggests no more than a few residual charred remains being deposited along with the rest of the fills.

However, a substantial amount of cereal remains was deposited in the enclosure ditch to the north of Site 3. This evaluation fill (451) may possibly have been an earlier midden deposit that was redeposited into the ditch. The cereal grains were mostly wheat, though there was also some barley. A few rachis remains suggest that the free-threshing wheat was bread wheat, but there are also a small number of remains of spelt or glume wheat chaff. These are likely to be residual from the Iron Age use of the area, though there is some evidence at a few other sites for continuing spelt cultivation in the Saxon period (Green 1979a, Murphy 1985). Weed seeds were a small part of this assemblage (6%) and most were a small-seeded legume which could not be identified but was similar to medick or clover. These plants can grow as weeds, but also have a value as forage and fodder. The crop assemblage resembles the remains of crops processed to the stage where they could be put in storage or prepared for consumption. If this deposit was a midden in origin it is likely that it was a domestic one.

The fills of the final phase of enclosure ditch in Phase 2c also produced plant assemblages which varied from small amounts of residual material with one or two items per litre to deposits with higher amounts of residual material or possible dumps of waste. One of the fills with greater amounts of material was evaluation context 564, which, in addition to free-threshing wheat and hulled barley, had a very few grains and chaff fragments of rye (*Secale cereale*). A single thorn of sloe or hawthorn (*Prunus spinosa/Crataegus* sp.) may be derived from fuel and suggests the local presence of one of these hedgerow/woodland edge species. There were also a few fragments of hazel nut (*Corylus avellana*) shell. Context 6050 (Site 4) was very similar in composition and abundance of material.

A possible dump of material (context 15428) with a still greater abundance of cereal remains also had primarily rye, rather than wheat or barley, and is the only context from the site where rye is the most abundant cereal. There were also some large legumes which may have been pea, though only two could be identified as such. This context (15428, Site 8) was comparable to context 451 in abundance of remains and may also have been a dump of domestic waste.

Features associated with the buildings

Two posthole fills from the building 7023 produced moderate amounts of free-threshing wheat with little in the way of other cereals, apart from a few grains of barley, and only a few weeds.

One postpipe fill (2154; posthole 2151, Building 2664, Figure 3.19), and one posthole fill (2644; posthole 2642, Building 2666, Figure 3.25) both produced more abundant charred remains than any of the fills from the enclosure ditch, or indeed from the two posthole fills analysed from building 7023. In both of these samples barley is the main cereal, and in one of them (2154) there are some grains that have germinated, though this could be the result of poor storage. There are also some large legumes, especially in context 2644, and some oat and rye, especially in context 2154. A small amount of free-threshing wheat is also present, but these postpipe assemblages are clearly different from the posthole assemblages from building 7023. There is little, however, to suggest a different use or status between building 2666 and building 2664.

A further posthole (6617 Site 4) from a barn or storage building produced a substantial assemblage of mainly barley, some of it sprouted. Other grains may also have sprouted but charring has made it impossible to be certain. Many of the grains are distorted, however, and it is possible that many more had germinated than could be identified as such. As with the postpipe 2154 it is possible that these sprouted grains could have resulted from grain spoiling during storage, possibly adding weight to the interpretation of these as storage buildings. The grain would still need to have been exposed to fire to become charred, however, so some form of waste disposal of the damaged grain by burning would have to have been carried out. Burning would destroy pests that might contaminate future stored crops. Alternatively it is possible that some form of malt roasting was being carried out, but there was no evidence for any form of nearby malting kiln. (The malting oven on Site 5 (see below) was almost 200 metres away.)

A sample from a beamslot fill (9060, Site 6) of Building 9184 compared more closely with the postholes from building 7023. Here again there was only a moderate amount of material, and wheat was the main cereal, although there were also a few large legumes including a possible bean.

Malting oven (Table 4.44)

Several samples were taken from various parts of the Phase 2c stone-built malting oven (Site 5). Three samples (4014, 4015 and 307) came from the floor of the oven chamber, one (4037) from the bottom of the flue, and two (4042 and 4043) from near the bottom of the wall inside the oven chamber. The latter two were not analysed as they produced only small amounts of material.

The three samples from the floor of the oven were all very abundant in grain and were also very similar in composition. Barley represented about 90% of identifiable grains in all three samples. Oats were a small percentage in 4014 and 4015, and wheat was also a small percentage in 4015 and 307. It is clear, however, that these were minor contaminents. The barley was probably all hulled, and there were some twisted grains, which are characteristic of 6-row barley. In theory a population of all 2-row barley would have only straight grains and a population of all 6-row barley would have twisted and straight grains present in a ratio of 2 twisted grains to 1 straight. A mix of the two would be

identifiable by a higher ratio of straight grains. The barley in these samples was too distorted to identify many grains as twisted or straight, however, so it remains possible that there was a mix of both types.

Roughly one quarter to one half of the barley could be identified as sprouted. Some of the wheat and oat grains had also germinated. Sprouting is not always easily detectable in charred grain. In some cases a distinct furrow is formed down the dorsal side of the grain but in grain that has only just germinated this may not be apparent. Charring often causes the embryos and the sprouts (coleoptiles) to detach from the grain and also often causes the sprouts to break, thus making it impossible to determine how long they were. Detached cereal sprouts were fairly abundant in these samples, but could not be counted because they were broken. It seems fairly clear, however, that the oven was indeed used for malting, and there is no evidence for any other use.

Malt is made from grain which has been germinated and allowed to grow just enough for the enzymes to begin the process of converting the starch to sugar. This process is called chitting. Once the grain has been chitted the process is arrested by lightly roasting the grain enough to kill the sprouts but not enough to damage the enzymes which will continue the process of converting starch into sugar during brewing. The malted grains are then crushed or ground and the malt can then be stored until required for brewing. Grain being chitted needs to be turned regularly to ensure even germination. In theory malted grain would have sprouts of roughly equal length, but in practice the maltsters may not always have been fussy about evenness of germination. The whole sprouts that were present in these assemblages seemed to vary in length and some of the barley grains (though only a few) were highly shrunken as if the germination process had gone too far.

Any cereal can be used to make malt but barley was favoured at least partly because the low nitrogen content improves the keeping qualities of the ale, though flavour may also have been a factor. Medieval assemblages of grain interpreted as malt seem to have often been of mixed cereals, however, and not necessarily barley. One example is the malting kiln at Oversley Castle, Warwickshire, which contained a mix mainly of oat and wheat with a little rye and practically no barley (Moffett 1997). This was actually a fairly low-status settlement associated with the castle and it may be that malt was made from whatever grain was to hand. The purity of the possible barley malt at Higham Ferrers suggests that either a high-quality product of the right flavour may have been desired, or that the other cereals had other uses.

The number of weed seeds is fairly low, between 3% and 11%, suggesting the crop was probably fairly well-cleaned before malting. The most common seeds were cabbage/turnip/mustard/charlock (*Brassica/Sinapis*) and stinking mayweed. Stinking

Table 4.43: Charred plant remains Phase 2

	451	2154	2644	6617	6901	6917	15218
Context no	451	2154	2644	6617	6901	6917	15218
Sample no	50	64	60	106	122	121	801
Phase	2b	2b	2b	4	2b	2b	2b
Sample size (litres)	40	10	10	10	10	10	40
Total flot size (mls)	200	60	600	60	4	8	145
Amount analysed	25%	100%	140 ml	50%	100%	100%	100%
Items per litre	28	67	62	74	5	5	<1
Feature	deposit in enclosure ditch	postpipe Building 2665	postpipe Building 2666	barn/store house posthole	posthole fill Building 7023	posthole fill Building 7023	fill of enclosure extension ditch
min = item partly or completely mineral-replaced							
Crop species							
Triticum dicoccum/spelta glume bases	2						
Triticum cf. *spelta* glume bases	1						
Triticum spelta/aestivum basal or sub-basal rachises	1						
Triticum aestivum L. rachises	3						
Triticum sp(p) free-threshing rachises	4	4	1				
Triticum sp(p) free-threshing	83	12	2		13	12	1
Triticum sp(p) rachises	2						
Triticum sp(p) glume bases	3						
Triticum sp(p)	62		1	6	4	28	2
Triticum/Secale							1
Secale cereale L rachises							
Secale cereale L		24	4	2	1	1	
Secale/Hordeum rachises							
Hordeum vulgare L rachises	2	1	4				
Hordeum vulgare L hulled, twisted		17		3			
Hordeum vulgare L hulled, straight		7					
Hordeum vulgare L hulled		213	44	121	1	2	2
Hordeum vulgare L hulled germinated		13		16			
Hordeum vulgare L	20			112	1	4	1
Hordeum vulgare L germinated	4			7			
Avena sp.		46	7	13	2	1	
Avena sp. germinated		14					
Avena/large Poaceae	1						
Avenae panicle nodes				1			
Cereal indet.	67	35	16	76	18		
Vicia faba L							
Pisum sativum L							
large *Vicia/Lathyrus/Pisum*	5	2	26				
Wild species							
Ranunculus acris/repens/bulbosus							1
Urtica urens L							
Corylus avellana L (nutshell fragments)							
Chenopodium sp				1	1		
Chenopodiaceae		187	7	7			2
Stellaria media type		1		1			
Agrostemma githago L		13	2	1			
Agrostemma githago L calyx tips							
Silene sp							
Polygonum aviculare L.		1		1			

15221	564	6050	6193	6621	9060	15149	15428	
804	5	153	127	109	502	803	810	
2b	2c	2c	2c	2c	2c	2c	2c	
40	40	40	40	30	40	40	10	
65	150	30	30	18	32	18	60	
100%	50%	100%	100%	100%	100%	100%	100%	
<1	6	7	2	2	4	1	35	
primary fill of enclosure ditch	middle fill of final enclosure ditch	fill of final enclosure ditch	fill of final enclosure ditch	fill of final enclosure ditch	beam slot fill of barn/storehouse	middle fill of final enclosure ditch	fill of final enclosure ditch	**Common name**
								emmer/spelt
								spelt
								spelt/bread wheat
		3			1		3	bread wheat
	4	1					1	free-threshing wheat
1	26	28	2	7	13		57	free-threshing wheat
	2							wheat
		2						wheat
2	8	84	13	17	21	10	22	wheat
	3	2	1		3		13	wheat/rye
	2	1					18	rye
	3	3			1		146	rye
			2					rye/barley
		3	2					barley
		1						hulled barley
								hulled barley
1		7		1			1	hulled barley
								hulled barley sprouted
	6	16	4	3	4		4	barley
			1					barley sprouted
2	3	5	1	1	3			oat
								oat sprouted
2					9	2		oat/large grass
								oat tribe
	28	71	13	20	39	3	42	cereal
					1cf			bean
							2	pea
					3	2	25	vetch/vetchling/bean/pea
								Common name
								buttercup
					1cf			small nettle
	5	1	1				1	hazel
		1						fat hen/goosefoot
					10			goosefoot family
								chickweed
	2		1					corncockle
	1							corncockle
		1						campion/catchfly
	1							knotgrass

Table 4.43 (continued): Charred plant remains Phase 2

Context no	451	2154	2644	6617	6901	6917	15218
Sample no	50	64	60	106	122	121	801
Phase	2b	2b	2b	4	2b	2b	2b
Fallopia convolvulus (L) A Löve		5	1	4			
Rumex actosella L				2			
Rumex sp	2	4	2	2			
cf Polygonaceae							
Brassica/Sinapis		1			1		
Potentilla sp							
Prunus spinosa/Crataegus thorns							
Vicia hirsuta (L) Gray				1			
Vicia sativa L							
small-medium *Vicia/Lathyrus*		2	2	1			
Melilotus/Medicago/Trifolium/Lotus	33			2			
Daucus carota L							
Apiaceae		2					
Hyoscyamus niger L							
Lithospermum arvense L.	2						
Galeopsis sp				1			
Plantago major L				1			
Plantago lanceolata type	2						
Euphrasia/Odontites							
Galium cf *aparine*				1			
Galium sp	1	6					
Lapsana communis L		1					
Anthemis cotula L	2	35	17	6	2	1	2
Asteraceae indet				2		1	
Juncus sp				1			
Eleocharis palustris/uniglumis							2
Carex sp							4
cf *Lolium temulentum* L							
Cynosurus cristatus L				1			
Bromus hordeaceus/secalinus	1						
Phleum pratense L				4			
Poaceae culm nodes	1	1					
Poaceae indet	5	17	2		3		2
Unidentified		7	4				2
fragments							
insect case							
Total items	309	671	143	396	47	50	22

mayweed is usually found on heavy soils, and, as noted above, it produces many seeds per head.

The flue sample is different from the oven chamber samples. There was less abundance of grain in the flue and the grain is mainly wheat, not barley. There was no sign that this wheat had sprouted. The flue samples also had many tiny pieces of silicified cereal chaff, some of it identifiable as wheat, with just a few awn fragments of barley. The pieces were too tiny and fragile to pick out of the sample, and counting them would be meaningless anyway as they were so fragmentary. They indicate, however that an abundance of wheat chaff was burned in the flue. This chaff appeared to be glume, lemma and awn fragments with no charred or silicified rachis remains or culm nodes. This may represent the light chaff by-product of winnowing the crop after it is threshed. This light chaff is very papery and would burn very quickly once it was alight. It would need to be used in very large quantities to be useful as fuel and would need to be continually replenished. It would be very impractical by itself as fuel for the malting kiln. However, light chaff would be very useful as tinder for starting fires. Since this chaff would mostly burn away in a fire it is almost certain that it is very under-repre-

15221	564	6050	6193	6621	9060	15149	15428	
804	5	153	127	109	502	803	810	
2b	2c	2c	2c	2c	2c	2c	2c	
							2	black-bindweed
								sheep's sorrel
1	3				1		1	dock
		4	26					knotweed family
								cabbage/turnip/ mustard/ charlock
					1			cinquefoil
	1							sloe/hawthorn
								hairy tare
1min				1				vetch
3	2			1	2		1	vetch/tare/vetchling
		1			2	9	1	melilot/medick/clover/ bird's foot trefoil
						3		wild carrot
								carrot family
		1						henbane
								field gromwell
								hempnettle
					1			greater plantain
								ribwort plantain
					9	1	1	eyebright/red bartsia
	1							cleavers
1					2	3	2	cleavers/bedstraw
								nipplewort
2	5	19	1		15		1	stinking mayweed
								daisy family
								rush
		1						spikerush
			1					sedge
	1							? darnel
								crested dog's tail
		1			1			soft/rye brome
					5			timothy
								grass stem nodes
2	5	3	1		8	1	1	unidentified grasses
1	7	3		1		5		unidentified seeds & other
1min								
18	119	263	70	52	154	39	345	

sented relative to the charred grains in the sample. Probably charred wheat grains were only a minor component of what originally was burned, and are present because a few grains were collected along with the chaff when it was gathered up.

The malting oven appears to have been deliberately destroyed rather than abandoned. The former is perhaps more likely since a stone built oven represents a considerable investment of resources. The preservation of the grain is fairly uniform in all the samples and this suggests it represents material from a single burning event rather than an accumulation from several firings.

Discussion

All of the assemblages from the enclosure ditch and the buildings have in common the fact that their composition is primarily cereal grain, most often wheat, but sometimes barley and in one case rye. Weed seeds are relatively few and this suggests that these grain assemblages are cleaned, or nearly cleaned, grain which has been processed and is ready for use or storage. There is no indication of any crop processing from any of these samples, though it should be borne in mind that grains survive charring significantly better than weed seeds or chaff and could be over-represented

Table 4.44: Charred plant remains Phase 2c malting oven

Context no	307	4014	4015	4037	
Sample no	1	4	3	6	
Phase	2c	2c	2c	2c	
Sample size (litres)	10	30	10	10	
Total flot size (mls)	500	3120	1170	90	
Amount analysed (mls)	105	180	73	100%	
Items per litre	146	96	177	25	
Feature	malting kiln	malting kiln	malting kiln	malting kiln	
Crop species					**Common name**
Triticum sp(p) free-threshing	14	6	40	18	free-threshing wheat
Triticum sp(p) silicified chaff fragments				many	wheat
Triticum sp(p)	24	12	12	104	wheat
Triticum sp(p) germinated			3		wheat sprouted
Triticum/Secale				2	wheat/rye
Secale cereale L	3		3	3	rye
Hordeum vulgare L hulled, twisted	49	45	43		hulled barley
Hordeum vulgare L hulled, straight	5		20		hulled barley
Hordeum vulgare L hulled	456	575	486		hulled barley
Hordeum vulgare L hulled germinated	153	285	136		hulled barley sprouted
Hordeum vulgare L	382	1455	444	20	barley
Hordeum vulgare L germinated	38		20		barley sprouted
Avena sp.	20	58	35	3	oat
Avena sp. germinated	32	39	60		oat sprouted
Avena/large Poaceae	20	2		5	oat/large grass
Cereal indet.	196	330	270	82	cereal
Cereal coleoptiles	100+	100+	100+		cereal sprouts
Linum usitatissimum L	1				flax
Wild species					**Common name**
Chenopodiaceae	6	10	5		goosefoot family
Stellaria media type			2	1	chickweed
Agrostemma githago L			2		corncockle
Polygonum aviculare L.	1				knotgrass
Fallopia convolvulus (L) A Löve		1			black-bindweed
Rumex sp		2			dock
Brassica/Sinapis	18	26	48		cabbage/turnip/mustard/ charlock
Vicia hirsuta (L) Gray			1		hairy tare
small-medium *Vicia/Lathyrus*	3	5	14		vetch/tare/vetchling
Plantago lanceolata type			1		ribwort plantain
Euphrasia/Odontites	3	3	15	2	eyebright/red bartsia
Galium sp	1				cleavers/bedstraw
Centaurea sp	1		1		knapweed/cornflower
Anthemis cotula L	22	27	70	4	stinking mayweed
Asteraceae indet		2	1		daisy family
Carex sp			1		sedge
Cynosurus cristatus L		1			crested dog's tail
Bromus hordeaceus/secalinus	5	1	7	1	soft/rye brome
Phleum pratense L		1			timothy
Poaceae indet	7		13	2	unidentified grasses
Unidentified		7	19	1	unidentified seeds & other fragments
Total items	1460	2893	1772	248	

relative to chaff and weeds. As in the previous phase, it is possible that the charred grain results mainly from domestic activities such as grain roasting, or simply disposing of rubbish in a fire. However, since some of the most abundant samples came from postholes of buildings possibly used for storage, it is worth considering whether some other non-domestic activity has resulted in charred grain. A threshed and cleaned crop product for storage would differ hardly at all from one being used for domestic consumption, apart, perhaps, from some final hand cleaning to remove the last weed seeds, bits of grit and other contaminants. The difficulty is how a few remains of a stored crop would be exposed to fire, since there is no evidence for any disaster or burning of grain on a large scale. One can only speculate that the remains of old crops might sometimes have been burned, especially if they were mouldy or infested with pests. Grain weevil holes can be seen in charred grain, but many others kinds of spoilage cannot.

The flue sample from the malting kiln is the only one that indicates a crop processing product other than cleaned grain. It is unlikely that light chaff would be transported in bulk quantities very far from where it was produced. It may be, therefore, that some crop processing was taking place on or near the site. Smaller quantities of light chaff might have been brought to the site from elsewhere for other purposes, such as packing material for breakable objects. Since we cannot know how much of this highly combustible material may have been burned away it is impossible to say how large an amount was used.

Phase 3 (Table 4.45)

Samples from fills (7027 and 7077) two hearths (7026 and 7076) from Site 4 and the fill (15305) from the Site 8 SFB 15300 were analysed, as well as the fill (2605) from the child's grave (2604), a fill (2006) of pit 2009, two postpipes from possible fence posts (2291 and 2356) and fill (2004) of paddock gully (2010) from Site 2.

Gully fill (Site 2)

The fill (2004) of gully 2010 had mainly free-threshing wheat, with some barley, a few oats, a couple of grains of rye, and some large-seeded legumes that were not well-preserved enough to identify. This sample also produced some rachis fragments of rivet/macaroni wheat (*Triticum turgidum/durum*) and of bread wheat (*Triticum aestivum* s.l.). Rivet/macaroni wheat has been found on a number of medieval sites in southern Britain (Moffett 1991) and is also found in smoke-blackened thatch of late medieval and post-medieval houses (Letts 1999). Pre-Conquest remains have been more doubtful, but late Saxon rivet/macaroni is present at West Cotton, though it cannot yet be dated more precisely than 950-1100 AD (G. Campbell 1994 and forthcoming). A very few fragments of rivet/

macaroni wheat rachis were found at Stratton in Bedfordshire, from a context loosely dated as 9th-11th centuries (Moffett and Smith in prep). Possible rivet wheat (*Triticum* cf. *turgidum*) occurs in a very small amount in a Saxo-Norman pit at West Walton (Murphy 1993). The rivet/macaroni wheat from Higham Ferrers was radiocarbon dated by AMS to cal AD 770-100 (1150+/-45 BP) (OxA-10126). This is the first radiocarbon dated evidence of pre-Conquest rivet/macaroni wheat in England. Rivet and macaroni wheat are generally not distinguishable from their rachis remains, but in England rivet wheat is the more likely crop as it is known from post-medieval records and is also more tolerant of the climate.

There were also a couple of large-seeded legumes in the sample and a single seed of opium poppy (*Papaver somniferum*). It appeared that some of the seeds were mineralised.

The sample from 2004 was large and could not be fully analysed in the time available, but because of the diverse nature of the material it was decided to scan the remaining unsorted fraction of the sample for the presence of other species and in hopes of finding an identifiable specimen of the large-seeded legume. The items identified in this process were not individually counted but are indicated as present in the sample by an asterisk in Table 4.45.

The results added some 18 taxa to the list of species from the gully fill and identified one seed of a large-seeded legume as a large-seeded type of common vetch (*Vicia sativa*). The large-seeded wild subspecies of common vetch (*Vicia sativa* ssp. *segetalis*) grows in grassy places and disturbed ground, and could easily grow as a crop weed. The cultivated subspecies (*Vicia sativa* ssp. *sativa*) has on average somewhat larger seeds. Unfortunately the two subspecies overlap in size and only with well-preserved material at the extreme ends of the size ranges is it possible to tell the two apart. The material from Higham Ferrers is too poorly preserved to be accurately measurable, but appears on the whole to be more within the size range for ssp. *segetalis*, though this does not wholly rule out a small-seeded variety of ssp. *sativa*.

Pit fill (Site 2)

Opium poppy and the *V. sativa*-sized legumes were not found in the fill (2006) of pit 2009, but otherwise the assemblage is fairly similar to 2004. The amount of material is less, though the relative richness of the sample is unknown as the size of the soil sample was unrecorded.

Postpipes

The postpipe (2291) produced abundant grains of hulled barley with only a few grains of oat and wheat and no chaff remains. About a third of the items in the sample were weed seeds, mainly the goosefoot family (Chenopodiaceae), *Brassica/Sinapis* and stinking mayweed. The other postpipe (2356)

Table 4.45: Charred plant remains Phases 3 & 4

	2004	2006	2356	2605	2291	7027
Context no	*2004*	*2006*	*2356*	*2605*	*2291*	*7027*
Sample no	*56*	*14*	*61*	*57*	*24*	*110*
Phase	*3*	*3*	*3*	*3*	*3*	*3*
Sample size (litres)	40	?	20	10	10	40
Total flot size (mls)	110	40	10	50	75	50
Amount analysed (mls)	20	19	100%	100%	26%	100%
Items per litre	109	?	11.5	18.5	161	1
Feature	gully	pit	post pipe	child grave	post pipe	domestic
*=present in unsorted part of	lower fill					hearth
sample; min=mineral-replaced						

Crop species

	2004	2006	2356	2605	2291	7027
Triticum turgidum/durum rachises	5					
Triticum cf turgidum/durum rachises	1	1				
Triticum turgidum/durum glume bases	2					
Triticum spelta/aestivum rachises	1	1				
Triticum aestivum L. rachises	12			1cf		
Triticum sp(p) free-threshing rachises	27	3				
Triticum sp(p) free-threshing	140	15	20			4
Triticum sp(p) rachises	8	1				
Triticum sp(p)	35	7	15	19	2	6
Triticum sp(p) germinated						
Triticum/Secale		1		1		
Secale cereale L rachises	2	9				
Secale cereale L	*	6	7	9		
Secale/Hordeum rachises		3				
Hordeum vulgare L 6-row rachises	1					
Hordeum vulgare L rachises	6	4				
Hordeum vulgare L hulled, twisted			4		4	
Hordeum vulgare L hulled, straight					4	
Hordeum vulgare L hulled	4	8	30	17	154	
Hordeum vulgare L hulled germinated					1	
Hordeum vulgare L cf naked				1		
Hordeum vulgare L	57	9	14	19		3
Hordeum vulgare L germinated						
Avena sp.	10	2	11	8	9	1
Avena sp. germinated						
Avena/large Poaceae	22		4			
Avenae panicle nodes	1					
Cereal indet.	148	59	36	55	121	15
Cereal/large Poaceae culm nodes	2					
large *Vicia/Lathyrus/Pisum*	2		1	3	2	
Papaver somniferum L	1					
Ficus carica L						
Linum usitatissimum L						

Wild species

	2004	2006	2356	2605	2291	7027
Ranunculus acris/repens/bulbosus	1					
Corylus avellana L (nutshell fragments)	*			1		
Chenopodium sp		1	20			
Chenopodiaceae	7				69	
Stellaria media type	1					
Stellaria palustris/graminea	*					
Agrostemma githago L	*min	3	5	2	1	
Agrostemma githago L calyx tips	*	1				
Silene sp	2					
Polygonum aviculare L.	*		1			
Fallopia convolvulus (L) A Löve		1		3	2	
Rumex actosella L	*			1		

7077	15305	15494	15556	15557	
115	809	811	813	812	
3	3	4	4	4	
10	40	40	40	40	
18	30	160	30	150	
100%	100%	50%	100%	50%	
7	5	20	7	12	
domestic hearth	sfb fill	oven base deposit	lower pit fill	rubbish pit fill	
					Common name
			1		rivet/macaroni wheat
					?rivet/macaroni wheat
					rivet/macaroni wheat
					spelt/bread wheat
					bread wheat
		1			free-threshing wheat
	20	50	23		free-threshing wheat
					wheat
2	52	81	37	2	wheat
		1	1		wheat sprouted
	2	7			wheat/rye
					rye
	2	24	3	3	rye
					rye/barley
					6-row barley
					barley
					hulled barley
					hulled barley
	4	4	11	49	hulled barley
		8	20		hulled barley sprouted
					? naked barley
1	23	12	43	99	barley
		2			barley sprouted
	6	23	12	6	oat
		16			oat sprouted
	2		4		oat/large grass
					oat tribe
2	68	39	20	44	cereal
					cereal/large grass
	1		1		bean/vetch/vetchling/pea
	1min				opium poppy
		1min			fig
	3				flax
					Common name
					buttercup
					hazel
				4	fat hen/goosefoot
18	1	7	7		goosefoot family
					chickweed
			2		marsh/lesser stitchwort
		18		1	corncockle
					corncockle
					campion/catchfly
					knotgrass
				1	black-bindweed
2					sheep's sorrel

171

Table 4.45 (continued): Charred plant remains Phases 3 & 4

Context no	2004	2006	2356	2605	2291	7027
Sample no	56	14	61	57	24	110
Phase	3	3	3	3	3	3
Rumex sp	6	3		2	5	1
cf Polygonaceae				1		
Malvaceae						
Brassica rapa/nigra			17			
Brassica/Sinapis	*min	1			22	
Cruciferae						
Lysimachia/Anagallis			3			1
Rubus sp	*					
cf *Rosa* sp			1			
Agrimonia eupatoria L						
Crataegus sp						
Vicia hirsuta (L) Gray	*					
Vicia tetresperma (L) Schreber	1					
Vicia sativa L	*					
small-medium *Vicia/Lathyrus*	48	1	3	6		1
Melilotus/Medicago/Trifolium/Lotus	13	3				1
Euphorbia helioscopa	*					
Conium maculatum L						
Bupleurum rotundifolium L	6		1cf			
Daucus carota L			2			1cf
Apiaceae	1			1		
Hyoscyamus niger L						
Lithospermum arvense L.	*min					
Ballota nigra/Marrubium vulgare						
Galeopsis sp		1cf				
Plantago major L	6				1	
Plantago lanceolata type	*		1cf			
Euphrasia/Odontites	20		1	1	1	
Galium cf *aparine*	6			1	1	
Galium sp	12	2				
Sambucus nigra L	*min					
Valerianella dentata (L) Pollich	*					
Centaurea cyanus L						
Centaurea sp	*					
Lapsana communis L	*					
Anthemis cotula L	67	18	11	18	31	6
Tripleurospermum sp						
Asteraceae indet	1					
Eleocharis palustris/uniglumis	1					
Carex spp	3					3
Cynosurus cristatus L						
Poa annua L	*			4		
Bromus hordeaceus/secalinus		4	1			
Phleum pratense L	35	6	1	2		
Poaceae culm nodes	*			1		
Poaceae indet	42	18	10	5	3	2
Sparganium sp						
cf *Claviceps purpurea*	*					
Unidentified	16	2	11	3	3	
Total items	782	193	229	184	436	44

| 7077 | 15305 | 15494 | 15556 | 15557 | |
| 115 | 809 | 811 | 813 | 812 | |
3	3	4	4	4	
1	3		3	2	dock
					knotweed family
				1	mallow family
					wild turnip/black mustard
2	8	11			cabbage/turnip/mustard/ charlock
				1	cabbage family
5	1				loosestrife/pimpernel
					bramble/raspberry
					? rose
			1		agrimony
1cf					hawthorn
					hairy tare
					smooth tare
					vetch
2	1	2	9	1	vetch/tare/vetchling
5	1		1	3	melilot/medick/clover/ bird's foot trefoil
	1				sun spurge
		4			hemlock
					thorow-wasx
		1cf			wild carrot
					carrot family
	2				henbane
					field gromwell
				1	black horehound/white horehound
					hempnettle
					greater plantain
			1		ribwort plantain
		6	21	4	eyebright/red bartsia
					cleavers
	1	57	2	1	cleavers/bedstraw
					elder
					cornsalad
			1cf		cornflower
					knapweed/cornflower
					nipplewort
2	4	3	22	7	stinking mayweed
			1		mayweed
					daisy family
1			1		spikerush
7		2	2	1	sedge
				3	crested dog's tail
1			6	4	annual meadow grass
	1	8			soft/rye brome
	?			?	timothy
					grass stem nodes
6	3	9	23	1	unidentified grasses
		1			bur-reed
					? ergot
12	3	3	6	4	unidentified seeds & other fragments
69	215	399	284	245	

has less abundant remains, though still more than would be expected as 'background' residual material. This sample appeared to be a rather mixed deposit of barley and wheat with a few grains of oats and rye.

Child's grave (2604)

The child's grave also had a very similar mix of cereals. It possible that wheat and barley were being grown as a maslin (mixed crop), but it is also possible that the material in these deposits has been reworked from several sources.

SFB (15300)

The sunken feature building infill (15305), like the sampled contexts from Site 2, had a mixed assemblage of wheat and barley, but only half as many weeds (15%). There were also a few flax seeds, a large legume, and a mineralised seed of opium poppy. It did not have a great abundance of charred plant remains and it is probable that these were associated with the disuse of the building, although the assemblage does appear to be domestic waste.

Hearths (within Building 6811)

The fills (7027 and 7077) of two domestic hearths (7026 and 7076) both had relatively few remains, and there were more weeds, especially in 7077 which had mostly weed seeds. The weed species were the same as those in the more cereal-dominated assemblages, though fewer because the assemblages were small. It is possible that these represent a final domestic stage of hand crop-cleaning before use, but the assemblages are too small for much interpretation.

Discussion

Weed seeds seem to be just under a third of the items in all of these samples from Site 2, which is more than the samples from Phase 2 and suggests a possible change of crop-related activities or methods from the previous phase. The Phase 3 samples generally seem to be rather weedier than those from both Phases 1 and 2, though where assemblages are small it is difficult to compare the percentages of weeds. Chaff remains are very few at all periods and this suggests that there may not have been much burning of the straw and chaff products of crop processing. These products are rarely found on sites at any period, however, as the fragments of free-threshing cereal chaff are more likely to burn away while grains and weed seeds sink to the lower, oxygen-poor bottom and are thus charred rather than destroyed (Boardman and Jones 1990). Thus weed seeds might be the only remaining evidence for the presence of these crop processing products. Increased numbers of weeds might result from burning crop processing waste, but might also be the result of less meticulous husbandry. Chaff and straw have many uses and it may also be that they were kept carefully from fire, except when deliberately used for tinder or fuel.

Phase 4 (Table 4.45)

A deposit (15494) from the base of an oven (15493), and fills (15556 and 15557) from two pits, all from Site 8, were analysed.

Oven

The fill of the oven (15493) produced fairly abundant remains. Free-threshing wheat was the most abundant. Rye, oats and barley were present roughly equally and made up about a third of the identified grain between them. A few of the grains had sprouted but they may have spoiled in storage. There was also a single mineralised fig seed (*Ficus carica*).

Pit fills

Both of these pits were near areas of occupation and contained moderate amounts of charred plant remains. Like some of the samples from Phase 3, wheat and barley were present as a mix in 15566 and about a third of identifiable seeds were weed seeds. There were somewhat fewer weed seeds in 15557 and nearly all of the grain in it was barley, with no sign of sprouted grains.

Discussion

There is nothing in the archaeobotanical remains to distinguish the medieval Phase 4 from the late Saxon Phase 3, although such an assertion is qualified, with only three samples deriving from Phase 4 activity.

Phase 5 (Table 4.46)

The sampling from this phase mainly reflected the activities centred on the pottery industry. Two samples were analysed from ash lenses in the Site 6 pot kiln (9075 and 9099). Another sample was analysed from the floor of the potter's workshop (9212). Samples were also analysed from a quarry pit fill (15199), a shallow rubbish pit (15255) and an oven base (15380), all from Site 8.

Kiln 1

Both ash lenses had very similar assemblages, and were roughly half cultivated legumes and half arable weed seeds. The weeds were the same as those found with the cereal crops of previous periods. There were scarcely any cereal grains in these samples, however, and instead the crops were bean (*Vicia faba*), pea (*Pisum sativum*) and vetch (*Vicia sativa*). There was also a single, rather doubtfully identified, legume that could have been a lentil (*Lens culinaris*). The beans were all a small-seeded and sometimes rather rounded type like the 'Celtic' bean (*Vicia faba* var *minuta*). The vetch was large seeded and probably cultivated (*Vicia sativa* ssp *sativa*), but the large seeded wild type (*Vicia sativa* ssp *segetalis*) overlaps in size with cultivated vetch, and with relatively few identifiable charred seeds it was not possible to be completely certain.

Use of cultivated vetch as a fodder crop is documented for the medieval period (Campbell 1988) and some medieval archaeobotanical remains have been found (e.g. Moffett 1995), though perhaps the earliest unequivocal archaeobotanical example of cultivated *Vicia sativa* ssp. *sativa* is from the early 12th century at West Cotton (Campbell forthcoming). Vetch was probably not used for human consumption, except, perhaps in times of famine; it is possibly toxic to humans in large quantities (Ressler 1962).

Legumes are relatively rare in charred assemblages as they seem to be less often exposed to fire than cereals. They are often difficult to identify with confidence in charred material as they tend to lose the testa (seed coat) during charring and with it the hilum, which is usually necessary for identification. Distinguishing peas from beans can be particularly difficult with the small-seeded beans of the medieval and earlier periods which are about the same size as peas and not always very different in shape. Most of the legumes not be identified, but of those that were, beans appeared to be the most common. Some of the beans were very small and may have been under-developed beans from the ends of the pods.

The weediness of the assemblages suggests that perhaps these assemblages are the remains of legume threshing waste used to start the fire the in pottery kiln. Although no pod remains were found, it is likely that these would survive relatively poorly in a fire as they are light and also large enough to stay in the upper, aerobic, part of the fire.

Workshop floor (9212)

The assemblage from the workshop floor probably also derives from legume threshing waste. There were a few more peas than beans, though most of the legumes could not be identified. There were also a few more cereal remains, including a few chaff fragments, but cereals were still not a significant part of this assemblage.

Quarry pit fill (15199 – fill of 15197)

The quarry pit fill produced few remains, and most of these appeared to be weed seeds. There were a few vetch seeds, and there were also a number of seeds which could only be identified as vetch or vetchling (*Vicia/Lathyrus*) which may have been cultivated vetch but which could also have been several species of wild legumes and were therefore placed (but possibly erroneously) under wild species in the Table 4.46. In any case the material in the quarry sample appears to show only a minor amount of residual material from the fill.

Rubbish pit (15255 – fill of 15254)

The rubbish pit was different from all the other analysed samples from this phase in that it had no cultivated legumes and appeared to be mainly wheat grains and weed seeds. This may be domestic waste similar to that seen in Phases 3 and 4. The small number of chaff fragments in this sample suggests that both rivet wheat and bread wheat were being consumed, but it is not possible to say in what proportion as the two wheats cannot be distinguished from the grains.

Oven base (15380)

Cereals were insignificant in this sample and legumes were again the main crops. Vetch, bean and pea were all found, and also some lentils, though only a few could be securely identified. Some of the peas were very small, suggesting that they, like the beans in the pottery kiln, were underdeveloped and may have come from the ends of the pods. Lentil does poorly in Britain as a seed crop for human consumption as it needs heat and sunshine for the seed to set well and ripen. However, there are post-medieval documentary records of lentil being grown as a fodder crop (Plot 1705). Small numbers of lentils are occasionally found in medieval deposits (e.g. Moffett 1995) and late Saxon lentils were found at Yarnton (Stevens 2004).

The most striking aspect of this assemblage was the number of wild species, and in particular the number of small-seeded legumes which could have been a number of plants such as melilot, medick, clover or bird's foot trefoil (*Melilotus/Medicago/ Trifolium/Lotus*). A few seeds of black medick (*Medicago lupulina*) were identified, but there was substantial variation in shape, and to a certain extent in size, among the small-seeded legumes, so it is probable that they are not all one species such as black medick. These small-seeded legumes account for approximately half the seeds of wild species in the sample. They are so abundant that it does lead one to wonder if perhaps, like the vetch and lentil, they also represent a leguminous forage or fodder crop.

Although most of the wild species are plants that can grow as weeds in many kinds of disturbed habitats as well as arable ground, there are also some which are more typical of calcareous grassland, such as greater knapweed (*Centaurea* cf *scabiosa*), hawkweed oxtongue (*Picris hieracioides*) and wild carrot (*Daucus carota*). There are more grass seeds than the other samples, though unfortunately the grasses are not distinctive enough to identify. Grasses grow in a variety of habitats besides grassland, so this is not a good indicator by itself, but taken with the herbaceous grassland species it does suggest that some of the non-cultivated species may derive from a different source than the segetal species such as corncockle (*Agrostemma githago*) and stinking mayweed. Perhaps the grassland plants were growing with the small-seeded legumes in a managed meadow which may have been cropped for hay. One can only speculate that handfuls of hay, as well as possibly legume threshing waste, may have been used to light the oven.

Table 4.46 Charred plant remains Phase 5

Context no	9075	9099	9212	15199	15255	15380	
Sample no	509	508	503	800	806	808	
Phase	5	5	5	5	5	5	
Sample size (litres)	10	10	10	10	20	40	
Total flot size (mls)	75	70	160	10	35	200	
Amount analysed	100%	100%	100%	100%	100%	50%	
Items per litre	20	19	32	4	12	68	
Feature	ash lens in pot kiln	ash lens in pot kiln	potters workshop floor	quarry pit fill	fill of shallow rubbish pit	oven base	

min=mineral-replaced

Crop species							Common name
Triticum turgidum/durum rachises			1		1		rivet/macaroni wheat
Triticum cf turgidum/durum rachises					1		? rivet/macaroni wheat
Triticum aestivum L. rachises					1		bread wheat
Triticum sp(p) free-threshing rachises			3				free-threshing wheat
Triticum sp(p) free-threshing			4		6		free-threshing wheat
Triticum sp(p)	1		3		66	7	wheat
Triticum/Secale					2		wheat/rye
Hordeum vulgare L hulled					3		hulled barley
Hordeum vulgare L					5	5	barley
Avena sp.		1	3		5	1	oat
Avena/large Poaceae					4	1	oat/large grass
Cereal indet.		4	11	1	64	9	cereal
Vicia sativa L cf ssp *sativa*	6		6	3		11	cultivated? vetch
Vicia faba L	23	24	17			4	bean
Lens culinaris Medik						6	lentil
? *Lens culinaris* Medik	1					21	? lentil
Pisum sativum L	3	3	14			9	pea
cf *Pisum sativum* L	4	8	12				?pea
large *Vicia/Lathyrus/Pisum*	80	59	149	1		165	vetch/vetchling/bean/pea

Wild species							Common name
Ranunculus acris/repens/bulbosus						1	buttercup
Papaver sp (not *P. somniferum*)						14	poppy
Urtica dioica L						7	common nettle
Chenopodiaceae	10	8	4	2	9	22	goosefoot family
Chenopodiaceae/Caryophyllaceae							goosefoot family/pink family
Stellaria media type					1		chickweed
Agrostemma githago L						1	corncockle
Silene latifolia ssp *alba* (Mill) Greuter&Burdet						9	white campion
Silene sp						1	campion/catchfly
Polygonum aviculare L.		1			1	2	knotgrass
Rumex actosella L							sheep's sorrel
Rumex sp	21	37	59	3	1	65	dock
Malva sylvestris L						2	common mallow
cf small *Malva* sp						1	mallow
Malvaceae				1		5	mallow family
Brassica/Sinapis	1					3	cabbage/turnip/mustard/ charlock
Vicia/Lathyrus	1	1		22	9		vetch/tare/vetchling
Medicago lupulina L						7	black medick
Melilotus/Medicago/Trifolium/Lotus	20	14	4	1	1	523	melilot/medick/clover/ bird's foot trefoil
Conium maculatum L						3	hemlock
Daucus carota L						59	wild carrot
Apiaceae						57	carrot family
Lithospermum arvense L.	1	1	1			18	field gromwell

Table 4.46 (continued) Charred plant remains Phase 5

Context no	9075	9099	9212	15199	15255	15380	
Sample no	509	508	503	800	806	808	
Phase	5	5	5	5	5	5	
Galeopsis sp			1				hempnettle
Plantago major L						15	greater plantain
Plantago lanceolata type			1				ribwort plantain
Euphrasia/Odontites				1	14	56	eyebright/red bartsia
Galium cf *aparine*	7					5	cleavers
Galium sp	4						cleavers/bedstraw
Sambucus nigra L						2	elder
Centaurea cf *scabiosa* L						5	greater knapweed
Centaurea sp						7	knapweed/cornflower
Lapsana communis L	1				1	10	nipplewort
cf *Leontodon autumnalis* L						1	autumn hawkbit
Picris hieracioides L						9	hawkweed oxtongue
Anthemis cotula L	11	13	8	4	29	17	stinking mayweed
Tripleurospermum sp						9	mayweed
Asteraceae indet		9	1			19	daisy family
Asteraceae indet flower head fragments						2	daisy family
Carex sp(p)	1		2			2	sedge(s)
cf *Lolium temulentum* L						4	? darnel
Poa annua L						3	annual meadow grass
? *Glyceria* sp						2	sweet-grass
Bromus hordeaceus/secalinus			1		1		soft/rye brome
Phleum pratense L		2			3		timothy
Poaceae indet			2		11	66	unidentified grasses
? tree/shrub buds			4				bud
Unidentified	7	2	8		2	52	unidentified seeds & other fragments
Total	203	187	319	39	241	1325	

Discussion

If the threshing waste from the legume crops was being used as tinder then it is likely that this was because it was available in some abundance. Threshing waste from several crops was probably combined, and may even have been stored as a useful product in its own right. It is likely that peas and beans would have been for human consumption but vetch and lentil are more likely to have been fodder crops. The relative paucity of domestic cereal remains familiar from the earlier periods is likely to be due to the changing use of the site. Domestic rubbish is probably still present, however, from the evidence of the rubbish pit. Rivet/macaroni wheat, bread wheat, barley and oat were all represented in the pit, and appear in small numbers in the other samples so it is likely that these crops were also in use on site.

Conclusion

The difference between the charred assemblages from Site 2 and Site 4 in Phase 1 is greater than the difference between Site 4 Phase 1 and the assemblages of Phase 2. Differences in activities are likely to be more significant in the resulting composition of cereal assemblages than mere chronological differences, especially when the same crops are involved throughout. These activities, however, are not always easy to define as the same crop product may become burned in a domestic fire due to activities relating to food preparation, or may have been the remains of a grain store burned as waste. The amount of charred material in the samples (except in the malting kiln) generally suggests burning due to minor accidents or rubbish disposal.

Bread wheat, rye, hulled barley, oat and flax were all cultivated throughout the Saxon period here, and peas and beans, though only a few of the legume seeds from the Saxon period could be identified. A single mineral-replaced seed of opium poppy was found in the late Saxon sunken feature building. Opium poppy was also found in the late Saxon/early medieval period at West Cotton (Campbell forthcoming).

The range of weed species from Phase 1 onwards included plants such as corncockle, thorow-wax and stinking mayweed which are often very typical of medieval cornfield assemblages. Some of the weed seeds may have been derived from hand cleaning of crops before final preparation for consumption. Many of the larger and heavier seeds, such as cleavers, corncockle and dock would be difficult to completely remove in processing. Some of the smaller seeds such as stinking mayweed, fat hen/goosefoot, and wild turnip/black mustard, can remain enclosed in capsules or attached to seed heads which may also have been difficult to remove except by hand cleaning. Such cleanings might easily be disposed of in a domestic hearth. Grain may have been burned as a result of minor spillages being swept into a hearth. There may also have been small accidents if grain was roasted prior to hand milling or as part of the process of preparing it for consumption. De Moulins (2006) suggests for the medieval period that weed seeds and some cereal grains may have dropped onto domestic floors from the roof thatch and then been swept into the hearth, and this is also a possibility here. There is an increase in the prevalence of weeds from Phase 3, which may suggest a change of husbandry practice, such as less efficient weeding, or less thorough crop processing. It may possibly also suggest that crop processing waste was being burned, of which only the weeds have survived.

Rivet or macaroni wheat appears in Phase 3 and seems from the radiocarbon date to indeed be pre-Conquest. The fragments of rivet/macaroni wheat rachis found in the Phase 1 sunken feature building were not radiocarbon dated and should probably be regarded as intrusive until further evidence shows otherwise.

The later medieval period, Phase 5 shows a complete change of emphasis from cereals to legumes, but this too, is likely to be a function of site activities rather than representing a major change in diet. As suggested above it seems likely from the weediness of the samples that legume threshing waste was burned in the pottery kilns. Probably this was legume waste rather than cereal waste simply because of availability, which does suggest that the economy of the site had changed. Legume crops were often grown in rotation with cereal crops because *Rhizobium* bacteria in the soil can fix atmospheric nitrogen if they can colonise legume roots (Davis *et al* 1992) and thus improve the fertility of the soil. This fertility-improving feature of legumes has been known to farmers for millennia. Vetch, lentil, and possibly some mix of small-seeded legumes may also have been grown for fodder, and could been part of a system of greater intensification of land use.

CHARCOALS *by Gill Thompson and Robert Francis*

Aims

The primary aims of this analysis have been to identify patterns of wood use and charcoal deposition at Higham Ferrers, both chronologically and spatially. The samples selected for analysis were chosen to span the five phases of occupation at the site, and to include a variety of types of deposit, including:

- charcoal from two hearths and three pits (possibly domestic fuel and refuse)
- sweepings on the floor of a pottery-making workshop
- the ashy residues recovered from the bottom of a ceramic kiln
- charcoal from a malting oven

Overall charcoal assemblage (Tables 4.47-4.48)

Thirteen samples were submitted for analysis and fragments from nine of these were identified (Table 4.49). These samples had been recovered by flotation and, except for sample 810, the flots had previously been sorted for other charred plant macroremains.

The charcoal assemblages were initially assessed in terms of their size, degree of fragmentation and their concentration in relation to the quantity of deposit which had been processed by flotation. This was achieved by weighing the total charcoal sample, sieving it into four fractions: >8 mm, 4-8 mm, 2-4 mm and <2 mm, then weighing each fraction (Table 4.48).

Samples 3, 801 and 808, from contexts 4015, 15218 and 15322 respectively, were weighed in total, but not subdivided because it had been decided not to identify the material from these contexts. This was because contexts 15218 and 15322 were ditch fills of uncertain taphonomy; context 4015 (the malting oven) was represented by two charcoal samples (3 and 5) and sample 5 comprised significantly more material than sample 3. Sample 502, from context 9060 which was from a beam slot for a building, was not sub-divided nor analysed as it was a very small sample.

Samples 110 and 115, from contexts 7027 and 7077 respectively, were analysed, but not subdivided by size as the assemblages contained very few fragments, as indicated in Table 4.48.

The samples ranged in weight from less than 3g up to nearly 250g. Two of the largest samples were from pits (6344 and 7236) and another significant sample weighing more than 100g came from the malting oven. This material from the malting oven was also the most concentrated deposit, as its concentration index was significantly higher than all the other deposits. This was probably due to the large quantities of charred grain in the assemblage.

If the weight of each size fraction is considered in terms of its proportion for the overall sample, it is clear that some charcoal assemblages have a fairly equitable distribution of large, medium-sized and small fractions. These include the burnt lens 15428 and pits 6344 and 6979. However, the charcoal recovered from pit 7236 may have had a different taphonomy, as there is much more comminuted material in the <2 mm size class. The charcoals in the layers 9212 and 9099 have been broken up, and the samples include relatively few large pieces of charcoal, and relatively large fractions of unidentifiable small fragments in the <2 mm size class.

Charcoal Identification

Methodology

The fragments to be identified were selected from each of the three identifiable size fractions mentioned earlier: >8 mm, 4-8 mm and 2-4 mm, in order to check whether there had been differential fragmentation, with certain types of wood being better represented in the smaller or larger size categories.

Cumulative subsampling of groups of 30 fragments was carried out in order to characterise the taxonomic diversity of the assemblage. Initially, 30 fragments were randomly selected, comprising up to ten from each of the size fractions. The number of taxa represented (excluding 'Indeterminate') was calculated and a further 30 fragments were analysed, cumulatively calculating the number of taxa present, until the number had stabilised and no new charcoal types were added to the list. There were some instances where fewer than ten fragments were available for analysis and in these instances, all the material was examined.

Standard methods of specimen preparation (Leney & Casteel 1975) were followed, fracturing individual fragments in three planes and viewing the wood anatomy using a Leica MZ11 low power stereomicroscope at x10-40 and an epi-illuminating Olympus BX41m microscope at magnifications of x100-500. The wood anatomy was compared with published sources (Schweingruber 1982; Hather 2000) and with the modern charcoal reference collection from the Department of Archaeological Sciences at Bradford.

The taxonomic diversity is recorded in Table 4.49 and the proportions of the various taxa are presented in Table 4.50. This presents the total number of fragments analysed and their proportion within the whole assemblage. Equal weight is given to large, medium and small fragments.

The figures in the table are for the number of taxa (excluding Indeterminates) found in each cumulative subsample, i.e. subsample 1 is up to 30 fragments, subsample 2 is up to 60 fragments, subsample 3 is up to 90 fragments etc.

Discussion

The samples analysed varied in their taxonomic composition, from just one taxon to at least six taxa (plus indeterminate fragments). Five of the nine samples analysed were dominated by oak (*Quercus* sp.), and oak was indeed dominant overall, occurring in all nine contexts. It is noteworthy that the three pit samples were each dominated by a single taxon. All three pit samples were predominantly oak, with pits 6344 and 7236 being exclusively oak and the phase 2b pit, 6929, being almost entirely oak, with a single fragment of *Prunus*. This is consistent with the charcoals from individual fires being deposited quickly in the pits, without subsequent mixing with debris from other fires. Another sample dominated by oak was from the malting oven (context 4015) where the charcoal might possibly have been produced by the fire used to heat the grain. This sample, though, also included a small proportion of hazel and maple. The other contexts with mainly oak charcoal were the burnt lens within the ditch (context 15428) (77% oak) and the hearth context 7077 (60%). By contrast, the most diverse assemblages were from hearth context 7027, with six taxa identified, layer 9212 with five taxa, and layer 9099 with only four.

Samples 503 (debris over workshop floor, context 9212) and 508 (ash layer from base of pottery kiln flue, context 9099) comprised mostly roundwood of

Table 4.47: Catalogue of charcoal samples

Site	Sample no.	Context no.	Feature no.	Feature type	Revised Phase	Notes
4	102	6344	6343	pit	1: 5th-6th c	one of a series of pits close to SFBs
4	110	7027	6811	hearth	2c: late 8th - e 9th c	hearth in posthole building
4	115	7077	6811	hearth	2c: late 8th - e 9th c	hearth in posthole building
4	117	6979	7023	pit	2b: mid 8th - late 8th c	pit close by posthole building
4	120	7236	7235	pit	3: mid 9th - 11th c	also contained slag, animal bone, burnt stone, fired clay
5	3	4015	4010	malting oven	2c: late 8th - e 9th c	deposit from within chamber
5	5	4015	4010	malting oven	2c: late 8th - e 9th c	deposit from within chamber
6	502	9060	9184	gully	2c: late 8th - e 9th c	beam slot of building
6	503	9212	9008	layer	5: late 14th - late 15th c	debris over workshop floor
6	508	9099	9200	layer	5: late 14th - late 15th c	ash layer from base of pottery kiln flue
8	801	15218	15165	ditch fill	2b: mid 8th - late 8th c	enclosure ditch extension
8	808	15322	15323	ditch fill	5: late 14th - late 15th c	shallow ditch
8	810	15428	15190	burnt lens in ditch	2c: late 8th - e 9th c	from final variant of enclosure ditch

Shading indicates that material was identified.

Table 4.48: Weight data for charcoals

Phase	1	2b	2b	2c	2c	2c	2c	2c
Feature type	Pit	Pit	Ditch fill	Malting oven	Malting oven	Hearth	Hearth	Burnt lens in ditch
Sample no.	102	117	801	3	5	110	115	810
Context no.	6344	6979	15218	4015	4015	7027	7077	15428
Feature no.	6344	7023	15165	4010	4010	6811	6811	15190
Volume of soil processed (litres)	40	16	40	9	10	40	10	5
Weight of >8mm fraction (grammes)	52.4	20.4			0.4			5.0
Weight of 4-8mm fraction (grammes)	58.3	21.2			4.4			3.0
Weight of 2-4mm fraction (grammes)	60.6	26.5			27.7			2.0
Weight of <2mm fraction (grammes)	72.4	28.6			86.8			4.0
Total weight of sample (grammes)	243.7	96.7	14.8	18.2	119.3	3.3	2.7	14.0
Charcoal concentration (grammes of charcoal per litre of soil floated)	6.091	6.04	0.37	2.02	11.93	0.082	0.27	2.74

Table 4.49: Charcoal: Sample diversity: cumulative sub-sampling data

Phase	1	2b	2c	2c	2c	2c	3	5	5
Feature type	Pit	Pit	Malting oven	Hearth	Hearth	Burnt lens in ditch	Pit	Layer	Layer
Sample no.	102	117	5	110	115	810	120	503	508
Context no.	6344	6979	4015	7027	7077	15428	7236	9212	9099
Feature no.	6343	7023	4010	6811	6811	15190	7235	9008	9200
Subsample									
1	1	2	2	3	2	2	1	4	4
2		2	3	5	3	3		5	4
3			3	6	3	3		5	
4				6					

Table 4.50: Charcoal: Taxonomic composition of the assemblages

Revised phase	1	2b	2c	2c	2c	2c	3	5	5
Feature type	Pit	Pit	Malting oven	Hearth	Hearth	Burnt lens in ditch	Pit	Layer	Layer
Sample no.	102	117	5	110	115	810	120	503	508
Context no.	6344	6979	4015	7027	7077	15428	7236	9212	9099
Feature no.	6343	7023	4010	6811	6811	15190	7235	9008	9200
Acer			1 (1.53%)	16 (40%)					
Betula								1 (1.44%)	
Corylus			6 (9.23%)	2 (5%)	2 (6.6%)	2 (3.50%)			
Fraxinus								1 (1.44%)	1 (3.22%)
Pomoideae				9 (22.5%)				30 (43.47%)	10 (32.25%)
Prunus		1 (1.66%)		2 (5%)	10 (33.3%)	7 (12.28%)		27 (39.13%)	13 (41.93%)
Quercus	30 (100%)	59 (98.33%)	57 (87.69%)	9 (22.5%)	18 (60%)	44 (77.19%)	30 (100%)	7 (10.14%)	1 (3.22%)
Salix / Populus				1 (2.5%)					
Indeterminate			1 (1.53%)	1 (2.5%)		4 (7.01%)		3 (4.33%)	6 (19.35%)
Total no. of fragments analysed	30	60	65	40	30	57	30	69	31

2c *Gully*	3 *Pit*	5 *Ditch fill*	5 *Layer*	5 *Layer*
502	120	808	503	508
9060	7236	15322	9212	9099
9184	7235	15323	9008	9200
40	40	18	10	10
	9.8		2.8	0.4
	22.4		5.5	0.9
	62.0		6.5	2.0
	103.0		19.2	9.5
6.5	197.2	27.2	34	12.8
0.16	4.93	1.51	3.35	1.25

a diameter generally between 1-9 mm. The small size of these twigs suggests that the charcoal is more likely to be the debris from kindling or fuel wood rather than burnt structural material. This young wood proved hard to fracture and identify. Context 9212 (debris over the workshop floor) also contained small quantities of charred thorns, c.3–4 mm in length. Context 9212 included charcoals from *Prunus* and the Pomoideae. The *Prunus* may be that of *Prunus spinosa*, which has thorns, and there are also two thorned taxa within the Pomoideae sub family: *Crataegus* sp and *Malus sylvestris*. Unfortunately due to the small size of these fragments it was impossible to identify the Prunus fragments to species, and the Pomoideae are renowned for the difficulty of separating the species on the basis of their wood anatomy (Gale and Cutler, 2000, 183).

RADIOCARBON AND ARCHAEOMAGNETIC DATING RESULTS *(Figs 4.31)*

Radiocarbon dating

A total of six radiocarbon dates were obtained from the various sites.

Phase 2c Human bone
Wk 12318 (University of Waikato, New Zealand)
Sample ID   HFKML 01 Cxt 6678
Description   Left Calcaneus bone from human skeleton
NZA   13004
d13C (o/oo)   -19.7 +/- 0.2 ‰
%
Radiocarbon age   1216 +/- 41 BP
delta-14C   -127.6 +/- 4.2 ‰
DELTA- 14C (o/oo)   -140.5 +/- 4.4 ‰

Per-cent modern   86.0 +/-0.4
Calibrated Age: 68.2% confidence interval (1 sigma)
          770 AD to 890 AD
Calibrated Age: 95.4% confidence interval (2 sigma)
          680AD (93.2%) 900AD
920AD (2.2%) 940AD

Phase 2c Human jawbone
R 28471/1   (Rafter Radiocarbon Laboratory, Institute of Geological and Nuclear Sciences Ltd, New Zealand)
Sample ID HFKML01 <355>
Description: Human bone
NZA 19399
d13C (o/oo) -19.51
Radiocarbon age 1235 +/- 35 BP
delta-14C (o/oo) -138.5 +/- 3.8
DELTA-14C -148.1 +/- 3.8
Per-cent modern 85.19 +/- 0.38
CALIBRATED AGE in terms of confidence intervals (Smoothing parameter: 1)
2 sigma interval is 683 AD to 889 AD 1267 BP to 1061 BP (98.2% of area)
1 sigma interval is 718 AD to 746 AD 1232 BP to 1204 BP (17.0% of area)
 plus 767 AD to 823 AD 1183 BP to 1127 BP (34.8% of area)
 plus 839 AD to 865 AD 1111 BP to 1085 BP (13.2% of area)

Phase 2c Human Jawbone
R 28471/2   (Rafter Radiocarbon Laboratory, Institute of Geological and Nuclear Sciences Ltd, New Zealand)
Sample ID HFKML01 <356>
Description: Human bone
NZA 19400
d13C (o/oo) -19.67
Radiocarbon age 1344 +/- 40 BP
delta-14C (o/oo) -150.4 +/- 4.2
DELTA-14C -159.6 +/- 4.2
Per-cent modern 84.04 +/- 0.42
CALIBRATED AGE in terms of confidence intervals (Smoothing parameter: 1)
2 sigma interval is 641 AD to 725 AD 1309 BP to 1225 BP (76.9% of area)
 plus 739 AD to 770 AD 1211 BP to 1180 BP (14.5% of area)
 1 sigma interval is 656 AD to 690 AD 1294 BP to 1260 BP (47.7% of area)

Phase 2c Malting oven grain
R 26416 (Rafter Radiocarbon Laboratory, Institute of Geological and Nuclear Sciences Ltd, New Zealand)
Sample ID   <1> 307 HFKML00
Description   Charred cereal grain – *Hordeum Vulgare*
NZA   13004
d13C (o/oo)   -22.75
Radiocarbon age   1196 +/- 85 BP
delta-14C   -139.7 +/- 9.2
DELTA- 14C (o/oo)   143.6 +/- 9.1
Per-cent modern   85.64 +/- 0.91
Calibrated Age: 68% confidence interval (1 sigma)
          710 AD to 963 AD
Calibrated Age: 95% confidence interval (2 sigma)
          662 AD to 1014 AD

Phase 3 Human bone (child burial)
OxA -10125
Sample ID   HSF99/79/16
Description   Human bone
d13C (o/oo)   -18.9 ‰
Radiocarbon age   1095 +/- 45 BP
Calibrated Age: 95.0% confidence interval (2 sigma)
      780 AD to 1030

Phase 3 Rivet wheat (*Triticum turgidum*) rachis
OxA -10126
Sample ID   HFKM95
Description   *Triticum turgidum* rachis
d13C (o/oo)   -26.1 ‰
Radiocarbon age   1150 +/- 45 BP
Calibrated Age: 95.0% confidence interval (2 sigma)
      770 AD to 1000 AD

Age, delta-14C, DELTA-14C and absolute per cent
Modern are as defined by Stuiver and Polach
Radiocarbon 19: 355-363 (1977).
1998 Atmospheric delta 14C and radiocarbon ages from:
Stuiver, M., Reimer, P.J., Bard,E., Beck, J.W., Burr, G.S.,
Hughen, K.A., Kromer, B., McCormac, F.G., v.d. Plicht, J.,
and Spurk,M. 1998, Radiocarbon 40(3):1041-1083

Archaeomagnetic dating *by Paul Linford*

Introduction

During the excavation of Site 6, in 2002, the
exposure of a well-preserved late medieval pottery
kiln provided an opportunity to conduct a
programme of archaeomagnetic analysis, to
produce absolute dating to set beside both the
typological date ranges of the pottery, and historical
references to pottery production in Higham Ferrers.

Methodology

The feature was given the CfA archaeomagnetic
feature code HF. Samples were collected from it
using the disc method (see Appendix 3, section 1a)
and orientated to magnetic north using a compass.
Subsequently the International Geomagnetic
Reference Field (IGRF 2000) was used to establish
that magnetic north was 3.2° west of true north at
the site on the date when the samples were taken
and the sample orientations were corrected accord-
ingly. Twenty-three samples were collected from the
pedestal and wall lining of the kiln as indicated in
the sketch plan shown in Figure 2 (Samples 01 and
09 fragmented on extraction, the number 15 was not
used as a sample identifier). All but two of the
samples were of very well fired clay: those from the
pedestal (samples numbers <=18) were yellow/grey
in colouration; those from the wall lining (sample
numbers > 20) were a more orange colour. The two
exceptions, 19 and 20, were discovered on cleaning
in the laboratory, to be of a whitish stone that had
been incorporated into the wall lining.

The natural remanent magnetisation (NRM)
measured in archaeomagnetic samples is assumed
to be caused by thermoremanent magnetisation
(TRM) created at the time when the feature of
which they were part was last fired. However, a
secondary component acquired in later geomag-

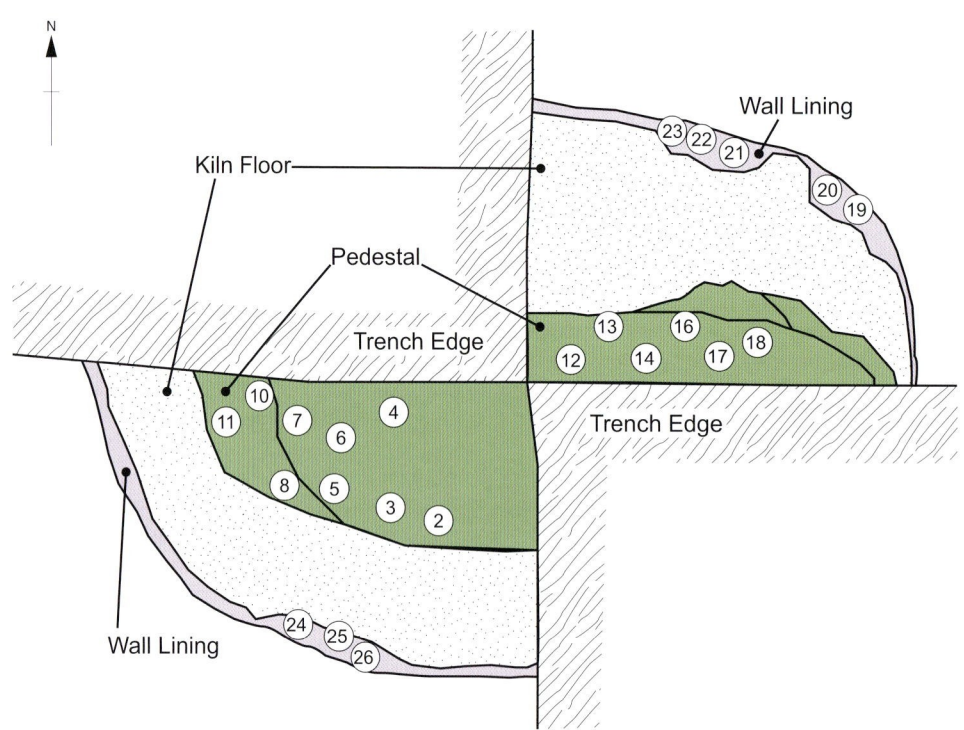

Fig. 4.31   Site 6: Sketch plan of Kiln 1 showing the locations of the archaeomagnetic samples

netic fields can also be present, caused by diagenesis or partial reheating. Additionally, the primary TRM may be overprinted by a viscous component, depending on the grain size distribution within the magnetic material. These secondary components are usually of lower stability than the primary TRM and can thus be removed by partial demagnetisation of the samples.

A typical strategy used in archaeomagnetic analysis of a feature is first to measure the NRM field recorded in all the samples. Then a number of representative samples are selected for pilot partial demagnetisation depending upon their material composition and NRM characteristics. Partial demagnetisation involves exposing the sample to an alternating magnetic field of fixed peak strength then measuring the resulting changes in its magnetisation. This procedure is repeated with increasing peak field strengths to build up a complete picture of the coercivity spectrum of the sample. The equipment used for these measurements is described in section 2 of the appendix.

After inspection of the coercivity spectra of the pilot samples, optimum field strength is selected where it is judged that the maximum amount of

Plate 4.6   Kiln 1 during archaeomagnetic sampling, viewed from the west. The quadrant containing samples 01-11(see Fig. 4.31) is visible in the centre of the picture

secondary magnetisation has been removed, whilst preserving the majority of the primary magnetisation. The remaining samples are then partially demagnetised using this optimum peak alternating field strength. In some cases the set of samples can be partitioned into groups with different material composition or magnetic characteristics. When this occurs several different field strengths may be used, each one judged to be the optimum for a particular group.

A mean TRM direction is calculated from the sample measurements made after partial demagnetisation at their optimum field strength. Some samples may be excluded from this calculation if their TRM directions are so anomalous as to make them statistical outliers from the overall TRM distribution. A "magnetic refraction" correction is often applied to the sample mean TRM direction to compensate for distortion of the earth's magnetic field due to the geometry of the magnetic fabric of the feature itself. Then the mean is adjusted according to the location of the feature relative to a notional central point in the UK (Meriden), so that it can be compared with UK archaeomagnetic calibration data to produce a date of last firing for the feature. Notes concerning the mean calculation and subsequent calibration can be found in sections 3 and 4 of the appendix.

This measurement and calibration strategy was applied to the analysis of the samples from Higham Ferrers. All the samples used to calculate the mean TRM direction were taken from the pedestal, a horizontal surface, so a magnetic refraction correction of 2.4o was added to this mean's inclination before calibration.

Results

Sample NRM measurements and measurements after partial demagnetisation are recorded in Table Appendix 3.1. (Table and Figure numbers refer to Tables and Figures in Appendix 3 below). Figure Appendix 3.1 depicts the distribution of the sample TRM directions before and after partial demagnetisation. Table Appendix 3.2 records the pilot demagnetisation measurements made on samples 03, 14 and 25 whilst Figures Appendix 3.2-3.4 illustrate these results graphically.

The maximum stability of the TRM in each pilot sample was estimated using the method of Tarling and Symons (1967). The maximum stability parameters and ranges over which they persist are listed for each sample in Table Appendix 3.3. In this method, any sample with a maximum stability parameter greater than 2 is judged to record a stable TRM direction and a parameter value over 5 suggests extreme stability. The figures in Table Appendix 3.3 indicate that the magnetisations of all the pilot demagnetisation samples are extremely stable.

However, it can be seen from Table Appendix 3.1 that the stone samples, 19 and 20, have extremely low magnetisation intensities and highly anomalous directions. These results indicate that the stone did not contain a suitable magnetic mineralogy to acquire a stable remanent magnetisation. These two samples were thus excluded from further analysis.

It is also clear from Figure Appendix 3.1 a, that the other samples that came from the kiln wall lining (sample numbers > 20) all have steeper inclinations than those taken from the pedestal, which cluster to form the main grouping. Furthermore, inspection of the pilot demagnetisation results from sample 25 (see Figure Appendix 3.4), suggests that this effect is not due to perturbation by low stability viscous remanence. Such anomalous steepening of the inclinations of samples taken from strongly magnetised features has been noted previously. Samples taken from the walls of kilns have been found to have inclinations often several degrees steeper than those of samples taken from the floors of the same kilns. The phenomenon is not well understood but it has been suggested that it is due either to magnetic refraction caused by the shape of the structure (Aitken and Hawley, 1971; Schurr et al. 1984), or to the magnetisation of those parts of the feature that cool first distorting the magnetic field through the feature (Tarling *et al*, 1986). Owing to this uncertainty, the remaining kiln wall lining samples were omitted from the present analysis, directed towards dating the Higham Ferrers kiln, but have been retained for possible future research into the phenomenon of magnetic distortion.

Inspection of the most stable ranges of the pilot samples in Table Appendix 3.3 suggested that the optimum field strength for partial demagnetisation of the remaining samples (all from the kiln pedestal) was 5mT. The results of measurements made after applying this demagnetising field are tabulated in Table Appendix 3.1 and depicted in Figure Appendix 3.1 b.

The mean TRM vector for the feature was calculated from the measurements made on the 15 pedestal samples after this 5mT partial demagnetisation:

At site: Dec = 2.3° Inc = 56.5° α_{95} = 2.0° k = 372.8
At Meriden: Dec = 2.0° Inc = 56.6°

Figure Appendix 3.5 shows the comparison of the mean TRM vector with the UK archaeomagnetic calibration curve depicted on a Bauer plot. The date of the last firing of the kiln deduced from it is:

1395 AD to 1425 AD at the 63% confidence level.
1385 AD to 1435 AD at the 95% confidence level.

Conclusions

Archaeomagnetic analysis of the Higham Ferrers kiln has shown it to be well fired but with some magnetic distortion to the remanence directions of the samples taken from the wall lining. However, after rejecting these samples, it was still possible to obtain a mean TRM vector of good precision using the 15 samples taken from the central pedestal of the structure. From this mean TRM it was possible to deduce an archaeomagnetic date for the last firing of the kiln, indicating that this event occurred in the early part of the 15th century AD. This date suggests that the kiln analysed in this report is not the one referred to in the documentary evidence and that Late Medieval Reduced Ware production at Higham Ferrers might thus have begun earlier than previously supposed.

Archaeomagnetic Date Summary

Archaeomagnetic ID:
HF
Feature:
Late medieval clay lined pottery kiln
Location:
Longitude 0.6oW, Latitude 52.3oN
Number of Samples (taken/used in mean):
23/15
AF Demagnetisation Applied:
5mT
Distortion Correction Applied:
+2.4°
Declination (at Meriden):
2.3° (2.0°)
Inclination (at Meriden):
56.5° (56.6°)
Alpha-95:
2.0°
k:
372.8
Date range (63% confidence):
1395 to 1425 AD
Date range (95% confidence):
1385 to 1435 AD
Independent date estimate:
1350 AD to 1550 AD (for pottery typology)

Chapter 5: Discussion

INTRODUCTION

The original project research design presumed (with good reason in the light of the available information at the time) that the site was that of a single settlement evolving – possibly without interruption – through five centuries. At the time the generic process of transition from early Saxon settlements through to prototypical nucleated 'villages' was a keenly debated issue. Concepts such as the 'Middle Saxon shift' – first espoused by Arnold and Wardle (1981) were attempts to explain the apparent absence of mid-Saxon and early Saxon antecedents for late Saxon nucleated settlements and early medieval villages. They suggested a shift of settlement from light to heavy soils, and a concurrent coalescing of scattered settlement into nucleated sites, driven by changes in land use (ibid. 149). The pre-excavation assessment of the evidence at Kings Meadow Lane appeared to show a well-preserved example of this process, displaying evidence of an organic evolution, and visible 'shift' of settlement, over a period of at least five centuries.

Over the last decade or so, the great amount of early and middle Saxon settlement excavation has emphasised the fluidity of early Saxon settlement; maybe the term should be more Middle Saxon 'coalescence', describing a period (broadly from the mid 7th century to the 9th century) when a number of distinct but interrelated factors caused rural society to agglomerate (see Hamerow 2002, 123-4).

Ironically, the archaeological evidence from Kings Meadow Lane shows more radical changes in settlement and land use between the 5th and 10th centuries than was first surmised, and on the face of it supports the scenario of a more abrupt settlement shift. However, it will be argued, that this has more to do with politics than with social economics.

The following discussion examines the evidence in a broadly chronological sequence. The evidence as a whole points to intermittent settlement and/or activity in the area of Kings Meadow Lane, with little in the way of continuity of settlement. The essential character of each phase is distinct in itself, and in each case, appears to have had little direct influence on subsequent occupation. Such similarities that are apparent arguably owe most to the overall topography of the area, namely the geographic factors of the two routes bracketing the area, and more broadly, the River Nene itself. Therefore, as the archaeological narrative of the Kings Meadow Lane area is essentially episodic, it is best to structure the discussion to suit.

EARLY SAXON SETTLEMENT (MID 5th CENTURY TO LATE 6th CENTURY)

Research context

As Reynolds (forthcoming) says, the framework of early archaeological research into early Saxon settlement and the course of migration was governed by the almost exclusive reliance on the most easily identified evidence, that is, the grave goods of pre-Christian burial sites. As is now accepted, grave goods may be as much about cultural shifts or fashion as genuine demographic movements. The development of DNA analysis may well in time enable such issues to be clarified, but as Miles argues, it is not as yet a 'magic wand' and it cannot yet determine without doubt whether a burial is that of a immigrant or a British native, regardless of what shape their brooch is (Miles 2005, 174-5).

The traditional view, inspired as much from a romanticised vision of the past as from hard evidence, that the incomers represented an organised invasion, with 'ready-to-rule' dynasties, poised to take over from the helpless and hapless natives, has long since been discredited by archaeological evidence (Yorke, 2001, 13). However, researchers instinctively persist in looking for an overall pattern – however nebulous – for the beginnings of early Anglo-Saxon settlement.

The sites at Kings Meadow Lane have provided an excellent example of one of the varieties of transition from Roman to Anglo-Saxon settlement. The subject is one that – after decades of debate – still evades any easy consensus, and various scenarios have been enthusiastically championed at different times. For a period in the 1980s it became popular to argue that there were instances of Anglo-Saxon incomers taking over working Romano-British villas – in other words – that there was a conscious effort to maintain key elements of the Romano-British infrastructure, and to imply an almost seamless process whereby a working Roman villa became an Anglo-Saxon one. The correlation between some of the Roman and Anglo-Saxon features on the site at Barton Court Farm, in Oxfordshire is particularly interesting and has been used by Hodges (1989, 17) to imply the continuity of a working estate, and, more recently, by Reynolds (1999, 41) to argue the opposite, that respecting some of the pre-existing landscape features was purely pragmatism on the part of the incomers.

However as the available database of sites and evidence has accumulated in the last few decades, the reality begins to look much less uniform than earlier scenarios would have it, and researchers seem to be moving perhaps reluctantly towards the conclusion that the transition process was more influenced by small-scale circumstance, the personalities of the incomers, and the reception accorded them by the native population. By their nature such factors cannot easily be deduced from the archaeological record. In this context, the evidence from Higham Ferrers points to such a opportunistic re-settlement, with Saxon incomers moving into a probably deserted, and possibly cleared area, but showing no interest in the relict Romano-British infrastructure.

Chronology of the Higham Ferrers settlement

It is not within the remit of this volume to examine in detail the decline and abandonment of the Roman settlement (Lawrence and Smith, forthcoming), but the evidence seems to point to a definite interval between the end of the Roman town and the advent of the Saxon settlers. The artefactual evidence seems to indicate that the Roman town was no longer a functioning small town by the end of the 4th century. No Roman-British coinage dating to the second half of the 4th century was found, although it is accepted that the importance of this factor can be overstated – it does not necessarily represent conclusive proof of abandonment, only the breakdown of the money economy. As the Roman town 'centre' was situated to the south of the excavated areas, there is no certainty that the entire town was deserted, but it seems most probable the Saxon incomers were confronted by a derelict and overgrown site, all but deserted for the previous few decades.

As a whole the artefactual dating from the SFB deposits – suggested by the presence of early Saxon decorated pottery – indicates that Saxon occupation in the area of Kings Meadow Lane began no earlier than the mid 5th century and, in its first phase, extended well into the 6th century. Interestingly, the pottery from the secure contexts of the SFB fills suggests that the incomers settled in the area of Sites 1 and 2 at first, well away from the Roman settlement, and only later was there settlement within the derelict Roman town itself. This reinforces the impression given by the location of the SFBs identified on Sites 9 and 10 that they were not sited with particular consideration to the layout of the Roman settlement itself, although it may be significant that two of the SFBs were situated either side of the road. It would be tempting to deduce that they were respecting an existing, and perhaps still used, road, but it may just mean that they were using the margins of the derelict road as relatively clear areas within which to site their buildings, and in the case of the SFB to the east of the road, its location may have been a response to the shelter afforded by the Roman building to the north-east.

Notwithstanding these uncertainties of detail, overall the site of the early Saxon occupation and its character is consistent with a scenario of a family or small group of possibly first-generation immigrants making their way up the Nene Valley to a suitable spot – perhaps attracted by the easy river crossing at this point – ignoring the remains of the Roman town, and building their own community on cleared land further up the dry valley to the south-east.

Extent of the settlement

The SFBs fall into three spatial groups, on Site 1, on Site 4, and thirdly loosely scattered across the Roman settlement to the west, on Sites 9 and 10. Given the incomplete coverage of the fieldwork over the project area as a whole, and the occasional finds of 5th- and 6th-century Saxon pottery sherds in areas away from the known SFBs, for instance on Site 7, it would be a mistake to assume that these three groups represent all the Phase 1 activity in the area of Kings Meadow Lane.

Early-middle Saxon hand-built pottery has also been found at Wharf Road, approximately 1 km to the south of Kings Meadow Lane (Blinkhorn 2003b), and this included a single small fragment with combed decoration, indicating an early Saxon date. Other finds of early Saxon pottery have been recovered from later Saxon or medieval assemblages from sites within the historic core of the town (Jones and Chapman 2003, 132-3; see Blinkhorn, Chapter 4). While no focus of settlement or structural evidence have yet been identified, it is very likely that early Saxon occupation continued sporadically along the high ground along the southern bank of the Nene to the south of Kings Meadow Lane, just as it appears to have done to the north (see below).

Character of the settlement

Once settled, there is no archaeological evidence to suggest that any effort was spent in reviving or maintaining the boundary ditches of the Romano-British field system, at least not that part evident in the investigated areas.

It has been argued on the basis of recent research that the laying out and maintenance of carefully demarcated fields and property boundaries was a consequence of the creation of nucleated settlements. Where there was ample land and no competition, and a greater reliance upon low energy pastoral subsistence farming, rather than organised cereal farming, there was no need to expend effort in marking out land boundaries (Miles 2005, 183). The ownership of land did not represent status or identity; status derived from the portable wealth of personal adornments and livestock, and identity was derived from kin, or tribal group.

The lack of interest that the incomers showed towards the attractions of the Roman way of life is less of a puzzle when one considers, as Barnwell suggests (2003, 6), that the settlers were themselves, or just one or two generations removed from, immigrants from the northern fringes of the Roman empire on the continent, and as such had never become familiar with, or adapted to Roman ways in their homeland.

There is no overall focus to the early Saxon settlement at Kings Meadow Lane, although loose groupings are evident on Sites 1 and 4. Whether this represents two contemporary and distinct family groups or the same family group moving from one area to another is impossible to determine on the basis of the finds evidence. However, SFBs 6057 and 6356 are worthy of further consideration, given their close relative proximity and alignment (Pl. 3.2). On these grounds it is reasonable to suggest that the two SFBs were contemporary and functionally related. The distinct difference between the carefully sculpted deep pit of SFB 6057, and the shallow rudimentary pit, combined with a complex arrangement of structural postholes of SFB 6356, suggests that each was specifically designed for a different role. It is tempting to suggest that SFB 6057 was the family sleeping quarters, and SFB 6356 the family workshop, although this is based upon no hard artefactual evidence.

A notable absence from the catalogue of buildings in Phase 1 at Higham Ferrers is evidence for any 'halls', or rectangular post-built buildings. It cannot be ruled out that they may have been sited in unexcavated areas, although this seems a rather contrived explanation. Given the typically lightly-founded nature of such buildings, truncation by later ploughing might be a consideration if it were not for the evident survival of several Middle Saxon post-built buildings in the same general area.

Instances of buildings in settlements of this period being restricted to SFBs are not uncommon in the same broad region, as for example at Melford Meadows, Brettenham (Mudd, 2002, 113) or Brandon Road, Thetford (Dallas 1993, 13-14). A recently published suite of Early and Middle Saxon SFBs and halls found at Yarnton, north of Oxford, was subjected to an extensive programme of radiocarbon testing, showing that, while there were instances of SFBs in existence alongside halls as late as the 8th century, there were no instances of hall buildings being contemporary with the Early Saxon SFBs (Bayliss and Hey, 2004, 263).

Where SFBs and 'halls' co-exist, as at West Stow, for instance, the temptation is strong to assign specific roles to the two types of building; most conveniently that the halls were dwellings, and the SFBs were associated craft workshops. It was argued that the craft could be determined from the evidence within the pit. The fairly common occurrence of textile-related objects – particularly loomweights – within SFB pits led some to conclude that SFBs were weaving sheds. To support this Ahrens (1966, 224-5) suggested that the pit of an SFB would provide a more humid atmosphere which was a benefit in textile manufacture. Incidents such as the discovery of loomweights in a number of SFB pits at

Mucking seemed to reinforce the idea, although Hamerow maintained a cautious circumspection (Hamerow 1993, 19). Experiments at West Stow have since shown that the sunken pit of an SFB does not significantly increase the humidity within the building, so weaving could have taken place as easily in a hall as in an SFB (Tipper 2004, 171-2). Furthermore, the restricted light and space available in a traditionally conceived SFB would have surely hampered a craft like weaving. It is worth noting at this stage that no loomweights were found at Higham Ferrers; two spindle whorls and a pinbeater were the only weaving-related tools found in the early Saxon phase of settlement.

Once it is accepted that the fill of an SFB – most likely deposited *after* the building had gone out of use – may have no connection the SFB's role (Tipper 2004, 184), then, with the advantage of a greatly increased body of data, it can now be confidently argued that SFBs could have had a variety of different roles, both domestic and 'industrial'. The basic design was modified to suit whatever function was required for a particular building at a particular time (ibid, 185).

If the possibility that the footprints of Phase 1 post-built buildings were destroyed by later plough erosion is discounted then it is difficult to see that the SFBs at Kings Meadow Lane were exclusively workshops or small stores. The absence of halls at this time may have had more to do with the requirements and resources (both timber and human) of the inhabitants. An early Saxon settlement comprising solely SFBs may not have had sufficient population to build a hall, nor need to do so (Hamerow 2002, 51).

Material culture of the settlement

In terms of the economy of this settlement, the evidence from the material remains, almost exclusively recovered from the SFB hollows, is an unremarkable. The assemblage is entirely consistent with the settlement detritus of a self-contained group or extended family. Blinkhorn points out that no reconstructable pots, or large parts thereof, were recovered from any SFB hollow. This suggests that the source of the refuse within the hollows derived from secondary deposition, originating in domestic middens of some description.

Moffett (see Chapter 4) argues that the charred plant material from the SFBs on Sites 1 and 4 suggests some variation in associated activities. Little in the way of cereals was recovered from the SFBs on Site 1, suggesting that if cereals were being processed, it was not in the immediate vicinity. This absence of cereal remains could imply an emphasis in this part of the settlement on animal husbandry rather than cereal cultivation. In contrast, the relative abundance of clean cereal remains in Site 4 SFBs suggests that preparation for consumption was the activity carried out in or near the buildings. Does this varied evidence imply divisions of labour, or distinct roles in different parts of the settlement, or for different family groups, or just variations in domestic practice over time? All that can be said is that any or all of these options are possible.

The animal bone evidence (see Evans Chapter 4) suggests that numbers of cattle, sheep and pig were present in broadly similar proportions. The relatively high proportion of pig (compared to later phases) could suggest a more wooded landscape, and suggests that pig was the principal source of meat.

Regional context

In terms of the character of the settlement represented by the dispersed scatter of SFBs on either side of the Lane, there is little that sets it apart from other 5th- and 6th-century settlements in the region. The fieldwalking and excavation results from the extensive Raunds Project, 6 kilometres to the north-east (Fig. 5.1), also suggest a development of scattered settlement on the slopes above the River Nene, and alongside lesser watercourses in the area, avoiding both the wet floodplains, and the heavy Boulder Clay of the uplands (Parry 2006, pages).

Structural evidence of the Sunken Featured Buildings

Across the entire development area a total of eleven definite Sunken Featured Buildings (SFBs), and one probable SFB, were identified and except in two cases, fully exposed and excavated. There was some variation in the preservation of the SFBs, and the clarity of their groundplan. Two of those within the Roman settlement were particularly difficult to define against the background 'noise' of Roman features and layers; one other had been truncated by a modern service trench.

These exceptions aside, generally the features of each SFB, comprising the pit and associated postholes (both within the pit and in close proximity) had suffered only moderate disturbance from medieval and modern ploughing.

Current thinking

The argument over the form and function of SFBs in this country has developed over the last 80 or so years, and will not be revisited in detail here. However, the evidence from Higham Ferrers, along

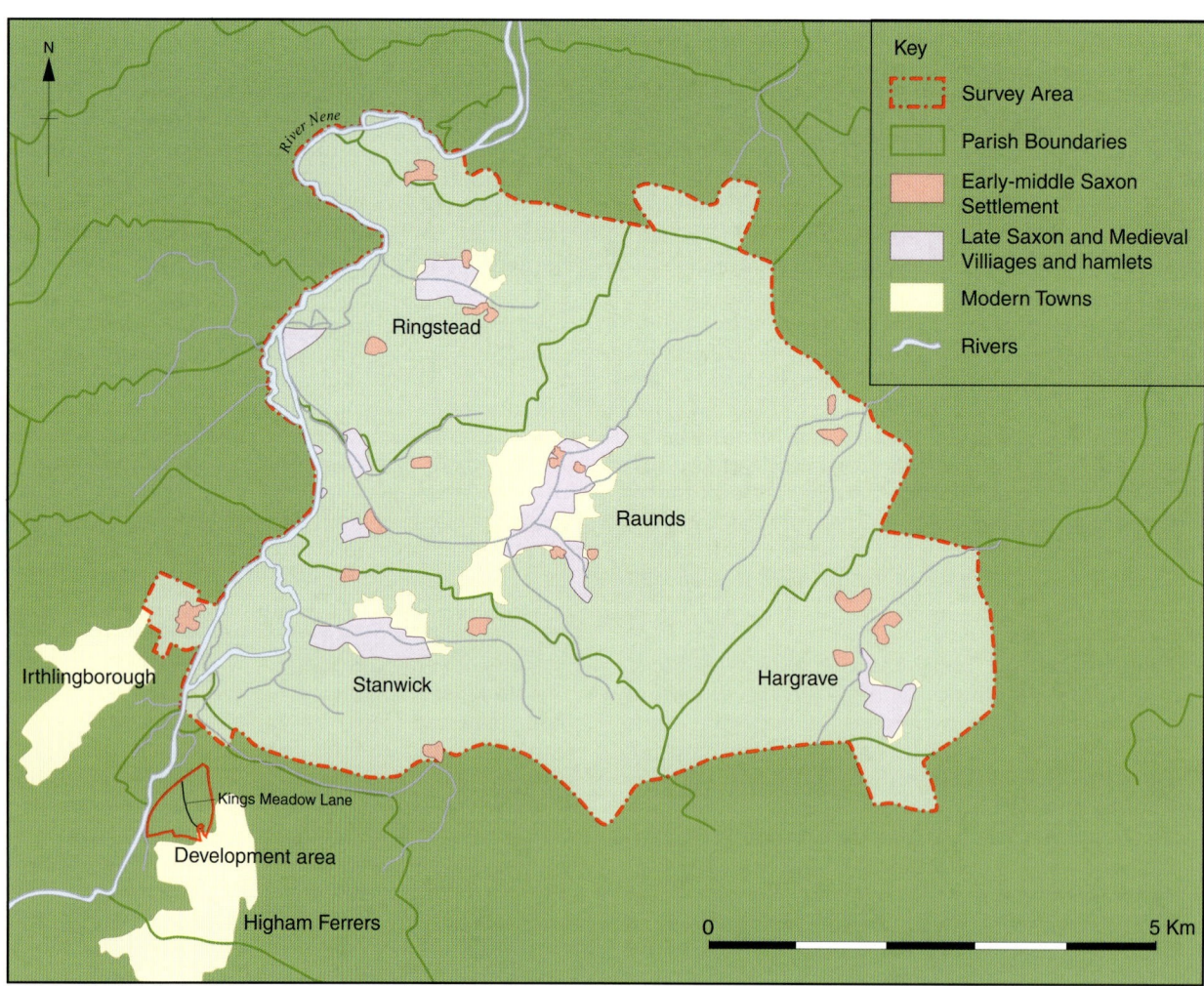

Fig. 5.1   The Raunds survey: extent of Early, Middle and Late Saxon settlement (after Parry 2007)

with recent advances in their understanding (see Tipper 2004), make at least a brief resumé of the evolution of the subject worthwhile, to set the Higham Ferrers evidence within a meaningful context.

The earliest identification in the archaeological record of the *Grubenhaus* type of building, later to be known as the Sunken Featured Building was made by ET Leeds in the 1920s, from his excavations at Sutton Courtenay (Leeds 1923). In the prevailing ethos of the time, his conclusion that the incoming Saxons were poverty stricken wretches who lived in total squalor in scruffy holes in the ground rather set the tone of interpretation for decades to come. Only in the late 1950's did this disparaging view come under serious question, initially through the seminal paper of Radford (1957), which argued the need for area excavation as the only way to understand Anglo-Saxon settlements. In the ensuing decades, many hundreds of SFBs have been excavated, and their presence seems to be fairly ubiquitous in the 5th and 6th century, and yet their form and function still cause problems, principally centring round the debate as to whether the pit feature represents the sunken floor of the entire structure, or a space beneath a suspended wooden floor at ground level. Until the excavation work and reconstruction experiments at West Stow (West 1985), the tendency was to accept that the base of the pit was the floor, despite the difficulties of fitting a believable entrance into the hypothetical structure. In recent years the consensus has been moving towards the suspended wooden floor hypothesis, but it is not unanimously accepted (Tipper 2004, 17). The debate is not ended and it is worth bearing in mind that against this view, Hamerow (2002, 31) cites the numerous Northern European examples where there is no doubt on the part of the excavators/interpreters that buildings had sunken floors. Significant support for this view comes from modern examples, for example in Poland (ibid, 35, fig. 2.14)

The Higham Ferrers SFBs certainly add fuel to the debate on form and function, although the evidence is not decisive one way or the other. As Table 5.1 shows, six of the twelve SFBs at Higham Ferrers were of the 'two-post' construction, but there were enough variations in the detailed evidence from all twelve to suggest a degree of individual preference, or idiosyncrasy, on the part of their builders, or perhaps variation based on the different use or function of the buildings.

On the question of the sunken floor, none of the Higham Ferrers SFBs contained any evidence for either laid or trampled floor surfaces in their pit bases. If it is argued that the SFB pit was a sub-floor storage area, what use could be made of the very shallow pits under some SFBs? Two of the Higham Ferrers SFBs (1256 and 6356) had very shallow pits. While there is a slight uncertainty about the degree of feature truncation in the case SFB 1256, the shallowness of SFB 6356 is not due to later ploughing, since it was sited close by SFB 6057, which had a pit depth of 0.43 m. The positions of SFBs 6057 and 6356 in relation to each other, and the proximity of the exterior postholes (6564, 6566, 6568 and 6570), strongly suggest that these two structures were contemporary and related. It can be argued that the shallowness of some SFB pits may indicate that they were not intended for storage, but simply to provide an air-space under a suspended wooden floor. This would promote a drier and warmer atmosphere in the building and prevent, or at least delay, the onset of rot in the floor itself.

Such a hypothesis raises the question why sunken areas are apparently not found within other timber buildings such as halls. It could be argued that, where a wooden floor was required in a hall building, a space between floor and ground surface – whether for storage or ventilation/insulation – could be achieved more easily by raising the floor than by lowering the ground level. It is suggested that Building 7023 lls (phase 2b) may have had just such a suspended floor (see below).

SFB 6057 also contained evidence of what may have been an ad hoc repair to a sagging floor. In the middle of the pit there was an arrangement of flat

Table 5.1 Dimensions of Sunken Featured Buildings

SFB	Site no.	Length (m)	Width (m)	Depth (m)	Subsoil	Principal postholes	Subsidiary postholes
1256	1	2.6	2.5	0.09	Silty clay/ironstone	1	1?
1263	1	3.5	2.3	0.5	Silty clay/ironstone	2	
1266	1	3.3	2.8	0.32	Silty clay/ironstone	3	
1253	1	3.9	3.1	0.35	Silty clay/ironstone	4(6)	5
6057	4	2.9	2.4	0.43	Silty clay	2	
6345	4	4.5	2.35	0.22	Silty clay	0	
6356	4	2.3	2.18	0.12	Silty clay	2	8
6630	4	n/a	1.44	0.24	Silty clay	1	
8222	9	3.12	2.87	0.28	Sandy silt	2	
10210	10	3.25	2.5	0.3	Silt and ironstone	2	
12740	10	3.97	2.14	0.22	Silt/ironstone/RB occupation layer	0	
12800	10	3.84	3.04	0.32	Silty clay/ironstone	2	

stones. These showed no signs of burning, and are not thought to be related to a fire or hearth base. It is suggested they could have formed a post pad for a central floor support. It would probably have been a lot easier to remove part of the floor and set a post on stone pad than to have dug out a new deep posthole.

There are sufficient numbers of SFBs with only one 'gable' posthole, or no 'gable' posthole, to suggest that the term 'gable posthole' is actually misleading. Tipper (2004, 192) suggests that, where they occur, they may have been merely scaffolding, to be removed once the ridged roof structure was assembled and was self-supporting. Many of these postholes are too large in size to be interpreted simply as scaffold holes. West (1985, fig. 290) offered a variant of the suspended floor idea, when he showed a suspended floor supported by a longitudinal joist that was keyed into two gable end posts supporting the ridge. A more recent discovery at Dorchester, Oxfordshire has been interpreted as a 6th-century SFB, with slots preserved in the base of the pit possibly indicating the joists of a suspended floor (Keevill 2003, 323-4, 357 and fig. 8).

A further step along the same line of thinking, taking into account Tipper's recent researches, dispenses altogether with the roof support function of the gable postholes. Instead it is suggested that the hole, or holes, contained short stout posts to support a longitudinal floor joist over a storage pit (P. Lorimer pers. comm.). Plate 5.1 depicts a possible interpretation of this idea. The planks of a suspended wooden floor would most likely have spanned the shortest distance across the pit – from side to side, and without some central longitudinal support in the form of a joist, the planks could flex and twist independently of each other, making the floor impractical and hazardous in use.

The SFB postholes at Higham Ferrers are of substantial size and depth. If these posts had simply been for scaffolding, or even to support a ridge pole, they would surely have not needed to be so substantial. If, on the other hand, the postholes were

intended to support a floor joist, then they would have needed to be of substantial thickness and well-anchored in the ground to avoid sideways movement and being driven into the ground by the weight of objects and people above. Would the absence of gable end posts compromise the roof ? Not necessarily; at Catholme the interpretation of the roof structure of one of the earthfast post-built buildings suggested that a ridge plate was unnecessary. Racking – that is collapsing together of the roof rafters – could be prevented by the presence if thatching laths or withies (Losco-Bradley and Kinsley 2002, 99).

An added complication to the discussion is the possibility that the SFB pit could have represented only a fraction of the internal area of the building. If the external walls of the building had been lightly founded, then all trace of the overall footprint of the building could be erased by later ploughing. The example of the structure of SFB 1256 (Site 1 – Fig. 3.5) may be significant in this respect. In addition to the structural postholes close to either end of the pit, a further isolated large posthole (1354 – see Fig 3.3) was identified approximately 2.3 m to the north-east of the SFB, and on the same axis. Posthole 1354 may be completely unrelated chronologically – no finds were recovered from its fill – but it is possible that it represents a gable end of a much larger building, of which the SFB pit was only a feature of one end.

Another aspect of SFB 1256 that is worthy of note is that, alone of all the SFBs, the structural postholes appeared to be situated outside the SFB pit. In this instance it is not certain whether this represents a different design and construction technique, or the result of truncation by ploughing. The fact that the pit was very shallow and its edges indistinct suggest that ploughing may have played a part. That the other three SFBs in Site 1 do not show signs of severe truncation need not necessarily be an obstacle. The 18th-century estate map (Pl. 1.3) indicates a field called 'Vine Hill' at this location. There is a suggestion from the map that it contained

Plate 5.1 Conjectural early Saxon SFB reconstruction

ridge-and-furrow cultivation oriented WSW-ENE. It is therefore quite possible that the area of SFB 1256 had been eroded by a furrow, while leaving SFB 1263 to the north, and SFB 1253 to the south-east, undamaged and protected by a 'ridge'.

Structural parallels

Table 5.2 catalogues the variation in dimensions of the SFBs from a number of sites of varying size across central and southern England. The variations in sizes of the Higham Ferrers SFBs seems slightly less than elsewhere, although as a group they fit comfortably within the general range of sizes observed on the other sites.

Associated features

In the area of Site 1 a single datable pit was found in the vicinity of one of the SFBs (Fig. 3.3). A scatter of postholes was also identified, planned as soil marks, and a sample excavated. No dating material was found in their fills, and no coherent structure(s) seemed to be defined. Although they could well belong to the Phase 1 activity, the evidence of some prehistoric activity on the site sounds a note of caution.

On Site 4, to the south and west of the group of SFBs, an arrangement of postholes pits and short gullies appeared define small paddocks and possibly some structures although no clear patterns were identifiable (Fig. 3.35). A line of substantial pits (7326) extended to the north-west; each contained a noticeable proportion of charcoal and burnt silty clay, although in no case did this burning appear to have taken place in situ.

A large scatter of postholes was identified to the south of the SFB group. They have been assigned to Phase 2b, in association with Building 7327, immediately to the south, but it is quite possible that some of the postholes belong to Phase 1, though none produced any dating evidence.

The shallow gully across the south-west end of Site 4 (7306) has been assigned to Phase 1 on stratigraphic grounds alone. Its north western end faded out beyond the line of the Phase 2b enclosure exten-

sion ditch, and its south-east end extended beyond the trench. While it might represent a boundary differentiating the SFB group to the north-east and another (unrevealed) group to the south-west of the site, the absence of other boundaries of such nature in Phase 1 raises the possibility that it could be an early element of the Phase 2a activity (see below).

THE MIDDLE SAXON EVIDENCE (7th–9th CENTURY)

Introduction

The Middle Saxon period, from around the end of the 6th century to the 9th century has tended to suffer in the eyes of researchers through its relative lack of easily identified material remains, in comparison to the early Saxon period, and its lack of easily understood social structure. Attention traditionally focussed on pagan burial studies of the early Anglo-Saxon period, later augmented by studies of their buildings, in particular the Sunken Featured Buildings. Research interest has also focussed on the Later Saxon period, but from the standpoint of the immediate post-Conquest state of English society, and looking back to the roots of nucleated village society.

The intervening period has proved the most elusive and difficult to characterise. The temptation has been (as it surely is with any archaeological period) to look for patterns and models by which the evolution of settlement structure can be explained. However, as Reynolds argues (2003, 99) this has led to a few classic sites, for instance West Stow, Mucking and West Heslerton, being used to explain all lowland settlement forms. Reynolds argues that it is as unrealistic to look for uniformity in Anglo-Saxon society as it is in society of any age (2003, 99). If anything uniformity is surely more unlikely in a Middle Saxon context, at a time of fluid, evolving kingdoms based upon quite disparate groups with different cultural and political agendas, dealing with very unpredictable circumstances.

In this context it is worth bearing in mind (but not unquestioningly accepting) parallels drawn

Table 5.2: Comparison of 5th–7th century SFB dimensions (after Tipper 2004, Table 21)

Site	No. of SFBs	Geology	Length (m)	Width (m)	Depth (m)
Abbots Worthy (Dorset)	5	Chalk	2.5 - 3.1	1.75 - 2.75	0.11 - 0.95
Barrow Hills (Oxon)	45	Gravel	2.8 - 6.5	2.1 - 4.45	0.11 - 1.03
Bishopstone (Sussex)	3	Chalk	3.7 - 4.4	2.7 - 4.0	0.4 - 0.9
Mucking (Essex)	207	Gravel	2.18 - 7.47	1.7 - 5.4	0.1 - 0.9
Old Down Farm (Hants)	6	Chalk	2.4 - 3.76	1.7 - 2.9	0.2 - 0.72
Puddlehill (Beds)	9	Chalk	3.6 - 11	2.45 - 4.55	0.2 - 1.0
West Heslerton (Yorks)	130	Various	1.65 - 6.59	1.01 - 5.4	0.07 - 1.19
West Stow (Cambs)	69	Sand	2.4 - 5.8	2.0 - 4.9	0.15 - 1.1
Higham Ferrers (Northants)	12	Various	2.3 - 3.97	2.14 - 3.04	0.09 - 0.43

from cultural anthropology. Studies of the transition of egalitarian groups and tribes to hierarchical chiefdoms highlight the ways in which increasingly complicated social structures develop, and inevitably encourage more central control and social organisation (see for instance Diamond 2006, 265-92). Although for each small group this process may well move at a different rate to its neighbours, sooner or later all groups will be drawn in.

Archaeological context and current research (Fig. 5.2)

Increasingly through the 7th and 8th centuries power or influence was expressed not just by personal loyalty but by territorial control. In archaeological terms, this is most often evident in the use of ditches and linear earthworks, from the peasant's fence and gully separating the edge of his paddock from his neighbour's, up to the grand boundary of Offa's Dyke, the most spectacular surviving middle Saxon expression of power and control. In some cases the ditches define the settlements, in the sense that they provide a sense of where the settlement is and how far it extends. Some display a discipline and rigour in their layout that would not go amiss in a fully-nucleated medieval village, as for example Wicken Bonhunt (Essex) or Cottenham (Cambridgeshire).

However, it is suggested that the evidence from Higham Ferrers points to a more politically motivated rationale for the ditches and earthworks, to create both a controlled and exclusive space, and to present a visually impressive spectacle to outsiders.

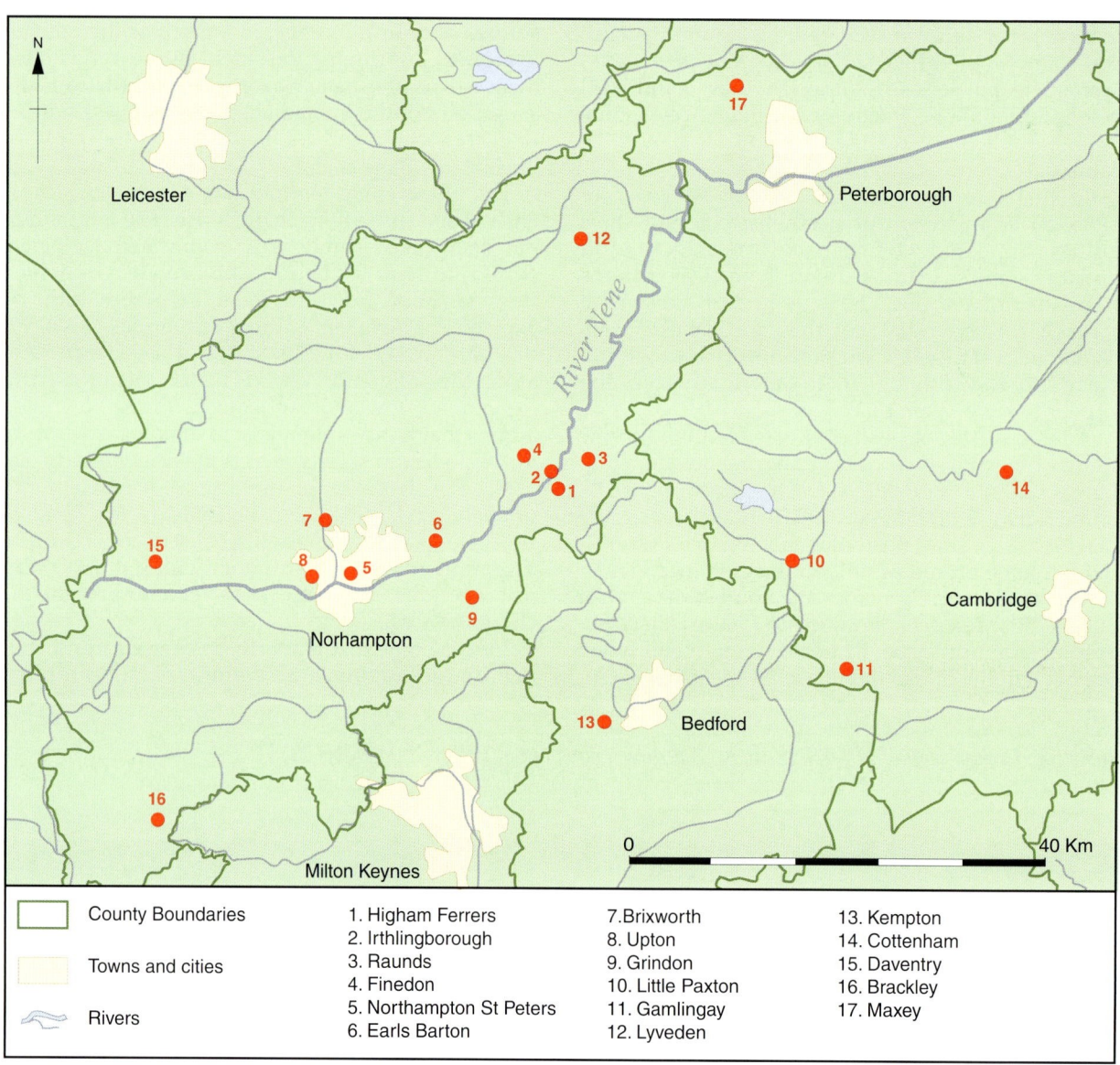

Fig. 5.2   Middle Saxon sites in the region mentioned in the text

Chronology of the evidence

There is no stratigraphic evidence that can demonstrate that the activity assigned to Phase 2 postdates the SFBs, but the artefactual evidence supports the contention that the SFB groups, or at least the grouping on Site 4 and mostly probably all the SFBs, were deserted before the Phase 2 complex was established. The pottery dating shows a clear absence of (non-intrusive) later pottery in the SFB pit fills of Site 4, and only a few sherds of early pottery in later features. Arguably, this supports the idea that there was a significant gap, possibly around half a century, between occupation phases, as suggested by the pottery itself. It is therefore reasonable to conclude that the activity of Phase 2 begins, on what was effectively a 'green' site, with the construction of the horseshoe enclosure, and the first building(s). At the end of Phase 2 the archaeological indicators point to the enclosure complex and all associated elements being dismantled, filled in, or destroyed in a single operation. In essence the 'green' site is restored.

To fix chronological dates to the start and end of Phase 2 is less straightforward, but, as Figure 5.3 shows, a combination of artefactual and scientific dating applied to the stratigraphy allows the overall chronology to be proposed with reasonable confidence.

From this it is possible to suggest that the site was laid out at sometime between the late 7th century and the early 8th century, and that it was dismantled and totally cleared towards the end of the 8th or early in the 9th century. The Maxey Ware pottery has a distinctly earlier date range, but almost none of it came from within the complex itself, unlike the Ipswich Ware. Nearly all of the Maxey Ware came from a context that may represent the redeposition of midden material (see below).

The end date of Phase 2 is defined by radiocarbon dates for human remains deposited in the enclosure ditch during its backfilling. Combined with the radiocarbon date for the last use of the malting oven, the dating of the Ipswich Ware pottery (Blinkhorn Chapter 4 above), and in the light of the known history, a date of the late 8th century to the early 9th century is a reasonable estimate for the end of Phase 2. As is noted in Chapter 2, while the beginning and end of the complex is fairly well defined, determining the boundaries of the subphases within Phase 2 is more problematic. The limits suggested in Figure 5.3 are cautiously proposed.

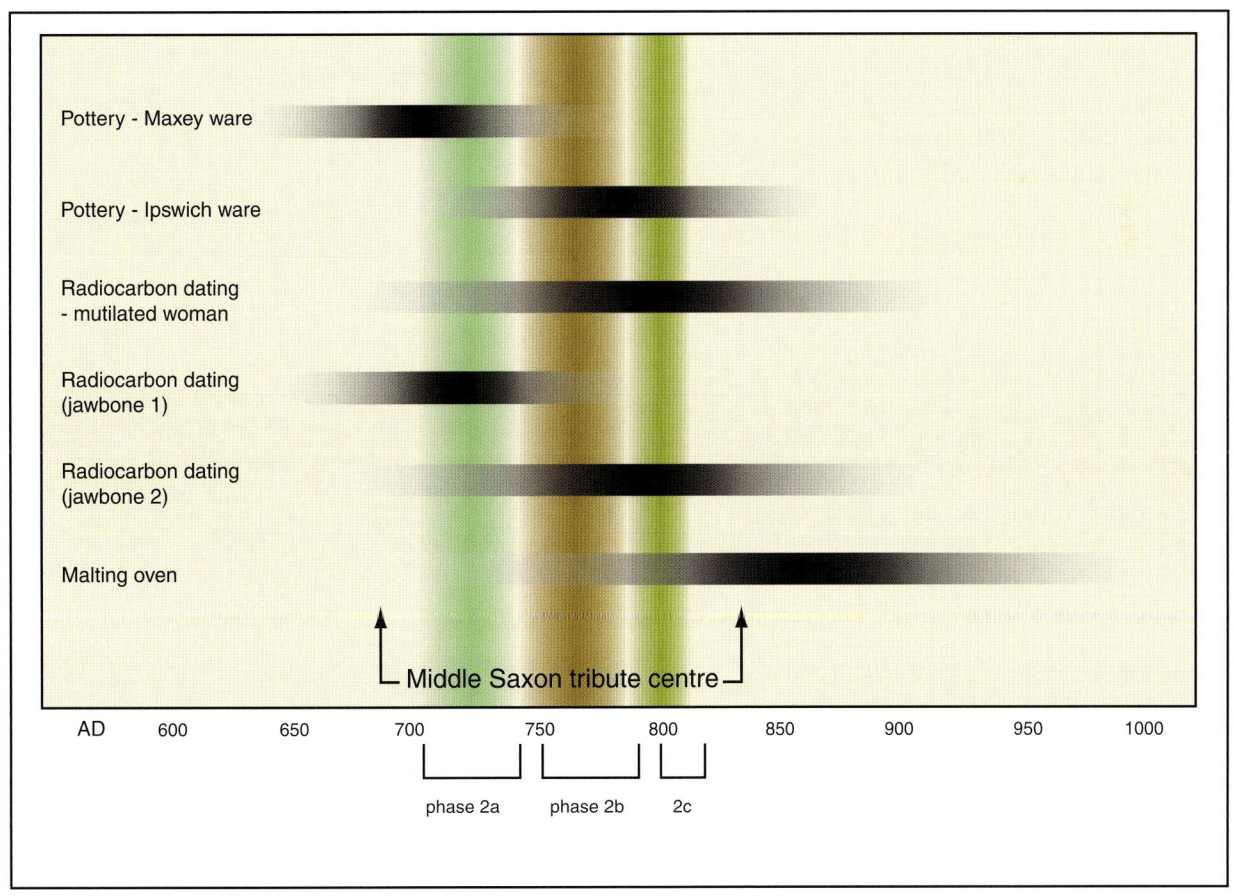

Fig. 5.3   The suggested chronology of the estate centre and associated artefactual and scientific dating ranges

193

Extent of the complex

The area around Kings Meadow Lane lay at the junction of important routes to the north and south along the Nene, and to the south-east. It is suggested that the presence of such a complex at a nodal point in the region was highly significant. It does, however, pose the question: did the route network pass through Higham Ferrers because of its importance or was it important because of the junction of major routes? It may well be that, in the larger scale of things, the Middle Saxon complex influenced the roads as much as they influenced the complex. (Foard and Ballinger 2000, 12).

The target areas of development project meant that – with the exception of Site 5 and the immediate surroundings of the malting oven, no part of the area to the south-west of Kings Meadow Lane was available for area investigation. It is considered most likely that the western enclosure extension ditch terminated at the line of the Lane. The small excavation alongside the north-eastern side of the Lane confirmed that the ditch ran at least that far (see section 595 Fig. 3.22), although there was no opportunity to excavate a similar slot on the south-west side of the Lane, or investigate the land immediately to the south-west of the Lane. The only observation that can be made is that there was no evidence in the geophysics plot, or in the area stripped around the malting oven, for a ditch comparable in dimensions. The linear feature revealed alongside the oven may in fact be earlier or later in date. It can be concluded with confidence therefore that if the enclosure complex did extend to the south-west, and did have similarly substantial perimeter ditches, they did not cross any of the areas examined.

Nevertheless, the presence of the malting oven on the south side of the Lane is a strong indicator that there were other elements of the complex on that side too. If so, how far to the south could the complex have extended? The land in question has never been available for archaeological investigation, so all that can be surmised is that the Lane may have acted as an armature, with buildings and structures associated with the complex on both sides of the Lane.

Elements of the complex

Ditches

The large horseshoe shaped enclosure of Phase 2a and its extensions and alterations in Phase 2b and 2c were clearly fundamental elements of the complex. Its idiosyncratic shape is perhaps a reflection of the fact that the enclosure was laid out on a 'green' site, and not carved out of an existing field system. In that sense its shape may well be specifically related to its intended function. Moreover, it is arguable that its situation was not an accident either. It is suggested that the enclosure was situated so that the interior would be visible from the royal site of

Irthlingborough across the river. The authors confirmed that this was the case at the time of the excavation, during the short interlude between the cutting down of the woodland on the eastern side of the river and the construction of the housing. The importance of the enclosure's visibility is considered further below.

While the original horseshoe ditch enclosed a large area of some 0.8 ha, even allowing for later truncation by plough damage, the ditch was modest in its dimensions, at no point wider than c 2 m or deeper than c 1 m. Unless the ditch was intended as no more than a nominal marker, it is reasonable to suggest that there was a bank, very possibly augmented by a fence or hedge. Only on the east side of the enclosure in Site 8 was there evidence of redeposited subsoil – on the outside of the ditch – that could be construed as the remains of a bank. A fence or hedge would have been necessary to augment any bank, if the interpretation of the enclosure as a stock-holding corral, is correct. A fence could have comprised close-fitting posts, although wattle screens would have served adequately, if not as impressively, as would a hedge, once it had grown.

While all the identified buildings of this period were located to the south of the horseshoe enclosure or between the extension ditches, there is some evidence that there was also a focus of occupation to the north of Site 8, outside the enclosure. Evaluation Trench 14 picked up the enclosure ditch and a significant quantity of Maxey Ware sherds from its fill. Interestingly, the composition of the vessel forms suggested domestic cooking use, whereas the Ipswich Ware, the predominant ware from within the complex, was generally in the form of pitchers and large storage vessels (see Blinkhorn, Chapter 4 above). The presence of this relatively early Maxey Ware in the late fill of the recut of a small stretch of the ditch, coupled with its almost complete absence from either the rest of the ditch or the north end of Site 8, could suggest that the pottery may represent redeposited material from a midden of a small farmstead pre-dating (or conceivably co-existing with) the enclosure complex in phase 2a. Further support for this hypothesis comes from the assemblage of lava quern fragments from the same evaluation trench (see Roe, Chapter 4 above)

The modification of the enclosure complex in phase 2b suggests that the whole area to the south of the horseshoe enclosure was now incorporated within the controlled space, and with the additional substantial buildings, a much more elaborate and sophisticated operation is implied. However, no subdivisions of the area were evident, except for the enclosure against the south-west end of the western extension ditch, around building 7023.

Buildings

There is a problem in the dating of the hall buildings discovered in Sites 2, 4, and 6. SFBs typically provide significant assemblages of material from the pit deposits, although it is becoming increasingly accepted that these deposits accumulate or are deposited (probably from surface middens) after the building goes out of use and is dismantled (Tipper 2004, 184). Nevertheless they can provide a fairly accurate date for the building, and clues to the activities going on in the vicinity.

In contrast, hall buildings, typically defined by lines of postholes and sometimes beamslots, rarely produce sufficient artefactual material to allow close dating of the structure. Furthermore, in many cases, there are few if any pits or other cut features that can confidently be associated with the individual halls. It is a problem that is well known and not open to easy solution (Reynolds 2003, 102). Attempts to devise a comparative chronology based on building styles (for instance James *et al* 1984) are difficult to sustain as more regional variation becomes apparent, and in this respect at least the halls at Higham Ferrers are a good example, demonstrating a fair degree of consistency in groundplan, but a variety of building styles within what is a broadly contemporary group (Table 5.3). It is reasonable to suggest that the buildings must owe their differences to intended function and/or status, although it should not be forgotten that the individual skill or preference of the builder(s) probably played a part as well.

In contrast to the variety of building styles in evidence, Table 5.3 highlights a striking consistency in the building width – around 6 m. The reason for this may be purely down to practicalities. The most common timber frame material was oak, derived from fairly young trees growing among underwood. The underwood suppressed the growth of the lower branches of the tree, resulting in a straight trunk up to approximately 6 m tall, from where the crown branched out (Rackham 1987, 87). If the tie-beams running across the building at eaves height could be fashioned from a single straight timber it would make for a much stronger structure.

Buildings 2664, 2665, and 2666 (Figs 3.19, 3.24-3.25)

These three buildings are best seen as a related group, the first two representing an original building (2664) and its rebuild and repositioning (2665), to accommodate the third building 2666.

Building 2664 (Site 2) – This is the first building in the sequence. The evidence of the best preserved end of the building suggests that the side walls consisted of earthfast posts, with the spaces between likely to have been infilled with plastered wattle panels. There was no evidence that a sill beam was incorporated into any of the walls. A central line of aisle postholes is clear, possibly denoting a fairly substantial roof structure. There was no evidence of an internal hearth, although it is accepted that the scouring effect of medieval and post-medieval ploughing may have removed the evidence for one.

Only the western part of the building was clearly identified and excavated. Among the scatter of the planned but unexcavated postholes to the east can be defined a possible continuation of the north wall, although this is uncertain, as they could also represent – along with a line of postholes to the west of the building – a fenceline across the open end of the horseshoe enclosure. The distinct gap in the posthole line of the south wall of Building 2664 appears to represent a (central) doorway, which would be consistent with a total length of the building as shown.

Building 2665 (Site 2) – This building seems to represent a rebuilding of 2664, slightly shifted to the north to accommodate building 2666 (see below). If the prime motive was to move Building 2664 out of the way of the intended site of Building 2666, than it as much represents recycling as rebuilding. The east end wall of 2665 is as difficult to accurately locate as that of 2664 due to later activity, but again there is a clear gap along the south wall denoting a ?central doorway.

The construction of building 2665 appears to involve a elaboration of the construction technique applied to 2664, at least with regard to the side wall construction. There is clear evidence of a sill beam along the north wall of 2665, and from the estimate of likely plough truncation, a corresponding beam along the south wall can be postulated, although no trace remains. The relationship of the upright wall timbers to the sill beam does deserve special attention. The postholes do not align squarely along the centreline of the beam slot, but against the inside edge. Although it cannot be proved, it is possible

Table 5.3: Dimensions of Phase 2 post-built buildings

Building	Site	Phase	Length (m)	Width (m)	Internal hearth?	Number of postholes	Average posthole depth (m)
2664	2	2a	12.0	6.0	N	50	0.18
2665	2	2b	12.0	6.0	N	21	0.20
2666	2	2b	20.0	5.0	Y	26	0.30
7023	4	2b	19.0	6.5	N	51	0.22
7237	4	2b	18.0	6.5	N	30	0.11
9184	6	2b	9.0?	6.5	N	9	0.16

therefore that the uprights were lap-jointed over the sill beam, spreading the wall and roof load along the beam, but avoiding the more complicated and time-consuming process of cutting mortises for each wall upright.

However, the ends of the uprights continued down below the beam, as there is clear evidence of dark silt-filled postpipes in the north wall postholes, in contrast to the lack of similar deposits in the beamslot itself. Evidently, when the building went out of use, the sill beam was salvaged, whereas at least the bases of the uprights were left in situ, presumably because they were rotten.

As with building 2664, there was a central line of aisle postholes. It is no coincidence that building 2665 half-overlaps the footprint of building 2664. Re-use of the aisle posts of the earlier building as part of the new outer wall is possible, and it may be that, being 'interior' posts, that they would be in better condition than the exterior wall posts, being less exposed to the elements. Of course, it is also possible that the in situ southern side posts of 2664 were reused in the centre line of building 2665, although it is unlikely as they would probably be shorter that required. Such an overlap between one building and its successor is possibly not unique; at Hartlepool, excavation within the monastic precinct revealed the partially overlapped beamslot trenches of possible monastic cells (see figure 86 in Welch 1992, 124; and Daniels 1988, figs 14 and 21). In that case, the relative position of the two buildings suggests that the outer wall of the later building was set over the centre line of the earlier building.

The similarity in layout and the lack of hearth or other evidence of domestic occupation suggests that Building 2665 served the same function as Building 2664. Both buildings produced no artefactual evidence but the high concentration of cereal remains from one of the posthole fills (see Moffet, Chapter 4 above) suggests a storage function would be likely.

Building 2666 (Site 2) – This appears to be the third building in the sequence, set at an angle to Building 2665, and aligned with the western extension to the enclosure. The alignment of 2666 with the extension ditch puts its construction into Phase 2b, along with Building 2665. The two buildings are associated by their close proximity, but the design and construction method of Building 2666 is very different from 2665 or its predecessor.

All four walls in the essentially rectangular structure are defined by beamslots with postholes of various sizes. As for interior features, the layout is similar to its companion buildings, namely a central doorway on one side, and a line of aisle posts, incomplete due to the truncation by Phase 3 ditch 2547. A patch of fire-reddened subsoil between two of the aisle postholes was identified as the probable site of the hearth in the northern part of the building.

The most intriguing feature of building 2666 is that the beamslots and postholes on the south-east side, or front, of the building are much more substantial – both in plan and section – than those on the north-west side or back (see Fig. 3.25). It should be remembered that the truncation caused by ridge-and-furrow cultivation in this area cut across Building 2666, rather than along it, and therefore it cannot be responsible for this structural characteristic.

One possibility was that the back wall appears to be less deeply founded because it was dug into a long-since eroded bank that ran along the east side of the enclosure ditch. It is true that there is a 3 m wide margin devoid of features between the ditch and the building, but elsewhere along this ditch the margin between ditch and structures was much less (see Building 7023, below), and all the indications from elsewhere in the enclosure complex are that if there was a bank it was on the outside of the ditch.

The possibility is that this building was constructed with an imposing facade to the front, the east side, while the back and end walls were more rudimentary. This has been a common characteristic of English architecture since the medieval period. A modern – if exaggerated – parallel might be a film or theatre set.

Buildings 7023 and 7327 (Site 4) (Figs 3.27-3.28)

These two buildings were sited at a right angle to each other and very probably should be treated as a pair, comparable to Buildings 2665 and 2666 above.

Building 7023 – As with the other hall buildings, there is an almost total lack of artefactual evidence recovered from the postholes. The exceptions are two small fragments of residual Phase 1 pottery, doubtless deriving from the focus of Phase 1 activity to the north-east. Consequently, the dating for the building relies upon its proximity to the ditch and the material derived from it. There is a discernible preponderance of both pottery and animal bone in the phase 2b and 2c fills of the ditch alongside the building, suggesting that it was in use possibly from the mid 8th century to the early 9th century. The fact that the human remains also came from the area immediately alongside the building may not be coincidental; this aspect is discussed further below.

To judge from the posthole arrangement, the building was the most substantial and elaborate in its construction, and had two distinct rooms. While they were possibly built separately, there is some evidence to suggest otherwise. A doorway midway along the east frontage of the building is possibly represented by the gap between postholes 6457 and 7211 (Fig. 3.27). Another doorway is suggested in the south end wall by the gap between postholes 6898 and 6900.

The northern room of the building displays some different characteristics from its southern counterpart. The posthole spacing is noticeably closer, possibly implying a different, and perhaps more lavish, construction. A possible doorway may be represented by the gap between postholes 6934 and 6936.

At the time of excavation, there was a distinct slope in the ground surface across the footprint of the building; the drop in level from the north-east corner to the south-west corner measured in the region of 1.2 m. If the ground in the immediate area was originally levelled up to form a platform before construction began, and has since been eroded away by ploughing, one would expect the downslope postholes to be much shallower features than those at the upslope end; this is not the case, the variation in the depth of the postholes is between 0.15 m and 0.30 m at both ends of the building. Therefore it would seem that the building was laid out and the postholes dug on a site that was on a similar slope to today. An internal floor surface with such a slope would surely have been very impractical. It can be suggested that a suspended wooden floor would have been a way around such a problem, and could have rested upon a ring beam attached to the wall posts. Such an arrangement could also help to explain the central beamslot, which could have housed a longitudinal joist to support the suspended floor itself, assuming, as is likely, that the floorboards ran across the building rather than along it. Alternatively, or perhaps as well, it could have supported a line of posts or a partition wall intended to strengthen a ceiling or conceivably a first floor. The evidence of structure B at Maxey could be interpreted in this way (see Addyman 1964, fig. 11, reconstruction B2).

In contrast to the other possible 'high status' building (2666) there was no evidence of an internal hearth in building 7023. Such an absence is not at all rare in middle Saxon building footprints, and it is usually assumed that later ploughing has removed the hearth base. The presence of just such a hearth signature in building 2666 requires that the issue be given more thought. One proposed solution to this problem has been the construction of hearths set in soil-filled wooden trays resting on the suspended floor of a hall, as seen in the reconstructions at West Stow. Setting the hearth in a raised bed of soil prevents heat damage to a wooden floor, and gives a bed to stand pots on. Of course, such an arrangement has yet to be discovered in the archaeological record, but it does suggest a simple answer to the problem of absent hearths.

The apparent large gaps in the north-west wall are almost certainly due to the difficulties of identifying postholes in plan where they were cut into the Roman ditch fill. The internal postholes, while broadly respecting the building's alignment do not seem to clearly define one structure; they are most likely to be supplementary structural supports or internal screens or partitions.

Associated features – There is clearly a close relationship between Building 7023 and the enclosure extension ditch to the west. Possibly complementing this, and separating this building from the others within the complex, is the interrupted ditch 7308/7309, which terminated, or petered out, just before the enclosure ditch, and included what can be interpreted as a gateway or entrance, defined by the two postholes 6126 and 6122. The curving orientation of the two ditches suggests that they continued to the south, possibly linking up with the Lane. In this way building 7023 was part of the complex, and yet divided from it within its own exclusive area.

Building 7327 – To the north-east of Building 7023, and orientated at right angles to the enclosure extension was a large, but relatively insubstantial building 7327 , judging by the modest dimensions of the wall postholes. Not all posts were identified, although whether this was a result of the excavation conditions or truncation is unclear. The interior of the building revealed just one aisle posthole, and although there may originally have been more, it is clear this structure was much more lightly built than some of the other buildings.

The building's proximity and alignment to the enclosure extension ditch and Building 7023 suggests it should belong within Phase 2b, although no clear artefactual evidence was recovered from the building's postholes. Judging by the lightweight nature of the construction, and the absence of an internal hearth or other evidence of domestic activity, Building 7327 seems most likely to have been a storage barn of some sort.

The extensive scatter of postholes to the north-east and south-east of the building are cautiously assigned to the same phase, if only because the scatter does not encroach upon the building's footprint, implying that they were contemporary. However, it is quite possible that some may relate to the Phase 1 SFBs to the north-east of the scatter (see Fig. 3.35).

Building 9184 (Site 6) (Fig. 3.29)

The building was partly exposed under the north baulk of Site 6. The combination of beamslot and posthole construction, evident in the southwest end wall, is similar to that adopted in Building 2665 (see above), although in this case the degree of later truncation was such as to remove any meaningful sectional detail. The other notable aspect of this building is the central linear feature. While this could be some sort of footing for a central support, it is doubtful as it only extends a short distance along the line of the building. The scarcity of finds and the absence of signs of domestic use (charcoal, burning etc) might lead to the tentative conclusion that it is a storehouse or barn. However it is pertinent to note that an environmental sample from the beamslot produced a very similar result to a sample from Building 7023, namely, a scarcity of plant remains in general and cereals in particular. It is therefore possible that Building 9184 and 7023 had a similar role in the complex.

Purpose and longevity of the buildings

It is reasonable to suggest that the six revealed buildings of Phase 2 broadly fall into one of two groups; those intended for occupation (living/working/meeting), and those intended for storage of material or livestock. If one accepts that the evidence of a hearth implies human occupation, then only one of the six buildings (2666) was occupied. However, the possibility of a raised hearth (see above), means that Building 7023, which is the most elaborate building, can also belong to that group. In both cases these buildings were situated alongside the Phase 2b/c extension ditch, which provided a convenient rubbish dump for domestic refuse. The other four buildings displayed very simple layouts, and, by comparison, relatively lightweight construction, encouraging a conclusion that they were most likely storehouses, or possibly animal shelters.

Aside from the presence or otherwise of evidence for a hearth, the difficulty of distinguishing between an occupied dwelling and a barn may explain why so few have been apparently identified as barns in this country. However, parallels have been found abroad, for instance at Odoorn (5th century) and at Gasselte (9th century) both in Drenthe, in the modern Netherlands (see Hamerow 2002 fig. 2.15). Typically the buildings displayed central doorways and no internal features other than a single line of (roof-supporting) central posts. Occasional finds of large quantities of carbonised grain support their identification.

How long the buildings of the Kings Meadow Lane complex stood or remained in use is not easy to determine, except possibly by association with ditches that are dated by artefact assemblages or scientific methods. If we exclude the example of Building 2664, which was dismantled for a functional reason, the life of a post-built timber building at this time would be very largely dependent upon ground conditions: Hamerow has suggested a lifespan of around 30-35 years for the timber halls at Mucking (1993, 90). Welch (1992, 29-30) has suggested that social custom could also have been a factor; halls would have been rebuilt once a generation when a son inherited the estate from his father, or approximately every 40 to 50 years. So on the reasonably well-drained soil of the slopes above Kings Meadow Lane, there is no reason why the buildings belonging to the enclosure complex could not have lasted throughout sub-phases 2b and 2c – perhaps as long as 70-80 years.

Material culture of the complex

No contemporary rubbish pits were identified near any of the buildings or indeed anywhere in the Phase 2 complex at all. While rubbish pits have been found in close association with hall buildings on a number of sites, they are usually interpreted as being originally small quarry pits or water holes – for instance at Maxey (Addyman 1964, 68). The extension ditches at Kings Meadow Lane, while open, appear to have been generally kept reasonably clear of domestic rubbish, although adjacent to Buildings 7023 and 2666 the ditches appear to have been used as rubbish dumps. The amount deposited was fairly meagre in each case, however, which either suggests a disciplined rubbish disposal regime (to a point or area beyond the site) or suggests that there was not a great deal of routine domestic activity going on in the enclosure complex. Judging by the assemblages of metalwork, worked stone, worked bone, and animal bone (see Chapter 4), we are looking at a resident population seemingly modest in numbers and neither routinely engaging in crafts typical of a self-supporting settlement, such as weaving, nor apparently indulging in conspicuous consumption.

However, the pottery assemblage invites a very different interpretation. Blinkhorn argues that the Middle Saxon pottery – measured by the prevalence of Ipswich Ware – is suggestive of a very important site, and high status trade coming into it. Yet perhaps the most telling part of Blinkhorn's conclusion is that, despite the scale of incoming high status trade, whatever was being traded was passing through, not being consumed on site, or at least not in such a way as to leave any archaeological signature.

Historical context

Middle Saxon administration in the region of Higham Ferrers

Although no known contemporary documentary sources specifically identify Higham Ferrers, ('Heihham' is mentioned in 1050) or refer to settlement at this site, there are aspects of the known history of Higham Ferrers that could represent 'echoes' of its Middle Saxon significance. Offa's confirmation of a charter at Irthlingborough in 786 is clear evidence of its royal status. Though the medieval importance of Higham Ferrers has never been in doubt, recent research – in particular by Glenn Foard (1985), and David Hall (1988) – has sought to shed light on Higham Ferrers's pre-Conquest past by looking for a legacy of its Middle Saxon role in its late Saxon and early medieval manorial organisation and administration.

Foard (1985) has suggested that the judicial role of the royal estate, originally centred on Irthlingborough, but by 1086 on Finedon, is hinted at by the 'thing' element of the medieval version of 'Finedon' – Thingdene (Jamison 1923, 196). Hall has shown (1988, 106-7) that in the late Saxon period Higham Ferrers was a multiple estate, and included – amongst other elements – Raunds (itself a multiple estate). Did the late Saxon and early medieval importance of Higham Ferrers derive from its associative role to the 'twinned' site of Irthlingborough, across the river?

Foard also raises the possibility that the importance of Higham Ferrers may have its origins as far back as the Roman period. Some evidence suggests a correlation between Roman small towns and middle Saxon estate centres, implying that

although the imperial administrative system, which we must assume was based upon the walled towns, did not survive the 5th century, a subsidiary system of administration, in some ways related to the unwalled 'small towns', did survive. (Foard 1985, 202).

This was written before any meaningful excavation of the Roman site; provisional results from the modern excavations suggest that it was in fact a centre of some considerable importance (Lawrence and Smith, forthcoming).

Politics and power in the region in the 7th and 8th centuries

In considering the broader view of the political situation in the region in the Middle Saxon period, it must be accepted that, frustratingly, the area of the East Midlands which includes Higham Ferrers is arguably the most obscure and poorly understood area of Lowland England at this time, principally because of a dearth of any detailed historical framework – in contrast to, say, Northumbria or Wessex.

There are two principal accounts of the middle Saxon period; Bede's *Historia ecclesiastica gentis Anglorum* was written in the early 8th century in the monastery at Jarrow, and understandably very much from a Northumbrian point of view. As such it is very sketchy about events in Mercia. The second great surviving 'history' is the Anglo-Saxon Chronicle, a modern term of convenience applied to a corpus of annals originally compiled under the orders of King Alfred in the late 9th century from aural histories and other documentation. Although the Chronicle purports to trace the story of England from the time of Julius Caesar, it is clear that it is by no means comprehensive or dispassionate. Alfred was attempting – at a time of great external threat – to legitimise the role of Wessex as the rightful heir to the embryonic nation state.

In terms of its geopolitical location, it would appear that Higham Ferrers lay towards the southeast edge of what is called Outer Mercia – secondary territories absorbed by Central Mercia in the 6th or 7th centuries. The extent of those areas is defined as much by elimination of the known areas surrounding Outer Mercia. Between Outer Mercia and East Anglia lay the ill-defined territory of the Middle Angles, a collective term for a number groups or tribes, whose names we know, but whose geographical extent is also a matter of conjecture.

Political evolution of kingdoms (Fig. 5.4)

The key to understanding the emergence of the Middle Saxon kingdoms in general, and Mercia in particular, is that the geographical extent of a kingdom was defined not by territory but by acceptance. The definition of a member of the Mercian kingdom in the 7th and 8th centuries was not a person who lived in a defined geographical area but one who accepted the authority of the Mercian king. As Bede defined it, a *gens* like that of the Mercians was ruled by a king, and everyone who recognised his authority was a member of his *provinciae* (Yorke 2001, 20-1). It therefore follows that the power of a king, whether it derived from military force, personality or charisma, was critical to the fortunes of a kingdom. As long as the king and his descendants and heirs maintained a strong, assertive profile the identity of the kingdom would be clear. But it would only take a slight interruption of succession, or the reign of an inadequate king, for the security of the kingdom to be under threat, both from rival factions within the kingdom and from enemies without. Such befell Mercia in the short space of time between the death of Offa and the accession of Coenwulf, with the attempts by Kent and East Anglia to secede from Mercian control. Although, through the efforts of Coenwulf, that attempt was largely unsuccessful, the precedent had been set, and within a few decades Mercian power collapsed (Williams 2001, 304).

Aethelbert, Offa, and Coenwulf

It is in the nature of the fluid and fluctuating Middle Saxon kingdoms that – like the groupings of the early Saxon period – their government was relatively untrammelled by fixed conventions, structures and institutions. The personality, longevity and strength of a king, coupled with good luck, were critical to both his and his kingdom's fortunes. A ruler needed to be strong and assertive if he was to last for any time at all, but if he was he could still to a large degree fashion the practicalities of government of his kingdom to his own design.

The proposed lifespan of the enclosure complex coincides more or less with the reigns of three Mercian kings; Aethelbald (716-757), Offa (757-796) and Coenwulf (796-821), who ruled Mercia during its age of supremacy in the tripartite contest with Northumbria and Wessex. (Beornred, Aethelbald's immediate successor, ruled for a few months in 757 before he was expelled by Offa, and Offa's son, Ecgfrith, ruled for 141 days in 796 before making way for Coenwulf.)

Aethelbald's style can best be summed up as selectively aggressive abroad and reasonably enlightened at home. He was personally somewhat self indulgent and disrespectful, until encouraged to modify his dissolute lifestyle by the increasingly influential church. As Zaluckyj says, the very fact that the church was able to criticise him says much for their growing power and confidence and his acknowledgement of that (Zaluckyj 2001, 142). It is possibly significant that relations between Mercia and the East Angles appear to have reached something of a high point of cordiality during Aethelbald's reign. From this we may infer that

Higham Ferrers and its region, situated between the two, must have been in a relatively stable situation, stable enough to allow the establishment and development of royal estate centres. However, Aethelbald's reign was eventually ended by his assassination at the hands of his own bodyguard in 757. Possibly the killing was part of a dynastic coup by his successor Beornred (Zaluckyj 2001, 143).

Offa, probably a second cousin to Aethelbald and therefore technically of the same dynasty, removed his predecessor Beornred and set about consolidating Mercian power. He was the first Mercian king to pay close attention to developments on the continent, and sought to emulate the renown of

Charlemagne. The two were friends of a kind, although Offa needed Charlemagne far more than Charlemagne needed Offa (ibid. 158). In contrast to his lofty ambitions for the future role of Mercian kingship, Offa was quite willing to go to any lengths to remove actual or potential threats to either his, or his designated heir's, security. He can be seen as a combination of ruthless gangster and aspirational ruler, and this has resulted in widely differing judgements of his rule by modern researchers. Zaluckyj calls his rule 'truly innovative and forward looking' (ibid, 162), while in contrast Keynes (1999, 341) argues that he was driven by nothing more sophisticated *'than a lust for power, not a vision of*

Fig. 5.4   The geopolitical landscape of England in the 8th century

English unity; what he left was a reputation, not a legacy'. It has been suggested that the Mercian kings of the 7th and 8th centuries never developed their concept of kingship beyond that of earlier times, and that Mercia never really evolved beyond a confederacy of sub-kingdoms, with an inherent tendency to go their separate ways if the power of the king weakened (Keynes 1999, 307). However, this may be due to an inherent lack of unity at the heart of the Mercian kingdom. Offa adopted an aggressive stance beyond Mercia, and a ruthless stance within it, trying to secure the throne from ever more threatening actions. However, the practice of setting up sub-kings or ealdormen to rule over the newly annexed Mercian provinces, a practice harking back to the 7th century, sowed the seeds of its own demise, as by the late 8th century the descendants of these ealdormen having some pedigree behind them, expected and sought a larger share of the ruling power (Yorke 1990, 126). Perhaps, as Yorke suggests, the very fact that no single all-powerful dynasty appeared in Wessex until the middle of the 9th century, and then under the pressure of the Viking threat, meant that inter-dynastic rivalry always had a low level outlet, and never reached the intensity that it did in Mercia (ibid. 178).

The last of the three kings, Coenwulf, has tended to be lost in the glare of his notorious predecessor, yet he maintained the integrity of Mercia, and only in his later years did his failure to reach a *modus vivendi* with the church become a serious flaw in Mercia's hegemony over subject territories, like the restless territory of Kent (Yorke 1990, 121). However despite these shortcomings, the heartland of Mercia was essentially maintained and it was not until the years after Coenwulf's death that the kingdom was riven by both external and internal threats and began to disintegrate.

Purpose of the complex

In considering the evidence for Phase 2, there are some very clear indicators that this is not a settlement that evolved organically from an earlier Saxon core. There is no clear stratigraphic relationship between the Phase 1 SFB groups and the Phase 2 activity, and the pottery assemblages from the two Phases give at least some support to the contention that there was a gap of around 50 years, or perhaps more , between the two Phases. When the complex was laid out in the late 7th or early 8th century, it was on a 'green' site. This in itself suggests that the complex was built to plan and with a predetermined design, and this implies that there was a clear purpose for the complex – the control of the resources.

The motivation for such an enterprise at that time is clearly a key to understanding the site. Broadly speaking it could derive from three sources: regional social and economic pressures, the church, or political administration. It seems unlikely that

the motivation for such an enterprise would have come from social and economic pressures. These factors do not appear overnight, and would tend to make their influence felt over a period, encouraging evolutionary change to a settlement.

Before any fieldwork took place in the area, one of the hypotheses suggested by Brown and Foard, based upon the fieldwalking and cropmark evidence, along with the early evaluation results, was that the Higham Ferrers horseshoe-shaped enclosure bore resemblance to the large oval churchyard enclosures sometimes evident in Northamptonshire, for instance at Daventry (Brown and Foard 1998, 77, fig. 9, D). While there was no indication of a minster or Christian shrine within the enclosure, could it nevertheless have been a sacred site of some kind? Although the fieldwalking did not identify any concentration of finds within the enclosure – in fact quite the opposite (see Fig. 2.1) – the area was intensively trenched to test for any signs of contemporary structures or other activity (Fig. 3.17). This revealed no finds, and no contemporary structural evidence.

A more prosaic explanation is that the enclosure was a stock pen, but it is questionable whether a single farmstead would require an enclosure of this size. The human resources required to dig an enclosure ditch on this scale would surely have been well beyond the capabilities of even an extended family.

While the number and range of rural settlements of this period that has been investigated has grown impressively in the last few decades, so that we are no longer solely reliant upon the traditional type sites of West Stow and Mucking, seeking a parallel for the Middle Saxon complex at Higham Ferrers has thus far been a rather fruitless task. One of the problems is that, while large enclosures have been identified by aerial observation and photography, and their dates provisionally established by field-walking, the sites are rarely excavated, and when they are it is often on a very small scale. At Barton-on-Humber a large oval, and apparently empty, enclosure has been identified to the east of the Anglo-Saxon church (Rodwell and Rodwell 1982, 290, fig.4). Its defensive potential has been noted (Reynolds 2003, 117), but how much its role was tied to the church and what that role was, is open to question. Also, in cases such as Bramford, Cottam, and Poundbury, the enclosures themselves are essentially complete – not open-ended as at Higham – and surround at least some of the associated buildings, suggesting that the role of the enclosures may have had a defensive element. Other examples show settlement and parts of large linear ditches as at Wickham Bonhunt in Essex (Reynolds 1999, fig. 62). In this instance the ditches clearly extend beyond the site – and beyond the settlement, but do they form any sort of unified enclosure? Without further investigation it is impossible to know.

The 7th-century enclosure at Yeavering seems to offer the only other fully revealed parallel to that at Kings Meadow Lane (Fig. 5.5). Yeavering was

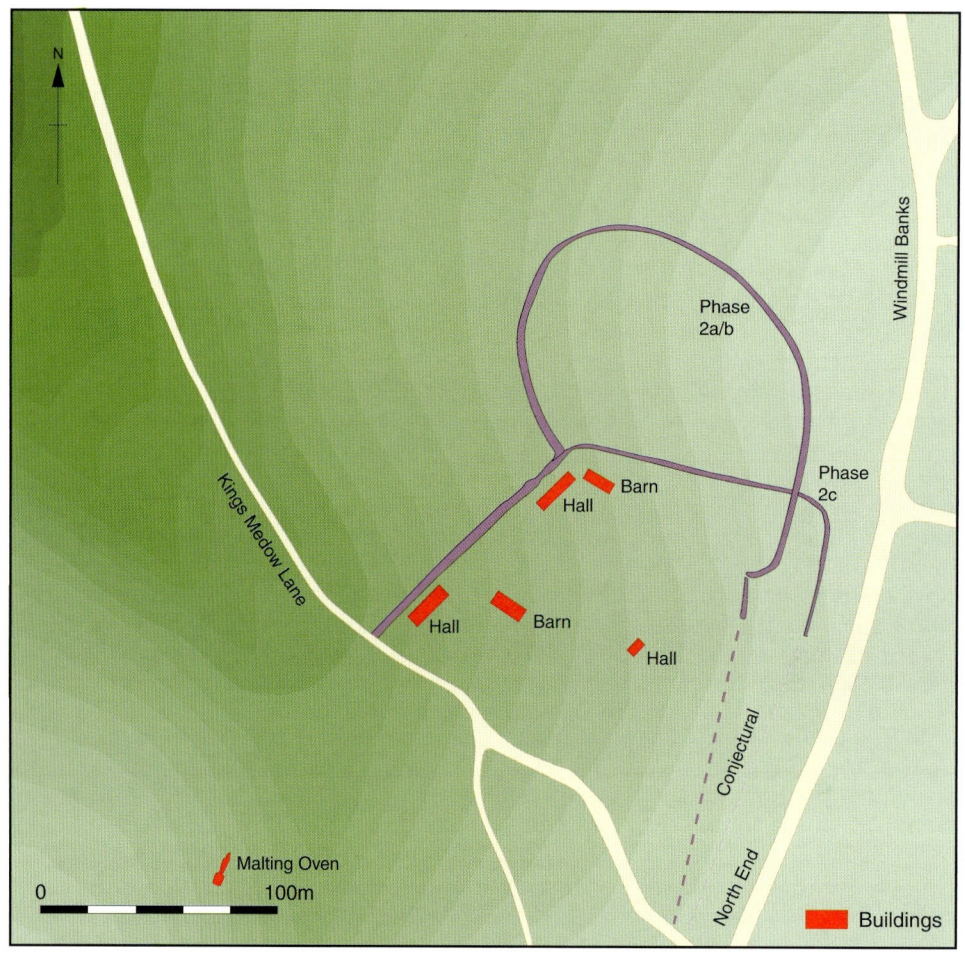

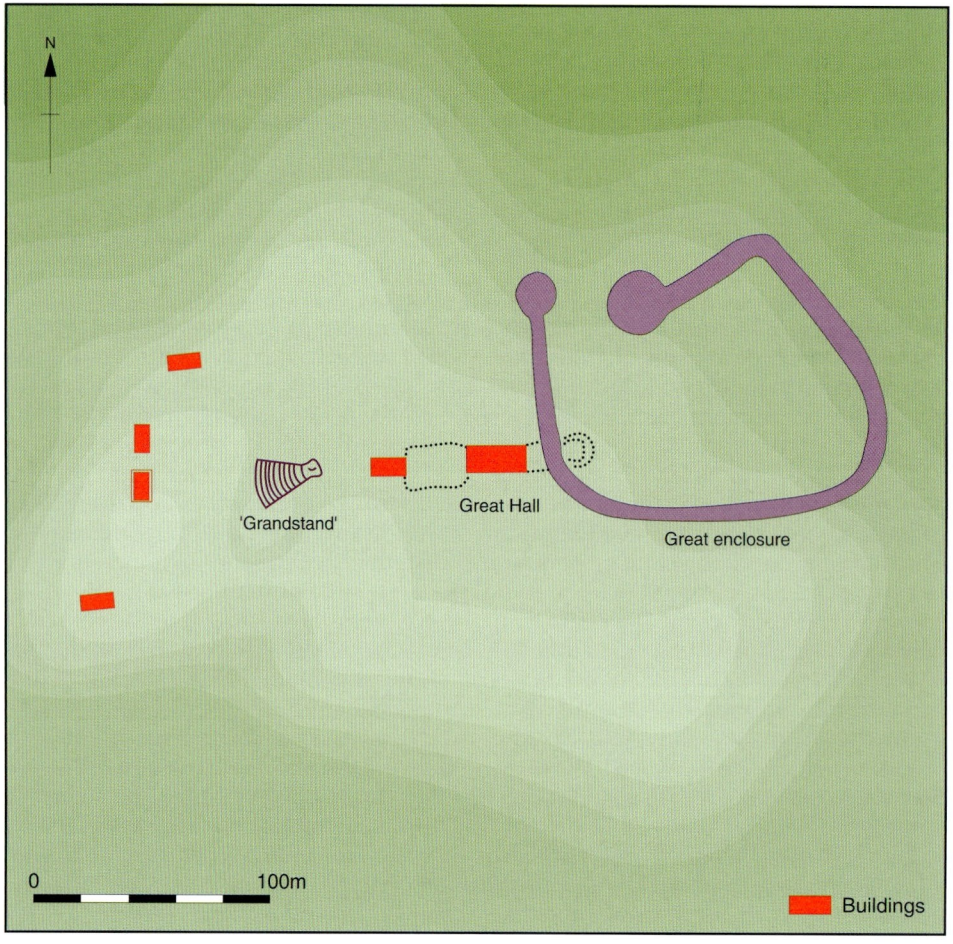

excavated in the 1950s and 1960s, and essentially comprises a very large ditched enclosure, as at Higham Ferrers devoid of any internal structure, and in conjunction a group of specialised buildings, some apparently of very high status. Dating to the mid-7th century, the complex is interpreted as a royal centre, a temporary residence for a peripatetic king and his retinue. (For a summary see Gittos 1999, 497.)

Figure 5.5 compares the basic layout of the two sites. However, aside from the most obvious point of comparison – the large empty enclosure – the differences between Higham Ferrers and Yeavering are too pertinent to ignore, and argue against the two sites operating in very similar ways. At Yeavering there is a strong ritual/religious aspect to the distribution of the buildings, and one is tempted to suggest that the so-called 'Great Enclosure' is as much a personal statement of royal prestige as are the buildings and the 'grandstand'. The structural evidence at Higham Ferrers seems to point towards a high-status occupation and powerful motivation, but the artefactual evidence is somewhat ambiguous. There is little evidence of high-status consumption on the site itself, and yet the elaborate malting oven alone indicates that the relatively large scale production of ale was an important activity, and this must have been for someone in the vicinity. In other words, the landscape elements – the large ditches, the timber hall buildings, the malting oven – would all have required substantial human and material resources to create and develop; they were designed to provide, in a controlled part of the landscape, certain services for an authority.

One aspect of consumption patterns on Anglo-Saxon sites which one might expect to indicate an elevated status is the frequency or otherwise of mammal or bird bones as the residues of hunting. Interestingly, most middle Saxon sites – even those that are evidently of elevated status such as royal hunting lodges (Bond 1999, 244) – produce very low percentages of deer bone, often less than 1%. This is curious, as hunting was very much celebrated in culture of the time. Maybe the chase was more important than the prize!

At Higham, there is a sharp increase of wild bird bones in Phase 2, but a very meagre percentage of deer bones (four of the six red deer fragments from Phase 2 were of antlers, and so may have found their way on site as a by-product of antler working. The evidence suggests that there may have been hunting as a means to supplement the diet, but that it was opportunistic and cannot really be classed as evidence of high status hunting expeditions. The larger game animals and the larger game birds were very much the preserve of the royal elite (Hagen 2006, 139) and the evidence as a whole suggests the

ruling authority was not resident in this part of the complex.

From the archaeological evidence and the possible parallels, it is suggested that the enclosure complex at Higham Ferrers represents part of a royal centre, which included Irthlingborough situated directly across the River Nene. The complex at Higham Ferrers functioned as a collection centre for tribute from the region, the enclosure acting as a stock pen, and most of the buildings serving as storehouses or barns for the collection of other goods. The tribute – or rent – was essentially to sustain and benefit the king and his retinue, who could number well over a hundred, during their sojourn in the royal centre. Such was the traditional importance of the feast in Saxon culture that the king had to ensure all the necessary supplies. As Hagen says *'The king could not have his status compromised by attending a feast at which the supplies were insufficiently lavish, or the mead might run out'* (2006, 409). However the control of the food supply and its distribution in the kingdom would also be a very effective political lever. Similarly donations of rents received (or the rights to collect them) reinforced the loyalty of, say, churches. Offa granted his food rents for two days per year for three years to the Church of Worcester (Loyn 1970, 304).

The presence of a substantial stock of cattle sheep and pigs in the vicinity of the enclosure seems to be reflected in the animal bone assemblage for Phases 2a and 2b (Fig. 4.30), although this cannot shed light on any process of the onward redistribution of animals that may have taken place. The presence of all three major species in some numbers supports the idea that the enclosure was probably partitioned, presumably by system of moveable hurdles. As for other goods and commodities, that would have been stored or passed through the site there is no direct archaeological evidence to hand, only the presence of evident storage capacity in the form of large storage buildings. We can only speculate on the types of goods collected and stored in this complex; itemised rents from the period suggest a wide variety, mostly in the form of food or drink, but other forms of tribute might be wool, cloth or leather. The king's lifestyle was indeed 'a moveable feast'; a peripatetic king would have no use for items such as iron pots – often required as rent in medieval times by static landlords such as monasteries. A list from the Laws of Ine in the late 7th century includes 'ten vats of honey, three hundred loaves, twelve ambers of Welsh ale, thirty of clear ale, two full grown bullocks or ten wethers, ten geese, twenty hens, ten cheeses, an amber full of butter, five salmon, twenty pounds of fodder and a hundred eels' (Robertson 1939, 58); the royal food rent at Berkeley in 883 required clear ale, beor, honey, bullocks, swine and sheep (Finberg 1972, 49-50).

Fig. 5.5 (facing page)
Comparison of the enclosure complexes at Higham Ferrers (8th century), and Yeavering (7th century)

Plate 5.2   Reconstruction of the malting oven

The most vivid evidence of the importance of food processing on the site was the malting oven (Pl. 5.2; see Chapter 4 for structural and operational analysis), surely far too elaborate and substantial a structure to have been part of someone's domestic brewing operation. Malt and ale are often cited in Saxon rents demanded by secular and church authorities (Finberg 1972, 208-9). It would be far more efficient for the tribute payers to bring their grain for malting at a central place, where the process could be properly controlled. Other beverages that could have formed part of the tribute, as brought or processed on site, include wine, mead, and beer, the first being the most prestigious (ibid. 199).

Butter does not appear to have formed a common element of food rents – presumably because of its short 'shelf life', whereas cheese – most stable, protein-rich, easily preserved and portable – did form a notable element. It is probably no surprise therefore that Offa took forty cheeses as part of the food rent for an estate at Westbury, Gloucestershire, granted to the church (Hagen 2006, 304, from D. Whitelock *English Historical Documents Vol.1*, 467)

An early signifier of a society's progression from disconnected groups or tribes is the growing central control of the provision and distribution of food (Diamond 1997, 90). A person's social identity, once expressed at the tribal level by military service and the giving and receiving of gifts, is increasingly expressed – at the level of the kingdom – by the routine giving of a defined tribute or tax, in the form of foodstuffs and other materials to sustain the kingdom's ruler. The Higham Ferrers complex can therefore be seen as an early form of regional administrative centre.

Plate 5.3   Reconstruction of the enclosure complex in the mid 8th century

Plate 5.4   Reconstruction – the enclosure complex in the landscape

205

The resident population of the complex was probably not numerous, and it is possible that the complex was uninhabited for parts of the year. From the remains of the malting oven and the human remains from the final phase of the complex (see below) it is clear that the complex provided other services, in the form of ale production and the administration of the law as well as tribute collection

Plates 5.3 and 5.4 show how the complex could have appeared in the second half of the 8th century. Alongside Kings Meadow Lane, access is restricted by a fence to a formal entrance way; the emphasis in the excavated evidence seemed to be on the delineation of a controlled space, so some form of physical barrier would have been likely along the road.

Final phase of the complex

At some point in the second half of the 8th century the complex was fundamentally reorganised. The oval enclosure was abandoned and allowed to silt up; the western enclosure extension ditch was re-cut and extended to run eastwards across the site, and then turn and head to the south, parallel with the line of Windmill Banks. The overall shape of the enclosure was changed dramatically, but the exclusivity of the enclosed area remained. Does this change imply cessation of any animal penning function for the complex? That is possible, although it is notable that the number of cattle bones remains high during this final phase (see Fig. 4.31), which might suggest that stock penning was still a function, but relocated. However, many of the cattle bones of this final phase were found in a single dump of bone in the backfilling material of the enclosure extension ditch. Conceivably the opportunity was taken while clearing and dismantling the complex to slaughter and butcher the remaining cattle in one operation.

End of the complex

The stratigraphic evidence strongly suggests that the third and final version of the enclosure complex went out of use abruptly, either at the end of the 8th century or perhaps as late as the early 9th century. This date range is derived from the radiocarbon dates from human remains found in the backfilled enclosure ditch, and the comparable date recovered from the last firing of the malting oven. By the late 8th century the horseshoe-shaped enclosure (Phase 2a and 2b) had long since been abandoned and possibly allowed to silt up naturally. However the evidence of the Maxey ware assemblage from the ditch section on the north-east of the enclosure suggests that at least part of the horseshoe ditch was deliberately infilled.

All the stratigraphic evidence suggests that the Phase 2c enclosure ditch was backfilled in its entirety in one operation. On the east side of the complex (Site 8), similar signs of a sudden infilling

of the ditch are apparent. The group of eight bone needles (SF 4003 – 4010, Pl. 3.4), probably tied together with a thong through the eyes, was dropped or thrown into the ditch before its backfill,possibly as a termination deposit.

It is suggested, although it cannot be clearly demonstrated, that those timber framed buildings that still survived were dismantled or demolished in the same operation. It is accepted that the dating of the buildings is difficult; however there is indirect support for thinking that at least the principal hall building (7023) survived until the end; the sections cut through the Phase 2c ditch alongside the building produced significantly more pottery and animal bone from both the middle and upper layers, than did the sections to the north-east or south-west of the building. If the building had continued in use after the infilling of the ditch a further deposit of domestic rubbish might have been expected in the upper fill of the ditch, which represented silting in the post-backfill subsidence; this was not the case. Furthermore, the suggested use of this building (see below) implies also that it would have remained in use until the very end of the complex.

Not only were the ditches and the buildings on the north-east side of the lane backfilled and dismantled, but the evidence suggests that the malting oven to the south-west of the lane was deliberately destroyed, rather than simply abandoned to decay slowly. All of the fired clay fragments found within the oven chamber displayed unabraded surfaces and breaks, suggesting a deliberate demolition rather than slow erosion of an abandoned structure by the elements. The radiocarbon dating of the grain (Cal 662 -1014 at 98% confidence – 710 to 963 at 78% confidence), representing as it does the final use of the oven (see Moffett Chapter 4), is consistent with the suggested end date of the complex.

The completeness and abruptness of the complex's demise suggests a premeditated decision and action, rather than a gradual 'shutting down'. To dismantle and clear all traces of the complex from the landscape surely suggests more than a simply abandonment. A political motive is a strong possibility, perhaps symbolically representing the removal of the political status hitherto enjoyed by the royal estate, or the incumbent thereof. However, the archaeology evidence of the end of the complex is given an intriguing twist by the contents of the enclosure ditch backfill alongside Building 7023.

The woman in the ditch and the end of the enclosure

A large amount of information has been recovered from the skeletal remains and the circumstances surrounding their presence in the ditch. The detailed osteological report on the human bone can be found in Chapter 4, but it is worth summarising the findings here, along with the circumstances surrounding the burial, before attempts are made to arrive at any conclusions.

The partial skeleton of a woman aged approximately between 30 and 40 years was found at the base of the final backfill of the enclosure ditch. The body was in a prone, foetal position, quite possibly due to her being bound and contained within a sack. Some parts of the skeleton were missing, including the head, both arms, shoulder blades, and the 4th lumbar vertebrae. Tooth puncture marks, probably caused by a small dog, were found on the vertebrae adjacent to the missing one. A radiocarbon date of Cal 770AD–890AD at 68.2 % confidence or Cal 680AD–900AD at 95.4% confidence was recovered from the skeleton; this date is consistent with other indicators of the end of the enclosure complex.

In the same backfill, within a few metres, were found two adult male mandibles. Radiocarbon dates were recovered from both jaws; one produced a date almost identical to that of the woman – around the late 8th century, the other produced a date about 70 years earlier. Three more disarticulated human bone fragments were recovered from the same ditch fill a few metres to the south-west, in amongst a dense deposit of animal bones, comprising mainly cattle.

Two articulated dog skeletons were also found in the ditch backfill (see Evans Chapter 4). In both cases, the close grouping of the bones suggested that each body was contained in a bag.

It is suggested that the bodies or parts thereof had been brought to the ditch in sacks. To explain the partial dismemberment of the woman's body, and the evidence of gnawing by animals, it is argued that she was the victim of an execution. After her death her body was left hanging and exposed – possibly for a few weeks – before her burial. With one of the jawbones producing a radiocarbon date significantly earlier than the other dated human bones, and yet being deposited in the same fill of the same ditch under the same circumstances, it is difficult to avoid the conclusion that the bodies or body parts were collected from a single site, and that the site is likely to have been a formal execution site and an integral part of the estate centre. It follows that, if as seems likely, the process of backfilling the enclosure ditch was part of the total clearance of all elements of the estate centre, then this clearance also included the clearance of a nearby execution site.

The presence of the two partially articulated dog skeletons in the same backfill adds further intrigue to the scenario; like the human remains, the skeletons are incomplete, and appear to have been collected up and dumped in bags, although neither dog displayed obvious signs of being deliberately killed. It is reasonable to suggest that the dogs' carcasses derive from the same place as the human remains. One of the dogs had suffered severely from rickets, suggesting that it was never a 'working' dog. Indeed, it must have been closely cared-for to have survived at all. Could it have belonged to the woman? It is not beyond the bounds of possibility, though it cannot be confirmed through archaeology, that the woman's crime was witchcraft, and that the deformed dog representing something akin to a 'familiar'.

The study of Anglo-Saxon burial practices has only recently begun to focus on what has been termed as 'deviant burials' – a term coined first by Helen Geake (1992) – meaning those burial remains of an atypical or non-normative character, as determined by their archaeological remains. More recently this area of study has been developed to examine the judicial character of Anglo-Saxon England (Reynolds, forthcoming), and how that may be represented in the archaeological record. Reynolds argues that historically the assumption has been that Anglo-Saxon judicial organisation existed only in urban centres, and that where 'deviant' burials were found, they were considered to be random acts of war, murder, or unspecified ritual probably associated with overt or furtive paganism.

It is increasingly evident that a sophisticated judicial system could be maintained, responsible to a central authority yet decentralised in its operation (ibid). The geography of judicial administration was dependent on the principal judicial agents, that is kings and kings' officials, wherever they may be, rather than a institution or building in a particular urban centre.

In some instances evidence of this judicial administration comes before any indication of urbanism in a region:

The centralised functions of 'folk' significance like Sutton Hoo and Yeavering evidently gave way during the middle Anglo-Saxon period to dispersed administrative functions, a process no doubt driven by the increasingly geographical extent of kingdoms and the need for more formalised systems of governance." (Reynolds forthcoming)

Table 5.4: Radiocarbon dates associated with the end of the complex

Material	Radiocarbon Date recovered
Mutilated woman	Cal 770AD - 890AD at 68.2 % confidence. Cal 680AD - 900AD at 95.4% confidence
Jawbone 1	Cal 774AD - 811AD at 65% confidence. Cal 683AD to 889AD at 98% confidence
Jawbone 2	Cal 656AD-690AD at 47% confidence. Cal 641AD -772AD at 92% confidence
Malting oven grain	Cal 710AD to 963AD at 78% confidence. Cal 662AD -1014AD at 98% confidence

Once executed, the dismemberment of criminals, and the display of the whole body (or parts thereof) for all to see, was not at all unusual (Meaney 1995, 30), and there is no evidence to suggest that women could not be subject to the same treatment as men. The display of the body of an execution victim would be intended as a warning to others, and therefore the body would be sited where it could not fail to be seen. This was often on a hill – for late Saxon and medieval examples see Steane 1985, 27 – but to achieve the same effect the 'display' site could be alongside a road. What better place to display those who had committed a crime against the royal authority than alongside the road that ran through the royal centre?

The fact that the human bone evidence suggests that execution victims were left to be dismembered by scavengers raises the implication that execution victims were not routinely buried soon after death. Perhaps exposure and dismemberment were reserved for the perpetrators of particularly severe crimes. That the execution and subsequent slow bodily decay, encouraged by scavengers, was seen as a dreadful fate is described with suitably mordant relish in a 10th-century poem 'The Fortunes of Men' included within the Exeter Book (Exeter, Cathedral Chapter Library, MS 3501, quoted in Reynolds 1999, 104):

One shall ride the high gallows and upon his death hang until his soul's treasury, his bloody bone-framed body, disintegrates. There the raven, black of plumage will pluck out the sight from his head and shred the soulless corpse – and he cannot fend off with his hands the loathsome bird of prey from its evil intent. His life is fled and deprived of his senses, beyond hope of survival, he suffers his lot, pallid upon the beam, enveloped in the midst of death. His name is damned.

In conclusion the archaeological evidence suggests that the woman was executed – probably for a serious crime, and quite possibly for reasons relating to events surrounding the end of the estate centre. Within weeks of her execution, the decision was taken, not just to abandon the complex, but to eradicate all elements of it from the landscape, including the buildings and other structures like the malting oven. During the process of clearance, the execution site, an established permanent site within the complex, and possibly situated close to the trackway, was also cleared, and the human remains lying there were bagged up and dumped in the ditch.

Conclusion

If the parallels of the Higham Ferrers complex with that at Yeavering are valid, does this imply that an outdated and obsolete form of regional administration was still being used by the most renowned king of Mercia more than a century later? The answer might be a (cautious) 'yes' if we could be sure that similar estate centres did not exist – either in Outer Mercia or indeed in Northumbria – in the intervening period. It is true that there are no known lowland English parallels for the complex at Higham Ferrers, but that doesn't mean they never existed. Had the principal focus of the late Saxon settlement at Higham Ferrers not been established a kilometre to the south, it is highly likely that the enclosure complex, along with all of its constituent parts and buildings, would have been completely destroyed by later development, or at very least left as unintelligible islands of archaeology. It is quite possible that sites already excavated and interpreted as (say) rural settlements might in fact be surviving elements of something on the scale of the complex at Higham Ferrers.

Rural settlement archaeology almost inevitably focuses on the development of the settlement through its economic development. The site therefore becomes understood in this way only. Higham Ferrers has offered the possibility that the socio-political development of Middle Saxon rural society may also be accessible through archaeological remains.

In this instance the authors believe that at Higham Ferrers, for a large part of the 8th century, there existed as complete an example of the administrative part of a Middle Saxon royal estate centre as has been revealed in modern times. It is certainly not suggested that the Higham Ferrers complex was unique, far from it. It may well be that small sites that have uncovered a few Middle Saxon buildings could have partially revealed similar administration centres. Such is the confidence and clarity with which the Higham Ferrers enclosure complex was laid out in the landscape, it is difficult to countenance the idea that it could have been a one-off design.

LATE SAXON SETTLEMENT

Introduction

The clearance of the landscape and structures of the complex produced something akin to a clear canvas upon which subsequent settlers could define their own boundaries. The new settlement appeared to comprise piecemeal and opportunist development, principally situated towards the high ground to the north, and with an increasing tendency to align with the north-south road.

Chronology of Phase 3

As with the other phases, the dating range for this period is qualified by the usual restraints, although in general sufficient stratigraphic relationships are evident, which, combined with the concentrations of fairly distinct Late Saxon pottery (principally St Neots ware), allow buildings and other features to be assigned to this phase with reasonable confidence.

Structural evidence

The evidence suggests that a focus of structural activity lay in the north-eastern part of Site 4, with associated activity in Site 2, and comprises at least two, and possibly three buildings, and a spread of small ditches, possibly defining paddocks.

Building 6811 (Site 4)

The building was situated in the north-east part of Site 4, and displayed what appeared to be an L-shaped layout, despite heavy truncation by later ploughing over the northwest corner of the building has removed enough of the postholes on the north-western side to make confirmation of the L-shape difficult. There was no evidence that the structure was originally a rectangle, later augmented with a cross-wing. There are very few examples of late Saxon buildings originally laid out in this way, although one of the later (9th-century?) buildings at Catholme was interpreted as one originally laid out in an L-shape (see Building AS43 in Losco-Bradley and Kinsley 2002, figure 3.58 and 3.87).

A sequence of well-used hearths was suggested by substantial spreads of burnt silty clay and ash in the north wing of the building, implying that at least part of the building served as a dwelling.

Building 7321

To the north-west of Building 6811, and on the same alignment, the structure 7321 is distinctive in the evidence of the apparent use of a combination of beamslots and what appear to be raking struts, at least on the south wall. The absence of internal features, and the presence of a cluster of postholes and a hearth around the east end of the building hints at a workshop function rather than a dwelling.

There is no suggestion that the complex of buildings is aligned on any boundary running across from the Lane to the north-south road. Also, there is no real evidence that the landscape has been formally divided at all at this stage.

Building 15300 (Site 8)

The east-west oriented pit of a Sunken Featured Building was first identified in the evaluation (Site 3), and the exposed (eastern part) was subsequently fully excavated in the excavation. It displays some of the hallmarks of Early Saxon Sunken Featured Buildings – a flat-bottomed pit with a posthole set in the approximate mid-point of the revealed east end. Were it not for the fact that the pit was cut into the infilled Phase 2 ditch, the two sherds of St Neots ware pottery dating to the 10th or 11th century, recovered from the pit fill, may have been assumed to be intrusive.

Late Saxon SFBs are not uncommon, but in England they are found almost exclusively in urban contexts, where space was at something of a premium, and the pit represented a proper cellar (Tipper 2004, 14). Many of these features show evidence for more sophisticated details, like shuttering for the pit walls, and trodden or even cobbled sunken floors. Neither of these elaborations was evident with Building 15300. However, Hamerow cites examples of sunken floored weaving sheds dating to as late as the 12th century in Saxony (2002, 33), so their demise in (rural) England may be a lot a less abrupt than is thought. It seems likely that Building 15300 was intended for a specific function, although there is precious little evidence to indicate what that may be. Only an iron object (SF 4029) of indeterminate (but possibly intricate) function was found in the pit fill (see Fig. 4.21, 64).

A scatter of small ditches appear to relate to Building 15300, although again they do not obviously indicate formal planning of property boundaries. To the south the circular structure – possibly representing a drainage gully surrounding a hayrick built around a central post – may also be associated with this building (although it could equally well be part of the complex centred on Building 6811).

Little can be said about the southern group of Phase 3 features. They suggest a possible focus of activity south of Site 4, alongside the Lane, but the absence of similar activity to the south-east in Site 7 suggests that the development alongside the Lane at this time was piecemeal and low-density.

Historical context

It is during this phase that Higham Ferrers is first mentioned (in Domesday as a manor that in 1066 belonged to Gytha, Countess of Hereford). Hall has shown (1988, 106-7) that in the late Saxon period Higham Ferrers was a multiple estate, and included – amongst other elements – Raunds (itself a multiple estate). He has also asserted that it is in this period that the strip field system was developed, overriding the remnants of the middle Saxon land division. Interestingly there's no archaeological evidence to suggest that happening on the site in Phase 3. As Hall suggests, less attractive (or unneeded) land could be left as pasture or scrub, to be incorporated into the field system at a later date (ibid, 108). The fact that there's no real indication until Phase 4 that the area is being formally partitioned may be due to the fact that, once the late Saxon settlement was established to the south (where the present centre of Higham Ferrers is) the relatively remote vicinity of Kings Meadow Lane may not have been particularly attractive.

The contention that the settlement shifted (either abruptly or slowly) from the Kings Meadow Lane area to its medieval core site was largely based upon the pre-excavation understanding. However, there is a case for saying that, as the Middle Saxon complex was an administrative establishment, there was no settlement to move after the destruction of the complex. Therefore it could be said that the medieval core is on the site of the original village settlement, and is not a transposed one.

Whether the present settlement was established before the demise of the Kings Meadow Lane complex is a difficult question to answer. The presence by 1086 of a priest and a market (attached to the manor) seems to be proof that the medieval church and market place were in place by the conquest, and therefore cannot realistically be considered representative of a new foundation – usually of a post-conquest date. It is not surprising that little archaeological investigation has been possible in the historic core of the town. Foard argues (2000, 13) that the most likely context of the settlement shift is part of the general re-planning undertaken at that time, evident in the adjacent villages in the Raunds area (Parry 2006), and possibly even driven by the fragmentation of the Irthlingborough estate.

Archaeological evidence from within the medieval core of Higham Ferrers to support this

scenario is unsurprisingly scanty, given the keyhole nature of the fieldwork that has taken place (see Chapter 2). However, a relatively recent excavation at College Street, on the northern outskirts of the historic core, revealed some helpful results. The excavators concluded that occupation on the site was not established until the 12th century (Jones and Chapman 2003, 129). Crucially, no early Saxon pottery, and only very few sherds of middle Saxon pottery were found, implying a presence in the near vicinity, but no more than that. A small assemblage of late Saxon pottery was found, suggesting that later occupation was centred to the south (ibid. 132-3). This seems to confirm that the origin of the settlement lay to the south, and occupation spread northwards in the late Saxon period.

Hall's examination of the 1567 fieldbook for Higham Ferrers shows that, in addition to the three open fields, there remained a large block of

Fig. 5.6   Extent of the medieval parish of Higham Ferrers

demesne – the manorial home farm. The proportion of the demesne to the open field is the same as stated in Domesday, and from this Hall concludes that the arrangement visible on the ground in 1567 is essentially the same as that of the Late Saxon period. He speculated that the intact block of demesne could represent the continuation of a Roman estate belonging to the settlement overlooking the Nene on the western outskirts of Higham Ferrers. With the hindsight of the excavations, one might equally well speculate that the demesne defined by Hall owes as much to the presence of the Middle Saxon complex. Figure 5.6 shows the extent of the demesne in relation to the open fields and to the Roman and middle Saxon sites.

Character of the settlement

The evidence suggests that the Phase 3 activity could be characterised as essentially roadside sprawl on re-colonised waste ground, beginning to align with both the northern route, as well as the north-western route. The relative influence of the two roads – Kings Meadow Lane and Windmill Banks roads is beginning change, although at this stage one might suggest that the two roads are equally important.

The archaeology is certainly consistent with an unplanned and opportunistic accretion of sprawling farmsteads. How much of a hiatus there may have been between the end of Phase 2c and the beginning of occupation in Phase 3 is impossible to say. It seems unlikely that reoccupation would have taken place within less than a generation or two, and it is not inconceivable that part or all of the site may have been considered a taboo area, in the light of what had transpired there at the end of the 8th century.

The identity of these early medieval settlers is worthy of consideration. By the 10th century this area had been effectively subsumed into the sphere of influence of the Danish incomers. Two metal finds, both from the vicinity of the Phase 3 activity on Site 8, hint at Norse influences, if not an actual Norse presence. An irregular shaped fragment of copper alloy sheet (Sf 4014: Cat.No. **46**; Pl 4.1) displayed a small area of interlace design, possibly Scandinavian in origin. The other is a Viking coin of St Edmund (SF 4028) dating to AD 885-915 (Pl. 4.2).

Child burial (Pl. 5.5)

That this part of the northern outskirts of the formative Higham Ferrers must have been somewhat remote is perhaps given support by the neonatal

Plate 5.5   Child burial

burial situated on Site 2, towards the north-western edge of the complex of small paddocks. The grave was little more than a scoop in the ground, and, possibly due to animal disturbance, or maybe because of the truncation by post-medieval ploughing, there was some disturbance to the bones (see Witkin Chapter 4). The surviving bones were radiocarbon dated, producing a date of 780 – 1030AD (95% confidence). The earlier end of this range just overlaps with the possible date range of Building 2666 (see above), so it is technically possible that the burial took place inside a standing building.

While there are a handful of examples of foetal or neonatal burials in early Saxon SFB pits – such a practice seems to have largely died out by the 8th century (see Hamerow 2006, fig. 1). How far these are instances of special deposition or 'foundation deposits' with a ritual or quasi-religious motive is unclear, but by the later Saxon period the growing authority of the Church brought pressure to bear to abandon what were considered pagan practices. It should be noted that there is a continental tradition of infant burials in NW European longhouses as late as the 10th century. Nevertheless, a burial date around the end of the 10th century (Phase 3) for the Higham Ferrers examples seems much more likely.

This burial is characteristic of the discreet interment of an unbaptised and possibly stillborn child (see Witkin, Chapter 4). The church taught that a baby who died before baptism would not reach heaven, and many believed that its spirit would return to trouble the living. Law 2 of King Ine of Wessex at the end of the 7th century gives us an idea how important it was to the newly Christian kings for their subject people to accept the new religion.

A child shall be baptised within 30 days. If this is not done, 30 shillings shall be paid in compensation. If it dies without being baptised, he [the father] shall pay everything he owns. (quoted in Crawford 1999, 85)

By the 10th century the scale of the penalty was reduced, but it was still a penalty. It seems that, in this case, the unbaptised (stillborn?) child was taken to a secluded spot and buried surreptitiously, away from view in a very shallow and rudimentary grave, just beyond the edge of the paddocks.

MEDIEVAL – 12th TO 14th CENTURY

Introduction

The processes of settlement migration begun in Late Saxon period are fully realised by the 12th century, and this applies not only to the migration of Higham Ferrers as a whole to the new (and present) focus on the high ground to the south, but also – within the project area – to the concentration of occupation close to the two roads, and particularly the N-S route, Windmill Banks.

It is also during this phase that the land divisions evident in their developed form in the 1737 map are first identified archaeologically in their embryonic form (Pl. 1.3). From this point on there is a clear distinction between the agricultural land to the west and settlement (of whatever character) to the east. Archaeologically, this means that the occupation evidence is confined almost exclusively to Sites 7 and 8, with traces of field ditches and or plough furrows in Site 4. While both Sites 7 and 8 contain evidence of occupation activity, the character of occupation on both sites is distinct. The implications of this are considered below.

Nature of the settlement

Site 7

The arrangement of ditches evident in this Phase suggests an orientation onto Kings Meadow Lane, with the curve of the Lane at this point being echoed by the composite gully 9371/9385. Two possible enclosures were partially revealed. In the northern one, the single identified building (9528) showed no sign of being a dwelling, and, given the meagre scatter of pottery and bone in the vicinity, a likely function is a small barn or outbuilding, dating to early in this period, perhaps associated with a house fronting onto the Lane. Any building(s) associated with the southern enclosure were presumably beyond the site boundary.

While the impression gained from the evidence on Site 7 in this period (as in all the other periods on this site) is somewhat clouded by the safety problems surrounding its excavation (see Chapter 3 – Phasing), the interpretation is that the roadside settlement represented here is fairly low status overspill from the new centre to the south.

Site 8

In contrast to the southern area (Site 7), there are plenty of signs of domestic and craft activity, in the form of well used surfaces, hearths or oven bases, and well-constructed drains. The provisional suggestion, based on the limited results of the evaluation (Site 3), was that the evidence represented an ad hoc 'squatter' dwelling. Clearly the more comprehensive evidence recovered at the excavation stage suggests a much more elaborate and sophisticated establishment.

The purpose of the quarrying is worth consideration. Further down the slope to the south, the natural subsoil varies from pockets of silty clay to beds of ironstone. The distinctions are reasonably clear, and the quarry pits (of Phase 5) invariably are targeted on the clay. On Site 8 – and particularly the central area -the character of the natural is a lot more intermixed, with bands of limestone sealed or interspersed with pockets and/or layers of silty clay. This suggests that the pits represent stone quarrying. Whether this quarrying was to provide material to construct buildings on the site or nearby is unclear, but despite the lack of clear structural evidence, these quarries do not seem to have been far from domestic activity. The presence of pieces of daub in the quarry backfill, close to the oven 15294, suggests the contemporaneity of domestic activity and quarrying.

The only reasonably coherent building identified on the site was the small rectangular structure 15294. It had what appeared to be a sunken stone surfaced floor (possibly a hearth base) at one end. The drain that crossed the building (falling from east to west) is higher than the sunken floor, which either suggests the building goes out of use before the drain is constructed, or the buildings function changes, not longer requiring a sunken floor. The drain appears to be emptying into the ground over the infilled Phase 2b ditch, but there's no evidence to indicate where the drain is emptying from.

The absence of clear evidence of substantial buildings other than 15495 is made more puzzling by the number of well constructed stone-lined drains, mostly surrounding or incorporated into, a central cobbled yard surface to the north of building 15495. Why would they need drains like this on what must have been at least reasonably well-drained ground? Assessing the direction of fall of the drains gives some clues to determine where they were draining from and to. In the northern part of this area, over the infilled quarry pits two drains are running eastwards into a large pit or sump, but in neither case is there any evidence of what each drain was leading from.

In the southern area, around Structure 15495, the drains appear to be running to the west, to the area over the infilled Saxon ditch of Phase 2b. Was this still a slightly lower area, and did it serve as a sump? One is drawn inevitably to the conclusion that there was some fairly elaborate building or range of buildings on the site or nearby, and associated yards (a farmhouse and outbuildings?). For reasons which are not clear, the activities underway on this site required an elaborate surface water drainage system (although it should be pointed out that that the area in question did not in any way appear to be susceptible to waterlogging during the excavation.

The finds evidence from this area at this time shows an unremarkable assemblage of metal items, principally of a domestic and personal character, in association with an equally unremarkable pottery assemblage. Indeed, if it were not for the elaborate yard surfaces and drains, the original evaluation interpretation, that it represented a short-lived 'squatter' dwelling would still be valid. As a piece of roadside development the sense of isolation from Higham Ferrers (or even Kings Meadow Lane) is artificially heightened by the destruction of all the archaeological deposits in a broad roadside swathe from Site 8 down to Site 7. It is surely most likely that other dwellings and tenements would have accumulated alongside the road in between.

Site 4

The evidence from Site 4 indicates the continued use of the area as arable land, albeit now in a more planned way in comparison to Phase 3, with the addition of boundary ditches, the orientation of which appears to be influenced by the line of Kings Meadow Lane and a possible NE-SW boundary linking the Lane and Windmill Banks, inferred from the ditch 7239 and that of ditch 6854. The junction of the latter with ditch 7024 (see Fig. 3.35) is the location of a possible building (7025) – interpreted from the lack of finds in its vicinity as an outbuilding, although serving what domestic focus is hard to determine.

Historical context

Historically, this period sees Higham become known as Higham Ferrers, become the borough and a property of the Duchy of Lancaster and reach something of a zenith of popularity and regional dominance. The development of the castle, the establishment of Chichele College, and the burgeoning prosperity of the borough seems to jar with the archaeological evidence in the Kings Meadow Lane area. Even though the character of the remains on Site 8 is difficult to determine, it is safe to say that it is not especially high status, or representative of extensive occupation. The historical documentation seems to indicate that, through design or circumstance, the north end of the borough became something of an enclave for the agricultural tenements, while those with commercial or industrial interests clusterd round, and to the south of, the medieval market square. By 1591 the northern borough boundary was established well to the north of the project area, and yet the area known as Bond End seems to have been considered as vitually a separate community, with its own bakehouse, prompting the suggestion from Foard and Ballinger (2000, 34-5), that in the early medieval period (before the borough was established) Bond End could have been a separate settlement.

LATE MEDIEVAL PERIOD (14th and 15th CENTURIES)

Kilns and the Higham Ferrers pottery industry
by Paul Blinkhorn and Alan Hardy

The archaeological evidence of this period is – on Sites 6 and 8 – almost entirely related to the activities surrounding the pottery industry, and associated processes (clay quarrying). On Site 4 there is finally clear evidence of a boundary ditch linking Kings Meadow Lane and the Windmill Banks, and on Site 7 a suggestion that the property orientation is beginning to swing to the south, implying the creation of the triangular green in the junction of the two roads, later to be known as Walnut Green.

Structure of the kilns

Kiln 1

This was by far the best-preserved of the kilns. It comprised a pit with a central pedestal, and two opposed stoke pits, each separated from the firing-chamber by an flue arch. While the roof of the firing chamber was missing, the two flue arches survived in situ (Pl. 3.9) The kiln is a classic example of Musty's type 2c (ibid. – see McCarthy and Brooks 1988, figure 16). A number of examples of kilns of this type are known from the medieval Britain, with Musty's corpus showing that they are limited to the midlands and south of England, including one from Brill in Buckinghamshire which is dateable to the 14th – 15th century (Jope 1953-4).

Within the firing chamber the flat top of the pedestal is clearly far too small to have accommodated more than a handful of pots, so one must conjecture some arrangement of ceramic fire bars, spanning the gap around the pedestal. No evidence of these bars was found in the kiln or the surrounding area, so it must be assumed they were removable.

The question of the nature of the superstructure of the Higham Ferrers kilns is a vexed one. While past assumptions – based on post-medieval or Mediterranean examples past and present, has assumed that the kiln chamber was topped with a clay (or brick) dome, in virtually all cases there is no archaeological trace of a superstructure.

While there is a believable case for there having been no more substantial covering to the kiln chamber on Site 6 than a pile of turves, there is

support for a 'rigid roof' hypothesis from two principal areas at Higham Ferrers. Both kilns were producing Reduced Ware. To achieve the sufficient and consistent reduction during firing it must have been possible to seal the chamber as efficiently as possible (McCarthy and Brooks 1988, 52). Arguably this would be difficult to achieve with a loose covering of turves.

Several large pieces of structural daub – each with a smoothed side, were found among the waster dump in the both the central chamber and the stokeholes of Kiln 1. They may have come from a superstructure, although it is accepted that some parts of the firing chamber lining and the central pedestal had fallen off, and therefore may account for some of the recovered pieces. The reconstruction (Pl. 5.6) shows the full clay dome with just a central chimney or vent. This would be very effective in maintaining both the heat and the reduced oxygen environment, although access to the chamber could be difficult. However, Musty (ibid.) argued that a permanent clay dome was not necessarily an obstruction to stacking the pots in the kiln prior to firing. He cited experimental pottery-making which showed that it was possible for an individual to crawl into the kiln through the firing-arch, and then stack the kiln by having pots passed in through the arch and the vent at the top of the dome. This could be a time-consuming method, however, taking many hours, and it was more efficient to have some sort of removable clay 'door' at the flue entrance to allow the potter to walk into the kiln. An open-topped kiln with a temporary roof would have facilitated stacking and removing the pots still further.

Plate 5.6   Reconstruction of the medieval pottery kiln

Musty (1974, 54) cites experimental firings where reduced pottery was made in an open-topped kiln which was sealed with clay plates and sods, and then sealed with clay when the desired temperature (*c* 900°C) was reached. Certainly, high temperatures and a low-oxygen firing environment could not have been achieved without some form of capping on the kiln, but it cannot be said with certainty if the kilns found on Sites 6 and 8 had temporary or permanent roofs.

The kiln was most probably fuelled with faggots (tightly-bound bundles of thin brushwood). The charcoal report (see Thompson and Francis, Chapter 4) notes the predominance of twig material from fruit trees (including apple) within the samples taken from the floor of Kiln 1 and the floor within the building 9008, immediately to the west of the kiln. Le Patourel (1968, 117) noted that at Laverstock in Wiltshire, manorial records show that men with the surname 'Potter' were purchasing roods of brushwood from a number of manorial centres, and there is a record of 14th – century tile-makers purchasing 1,000 faggots for the firing of ten tile-kilns. The 'Potter' surname also applied to some metal workers, usually those involved with copper alloys, although they would not have required large quantities of faggots for any of their processes. Faggots would have a double advantage over large pieces of timber in that they were considerably cheaper, and would have burned quickly and thus at a higher temperature. This method of fuelling the kiln seems to have been used at both Brill (ibid. 18) and at Lyveden in north-east Northamptonshire (Musty 1974, 56), although in the case of the latter, a single large diameter (*c* 175mm) piece of oak was also noted. The environmental evidence (see Challinor Chapter 4) shows that most of the charcoal fragments from the kiln were 1 – 9 mm in diameter, indicating that brushwood faggots were indeed the source of fuel.

There seems to be very little consistency in the wood species exploited for fuel. The Lyveden potters utilised hawthorn and oak, whereas those at Laverstock used oak, willow, hazel and birch (ibid.). The fact that most of the identifiable wood from Kiln 1 at Higham Ferrers was species of fruit tree would suggest choice was more a reflection of the local availability than species preference.

Kiln 2

While very little of the kiln in Site 8 survived, it is reasonable to conclude that it was of very similar construction to kiln 9200 in Site 6. The fact that it was constructed at ground level, not within a purpose-built pit, is worthy of note (and explains why so little has survived). Typically, the sinking of the stoke holes and chamber below ground was done to improve the efficiency of the firing and avoid the depredations of the elements. Why this was not done at Site 8 is unclear, especially as its location (further up the slope) is arguably even more exposed to the elements than Kiln 1 on Site 6.

Setting the base of the kiln at ground level necessitated the construction of a lining for the stokeholes – in this case of limestone blocks, some of which survived.

Possibly the effort of sinking it below ground was considered excessive – which begs the question, is it actually the case that medieval kilns were typically sunken below ground, or is that an erroneous impression influenced by the fact that above-ground kilns are much more likely to be heavily (or completely) truncated by later activity?

1965 "kiln" reconsidered (Fig. 5.7)

A small excavation (c. 40 sq m) was carried out by David Hall in 1965 in the corner of Chamberlain's factory car-park, in response to factory development. The location of the site was immediately to the west of Site 6. Various stone features and cut features were revealed in a sequence of interconnected excavation trenches or sondages, along with large quantities of Reduced Ware pottery. The features were interpreted as a stone-built kiln and associated stokehole, and contemporary features including a NE-SW wall and ditch, and a square pit to the north-west. The great quantity of recovered wasters gave a consistent typological date of the early 15th century.

Brief publication of the discovery, including a description and summary quantification of the pottery, but excluding a site plan appeared some years later (Hall 1974). Copies of the original site drawings have been obtained, and are sufficient to understand the basic layout of the features discovered.

The excavation of Site 6 and the extensive structural remains of kiln 9200 prompts a reconsideration of the interpretation of the remains discovered in 1965. The circular stone shaft was interpreted as the kiln itself and a shallow ditch extending to the south-west was considered to be the remains of a single flue. The fact that the bulk of the pottery was recovered from these two features clearly influenced the interpretation. The circular stone shaft (FI) and the slight gully running to the south-west bear some similarity to a Musty Type 1 kiln and flue, but does not fit comfortably with any known late medieval kiln type, and bears no similarity at all with the kiln discovered in 2002.

Therefore, benefiting from the full excavation of kiln 9200, it is possible to offer an alternative interpretation of the 'kiln' features from the 1965 excavation. From the available data, the circular stone feature has some of the characteristics of a stone-lined well, although the excavator asserts that it was too shallow to be a well (Hall, pers. comm.). If not a well, the circular stone feature could have been for storing clay, or possibly where the clay blunging was carried out to remove impurities and stones (McCarthy and Brooks 1988, 19). Alternatively it is possible that the circular feature could have been, for instance, a lead-lined cistern; a means of storing water, close to the

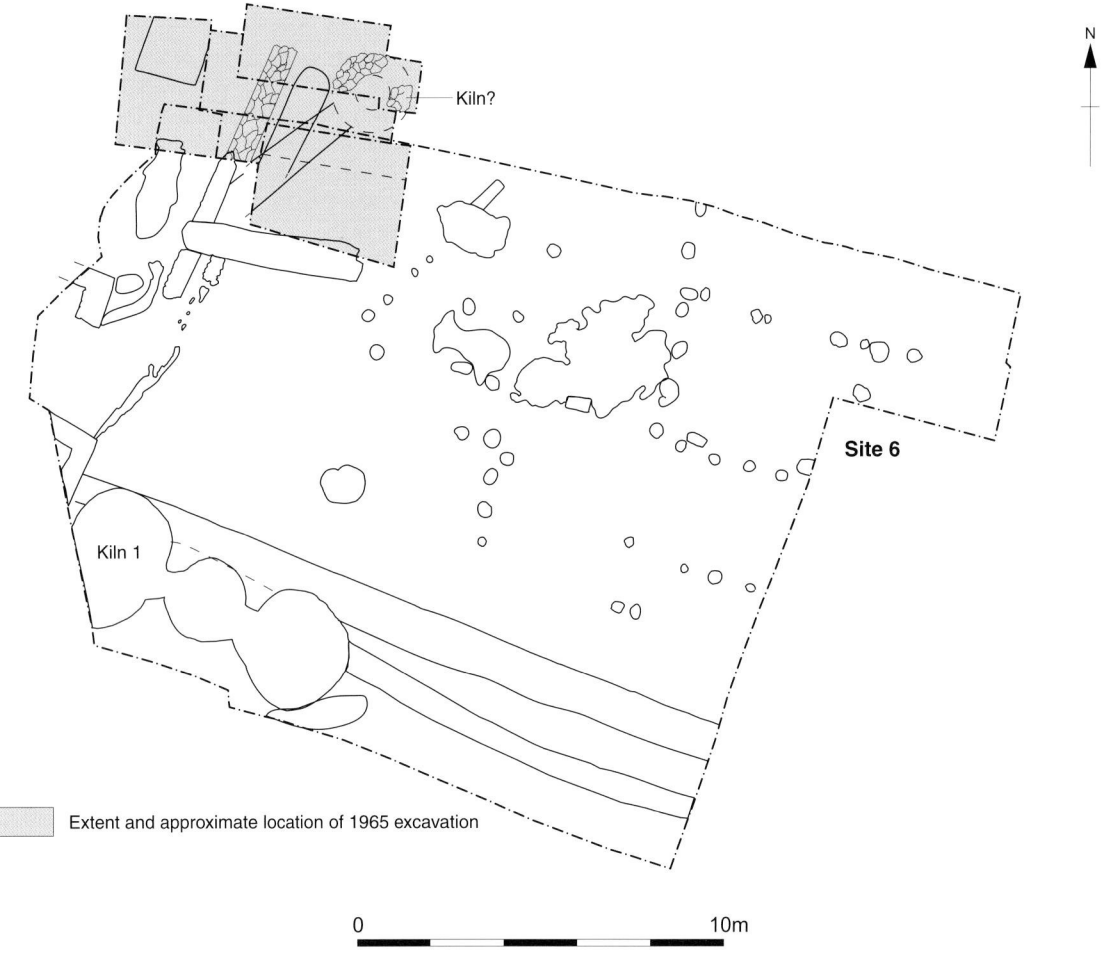

Fig. 5.7   Site 6 with the 1965 excavation plan superimposed

workshop, would have been necessary;. It is suggested that both the stone feature and the shallow gully were exploited as convenient dumps for kiln waste when the production site was abandoned and cleared. It is significant to note that the character of the wasters recovered in 1965 is indistinguishable from those recovered from the vicinity of Kiln 1 (see Blinkhorn, Chapter 4).

Unfortunately, the location of the site on the original 1965 drawings is insufficiently precise to accurately locate it in relation to the excavation of Site 6. It must be assumed that the 1965 site lay very close to the northern edge of Site 6, as no trace of the 1965 excavation was found during the latter work, although some modern disturbance was noted in the north-west part of Site 6. Two of the features revealed in the 1965 excavation appear – from their dimensions and orientation – to be continuations of features revealed in Site 6. A SW-NE oriented wall (F2), and a parallel ditch (F3) appear to correspond to features 9005 and 9206 respectively. Figure 5.7 depicts the conjectural location of the 1965 features in relation to the 2002 excavation.

Medieval pottery industry in Higham Ferrers

Extent of the industry

While two definite kilns were positively identified, there is some archaeological evidence that more may have been situated in the area between Kings Meadow Lane and Windmill Banks. The occurrence of Reduced Ware sherds in the vicinity of the northern kiln (15275) showed a definite concentration of material to the south of the kiln, towards the southern edge of Site 8, which may suggest that a further kiln or kilns once existed in the area since terraced by the 20th century factory construction.

Two pieces of documentary evidence, from the Hundredal Court Rolls, shed light on the Higham Ferrers pottery industry in the 15th century. In 1436 William Potter *'took a messuage not built, together with a selion of land in an adjacent croft, in which croft there is a kiln for making pots and other earthen vessels'* (Sergeantson 1917, 44). This seems to imply that he took over a going concern, with the intention of expanding the business. Repairs to a pottery kiln are also mentioned in 1467 (Serjeantson 1917, 37). The archaeomagnetic date range for the last firing obtained from Kiln 1 on Site 6 is 1385 – 1435 (95% confidence), slightly at odds with the documentary reference to William Potter, although conceivably the kiln cited is Kiln 1 on Site 6.

Other than William Potter himself, how many other people were involved in the pottery business at Higham Ferrers? Blinkhorn (Chapter 4) shows that there were distinct differences between the range of vessel sizes made in Kiln 1 and Kiln 2, and suggests that two different potters may have been at work. Was William Potter one of them, or did he subcontract out the actual potting?

In the late medieval period pottery production was a fairly low-status industry, providing only at best a moderate income, and attracting workers from the lower end of the social scale. Certainly, in medieval Britain, few potters appear to have had sufficient wealth and status to enable them to reach the rank of Freeman, and there was never an earthenware potters' Guild (see McCarthy and Brooks 1988, 77). In prospering towns, such a low status business, inherently filthy and carrying the risks of fire, would have been exiled to the peripheries of the built-up area. It is no surprise that pottery production at Higham Ferrers was situated well to the north of the town centre. However, this may have been as much due to the preference of the potter as to discrimination by his industrial peers. The efficient functioning of the kilns required a plentiful (and convenient) supply of wood and clay.

Analysis of the petrology of some large fragments of clay from the collapsed structure of Kiln 1, in addition to samples of the pottery from both Kiln 1 and the assemblage recovered in 1965 has provided some pertinent details of the material used (Vince, forthcoming). There was some variation in the clay used to make the pots, suggesting that – even if the 1965 site did not reveal a kiln as such, the pottery recovered was not part of the same waster dump as that found in and over Kiln 1. The analysis has also shown that the clay used in the kiln structure was not the same as that used to make the pots. One of the samples contained moderate sized fragments of calcareous rocks, shelly marl and calcareous sandstone. This may suggest (not unsurprisingly) that the superstructure was constructed of clay either derived from less 'pure' deposits, or less thoroughly washed before use than that used for the pots themselves.

Some idea of the economics and logistics of obtaining clay for potting can be found in the details of medieval clay-digging licences. The potter usually had to pay the lord of the manor for licence to dig clay, but the physical nature of clay-pits varied considerably. Le Patourel (1968, 114) noted some of the more common descriptions of clay-workings, which included pits from four feet square up to twenty feet square, and other pits in the form of long ditches from two to four feet wide and up to four perches long. Clearly, on mixed subsoil as at Higham Ferrers, the pit size and shape would tend to be influenced by the depth and extent of the clay

'seam'. Clay pits were often – as at Higham Ferrers – dug in the open fields; at a time of low grain prices, a licence to dig clay could earn a lord more than growing corn on the same land (ibid.).

It is suggested that the croft or tenement that contained the kiln on Site 8 fronted onto the north-south road, Windmill Banks, although it still not clear where the line of the road falls in relation to its modern position. Judging by the continued absence of significant features in the eastern part of Site 8 in the late medieval period, and the impression given by the 1737 map, it was still a rough and undefined droveway, rather than a precisely delimited road.

The abandonment of the kilns appears to have taken place by late in the 15th century. There is some evidence to suggests that the first in the sequence of NE-SW boundary gullies that clip the side of Kiln 2 was dug soon after, as its fill contains a high proportion of wasters from the pottery operation. It is reasonable to suggest that the two ditches identified along the south-east side of Site 4 represent the continuation of this boundary definition down to the line of Kings Meadow Lane.

However much activity and industry there was in the late medieval period, it is far from clear that the area of Kings Meadow Lane was considered to be any part of urbanised centre of Higham Ferrers, despite it still being part of the borough. Regardless of the cartographic accuracy of the Norden map of 1590, the northern extent of Higham Ferrers is depicted as the junction of what is now College Lane and Kimbolton Road; Kings Meadow Lane is not even shown. It seems that once the pottery industry had closed down the area quickly reverted to waste ground or agricultural use.

17th CENTURY – 20th CENTURY

Introduction

With the disappearance of the pottery industry, the archaeology shows that the Kings Meadow Lane area reverted to farmland, bordered by sporadic settlement along the north side of the Lane and the west side of Windmill Banks. The correlation between the archaeological evidence of buildings and boundary ditches and the earliest maps of the area (including Pl.1.3) is reasonably consistent.

Site 7

In the south-east corner of Site 7 the stone footings of one of the cottages that fronted onto Walnut Green from the 18th century were exposed, with associated cobbled surfaces and a large feature (not fully excavated, that nevertheless produced a substantial quantity of horn cores.

Site 8

In the south-east corner of Site 8 remains were found of cobbled yards, and a stone lined well. Both

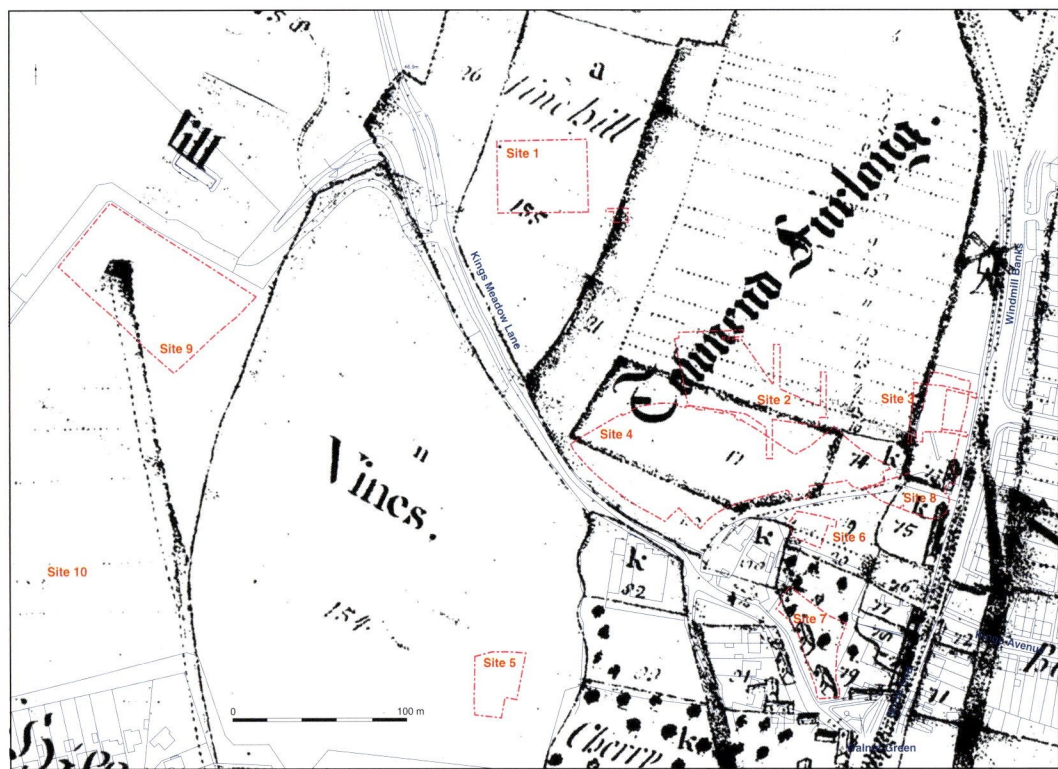

Plate 5.7 Detail of 1737 estate map and with superimposed site outlines (Northampton Record Office, Map 1004, reproduced with permission of Sir Philip Naylor Leyland Bt. and the Milton (Peterborough) Estates Company)

dated to the 19th century, and would appear to have been back yard elements associated with roadside cottages – presumably situated to the east of the site.

Of interest is the eventual definition of the line of the north-south road, implied by the archaeology in Site 8, evident in the 1737 estate map (Pl. 1.3) and the Inclosure Map of 1839. The road is entitled Kettering Turnpike Road in the latter, which might explain the more precise delineation of the road by this time. More recently the road was renamed Windmill Banks, on account of the 18th century windmill built at the top of the hill (and shown in the 1737 map). The name remains to this day, although the windmill is has long since been demolished.

Comparison of the principal elements of the post-Roman archaeology and the estate map of 1737 throws up some interesting elements. In the first instance the correlation between the Phase 6 archaeology and the cartographic display is reasonably accurate and informative, although it is notable that what could be construed from the map as substantial boundary ditches are not necessarily deeply cut features. One aspect that influenced pre-excavation interpretations of the relationship between the Phase 2 horseshoe enclosure and later activity was the apparent correlation between the east side of the horseshoe enclosure ditch and the east side of the Townend Furlong. From the archaeology of Phases 3 and 4 it is clear that the enclosure ditch did not survive as an earthwork beyond Phase 2. Any correlation must therefore be circumstantial.

Plate 5.8   Aerial view of development area after the Saxon and medieval excavations, looking north-west (Duchy of Lancaster copyright)

Appendices

Appendix 1: Catalogue of the human remains

Articulated remains:

Skeleton number: 2591
Completeness: Excellent
Preservation: Excellent
Age: 37-38 weeks *in utero*
Dental inventory:

Dental pathology: None
Pathology: None
Taphonomy: Gnaw marks on left femur

Skeleton number: 6678
Completeness: Good
Preservation: Fair
Age: 30-50 years
Nonmetric traits present:
Pathology: Slight degenerative joint disease on both knees, slight spinal degenerative changes on all elements present, Schmorl's nodes on T6-L4.
Taphonomy: Carnivore puncture marks on spinal processes of first and second lumbars.

Disarticulated remains:

Context number: 6050
Small finds number: 355
Skeletal element: Mandibular body
Preservation: Good
Age: 30-38 years
Sex: Male

Dental inventory:

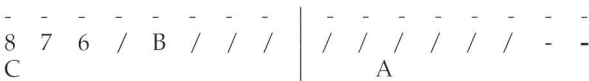

Dental pathology: Small occlusal caries on right third molar, dental abscess, moderate and considerable vertical periodontal disease

Context number: 6621
Small finds number: 356
Skeletal element: Mandible
Preservation: Good
Age: 24-30 years
Sex: Male
Dental inventory:

Dental pathology: Slight mesial and distal calculus, moderate horizontal periodontal disease, right third molars not present.

Context Number	Skeletal element	Side	Age	Sex	Non-metric trait	Pathology
6050	Iliac blade	Left	Adult	Unknown		
6621	Parietal	Right	Adult	Unknown	Parietal foramen	Healed porotic hyperostosis
6621	Femur shaft	Right	Adult	Unknown		
6621	Patella	Right	Adult	Unknown		

Appendix 2:
Charcoal assemblage: Raw data for charcoal identifications and composition in terms of fragment size

PHASE 1

Context no. 6344
Feature no. 6343, *pit, one of a series close to SFBs* (Figure Appendix 2.1 a)
Sample no. <102>

Size >8mm		Size 4–8mm		Size 2–4 mm	
Fragment number	Identification	Fragment number	Identification	Fragment number	Identification
1	*Quercus*	1	*Quercus*	1	*Quercus*
2	*Quercus*	2	*Quercus*	2	*Quercus*
3	*Quercus*	3	*Quercus*	3	*Quercus*
4	*Quercus*	4	*Quercus*	4	*Quercus*
5	*Quercus*	5	*Quercus*	5	*Quercus*
6	*Quercus*	6	*Quercus*	6	*Quercus*
7	*Quercus*	7	*Quercus*	7	*Quercus*
8	*Quercus*	8	*Quercus*	8	*Quercus*
9	*Quercus*	9	*Quercus*	9	*Quercus*
10	*Quercus*	10	*Quercus*	10	*Quercus*

PHASE 2B

Context no. 6979
Feature no. 7023, *pit close to posthole building* (Figure Appendix 2.1 b)
Sample no. <117>

Size >8mm		Size 4–8mm		Size 2–4 mm	
Fragment number	Identification	Fragment number	Identification	Fragment number	Identification
1	*Quercus*	1	*Quercus*	1	*Quercus*
2	*Quercus*	2	*Quercus*	2	*Quercus*
3	*Quercus*	3	*Quercus*	3	*Quercus*
4	*Quercus*	4	*Quercus*	4	*Quercus*
5	*Quercus*	5	*Quercus*	5	*Quercus*
6	*Quercus*	6	*Quercus*	6	*Prunus*
7	*Quercus*	7	*Quercus*	7	*Quercus*
8	*Quercus*	8	*Quercus*	8	*Quercus*
9	*Quercus*	9	*Quercus*	9	*Quercus*
10	*Quercus*	10	*Quercus*	10	*Quercus*
11	*Quercus*	11	*Quercus*	11	*Quercus*
12	*Quercus*	12	*Quercus*	12	*Quercus*
13	*Quercus*	13	*Quercus*	13	*Quercus*
14	*Quercus*	14	*Quercus*	14	*Quercus*
15	*Quercus*	15	*Quercus*	15	*Quercus*
16	*Quercus*	16	*Quercus*	16	*Quercus*
17	*Quercus*	17	*Quercus*	17	*Quercus*
18	*Quercus*	18	*Quercus*	18	*Quercus*
19	*Quercus*	19	*Quercus*	19	*Quercus*
20	*Quercus*	20	*Quercus*	20	*Quercus*

PHASE 2C

Context no. 4015 *deposit within the chamber of the malting oven*
Feature no. 4010, *malting oven* (Figure Appendix 2.1 c)
Sample no. < 5 >

Size >8mm		Size 4–8mm		Size 2–4 mm	
Fragment number	Identification	Fragment number	Identification	Fragment number	Identification
1	Indeterminate	1	*Quercus*	1	*Quercus*
2	*Quercus*	2	*Quercus*	2	*Corylus*
3	*Quercus*	3	*Quercus*	3	*Quercus*
4	*Quercus*	4	*Quercus*	4	*Quercus*
5	*Quercus*	5	*Quercus*	5	*Quercus*
		6	*Quercus*	6	*Corylus*
		7	*Quercus*	7	*Quercus*
		8	*Quercus*	8	*Quercus*
		9	*Quercus*	9	*Quercus*
		10	*Quercus*	10	*Quercus*
		11	*Corylus*	11	*Quercus*
		12	*Quercus*	12	*Quercus*
		13	*Quercus*	13	*Quercus*
		14	*Quercus*	14	*Quercus*
		15	*Quercus*	15	*Acer*
		16	*Quercus*	16	*Quercus*
		17	*Quercus*	17	*Quercus*
		18	*Corylus*	18	*Quercus*
		19	*Quercus*	19	*Quercus*
		20	*Quercus*	20	*Quercus*
		21	*Quercus*	21	*Quercus*
		22	*Quercus*	22	*Quercus*
		23	*Quercus*	23	*Quercus*
		24	*Quercus*	24	*Quercus*
		25	*Quercus*	25	*Quercus*
		26	*Corylus*	26	*Quercus*
		27	*Corylus*	27	*Quercus*
		28	*Quercus*	28	*Quercus*
		29	*Quercus*	29	*Quercus*
		30	*Quercus*	30	*Quercus*

Context no. 7027
Feature no. 7026, *hearth in posthole building* 6811
Sample no. < 110 >

Size >2mm		Size >2mm	
Fragment number	Identification	Fragment number	Identification
1	Pomoideae	21	Pomoideae
2	**Acer**	22	Pomoideae
3	Pomoideae	23	**Acer**
4	**Acer**	24	*Corylus*
5	Pomoideae	25	*Quercus*
6	**Quercus**	26	*Quercus*
7	*Acer*	27	*Quercus*
8	*Acer*	28	*Acer*
9	*Acer*	29	*Acer*
10	*Acer*	30	*Quercus*
11	*Acer*	31	*Acer*
12	*Acer*	32	*Acer*
13	*Quercus*	33	*Quercus*
14	*Prunus*	34	Pomoideae
15	Indeterminate	35	Pomoideae
16	**Acer**	36	**Quercus**
17	*Acer*	37	Pomoideae
18	*Quercus*	38	**Corylus**
19	*Salix / Populus*	39	*Prunus*
20	*Acer*	40	Pomoideae

PHASE 2C *(continued)*

Context no. 7077
Feature no. 7067, *hearth in posthole building* 6811
Sample no. < 115 >

Size >2mm

Fragment number	Identification
1	*Quercus*
2	*Quercus*
3	*Quercus*
4	*Quercus*
5	*Quercus*
6	*Quercus*
7	Pomoideae
8	Pomoideae
9	*Quercus*
10	*Quercus*
11	Pomoideae
12	*Quercus*
13	*Quercus*
14	Pomoideae
15	Pomoideae
16	*Quercus*
17	*Corylus*
18	Pomoideae
19	*Quercus*
20	*Quercus*
21	*Quercus*
22	*Quercus*
23	*Quercus*
24	Pomoideae
25	*Corylus*
26	Pomoideae
27	Pomoideae
28	Pomoideae
29	*Quercus*
30	*Quercus*

PHASE 2C *(continued)*

Context no. 15428 *burnt lens in ditch*
Feature: *from final variant of enclosure ditch* 15190 (Figure Appendix 2.1 d)
Sample no. <810>

Size >8mm		Size 4–8mm		Size 2–4 mm	
Fragment number	Identification	Fragment number	Identification	Fragment number	Identification
1	*Quercus*	1	*Quercus*	1	*Quercus*
2	*Quercus*	2	*Quercus*	2	*Quercus*
3	*Quercus*	3	*Quercus*	3	*Quercus*
4	*Quercus*	4	*Quercus*	4	*Quercus*
5	Prunus	5	*Quercus*	5	*Quercus*
6	Prunus	6	*Quercus*	6	*Quercus*
7	*Quercus*	7	*Prunus*	7	*Quercus*
		8	*Quercus*	8	*Quercus*
		9	*Prunus*	9	*Quercus*
		10	*Quercus*	10	*Quercus*
		11	*Quercus*	11	*Quercus*
		12	*Quercus*	12	*Corylus*
		13	*Quercus*	13	*Quercus*
		14	*Quercus*	14	*Quercus*
		15	*Prunus*	15	*Prunus*
		16	*Quercus*	16	*Quercus*
		17	*Quercus*	17	*Quercus*
		18	*Quercus*	18	*Quercus*
		19	*Quercus*	19	Indeterminate
		20	*Quercus*	20	*Quercus*
				21	*Corylus*
				22	*Prunus*
				23	Indeterminate
				24	Indeterminate
				25	Indeterminate
				26	*Quercus*
				27	*Quercus*
				28	*Quercus*
				29	*Quercus*
				30	*Quercus*

PHASE 3

Context no. 7236
Feature no: 7235, *isolated pit* (Figure Appendix 2.1 e)
Sample no. <120>

Size >8mm		Size 4–8mm		Size 2–4 mm	
Fragment number	Identification	Fragment number	Identification	Fragment number	Identification
1	*Quercus*	1	*Quercus*	1	*Quercus*
2	*Quercus*	2	*Quercus*	2	*Quercus*
3	*Quercus*	3	*Quercus*	3	*Quercus*
4	*Quercus*	4	*Quercus*	4	*Quercus*
5	*Quercus*	5	*Quercus*	5	*Quercus*
6	*Quercus*	6	*Quercus*	6	*Quercus*
7	*Quercus*	7	*Quercus*	7	*Quercus*
8	*Quercus*	8	*Quercus*	8	*Quercus*
9	*Quercus*	9	*Quercus*	9	*Quercus*
10	*Quercus*	10	*Quercus*	10	*Quercus*

PHASE 5

Context no. 9212, *layer*
Feature: *debris from the ceramic workshop floor adjacent to wall 9008* (Figure Appendix 2.1 f)
Sample < 503>

Size >8mm		Size 4–8mm		Size 2–4 mm	
Fragment number	Identification	Fragment number	Identification	Fragment number	Identification
1	*Prunus*	1	*Quercus*	1	*Prunus*
2	*Prunus*	2	Pomoideae	2	Pomoideae
3	*Prunus*	3	Pomoideae	3	Pomoideae
4	*Prunus*	4	Pomoideae	4	Pomoideae
5	Pomoideae	5	Pomoideae	5	*Quercus*
6	*Prunus*	6	*Prunus*	6	Indeterminate
7	Pomoideae	7	*Fraxinus*	7	Pomoideae
8	Pomoideae	8	*Prunus*	8	Pomoideae
9	Pomoideae	9	*Quercus*	9	*Prunus*
		10	Pomoideae	10	*Prunus*
		11	Pomoideae	11	Pomoideae
		12	Pomoideae	12	Pomoideae
		13	Pomoideae	13	*Quercus*
		14	*Quercus*	14	*Prunus*
		15	Prunus	15	Pomoideae
		16	Pomoideae	16	*Betula*
		17	*Prunus*	17	Pomoideae
		18	*Prunus*	18	Pomoideae
		19	*Prunus*	19	Pomoideae
		20	*Prunus*	20	*Prunus*
		21	*Prunus*	21	*Prunus*
		22	*Prunus*	22	*Prunus*
		23	*Prunus*	23	Indeterminate
		24	*Prunus*	24	*Prunus*
		25	Pomoideae	25	*Prunus*
		26	Pomoideae	26	*Prunus*
		27	Pomoideae	27	Pomoideae
		28	*Prunus*	28	*Quercus*
		29	Pomoideae	29	Indeterminate
		30	Pomoideae	30	*Quercus*

PHASE 5 *(continued)*

Context no. 9099, *Ash layer*
Feature no. 9200, *base of the pottery kiln 2 flue* (Figure Appendix 2.1 g)
Sample < 508>

Size >8mm		Size 4–8mm		Size 2–4 mm	
Fragment number	Identification	Fragment number	Identification	Fragment number	Identification
1	*Prunus*	1	Indeterminate	1	Pomoideae
		2	Indeterminate	2	*Quercus*
		3	Pomoideae	3	*Prunus*
		4	Pomoideae	4	Pomoideae
		5	Indeterminate	5	Indeterminate
		6	*Prunus*	6	Pomoideae
		7	*Prunus*	7	Pomoideae
		8	*Prunus*	8	Pomoideae
		9	Indeterminate	9	Fraxinus
		10	*Prunus*	10	Pomoideae
				11	Pomoideae
				12	*Prunus*
				13	Pomoideae
				14	*Prunus*
				15	*Prunus*
				16	*Prunus*
				17	*Prunus*
				18	*Prunus*
				19	Indeterminate
				20	*Prunus*

Fig. Appendix 2.1 (facing page)   Charcoal assemblage:
Pie charts showing sample composition by weight in terms of fragment size: a) Context 6344, Pit 6343, Sample composition by weight in terms of fragment size: a) Context 6344, Pit 6343, Sample <102>; b) Context 6979, Pit 7023, Sample <117>; c) Context 4015, Malting oven 4010, Sample <5>; d) Context 15428, Burnt lens 15190, Sample <810>; e) Context 7236, Pit 7235, Sample <120>; f) Context 9212 (layer), Floor 9008, Sample <503>; g) Context 9099 (layer), Feature 9200, Sample <508>

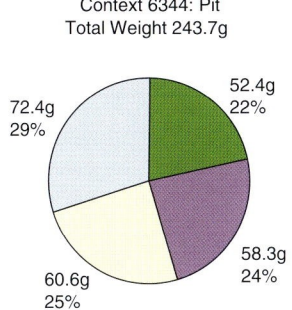

Context 6344: Pit
Total Weight 243.7g

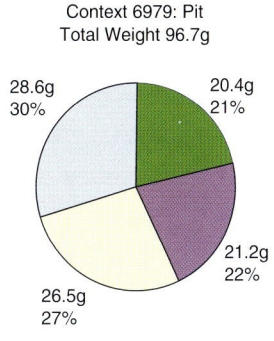

Context 6979: Pit
Total Weight 96.7g

(a) Context 6344, Pit 6343, Sample <102>

(b) Context 6979, Pit 7023, Sample <117>

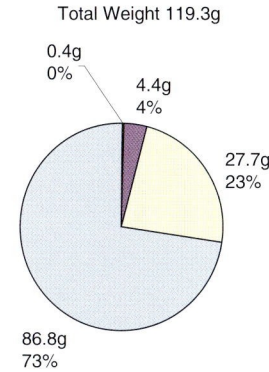

Context 4015: Malting oven
Total Weight 119.3g

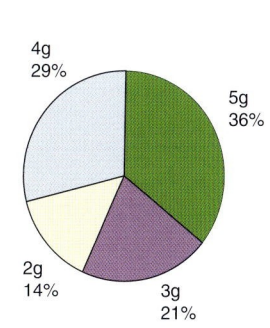

Context 15428: Burnt lens
Total Weight 14g

(c) Context 4015, Malting oven 4010, Sample <5>

(d) Context 15428, Burnt lens 15190, Sample <810>

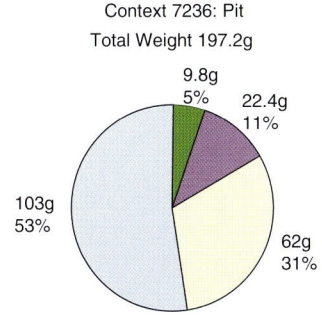

Context 7236: Pit
Total Weight 197.2g

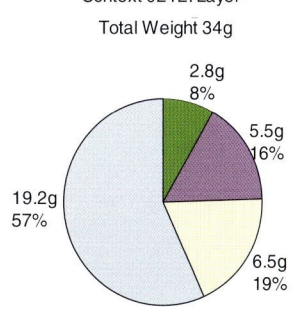

Context 9212: Layer
Total Weight 34g

(e) Context 7236, Pit 7235, Sample <120>

(f) Context 9212 (layer), Floor 9008, Sample <503>

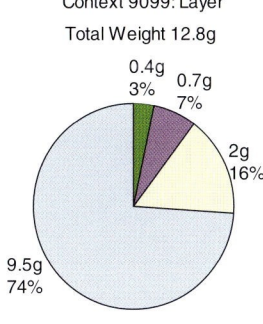

Context 9099: Layer
Total Weight 12.8g

- > 8mm
- 4 - 8mm
- 2 - 4mm
- < 2mm

(g) Context 9099 (layer), Feature 9200, Sample <508>

Appendix 3: Archaeomagnetic dating

A Archaeomagnetic data

Table Appendix 3.1: NRM measurements of samples and measurements after partial AF demagnetisation for feature HF. J = magnitude of magnetisation vector; AF = peak alternating field strength of demagnetising field; R = sample rejected from mean calculation

		NRM Measurements			After Partial Demagnetisation				
Sample	Material	Dec^0	Inc^0	$J(mAm^{-1})$	$AF(mT)$	Dec^0	Inc^0	$J(mAm^{-1})$	R
HF02	Clay	4.5	56.1	1712.5	5.0	3.5	54.9	1598.6	
HF03	Clay	1.4	47.0	2748.1	5.0	1.2	46.9	2495.3	
HF04	Clay	6.3	54.2	3297.0	5.0	7.1	53.0	3041.6	
HF05	Clay	2.2	52.4	2375.4	5.0	0.8	53.7	2209.8	
HF06	Clay	1.9	53.2	2524.5	5.0	0.1	52.7	2393.9	
HF07	Clay	-2.3	57.7	200.5	5.0	-2.1	57.0	176.9	
HF08	Clay	4.8	55.9	4078.4	5.0	5.9	57.6	3820.0	
HF10	Clay	-3.4	54.2	942.4	5.0	-4.6	53.5	886.3	
HF11	Clay	2.9	53.0	1428.4	5.0	1.2	53.6	1285.9	
HF12	Clay	-5.1	50.6	29.7	5.0	-0.6	48.2	26.4	
HF13	Clay	-2.7	55.4	1731.0	5.0	-4.2	54.9	1659.5	
HF14	Clay	13.3	57.3	2835.1	5.0	13.7	56.9	2672.4	
HF16	Clay	7.1	58.7	2036.6	5.0	6.5	57.9	1927.7	
HF17	Clay	-0.1	56.4	468.5	5.0	-0.7	56.1	442.2	
HF18	Clay	8.3	54.6	2945.8	5.0	8.7	53.0	2943.6	
HF19	Stone	63.2	-20.5	5.1	-	-	-	-	R
HF20	Stone	-136.6	46.1	5.0	-	-	-	-	R
HF21	Clay	-8.4	61.2	3896.5	-	-	-	-	R
HF22	Clay	-0.5	60.7	2182.4	-	-	-	-	R
HF23	Clay	-14.9	63.7	54.6	-	-	-	-	R
HF24	Clay	-13.7	74.8	4753.3	-	-	-	-	R
HF25	Clay	-6.5	69.1	3522.5	-	-	-	-	R
HF26	Clay	-8.3	73.8	2714.9	-	-	-	-	R

Table Appendix 3.2: Incremental partial demagnetisation measurements for samples HF03, HF14 and HF25.

	HF03			HF14			HF25		
$AF(mT)$	Dec^0	Inc^0	$J(mAm^{-1})$	Dec^0	Inc^0	$J(mAm^{-1})$	Dec^0	Inc^0	$J(mAm^{-1})$
0.0	0.6	47.8	2693.3	13.7	57.6	2830.3	-6.9	67.2	3535.1
1.0	1.0	47.8	2667.0	13.7	57.2	2811.7	-6.7	66.5	3522.6
2.5	1.2	47.7	2619.5	14.0	56.9	2771.8	-6.6	66.4	3486.1
5.0	1.2	46.9	2495.3	13.7	56.9	2672.4	-6.7	66.3	3404.5
10.0	0.7	46.1	2147.6	14.1	56.7	2268.3	-6.5	66.4	3060.8
15.0	-	-	-	13.9	56.2	1801.6	-6.0	66.8	2616.9
20.0	0.3	43.6	1459.8	13.6	55.6	1351.3	-5.1	66.5	2092.6
30.0	-0.4	42.1	985.3	13.8	54.9	760.3	-6.2	66.2	1495.5
50.0	-0.1	39.7	470.6	14.9	54.4	320.2	-4.9	65.9	965.1
75.0	0.0	35.6	199.8	16.5	47.3	168.3	-5.4	64.9	727.7

Table Appendix 3.3: Assessment of the range of demagnetisation values over which each sample attained its maximum directional stability for feature HF, using the method of Tarling and Symons (1967).
The declination and inclination values quoted are for the mean TRM direction for the sample calculated for all demagnetisation measurements in its range of maximum stability.

Sample	Range min. (mT)	Range max. (mT)	Max. Stability	Dec^0	Inc^0
HF03	0.0	2.5	23.4	0.9	47.8
HF14	2.5	10.0	53.4	13.9	56.8
HF25	2.5	10.0	123.2	-6.6	66.4

B Standard Procedures for Sampling and Measurement

1) Sampling

One of three sampling techniques is employed depending on the consistency of the material (Clark, Tarling and Noel 1988):

a) **Consolidated materials:** Rock and fired clay samples are collected by the disc method. Several small levelled plastic discs are glued to the feature, marked with an orientation line related to True North, then removed with a small piece of the material attached.

b) **Unconsolidated materials:** Sediments are collected by the tube method. Small pillars of the material are carved out from a prepared platform, then encapsulated in levelled plastic tubes using plaster of Paris. The orientation line is then marked on top of the plaster.

c) **Plastic materials:** Waterlogged clays and muds are sampled in a similar manner to method 1b) above; however, the levelled plastic tubes are pressed directly into the material to be sampled.

2) Physical Analysis

a) Magnetic remanences are measured using a slow speed spinner fluxgate magnetometer (Molyneux et al. 1972; see also Tarling 1983, p84; Thompson and Oldfield 1986, p52).

b) Partial demagnetisation is achieved using the alternating magnetic field method (As 1967; Creer 1959; see also Tarling 1983, p91; Thompson and Oldfield 1986, p59), to remove viscous magnetic components if necessary. Demagnetising fields are measured in milli Tesla (mT), figures quoted being for the peak value of the field.

3) Remanent Field Direction

a) The remanent field direction of a sample is expressed as two angles, declination (Dec) and inclination (Inc), both quoted in degrees. Declination represents the bearing of the field relative to true north, angles to the east being positive; inclination represents the angle of dip of this field.

b) Aitken and Hawley (1971) have shown that the angle of inclination in measured samples is likely to be distorted owing to magnetic refraction. The phenomenon is not well understood but is known to depend on the position the samples occupied within the structure. The corrections recommended by Aitken and Hawley are applied, where appropriate, to measured inclinations, in keeping with the practise of Clark, Tarling and Noel (1988).

c) Individual remanent field directions are combined to produce the mean remanent field direction using the statistical method developed by R. A. Fisher (1953). The quantity α_{95}, "alpha 95", is quoted with mean field directions and is a measure of the precision of the determination (see Aitken 1990, p247). It is analogous to the standard error statistic for scalar quantities; hence the smaller its value, the better the precision of the date.

d) For the purposes of comparison with standardised UK calibration data, remanent field directions are adjusted to the values they would have had if the feature had been located at Meriden, a standard reference point. The adjustment is done using the method suggested by Noel (Tarling 1983, p116).

4) Calibration

a) Material less than 3000 years old is dated using the archaeomagnetic calibration curve compiled by Clark, Tarling and Noel (1988).

b) Older material is dated using the lake sediment data compiled by Turner and Thompson (1982).

c) Dates are normally given at the 63% and 95% confidence levels. However, the quality of the measurement and the estimated reliability of the calibration curve for the period in question are not taken into account, so this figure is only approximate. Owing to crossovers and contiguities in the curve, alternative dates are sometimes given. It may be possible to select the correct alternative using independent dating evidence.

d) As the thermoremanent effect is reset at each heating, all dates for fired material refer to the final heating.

e) Dates are prefixed by "cal", for consistency with the new convention for calibrated radiocarbon dates (Mook 1986).

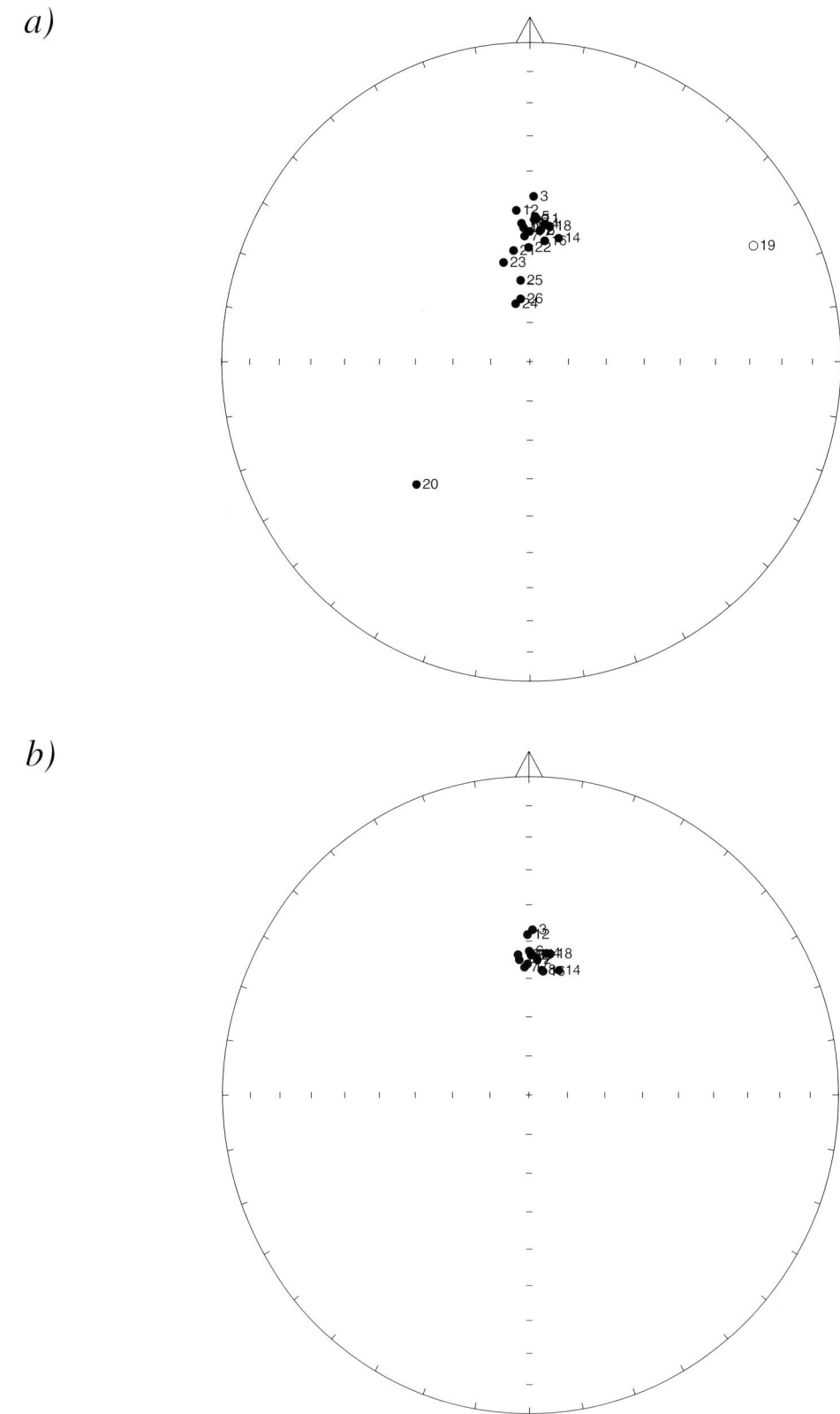

a)

b)

Figure Appendix 3.1

a)

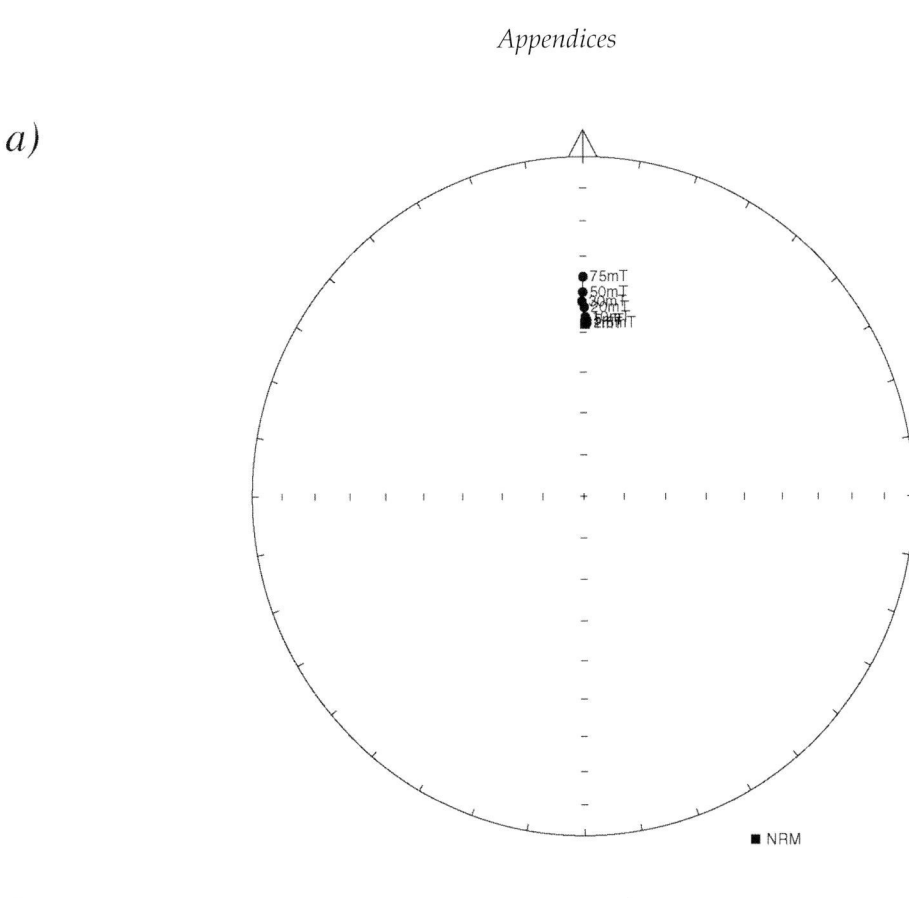

b)   *c)*

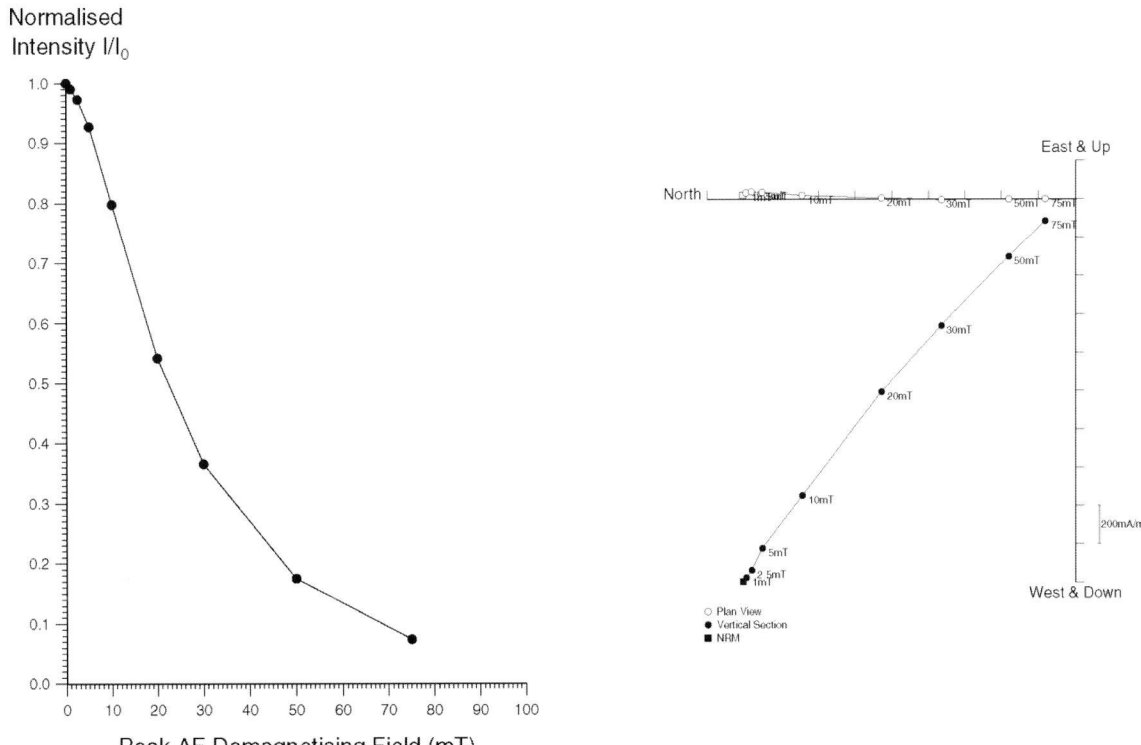

Figure Appendix 3.2

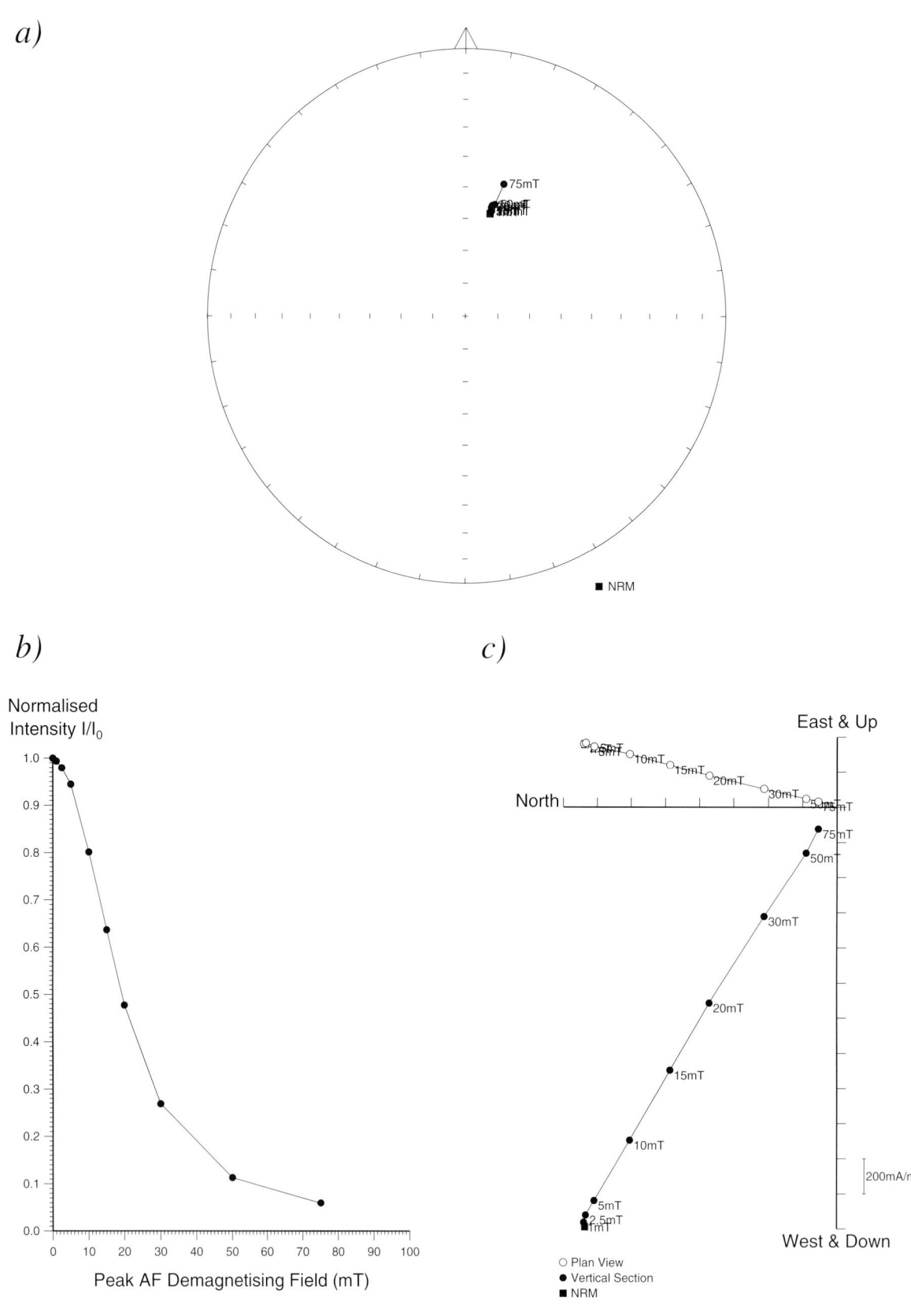

Figure Appendix 3.3

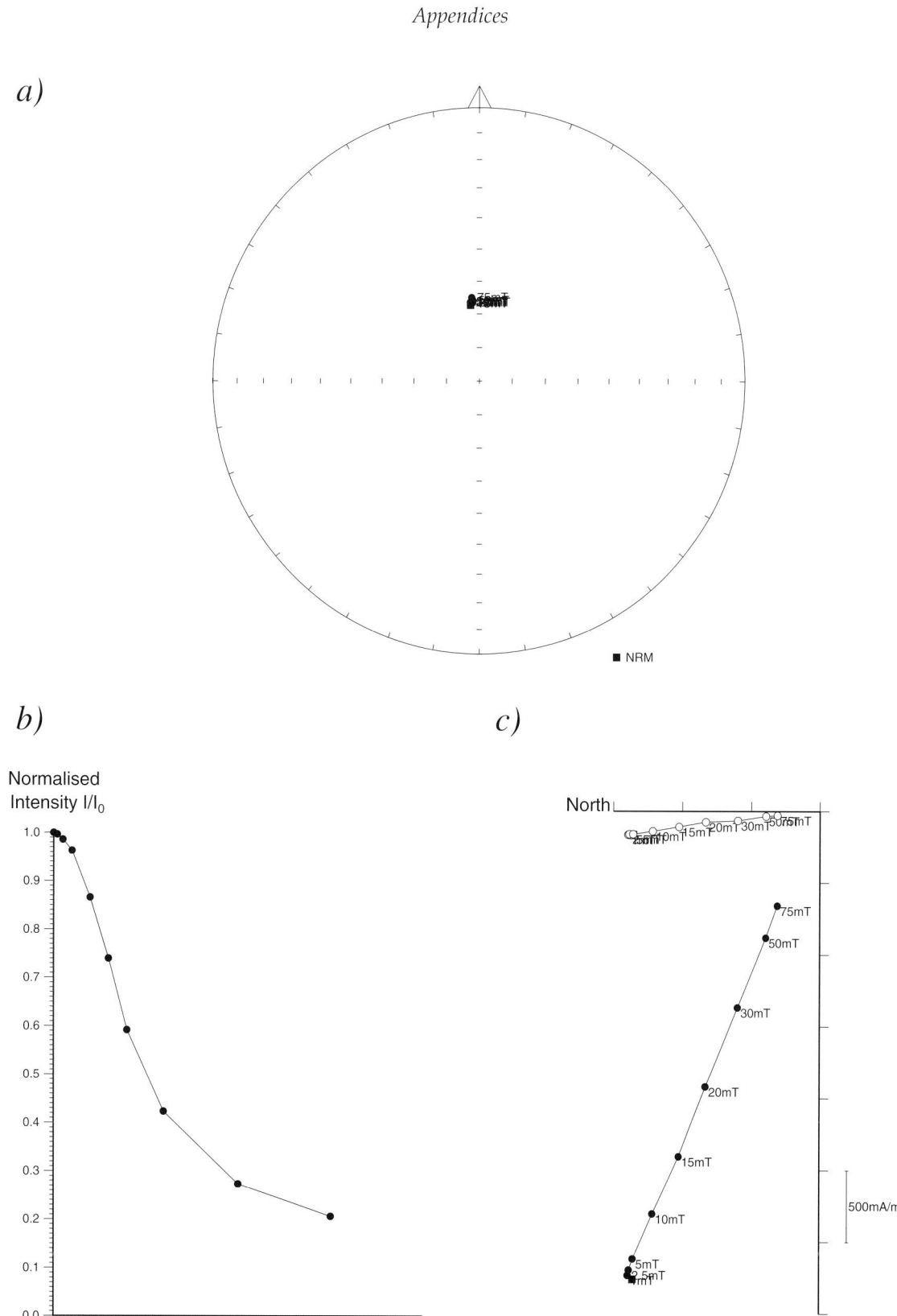

Figure Appendix 3.4

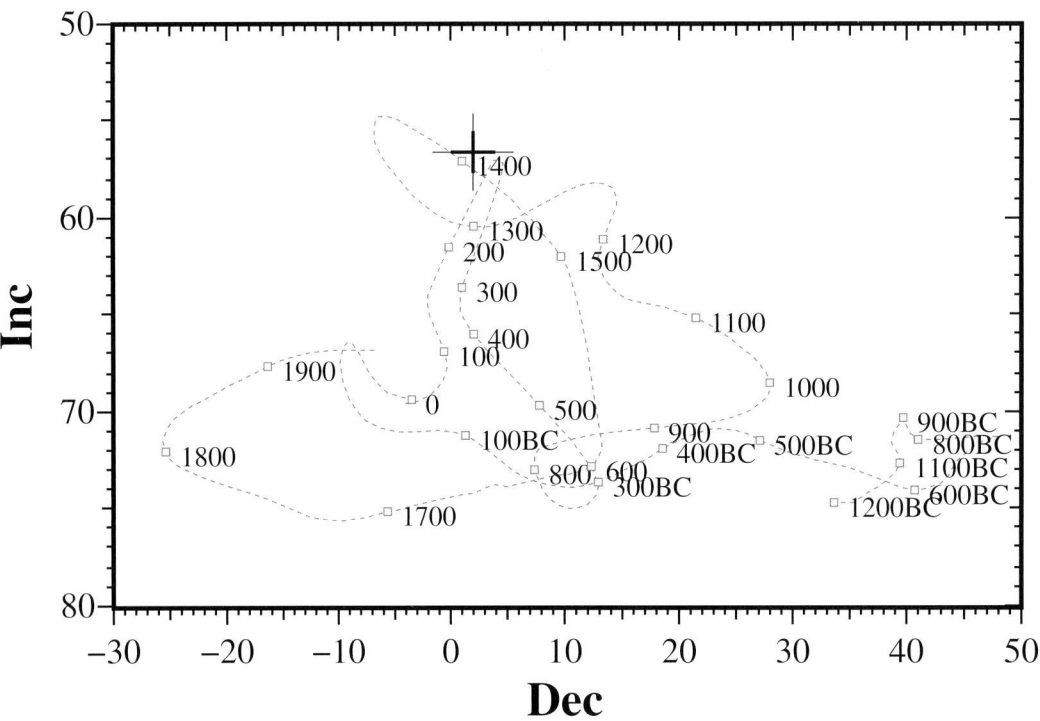

Figure Appendix 3.5

Bibliography

Addyman, P V, 1964 A Dark Age settlement at Maxey, Northants, *Medieval Archaeol* **8**, 20-73

Ahrens, C, 1966 Vorgeschichte des Kreises Pinneberg und der Insel Heligoland: Die vor- und frügeschichtlichen Denkmäler und Funde in Schleswig-Holstein , 7 in K. Kersten (ed.) *Veröffentlichungen de Landesamtes für Vor- und Frühgeschichte in Schleswig* Neumünster 205-32

Aitken, M J, 1990 *Science-based dating in archaeology*, Longman, London

Aitken, M J, and Hawley, H N, 1971 Archaeomagnetism: evidence for magnetic refraction in kiln structures, *Archaeometry* **13**, 83-85

Albarella, U, and Davis, S, 1994 The Saxon and Medieval bones: animal bones excavated 1985–1989 from West Cotton, Northamptonshire, London: English Heritage AML report 17/94

Andrews, P, 1990 *Owls, caves and fossils*, Chicago

Archibald, M M, Metcalf, D M, and Rigold, S E, 1979 The coins, counters and a token, in J H Williams 1979, 243-6

Archibald, M M, and Metcalf, D M, 1985 The coins, in Williams *et al*, 1985, 64

Arnold, C, and Wardle, P, 1981 Early medieval settlement patterns in England, *Medieval Archaeol* 25, 145-9

As, J A, 1967 The a.c. demagnetisation technique, in D.W. Collinson, K. M. Creer and S. K. Runcorn (eds) *Methods in Palaeomagnetism*, Amsterdam

Aufderheide, A C, and Rodríguez-Martín, C, 1998 *The Cambridge encyclopaedia of human paleopathology*, Cambridge

Ayers, C, Ingrem, C, Light, J, Locker, A, Mulville, J, and Serjeantson, D, 2003 Mammal, bird and fish remains and oysters, in Hardy *et al*, 2003, 341-432

Baker, D, Baker, E, Hassal,J, and Simco, A, 1979 Excavations in Bedford 1967-1977, *Bedfordshire Archaeol J* **13**

Baker, E, and Hassall, J, 1979 The Pottery, in Baker D *et al*. 1979, 147-240

Barnwell, P, 2003 Britons and Warriors in Post-Roman South-East England, in D Griffiths *et al* (eds) 2003, 1-8

Bartlett, A D H, 2000 Kings Meadow Lane, Higham Ferrers, Northamptonshire: Report on Archaeogeophysical Survey,Unpublished report, Bartlett-Clark Consultancy

Bartlett, A D H, 2001 Kings Meadow Lane, Higham Ferrers, Northamptonshire: Report on Archaeogeophysical Survey, Unpublished report, Bartlett-Clark Consultancy

Bayliss, A, and Hey, G, 2004 Chapter 13: Scientific Dating, in Hey 2004, 255-66

Beamish, H F, 1990 A medieval pottery production site at Jack Ironcap's Lane, Great Brickhill, *Rec Buckinghamshire* **31**, 88-92

Behrensmeyer, A K, 1978 Taphonomic and ecologic information from bone weathering, *Palaeobiology* **4**, 150-162

Bellamy, B, 1983 Medieval pottery kilns at Stanion, *Northamptonshire Archaeol* **18**, 153-61

Beresford, G, 1987 *Goltho: the development of an early medieval manor c. 850–1150*, English Heritage Arch Report **4**, London

Beresford, M W, 1957 *History on the Ground*, London

Bewley, R H, 1987 Ewanrigg, *Current Archaeol* **103**, 230-33

Bewley, R H, with Longworth, I H, Browne, S, Huntley, J P, Varndell, G, *et al* 1992 Excavation of a Bronze Age Cemetery at Ewanrigg, Maryport, Cumbria, *Proc Prehist Soc* **58**, 325-54

Biddle, M, 1990 *Object and Economy in Medieval Winchester*, Winchester Studies **7**, 2 vols, Oxford

Biddle, M, Hiller, J, Scott, I, and Streeten, A, 2001 *Henry VIII's Coastal Artillery Fort at Camber Castle, Rye, East Sussex*, English Heritage and Oxford Archaeological Unit, Oxford

Binford, L, 1981 *Ancient Men and Modern Myths*, New York

Blackburn, M A S, and Pagan, H, 2002 The St Edmund coinage in the light of a parcel from a hoard of St Edmund pennies, *Brit Numismatic J* **72**, 1-14

Blair, J, 2005 *The church in Anglo-Saxon society*, Oxford

Blinkhorn, P W, 1997 Pottery, in I Soden, Saxon and medieval settlement remains at St. John's Square, Daventry, Northamptonshire, July 1994–February 1995, *Northamptonshire Archaeol* **27**, 51-99 (71-79)

Blinkhorn, P W, 1999a Middle and Late Saxon Pottery, in Chapman 1999, 55-57

Blinkhorn, P W, 1999b Of cabbages and kings: production, trade and consumption in middle Saxon England, in M Anderton (ed.) *Anglo-Saxon trading centres and their hinterlands. Beyond the emporia*, Cruithne, Glasgow, 4-24

Blinkhorn, P W, 1999c The trials of being a utensil: pottery function at the medieval hamlet of West

Cotton, Northamptonshire, *Medieval Ceramics* **22-23**, 37-46

Blinkhorn, P W, 2000 The pottery, in P W Blinkhorn and G Pugh, *Excavation of the medieval waterfront at King Stable Street, Eton, Berkshire*, Oxford Archaeol Unit Occasional Paper **7**, 19-24

Blinkhorn P W, 2002a The pottery, in S Morris, Evaluation on land off College Street, Higham Ferrers, unpublished Northamptonshire Archaeology report

Blinkhorn, P W, 2002b The Anglo-Saxon pottery, in S Foreman, J Hiller and D Petts, *Gathering the people, settling the land. The Archaeology of a Middle Thames Landscape*, Oxford Archaeology Thames Valley Landscapes Monog **14**, 35 and CD-ROM

Blinkhorn, P W, 2003a The pottery, in A Hardy, A Dodd and G D Keevill, *Aelfric's Abbey: Excavations at Eynsham Abbey, Oxfordshire, 1989-92*, Oxford Archaeology Thames Valley Landscapes Monog **16**, 159-206

Blinkhorn P W, 2003b The pottery, in S Morris, Land off Wharf Road, Higham Ferrers, Northamptonshire: Archaeological evaluation, unpublished Northamptonshire Archaeology report

Blinkhorn P W, 2003c The pottery, in Jones and Chapman, 2003, 131-32

Blinkhorn, P W, forthcoming a The pottery, in I Meadows, *Excavations at Warmington, Northants* Northamptonshire Archaeology

Blinkhorn, P W, forthcoming b The post-Roman pottery, in M Audouy *Excavations at North Raunds, Northamptonshire*, English Heritage Monog Ser

Blinkhorn, P W, forthcoming c Pottery from West Fen Road, Ely, Cambridgeshire

Blinkhorn, P W, forthcoming d Post-Roman pottery from Tempsford, Beds Bedfordshire Archaeology

Blinkhorn, P W, forthcoming e Pottery from Dando Close, Wollaston, Northants *Northamptonshire Archaeol*

Blinkhorn, P W, in prep *The Ipswich Ware Project: Ceramics, Trade and Society in Middle Saxon England*, Medieval Pottery Res Group Monog

Boardman, S, and Jones, G, 1990 Experiments on the effects of charring on cereal plant components, *J Archaeol Sci* **17 (1)**, 1-11

Boessneck, J, 1969 Osteological differences in sheep (*Ovis aries Linné*) and goat (*Capra hircus Linné*), in Brothwell and Higgs (eds) 1969, 331-358

Bond, C J, 1999 Hunting, in Lapidge *et al* 1999, 244

Brooks, S, and Suchey, J M, 1990 Skeletal age determination based on the *os pubis*: a comparison of the Acsadi-Nemeskeri and Suchey-Brooks methods, *Human Evolution* **5**, 227-238

Brothwell, D, 1981 *Digging up bones*, 3rd edn, New York

Brothwell, D, and Higgs, E S (eds) 1969 *Science in Archaeology*, Thames and Hudson, London

Brown, D H, 1997 The social significance of imported medieval pottery, in C G Cumberpatch and P W Blinkhorn (eds.) *Not So Much a Pot, More a Way of Life*, Oxbow Monograph **83**, Oxford, 95-112

Brown, T, and Foard, G, 1998 The Saxon landscape: a regional perspective, in P Everson and T Williamson (eds), *The Archaeology of Landscape*, Manchester, 67-94

Browne, M P, and Farr, C A, (eds) 2001 *Mercia, an Anglo-Saxon kingdom in Europe*, Leicester

Bryant, G F, and Steane, J M, 1969 Excavations at the deserted medieval settlement at Lyveden. A second interim report, *J Northampton Museum and Art Gallery* **5**

Buikstra, J E, and Ubelaker, D H, 1994 *Standards for data collection from human skeletal remains*, Arkansas

Calthrop, C M, 1923 Higham Ferrers, in *VCH Northamptonshire* Vol. **3**, 263-79

Campbell, B M S, 1988 The diffusion of vetches in Medieval England. *Econ Hist Rev* (2nd series) **41 (2)**, 193-208

Campbell, G, 1994 The preliminary archaeobotanical results from Anglo-Saxon West Cotton and Raunds, in Rackham 1994, 65-82

Campbell, G, forthcoming The charred plant remains from West Cotton

Carver M O H (ed.), 1992 *The Age of Sutton Hoo: the seventh century in north-western Europe*, Woodbridge

Cauvain, P, Cauvain, S, and Green, M, 1989 Prehistoric, Romano-British and Fourteenth century Activity at Ashwells, Tylers Green, Bucks, *Rec Buckinghamshire* **31**, 111-20

Chamberlain, A, 1994 *Human remains*, London

Chambers, R A, and McAdam, E, 2007 *Excavations at Barrow Hills, Radley, Oxfordshire. Volume II: the Romano-British cemetery and Anglo-Saxon settlement*, Oxford Archaeology Thames Valley Landscapes Monograph

Chapman, A, 1999 Excavation of the town defences at Green Street, Northampton, 1995-6, *Northamptonshire Archaeol* **28**, 25-60

Chapman, A, forthcoming *West Cotton, Raunds: a study of settlement dynamics. Excavations at West Cotton, Nothamptonshire 1985-9*

Clark, A J, Tarling D H, and Noel M, 1988 Developments in archaeomagnetic dating in Britain. *J Archaeol Sci* **15**, 645-667

Clark, J, 1995 *The medieval horse and its equipment*, (Medieval finds from excavations in London: **5**, Museum of London/ HMSO)

Cole, J, 1838 *The history and antiquities of Higham Ferrers with historical notices of Rushden and Irthlingborough in the county of Northampton*, London

Cowgill, J, de Neergaard, M, and Griffiths, N, 1987 *Knives and scabbards*, (Medieval finds from excavations in London: **1**, Museum of London/ HMSO)

Crawford, S, 1999 *Childhood in Anglo-Saxon England*, Stroud

Creer, K M, 1959 A.C. demagnetisation of unstable Triassic Keuper Marls from S. W. England, *Geophys J R Astr Soc* **2**, 261-275

Dallas, C, 1993 *Excavations in Thetford by B.K. Davison between 1964 and 1970*, EAA **62** Norwich

Daniell, C, and Thompson, V, 1999 Pagans and Christians: 400-1150, in P C Jupp and C Gittings (eds), *Death in England*, Manchester, 65-89

Daniels, R, 1988 The Anglo-Saxon monastery at Church Close, Hartlepool, Cleveland *Archaeol J.* **145**, 158-210

Davies, S, 1992 A Rapid Method For Recording Information About Animal Bones From Archaeological Sites, London: English Heritage AML report **19/92**

Davis, B, Walker, N, Ball, D, and Fitter, A, 1992 *The Soil*, London

De Moulins, D, 1996 King's Meadow Lane, Higham Ferrers (HFKM 95) assessment of the charred plant remains (Unpublished report)

De Moulins, D, 2006 The weeds from the thatch roofs of medieval cottages from the south of England. *Vegetation History and Archaeobotany* **16 (5)**, 385-98

Denham, V, 1985 The pottery, in J H Williams *et al*, 1985, 46-64

Department of Culture Media and Sport 2001, *Treasure Annual Report* 2000, London

Diamond, J, 1997 *Guns, Germs and Steel: The Fates of Human Societies*, New York

Dickinson, T, and Griffiths, D, (eds) 1999 *The making of kingdoms. Anglo-Saxon Studies in Archaeology and History* **10,** Oxford

Domínguez-Rodrigo, M, and Piqueras, A, 2003 The use of tooth pits to identify carnivore taxa in tooth-marked archaeofaunas and their relevance to reconstruct hominid carcass processing behaviours, *J Archaeol Sci* **30**, 1385-1391

Douglas-Irvine, H, 1923 Irthlingborough, in *VCH Northamptonshire* Vol **3**, 207-215

Drennan, R D, 1997 *Statistics for Archaeologists*, London

von den Driesch, A, 1976 *A guide to the measurement of animal bones from archaeological sites*, Peabody Museum

von den Driesch, A. and Boessneck, J. 1974. Kritische Anmerkungen zur Widerristhohen-Berechnung aus langmassen vor- und fruhgeschichtlicher Tierknochen. *Saugetierkundliche Mitteilungen*, **22** (**4**), 325-48.

Egan, G, and Pritchard, F, 1991 *Dress Accessories c.1150 – c.1450* in Medieval Finds from Excavations in London: **3**, Museum of London/HMSO

Ellis, B M A, 1995 Spurs and spur fittings, in Clark 1995, 124-50

Farley, M, 1980 Middle Saxon occupation at Chicheley, Buckinghamshire, *Rec Buckinghamshire* **22**, 92-104

Farley, M, and Lawson, J, 1990 A fifteenth century pottery and tile kiln at Leyhill, Latimer, Buckinghamshire, *Rec Buckinghamshire* **32**, 35-62

Fenton, A, 1978 *The Northern Isles*, Edinburgh

Finberg, H P R, 1972 *The Early Charters of the West Midlands*, Leicester

Fisher, R A, 1953 Dispersion on a sphere, *Proc. R. Soc. London A* **217**, 295-305

Foard, G, 1985 The administrative organisation of Northamptonshire in the Saxon period, *Anglo Saxon Studies in Archaeology and History*, **4**, 185-222

Foard, G, 1992 *Duchy of Lancaster Land, Higham Ferrers: Archaeological Assessment*, Unpublished report

Foard, G, 1994 *Higham Ferrers: A Research Framework*, (Northants Heritage 27.x.94)

Foard, G, 2004 An archaeological resource assessment of Anglo-Saxon Northamptonshire, *Draft Archaeological Resource Assessment for the East Midlands* www.le.ac.uk/ar/east_midlands_research_framework.htm

Foard, G, and Ballinger, J, 2000 *Northamptonshire Extensive Urban Survey: Higham Ferrers*, Northampton

Fock, J, 1966 Metrische Untersuchungen an Metapodien einiger europäischer Rinderrassen, Unpublished Dissertation, Munich

Foreman, S, Hiller, J and Petts, D, 2002 *Gathering the people, settling the land. The archaeology of a middle Thames landscape. Anglo-Saxon to Medieval*, Thames Valley Landscapes Monograph No. **14**, Oxford

Ford, S, 1995 The Excavation of a Saxon Settlement and a Mesolithic Flint Scatter at Northampton Road, Brixworth, Northamptonshire *Northamptonshire Archaeol* **26**, 79-108

Gale, R, and Cutler, D, 2000 *Plants in archaeology: identification manual of vegetative plant materials used in Europe and the Southern Mediterranean to c.1500*, the Royal Botanic Gardens, Kew and Westbury Publishing, Otley.

Geake, H M, 1992 Burial Practice in Seventh- and Eighth-Century England, in M O H Carver (ed.) *The Age of Sutton Hoo: the seventh century in north-western Europe*, Woodbridge 83-94

Geddes, J, 1985 The small finds, in J N Hare, *Battle Abbey. The eastern range and the excavations of 1978-80*, English Heritage Archaeological Report No **2**, London, 147-77

Gittos, H, 1999 Yeavering, in Lapidge *et al*, 1999, 497

Goodall, I H, 1990 Locks and Keys, in Biddle 1990, 1001-1036

Grant, A, 1982 The use of tooth wear as a guide to the age of domestic ungulates, in Wilson *et al*, 1982, 91-108

Green, C, Green, I, and Dallas, C, with Wild, J P, 1987 Excavations at Castor, Cambridgeshire in 1957-8 and 1973, *Northamptonshire Archaeol* **21**, 109 – 48

Green, F J, 1979a Plant remains, in C M Heighway, A P Garrod, and A G Vince, Excavations at 1 Westgate Street, Gloucester, 1975, *Medieval Archaeol* **23**, 159-213

Green, F J, 1979b Medieval plant remains: Methods and results of archaeobotanic analysis from excavations in Southern England with especial reference to Winchester and urban settlements of the 10th – 15th centuries, Unpublished M. Phil. thesis, Southampton University.

Griffiths, D, Reynolds, A, and Semple, S, (eds), 2003 *Boundaries in Early Medieval Britain. Anglo-Saxon Studies in Archaeology and History* **12** Oxford

Gryspeerdt, M, 1981 The pottery, in J H Williams, Excavations in Chalk Lane, Northampton *Northamptonshire Archaeol* **16**, 87-135 (108-118)

Hagen, A, 2006 *Anglo-Saxon Food and Drink: production, processing, distribution and consumption,* Norfolk

Hall, D N, 1974 Medieval pottery from the Higham Ferrers Hundred, Northamptonshire, *Journal of the Northamptonshire Museum and Art Gallery* **10**, 38-57

Hall, D N, 1988 The Late Saxon countryside: villages and their fields, in D Hooke (ed.), *Anglo-Saxon Settlements*, Oxford, 99-122

Hall, D N, 2000 The ceramic sequence, in R Mortimer, Village development and ceramic sequence: the middle to late Saxon Village at Cottenham, *Proc Cambridge Antiq Soc* **89**, 21-33

Hall, D N, 2001 Medieval pottery from Forehill, Cambridgeshire, *Medieval Ceramics* **25**, 2-21

Halstead, P, 1985 A study of mandibular teeth from Romano-British contexts at Maxey, in F Pryor, *Archaeology and Environment in the Lower Welland Valley*, EAA **27**, 219-24

Hamerow, H F, 1991 Settlement mobility and the 'Middle Saxon Shift': rural settlements and settlement patterns in Anglo-Saxon England, in *Anglo-Saxon England* **20**, 1991, 1-17

Hamerow, H F, 1993 *Excavations at Mucking Volume 2: The Anglo-Saxon Settlement,* English Heritage Archaeol Rep **22**

Hamerow, H F, 1999 Angles, Saxons and Anglo-Saxons: rural centres, trade and production, *Studien zur Sachsenforschung* **13**, 189-205

Hamerow, H F, 2002 *Early Medieval Settlements. The Archaeology of Rural Communities in Northwest Europe 400-900,* Oxford University Press, Oxford

Hamerow, H F, 2006 Special Deposits in Anglo-Saxon Settlements, *Medieval Archaeology* **50**, 1-30

Harcourt, R A, 1974 The dog in prehistoric and early historic Britain, *J Archaeol Sci*, **1**, 151-175

Hardy, A, Dodd, A, and Keevill G D, 2003 *Aelfric's Abbey: Excavations at Eynsham Abbey, Oxfordshire, 1989-92,* Thames Valley Landscapes **16**, Oxford

Hardy, A, and Lorimer, P, 2004 *The Roots of an English Town. Exploring the archaeology of Higham Ferrers*, Oxford Archaeology, Oxford

Hassall, J, 1976 Medieval pottery and a possible kiln site at Everton, *Bedfordshire Archaeol J* **10**, 69-75

Hather, J, 2000 *The identification of the northern European woods*, London

Healey, H, Malim, T, and Watson, K, 1998 A medieval kiln at Colne, Cambridgeshire, *Proc Cambridge Antiq Soc* **87**, 49-58

Hey, G, 2004 *Yarnton: Saxon and medieval settlement and landscape: Results of Excavations 1990-96,* Oxford Archaeology Thames Valley Landscapes Monograph **20**, Oxford

Hillman, G C, 1981 Reconstructing crop processing from charred remains of crops, in R Mercer (ed.), *Farming practice in British prehistory*, Edinburgh, 3-162.

Hillson, S, 1996 *Dental anthropology*, New York

Hinton, D A, 1990 Hooked tags, in Biddle 1990, 548-52

Hinton, D A, 1996 *The gold, silver and other non-ferrous alloy objects from Hamwic*, Southampton Finds Volume **2**, Southampton City Museums

Hinton, D A, and Parsons, A L, 1996 Pins, in Hinton 1996, 14-37

Hodges, R, 1989 *The Anglo-Saxon achievement; archaeology and the beginnings of English society,* London

Hoffman, R, 1987 Introduction, in E J Crossman and J M Casselman, *An annotated bibliography of the Pike Esox lucius: the proto-history of pike in western culture*, Royal Ontario Museum, Toronto

Hollis, F, 1946 The horse in agriculture, in B Vesey-Fitzgerald (ed.) *The book of the horse*, London, 160-83

Hope-Taylor, B, 1977 *Yeavering; An Anglo-British centre of early Northumbria*, London

Hutchings, N, and Farley, M, 1989 A fifteenth- to sixteenth-century pottery industry at Tylers Green, Penn, Buckinghamshire, *Rec Buckinghamshire* **31**, 105-10

IGRF, 2000 International Geomagnetic Reference Field – Epoch 2000. Revision of the IGRF for 2000–2005 *www.ngdc.noaa.gov/IAGA/wg8/igrf2000.html*

James, S, Marshall, A, and Millett, M, 1984 An early medieval building tradition, *Archaeol J* **141**, 182-215

Jamison, C, 1923 Finedon, in *VCH Northamptonshire* Vol. **3**, 196-202

Johnston, G, Foster, P J, and Bellamy, B, 997 The excavation of two late medieval kilns with associated buildings at Glapthorn, near Oundle, Northamptonshire, *Medieval Ceramics* **21**, 13-42

Jones, C, and Chapman, A, 2003 A medieval tenement at College Street, Higham Ferrers, Northamptonshire, *Northamptonshire Archaeol* **31**, 125-35

Jope, E M, 1953-4 Medieval pottery kilns at Brill, Buckinghamshire: Preliminary Report on Excavations, in 1953, *Rec Buckinghamshire* **16**, 39-41

Jope, E M, and Ivens, R J, 1995 A later medieval pottery kiln at Potterspury, Northamptonshire, *Northamptonshire Archaeol* **26**, 141 – 8

Keene, S, 1990 Eyed weaving implements, in Biddle 1990, 232-33

Keevill, G D, 2003 Archaeological investigations in 2001 at the Abbey Church of St. Peter and St. Paul, Dorchester-on-Thames, Oxfordshire, *Oxoniensia* **68**, 313-362

Keynes, S, 1999 Mercia, in Lapidge *et al* 1999, 306-8

Kilmurry, K, 1980 *The pottery industry of Stamford, Lincs. c. AD850-1250*, BAR British Series **84**, Oxford

Lambrick, G, and Robinson, M, 1979 *Iron Age and Roman riverside settlements at Farmoor, Oxfordshire*, CBA Research Report **32**. Oxford and London

Lapidge, M, Blair, J, Keynes, S, Scragg, D (eds) 1999 *The Blackwell Encyclopaedia of Anglo-Saxon England,* Oxford

Lawrence, S, and Smith, A, forthcoming *Excavations on the site of a Roman settlement at Higham Ferrers, Northamptonshire,* Oxford Archaeology, Oxford

Le Patourel, H E J, 1968 Documentary evidence and the medieval pottery industry, *Medieval Archaeol* **7**, 101-26

Leeds, E T, 1923 A Saxon village at Sutton Courtenay, Berkshire, *Archaeologia* **73**, 147-92

Leney, L, and Casteel, R W, 1975 Simplified procedure for examining charcoal specimens for identification, *J Archaeol Sci* **2**, 153-59

Letts, J, 1999 *Smoke blackened thatch, a unique source of late medieval plant remains from southern England*, London and Reading

Levine, M A, 1982 The use of crown height measurements and eruption-wear sequences to age horse teeth, in Wilson *et al*, 1982, 223 – 250

Losco-Bradley, S, and Kinsley, G, 2002 *Catholme: an Anglo-Saxon settlement on the Trent Gravels in Staffordshire,* Nottingham

Lovejoy, C O, Meindl, R S, Pryzbeck, T R, and Mensforth, R P, 1985 Chronological metamorphosis of the auricular surface of the ilium: a new method for determination of adult skeletal age-at-death, *American Journal of Physical Anthropology* **68**, 15-28

Loveluck, C, 2001 Wealth, waste and conspicuous consumption. Flixborough and its importance for middle and late Saxon settlement studies, in H Hamerow and A MacGregor (eds), *Image and Power in the Archaeology of Early Medieval Britain, Essays in honour of Rosemary Cramp*, Oxford, 79-130

Loyn, H R, 1970 *Anglo-Saxon England and the Norman conquest*, London

Lyman, R L, 1996 *Vertebrate Taphonomy*, Cambridge Manuals in Archaeology, Cambridge

Margeson, S, 1993 *Norwich Households. Medieval and post-medieval finds from Norwich Survey excavations 1971-78*, EAA **58**, Norwich

Matolcsi, J, 1970 Historiche Erforschung der Körpergrosse der Rinder auf Grund von Ungarischen Knochenmaterial, *Zeitschrift für Tierzüchtung und Züchtungsbiologie* **87**, 89-128

McAdam, E, 2007 The Saxon settlement, in Chambers and McAdam 2007

McCarthy, M, 1979 The pottery, in J H Williams 1979, 151-229

McCarthy, M R, and Brooks, C M, 1988 *Medieval pottery in Britain AD 900-1600*, Leicester

Meadows, I, 1992 Excavations by E Greenfield at Bozeat, Higham Ferrers and Great Oakley, *Northamptonshire Archaeol* **24**, 77-94

Meaney, A, 1995 Pagan English sanctuaries, place-names and hundred meeting-places, *Anglo-Saxon Studies in Archaeology and History* **8**, 29-42

Miles, A, 1962 Assessment of age of a population of Anglo-Saxons from their dentition, *Proc Royal Society of Medicine* **55**, 881-886.

Miles, D, 2005 *The Tribes of Britain* London

Millett, M 1987 The question of continuity: Rivenhall reviewed, *Archaeol Jour* **144**, 434-438

Moffett, L, 1991 The archaeobotanical evidence for free-threshing tetraploid wheat in Britain, in *Palaeoethnobotany and Archaeology*, International Workgroup for Palaeoethnobotany, 8th Symposium at Nitra-Nové Vozokany 1989, Acta Interdisciplinaria Archaeologica **7**, Nitra: Slovak Academy of Sciences, 233-243.

Moffett, L, 1993 Charred plant remains, in D Knight, Excavations of an Iron Age Settlement at Gamston, Nottinghamshire, *Trans Thoroton Soc Nottinghamshire* **96** (for 1992), 16-90 (79-82).

Moffett, L, 1994 Charred cereals from some ovens/kilns in late Saxon Stafford and the botanical evidence for the pre-burgh economy, in Rackham 1994, 55-64

Moffett, L. 1995 Charred plant remains, in T G Allen, A Medieval grange of Abingdon Abbey at Dean Court Farm, Cumnor, Oxon, *Oxoniensia* **59**, 219-447 (398-406)

Moffett, L. 1997 Plant remains, in Jones, C., Eyre-Morgan, G., Palmer, S and Palmer, N, Excavations in the Outer Enclosure of Boteler's Castle, Oversley, Alcester, 1992-3, *Trans Birmingham Warwickshire Archaeol Soc* **101**, 74-85

Moffett, L, 2007 Charred cereals and other plant remains, in Chambers and McAdam, 2007, 290-295

Moffett and Smith, in prep, Crops and weeds from Saxon and medieval settlements at Stratton, Bedfordshire, England

Molyneux, L, Thompson, R, Oldfield, F, and McCallan, M E, 1972 Rapid measurement of the remanent magnetisation of long cores of sediment, *Nature* **237**, 42-43

Mook, W G, 1986 Recommendations/Resolutions Adopted by the Twelfth International Radiocarbon Conference, *Radiocarbon* **28**, 799

Moore, W R G, 1974 Yardley Gobion, *Northamptonshire Archaeol* **9**, 112

Moorhouse, S, 1974 A distinctive type of late medieval pottery in the Eastern Midlands: a definition and preliminary statement, *Proc Cambridge Antiq Soc* **55**, 46-59

Moorhouse, S, 1981 The medieval pottery industry and its markets, in D W Crossley (ed.) *Medieval Industry*, CBA Research Report **40**, 96 – 125

Morton, J, 1712 *The Natural History of Northamptonshire*

MPRG, 1998 *Guide to the Classification of Medieval Ceramic Forms*, Medieval Pottery Res Group Occ. Paper **1**

MPRG, 2001 *Minimum Standards for the Processing, Recording, Analysis and Publication of post-roman Ceramics* Medieval Pottery Res Group Occ. Paper **2**

Mudd, A, 2002 *Excavations at Melford Meadows, Brettenham, 1994: Romano-British and early Saxon occupations*, EAA **99**, Oxford

Murphy, P, 1985 The cereals and crop weeds, in West 1985, vol 1, 100-108

Murphy, P, 1993 Anglo-Saxon arable farming on the silt fens – preliminary results, *Fenland Research* **8**, Cambridge Archaeological Unit, University of Cambridge, 75-79

Musty, J, 1974 Medieval pottery kilns, in V I Evison, H Hodges and J G Hurst (eds) *Medieval Pottery from Excavations. Studies Presented to Gerald Clough Dunning with a Bibliography of his works*, London, 41-65

Mynard, D, 1980 A Tudor pottery kiln at Wood Newton, Northants, *Northamptonshire Archaeol* **15**, 160-2

Mynard, D C, Petchey, M R, and Tilson, T G, 1983 A medieval pottery at Church End, Flitwick, Bedfordshire, *Bedfordshire Archaeol* **16**, 75 – 84

Mynard, D C, and Zeepvat, R J, 1992 *Excavations at Great Linford, 1974-80*, Buckinghamshire Archaeol Soc Monog Ser **3**

Myres, J N L, 1977 *A Corpus of Anglo-Saxon pottery of the Pagan Period*, 2 volumes, Cambridge

NAU, 1991 Archaeological evaluation on Duchy of Lancaster land at Higham Ferrers, Northants, Unpublished client report, Northamptonshire Archaeological Unit

Nenk, B S, Margeson, S, and Hurley, M, 1992 Medieval Britain and Ireland in 1991, *Medieval Archaeology* **36** 184-308

North, J J, 1994 *English hammered coinage. Volume 1 Early Anglo-Saxon to Henry III c.600-1272*, 3rd ed. London, 1994

OA, 2002 Kings Meadow Lane, Higham Ferrers, Northants: Post-excavation Assessment and Research Design, Unpublished report, Oxford Archaeology,

OAU, 1994 Kings Meadow Lane, Higham Ferrers, Northants, Archaeological Evaluation, Unpublished client report, Oxford Archaeological Unit

OAU, 1995 Higham Ferrers, Kings Meadow Lane, Northants: Archaeological Project Outline, Unpublished client report, Oxford Archaeological Unit

Orton, C, 1998-99 Minimum Standards in Statistics and Sampling *Medieval Ceramics* **22-23**, 135-8

Ottaway, P, 1992 *Anglo-Scandinavian ironwork from Coppergate*, The Archaeology of York, The Small Finds, **17/6**, York

Ottaway, P, and Rogers, N, 2002 *Craft, industry and everyday life: Finds from Medieval York*, The Archaeology of York, The Small Finds, **17/15**, York

Parkhouse, J, 1976 The Dorestadt quernstones, *Berichten van de Rijkdienst voor het Oudheidkundig Bodemonderzoek* **26**, 181-8

Parry, S J, 2006 *Raunds Area Survey: An archaeological study of the landscape of Raunds, Northamptonshire 1985-94*, Oxford

Pearson, T, 1994 The pottery, in A G Johnson, Excavations in Oundle, Northants: work carried out at Stoke Doyle Road, 1979, Black Pot Lane 1985 and St. Peter's Church 1991, *Northamptonshire Archaeol* **25**, 99-118 (102-104)

Philp, B, 1984 *Excavations in the Darenth Valley, Kent*, Kent Monograph Series **4**, Dover

Plot, R, 1705 *The Natural History of Oxford-shire*, 2nd ed., Oxford and London.

Powlesland, D, 1990 West Heslerton: The Anglian settlement. Interim report on excavations in 1989, *Medieval Settlement Research Group Annual Rep* **4**, 46

Prummel, W, and Frisch, H-J, 1986 A guide for the distinction of species, sex and body size in bones of sheep and goat, *J Archaeol Sci* **13**, 567–77

Rackham, J, 1994 *Environment and Economy in Anglo-Saxon England*, CBA Research Report **89**, York

Rackham, O, 1987 *The History of the Countryside*, London

Radford, C A R, 1957 The Saxon house: a review and some parallels, *Medieval Archaeol* **1**, 27-38

Ressler, C, 1962 Isolation and identification from Common Vetch of the Neurotoxin _-Cyano-L-alanine, a possible factor in Neurolathyrism, *The Journal of Biological Chemistry* **237** (3), 733-735

Reynolds, A. 1997 The definition and ideology of Anglo-Saxon execution sites and cemeteries, in G De Boe and F Verhaeghe (eds), *Death and burial in Medieval Europe*, Papers of the Medieval Europe Brugge 1997 Conference, Volume **2**, 33-41

Reynolds, A, 1999 *Later Anglo-Saxon England: life and landscape*, Oxford

Reynolds, A, 2003 Boundaries and Settlements in later Sixth to Eleventh-Century England, in D Griffiths *et al*, 2003, 98-135

Reynolds, A, forthcoming *Anglo-Saxon Law in the Landscape* Oxford

Riddler, I, 2002 The bone and antler objects, in Foreman, *et al* 2002, 39-41 (see also CD ROM/specialist reports/bone/worked bone)

Roberts, C, and Cox, M, 2003 *Health and disease in Britain. From prehistory to present day*, Stroud

Roberts, C, and Manchester, K, 1995 *The archaeology of disease*, 2nd ed, New York

Robertson, A J, 1939 *Anglo-Saxon Charters,* Cambridge

Rodwell, W J, and Rodwell, K A, 1982 St Peter's church, Barton-on-Humber: excavation and structural study, 1978-81, *Antiq J* **62**, 283-315

Rodwell, W J, and Rodwell, K A, 1985 *Rivenhall, investigations of a villa, church, and village, 1950-77*, CBA Res Rep **55**

Roe, F, 2002 The worked stone, in Foreman *et al* 2002, 37-9

Rogerson, A, and Dallas, C, 1984 *Excavations in Thetford 1948-59 and 1973-80* EAA **22**, Dereham

Scheuer, J L, Musgrave, J H, and Evans, S P, 1980 The estimation of late foetal and perinatal age from limb bone length by linear and logarithmic regression, *Annals of Human Biology,* **7** (3), 257-265

Schurr, K, Becker, H, and Soffel, H C, 1984 Archaeomagnetic study of medieval fireplaces and ovens and the problem of magnetic refraction. *J. Geophys.* **56**, 1-8

Schweingruber, F, 1982 *Microscopic wood anatomy,* 2nd edition, Teufen

Scott, I R, 2001 Other Finds: metalwork and organic materials, in Biddle, Hiller, Scott and Streeten 2001, 257-282

Scott, I R, 2002 The metalwork, in S. Foreman, J Hiller and D Petts 2002, 35-7 (see also CD ROM/specialist reports/metalwork)

Scott, I R, forthcoming Small finds, in Lawrence and Smith forthcoming

Serjeantson, D, 1996 The animal bones, in E S Needham and T Spence (eds) *Runnymede Bridge Research Excavations*, Vol. 2: *Refuse and Disposal at Area 16, East Runnymede*, British Museum, London, 194-223

Serjeantson, R M, 1917, *The court rolls of Higham Ferrers*, III, Northampton

Shaw, M, 1991 Saxon and earlier settlement at Higham Ferrers, Northamptonshire, *Medieval Settlement Research Group* **6**, 15-19

Shaw, M, and Steadman, S, 1992 Archaeological evaluation at Higham Ferrers Castle, Northamptonshire, Unpublished report, Northamptonshire Archaeology

Shay, T, 1985 Differentiated treatment of deviancy at death as revealed in anthropological and archaeological material, *Journal of anthropological archaeology* **4**, 221-241

Silver, I, A, 1969 The ageing of domestic animals, in Brothwell and Higgs, 1969, 283-302

Sledzig, P S, 1998 Forensic taphonomy: postmortem decomposition and decay, in K J Reichs (ed), *Forensic osteology. Advances in the identification of human remains*, Illinois, 109-119

Slowikowski, A M, 1991 A previously unrecognised sherd of Tating-type ware from excavations in Bedford in 1976, *Bedfordshire Archaeol* **19**, 130

Slowikowski, A M, forthcoming Late medieval reduced ware: A regional synthesis

Spandl, K, and Durden, T, 1999 Higham Ferrers post-excavation assessment and project design, Oxford Archaeological Unit.

Stace, C, 1997 *New Flora of the British Isles*, 2nd ed. Cambridge

Steane, J M, 1974 *The Northamptonshire Landscape,* London

Steane, J M, 1985 *The Archaeology of Medieval England and Wales,* Beckenham

Steane, J M, and Bryant, G F, 1975 Excavations at the deserted medieval settlement at Lyveden, Northants *J Northampton Mus and Art Gallery* **12**

Stenton, F M, 1971 *Anglo-Saxon England,* Oxford

Stevens, C, 2004 Charred plant remains, in Hey 2004, 351-364

Suchey, J M, and Brooks, S, 1990 Skeletal age determination based on the *os pubis*: A comparison of the Acsádi-Nemeskéri and Suchey-Brooks methods, *Human Evolution* **5**, 227-238

Tarling, D H, 1983 *Palaeomagnetism*, Chapman and Hall, London

Tarling, D H, Hammo, N B, and Downey, W S, 1986 The scatter of magnetic directions in archaeomagnetic studies, *Geophysics* **51**, 634-639

Tarling, D H, and Symons, D T A, 1967 A stability index of remanence in palaeomagnetism. *Geophys. J. R. astr. Soc.* **12**, 443-448

Taylor, G, 2003 An early to middle Saxon settlement at Quarrington, Lincolnshire, *Antiq J* **83**, 231-80

Teichert, M, 1975 Osteometrische Untersuchungen zur Berechnung der Widerristhöhe bei Schafen, in A T Clason (ed), *Archaeological Studies*, Elsevier, Amsterdam, 51-69

Thompson, R, and Oldfield, F, 1986 *Environmental Magnetism*, London

Timby, J, 1995 Pottery, in S Ford 1995, 88-94

Tipper, J, 2004 *The* Grubenhaus *in Anglo-Saxon England,* Landscape Research Centre Archaeological Monograph **2**, London

Todd, T W, 1920 Age changes to the pubic bone: 1 The male white pubis, *American Journal of Physical Anthropology* **3** (3), 285-334

Todd, T W, 1921 Age changes in the pubic bone, *American Journal of Physical Anthropology* **4** (1), 1-70

Trotter, M, 1970 Estimations of stature from intact long limb bones, in T D Stewart (ed), *Personal identification in Mass Disasters*, Washington, 71-83

Turner, G M, and Thompson, R, 1982 Detransformation of the British geomagnetic secular variation record for Holocene times, *Geophys. J. R. Astr. Soc.* **70**, 789-792.

Ulmschneider, K, 2000 Settlement, economy and the 'productive' site: Middle Anglo-Saxon Lincolnshire AD 650-780, *Medieval Archaeol* **44**, 53-79

Vince, A, 1995 Petrological discussion, in S Ford 1995, 92

Vince, A, 2006 Characterisation of late medieval Reduced Wares from the south-east Midlands, in A Slowikowski forthcoming

Wade-Martins, P, 1980 *Excavations in North Elmham Park, 1967-72,* EEA **9**, Dereham

Watt, J, 1994 Lava querns, in K Steedman, Excavation of a Saxon site at Riby Crossroads, Lincolnshire, *Arch Jour* **151**, 212-306

Welch, M, 1992 *The English Heritage book of Anglo-Saxon England* London

West, S E, 1985 *West Stow. The Anglo-Saxon Village* Vols 1 and 2, EAA **24**, Ipswich

Wheeler, A, 1969 *The fishes of the British Isles and N W Europe,* Michigan

Whitelock, D, 1979 *English Historical Documents Vol. 1 c. 500 – 1042,* 1955, 2nd ed 1979, reprinted 1996, London

Wilkinson, D W (ed), 1992 *Oxford Archaeological Unit Field Manual*, Oxford

Williams, G, 2001 Military institutions and royal power, in M P Brown and C A Farr 2001, 295- 309

Williams, J H, 1979 *St Peter's St, Northampton. Excavations 1973-76,* Northampton Development Corporation Monog Ser **2**

Williams, J H, Shaw, M, and Denham, V, 1985 *Middle Saxon Palaces at Northampton*, Northampton Development Corporation Monog Ser **4**

Wilson, B, Grigson, C, and Payne, S, (eds), *Ageing and sexing animal bones from archaeological sites,* BAR British Series **109,** Oxford

Wilson, D M, 1984 *Anglo-Saxon art. From the seventh century to the Norman Conquest,* London

Woodland, M, 1990 Spindle-whorls, in Biddle 1990, 216-25

Yorke, B, 1990 *Kings and Kingdoms of Early Anglo-Saxon England,* London

Yorke, B, 2001 The Origins of Mercia, in M P Brown and C A Farr 2001, 13-22

Zaluckyj, S, 2001 *Mercia: The Anglo-Saxon Kingdom of Central England*, Almeley

Index